Selling Culture

THE HAYMARKET SERIES

Editors: Mike Davis and Michael Sprinker

The Haymarket Series offers original studies in politics, history and culture, with a focus on North America. Representing views across the American left on a wide range of subjects, the series will be of interest to socialists both in the USA and throughout the world. A century after the first May Day, the American left remains in the shadow of those martyrs whom the Haymarket Series honors and commemorates. These studies testify to the living legacy of political activism and commitment for which they gave their lives.

Selling Culture

Magazines, Markets, and Class
at the Turn of the Century

RICHARD OHMANN

VERSO

London • New York

First published by Verso 1996
© Richard Ohmann 1996
All rights reserved

The right of Richard Ohmann to be identified as the author
of this work has been asserted by him in accordance with
the Copyright, Designs and Patents Act 1988

Verso
UK: 6 Meard Street, London W1V 3HR
USA: 180 Varick Street, New York NY 10014–4606

Verso is the imprint of New Left Books

ISBN 1–85984–974–1

British Library Cataloguing in Publication Data
A catalogue record for this book is available from the British Library

Library of Congress Cataloging-in-Publication Data
Ohmann, Richard M. (Richard Malin), 1931–
  Selling culture: magazines, markets, and class at the turn of the
century / Richard Ohmann.
    p.   cm. — (The Haymarket series)
  Includes bibliographical references and index.
  ISBN 1–85984–974–1 (hardcover).
    1. Advertising—Social aspects—United States—History.
2. Advertising, Magazine—Social aspects—United States—History.
3. Marketing—Social aspects—United States—History.   4. Popular
culture—United States—History.   5. Mass media—Social aspects—
United States—History.
  H5813.U6035 1996   95–42615
    659.1'042'0973—dc20   CIP

Typeset by M Rules
Printed in Great Britain by Biddles Ltd, Guildford and King's Lynn

Contents

Preface

I hope to have argued persuasively in this book that a national mass culture was first instanced in the United States by magazines, much like those of the present time, reaching large audiences and turning a profit on revenues from advertising for brand named products; that this highly consequential change in the making of culture took place very rapidly just before and after the end of the last century; that it did so through the energies and innovations of diverse agents – publishers, editors, writers, readers, ad men, merchandisers, sales executives, and others – acting to achieve disparate but compatible goals of their own; that their efforts succeeded because they responded to the needs of big business at a time when industrial capitalism's greatest achievements had led to its deepest crisis; and that the combined but largely uncoordinated work of these people reestablished the American social order on a new basis. There is much more in this book about the magazines themselves than this précis suggests, and more about the core group of their readers, in whose formation as a new social class the magazines played a role. The story I tell is complicated, but it is a single story with a main plot that I have tried to make accessible for readers with various backgrounds and interests.

Some of those readers will know far more than I do about parts of my subject; in fact, only in chapters 9 and 10 do I explore intellectual terrain on which I have some claim to expertise, by virtue of professional training. The rest of the study blends economic, business, social, and cultural history with theory drawn from those areas, from cultural studies, and from the broad marxist tradition. To describe my project that way is to invite the label "interdisciplinary." I have indeed pillaged – gratefully! – the works of scholars in several disciplines. But my aim is not to have worked between or bridged disciplines; it is to have put forth an analysis that integrates much of what scholars (including myself) have learned about a transformative moment in the history of the United States, the history of culture, the history of capitalism. Since I have tried to make total sense of these changes, I will of course have failed. Right now, I am pretty cheerful about the attempt and about the uses of such a failure. I hope the reader shares my pleasure and finds ways to improve on the understanding advanced here. Short of that, I hope she or he learns something of use about magazines.

Over the fifteen years during which I have intermittently worked on this study, many friends have helped: given me bibliographies, challenged my ideas, offered ideas of their own, read parts of the manuscript, encouraged me. A large number of them – all but one in the list below – are or have been colleagues at Wesleyan University or at its Center for the Humanities. Those who made specific contributions include Nancy Armstrong, Gerald Burns, Mary Ann Clawson, Michael Denning, Ellen D'Oench, Ann duCille, Alex Dupuy, Patricia Hill, Joan Jurale, James Kavanagh, Stanley Lebergott, Donald Meyer, the late Carol Ohmann, Joel Pfister, Claire Potter, Roy Rosenzweig, Ronald Schatz, Michael Schudson, Richard Slotkin, Michael Sprinker (who is also my able editor at Verso), William Stowe, Elizabeth Traube, and Richard Vann. At least another two dozen colleagues have stimulated my thoughts, brightened my working days, and made Wesleyan an extraordinary place to do cultural studies. Among many students who did the same, I would like to mention Peter Blier, Joseph Entin, and David Krasnow, research assistants and intellectual provocateurs. The work of Jaqueline Rich and Patricia Camden on my manuscript has been heroic. Many not at Wesleyan have given assistance, too. Marion Hirsch, Reference Archivist at Duke University's John W. Hartman Center for Sales, Advertising, and Marketing History meticulously checked my uses of material from the J. Walter Thompson Company Archives, rescuing me from small errors and confusions. I hope I have properly acknowledged other help in the endnotes.

A fellowship from the Rockefeller Foundation started me off on this project, though I did not yet realize what it was. Once the obsession took hold, two sabbaticals from Wesleyan helped me sustain and, finally, exorcise it. Thanks, thanks, to all.

1

The Experience

It is easy to imagine, and one will have to, because the Johnsons left no record of it.

When the morning mail arrives, on a muggy autumn day in 1895, Mrs Johnson is alone in the house on Cleveland's East 107th Street, at work on a new dress. Welcoming the diversion, she comes down from the sewing room and settles for a moment on the porch, where a slight breeze moves the unseasonably warm air. She reads a letter from her sister in Fort Wayne, glances at a couple of bills and puts them aside, and picks up the October issue of *Munsey's Magazine*. The cover engraving (in shades of red) shows an elegant woman in a top hat, side-saddle on a spirited horse, riding down a rural lane. The woman is at ease, riding crop and reins held loosely in her white-gloved hands. She ignores the horse and the road, gazing out into the landscape and showing us her aristocratic profile. Mrs Johnson has not been on a horse since she came with her family from Wellington, Ohio to Cleveland as a girl, and those were farm horses; still, she feels a subterranean kinship with the rider – the freedom; the style.

Prolonging her mood, she opens the magazine to her favorite department: "The Stage." Here are halftones of Lillian Russell, Ada Rehan, Della Fox, Vesta Tilley, Olga Nethersole, Lillian Thurgate, and Lily Hanbury – handsome women whose attitudes suggest a wealth of feeling and experience that Mrs Johnson cautiously envies. She admires, too, the gossipy sophistication of the theater notes: the anecdote of Miss Russell's discovery by D'Oyly Carte, and her current enthrallment with "the fad for bicycling"; the dearth of good new plays, in both London and New York; how Beerbohm Tree put an impertinent young man in his place. Mrs Johnson glances over the names of the producers and plays that constitute the young New York season. She will absorb this information later, for discussion with her friend Mrs Condit, who does amateur theatricals and goes to New York once a year with her lawyer-husband. Later, too, she will consult her other favorite departments: "The World of Music," "Literary Chat," "In the Public Eye" (profiles of or notes on Theodore Roosevelt, William Morris, Susan B. Anthony, the British royal family, E. L. Godkin, and so on – the equivalent of *People*

Magazine today), and, with more of a sense of duty than of pleasure, "Artists and Their Work." She specially looks forward to the hour she will spend tonight with the final installment of Robert McDonald's "A Princess and a Woman" (dashing Americans, now caught up in a Carpathian intrigue). And during the month, she will return to the magazine for the other fiction, including a new serial, "Robert Atterbury," by Thomas H. Brainerd. She will carefully read the article on the Strauss family ("The Waltz King"), duly noting that "Americans hold Strauss and his music in great esteem" (p. 17); this kind of information helps her find bearings in a cultural landscape that she knows mainly through magazines and those friends who belong to it by birth and education.

She must get back to her sewing; but not quite yet – there's time to skim the ads first. She only half-notices, but with reassurance, those for Sapolio, Pears' Soap, Cleveland's Baking Powder (commended by Fannie Farmer and six other teachers of cookery), Quaker Oats, Garland Stoves and Ranges ("The World's Best," is all the ad says). She already uses these products: she has a Garland range; the ads confirm her good sense. She lingers a bit longer over the ad for the Charter Oak ladies' bicycle: would Miss Russell perhaps ride one of these? No matter – still too expensive at $65, but they have been coming down in price, and she'll have one before long. Eventually she will study the ads for clothing, wallpaper, parquet floors; but the only ad she reads thoroughly now, and with something like the intent to purchase, is for the Autoharp. "*Why should you get an Autoharp?* Because you can learn to play the popular music – Operas, Hymns, Waltzes, Marches, Galops, Mazurkas, Schottisches, Yorkes, College Songs – almost at sight. No teacher is necessary, as our instruction book is complete . . . ." Yes, she would like very much to play "My Pearl's a Bowery Girl," "Her Eyes Don't Shine Like Diamonds," and those Victor Herbert marches; sheet music comes at $1 per dozen. The Autoharp itself costs as little as $5, and looks almost like the one for which the Condits paid $25 last year. Mrs Johnson would like her daughter Margaret to have the same advantages as Elsa Condit; she will speak to her husband about it. Meanwhile, her eye can't help taking in the Pre-Raphaelite lady on the opposing page, languidly scattering violets and signifying the glamour that goes with use of Vio-Violet, the new Lundborg perfume. She would never buy it for herself ("$1.75 per bottle"), but maybe a hint to Mr Johnson before their anniversary? She noticed Vio-Violet on the shelf at Halle Bros, when she was downtown yesterday. With this thought she pulls herself away from *Munsey's* and goes back upstairs with a keener sense of herself, her possibilities, her world.

When Margaret gets home from school, she too picks up *Munsey's*, deferring errands and homework long enough to finish "A Princess and a Woman," and to pore over the ads for accessories and corsets. A year ago she would have scorned these, but some of her friends are fashion-conscious now, and Margaret has come to see herself partly through their eyes. She does not look like the singers and fashion models; she is too large in the waist, too small in the bosom. Beauty will be a project for her, with help from magazines like this, even more than from the more detailed but more prudish *Ladies' Home Journal.* Her mother endorses the project only with mixed feelings, but Margaret now takes her lead more from those public images and her friends than from Mrs Johnson. Off to the store now, but she will return to *Munsey's,* reading every story, crying a little at the way Robert Atterbury selflessly breaks off from his fiancée, Claire, when he learns he has tuberculosis; delighting in the romantic high jinks that take place in the train "On the Way North"; thinking it sad, but a little contrived, that each of "The Two Brothers" sacrifices his own life so that the other might survive with the two days' water supply they have left on their desert island in the Pacific. Margaret will read the poems, too, and find there other inflections of love and sentiment.

Tommy Johnson is the only other child in the family to look at *Munsey's.* When he gets home from his paper route he turns with excitement to "The World of Sport," knowing that football will be covered in this issue. He is not disappointed: terrific photos of a scrimmage at Princeton, "The Famous Yale Wedge," and Captain Thorne of Yale, looking self-possessed, manly, and noble in his "Y" turtleneck. The editor's rather cynical comments on increasing violence in the sport do not disturb Tommy's fantasies of starring for Yale, even though he half knows that he'll be lucky to get in to Western Reserve, right around the corner. (His father wants him to try for a more practical education at the Case Institute of Technology – also right around the corner – and Tommy likes the idea of being an engineer; but Case has no football team.) Tommy glances at a few ads, notably one for the American Cyclometer, but he has finished with *Munsey's,* except for a dozen or so returns to those football pictures. *Youth's Companion* and *Popular Science Monthly* are the magazines whose delivery gives an edge to Tommy's day.

Mr Johnson won't be home until tomorrow evening. He travels for Thompson Products Company,[1] but would not call himself a "drummer" because he is welcomed by the entrepreneurs and chief engineers to whom he sells machine tools, because he knowledgeably serves them as consultant and trouble-shooter after the sale, and because he draws his pay mostly as salary rather than commission: he thinks of himself as a professional, though his profession has no name and no degrees. Increasingly, it will be the province of formally trained engineers; though proud of his own training in the school of hard knocks and his one year of college, Mr Johnson senses the change; hence his ambition for Tommy.

Like his son, Mr Johnson turns first to "The World of Sport," taking in the football commentary, but turning with more interest to the sections on boxing and on shooting (he handled a gun well, himself, as a farm boy, and he usually manages a day in the field during duck season). He is a little disturbed by the tone *Munsey's* correspondent takes toward the upcoming Corbett–Fitzsimmons fight, which Mr Johnson has been eagerly anticipating:

> In its many years of existence, the "prize ring" has not advanced to any high moral plane. The champions of recent days have proved themselves to be men of the same stripe as their predecessors, and decent people are pretty well disgusted with their performances. (p. 100)

As a decent person in terms of job, home (it cost $2400), and social position, Mr Johnson probably should agree with the writer, but John L. Sullivan is a hero for him, not least because he is Irish (Mr Johnson has no use for papists, but as a second-generation Swede he has to admire anyone who makes good among the Yankees). For similar reasons, *Munsey's'* admiring reports on gentlemen golfers, tennis players, and yachtsmen tug Mr Johnson two ways. It may be true that Lord Dunraven's "sportsmanlike bearing has made many American admirers for him" (p. 102), but admiration for an idle rich yachtsman comes grudgingly to Mr Johnson. He prefers baseball to all other sports, and takes *Sporting Life*: though he would not make it a topic of conversation with Charles Condit, he finds many like-minded men at work and on the road.

Likewise, he skims the sections on art, music, theater, and literature, with a sense of looking in from the doorway. His wife wants him to be publicly conversant on these matters, but they win little response from him other than a quickening of the pulse as he takes in the photos of actresses and sopranos. He does share with Mrs Johnson, however, an interest in the celebrities "In the Public Eye." They admire Mr Roosevelt's manly work against corruption in New York, and exchange a few tut-tuts over William Morris's conversion to "the socialistic movement" (p. 42). Turning to another of his favorite departments, "Impressions by the Way," Mr Johnson notes with satisfaction another reprimand to British socialists, one of whom has recently drawn scorn from the American public, "his cloth cap and knee breeches being regarded as a symbol rather of the haughty aristocrat than of the professional foe of caste" (p. 124). Mr Johnson takes seriously the brief reports and opinions here at the back of the magazine. He duly records the editor's beliefs that the Tory victory does not presage the end of democracy in Britain, that it is bad form to overfeed your dinner guests, that the $8000 salary paid to US cabinet ministers is too little to attract and support in "suitable style" "the very best brains in the country" (Mr Johnson himself earns about $1200), that one can carry too far the current rage to preserve the childhood homes of great Americans, that the property of the wealthy is scandalously under-assessed, and that,

> Of war and pestilence, the two great scourges of the human race, the latter is to a certain extent a blessing in disguise; it carries off the weak and

the unfit, leaving the sounder constitutions to propagate a stronger type. But war is utterly cruel and unnatural; it reverses the selective process, leaving the weak and the unfit in safety, while it immolates the flower of a nation's manhood upon the lurid altar of military glory. (p. 125)

The only opinion that upsets him is yet *another* paean to New York yachtsmen (rich, yes; but skilled, hard-working sailors).

In general, he feels satisfied as he puts the magazine aside and talks with his wife for a while about domestic matters before going up to bed. He will make much less use of it than she, after this first perusal, reading with real interest only the articles on "The Red Cross in the Far East" (the Japanese are civilized, the Chinese, barbarians) and "American Patriotic Societies" ("a grand wave of patriotism is spreading over our beloved country" [p. 84]). The romantic fiction and poetry make him gag, and the ads seem to address his wife more than himself (there are a few for engines, heating systems, and lathes, but he gets his information on these from trade journals). On the whole, he prefers *Cosmopolitan*; it really informs him about science, industry, and social questions, and its fiction is a bit more tolerable. But Frank Munsey's product contributes a knowing attitude to Mr Johnson's social repertoire, and more to that of his wife. He is genuinely proud of the way she has built up her store of Culture over the years, even while raising four children and fashioning a home that speaks as well for the taste of these migrants to the city as Mr Johnson's advancement at work does for their sturdy stock and vigorous ambition.

Both Johnsons are also proud, in a small way, to have been participants in the success of Frank Munsey himself. They had seen his bold ads in the fall of 1893 – "No middleman; no monopoly," and so on. They bought a copy of this curiosity, the ten-cent magazine, and then they subscribed. Now they find themselves flattered in Munsey's personal column, "The Publisher's Desk," where he recounts the story of his victory over the American News Company (never mentioned here by name: always "the middleman," or "monopoly"). As he struggled to break the grasp of monopoly, "conservatism," and "conventionality" and get his dying magazine directly to news dealers and customers, he was "relying confidently on the sober sense of the people," their eyes not blinded by custom, willing to test the extraordinary proposition that they might buy a magazine of "standard size" and "standard excellence" for ten cents. The Johnsons are pleased to have been among the prescient ones, pleased to overhear Munsey offering them to advertisers as "wide awake, up-to-date people," and pleased to be among the more than 500,000 such readers that he claims (erroneously) have made *Munsey's* the "leading magazine in the world in circulation" (p. 128). It seems right that their steady, hard-won rise in American society should somehow be bound up with the triumph of the upstart Munsey over the old-fashioned monopolist, and that through his columns they should make a kind of contact with half a million families to whom they might be social equals and friends were they to live in Omaha, Baltimore, or Rochester rather than in Cleveland.

Fifteen years earlier, the Johnsons would have had to skimp to afford even a ten-cent, monthly, "general" magazine, had there been one. The nearest equivalents were the leading literary monthlies like *Harper's*, whose circulation of about 200,000 was perhaps the highest for a publication of this sort. *Harper's* sold for 35 cents a copy, $4 by annual subscription. Mr Johnson was earning $680 a year, assuming no lay-offs. He would not have considered spending half of 1 percent of his income on a magazine, and of course there was no chance of bringing into their rented house as many as the eight magazines they were to receive in 1895.

But the impossibility was more than monetary. Not much in the *Harper's* of 1880 would have appealed to the Johnsons. In the December issue, for instance, Mr Johnson might have turned to "The City of Pittsburgh," but would have found the twenty-page article and twenty engravings a bit elegant and unreal – industry from a leisured perspective. Other articles extended this perspective to sights even less likely to attract the Johnsons: the Lake District and its poets (Mrs Johnson had not yet applied herself to literature), San Francisco's Chinatown, the inner workings of British government. News of the great advance in women's education realized through their admission to "The Annex" at Harvard (later, Radcliffe College) would not have stirred or vexed the Johnsons as much as it did their social superiors in the East. The final installment of Henry James's *Washington Square* was quite over their heads, and the other fiction and poetry would have seemed effete. The four departments conducted by the editor (Henry Mills Alden) did not offer the cultural novitiate later provided by *Munsey's*, but treated of matters supposedly *already* grasped by readers. And instead of meeting the chatty, bluff voices of Munsey and his colleagues, the Johnsons would have had to make themselves fit audience for *this* voice:

> Ripe and golden as grains gleaned from a generous harvest field are the less than a score of poems gathered by Mr Longfellow into the little volume which he has prophetically christened *Ultima Thule*: like those grains, though ripe and golden, without any sign of decay; like them, carrying us back to the time when the young shoot sprang green and tender and full of promise from the sweet-smelling earth . . . (p. 151)

and so on for as many words again before the simile and the sentence play themselves out. *Harper's* implied and reached an audience of the leisured and affluent, with culture given by birth and education, rather than achieved in spare moments as an adjunct to new and precarious respectability. It would not have been at home on the porch at East

107th Street, had that porch existed in 1880.

To examine these two tattered magazines a century later is to look across a cultural divide at least as broad as that between *Munsey's* in 1895 and the *New Yorker* in 1995. The engraving on *Harper's'* cover is iconic, not representational. The publisher's name is inscribed on a pedestal that bears scattered, musty shards of culture: two piles of books bound in morocco, parchment scrolls, an artist's palette, papers, an inkstand. From behind the books rise two columns loosely draped in sashes, one with a cluster of flowers and the other with fruit and vegetables. On top stand two toga-clad children with baskets on their heads from which they are strewing blossoms. Wavelike scroll work extends toward the center from the tops of the columns, touching but not supporting a globe on which sits a third child, this one naked except for a polite wisp of cloth, blowing bubbles. The design has no direct social referent such as the classy horsewoman on *Munsey's'* cover. It makes no contact with the present moment; it has no historical coordinates. Even less does it proclaim an invitation to experience the trendy or the new. This cover remains the same from month to month, asserting the stability of a culture and of the class that lives it. Needless to add, there is no color on or in *Harper's*.[2]

Inside there are indeed illustrations, fifty-three wood and steel engravings. But these are presented as themselves cultural artifacts reflecting the tutored eye of the viewer – even those that take us to the open hearths of Pittsburgh. Most of the seventy-five illustrations in *Munsey's* are photoengravings, pointing viewers outward to some referent in the world. If they call attention at all to their technique, it is to the magical fidelity of the camera, only slightly diminished by halftone reproduction.

But to catch the full difference in visual presentation, you have to turn to the advertising sections. *Harper's* of 1880 carries 16 pages, after 160 pages of editorial material, not counting the back cover, which, sometime in the intervening 115 years, has become separated from my copy. And these are not ads at all, in the full sense: they are notices for new Harper books, and thus they brought no direct revenue to the magazine. Among them two illustrations from the books for sale are reproduced; otherwise, these pages offer only titles in bold type and discursive material in small print. *Munsey's* for October 1895 has 9 pages of ads at the front, and, after the 128 pages of text and illustration that the publisher boastfully calls "standard size," another 64 pages of ads. All told, there are 272 display ads (that is, larger than classified size, with either illustrations or bold type). Seventeen are full-page ads. Large or small, the majority project visual images, running from primitive logos to cartoons, idealized engravings, *art nouveau* designs, or photographs. The lived experience of 1895 is pictorially represented: typewriters, pianos, cutlery, bicycles, a pencil sharpener, electrical devices to cure all diseases, suburban houses, furniture, furnaces, shoes, corsets, jewelry, pens, tinned food, a meat grinder, boxes of soap. Sixteen ads portray men, and thirty-one

have representations of women, mostly people "like us" rather than
archaic or stylized icons. I thought of having the Johnsons turn to the
ads first – and why not, with this riot of imagery to seduce the eye?

One thing more about these two magazines and the ways they constitute their readers. Each achieves a certain consistency of voice, at which
I have hinted, in its editorial portions. But *Munsey's'* advertising section
evokes 300 commodities, a way of life conducted through them, and
accompanying images of self and family. *Munsey's* addresses a group of
people defined by what they might purchase. It speaks to them as a new
category of person: the consumer. (Readers of *Harper's* buy the books
and magazines of the Harper brothers; aside from that, total silence
about their participation in markets.)

And of course, this change thoroughly altered the transaction that
took place when one bought and used a magazine. In 1880 the
Condits, who did subscribe to *Harper's*, made a simple purchase: for $4
a year they received a certain amount of entertainment, edification,
self-congratulation, and prestige in the eyes of visitors to their home.
The Johnsons entered a more complex bargain. They bought those
same values, but their dollar-a-year fell far short of paying what it cost
to produce the magazine. To make up the difference, Frank Munsey
sold their attention, and a shot at their buying power, to advertisers.
The Johnsons bought the magazine, and, through the same medium,
they themselves were bought.

One can make a rough guess at the proportions. If Munsey was telling
the truth about circulation, and if most sales were by subscription, his
revenue from the sale of the October issue was around $44,000. At his
well-known advertising rate of a dollar per page per thousand of circulation, he would have received $36,500 for the ads. But assuming that he
charged more, proportionately, for small ads than for full-page ones, he
made just about as much *for* his readers as *from* them.

This was a new relationship, new in many more ways than I have so far
indicated. For now it will be enough to stress that the Johnsons did not
simply buy a cultural commodity with a certain use value for them; they
bought one that commodified *them* as well – presented their attention,
their needs, their aspirations, their anxieties, as use values to unseen
third parties. And fourth parties, for, as we shall see, a group of specialists in such commodification had rapidly emerged and come to stand
between manufacturers and cultural entrepreneurs like Munsey: advertising agents. Munsey offered to deliver the right kind of people, "wide
awake, up-to-date people" with money to spend, in specified large numbers. The agencies offered to shape and create needs among those
people. The Johnsons chose a particular bargain when they subscribed,
but were not party to these other negotiations that sought to package
their further choices; they were in fact hardly aware of them. Their role
was much more like that of the family who chose last night to watch

"Roseanne" instead of the ball game, than like that of the Condits in 1880. The Johnsons and the TV viewers got a cultural experience almost for nothing, meanwhile being counted, weighed up "demographically," and courted in ways both direct and oblique. Something had happened by 1895 that made them twentieth-century people. That something was the invention of mass culture.

I sit with a stack of old magazines in front of me. I am in a room built around 1780. The town history tells me that Noah Cooley was one of the original settlers of Hawley in 1771, that he "cleared land on a pond-source of Cooley Brook, built a shack, brought his bride, Esther Hyde, on horseback. Her dowry of household goods was brought by oxen on an ox cart."[3] Since Esther and Noah were not married until 1780, I assume that he had built the old part of this house by then, and that her household goods did not go into the shack, whose tiny foundation is still down there by the brook. I conjecture, also, that there was hardly a bought thing in that ox cart – a brooch, some needles and thread, a few utensils. And I am certain that the Cooleys lived (and died) mainly without commodities in this room until they found iron ore on their land and opened a mine and a foundry. Why would they be different from the nineteenth-century Massachusetts farmer quoted by Stuart Ewen, who "never spent more than ten dollars a year, which was for salt, nails and the like. Nothing to eat, drink or wear was bought, as my farm produced it all."[4]

Today, nothing in this room is *not* a commodity, except for the dust, the cats, and the cordwood; and of course I used commodities to cut, haul, and split the wood. (The cats can be as self-sufficient as the Cooleys, but on the whole they prefer to eat commodities.) Among the kinds of bought thing I can see from where I sit, many came into use about the time of these magazines, and partly through their mediation: the record player, electric lamps, machine-made furniture, the typewriter through which my fingers express these thoughts, the automobile outside my window. Others existed long before 1895 but only became national, homogeneously made and packaged commodities about then: bar soap, tea, cereal, canned soup – even a tin of Royal Baking Powder, nearly the oldest national brand of them all. One-fourth of *Munsey's*' back cover goes to an ad for this product. A woman's hand holds out a tin of it almost identical to the one on my shelf, with the ingenious device of a smaller can pictured in a circle on the large one, one smaller still in a circle on that, and so on to infinity. The ad makes no arguments, no offers, nor does it say how or where to buy Royal Baking Powder. In fact, only two words speak from the red field in back of the can: "*Absolutely Pure.*"[5] This familiar slogan, plus the woman's frilled cuff, plus the imaged can, plus innumerable repetitions, said a lot, in a code that the Johnsons deciphered without pause, but which would have been a challenge if not a mystery to the Cooleys, like encountering a new dialect.

Munsey's Magazine looks a bit crude to the late-twentieth-century eye, yet it seems unequivocally part of the world I inhabit. It helped create that world. It was harder to produce the Johnsons, who lived across a divide between epochs. What was it like for them, and for men like Frank Munsey? My sketch of the Johnsons strikes me as thin and surely anachronistic in ways beyond my ken. But sitting here, with three versions – 1780, 1895, 1995 – of what it was and is to be human imaged before me, the effort to understand that passage of consciousness, material life, and social being seems important. When did mass culture arise? Where did it come from? Why? What has it done for and to its various participants?

I will try to explain these things. The exposition will wind through many empirical domains; my maps of some are like fourteenth-century maps of the world. But everything connects with everything, and this is the only way to essay it.

2

The Origins of Mass Culture

In this study I try to answer the question: Where did mass culture come from? Behind that question lies another one, the question that led me to this subject in the first place, and that gives it more than antiquarian interest: What does mass culture do, in and to societies like ours? That second question will probably seem important to everyone, and indeed it occupies a central place in both scholarly and popular discourse about society. Everyone finds it striking that the average family has television on for six or seven hours a day, that in addition we listen to the radio for an average of three hours a day, that each of us sees or hears about five hundred commercial messages a day, and so on. Such experiences mark our lives as radically different from those of our great-great-grandparents, and from those of human beings today in those shrinking enclaves of the world not yet saturated with mass culture. But different in what ways, aside from the use of mass culture itself?

Tens of thousands of books and articles have addressed this question, and their authors rarely concur. That is in part because of the way most have put the question, as if one could extract from the entire social process just the movies we watch, the time spent reading newspapers and magazines, the football games, the hit records, the activity of the broadcasting networks and advertising agencies, and so on, and treat this conglomeration of doings and products as a single cause operating on the remainder of our lives. Confusing the issue even more, people who argue this question are usually trying -- openly or implicitly -- to evaluate mass culture or some part of it: Is it good or bad for "society"?

It is as if the central question of physiology were whether the mind is good or bad for the body: an inconclusive and miscast debate would go on in learned journals, with some arguing that the mind is good because it keeps the body out of danger, gives it instructions on what to feed itself, shows it how to get sexual pleasure, and so on; and others pointing out that the mind gives the body hypertension and heart attacks and psychosomatic illnesses and a host of damaging substances and bad habits. Just so, the debate on mass culture lines up on one side those who say that TV (for instance) educates and amuses people, democratically opens up the range of possibilities available to them, puts them in touch with the whole society or even the whole global village, makes them informed citizens, helps them to improve their material lives, and so keeps the economy going; and on the other, those who say TV creates illusions, corrupts morality and taste, promotes rape and murder, destroys literacy and the English language, isolates people from one another, puts them in debt by making them want things they don't really need, and turns them into political zombies. The optimists and the worriers both see mass culture as a profound force in our society, and they will never agree about its consequences, so long as the debate rests on such confusions about cause and effect and value.

Like mind and body, mass culture and this form of society are inseparable; it is impossible to imagine one without the other.[1] To ask what the effects of mass culture are and whether it is good or bad for us is to freeze events and stand outside them with a slide rule and a list of (someone's) do's and don't's, turning away from the complex social process in which individuals and groups try, over time, to make the best of the circumstances in which they find themselves. Asking whether we want the kind of mass culture we have is almost the same as asking whether we like the social relations of advanced capitalist society.

The expenditure of $40 billion a year on advertising is both a cause and an effect – really, many causes and effects. It represents the achievement of many aims by many people, along with the defeat or frustration of aims that others have pursued. More complicated still: Jane Jones may genuinely *want* the promises about a new sleeping pill that a TV commercial brings her. Her aims may harmonize with those of the pharmaceutical company and the ad agency; but only because the kind of life she leads, which is integrally bound up with TV advertising and the circulation of commodities, has given her money problems, anxiety at work, rebellious kids, and other experiences she doesn't want, all of which add up to insomnia. In a world made up of such situations it seems almost pointless to ask in a broad way what the function of advertising is.[2]

In this situation it helps to look back. Like mind and body, mass culture and advanced capitalism evolved together. By going back, we can consider what needs led some to produce and others to consume mass culture in the first place, and how that culture in turn opened up some avenues for social and personal development while closing off others. In this way it is possible to pry apart the fusion of cause and effect that we see whenever we look about us: the advertiser can sell Bill Black an image of himself as a carefree male (lost with his buddies in West Virginia, but here's a place we can get steaks and Löwenbrau), because he has already learned from a million other commercials to fill vacancies in his life through commodities, because advertisers have long since inscribed that nexus on his mind, because *they* have to expand sales to cope with the productive capacity that manufacturers have achieved partly by making Bill's job mechanical, which in turn makes him long for autonomy and market-free social relations, which desire has over decades been fixed to an image of the home as a place of care and refuge, which image in turn drew him into marriage with impossible hopes, and the burden of these hopes on his wife, along with her own ad-inflated aspiration to be superwoman, has made her resentful and no fun to be with. . . . And so on and on.

Of course there was never a bright day in September when some Edison of the marketplace invented all these connections and changed our society from traditional to modern. And there is no moment in the past to which we can look for an uncontaminated cause and a newborn effect. But it's my contention that causes, effects, needs, and strategies show themselves more plainly in times of rapid emergence than in times of elaboration and refinement. Broadcasting is a routine fact of our lives now, and alternatives to the technology and the social relations embedded in it are unimaginable, even though we see their pliability as television supplements radio, as cable companies challenge networks, as interactive TV emerges over the horizon. But in the early 1920s, nothing about the forms, technologies, uses, and power relations of broadcasting was settled, and everyone could see that a new shuffling of the social deck was in progress, with battles to be won and lost. I hope to find such clarity about mass culture, more broadly, by looking at an earlier time when some of its main structures and processes were initiated through a ten- or fifteen-year period of intense change.

One more caveat: even a satisfying answer to the questions, Why did mass culture appear at the end of the last century? and To what conflicts and needs was its appearance a reply? will not tell us what mass culture does now, any more than discovering the first meaning of a word tells us what that word means now. I hope to avoid the etymological fallacy. But by returning to a foundational moment one may at least strip from cause and function the obscuring shroud of dailiness, and see the appearance of mass culture as the result of particular human efforts to negotiate difficulties and seize opportunities. Perhaps we can see, too, what structural changes in society created those difficulties and opportunities. If so, we can consider why societies like ours have mass culture, in the only sense of *why* that is intelligible to me: one that refers us to the social process through which people create lives, relations, and institutions, of a particular kind.

Now I had better pause to designate what I perceive to be the constituent elements of "mass culture". Nothing original, here: I have in mind experiences or products like movies, top-forty radio, hit records, network TV shows, videos, daily newspapers, mass circulation magazines, major sporting contests, best selling books, and advertisements in various media for name brand products. I hope most readers will find the list unsurprising, and agree that this is approximately what they mean by "mass culture," too. If not, we can walk in step anyhow, so long as they recognize the phenomena I've listed as belonging together in a grasp-able and significant category, whatever they would prefer to call it.

Some, let me explicitly acknowledge, prefer the term "popular cul-ture," and the difference is more than terminological: it expresses conflicting emphases, traditions of analysis, and political outlooks. In my view each term points to truths as well as distortions. "Mass culture" rightly signals the homogenization, the overriding of local and subcultural distinctions, that has accompanied the expansion of media in our century, and rightly implies the power of the culture industries to shape audiences and groups of consumers. It wrongly implies a passivity and a static uniformity of audiences, and connotes a snobbish disparage-ment of popular tastes, or at worst of the people themselves. "Popular culture" restores the respect withdrawn by the other term; it credits popularity as authentic (not cynically imposed from above), and rightly implies a more active role for audiences in choosing and interpreting entertainments. But it erases the stark inequality inherent in late-twentieth-century cultural production, and often implies a politically mystifying celebration of marketplace democracy. Neither term is ade-quate. I choose "mass culture" because I want to keep questions of production and power in the foreground, and because the wrong impli-cations of the term seem to me less disabling than those of its alternative. I hope to give the popular its due, along the way, and carry forward my analysis without the condescension and paralyzing pessimism that too often attend its controlling idea.

Now, a definition: mass culture in societies like this one includes vol-untary experiences, produced by a relatively small number of specialists, for millions across the nation to share, in similar or identical form, either simultaneously or nearly so; with dependable frequency; mass culture shapes habitual audiences, around common needs or interests, and it is made for profit.

Each part of this definition both responds to and creates difficulties. I will comment briefly on them, both for the sake of clarity and to lay the groundwork for my attempt to date the emergence of national mass culture in the United States.

1. *Voluntary experiences*: I distinguish this concept of culture from a more anthropological one that would encompass the use of designer jeans, Whoppers and Big Macs, mini-vans, development homes – types of commodities that we *must* purchase in one brand or another to be fed, clothed, sheltered, and transported. I do not mean to dismiss, but only to bracket, questions of the way mass culture itself endows our consumption of necessities with freedom (spurious or not), so that each of us is to experience vistas of choice and self-definition whenever we buy clothes or fast food. Nor do I deny the converse: the element of determination

behind every "choice" to watch a particular TV program, buy the *National Enquirer* rather than the *Wall Street Journal*, listen to the news, or whatever. My use of the rather unsatisfactory term "voluntary" is meant only to mark off a category of *entertainment* from other activities of social reproduction.

2. *Produced by a relatively small number of specialists*: I exclude street games, gossip, square dancing, joke-telling, poker, jogging, smoking marijuana, even Mardi Gras in New Orleans – all those activities that people generate themselves, more or less independently of the market, on their own schedules, and in their own way. Mass culture comes at us from a distance, produced by strangers.

3. *For millions across the nation to share*: please allow some slack here. The point is not to explicate "mass" by setting an arbitrary minimum figure for size of audience. Clearly a particular Indians–White Sox game on a cold day in April instances mass culture even if it is not nationally televised, and only 750 fans show up. Motorcycle magazines belong to mass culture even if none of them has a million readers. My intent is to exclude genres like chamber music concerts and socialist newspapers whose total regular audience is small, as well as purely local phenomena like the Middletown, Connecticut sidewalk sale or the use of access channels on cable TV. Some vagueness at the boundaries won't hurt, so long as we are agreed about the central experiences of national mass culture.

4. *In similar or identical form*: Rap, yes; Christmas, no. (Or not yet.) This feature of mass culture is what gives it its centripetal, mythic function, making it a universal medium within national boundaries and increasingly across them.

5. *Either simultaneously, or nearly so*: perhaps over a twenty-year period, a million students read *Paradise Lost*, but that doesn't make it mass culture. Innumerable categories within the discourse of mass culture emphasize this simultaneity: the news, the top story, the celebrity, the smash hit, the best seller list, the top forty, the ten worst dressed women, the player of the week. Mass culture projects itself as a sequence of intense present moments, each filled with a number of noteworthy persons and events about which "everyone" knows.

6. *With dependable frequency*: the Challenger disaster was not itself mass culture, though of course TV coverage of it – "news special" – manifested one of the standard genres of mass culture. The dynamic of mass culture demands steady audiences, reassembled daily, weekly, or monthly – or, as with moviegoers and the readership for best sellers, irregularly but often. (The drive toward periodicity invades even these areas, with shows like "Tuesday at the Movies" on TV, and with book clubs; some popular genres of book are sold mainly on a schedule, to regular consumers: one subscribes to a series of romances, or eagerly awaits the appearance of the fifteenth Stephen King novel.)

7. *Mass culture shapes habitual audiences*: the producers' aim is to make

sure that the same audience *will* be there for tomorrow's episode of "General Hospital" or the next issue of *Newsweek*.

8. *Around common needs or interests*: this holds true especially for those productions that take their profit from advertising, and must guarantee delivery of skiers or stereo connoisseurs or beer-drinkers to advertisers of particular commodities; more generally, they must deliver an audience with the right "demographics." But it applies also to media like movies and books, where much hype is generated to bring back addicts of the supernatural or of gothic romance, time after time. It is important to note that, from the point of view of those who *make* mass culture, our only significant common needs are those that might be channeled into purchases.

9. *And it is made for profit*: in other words, my definition excludes phenomena like university education and the Catholic mass.

Let me repeat: the point of a definition like this one is not to dispute other people's categories or labels, nor to settle substantive questions by fiat. I wish only to be as clear as I can about the subject of this book, in an area filled with terminological variety and conceptual overlap. Of course I do also hope to have marked off an area of human activity that readers will recognize as a unified field, not the result of intellectual gerrymandering. And I hope I have succeeded in specifying, through the definition, features of mass culture that are truly distinctive rather than incidental. I mean the definition to be perspicuous, in pointing toward fruitful questions about important matters – more like "rational animal" than like "featherless biped," as a definition of "human being." And I mean it to indicate an area of experience that is recognizably contemporary, so that one may also find a time in the past when it did not exist, and a time when it came into being.

A time when it did not exist: I have encountered no claim that mass culture arose in the US before the end of the eighteenth century. To be sure, historians of particular cultural forms are fond of pushing back to firsts. James Playsted Wood traces advertising to street cries of the Greeks, "thousands of years ago."[3] Frank Presbrey says that Babylonian merchants used these techniques, and even entertains the possibility that they inscribed ads in stone. And he identifies as the first printed advertisement in English a poster by Caxton, offering for sale a set of rules for the conduct of the clergy at Easter.[4] Less ambiguously, the first book to be printed in the American colonies appeared in 1640, the first newspaper in 1690, the first magazine in 1741. But for many decades after even the last of these dates, there was nothing in the colonies or the new Republic that distantly resembled a modern mass culture.

It will be worthwhile to pause for a few comments on this time – "before" – to understand what then filled the structural position into which mass culture has since moved. The list of activities itself, that constituted entertainment for colonists in villages and small towns, is unsurprising. They sang, fiddled, danced. They did competitive and semi-competitive sports: foot racing, horse racing, shooting at the mark, hunting, fishing, wrestling, boxing, cudgelling, cricket, football. There were the quieter pleasures of riding, boating, sleighing, skating, and the rougher, tavern sports of bear baiting and cock fighting, along with cards, dice, backgammon, billiards, bowling. More rarely, a traveling wagon show (ancestor of the circus) would come through, and occasionally a traveling musician, juggler, acrobat, tightrope walker, or keeper of some exotic animal.[5]

Except for this last group of entertainments, none was staged by a "professional," or involved payment. Some of the others implied a separation of performers or contestants from the audience, but that division was only temporary, as fiddlers, racers, boxers melted back into the farm and village population when the event was over. The people organized their own recreations, and participated in them as neighbors.

Note, too, that many of the activities were closely related to work, and to common skills of survival. Hunting and fishing were productive labors, carried on in a sociable form. Boating, riding, horse racing and sleighing were techniques of work carried on apart from a productive goal. Foot racing and the sports of personal combat displayed strength and quickness developed through daily life, though to a specialized and unproductive purpose. The fissure between work and play had opened only a bit.

Furthermore, much of this recreation took place in the context of actual work – that part of work that called for cooperation beyond the individual farm and family. When people joined for barn raisings, house raisings, sheep shearings, and log rollings, they would stay for dancing and sports. In some such gatherings, the work itself was organized as a kind of game: at corn huskings, for instance, a young man who found a red ear could kiss whichever young woman he fancied. And of course fairs, where country people gathered to display, trade, and sell what they had produced, were the prime settings for a variety of recreations. Much entertainment took place as an almost spontaneous overflow of the energies of social production.

Civic and religious ceremonies provided most of the other occasions for public entertainment. In New England, for instance, the institution of lecture day – the mid-week sermon – persisted well into the eighteenth century, along with many religious holidays (though not so many as in Britain). Unlike the Sabbath, a lecture day carried with it no proscription of secular pleasure, once the sermon ended. Nor did election day, or court days, or training days (when the men of the district collected to drill and march as a militia). Recreation was embedded in such recognizably social functions; in spite of the constant and mainly futile objections raised by the Puritans, play was less a threat to the

religious life than an adjunct to social reproduction and communal solidarity. To be sure, a kind of entertainment that split off from basic
activities of work and citizenship had begun to develop in the larger
towns; there were some theatricals and concerts that drew a clear line
between performers and audience. These also helped to define class
lines, as did horse racing and the fox hunt in the southern colonies, and
assembly balls in north and south. But for the most part, entertainment
existed in the context of a whole way of life, and of what may well be
called "organic community."[6]

Newspapers and magazines were a negligible part of this culture.
There were but ninety-two of the former in 1790,[7] and no more then
seven of the latter.[8] Their circulations were small, and they tended to be
unstable enterprises, especially magazines. Books were another matter:
by the end of the eighteenth century, well over a thousand new titles
(books and pamphlets) appeared each year, and even by mid century
some came out in printings of several thousand. Until about the time of
the Revolution, however, most belonged to the earnest discourses of
religion and politics; they were not meant to be entertaining. And ordinary people read few of them: reading was for the Bible, *The Pilgrim's
Progress*, and a few other texts that one might live by. Culture was immediate, oral, participatory.

That began to change fairly early in the nineteenth century; people
entered into experiences that had some of the characteristics of mass
culture. For the first time, thousands of people who did not know each
other came together as audiences. In sport, for example, a crowd estimated at more than 50,000 watched the famous race between Eclipse
and Sir Henry, in 1823. The next year, a similar crowd lined New York
harbor to watch a boat race for a $1000 prize. Foot racing became a pro-
fessional sport, with paid admission, and in 1835 a much publicized
contest to see if any runner could run ten miles in less than an hour
drew twenty or thirty thousand people.[9] But sporting events were not formally organized and regulated, repeated daily or weekly for large paying
audiences, and surrounded with an aura of printed publicity and statistics until at least a decade after 1876, when the National Baseball League
was founded. These early spectacles were just that: more comparable to
the public feats of an Evel Knievel than to the continuous marketing of
events to fans that marks our century.

In fact, one might characterize most large public entertainments
around mid century as spectacles, thus emphasizing the way they stood
out from the fabric of daily life rather than merging into its pattern.
Many were irregular experiences billed as the greatest ever, within some
category, and the appeal was to people's sense of the extraordinary or
unique. Barnum's American Museum (opened in New York in 1842)
epitomized this kind of attraction, bringing under one roof 600,000
exhibits and acts whose only uniting theme was their oddity: famous

paintings, giants and midgets, serpents, George Washington's nurse, white elephants. Every visitor to New York had to take in this wonder; everyone in the country knew about it.

The American Museum was there every day; many events happened only once, or just once in a given place, or once a year. Thousands came together to watch balloon ascensions, Fourth of July displays, circuses. There was little distinction between art and entertainment. (This line would later be drawn with care, effort, and money by the patrons of art museums and symphonies, the studied culture of class.) Jenny Lind's mid-century tour drew multitudes who would never have heard of her had it not been for Barnum's hype. (Her ninety-five concerts grossed a total of $712,161.)[10] Tens of thousands met her boat at the wharf and milled around her hotel. There was a brisk market in souvenirs and commodities named after or associated with her. Her visit was the prototype of the sensational, never-to-be-matched event.

Scheduled entertainments, like theater, also ran to the spectacular. Shakespeare, farces, and melodramas mixed with acrobatic perform-ances, feats of strength, and equestrian dramas. And the regular repertoire itself was sold to audiences increasingly through the celebrity of famous actors and actresses: Kean, the Kembles, the Booths. Even highly stereotyped performances such as melodramas and minstrel shows offered themselves as novel, bizarre, sensational.[11]

There is no question that Americans began to learn the role of a mass audience through what might be called the Age of Barnum. They learned to pay for amusement, learned to expect that it would be pro-vided by professionals (and strangers), learned to accept publicity as the forerunner and framer of a major event, learned that they *must* have certain experiences – or at least know about them – to feel adroit in the medium of the social. They developed a vocabulary of the new and the celebrated. But this was not yet a national culture, and, more importantly, it came in staccato bursts of the extraordinary, rather than in measured, formulaic portions delivered to the neighborhood theater, the sports park, or the home itself. Also, these were face-to-face experiences, the audience all in one place, rather than dispersed and forming a crowd only through the mediation of the printing press or an electronic impulse.

What, then, of the print media? Without doubt, a transformation of newspapers and their place in the life of the nation occurred in the 1830s. Even before that, the small-town weekly had integrated itself into the lives of most Americans; Robert Gross notes that in 1827 the *Yeoman's Gazette* of Concord, Massachusetts had a circulation of 1100 in and around a town whose population was only about 1500. By 1840 there were 1400 of these papers around the country.[12] But a production resem-bling the modern daily emerged only after 1830, and did so in a dramatic way, much as happened later with the magazine.

Most urban dailies sold for six cents, up to that time, and sold a few hundred copies, chiefly to merchants and other affluent people, whose political views they represented. In 1833, a compositor named Benjamin Day hit upon the idea of bringing out his *New York Sun* at a penny; it was soon followed by the *Transcript* and by James Gorden Bennett's *New York Herald*. These papers revolutionized the business and brought together a new readership, as one can tell from the numbers: in 1830 the circulation of all eleven New York dailies amounted to about 25,000; by 1835 the three leading penny papers alone sold 44,000 copies a day. As penny papers sprang up around the country, the national circulation of all dailies went from 78,000 in 1830 to 300,000 in 1840.[13]

This boom derived from more than simply the drop in price. Day, Bennett, and the rest of the new editors sharply altered the nature of the product and its place in readers' lives. For one thing, they were the first to collect and convey news itself, in the modern sense – the first to send reporters out on beats, to keep track of crime and high society, to acknowledge the daily life of the city. Moreover, they largely divorced themselves from the political factions whose mouthpieces newspapers had been, proclaiming their independence and groping toward what would eventually become the practices of objectivity. Most readers ceased to consult newspapers primarily for business and editorial opinion, and went there instead for a conspectus on themselves and their immediate world. The ads, too, had a different appeal, speaking to readers as consumers of clothing, patent medicines, and the like, rather than as businessmen who needed to know about the arrivals of ships. Naturally, with the lower selling price of the papers, ads also paid a much greater share of costs. And, since the new editors had hit on the idea of selling readers to advertisers, they also aggressively pursued new readers: most strikingly, they sent newsboys to hawk papers in the streets, whereas earlier editors had depended on subscriptions. The newspaper itself became part of the spectacle of city life.

In all these ways it drew closer to a form we would recognize. Yet it still belonged to a different epoch. A total circulation of 300,000 in 1840 represented a quantum leap, but that still amounted to just one daily for every 57 people in the country. Most never saw or had a chance to buy one; this was a phenomenon of the city. And it was local in another sense, too: Though by the 1850s a few papers (Greeley's *Tribune*, the *Springfield Republican*) had readers scattered around the nation, most did not circulate far from home. And their content was different from place to place, aside from some of the political news. A reader in Baltimore saw none of the same text as a reader in Boston, and very likely none of the same ads.[14] Physically, these papers were drab: four pages of unbroken columns, with no large headlines and no graphics except for tiny, stylized logos in the ads. They made no appeal to the eye.

The developments that formed the modern newspaper and made it a national medium took place gradually over the next five decades. By 1860, some stories from papers like the *Herald* and the *Tribune* were reprinted around the country, as were dispatches from Civil War battle-grounds. The development of the telegraph after 1840 and the formation of the Associated Press in 1848 prepared the way for this spread of identical news. Journalism began to emerge as a profession, with its own practices and organizations, and its ethic of empiricism. Syndication of features became common in the 1880s; comics arrived in the 1890s. That was the first time Americans had available in the format of the newspaper a homogeneous national experience of *the* news, of opinion, of household advice, and of entertainment.

Gradually, through this period, the paper became modern in other ways too. Ad agencies began selling space to clients in "lists" of dailies from all over, so that national advertising became feasible. Advertisers were also responsible for constant pressure on the "column rule"[15] and for ingenious schemes to draw the eye of the reader. Publishers finally realized that their product, too, could sell itself visually, and by the 1890s halftone reproductions of photographs had supplanted engravings in this effort. Hearst and Pulitzer capitalized on and extended these prac-tices, along with the "yellow" journalism that made the newspaper unequivocally a form of entertainment, whatever else it was. Finally, it was only in the 1890s that advertising began to provide more than half the revenue for newspapers, and that ads for national brands took a prominent place alongside classifieds and ads for local merchants and department stores.[16] In short, the newspaper became a channel of national mass culture about the same time as did the magazine, in spite of a longer and richer evolution.

Anyone wishing to identify a form of national mass culture well before this time could make the strongest case for books (though it is a bit anomalous to imagine mass culture existing in just one medium). Such a case would not have to depend upon the presence and regular use of a Bible in most households, supplemented by a few other texts central to the old, theocentric culture. Nor would it have to rest on the almost uni-versal use of a household standby such as Webster's *Speller*, which had sold 30 million copies by 1860, nor even on the phenomenon of *Uncle Tom's Cabin*, which sold 300,000 within a year of its 1852 publication, 3 million before the Civil War, and perhaps more hardbound copies than any new book before or since. Rather, one could note that there was a surge of cheap, paperback publishing after 1841, when the weekly paper, *New World*, brought out a supplement that included the entire first vol-ume of a Charles Lever novel, for 50 cents. A rival paper, *Brother Jonathan*, quickly published the same novel at 25 cents, and a race was on that led to sales of many novels in newspaper format at 12½ cents, and some for as little as 6 cents. Major book publishers like Harper's met the compe-tition with paperbacks sold almost as cheaply, and for a while dozens of pirated novels by Scott, Bulwer, Balzac, Hugo, Sue, Dickens, and the like, as well as some by American writers, were available at prices anyone could afford. Few sold as many as 30,000 copies, and the original paper-back entrepreneurs went out of business within a few years. But the cheap book was now established, and a new readership for books created, so that publishing exploded as an industry through the rest of the 1840s and the 1850s:[17] the value of books made and sold in the United States tripled from 1840 to 1856, and, given the drop in price, the number of copies sold must have increased far more than that.[18] Over succeeding decades, a number of entrepreneurs exploited the techniques of inex-pensive production and the presence of a large audience habituated to reading. The famous dime novels began appearing in the 1860s, and the following two decades brought a flood of cheap "libraries" – that is, series of reprints – selling for anything from 10 to 50 cents a volume. In 1877 there were fourteen libraries, and the most frenetic publisher in this format, George Munro, was bringing out a novel a day.[19]

Nineteenth-century book publishing resembled modern mass cul-ture in other ways than sheer volume of production and low cost. People who liked a particular kind of experience could repeat it regularly and indefinitely. Individual authors kept their fans satisfied with repeat per-formances, across the cultural spectrum: Cooper's novels were selling 40,000 copies a year by 1860, and Mrs E.D.E.N. Southworth, the most popular novelist of the century, turned out fifty or so romances begin-ning in 1854, almost all of which sold over 100,000 copies. The other "scribbling women" were not far behind, and writers like Longfellow and Irving, remembered more generously today, appeared in innumerable editions that sold well. Books were everywhere available: before the Civil War there were 3000 booksellers, and after it, books began to make their way into department stores and other outlets (often at discount).[20] Subscription sales developed into an almost equally large system of dis-tribution, reminding one of book clubs and of series like Hawthorn Romances today. Some novels were expensively advertised, creating a modern sort of cultural imperative. And most books with large sales were novels (in many years, more than 1000 new and old novels were published): this was unequivocally a form of entertainment. Finally, books had almost the same material appearance in the mid nineteenth century as they do today.

For all that, one might almost as convincingly hold that book pub-lishing was the last culture industry to attain modernity. Not until after World War II did it become part of the large corporate sector, and adopt the practices of publicity and marketing characteristic of monopoly capital. Throughout the nineteenth century and well into the twentieth, publishing houses were either family businesses operating (at least, to hear them tell it) more for the love of books than for profit, or fly-by-night opportunists, or a mixture of both. Most ran their enterprises in a haphazard and highly individualistic fashion, and the history of cheap publishing can be viewed as little more than a series of coups and bankruptcies. Price wars periodically racked the industry, along with intense and ingenious races to be first on the streets with a new book. Distribution was chaotic, with leadership sometimes assumed by the publishers themselves, but often by wholesalers, jobbers, printers, local or regional correspondents, bookstores, even department stores buying out random lots of surplus books and selling them at a few cents apiece. Equally chaotic relations between publishers and authors marked the period, running from virtual slave labor to the payment of huge advances and royalties of over 20 percent. It was not uncommon for less well known authors to have to pay for or subsidize the costs of production; on the other hand, some famous authors like Longfellow *chose* to buy and keep the plates of their books, thus maintaining full control. Finally, nineteenth-century publishing was one of the few capitalist industries grounded in piracy.

I think it fairest to adopt neither of the two positions, but recognize that book publishing went through extremely uneven development for over a century. It achieved some of the methods of mass culture early, but failed to consolidate them into a stable and controlled enterprise with enduring relations to a mass public. The practice which, more than any other, made books a mass medium was the large-scale production of cheap paperbacks, and that came to an abrupt *end* in the 1890s, just as an integrated mass culture emerged.[21] Books were out of step with the rest of the culture industry: a telling statistic is that, across the entire period from 1850 to 1914, which surely embraces the rise of mass culture, book publishing's share of all manufacturing value declined from 1 percent to one-fourth of 1 percent, even as it was quadrupling in absolute value.[22] This makes sense: books came first, and for many decades they held the largest share of the cultural market; but when other forms of cultural production (newspapers, magazines, spectator sports) transformed themselves, and new ones (movies, records) appeared, books were crowded into a smaller corner of leisure time and of the market.

But I do want to claim that in the final fifteen years of the nineteenth century – the inaugural moment, I argue, of our national mass culture – book publishing, too, underwent some changes that brought it into greater conformity with the other modern culture industries. It undertook practices of rationalization and control, efforts to rein in the anarchic competition of earlier decades. Publishers gradually learned how to stabilize the sales effort. They acquired their own staffs of traveling salesmen, and greatly increased both the amount and the flamboyance of their advertising. They began to shape their product and create its market, rather than just publishing what appealed to them and hoping for the best. As a result, hardback sales of 100,000 and more became common in the 1890s. Given the economics of publishing, successes like these were necessary to cover the inevitable failures and to make substantial profits. Publishers concentrated their efforts more on achieving the big hit, and less on grinding out series of cheap books. These efforts were rewarded with marketing sensations like *Trilby, Ben Hur, Black Beauty, Freckles, Quo Vadis, David Harum,* and *The Red Badge of Courage.* This new emphasis in the industry was punctuated by the first regular publication of regional best seller lists in the *Bookman* in 1895, and national best seller lists in 1897.

At the same time, publishers were accepting, and even creating, checks on the cutthroat competition that had long characterized their business. Many of them supported a stronger copyright law, one that gave protection to foreign books for the first time, and thus eliminated the main source of free raw material for paperback publishers. It passed in 1891, finally ending piracy, and making for more durable and amiable relations with authors. They also reluctantly began dealing with literary agents, who first appeared at this time and whose intervention helped regularize relations with authors. It was in the 1890s, too, that publishers increasingly generated ideas for books themselves and pressed writers to execute their plans, rather than just competing for finished manuscripts. Most significantly, perhaps, publishers recognized the need to cooperate; by 1900 the leaders of the industry had formed the American Publishers' Association, and were encouraging retailers to form the American Booksellers' Association, which organized in 1901. The two groups immediately agreed on a system of retail pricing, of discounting to the trade, and of what we now know as remaindering, designed to end the fratricidal price competition that had long made the business so risky. This agreement failed, mainly because it did not include department stores, but a key principle of advanced capitalism had been established, and would eventually take hold.[23] In this context, the decline of paperback publishing in the 1890s can be seen as part of a successful attempt by major houses to get rid of ill-mannered entrepreneurial competitors. Book publishing was now a smaller part of the cultural environment, but it had acquired many of the characteristic forms and practices of a twentieth-century culture industry.

Few of the ambiguities and reversals that mark the development of book publishing obscure the birth of modern magazines. Their transformation was dramatic, and obvious to all; that is one reason for taking them as paradigmatic in this study. A typical magazine of the 1830s, to pick a starting point, claimed a circulation measured in hundreds, for a few pages of solid columns of print, with few or no ads. These magazines reached audiences that were at most regional; they rarely made a profit, and they usually died young. There were no national magazines at all before 1850. Even after the railroad linked the two coasts in 1869, and after the Postal Act of 1879 made cheap distribution possible, magazines were not a main feature of American culture, and they barely resembled their counterparts of the late twentieth century. Yet by 1900 they very much did, as I have indicated in my sketch of *Munsey's*. And "everyone" (I'll gloss those quotation marks later) was reading them. Any aficionado of historical discontinuities could delight in the events of 1893; even the sober historians of American magazines feel compelled to call it a "revolution."[24]

And although I think it bears a different kind of scrutiny than they have given it, 1893 was indeed a year when something happened. At that time the leading respectable monthlies – *Harper's, Century, Atlantic,* and a few others – sold for a quarter or 35 cents, and had circulations of no more than 200,000. In the middle of the panic of 1893, S.S. McClure brought out his new monthly at an unprecedented 15 cents. John Brisben Walker, editor of the old *Cosmopolitan*, quickly dropped his price to 12½ cents. And in October, with much hoopla, Frank Munsey cut the price of his faltering monthly from a quarter to a dime. Its circulation went from 40,000 that month to 200,000 the following February to 500,000 in April, and to a circulation that Munsey called the largest in the world by 1898. These entrepreneurs – Munsey most consciously – had hit upon a formula of elegant simplicity: identify a large audience that is not hereditarily affluent or elite, but that is getting on well enough, and that has cultural aspirations; give it what it wants; build a huge circulation; sell lots of advertising space at rates based on that circulation; sell the magazine at a price *below* the cost of production, and make your profit on ads. An unnamed publisher is reported as saying, with only slight exaggeration, "If I can get a circulation of 400,000 I can afford to give my magazine away to anyone who will pay the postage."[25]

But if this is the economic principle behind the mass magazine of our century (and up until recently, it has been), the decision to fix 1893 as the critical moment is only a narrative convenience. It credits McClure and Munsey with too much, and makes a development that could only have occurred over time seem instantaneous and magical. I would venture to say that no major form of cultural production ever springs at once from the brain of a single person: television plagiarized from radio and the movies; radio took its content from newspapers, vaudeville, and the concert hall; moviemakers drew upon a variety of entertainments like the photograph, stereopticon, and magic lantern, which appealed through their re-presentation of real life. Munsey and McClure also fused and elaborated practices that were well established before 1893.

For instance, the elite monthlies had earlier concocted the blend of genres that editors of the 1890s adapted for a wider audience: fiction, articles about the famous, historical pieces, cultural articles and reviews, and so on. Furthermore, some of them had long since abandoned their aristocratic scruples about advertising. The *Atlantic* began to take a few ads as early as 1860. Soon after *Scribner's Monthly* was founded, in 1870, its business manager, Roswell Smith, actively sought ads:

> The publishers of *Scribner's Monthly* will insert in each number of the magazine certain pages devoted to advertisements of a character likely to interest magazine readers. These will not increase the postage, while they will add materially to the ability of the publishers to render their magazine readable and attractive. The press of advertisements upon our first number shows how quickly the claims of the new monthly upon the business public are recognized. Our edition will be very large, and it will have a national circulation. It is now well understood that a first-class popular magazine furnishes to all men who seek a national market the very best medium for advertising that exists. It is both widely distributed to the prosperous and intelligent classes of society, and carefully read and preserved.[26]

Smith's claims were exaggerated but prescient, especially in his understanding that a "national market" was coming into existence, and that manufacturers might want to pay extra for the attention of a readership grouped by class – "prosperous and intelligent." *Scribner's* did not in fact attract a lot of advertising for a while; this was an idea whose time had not yet come. But after the magazine changed its name to the *Century* in 1881, its ad pages multiplied. This example shattered the reserve of some other class monthlies, *Harper's* in particular, which averaged about ten pages of ads in 1885, but about seventy-five pages in 1890, in which year it passed the *Century*.[27] Munsey could not have missed the point.

A second forerunner was the popular weekly. Usually spoken of as a "paper" rather than a magazine (and printed in newspaper format, though on better paper), it too found advertising quite acceptable. Advertising in *Harper's Weekly*, for instance, went from about half a quarto page per issue in its first year (1857), to a page in 1862, to two pages in 1867, and three pages in 1872. The weeklies also pioneered display ads: the 1 June 1872 issue of *Harper's Weekly* (circulation about 150,000) included pictorial ads for lawn mowers, corsets, furniture, jewelry, a toy engine, statuary, a freezer, a carriage, roofing, shotguns, engines, and sewing machines.

By the end of the 1880s, *Youth's Companion* (circulation about 400,000) had in effect an advertising department, which got up full-page pictorial ads for presentation to manufacturers, many of whom went along with the new idea. Most famously, it sold to Mellin's baby food the plan for a full-page and full-color ad, a lithograph of Perrault's "The Awakening of Cupid": both the color and the price ($14,000) were firsts.[28] This movement toward the visual characterized the whole content of the magazine, as well as that of other major weeklies like *Frank Leslie's Illustrated Newspaper*. There was apparently an insatiable appetite among subscribers for engravings of Civil War scenes; Leslie maintained the visual emphasis after the war, with many full-page engravings per issue. The balance began to shift in some of these periodicals, from pictures as secondary to the text (illustrations) to pictures as the heart of a feature, with the text as a gloss. Walker's *Cosmopolitan* was a leader in adding photoengravings to the visual display; Munsey developed this innovation into virtually the equivalent of the modern photo-essay.

The "mail-order journals" also anticipated Munsey's idea, and probably influenced it. So ephemeral were they that few libraries in the country have preserved any of them, and my supplier of old magazines, who had three warehouses full, had not heard of even the major titles. Thus I rely on Mott's definition of this genre: "a yearly subscription rate of twenty-five to fifty cents, poor printing (usually in the folio size), cheap serial fiction, and varied but undistinguished household departments."[29] The first of these was the *People's Literary Companion*, started in 1869 by E.C. Allen, who made Augusta, Maine a center for such publications. By the 1890s there were apparently hundreds of them; Allen himself put out twelve. They contributed two ideas to the composite of the modern magazine. First, not only were they cheap, but the publishers spent little effort soliciting renewals, preferring to continue sending the magazines free to one-time subscribers, and in effect selling this list to the advertisers who paid the freight.[30] Hence editorial content was completely subordinate to the advertising relationship. Second, these magazines apparently went to millions of people who could not have afforded and would not have liked the class monthlies. Allen and his competitors discovered that there was truly a mass audience for magazines: *Comfort*, the leader among them, carried perhaps a million "subscribers" through the 1890s and into this century. Munsey obviously did not consider it a monthly magazine when he made his boast, but he seems to have learned from it, in his definition of "the people" (see chapter 1).

If the credit given to Walker, McClure, and Munsey ignores periodicals directed at a working class audience, it also ignores those produced for women. Not only had *Godey's Lady's Book* been the circulation leader at mid century (followed closely by *Peterson's*, another women's magazine); it had latched onto a central ideology of that time – progress – in a version tailored to the advancement of women. It took up the cause of labor-saving devices like the sewing machine, anesthesia, women doctors, exercise and education for women. It was prettily illustrated, with engravings hand-colored by an army of 150 employees. Still, it was a crude production by later standards, and hampered by the primitive infrastructure of the society; its publication tended to be irregular, and its arrival even more so as it was shipped by boat and stage and vulnerable to bad weather as well as bad roads.[31]

These difficulties had long been surmounted in 1883, when Cyrus H.

Curtis decided to transform the women's pages of his *Tribune and Farmer* into a separate magazine called the *Ladies' Home Journal*. A combination of brilliant editorial conception (executed for a while by Mrs Curtis, then, after 1889, by Edward Bok) and vigorous advertising pushed the circulation of the *Journal* to 200,000 in 1885, 400,000 in 1888, and 600,000 in 1891. It sold for a nickel until 1889, then for the same ten cents, or a dollar a year, that Munsey "hit on" in 1893. It welcomed advertising, and displayed it handsomely, not all on separate pages at beginning and end, but set in amongst the editorial contents.[32] It may have been the first magazine to change its cover design with each issue (in the early 1890s), thus signalling the contradictory fusion of novelty and sameness which has since been crucial to the ideological subtext of magazines, and of mass culture in general.

The *Journal* not only took the lead in perfecting the format and economic formula of the modern magazine, but also approximated it in editorial content by 1893. Munsey and the others did not regard the *Journal* as a magazine; it and its editor were the butt of many jokes and lampoons during this period. This ridicule had a basis in both gender and class. Through its early years, the *Journal* gave its audience practical household advice, moral counsel of the Dear Abby sort, and instruction in how to be respectable. Readers and editors of the cultural monthlies found this blend embarrassingly intimate, lowbrow, and feminine. And indeed, the *Journal* did frankly address its audience as one that needed counsel in matters taken for granted at homes where the affinity was for *Harper's* or the *Atlantic*. It penetrated into areas of personal and social concern previously kept apart from Culture in the medium of magazines, if not in other sectors of American society. But Curtis, and especially Bok, understood that the kind of propriety (read, class standing) they nourished through instruction in fashion, home design, and entertaining, as well as through departments like "Side Talks with Girls," needed the counterpoint of literary culture. At first, the latter was difficult to bring into the magazine, since recognized writers did not want to be associated with the former. But Curtis inveigled writers like Louisa May Alcott, Elizabeth Stuart Phelps, Mrs A.D.T. Whitney, and Will Carleton into contributing, and advertised their names widely on his "List of Famous Contributors." Bok further extended the list to include Howells, Stockton, Addams, Kipling, Twain, Harte, Jewett, and more than one president of the United States, as well as many artists of note. By the mid nineties, the *Journal* was a previously unimaginable blend of intimate domestic chatter (though it dropped the subtitle, "And Practical Housekeeper" in 1889) and upper middle class literary culture. If one magazine should get more credit than another for discovering the twentieth century, it is the *Ladies' Home Journal*.[33]

What actually happened in 1893, then, was the broadening of a "revolution" already underway. Munsey, McClure, and Walker fused a number of business and editorial practices that were working well enough, but separately. They took from the weeklies the idea of a lively pictorial appearance, from these and a few of the monthlies a willingness to hustle ads and let them be splashy, from the women's magazines and the mail order journals the idea of a very low price that would attract a large audience of people with only a little extra money to spend. Some publishers of magazines from each of these genres had already discovered that such an audience could be delivered to advertisers at prices that would pay a major share of costs. And from the literary monthlies, the entrepreneurs of 1893 took the idea of offering this audience participation in a mainstream of national culture, though they rechanneled that stream in such a way that it no longer implied life membership in an elite club; it was no longer a culture rooted in family, old money, the past.

So there was no spontaneous generation of this mass cultural form, one day in 1893. But, having restored the change to the category of process, rather than invention, I must reemphasize the fact that this process ran its course very quickly, as historical changes go. I would say that there were no modern, mass circulation magazines in 1885, and that by 1900 there were in the neighborhood of twenty – enough to make them a highly visible and much noted cultural phenomenon. The numbers bear out the claim: at the end of the Civil War the total circulation of monthlies seems to have been at most 4 million. It was about 18 million in 1890, and 64 million in 1905. To bring these figures down to scale, in 1865 there may have been one copy of a magazine each month to every ten people in the country. By 1905 there were three copies for every four people, or about four to every household. And for a contrast, while monthly magazine circulation more than tripled between 1890 and 1905, the total circulation of newspapers and weekly periodicals rose only from 36 million to 57 million – the two forms together having less circulation than the monthlies.[34] By this measure, monthly magazines had become the major form of repeated cultural experience for the people of the United States.[35]

Because of that, and because this culture industry took shape so rapidly, the history of monthly magazines can stand as a paradigm case. Such a concentrated development gives focus to the questions with which I began this chapter: Where did mass culture come from? What does it do in and to societies like ours? But I hope I have also made the point that magazines are not otherwise a special case – that the same processes of commercializing the "product," regularizing its availability, and attracting large audiences to it took place also in public entertainments such as sport, newspaper publishing, and book publishing; and that they culminated in modern forms of cultural production at roughly the same time.

By 1900 people in cities could regularly watch "their" ball team play, follow it in the daily papers while keeping up with the news, and buy the latest best-selling novels. They could also go to amusement parks like Coney Island, stop in at a vaudeville house, see the moving pictures, or listen to ragtime on the gramophone – though these latter forms of entertainment would not rival the former for a few more years. I propose that the answers I am able to construct for my original questions, by analyzing the emergence of magazines, will also apply to mass culture in general.

3

Explaining Things

As noted at the beginning of chapter 2, an obviously important but broad, vague, and perhaps misleading question motivated this inquiry: What does mass culture do, in and to societies like ours? I bracketed it, and turned in hopes of simplification to a related question: Where did mass culture come from? But the briefest reflection on possible answers puts simplicity to flight: mass culture sprang from the mind of Edison, or Gutenberg. P.T. Barnum invented it. People needed it when they began to live in cities, and could no longer get entertainment and news face-to-face. The ideal of and popular demand for democracy in a large nation required mass culture. It came about in the course of a natural and inevitable progress toward efficiency and a more various life. The rich and powerful created it to keep workers and poor people amused and submissive. It developed, like everything else in this society, from the search for profit. It moved in to fill the space vacated by faith. It satisfied the need for distraction that arose when most people began to earn their livings through alienated work in factories and offices. All these and many more explanations have had their advocates. Not only that: most have some initial plausibility, and to an extent they are compatible with one another, because they work on different levels of analysis. Do we simply say, then, that mass culture had twenty-two causes, and list them as history textbooks used to list the causes of World War I? If not, how do we decide which ones are important, which minor, which secondary (that is, themselves caused by some primary cause or development), which false, which vacuous, which "merely" poetic, like Yeats's elegant account of the Industrial Revolution:

> Locke sank into a swoon.
> The garden died.
> God took the spinning-jenny
> Out of his side.
> > "Fragments"

All the vexed issues of historical causation (including whether there *is* such a thing) threaten to stop the inquiry before it starts. Such difficulties multiply in part because even the simpler question lacks precision. The practices lumped together as "mass culture" are various, and date from various times. For that reason I tried to identify characteristics shared by all the main forms of contemporary mass culture: an attempt at explication of a widely held, common-sense idea, not at coercive definition. Then, for the rest of the chapter, I scanned US history seeking an emergent form of cultural production and reception that first brought those features together in a working and sustainable process. The mass circulation magazine of the 1890s seemed the most plausible candidate. If so, one can reduce the question of mass culture's origin to more manageable proportions. Over the next few chapters, then, I propose to consider what conjunction of interests, needs, activities, and forces led to the invention and success of the modern magazine industry. An adequate explanation should account for the rapidity of this development and for its occurrence in the 1890s rather than earlier or later, as well as for the dynamics of the new magazine business, the kind of product it made, and the appeal of that product to a large audience. Such an explanation will not necessarily tell much about how mass culture attained its present shape, or about how it works in contemporary society (I return to these matters at the end of the book). Origins do not determine later outcomes. But neither are they inconsequential, as will become clear through the process of explanation itself.

This narrowing of the inquiry defers a host of difficulties for the moment, but not those that beset explanation itself. Does it come down to identifying causes? How can they be isolated from the continuous and infinitely complex stream of historical process? Is every cause not also an effect, every effect a cause of some subsequent effect? How to assign priority and weight? What counts as an explanation? What makes history happen? Although I harbor convictions, hypotheses, hunches, and doubtless prejudices on such matters, I will not advance them now, abstractly, but propose rather to give them gradual articulation while staying close to the concrete material of this study. That is, by considering for a while what historians have actually said in their attempts to explain the rise of the new monthly magazines, I hope to bring some of the broader issues into focus, as well as to simplify matters by discarding some kinds of explanation that don't explain much.

Not that all historians feel the need for explanation. John Tebbel, for example, refers to the emergence of the cheap monthlies as "perhaps the most remarkable phenomenon in the years just before and after the turn of the century,"[1] and lets it go at that, mentioning only the 10-cent price itself and the "liveliness and variety" of the magazines as causes of this "phenomenon." Beyond that, a reader may conclude on his or her own that Tebbel sees the events of the 1890s as part of the march toward a free, critical press which is the general theme of his book.[2]

Likewise, a number of those who write about specific magazines and editors, including those editors who have written about their own lives, say little about underlying causes. Understandably their preoccupation is the achievement of individual genius; to suggest that broader historical forces brought about the rise of magazines would be to diminish the importance of their subjects. Nor do I wish to deny that Bok, McClure, Munsey, George Horace Lorimer (of the *Saturday Evening Post*), and the others had unusual talent, vision, and energy. But a constellation of geniuses in no way explains the growth of the magazine industry at this historical moment. There are people with talent and energy at all times; in the years before 1890, some of them even edited magazines – Frank Leslie, Sarah Josepha Hale (of *Godey's*), Richard Watson Gilder (*Century*), William Dean Howells (*Atlantic*), E.L. Godkin (*Nation*), Allen Thorndike Rice (*North American Review*), to name a wide assortment of them. But neither singly nor collectively did they achieve the mass circulation magazine. An explanation that is available for any change at any time explains no particular change.

The new editors did achieve a new blend of content, even if it was not one whose perfection required genius. They and the historians rightly stress the editorial formulas that turned out to have such a broad appeal. They are unanimous in seeing the prestigious magazines of the 1880s as stodgy, bland, and impersonal, almost as if their editors wanted to repel readers – aside from the few who already belonged to the club – rather than attract them. The new editors found ways to break down this exclusiveness. I have mentioned Munsey's claim that he overcame "monopoly" by going directly to "the people," and others sound this same note. McClure credits his success partly to his youthful experience as a peddler in the Midwest, through which he gained "a very close acquaintance with the people of the small towns and the farming communities, the people who afterward bought *McClure's Magazine*." He had himself become one of "the people," so that later on he could be fairly certain that if he "bought and printed what interested [him]," it would also interest those Midwesterners, who were moreover "just like the people in New York or Boston."[3] Bok, too, has a vision of the audience for a national mass culture; though he speaks of them as "the public," he also feels that he knows them intuitively: "the American public loved a personality," and "the time had come. . . for the editor of some magazine to project his personality through the printed page" as "a real human being who could talk and not merely write on paper." That editor would not make the "grievous mistake" of his predecessors, writing "down" to the public; but would "rightly gauge" his "public psychology," flattering readers by aiming just slightly above what they know they want, speaking to them at once as an intimate and as a cultural leader.[4]

Algernon Tassin, the first of the magazine historians and the only one who wrote about the 1890s from personal memory, emphasizes this immediacy: Bok's "personal note," the "face-to-faceness" of Walker's confessions in *Cosmopolitan* about doings inside the offices of the magazine, and the way the magazines seemed to most Americans to move "closer to contemporary life."[5] Later historians also give credit to the rapport of the new editors with middle class people; Mott, for instance, holds that the editors responded to a "remarkably aggressive drive for self-improvement which characterized middle-class society in this decade,"[6] and no doubt that is a cause of their success. The question remains, though, Why then? Why did they arrive at the strategies of intimacy and improving advice only in the 1890s, if a large readership had been there waiting for the personal note? And where had that readership come from, since it had not earlier presented itself as a field for cultivation by editors and entrepreneurs? To cite tone and content in this way is to refer causation back to the emergence of a new kind of public, and hence to a change in the make-up of the society.

On that, the historians have a little to say, but I don't think it helps much. One explanation routinely invoked sounds plausible, but dissolves on critical scrutiny: that a broadly literate public demanded reading material. To be sure, there can be no print culture for millions unless millions can read. Yet the spread of literacy cannot explain why the magazines of the 1890s grew so fast. It is enough to note that the timing is wrong. In the Northeast, most women and almost all men could read at the beginning of the nineteenth century. Nationwide, basic literacy among white people reached nearly 90 percent by 1850. The increase of another 4.5 percent by 1900 can hardly have contributed greatly to the construction of an audience for magazines.[7] In any case, the social practice of reading – far more significant than the bare ability to read – was notoriously widespread early in the century, and remarked by traveler after traveler from abroad. Local newspapers were a staple of daily culture in the 1820s; in some towns their circulation was nearly universal.[8] And the explosion of the penny press in the next decade shows that the urban population was qualified, in point of literacy, to support a mass print culture long before any national media developed.[9]

A related cause, mentioned almost as a reflex by some of the historians, is the growth of public education. Theodore P. Greene, for instance, who says that the magazines of the 1890s "were obviously reaching entirely new readers" for such periodicals, speaks of the many new high schools established in the 1880s, and of the rapid expansion in their enrollments, as having "prepared the way for magazine-reading," along with the Chautauqua movement, libraries, and self-improvement efforts of all sorts. Yet in 1890 less than 10 percent of the appropriate age group was in high school, and the proportion of high school graduates in the adult population was tiny. Greene's other point – that both the high school movement and the flourishing of adult education "testified to an urge for wider horizons, for greater familiarity with the world and its standards, for needed orientation to a rapidly changing society" which magazines helped to satisfy – is helpful.[10] But it makes education more an effect than a cause, and that seems to me the right emphasis. People learn to read, and seek education, when there is reason to do so – when literacy opens up avenues of participation in the social process.[11] The movement toward universal secondary education became decisive well *after* print culture had saturated our way of life.[12]

If not the spread of literacy and education, did some other change constitute an audience that called the new magazines into being? A number of the historians call on a generalized prosperity, or more specifically a larger and more affluent middle class, to account for the success of magazines. This explanation has three sides: (1) many more people could afford to buy the magazines; (2) they had more money for the products advertised there, and so needed magazines as a guide to consumption; (3) they had more leisure to devote to reading. All these reasons carry weight, if one steps back to survey the hundred years or so of history that saw the transformation of American life. But they give little insight into the initial surge of monthly magazines and encounter the following objections:

1. Magazines came down in price to meet potential buyers, as opposed to buyers having to pay elevated costs. The magazine "revolution" resulted in little or no increase in circulation for the more expensive magazines. Mott may be closer to the truth in offering a contrary explanation: that the depression of the mid nineties fostered the growth of cheap magazines, as "prices that were acceptable in a more inflationary period now seemed too high."[13] One might even argue that the magazines were a stimulus to renewed prosperity, rather than vice versa.

2. The same difficulty blocks the second argument from prosperity. In the fullest and most interesting of the historians' analyses, Theodore Peterson notes that there has been a close relationship between consumer spending and magazine revenue throughout this century,[14] but these two figures were wildly out of kilter in the early and mid nineties.

3. Leaving aside serious questions about the much vaunted increase in leisure time, this hypothesis does not speak to the fact that at the end of the nineteenth century the reading of monthly magazines came to occupy a much larger *share* of whatever leisure was available than they had before, while daily newspapers and weekly magazines made no such gains.

Economic growth is clearly intertwined with the evolution of magazines and of mass culture generally, but as both cause and effect, and with no simple connection to the 1890s. Nor will it do to cite as a cause the prosperity of the audience.

Look at economic growth from the other side of the market, and a different set of possible causes comes into view. Some of the historians mention the industrialization of American society, the extension of transport (especially the railroad boom), and new marketing practices (department stores, mail order houses, and so on). At the end of this chain appears a proximate cause, the need for, and rapid growth of, advertising.[15] Here, I think, is an indisputable connection: no increase in advertising, no cheap magazines. But it is a connection that whets the appetite for more. Yes, advertising followed industrialization, but the latter had been booming since the Civil War, at least twenty years before national advertising assumed some of its modern shapes and filled the monthly magazines. What brought on the efflorescence of advertising? Hardly a hint from these authors, aside from Lyon's remark that the production of goods increased so rapidly that "new advertising techniques had to be developed," and those techniques called for a national medium to sell products nationally (p. 114). This seems to me close to the heart of the matter, but it's another answer that leads to more questions: Why *this* solution? Why then? What stimulated the growth in production? Why were older marketing techniques suddenly inadequate? This explanation needs buttressing by some broader account of historical change, even by a theory. The magazine historians do not provide either one, so even the plausible reasons they offer fit no pattern and add up to no comprehensible whole. A list of causes is just a list; one wants some way of thinking about history to draw the causes together, giving primacy to some and subordinating others.

Actually, if one draws back and considers the histories as a group, such a primary cause does make itself felt, if almost subliminally. Every one of the historians I have consulted and each of the editors except Bok speaks prominently of technology as a stimulus, giving it the status almost of a final cause, since no other has anything like so wide a currency in these books.[16] This bears some inspection. The agreement on a technological cause could be no more than a reflection of the fact that Munsey spoke of "the perfecting of printing machinery" in explaining his scheme to sell the magazine for a dime,[17] and that McClure (he is quoted again and again) said the development of photoengraving made cheap, popular magazines possible.[18] But I rather believe this explanation leapt to the historians' minds for the same reason that Munsey and McClure thought of it: a technological determinism is deeply embedded in the common sense of most people in industrial, capitalist societies. Watt made the steam engine, Arkwright the spinning jenny, Whitney the cotton gin, Edison the light bulb, Marconi the radio – and everything else followed. Given this way of thinking, it is natural to look for a set of inventions that brought us something as salient as mass culture.

This kind of explanation is perhaps understandable, though false, with respect to something as mysterious as broadcasting.[19] That it should rise to the surface as an account of how mass magazines were born can only show how ingrained and uncritical this habit of mind is. Indisputably, there could have been no magazines like those of the 1890s *without* certain innovations. But what were they? The two-cylinder rotary press, the Linotype machine, the Fourdrinier paper-making machine, the process for making paper from wood pulp rather than rags, the stereotype plate, the halftone process of photoengraving, and an assembly-line, continuous-flow scheme of print shop organization. There are two things to note about these developments. First, they are based on relatively simple mechanical or chemical principles; all of the technologies were available in principle long before the 1890s, and crude forms were available in fact. In so far as one can put specific dates to the latter, they are: rotary press, 1847; Linotype machine, before 1886; Fourdrinier process, 1799; paper from pulp, 1844; stereotyping, the 1860s; photoengraving, no later than 1878; the assembly line, the 1830s. If they begat the cheap magazine, why did gestation take so long? Second, an integrated technology like that needed to produce thousands of illustrated magazines in an hour did not come about accidentally or derivatively, as the unanticipated consequence of some lone inventor's eccentric tinkering. The various inventions and improvements all took place gradually and in a particular context: that of the commercially sponsored development of printing and media over a hundred years and, more broadly, of capitalist growth. Invention is supported and propelled by visions of use, and those visions with social backing – in this case, money – are most likely to be realized. As Raymond Williams argues, a technology is foreseen and intended.[20] It would make sense to argue that the growth of a commercial press caused the development of printing technologies, rather than the other way around,[21] and in support one could cite many instances such as the new rotary presses with record capacities built to order for *Century* in 1886 and *Munsey's* in 1898. But that would be artificial, too: the two developments sustained each other, inseparably. Munsey saw a chance for profit in high-speed printing, McClure in the halftone; technology stimulated their entrepreneurial spirits, as earlier commercial successes had opened the eyes of inventors to such technical possibilities.

So technology cannot be a primary cause – perhaps not a cause at all, in any clear sense – of the cheap popular monthly or of mass culture in general. Technological determinism, however, does at least have two features that I would want in a good explanation: it is a theory of how history happens rather than an ad hoc matching of causes to effects; and it assigns priority to some agents and forces. Without that second feature, a theory cannot achieve the first. It will either dissolve into an agnostic muddle – history is just one damn thing after another – or it will raise itself into a metaphysical principle that explains everything and hence nothing (usually through a tacit appeal to values that show "us" to be the chosen people). History is progress. History executes the divine will. History is a Darwinian struggle, with the fittest surviving. The teleology present in such ideas makes it clear that they will satisfy only those who want to believe them for other than historical reasons.

Of course the agnostic position *could* be right; history could make no sense and have no system. There is no way to refute such an anti-theory except by offering explanations that somehow do satisfy the need for explanation. Since this study, like almost all histories, aims to do just that, I will get on with it, and finish this chapter by sketching out three other ways of explaining the emergence of mass culture, which do have the characteristics I am looking for. To anticipate a bit: because the arrival of mass culture cannot be detached, as a particular event, from a broader change in the social order, its explanation must like any in social history account for a transformation of the relations that constitute a society; it must connect human action to social structure, as both cause and effect.[22]

Modernization Theory

Although modernization theory originated among social scientists, Richard Brown rightly points out that it offers to historians, too, an appealing explanatory power:

> For in an era when general history is becoming less and less comprehensible owing to the increasing specialization of scholarship, an interpretive framework that promises to integrate a wide range of historical phenomena – everything from agricultural technology to popular amusements and legal codes – deserves scrutiny. An idea that helps to explain the connections among events in economic, political, social, and intellectual history can be vitally important for our understanding.[23]

Not only does the idea of modernization integrate the whole social process of change, it also sounds like a theory in that it generalizes a series of changes over all developing societies, and thus is indeed an idea about how history happens – at least that part of history with which I am concerned in this study. Furthermore, it assigns to mass culture an important place in the process of becoming modern.

Thus Daniel Lerner, who most formally brought mass culture within the scope of the theory, outlined a model of development in which four processes work together: more people move to cities; more people learn how to read and write; more people buy newspapers, listen to radios, and so on ("impersonal communication"); and more people vote. The social system evolves in that order: urbanization, literacy, "media participation," and "electoral participation" – to give these processes the names Lerner used.[24] Both for Lerner and for other exponents of the theory, modernization embraces many other changes, such as a movement towards rationality and efficiency, increases in production, social specialization, national integration and a cosmopolitan outlook for citizens, and expanding aspirations (the expectation that one can better one's life). But let me stick for a moment to Lerner's sequence.

The difficulty with his model as an *explanatory* theory is that Lerner wanted to build it around "correlational hypotheses which can be tested," and so avoid "the genetic problem of causality" (p. 56). Yet if things always happen in a certain order, that fact implies that each activates the one after it, or that something deeper causes the whole series of changes. It is not surprising (nor, to me, disturbing) to find Lerner's language gravitating toward the causal. Urbanization, he held, was the "key variable" in the system, for "it is with urbanization that the modernizing process historically has begun in Western societies" (p. 58). Urbanization is "necessary to start modernization" (p. 59); specifically, the process begins when about 25 percent of the people live in towns with a population of 50,000 or more. It is hard not to see a cause in such formulations: urbanization "stimulates the needs" for participation in society; "only cities require a largely literate population," and "create the demand for impersonal communication" (p. 61) – that is, mass media. And so on through the steps of change: "increasing urbanization has tended to raise literacy; rising literacy has tended to increase media exposure; increasing media exposure has 'gone with' wider economic participation (per capita income) and political participation (voting)" (p. 46). Again, literacy "supplies media consumers, who stimulate media production" (p. 64), and a communication system is both a result and an "agent of change" (p. 56). There is no shortage of causal thinking in this account.

Of course neither a communication system nor cities nor the process of urbanization can literally be an "agent of change." Lerner needed some premise about who the human agents are behind these abstractions, and why they act as they do. That premise, implicit throughout his exposition, was clearly stated at the end: "the great dramas of societal transition occur through individuals involved in solving their personal problems and living their private lives" (pp. 74–5). Thus urbanization (the "key variable") is a "movement by individuals, each having made a personal choice to seek elsewhere his own version of a better life" (pp. 47–8). A plain truth – though one may want to recall Midland farm laborers deprived of subsistence by enclosure, Lancashire hand-loom weavers starved out in competition with power-loom owners, Irish peasants driven by repression and famine to Liverpool and New York, or peasants cheated by landlords and squatting in shack towns on the edge of Adana or Ankara in Lerner's much admired Turkey, and then add Marx's qualification: "not under circumstances they themselves have chosen." Still, a choice is a choice (if not coerced), and Lerner's version of modernization clearly posits the choices of millions as the force behind urbanization, media participation, and the other stages.

Modernization had a wide currency for a decade or so, and then fell into disfavor as an account of development in poor nations of the mid twentieth century. Many supporters lost interest as it became evident that the theory did not lead to practical policies for modernizing the Third

World and maintaining its allegiance to the First World. Critics attacked it for smuggling in Western values and measuring Latin America, Africa, and Asia by them. Neither of these difficulties would have bothered Lerner, for whom modernization was simply "an historical fact," in the West and elsewhere. But another line of criticism addressed the theory precisely on empirical grounds, maintaining that although it predicted the steady development of poor countries into relatively affluent (and democratic) ones, in fact the gap between rich and poor countries was increasing, resulting in an absolute deterioration for majorities in many of the latter. It became clear that the theory failed in this respect because it treated each society in isolation (except in so far as the West provided a model for poor nations) and thus could not address the impact of Western economic power upon development elsewhere. Hence, it was pretty much scrapped in the 1970s, and replaced by various "dependency" or "underdevelopment" theories, which held that multinational corporations and the governments of advanced capitalist countries distorted the economies of the Third World, and in fact *prevented* development on the Western model.[25]

But that's another story. Modernization theory suffered no such defeat as an account of how European and North American societies became modern in the first place; it is one among various contenders, and has articulate proponents like Richard Brown. His analysis is a good deal more intricate than Lerner's, as one would expect from a historian: it includes more dimensions of change, and posits no linear sequence, but rather describes US history as an uneven and sometimes interrupted movement from the first settlements to the end of the Civil War, when the society was prepared in many ways to become fully modern. For example, he emphasizes the commercial development of farming ("a base not only for industrialization but for other aspects of modernization" [p.124]), both as a form of modernity in itself and as a stimulus to factory production: when New England farmers could no longer compete, owing to poor land and climate, manufacturing became for them a "much more attractive investment opportunity" (p. 127).

But as even that formulation suggests, Brown is like Lerner in making the needs and choices of ordinary people basic. Thus, behind the changes in agriculture were "transportation facilities, improved technology, and, most fundamental, the attitudes of farmers" (p. 124). In explaining the growth of communications, too, Brown stresses attitudes: "The desire to manipulate the environment through the use of technology becomes a prevalent goal, since change (for the better) is viewed as a real possibility." Such "drives" propel self-conscious advances in communication, now "viewed as necessities" (pp.12–13). Brown does allow for intended advances by government and commerce, but makes these powerful intentions one with those of people in general. Along with economic development, "public interests necessarily rose to regional and national levels" (p. 165), and a national communication system met those interests. The government promoted railroads and the telegraph, but only because the war had created a "general recognition," through the "demand for news," that a national system of communication was necessary (p. 178), and "convinced Americans" that investment in it was critical (p. 180). Attitudes, drives, needs, broadly diffused among the people, generate the means of mass communication, and make history happen. As Lerner said, "Modernity is primarily a state of mind" (paperback edition, 1966, p. viii).

Modernization theory rose out of the pluralism that dominated American social science through the postwar period, and has close affinities with it. Like pluralism, it envisions society as a network of overlapping groups, interests, and influences, with power distributed rather evenly among them and highly mediated. This understanding covers mass culture, along with other main institutions. Thus the whole tradition of pluralist communications research, growing out of the work of Paul F. Lazarsfeld, carried the message – and backed it with tons of "effects studies" – that mass communications do not have much of an impact on behavior (for example, voting) or attitudes (public opinion).[26] People interpret the content of the media through values and beliefs already held, through patterns of life well established in family and community, and through the mediation of personal influences (by a respected neighbor, fellow worker, and so on). Mass culture reflects, or expresses, or at most reinforces the core values of a society; it plays a part in shaping the consensus around which society coheres, but a secondary part. The choices of news and entertainment that people make are real choices; people hold more sovereignty over the producers of culture than vice versa.

One can hear the reverberations of this position in Brown's language of "demand" and "need." And it is explicit in Lerner's account: "when most people in a society have become literate, they tend to generate all sorts of new desires and to develop the means of satisfying them." They do so through "media participation," which in turn "tends to raise participation in all sectors of the social system." The generating force here is, simply, "people" and their desires, "to which participant institutions have responded" (p. 62). In theory as in pluralist studies of the media, the people get what they want, and suppliers – themselves participants, too – merely meet their demands.

Marxism/The Frankfurt School

Marx and Engels had it the other way around. To begin with, "people" do not "generate" needs and ideas; the social order produces their consciousness. As Marx put it in a famous passage:

In the social production of their life, men enter into definite relations that are indispensable and independent of their will; these relations of production correspond to a definite stage of development of their material forces of production. The sum total of these relations of production constitutes the economic structure of society – the real foundation, on which rises a legal and political superstructure and to which correspond definite forms of social consciousness. The mode of production of material life determines the social, political and intellectual life process in general. It is not the consciousness of men that determines their being, but, on the contrary, their social being that determines their consciousness.[27]

Furthermore, this determination works through the agency, not just of "people," but especially of *some* people. To quote another well known statement:

The ideas of the ruling class are in every epoch the ruling ideas: i.e., the class which is the ruling *material* force of society is at the same time its ruling *intellectual* force. The class which has the means of material production at its disposal, has control at the same time over the means of mental production, so that thereby, generally speaking, the ideas of those who lack the means of mental production are subject to it.[28]

The "means of mental production" include the media, along with legislative bodies, courts, schools, the church, and so on. Thus, in the narrowest application of these ideas to the matter at hand, the "suppliers" of media experiences turn out to be paid servants of the ruling class, and "people" get what the suppliers want for them.

Historical materialism implies not only a theory of how mass culture works, but a clear enough idea of where it must have come from. To give the briefest possible account, since all of this is familiar to anyone acquainted with marxism: history moves because the forces of production – tools, technologies, skills, knowledge, the organization of work – are relatively dynamic; people are always using their creativity to modify their relation to nature, and hence themselves. But the social relations of production – laws, classes, institutions, and so on – are relatively conservative; those who benefit from a particular system use their power to preserve it. Eventually, the relations of production are no longer able to contain new productive forces or the class that has grown in conjunction with them. Out of the conflict comes a new mode of production, a new ruling class, and a new social system. Thus, within feudalism a small merchant class emerged, amassed capital through trade, finance, and colonial exploitation, inaugurated the system of wage labor, and used the social surplus (profit) to build more advanced forces of production, and so control the labor power of ever more people as well as an ever larger share of the surplus. By the mid nineteenth century, the bourgeoisie had mainly replaced the aristocracy as the dominant class, and established its own social order – in fact a *world* order, so that capitalism became the dominant system even in areas like North America where feudalism had not existed.

Like any ruling class, the bourgeoisie extended its power by controlling the means of mental production. And so the general theory offers an explanation of how mass culture arose, and how it works – even though Marx and Engels had not experienced it when they wrote. The bourgeoisie, which comes to own the means of communication along with other means of production, uses the media as a channel for its beliefs, values, and total understanding of the world. Its aim is to legitimate its rule, making its interests seem natural, inevitable, and universal, so that the other classes will accept their subordinate positions. Since the largest and most threatening of these, the working class, is not held in place by fixed hierarchies, as were medieval serfs, but is supposedly "free" within the market system and democratic polity which the bourgeoisie has created, the task of culture in maintaining the class system is proportionately greater. The bourgeoisie must create, in fact, a *mass* culture, to produce docile minds in the heads of millions. And it is able to do this by building on the very processes of mechanization it has used to revolutionize material production and the means of communications necessary to support it. Railroads, postal systems, steamships, steam presses, and the telegraph easily adapt to the creation and distribution of mass culture, as do later innovations like electric power and lighting, wireless transmission of sound and images, photoengraving, and motion pictures. Mass culture fuses the bourgeoisie's mastery of production and its need to master the consciousness of its subordinates.

In this summary I have already gone beyond what Marx and Engels said, or could have said – though they said surprisingly much of it, given that they had not actually experienced all these developments, or anything like a full-blown mass culture.[29] Communication, culture, even ideology were somewhat removed from the center of their intellectual project, and they did not systematically work out their ideas in this area. The next generation of marxist theorists, deeply involved in working class movements and struggles around production and party building, concentrated on economics and politics, and gave even less attention to culture. It remained for a third generation to elaborate a theory and analysis of culture. I focus here on one group of them, the Frankfurt School writers, principally Adorno, Horkheimer, and Marcuse. Between them and Marx and Engels there was not only a temporal gulf, but a gulf of experience and attitude, since this generation's ideas developed in an environment of defeat – first the defeat of revolutionary movements in all advanced capitalist societies except Russia, and then that of even liberal democracy in Nazi Europe.[30]

Marcuse and others said little about the origins of mass culture, and almost nothing about the mechanisms by which bourgeois ownership of what they called the "culture industry" translated into bourgeois dominance of working class consciousness. But they did offer a detailed account of how mass culture works to suppress critical or revolutionary tendencies, in a way that carried forward Marx and Engels's notion of working class ideas being "subject" to the ruling class. The Frankfurt School theorists held that the culture industry, along with the whole apparatus of mental production and commodity consumption, colonized and supervised leisure time so as to eliminate critical ways of thinking and even the inner life itself. It replaced an earlier, organic working class culture with one imposed from without, that created a host of false needs to be met by commodities and by the products of the culture industry. This hedonistic culture, both cause and consequence of weakening primary institutions like the traditional family, flattened consciousness almost into a state of narcosis, subduing the exploited, and blocking the desire to organize for socialism, at least among the traditional working class.

Of course this set of ideas did not remain static, and Marcuse for one backed away from its most pessimistic version after the movements of the 1960s revealed that opposition to capitalist society had some life in it. But the theory that I have pieced together by joining the tenets of the Frankfurt School to some basic ideas of classical marxism retains many advocates.[31] And in its view of mass culture as a powerful and intended *manipulation of the audience* for broad political purposes, it contrasts sharply and helpfully with modernization theory and the pluralist understanding of modern communications.

Marxism: Hegemony

A different strand of marxist thought emerged in the writings of Antonio Gramsci,[32] lay unnoticed for a while, and then, from the 1960s on, was picked up by a variety of activists and theorists in Europe, Britain, and the US. They have woven it into a rich fabric of explanation and analysis which in some countries is now the dominant understanding of culture: in Britain, especially, where a flourishing school of cultural studies has worked Gramsci's ideas in with native traditions of history and with other European elements.

The theory of hegemony shares with other marxisms the historical materialist view of how history happens, and of how capitalism happened, in particular. It places the same emphasis on forces and relations of production, on classes, and on class struggle. There it begins to diverge, especially from the marxism I described in the previous section of this chapter. The bourgeoisie did come to own the "means of mental production," but not as a system apart from material production. Rather, it has to establish and control new means of communication in order to carry out its scheme of production for markets, and of accumulation. In the early stages of capitalism, to be sure, the press was a partisan and overtly ideological instrument of various factions; and that was the situation within which Marx and Engels, understandably, made their claim about how the ruling class spreads its ideas. But the bourgeoisie developed and used the media, more and more through the second half of the nineteenth century, as adjuncts to its system of commodity production and distribution, as vehicles for information that it needed in this project, and especially as instruments of marketing.

Furthermore, the dynamic of capitalist growth means that the masters of production must constantly expand into areas previously outside the market. Culture itself was such an area. Businessmen increasingly found ways to turn information and entertainment into commodities, produced and marketed in much the same way and for the same ends as soap and stoves. Clearly this account is incompatible with any simple division of productive base and reflexive superstructure; mass culture is *part* of capitalist production. In passing, note also that at this point the theory makes it unlikely that the bourgeoisie would want, or be able, to use its control of the media mainly to proclaim its ideas and values to the subordinate classes, in any direct way. When cultural experiences are bought and sold in markets, propaganda becomes an expensive luxury for its producers, unless audiences want to consume and pay for it in preference to other experiences. So to whatever extent mass cultural products and forms do express ruling class ideology, the reason must be different from the one offered by manipulation theory.

The theory of hegemony holds that the capitalist ruling class, in gaining control of production, also comes to dominate most major institutions, from legal to military to cultural. In this way it defines the situations within which all people live their lives, and sets limits to the possible – or at least plausible – choices they can make, relations they can enter into, ideas they can have. In other words, the capitalist version of reality saturates the common sense (Gramsci's term) and daily activity of all classes. The ruling class thus dominates the others quite systematically, yet its domination works through means that are often indirect and even unintentional. To be sure, it means to keep society as a field open to its project of cultivation, and has the power to do so through direct coercion up to a point. But it prefers not to, and usually does not. For one thing, the legitimacy of the social order in the eyes of subordinate classes depends on their belief that they are free and that their institutions – including the media – are open (and most members of the bourgeoisie themselves share this belief). Thus the hegemonic process, when it is working well, is a system of rule that depends on widespread, active consent more than on force or manipulation.

Of course this is not yet a full explanation of how mass culture

developed and what it does. In particular, it needs a detailed elaboration
of how the hegemonic process was transformed in and after the 1890s,
and an account of how hegemony works through media institutions to
spread bourgeois ideology and enforce consent, when that may not be
the conscious aim of anyone involved in the process.[33] But I hope to have
said enough to show that the theory of hegemony meets my stated criteria, and that it is distinctly different from both modernization theory
and manipulation theory. From the former, it differs in describing the
media and mass culture as channels of domination, and in almost every
other way *except* that it too accords a significant role to audiences and
their needs and choices. That area of agreement constitutes one major
way in which hegemony theory differs from manipulation theory.
Another is in the position each takes on what the ruling class does – and
why – with its control of the media.

For in this the two marxist theories diverge, too: in manipulation
theory, control of a cultural industry implies direct and effective management of ideology, while hegemony theory admits more autonomy
on the part of various actors in and outside the industry, and sees ideology as the always-contested and often inconsistent product of various
interests and outlooks. So the two theories differ in their understandings
of agency and structure.

This is abstract. With luck, the rest of the study will sharpen the outlines of and differences among the three explanatory frameworks, and
test their claims with reference to my account of the magazine revolution. By test, I do not mean empirically verify or falsify; I have in mind,
rather, spelling out the implications of a theory, reflecting on its per-
spicuity in analysis of events and processes, and considering its capacity
for fruitfulness, for generating new knowledge.[34] But of course no historical account begins without theoretical presuppositions that influence
what the investigator will look for and find, what will seem to be evidence, what story will shape it. My own commitment, in advance, is to
some version of hegemony theory – as the reader will surely have
inferred from the argumentative edge of the foregoing exposition, and
from its very sequence (the third sister or brother or suitor is always the
one to pass the test or solve the riddle, after the first two fail). That
commitment derives from years of studying and teaching about and
puzzling over contemporary mass culture, a project that in turn followed from political activism and reflection in the late 1960s and after,
which left no doubt that mass culture plays a main role in reproducing
our social order, while also opening up terrains of resistance and stimu-
lating alternative projects.

As I began this study, more than a decade ago, it seemed to me that
the idea of hegemony would have power, too, in explaining the origins
of mass culture. Unlike modernization theory and its pluralist cousins,
marxism emphasizes contradictions and crises in the social order, and

transformative, epochal change rather than gradual and steady evolution. Certainly the period from the Civil War to the 1890s was one of intense conflict and crisis, easy enough to grasp as instancing the laws of capitalist motion. Capital must accumulate or fail. That project brings it into sustained struggle with the working class, and entails other contradictions such as that between the needs of the individual manufacturer and those of the capitalist class as a whole, with dire consequences including overproduction, overaccumulation in fixed capital and in the built environment with attendant bankruptcies and financial panics, the cycle of boom and bust. Events of the postwar era fell into a pattern predicted well if roughly by the theory, and could be read as partly confirming the general marxist explanation of historical change: that forces of production outrun relations of production until there is a tectonic plate shift in social structure.

Here, as I see it, orthodox marxisms tend to posit a final collapse out of which socialist revolution rises. Hegemony theory is more hospitable to the idea of transformative and epochal changes within capitalism, hegemonic shifts that throw up new historic "blocs" – and pertinently, that work themselves out partly in the realms of ideology and culture. Thus it seems to me especially promising as a framework for explaining the reconstitution of capital in its corporate form around 1900, the new prominence of mass culture and consumption, and (as I will argue) the emergence of a new class in a new relation to the big bourgeoisie.

This is not to say that theoretical presuppositions decide the outcome of the inquiry. On the contrary, as I revise these paragraphs at its end I think of some major surprises and revisions it has produced. But that, I suppose, is how one usually proceeds to study history: with a theory that will organize the investigation and point toward some kinds of evidence while deemphasizing other kinds, yet remain open to modification or even (but not in this case!) abandonment because of what one discovers and how one rethinks it.[35] Thus I hope this project will strengthen, elaborate, and critique the theory of hegemony, even as I construct a narrative of magazines and mass culture that would be impossible or at least very different had it built from another foundation.[36]

4

What Capitalists Needed

Magazines quickly became a national, mass cultural form. Sudden growth of this kind, apart from the deployment of a new technology, suggests pressures building up outside the particular area of production, and finding all at once a channel to burst through. Since I hold that the main engines of history are forces of production and the class conflict that develops with them, I look first in this direction. But I think that anyone, marxist or not, scanning the American landscape at the end of the last century for important forces bringing about major social changes would have to consider, early on, the forces of production. Historians of every persuasion agree that the way people made what they needed in our society changed utterly in the last half of the century, and almost everything else along with it. Because the point is not controversial, I will dwell on it only long enough to sketch the dimensions of change, and establish a context for some remarks on what is less obvious.

In 1850 six people out of every ten still worked on farms, and the value of what they produced for sale was about equal to the value of all manufactured things. And since both they and many people who worked in towns and cities made much of what they needed for themselves, rather than buying or selling it, manufacturing accounted for a good deal less than half of all production. By 1900, only 39 percent of Americans worked on farms, and home production for use had declined sharply in both town and country. Considering people as makers of goods and of material life, one can see them in the aggregate going out to work for wages, in shop and factory. Considering them as consumers – and the very concept and word appeared only during this period – one can see them turning to stores, mail order catalogs and specialized producers for what they used to make at home – soap, clothes, food, furniture, the home itself – and for many new products – gum, cameras, bicycles, telephones, electric lighting.

In economists' statistics, this change appears as spectacular growth. It is important to remember that their net catches only what passes through markets, and that economic growth so measured greatly exaggerates the increase in useful things produced. Yet the figures are telling: from 1869 to 1873, gross national product averaged $9.1 billion; from

1892 to 1896, it had more than tripled, to $29.6 billion (all figures are in 1929 dollars). The population was growing rapidly during this period, too; still, GNP per person almost doubled, from $223 to $434.[1]

GNP includes all kinds of production – manufacturing, agriculture, mining, services, and so on – and all these kinds increased significantly from the Civil War to the end of the century. But about half of the total gain came in manufacturing, where the rate of increase was much faster than elsewhere. In 1859, the value of manufactured goods was $1.9 billion; in 1899, $13 billion; this value grew two and a half times as fast as the population.[2] Factories and manufacturing shops multiplied across the landscape – from 140,000 of them just before the war to 512,000 in 1899. The number of people who worked there increased almost as rapidly, and the value of what they produced much more so, as factories became larger and machines more sophisticated. Another way to approach the same fact is to note that "productivity" was also rapidly increasing – the output of commodities per person-hour went up 64 percent between 1869 and 1899.[3] The United States had become an industrial nation, in short, and with incredible speed, accomplishing in fifty years or so what had taken closer to a hundred in Britain, where the first Industrial Revolution occurred. In fact, whereas American factories produced less than those of Britain or France or Germany in 1860, they produced almost as much as those of the three countries taken together in the 1890s.[4]

One more thing worth noting about this growth: while it generated a powerful new flow of cheap manufactured goods to people (for example, ready-to-wear men's clothing was practically nonexistent in 1860, but made up 90 percent of all men's clothing in 1890)[5] even more important in some ways was the development of a national "infrastructure" – a system of transportation and communication that made everything else possible. Railroads came first, far outreaching canals even before the Civil War, and extending the network from 30,000 miles of track in 1860 to 200,000 miles in 1900 (creating a need for iron and steel which led the US to world leadership in that industry before 1900). The telegraph was in widespread use by the 1860s, providing the fast communication necessary not only to operate railroads but to run a far-flung business enterprise. The telephone was well established by 1890, another boon to commerce. Electric power developed late, but quickly. It drew even with steam as a source by 1900, and this was nowhere more important than in transportation: electric powered streetcars provided 15 percent of urban transit in 1890, and 94 percent in 1902.[6] Such developments made it easy for people to get to work, for salesmen to travel everywhere, for raw materials to reach factories, for corporate managers to keep track of national operations, and for products to find national markets.

Capital

Production requires capital; it also creates capital, when things are going well. In a capitalist society that happens in various ways, but mainly through the reinvestment of profits by businesses and through the savings of people who themselves are receiving a share of the profits, or salaries much larger than needed for subsistence. Rapid growth in production, over and above growth in population, implies rapid growth in capital, too, unless everyone is working longer days or working at more and more furious rates of speed. We can ignore those latter possibilities, as capital did indeed pile up fast toward the end of the nineteenth century: it quadrupled from 1869 to 1899, and more than doubled in relation to the number of people in the country – from $1120 to $2530 per capita.[7]

Capital is wealth capable of producing more wealth. It includes people's houses (but not other private possessions), small stores, horse-drawn cabs, and the like. But the main wealth-producing capital was in manufacturing, mining, utilities, transportation, and agriculture. Capital on farms was a steadily declining portion of the total; the main accumulation of capital took place in big business. With their head start, railroads continued as both the largest repository of capital and the area in which most new capital was accumulating; in fact, nearly half of new private investment went into the railroads from 1880 to 1900.[8] But this leadership could not continue forever, as rail lines reached every corner of the country. Investment in them slowed down during the 1890s, while it spurted in manufacturing and mining. The wealth of the country flowed into steel, oil, electric power, transportation systems, and factories that mass-produced more and more of what people used.

Furthermore, the rate of *increase* in capital formation reached its historic high in the late 1880s and the 1890s. This seems to be true whether one considers the amount of new capital added every few years to what was there before,[9] or the percentage of the national product plowed back into capital. This second way of looking at capital formation deserves closer attention, because it captures the decisions a society (that is, those with the power to decide) makes about what to do with the fruits of its work. Other things being equal (which, of course, they never are), the more people consume, the less they put into new capital, and vice versa. Toward the end of the time when American capitalism was growing at the fastest pace ever, it was also putting aside the highest proportion of its income for the pursuit of future profits. The percentage reached 16.1 and 16.2 for the overlapping decades 1884–93 and 1889–98 respectively, the only time in our history (for which records are available) during which it was over 15 percent. By contrast, during the 1920s boom it was just over 10 percent, and through the prosperous decade just after World War II only 6 percent.[10]

To move still closer to the real-life meaning of this growth, consider now that just when capital accumulation was highest, the rate of increase in "flow of goods to consumers" was lowest: from 1881 to 1896.[11] People were, on average, eating and wearing and using more commodities year by year, but these measurable gains in material life were most gradual while gains in productive wealth were most rapid. The contradiction becomes even sharper when we observe that capital in manufacturing increased tenfold from 1859 to 1899; in the 1880s alone it more than doubled, and it rose another 50 percent in the 1890s.[12] Industry frenetically built up its capacity to make things, but the value of what it produced with this capacity grew less rapidly, and what it produced for consumers grew less rapidly still.

Economists conventionally treat these relationships as expressing the "rate of savings." This idea, like so many concepts of mainstream economics, calls up the vision of a homogeneous society, cooperating and competing in a shared project of development. Today we hear of the thrifty Japanese with their very high rate of savings (higher, in fact, than it has ever been in the US), and the spendthrift Americans with the lowest rate of savings among the advanced industrial nations. The picture is of ordinary people choosing (according to their personalities and preferences) to set aside more or less of their paychecks each week. This picture badly misrepresents the situation today, when the poorest fifth of the population has "negative wealth" – that is, owes more than it owns – and the poorer half owns less than 10 percent of all wealth, and about 2 percent of the income-producing wealth. I think it probably obscures late-nineteenth-century reality even more. One needs to ask, Where did the new capital come from? Who was being so thrifty?

First, it seems that business firms and corporations themselves – not private individuals – did most of this "saving." I have not found figures for the years before 1900, but in the first decade of this century corporations generated well over half of their new capital "internally" – that is, mainly through profits.[13] Every indication suggests that the rate was even higher before 1900: manufacturing capital grew at a faster rate then, while banks and other financial institutions had much smaller assets to use in loans, and a securities market for industrials barely existed before the late 1890s. So the remarkable enlargement of capital that characterized economic growth in this period came mainly from surplus value extracted through the labor process by industrialists – in marxian terms, capital is "dead" labor, labor from which capitalists and not workers get the return.

That is not the whole story. A good deal of new capital came from abroad: Europeans had begun investing in railroad bonds early on ($1.3 billion from 1863 to 1873), and they continued buying American securities, which began to include industrials ($1.8 billion came from Europe in the 1880s;[14] more than 10 percent of all new capital came from abroad, from 1882 to 1893).[15] We can assume that most of this money derived from the exploitation of *European* workers; certainly it was not the savings of ordinary Americans.

Further, ordinary Americans *gave* a rich mine of new capital to corporations, especially to the railroads. Federal and state governments granted 180 million acres of public lands to them, in all,[16] four times as much as to homesteaders,[17] and even that figure bypasses the fact that many "homesteaders" were really land speculators. So were the railroad companies: they turned their free land into capital both by selling it and by developing the rich resources it often contained. So government lands, acquired partly with tax money, contributed a good share to the growth of capital. This is not to say that it was a bad idea to subsidize the growth of the railroad system, but only that doing so in this way transferred wealth upwards.

The remaining portion of new capital came mainly as loans from banks and insurance companies, and through the sale of stocks and bonds. The assets of banks and insurance companies grew from about $2 billion in 1865 to well over $9 billion in 1890;[18] this money was available for lending to businesses and for stock purchases, as well as for small loans to farmers and homeowners, and it did represent "savings," in the common meaning of the term. But again, whose savings? I have no figures, but can only suppose that in 1890 as in 1990, most personal saving was done by the relatively well-off. Certainly that holds for the private purchase of stocks and bonds. Even though 4 million people owned some stock before the end of the century, an 1890 study showed that 1 percent of the people owned one half of such wealth.[19]

I have tried looking from several angles at the (dubious) statistics that measure the building of railroads, factories, warehouses, mining operations, and electric power systems – the building of industrial America. They are spectacular numbers, if you have a taste for that sort of thing. For those who don't, let me underline my conclusions. The most rapid capital formation in our or anyone's history was not a matter of "people" choosing to save rather than spend. Rather, it should be seen as saving by the already rich, in order to become richer; as their appropriation of wealth and sources of wealth from people who were not rich; as a concentration of the country's productive resources in the hands of a few, to a degree quite new in the US (though this hasn't changed much since 1900). The success of businessmen in this project brought material benefits to most people, at least in time. But most of the benefits – and the power – went to businessmen themselves during this period. Not only wealth, but income too became more unequal.[20] This was success indeed, but success that hid dangers to the beneficiaries. Would the ideas of democracy and equality continue to legitimate the social order, under such circumstances? Who would buy all those products? And did control over the economic process follow naturally from such growth?

Crises

I have been describing the broad movement of capital – a great success for businessmen that was simultaneously though less obviously a source of trouble. The crises that I will now briefly mention were far from subtle. All were evident to the leaders of industrial capitalism; some were plain to the whole nation. All were interconnected, though I list them separately.

1. Workers strenuously resisted the efforts of businessmen to squeeze them in the cause of profit, capital formation, and control of the work process. At best, the conditions of industrial work were hard and precarious enough. Most workers had no protection against lay-offs, nothing set aside for old age other than what they could save from their meager wages, no security in case of injury – and work was very dangerous for many, with deaths rising toward twenty thousand annually and injuries to a million, through this period. A sixty-hour week was common, and a longer one not rare. Some rebellions – most notably the May Day strikes of 1886 – organized around this last condition, the one that workers experienced every day, and the one that excluded them from the expansion of leisure – human time – that the growth of the economy might have made available to all.

Periodically, as depressions threatened profits, capitalists sought to guard their position by pressing workers even harder. The "Great Upheaval" of 1877 began when the Baltimore and Ohio Railroad cut wages by 10 percent, the second cut in a year. The battle at the Homestead works in 1892, through which Carnegie and Frick sought to break the union (the Amalgamated Association of Iron and Steel Workers), began soon after they announced a new wage scale that would cut the wages of the Amalgamated men by 18 percent. Many of the strikes that erupted in 1894 (for example, those of the coal miners and the Pullman workers) followed wage reductions.

These were massive conflicts. In 1877 there was virtually a nationwide general strike. In 1886 there were 1400 strikes involving half a million workers. In 1894, 750,000 workers went out on strike. And these were no polite walkouts of the sort we mainly know: repeatedly, the bosses called in Pinkerton guards, the militia, the army, and pitched battles resulted. The capitalists and the middle class spoke fearfully of anarchy, and one can't dismiss that as paranoia or scaremongering. In addition, the uprisings of farmers (more and more of whom were driven into tenancy or bankruptcy) made the new social order seem precarious. Businessmen could not moderate the system they had built, nor make it seem to others to be compatible with basic values of justice and dignity. "Robber barons": that such a phrase should have gained common currency as a label for the dominant class suggests how deep was the crisis of legitimacy.[21]

2. Business was extraordinarily risky. Laissez-faire ideology held that it should be so; but that did not help capitalists *enjoy* the unrestrained competition to which they were theoretically committed:

> You know how often I had not an unbroken night's sleep, worrying about how it was all coming out. All the fortune I have made has not served to compensate for the anxiety of the period. Work by day and worry by night, week in and week out, month after month.[22]

That's how one of the big winners, John D. Rockefeller, spoke of competition. We can be assured that wakeful nights were as common for the less successful.

Essentially, industrialists competed by enlarging their factories, buying more and better machines, and increasing both the amount and the efficiency of production. That was fine while the market for a new product was expanding; but early success drew new competitors into the field, and led all to expand past the eventual needs of consumers. With fixed costs high, it made sense to keep the machines running and try to undersell the competition: better some income than none. The result, in industry after industry, of expansion beyond the ability of existing markets to absorb the product was price cutting, idle capacity, and the constant threat of failure. Businessmen understood this. The journal of the iron and steel makers said, in 1884, "it might almost be rated the exception for half the works . . . to be in operation simultaneously." The president of the stovemakers' organization: "It is a chronic case of too many stoves and not enough people to buy them" (1888). And in the same year, the vice president of the millers' association: "our ambition has overreached our discretion and judgment. We have all participated in the general steeplechase for pre-eminence . . . . As our glory increased our profits became smaller, until now the question is not how to surpass the record, but how to maintain our position . . . ."[23]

And fail they did, in large numbers – about 10 percent of them each year, on average. Of course many of these were tiny enterprises, but larger ones went under, too. In the depression of the 1870s, bankruptcies among commercial firms rose from 5000 in 1873 to over 10,000 in 1878. There was a similar rate of collapse in the mid 1880s, and an even greater one in the depression of the 1890s, when three times as many commercial houses failed as had failed in the 1870s depression. In that of the 1890s, 156 railroads with capital of $2.5 billion and 28 percent of the nation's track went bankrupt; by 1897, 800 banks had failed.[24]

Again, business failure had a place in the official scheme of ideas – the fittest would survive and all would benefit – but capitalists were less enthusiastic in practice than in theory about Darwinian struggle.

3. As individual firms and industries overexpanded and overproduced, so, periodically, did the economic system as a whole. Speculation

exaggerated the cycle. Severe depressions resulted, roughly in the middle years of each decade from the 1870s through the 1890s. Each general bust heightened the risk of failure for individual businesses, and fueled workers' organized resistance to capitalist rule. (As many as 20 percent of workers were jobless, at times.) So on top of those risks and conflicts that characterized daily life for the big bourgeoisie, it lacked the means to regulate growth and forestall periodic disasters. It is striking, in fact, that during this time when the US economy expanded more rapidly than ever before or since, fourteen of the twenty-five years from 1873 to 1897 were years of depression or recession.[25]

Like the suicidal overproduction of specific goods such as flour and stoves, economy-wide overproduction was no secret to be exposed only by socialists or, later, by historical investigation. Congressmen, government agencies, and businessmen themselves decried the vast surpluses that industry was creating. The National Association of Manufacturers made overproduction the main theme of its organizational meeting in 1895. Like William McKinley, whom they invited as keynote speaker, they saw access to overseas markets as the "only promise of relief," thus acknowledging their inability to restrain competitive excess and resolve the crisis within the confines of the system they had so vigorously built.[26]

4. Finally, profits were falling, if one judges by the average return on shares of common stock. For industrials, railroads, and utilities that return fell steadily, from 8.8 percent (1871–78), to 8.4 percent (1874–83), to 7.0 percent (1879–88), to 6.0 percent (1884–93), and to 5.75 percent (1889–98).[27] At the same time, the productivity of capital was rising, but the general decline in *prices* from the Civil War to the end of the century more than offset the increase in output, and the actual return on capital fell to the lowest level it would ever attain until the depression of the 1930s. This was, of course, good news for workers, whose real standard of living improved modestly through the period even though their money wages stayed more or less level. But for capitalists, falling profits were one more indication that in spite of their great power and dynamism, they were unable to make their system work as they would have liked.

Power and Disorder

None of this should be taken to imply that American capitalists as a class were weak and vulnerable; in their spheres of daily operation the more successful ones had perhaps as much unrestrained freedom of action as any group of men ever, in a market society. They had built a colossal productive system, but, willy-nilly, in the uncoordinated way that Adam Smith had advocated. Through the increase of their wealth and their aggregate power, they had failed to exercise anything like systematic *class* control

over their environment. That failure is expressed in what I have just
summarized: smoldering worker rebellion, frightening risk, great instability, and declining profits, as well as in widespread skepticism about
their leadership. Nor had the new middle class, fast though it was growing, yet come to stand as an executor of capitalist designs, a buffer
between bosses and workers, and an encouragement and model to the
latter; it had, in fact, fluctuating and often negative attitudes toward big
business, culminating in the anti-trust sentiment of the 1890s.[28]

The capitalist class today may be characterized by rifts and conflicting
interests as much as it was in 1890. But consider what means of stabi-
lization and control are available to it and its allies, now, by comparison.
There is a strong central banking system to regulate credit. There is the
array of keynesian and monetary levers, which have worked pretty well
since World War II, even if less well recently. There is federal regulation
of a host of business practices; corporate leaders periodically howl about
this situation, but they helped establish it, and on the whole it stabilizes
their environment and limits the sorts of competition to which they
must respond. There is oligopoly in many more industries, and, more
importantly, there is the tacit system of collaborative pricing (for example, steel, autos) that has supplanted price competition. There is vertical
and horizontal integration of companies, allowing them to regulate
internally many processes that were subject to market vagaries in 1890.
There are big unions, and there is regulation by the government of
their conflicts with corporations, so that not only are "labor problems"
more measured and predictable, but once a contract is settled, the union
does much of management's work in enforcing it. There is (or was?) the
welfare state to keep the worst victims of capitalist inequality from starv-
ing or revolting, and also, along with the military establishment, to take
up some of the slack that has weakened American capitalism since 1929.
There are the mass media, sending myths that justify the status quo into
every home. And I could go on.

Late-nineteenth-century capitalists understood that they needed
broad controls over their world, in order to continue amassing wealth
peacefully. But they had not – could not have – hit upon any serviceable
methods. Concentrating on the immediate sphere of their operations,
production, they tried a variety of schemes to temper the chaos of competition. Gentlemen's agreements, trade associations, pools, cartels,
trusts, outright monopoly: all these and other strategies to restrict production, share markets, and keep prices up were repeatedly essayed,
but none succeeded more than fleetingly. And industrialists were hardly
more successful in achieving stable relations with their workers than
with their competitors. Their main weapon was force itself; and the use
of force failed to tame workers more than temporarily, while it periodically shook the faith of others in the legitimacy of big business.
Furthermore, the sometimes brutal effort to push exploitation to its

limits denied workers the means to buy many products of the machines they ran.

In short, businessmen were good at seizing the main chance, forging ahead with new enterprises and empires; but they were unable to find ways of cooperating, of stabilizing their milieu, of *ruling*. I hold with Gabriel Kolko on this point, and with Robert H. Wiebe.[29] The institutions that a national business class needed to carry on its affairs harmoniously did not yet exist. Two lacks were salient. There was only a decentralized and disorderly system of credit and finance; J.P. Morgan was himself the closest thing to a central bank, before 1914, and even his considerable resources of money, allies, influence, and determination were not sufficient. (All the major depressions were owed in part to financial disorder, and to the speculation and corruption that naturally accompanied it.) And the "political capitalism" (Kolko) that businessmen later managed to achieve, even while some bitterly resisted it, had barely begun to take shape in 1890, with timid regulation of railroads. Before the end of the century, capitalists took little interest in the political process, except as a source of giveaways and a target for bribes. When they did seek political remedies, these were often partial and local, answering the needs of one group by frustrating those of another.

Perhaps this disarray was inevitable in a nation that was not really one, a society composed of what Wiebe calls "island communities," lacking a national center and national institutions, only just united physically, with that unity more a cause of disruption than of coherence. Perhaps a self-conscious and united ruling class was an impossibility. In any case, it did not yet exist, and for all their power, businessmen had so far been unable to cope with the disorder they had created, while creating that power.

A Strategy

One strategy for control lay within the power of businessmen to execute. Rather than allying themselves with competitors, or swallowing them up, or making the government their executive committee, the masters of production could become engineers of consumption as well. They could, and did, turn the same kind of attention and energy that had made an agricultural society into an industrial one toward marketing. I am going to be specific about this in later chapters. But now, just for the moment, let us approach it conceptually and holistically, adopting the useful fiction that capitalists in their various enterprises moved with synchronized steps toward a common goal. In what ways did they address the crises I have itemized, by bringing sales under their systematic control?

If they could predict, or even guarantee, sales of a certain volume, they could calibrate production accordingly. There would be no more frenetic overbuilding of flour mills and stove factories in the blind hope of enough ready customers, and hence no desperate alternation between machines going full tilt and machines idle, between hiring and firing large groups of workers, between years of great profitability and years of loss or collapse. Or if they *had* overbuilt, they could remedy the mistake by reaching out to find more customers. Ideally, this would even out the frightening vicissitudes of their activities and their ledgers. And it would put them in a position to see everything at once – through the eyes of all the division heads and middle managers of the new large corporations – the whole of the process they must organize, from raw materials to factory, where the right number of machines and workers would be ready to turn out the right volume of product; from factory to a sophisticated distribution network reaching out to a known market. The flow of information would simultaneously run backward through these same stages, so that every decision about capital, labor, and materials would be founded on confident expectations about sales.

Although this strategy would not end competition, it could moderate it in two ways. First, through market research, salesmanship, and product differentiation, companies could divide customers up into "shares" of the market, and develop brand loyalties among them, so that competition would no longer be a voracious struggle ending in total domination or extinction. Second, the companies in any field that first achieved integration and rational management would squeeze out smaller competitors and make it hard for new ones to gain entry. That would mean a more stable environment with known dangers. And eventually it would lead to collaborative pricing, and the tacit agreement that prices could regularly go up but rarely go down (thus, in the fullness of time inflation would be a permanent feature of capitalism, but that's another story). Clearly these new arrangements also promised to stop the declining rate of profit and allow for accumulation at a satisfying pace.

Also, an emphasis on sales and consumption would gradually put capitalists in a new relationship with workers. They would of course continue to extract labor and surplus value from them at the work place, but in *realizing* that value through a vastly expanded sales effort they would approach those same workers on the other side of the factory gate, as consumers. They would urge workers – first those of the middle class, then all workers – to bring more and more commodities into their homes, and to share in the vision of a good life conducted through the use and display of these products. For decades the reality would fall a good deal short of the vision, but slowly rising wages (made possible by all that capital formation and the consequent rise in productivity) would support enough growth in consumption to keep the vision alive. And that, along with the softening posture of bosses to workers at the work place, would temper the harsh antagonism between the two classes. With luck, and in time, it would help enlist workers in the whole vast project of American capitalism, winning hearts and minds along with bellies.

While easing the contradictions of late-nineteenth-century capitalism, the turn toward marketing and its integration with production would give capitalists an olympian scope of action and saturate life with their needs and interests. Not only would they colonize the leisure of most citizens, as they had previously dominated work time; they would also integrate the nation into one huge market and market culture, seizing on recently created systems of transport and communication for this purpose. Before the people of the United States were a nation politically, businessmen had gathered their "island communities" into a nation organized around markets, money relations, and commodified culture.

That is the narrative whose early episodes ground the more particular stories I plan to tell in subsequent chapters. As I have outlined it here, it is at best bold, at worst crude and monolithic. I have excised all choices and actions except those of businessmen, as if the rest of the people had no projects and needs of their own, but were inert matter for capitalists to shape. I have compressed into one "strategy" an uneven, complex, and contested process that took decades to work through. I have written as if all capitalists hit on this strategy (they didn't), and as if they pursued it in harmonious collaboration (!). I have made it seem as if they had a conscious, broad, social design for the 1950s and after, which they began to effect in the 1890s with a prescience that no capitalist ruling class has so far exhibited. And I have made it sound as if the sales effort were the single solution to manufacturers' dilemmas.

That last stroke of Occam's razor answers to purposes of this study, which must keep marketing and advertising in the foreground because of their causality in the success of monthly magazines, my home ground. It responds also to my interest in those regions of the hegemonic process where historic agency is least coordinated, most widely dispersed among participants from different groups seeking different ends. Thus, I privilege the choices of businessmen in that sphere of their activity where each must look to the survival and profitability of his own company, in competition with other companies, and apart from conscious designs of class rule or social transformation.

While this emphasis directs attention to innumerable specific decisions such as that of Nabisco in 1898 to brand, package, and nationally advertise its crackers, it also lends itself to the most abstract understandings of historical change, by seeking to identify deep and general conditions that drove the myriad specific decisions and determined which ones would have a chance to succeed. Such conditions include overproduction, constraints on the realization of value, distortions and excesses in the formation of capital, falling rates of profit, and attendant financial crises, all of which periodically stall the normal work of capitalist accumulation and force a tectonic plate shift, a new regime of accumulation. That language and that abstraction suggest affinities between my argument and the theory of regular transformations within capitalism put forward by Michel Aglietta and the "regulation school." From their perspective, a new "social norm of consumption" was already "inscribed" in mechanized production and "Fordist" control of the labor process, so that collectively, businessmen *had* to meet the crisis of the 1880s and 1890s as they did, even though they could do so only in atomized disarray. The law of accumulation is a marxist counterpart of Smith's invisible hand.[30]

But it is just one character in the hegemonic story: many visible, human hands worked together in a conscious effort to establish and solidify the new social order. The very conditions of its possibility were laid down by concerted legal and political action, from the mid 1880s through the turn of the century. A series of court cases enabled its main institution, the modern corporation: determining that a corporation was legally a person with attendant contractual and political rights; establishing the shareholder form of ownership with limited liability; redefining property to include a right of return on intangible assets such as good will; facilitating the market in industrial stocks; and so on. New state laws (most notably in New Jersey) gave to corporations in general privileges, mobility, and powers previously granted chiefly to railroads. Federal law legitimated the corporation and its operation across state lines – its national scope – while mildly regulating it. Company lawyers and their allies fought for these new arrangements, which prepared the way for the mergers of 1898–1904 that helped resolve the crisis of competitive capitalism and brought the giant corporation into secure command of the economy.

Corporate leaders acted purposefully and collaboratively, along with political allies, to extend that command and negotiate the conflicts over regulation and trusts that marked the first decade of our century. In this sphere of activity they did enact a vision of social transformation and a new kind of class rule – political capitalism. In cooperation and combat with "professional-managerial class" reformers and with leaders of the old upper class such as Roosevelt, they established what Martin Sklar calls an "anti-competitive consensus," pushing aside both the ideology and many practices of the laissez-faire system. They hammered out a new ideology of order and efficiency, imagining the corporation as successor, through natural evolution, to the old entrepreneur, and as the vanguard of progress. They fought in the political arena, not just at factory gates, against unions. They agitated for American imperial power, to enlarge and protect international markets and investments. All this is familiar knowledge, and I do not mean to dismiss or diminish it by setting my inquiry on other hegemonic terrain.[31]

Furthermore, in such matters corporate leaders acted consciously as a class – or really, as a class-in-formation, since they were transcending the former position of some among them as entrepreneurs, and contesting

vigorously with small proprietors. They collaborated through such organizations as the National Association of Manufacturers, the National
Civic Federation, trade associations, and government commissions, as
well as in political parties, especially the Republican. They sat on one
another's boards. And of course they mingled in social organizations, cultural circles, private schools, elite suburbs. The ensemble of their
activities, as Sklar says, amounted to a social movement, one that in my
view produced a new hegemonic class within a transformed social order.

Having granted the vision and solidarity of that class in the political
arena, I want to reiterate that in daily work businessmen pursued no
vision beyond the usual one of survival and accumulation, and acted
more in antagonism than in concert. But their improvisation and oppor-
tunism in that sphere were no less consequential than their
self-organization in the other. A shift of their energy and resources to the
selling of products helped mightily to ease the crisis of the late nineteenth century and recreate American life on a new foundation.

5

Moving the Goods

Now I will elaborate on what it meant for "capitalists" to shift attention, resources, and energy to the sales effort. Those quotation marks are a signal that the agents of this historical change were a shifting, varied, and even motley cast of characters, which included captains of industry and finance, but also general merchants, factors, commission merchants, jobbers, specialized and general wholesalers, commodity dealers, founders of department stores, mail order sellers, chain store operators, advertising agents, and many others. I want to acknowledge the complexity and cross currents of the turn toward mass distribution, yet my purpose here is merely to sketch that complexity, and then devote most of the chapter to an analysis that looks for a unity among underlying processes. And I hope that it will help locate national advertising – the subject of the next chapter – within a much broader historical movement of transformation.[1]

Toward Modern Selling

In the early years of the Republic, three-quarters of the people worked on farms. They grew, processed, and cooked or preserved most of what they ate; built their own houses and barns; made most of their furniture and many of their tools and utensils; spun, wove, and sewed most or all of their clothes and bedding. For other needs they counted on local artisans, many doubling as farmers. Most of the remaining quarter of the workers were craftsmen, and they shaped and fabricated almost everything not produced at home.

It is important to remember the dominance of home production when thinking about the activities of selling. Before 1800 there was a good deal of *exchange* alongside direct production for use, but much of that happened through the informal cooperation of neighbors, through the barter of goods for goods and goods for services, and through small purchases made directly from the tinker or blacksmith or cordwainer who himself manufactured the goods. But specialized and separate activities of buying and selling had little place in economic life, and they served mainly the handful of townspeople (only 5 percent lived in towns of more than 2500, in 1790) and the smaller handful of affluent landowners.

With so few people, with so little commerce beyond village trading, and in light of the society's colonial roots, it is easy to understand that those who did preside over buying and selling – apart from making and using – operated in a far wider and less specialized arena than anyone does today. They were the all-purpose merchant capitalists, hardly distinguishable in their operations from those who for centuries had spread European commerce and hegemony through the rest of the world. They owned ships, bought cargoes on speculation. They were both importers and exporters. They acted as agents for other merchants. They insured cargoes. They lent money to finance local construction and manufacturing in the river and sea ports where they resided. They sold both at retail and at wholesale. And they traded all kinds of products, from hogs and whiskey to lace and tea.[2] These were powerful families; they organized the economic life of the nation. But they were far more than merchandisers, and their selling activities were amorphous, variable, and largely improvised.

Furthermore, in spite of the broad scope of their operations, these merchants dealt almost entirely with a network of people known to them. Each

> tried, where possible, to have members of his own family act as his agents in London, the West Indies, and other North American colonies. If he could not consign his goods and arrange for purchase and sale of merchandise through a family member or through a thoroughly reliable associate, the merchant depended on a ship captain or supercargo . . . . The merchant knew the other resident merchants in his town, who collaborated with him in insuring and owning ships, as he did the shipbuilders, rope-makers, and local artisans who supplied his personal as well as his business needs. Finally, he was acquainted with the planters, the farmers, and country storekeepers, as well as the fishermen, lumbermen, and others from whom he purchased goods and to whom he provided supplies.[3]

In short, at this time selling practices were embedded in a network of familiar social ties and were geared to directly perceived needs. Merchants who sold things to Americans also bought their produce and their small manufactures, so that distribution was intimately related to production. And, to repeat, although merchants played a magisterial role in the money economy, that economy did not encompass most of the productive work of Americans.

Through the first eighty years of the nineteenth century, this system of moving the goods entirely changed, in part because the population multiplied tenfold, and because the nation spread away from its coast-line, but mainly because production itself changed, in the way summarized in chapter 4. Suffice to say that by 1880 the transition was far advanced, from domestic and artisanal production to a factory sys-tem that turned out producer and consumer goods in large quantities. Production of some was highly mechanized: cigarettes, textiles, flour, film, paper, soap, canned goods, cereals, oil, paint, sugar, beer, for exam-ple. But even where technology was simple, most production took place in large units with many workers performing specialized tasks. A huge railroad system made it possible to bring raw materials from a distance and ship finished goods out to all parts of the country. Most people worked for wages, and produced very little at home, directly for use.

The old general merchants were unable to carry on their multiple functions through even the first stages of this change. An exceedingly complex evolution took place in sales, which may be schematized thus: retail and wholesale selling became more and more distinct functions. Shopkeepers bought from wholesalers, and wholesalers dropped out of retail sales (though there are major exceptions, like Marshall Field). Meanwhile, wholesaling became much more specialized, as to both the function and the range of goods handled. Middlemen came to deal only in textiles, or cotton, or hardware. And they reduced the number of economic transactions they handled. There were now specialized importers, exporters, factors, brokers, commission merchants, auction-eers, jobbers, warehousers, manufacturers' agents, and so on. Goods moved through complex series of transactions, from producer to con-sumer, with credit flowing along the line in equally complex ways.

That last point deserves some emphasis. For most of the time up until the Civil War, cash was scarce in the United States, there was no stock market for industrials, and commercial banking had not developed much as a source of capital for manufacturers. So it was natural that, as the old all-purpose merchants narrowed the scope of their selling oper-ations, they retained one that had no intrinsic connection to selling: the extension of credit. This activity assumed multiple forms (like all those so schematically presented here), running from brief advances to man-ufacturers secured by their inventories, to collaborations between wholesalers and industrial firms in enlarging the plants of the latter, to outright formation of companies with capital gathered by merchants, as with the Waltham and Lowell textile mills and the Cambria and Bethlehem rail mills.[4] In effect, merchants continued to act as the cen-tral coordinators and financiers of industrial growth, even as they specialized their selling activities to a fineness.

The situation – think of it as a large number of small- to medium-sized producers reaching out to an enormous number of small shopkeepers, through an elaborate network of independent middlemen – grew more and more unstable after 1860 or so. The broadest way to understand that instability is to say that industrial capitalism had burgeoned within a mercantile capitalist framework that could no longer contain its energies; or again, that a severe contradiction had arisen between production and distribution. I'll mention a few particulars of this crisis.

First, of course, mass production itself put a strain on the Rube Goldberg apparatus of distribution. Manufacturers needed to keep the machines running in order to turn a profit on fixed capital, and the wholesaler network couldn't keep up. Second, industrial firms grew larger and larger; by the 1880s some had become oligopolists in their sectors and this tendency toward concentration accelerated rapidly through mergers, reaching a crescendo in the years just before and after 1900. On the other side, industrialization created armies of workers who had to buy most of the things they used, and massed these consumers together in cities. So the larger producers faced their own and other workers as a potential mass market, across a crowd of middlemen and a vast array of small stores. The shopkeepers and country merchants were very like their predecessors of the eighteenth century. The middlemen had altered their tasks, but still carried them out in much the same personal and improvised ways, and through the same kind of organization – basically the family firm. Advanced, concentrated production; old-fashioned, diffuse marketing: the imbalance had grown more uneven because manufacturers had less and less need for the services of wholesalers in providing capital. A combination of Civil War profits, the spoils of high-tech production, the emergence of banks willing to lend to industrialists, and the increased use of the joint stock company gave big manufacturers more autonomy and the potential to take leadership in the economy.

Mass Marketing

They did assume leadership in time, but they were not the first to undertake the rationalization and control of markets. That effort was launched first by agents in the other two sectors – by middlemen and retailers. Here, as at so many points in this study, it seems that the needs of industrial capital realize themselves through mediation by new kinds of entrepreneurs, who see or stumble upon opportunities where capitalists have noticed only barriers and frustrations. Such mediations often lead the way, and make wealthy capitalists of their inventors, but only when they fit in with and help advance the project of industrial capitalists. People like John Wanamaker and Montgomery Ward did not act under the direction of manufacturers, but their success could have happened only in the space created by large scale capitalist production. I will turn now to the revolution in selling, and mention half a dozen contributors to it. They emerged in different quarters of the economy and pursued different courses of action, but I will argue that they all contributed to a single, underlying process: turning sales into big business.

In the 1850s, some wholesalers began to reassemble into one business all the transactions that took place between manufacturer and retail store. They took on full lines of goods (hardware, for example, or dry goods or drugs). They took advantage of the railroads and telegraph to extend their trade through large parts of the country. And they became jobbers, taking ownership of the goods for cash, and usually selling for cash or for very short-term credit. Their goal was to move large quantities of merchandise, and move it fast; by the 1870s, they measured the performance of their various departments by the rate of "stock-turn." As the word "department" suggests, they also became complex business organizations, in contrast to all the middlemen of the first half of the century. An executive branch was flanked on one side by hundreds of salesmen fanning out through the cities and small towns to influence *and meter* demand, and on the other side by departmentalized buyers, who acquired large amounts of merchandise from producers around the country and in Europe – and who increasingly influenced production by contracting in advance to buy the whole output of a manufacturer, or a large portion of it, meanwhile setting specifications to which the manufacturer would work. In other words, these jobbers not only shortened and rationalized the chain of distribution, they also constituted a medium through which information easily passed from retailer to producer and back again. And of course they helped lower the final prices of commodities, bringing more of them within the range of more customers.

Mass wholesaling emerged as a significant business practice in the 1850s and reached the height of its development just after 1880.[5] Another innovation began earlier in the retail sector and continued to grow in importance for many decades after wholesaling peaked. That was the department store, though the institution did not assume its modern form until the 1870s (and the *term* came into wide use only in the 1890s). Some dry goods stores in New York began to expand their sales to previously unheard-of levels in the 1830s, and their premises a bit later: A.T. Stewart's famous Marble Dry Goods Palace in 1846; Arnold Constable's Marble House in 1857; Lord & Taylor's new marble structure in 1860. These elegant, spacious, five-story buildings, among the largest of any sort in New York, gave visible evidence that selling had become a new kind of activity. These retailers bought in volume, sold cheap, had hundreds of employees, and served tens of thousands of customers – a far cry from the one- or two-person shop that had dominated retailing since the earliest days.

But in two ways, these flourishing businesses had, in 1860, still fallen short of their modern articulation. In most of them, retail sales were an adjunct to wholesaling; for some, that balance continued for decades – A.T. Stewart and Marshall Field, for instance.[6] And although some of the big stores had developed a departmental structure, both in their buying and at their sales counters, they still limited their wares primarily to dry goods. The transformation of the dry goods "palace" into a kind of universal market, with retailing in command, took place between 1860 and the 1890s, with Macy's and Lord & Taylor leading the way.

For instance, when Rowland Macy started his New York store in 1858, he specialized almost entirely in "fancy dry goods": ribbons, lace, artificial flowers, feathers, and so on, to be used in finishing dresses and hats.[7] By 1860 he sold furnishings, towels, underwear, blankets, curtains, and parasols. Through the 1860s, the line expanded rapidly to include handbags, tea sets, picture frames, dolls, games, soaps, perfumes, hats, bracelets and other jewelry, bronze and ivory ornaments, clocks, silverware, housewares, utensils, brushes, baby carriages, books, and candy. And by the 1890s, his very much enlarged store carried glassware, furniture, rugs, gardening sets, sporting goods, guns, bicycles, sewing machines, hardware, shoes, paintings, boys' and men's clothes, watches, stoves, photographic supplies, and many other lines. It would probably be easier to list the items *not* sold at Macy's. Meanwhile, the store had become an integrated, multi-unit, modern company, with dozens of departments working as semi-autonomous operations, reporting to a hierarchy of managers. It was a gigantic enterprise, employing 3000 people and passing $8 million in annual sales before the end of the century. Remember that there were about ten other big department stores in New York at this time, and a proportionate number in other large cities. They quite dominated urban retailing amid the ruins of many small businesses, and after protracted legal battles.[8]

They built their unprecedented trade through a variety of practices, many new at the time, all standard now. They bought in large quantities, more and more often directly from manufacturers; and like the big jobbers, they ordered goods made to specification, and even went into manufacturing themselves, though not in most departments. They admitted all customers, with no obligation to buy. They sold cheap. Their prices were fixed: no haggling, one price for all. Some, like Macy's, accepted only cash, but many extended credit widely. They also followed the lead of Marshall Field, Wanamaker's, and Macy's by guaranteeing goods, and offering the customer's money back for any purchase returned as unsatisfactory. They advertised lavishly in local newspapers (Macy's ad budget averaged more than 1.5 percent of sales through the 1890s). And to the customers drawn by advertisements and low prices, the big stores offered an experience of luxury and plenty: not only the elegant buildings and glittering array of commodities, but services that made the humblest shopper feel like Mrs Astor. Marshall Field, for instance, had writing rooms with desks and paper supplied, a library, restrooms with maids, a nursery, a medical room, waiting rooms for men, original art to gaze at, and of course a large restaurant.[9] Macy's, though less elegant than Marshall Field, did not exaggerate in calling itself a "shopping resort."[10] A plethora of cheap as well as expensive goods surrounded by a glow of affluence characterized the experience of city shopping.

A mass urban market grew up rather quickly in the years before and after the Civil War. It is important to remember, however, that while cities boomed the rural population also continued to grow (until 1910), and remained larger than the urban until about the time of World War I. Farm income more than tripled between the Civil War and the end of the century. For obvious reasons, no retail palaces could serve this large market, which remained dependent on the general, country store for items not produced by farmers for their own use (and they produced more for market and less for use throughout this time). "Dependent" is the right word, too, especially in the South and the West, where store-keepers extended credit to farmers against the harvest and often held them virtually in bondage. In addition, store prices were high, reflecting as they did the wholesaler's and jobber's mark-up as well as that of the country merchant himself, and the cost of the credit which was generally added on at each stage of distribution, so that retail prices were often more than double manufacturer's prices.[11] And of course the stock in these general stores included only a drab assortment of basic and usually generic goods. Though the country store did often serve as a social center and the locus of neighborly courtesies, farmers had good reason to feel cheated, and they did.

Once railroads and the postal system linked all parts of the country, the opportunity arose for a new kind of selling to this scattered but very large market. In the 1860s, a number of entrepreneurs began selling by mail; more precisely, they advertised and received orders by mail, but sent the goods by railway freight or express (the modern parcel post system came into effect only in 1913). They sold a broad range of products in this way, from jewelry to medicines to musical instruments to farm machinery. They advertised widely in national magazines; indeed, as noted in chapter 2, a whole genre of magazines prospered in the 1870s and 1880s, which were little more than vehicles for mail order ads, and which were virtually given away (*People's Literary Companion, Comfort, Fireside Visitor, Chicago Fireside Friend*, and so on). But these earlier mail order merchants sold only one line of goods, for the most part; their individual operations were small, even though as an ensemble they offered farmers an important alternative to the general store.

Aaron Montgomery Ward first conceived the idea (in 1872) of conducting a sales operation by mail that would parallel and surpass that of the country store. It is interesting to note that his venture built consciously on farmers' discontent: he made it his project to buy for cash from the manufacturer and sell for cash to the farmer at very low prices made possible by volume buying and the elimination of middlemen and credit. He had the endorsement of the Grange (the powerful organization of farmers), carried on the cover of his catalog into the 1880s. And almost from the beginning, he offered a money-back guarantee. The business succeeded immediately: by the early 1890s, Ward was putting out a 540-page catalog listing 24,000 items, and selling more than a million dollars' worth of goods annually.

The other great mail order house began with no populist mission, and in an almost comically contrasting way. Richard Sears cooked up one shady scheme after another for selling watches and jewelry, beginning in 1886. He repeatedly folded up one "business" and started another, never believing that mail order was more than a passing fad. And even when Sears, Roebuck and Company was clearly a major enterprise, Sears hyped his goods wildly and erratically, often bringing in floods of orders that outran both inventory and the capacity of staff to respond. This drove Roebuck to distraction; he got out in 1895, making way for Aaron Nussbaum and Julius Rosenwald, who managed to counterbalance Sears's maniacal brilliance, and organize the company for its permanent expansion.

Yet Sears, Roebuck and Montgomery Ward became very similar operations in spite of these differences in purpose and temperament (as did other mail order houses that pursued the two giants at a distance). Like Ward, Sears bought in quantity and for cash from manufacturers, usually contracting for their entire output of a particular line and often dictating the specifications of products. Eventually, Sears went more into direct control of production: by 1906 it owned part or all of sixteen factories. The company sold at fixed, rock bottom prices, for cash, and with a free return policy for any merchandise that failed to please the customer. (Briefly, around 1900, it even sent goods in advance of payment.) It advertised broadly if crudely; from 1898 to 1905 advertising expenses ranged between 6 percent and 13 percent of sales.[12] The bulk of this money went into the famous catalog, but Sears also used the "mail order magazines," and even some prestigious monthlies like *Cosmopolitan*.

The difference in scale between advertising by Sears and Ward on the one hand and major department stores on the other reflects the difference between presenting one's entire line of goods to isolated farmers and attracting city people into a nearby store where they might inspect the goods themselves. Otherwise, the mail order houses created a space of desire and purchase homologous to that of the department stores. Thus, the 1895 Sears catalog arranged its wares in departments much like those of Macy's: crockery, bicycles, guns, revolvers, fishing tackle, sporting goods, baby carriages, furniture, buggies, harnesses, saddlery, sewing machines, boots, shoes, clothing, pianos, organs, other musical instruments, optical goods, watches, jewelry, diamonds, silverware, and clocks.[13] One additional department, farm implements, never made an appearance on 14th Street. Missing from the list (unaccountably, to me) are dry goods, but by 1900 the Sears catalog had added this line, the initial *raison d'être* of department stores.[14] So, by the 1890s, city and country people had comparable arrays of inexpensive commodities available to them. And the sellers were all big businesses: like Marshall Field, both Ward and Sears passed $10 million in annual sales around 1900.

One other form of mass retailing deserves a brief mention: the chain store. Structurally, retail chains came to occupy a demographic space between that of the mail order houses and the department stores. Woolworth's began in medium-sized towns like Utica and Lancaster; A&P launched its first tea stores in lower Manhattan. For the most part, chain stores operated in small towns and in city neighborhoods away from "downtown." Otherwise, they resembled department stores and mail order houses: quantity buying; increasing control over manufacturing, processing, and packaging; fixed, low prices; cash business only. Many relied heavily on advertising, though not F.W. Woolworth, who felt that his store windows were advertisement enough, along with the opportunity for customers to *feel* the enticing objects that could be bought for a nickel or a dime. Although most chains (apart from "variety" stores like Woolworth's) sold only a few lines, together they covered most areas – hardware, paint, housewares, shoes, clothing, drugs, and so on. The one area in which they claimed the mass retailing field for themselves was of course food. (Both Sears and some of the department stores tried selling groceries, but never carried the effort very far.) Chain stores equaled and passed the other types of mass retailer only in the 1920s and after, but they had established themselves firmly by 1900, when A&P had 200 stores, Woolworth 59; and each attained annual sales of $5 million.[15]

To recapitulate: after the Civil War, some wholesalers took an initiative that made them sole middlemen between manufacturers and retailers, and made them mass marketers as well. Simultaneously at the retail end, department stores, mail order houses, and later chain stores began taking over from middlemen, presenting customers with rich displays of goods, and developing into multimillion dollar businesses. Now I want to turn to a third movement, which completed this revolution in sales and consumption. It parallels the other two, in a kind of structural tidiness, because it originated with *manufacturers*.[16]

Companies making consumer products went into sales for one basic reason, already detailed in the last chapter: they *had* to, in order to cut down the risks of their highly competitive environment and to smooth out the process of accumulation. Beneath this generalization lie a number of more specific causes that led some manufacturers to build distribution networks, while others continued to rely upon the old system, and restricted their efforts to making the goods:

1. The pioneers had learned how to make their products in large quantities, very rapidly, and with heavy use of fixed capital: machines that had to be kept running to pay for themselves (you can't lay off a machine when business is slack). Such methods of production, involving

high-speed or continuous process machines and a large input of energy, began to develop in sugar refining, brewing, and oil refining by the 1860s. A real explosion in high speed production occurred in the early 1880s: flour, cereals, canned goods, film, cigarettes, matches, followed a bit later by chewing gum and soft drinks. Leaders found themselves producing more than they could distribute by traditional methods. For instance, when James Buchanan Duke acquired his first two Bonsack cigarette machines (and exclusive rights to their use), he could immediately make more cigarettes than all Americans smoked. He had to build a sales network and advertise heavily to turn his product from a novelty into a necessity. Likewise, Henry P. Crowell built an integrated mill to make oatmeal in 1882, but Americans didn't eat much oatmeal – a difficulty overcome on the sales side by the creation of Quaker Oats.[17]

2. Some companies, whether their production was enormous or simply large, had problems that general wholesalers couldn't handle. Some needed temperature control (meat, bananas, beer). Some needed elaborate customer services (sewing machines, reapers, binders, office equipment). These, too, took over the distribution of their own wares.

3. Most producers of consumer goods who integrated forward to wholesaling or retailing made inexpensive things that sold to large numbers of customers. For these firms, the growing cities offered big, concentrated markets. After a certain point, they could reach these markets more efficiently and cheaply by setting up their own sales departments. Examples: Standard Oil, US Rubber (boots and shoes), Sherwin-Williams (paint), Cluett, Peabody (collars and cuffs), Parker Pens, and Eaton, Crane, and Pile (stationery).[18]

4. The move from production into sales facilitated oligopoly in many sectors. Likewise, where oligopoly came first, through merger, the newly formed giants soon found that if they did not integrate forward into sales (as well as backward), their size alone did not protect them from the choice between suicidal price wars and the strain of buying out competing companies. But if they did organize their own sales operations, their size permitted great economies, as well as major ad campaigns: examples include the Distillers Corporation, the National Biscuit Company, and the American Cotton Oil Trust (fertilizer, feed, washing powder, lard, soap); while the road to monopoly capital was littered with failed mergers that did not integrate, especially in food, textiles, clothing, leather goods, bicycles, and paper products.[19]

Companies that established nationwide sales networks for one or all of these reasons were not, however, the only ones to succeed in capturing big national markets. Many who continued to rely on independent wholesalers and jobbers also succeeded, and a partial list of these is instructive: Kellogg, Postum, Cream of Wheat, Baker (chocolate), Van Camp, Calumet, Horlicks, Beech-Nut, Pacific Coast Borax (Twenty Mule Team),

Parke-Davis, I.W. Lyon and Son (tooth powder), Western Clock Co. (Baby Ben), Whitman's (candy), Bissell (carpet sweepers), Ingersoll, Elgin, Gillette, B.V.D.[20] Evidently, these companies were not leaving sales to chance or the whim of the jobber. Their brand names are lodged in the memory because they, like most of the integrated corporations, reached out into the consumer's mind through advertising. There were more ways than one for manufacturers to control sales, and advertising was more nearly universal than wholesaling or regional offices. To guarantee consumer demand for a small household item was, in fact, to make it almost irrelevant whether the producer or the jobber handled distribution.

Looking back to the 1880s, a major soap maker showed how clearly manufacturers understood this:

> Twenty-five years ago the manufacturer went to the jobber, related the merits of his goods, and arranged the terms. The jobber said: "Send me two cars at the agreed terms." The jobber then went to the retailer and told him that he had goods of exceptional quality, stated the terms, and the retailer ordered several cases. When the consumer came to the retailer, she asked for an article but did not specify the brand. She relied upon the retailer, who supplied her from his stock on hand. The method of twenty-five years ago is reversed today. The manufacturer goes first to the consumer. By advertising he burns it into the consumer's mind that he wants a certain brand. Through premiums, gifts or bribes if you please, he induces her to try his brand. At tremendous expense the manufacturer educates her to ask for Fels Naphtha, Ivory, Rub-No-More, Arrow collars, etc., as the case may be. The demand created, the retailer goes to the jobber asking him to furnish the articles called for. Then the jobber goes to the manufacturer.
>
> Our company sells through the jobber, and we do the rest. We create the desire for our product through advertising.[21]

As producers learned to engineer sales, they sometimes took the wholesaler's function into their own organization, and when they didn't, they reduced that function to one of taking orders and delivering the goods, rather than selling.

Meanwhile, mass retailers preempted the wholesaling function from the other side, and increasingly dictated what would be produced for their counters and catalogs. A new kind of economy had arisen, dominated by large corporations that in one way or another made sales their business.

Dimensions of the Change

In writing about these events I have wanted to emphasize their variety and disconnectedness, even their chaotic quality. Men like Duke,

Woolworth, Procter and Gamble, Sears, and Macy followed no grand designs. They did not foresee even their own successes, much less understand their efforts as a reorganization of society. There was a hit-or-miss spontaneity to their schemes, as they followed intuitions and sought only their own advancement. When something worked, they did more of it. At the same time, I have wanted to make a seemingly opposite point: that these events do constitute one story, that of ingenuity, resources, and organizational energy shifted from production to sales. Now I will stand back a bit farther from the story, and gloss some of its historical meanings in a way that will, I hope, prepare for my account of advertising and mass culture.

Behind the process that led to planned mass marketing, we can see a double transformation of American society that took place with great speed, by historical standards. Within a hundred years the society moved through three forms of economic organization. At the beginning of the century, general merchants supervised economic life. They, along with the big landowners (especially in the South), made up a rather diffuse ruling class. One may wonder whether to call this system mercantile capitalism: merchants did not own the major means of production (land and tools), and some have argued that the US in 1800 is best understood as a "domestic mode of production." I don't think much is at stake here, so long as we remember that the US, with no feudal past, was a remote outpost of European mercantilism and integrated within that world system. Capitalism was marginal to the lives and production of most farmers and artisans, but the capitalism that did exist was mercantile, and merchants presided over the social surplus.

They helped move some of it into mills, factories, railroads, and so sponsored a new class that in turn became dominant, by 1870. Industrial entrepreneurs freed themselves from dependence on merchants (wholesalers). They owned most of the productive apparatus in the manufacturing sector, which was creating more market value than farmers, and which was the dynamic force in capital formation and social change. Industrialists brought into being a new counterpart class, a wage-earning proletariat. And their project led to intense crises along with power and wealth, as noted in the last chapter.

Out of those crises emerged a third form of American capitalism, dominated by large corporations and their owners. These corporations no longer limited themselves to manufacturing, but organized the entire economic process, from farming and the extraction of raw materials all the way through to retail sales or sales of producer goods. Some originated *in* retailing, a few in extraction, most in manufacturing. But almost all the successful ones shortened the chain between production and final sales, taking internal control of what had been risky and chaotic market processes. Manufacturers went into distribution and advertising; mass retailers took over the wholesaling function and increasingly directed production of the commodities that adorned their shelves and catalogs.[22] They substituted planning and control for the old system of producing the goods and hoping for the best.

The movement from production to sales ties in with all the main features of the modern corporation, whether analyzed by mainstream historians like Chandler or by marxists like Baran and Sweezy. The many units and complex internal hierarchies of these corporations were necessary to monitor and coordinate production and sales. The corporations were able to achieve *autonomy* – control from inside, generation of their own capital – partly because they stabilized and controlled distribution. They could abandon the old war of all against all, with its destructive bouts of price cutting and market cornering, because they found more steady and reliable ways to maintain a market share and expand with the whole economy rather than through cutthroat competition. Hence the "corespective" behavior of oligopolists, the competition through cost cutting rather than price, the tacit price fixing, the rising rate of profit for all. Monopoly capitalism is *marketing* capitalism.

In fact, Baran and Sweezy argue that through market research, spurious product differentiation, and advertising, the sales effort – once a mere adjunct of production, helping the manufacturer to dispose profitably of goods designed to satisfy recognized consumer needs – increasingly invaded factory and shop, dictating what was to be produced according to criteria laid down by the sales department and its consultants and advisers in the advertising industry.[23] Things had not "progressed" nearly so far in 1900. Yet I have indicated how much the mass retailers influenced production around that date, sometimes taking it on directly, and often setting the specifications to which independent factories would work. And manufacturers had already begun the process of creating needs not previously felt – for gum, cigarettes, oatmeal, soft drinks, and so on. From there it did not take a revolution to carry the process one step further, first determining what needs could be fostered or created, and then making the product to go with the ad campaign. A few ventures such as Gillette were sales-driven from the start. What laid the foundation for our present consumer culture was the integration of sales and production, well underway ninety-five years ago.

Along with that integration, and inseparable from it, came the integration of the United States itself as more than a loose political affiliation. Canals, railroads, steamship lines, the telegraph, and the telephone were the infrastructure, gradually laid down through the nineteenth century. But the unification of production and daily life came through the sales effort. Schematically: department stores sold much the same classes of commodities in the city center as mail order houses did on the farm, and chain stores in the neighborhoods and small towns. Manufacturers who went into sales advertised and distributed nationally, so that both Ivory Soap and its intrusive symbolism were available on 23rd Street as well as in Hoxie, Kansas, bringing these distant and disparate communities into the same commercial culture.

Monopoly capital united us as consumers. But of course it further divided us as producers. A corporate ruling class consolidated itself, through stocks, bonds, banks, political networks, cultural organizations, marriages, schools, the social register. Increasingly, it delegated management of its enterprises to hired employees, who, along with the growing force that managed money, the law, education, government agencies, and other key institutions of the new society, emerged as an identifiable middle class – the "professional-managerial class," as I call it.[24] Shopkeepers and farmers remained, but declined in relative importance after 1900. The industrial working class swelled with immigrants and with country girls and boys who gave up on farm life; and the sales effort created an army of deskilled wage workers harder and harder to distinguish from their counterparts in factories. How different was the $8-a-week laborer in Sears's wallpaper factory from the $5-a-week stock clerk at Sears's warehouse on Fulton Street?

All these classes – and even farmers – moved farther and farther into the money economy through the last half of the century. Production for exchange eased out production for use. To look at the transition another way, before mid century, most people still grew and prepared most of their own food, made most of their own clothing, produced their own lighting and heat, built their houses, made some furniture and tools. (Even in cities, many had gardens, kept chickens and pigs, made candles and soap.) The early development of mass marketing fit itself into home production, rather than displacing it. Farm implements sold by mail were, of course, used to produce food and cotton. One of the earliest foodstuffs to be branded and sold in the new way was flour, which then became bread and pastries through further home labor. Department stores dealt mainly in dry goods through the 1870s and even later: factories made the textiles, but the purchaser then continued the process of production at home, to make dresses, hats, cloaks, upholstery, bedding, drapes. Ditto for the notions that were a staple of five-and-dime stores. Men's ready-made clothing was uncommon before mid century; ready-made clothes for women came still later. Only toward the end of the century could one buy a full array of cheap finished products through the mail and at stores. And needless to say, that manifestation of goods for sale was no more than the other face of a change which by 1900 put most people's labor power to work for wages, in factories and shops, stores and offices.

The displacement of home production amounted also to a redefinition of gender, especially for women, as the last paragraph suggests. From acting as part of a semi-autonomous productive unit, women gradually gave up parts of their work and skill to industrial capitalists. Many –

farm daughters and immigrants especially – became wage workers themselves. Whether a woman did that or not, she entered the money
economy as a purchaser and manager of commodities. This is not to say
that women were released from the burden of domestic work; there was
(and is) still plenty of that, except for those women of the two highest
classes who could afford maids and cooks. But the nature of the work
changed, becoming less universal, less skilled, more involved with products made at a distance by others. The male gender altered, too, as men
left the home and went to work for bosses, but they kept a visible place
in production. Women's productive activities were devalued and made
almost invisible, because left out of the new money economy. But women
as consumers were visible indeed. The Sears and Montgomery Ward
catalogs, going as they did to family farms, were almost gender-neutral.
Other mass marketers understood well with which gender they traded.
Most ads for branded products targeted women, in *McClure's* and
Munsey's almost as much as in the *Ladies' Home Journal.* Woolworth stores
drew mainly women and children, and food chains were a female preserve until quite recently. Department stores, in particular, created a
social space for women: as late as the 1950s, 80–85 percent of spending
there was done by women.[25] The services and amenities they provided
made women feel at home – or at a higher-class home than their own.
Some stores, like Macy's, hired mainly female clerks to put customers at
ease; others, like A.T. Stewart, hired attractive young men to eroticize
shopping. Either way, the appeal was to women. When stores began to
include men's clothing departments, they invariably placed them near
store entrances or in separate buildings, to save men the discomfort of
wandering deep into this female world.

Gender aside, consuming was a way of life that had to be learned, and
taught. Moving from dependence on traditional skills, family labor, local
artisans, and village merchants, to reliance on products that were made,
plugged, and often sold by strangers was exciting but scary. As manufacturers and retailers invited people into these new relations of
distribution, they sought in various ways to build trust. At department
stores, for instance, free entry and departure set people at ease. Home
delivery accommodated and flattered the customer. The policy of fixed
prices – universal among mass retailers – made for a clean if impersonal
transaction. Cash only did likewise, where it was practiced, and also
ended the often messy and demeaning dependency of customers on
merchants. Most important of all, the money-back guarantee allayed
fears of being gypped, and represented the company as honest, reliable, and permanent. Nor was this policy hypothetical: both department
stores and mail order houses took back significant percentages of what
they sold, making good on their guarantee of satisfaction, and keeping
the customer "always right."[26]

These were straightforward business practices, which made shopping a safe, simple habit. Around them emerged a wider set, less plain and comprehensible. Perhaps I can best generalize by saying that companies tried to familiarize and humanize their relations with customers. Branding contributed much to this effort, along with trademarks and uniform packaging. Even if ten brands of soap were much alike, to know that Pears' or Ivory was one's *own* brand was to feel more at home amidst the dazzling variety. As Susan Strasser puts it, branding allowed distant manufacturers to establish "reputations and relationships with consumers as surely as the corner grocer did through personal contact and personality." It also substituted brand loyalty for competitive pricing, when it worked successfully.[27] Wholesalers began branding products early on, as did a few manufacturers. Department stores, mail order houses, and many of the chains followed suit. And in a wider sense, these retailers' names and symbols (Macy's red star, for example) served as brand names, giving an identity to all the products in the store or catalog.

Hand in hand with branding went advertising, which proliferated through the 1890s, and which will be my subject in chapters 6 and 8. Manufacturers advertised in national magazines, department stores in local newspapers, mail order houses through their own catalogs – and there were billboards, signs, posters, advertising cards, and a host of other forms. In many ways, advertising sought to make the potential customer feel herself part of a personal relationship. The voice in most national advertising, which I will discuss in chapter 8, became informal, helpful, neighborly, sometimes humorous. Rowland Macy struck a similar note in local ads, writing copy that ran from the casually homiletic –

THERE is an ART or SCIENCE
In spending money, and few know how to spend
to the best advantage. Buy the best the market
affords. Buy for cash. Buy cheap and you are wise.

– to the self-mocking –

R.H. MACY,
Nos. 204 and 206 6th-av.,
HAVING GONE IN, WAY UP TO HIS NECK, TO
WAX DOLLS, CRYING BABIES,
BABIES THAT CAN'T AND WON'T CRY,
BABIES THAT CAN AND BABIES THAT CAN'T OPEN
THEIR EYES OR SHUT 'EM,
. . .
HAS NOW DETERMINED TO GET OUT![28]

But the prize for homiest corporate voice should probably go to Richard Sears, who filled every inch of space in his catalogs with enthusiastic copy, and told customers why they should accept Sears, Roebuck and Company as a trustworthy friend:

> We shall always aim to make the ordering of goods from us pleasant as well as profitable to the purchaser. Our army of employes [sic] are instructed to handle every order and letter with care, in fact, to treat every customer at a distance just as they would like to be treated were they in the customer's place and the customer in theirs. . . . As we have thousands of customers in every state and territory, you will no doubt find one of them a neighbor, who can explain to you how thoroughly we live up to all our representations and how carefully we watch the interests of our customers. . . .[29]

And:

> Don't be afraid that you will make a mistake. We receive hundreds of orders every day from young and old who never before sent away for goods. We are accustomed to handling all kinds of orders. Tell us what you want in your own way, written in any language, no matter whether good or poor writing, and the goods will promptly be sent to you.[30]

Friendly letters poured in in response, bearing orders. Sears invited customers to visit the plant when in Chicago, and they did.

Fixed prices and return policies invited trust through contracts offered by the marketer and accepted by the customer. Advertising and catalog copy did so in a discourse initiated by the company and sent out to people it regarded as the masses, though it addressed them in a quasi-personal way. Distant and unequal relations gradually replaced the transactions of city shop and country store, where one bought from a neighbor, negotiated prices and terms, gossiped, or discussed crops and weather. New relations of selling occupied a new social space that was more abstract, in some ways imaginary.

Meanwhile, marketers built physically real spaces of a new kind. Department stores were paradigmatic. Elegant, imposing "palaces" dominated the cityscape. Behind large, plate glass windows, increasingly theatrical displays lent an aura of glamour to commodities and drew shoppers to entrances where no steps slowed access, and where revolving doors eased passage. Inside were domes, great staircases, galleries, open spaces, elevators and later escalators, indirect lighting, mirrors, fountains, restaurants, hundreds or thousands of people, and magical tableaux of commodities in glass cases meeting every need and instilling needs not previously realized. The early synonyms for store – palace, house, emporium, resort – suggest the exuberance felt by the owners, and there is no reason to doubt that customers shared that feeling. In entering the store one entered a world apart, vistas and labyrinths constructed on a different logic from that of the streets outside. Here one could wander from gloves to bicycles to the writing room, through an organized confusion united perhaps by a Japanese or Middle Eastern or cathedral theme, by the aura of shopping, and by the purposeful errands of cash boy and cash girl – later by the ring of the cash register. A woman who came for cutlery might leave with fine lace and a doll, and feel a kind of liberation from dull instrumentality. The principle of *seduction* was overcoming that of *supply*,[31] as retailers created an "environment of desire."[32] Dreiser described its allure:

> Carrie passed along the busy aisles, much affected by the remarkable displays of trinkets, dress goods, stationery, and jewelry. Each separate counter was a show place of dazzling interest and attraction. She could not help feeling the claim of each trinket and valuable upon her personally, and yet she did not stop. There was nothing there which she could not have used – nothing which she did not long to own. The dainty slippers and stockings, the delicately frilled skirts and petticoats, the laces, ribbons, hair-combs, purses, all touched her with individual desire, and she felt keenly the fact that not any of these things were in the range of her purchase.[33]

Space at Woolworth's was humble by comparison, but similar in design. Variety stores, like department stores, lured people in through window displays, and trusted that novelty and profusion would set off unanticipated impulses to buy. Ward and Sears collected their goods out of sight in Chicago plants, but their catalogs brought into the very hands of farmers and townspeople the same dazzling array, in two-dimensional images spread over more than a thousand pages. Advertising sections of national magazines did the same. By 1900, everyone in American society had access to at least some of these social spaces where displays provoked the imagination to new visions of self, family, status, the good life.

I say "everyone": commodified life took root among the wealthier classes first, but marketers cultivated at least the feeling of democracy. Macy's advertising insisted that the store "caters *ABSOLUTELY* to *ALL* classes."[34] At Field, Leiter and Company – predecessor of Marshall Field – working women could gaze at Mrs Potter Palmer, Mrs Cyrus McCormick, and Mrs Abraham Lincoln alighting from their carriages,[35] and Field's clerks were instructed to treat both classes of women with the same courtesy. Sears, as noted above, explicitly told rural folk that their syntax and manners raised no barriers or eyebrows. Woolworth courted the business of immigrants and blacks (though he refused to *hire* the latter).[36] Rural African Americans could receive mail order catalogs. *Munsey's Magazine*, at ten cents a copy, went mainly to middle class people but was within reach of farmers and workers, at least for an occasional peek into a world that might later be available. The new social spaces opened the prospect – the mirage – of a society made classless through consumption.

Finally, though shopping was more and more a necessary activity for social reproduction and individual survival, marketers represented it as a form of *leisure*, something women did in their spare time and for pleasure. An ideology of freedom grew around consumption, and helped sharpen the division between work and leisure. I hope I have shown how pragmatism and fantasy, self interest and illusion, mingled in this ideology, and to what extent imaginary social relations grew up amidst the real relations of production, exploitation, and hard sell. It is worth noting that the resistance to mass retailing – often bitter and well organized – came entirely from the wholesalers and small store owners who were being pushed aside, not from the consuming "public."

Like all social formations, monopoly capitalism presented surface appearances that mystified its underlying forces. But the connection between retail palace and industrialists' struggle for survival and dominance was perhaps more opaque than that between medieval cathedral and the rule of feudal lords. In the 1890s, when national advertising and a national mass culture came into being, the transition to monopoly capitalism was far from complete. Its emergence, rather than its ascendancy, formed the arena for the developments I will consider next.

6

Advertising: New Practices,
New Relations

In 1784, the *Pennsylvania Packet and Daily Advertiser* did indeed become a daily newspaper, the first in the young Republic. It had begun in 1771 as a weekly, then gradually shortened the intervals between issues, driven toward more frequent publication by the amount of advertising its editor was able to bring in.

As was customary, page one (of four pages, total) in the first daily issue went entirely to ads. The first five ads gave notice of sailings for Liverpool, Dublin, Cork, Gothenburg, and London; the sixth offered a ship for sale. Three ads proclaimed the services of "brokers," really all-purpose merchants and bankers. Half a dozen ads or so offered assortments of merchandise for sale, from "coarse and fine blankets" to "Old Cognac Brandy in boxes of 12 bottles each." Such notices were often connected to the arrival of a particular ship from abroad, with mixed cargo to be retailed in batches that were quite miscellaneous by modern standards. There were three ads for real estate, a number of official notices (legal actions to be taken unless debts were paid, and so on), three offers of rewards for information leading to the recovery of stolen goods, two notices of books just published, an ad for sugar, one for a dancing school, and a few other odds and ends.

The page looked much like a page of classifieds today: little variety in typeface or size, and no graphics except for crude woodcuts of ships to accompany the sailing notices. The advertisements directed readers' attention to specific lots of goods ("One hundred and nine tierces of best Carollas RICE, just arrived in the ship Philadelphia, Captain Strong, from Charleston"), to the services offered by a particular local merchant ("Buys and sells on commission, all kinds of Merchyndize . . ."), or to unique opportunities (sale of a deceased man's household goods at auction).[1] They were in fact similar to news items; most of them reported unique situations or upcoming events, like the sale of precisely that shipment of Carollas rice. And so it is with most local advertising today: a sale on lawn mowers at Sears, through Saturday; the old Garner place on the market at an asking price of $165,000; and so on. Although newspapers changed dramatically, beginning with the penny press of the 1830s, eventually drawing most of their revenue from ads, and although urban merchandising changed beyond recognition, local advertising has remained much the same kind of discourse, and about the same sorts of thing.

Sporadic efforts in the direction of national advertising began well before mid century. Proprietors of lotteries often ran newspaper ads in various cities, in the 1820s and before. Book publishers did the same, or advertised in weekly magazines that had broad circulation, like the *Nation*; *Harper's* showed book publishers another way, by starting its own weekly magazine, followed by its monthly. Developers and speculators widely advertised western land. Barnum promoted his museum and circus around the country. Frank Presbrey suggests (p. 264) that advertising for Union war bonds in thousands of newspapers constituted the first truly national campaign. These examples do not bring us much closer to modern advertising, though, since they still refer to transitory offers.

The missing element, of course, was the brand name product, sold not by just one shopkeeper, but repeatedly available "everywhere." The idea of selling such products nationally was an old one. Walter Baker & Co. developed its trademark for cocoa in 1785, and persistently displayed that icon throughout the nineteenth century. This was an idea before its time in the US, though not in England. Few manufacturers picked up on it, apart from the makers of patent medicines; and ironically, their efforts helped spoil the idea for other businessmen, since the mendacious copy with which they filled newspaper and magazine columns through the middle decades of the century put advertising out of bounds for many respectable producers.

As late as the 1880s, the practice of branding and nationally advertising products was one way of doing things among many, not a standard system of marketing. Manufacturers were still "discovering" this idea. Paradigmatically, if a bit absurdly, Harley Procter, listening to a reading of the Forty-fifth Psalm in church, suddenly thought of naming his soap "Ivory" and advertising it nationally, which he did in 1880.[2] Ivory was one of just four products, apart from patent medicines, advertised in the modern way through the 1880s. Of these, Royal Baking Powder was far and away the leader, with an annual advertising budget approaching $500,000, though its campaign was unimaginative, consisting mainly of the same quarter-page ad placed on the back covers of many national magazines, month after month. The other two leaders were Pears' Soap, which budgeted $35,000 in 1888, and a cleaning powder called Sapolio, whose makers spent $70,000 in 1885, the year they hired one of the famous early ad men, Artemas Ward (not the humorist), to work full time writing their copy. It is striking, then, that by 1899 there were about a hundred national campaigns, each costing over $100,000 a year.[3]

Clearly there was an advertising revolution in the 1890s. An editorial in the *New York Sun* called it that, as early as 1896, noting that "The development of the art of advertising during the last four or five years has been remarkable."[4] And a few years later, in one of the early how-to-do-it texts on advertising, Earnest Elmo Calkins and Ralph Holden could look back over this transformation and write, "Men not very old have witnessed the entire development of modern advertising from being an untrustworthy instrument of quacks and charlatans to its place as an engine in the conduct and expansion of business."[5] Calkins and Holden, themselves under forty, had taken part in it as founders of an agency, not just witnessed it. But even if self-congratulatory, their assessment is unquestionably correct.

I wish I could with confidence translate these contemporary observations into numbers. The most commonly used figures do show a 128 percent increase in advertising expenditures during the fifteen years from 1890 to 1904. That amounts to an 18 percent rise in the proportion of the GNP represented by advertising, and puts advertising's share of GNP for 1904 at 3.4 percent, a level matched only during the 1920s, and one considerably above the present level.[6] That would indeed suggest a key role for advertising as an "engine" of expanding production. Unfortunately these figures, although given an imprimatur by inclusion in the Census Bureau's *Historical Statistics of the United States*, are open to challenge. Daniel Pope, the most thorough historian of advertising, constructs a revised set of figures that show ad expenditures remaining fairly constant through this period as a proportion of GNP, and at a considerably lower level than was later attained.[7] Only two things seem certain: absolute expenditures on advertising grew rapidly; so did expenditures per capita.[8] Both facts mean that any urban person living through this time – and any rural person who read and shopped – had striking visual evidence of a burgeoning cultural practice, and came to participate more often in it.

Even if reliable, figures like these would not reflect just the phenomenon with which I am concerned: the increase in manufacturers' national advertising of branded products, especially in magazines. To my knowledge, there are no statistics that divide national from local advertising for this period. One may make an informed guess by extrapolating from numbers in the *U. S. Census of Manufactures*, reporting on revenue for all serial publications. From 1909 on, this series distinguishes newspaper from magazine advertising. If we assume that magazine advertising increased in relation to newspaper advertising at the same rate from 1890 to 1909 as from 1909 to 1919, then we can estimate magazine advertising at $16 million in 1890 and $37 million in 1904.[9] For the latter year, this figure seems in line with estimates of ad revenue for individual monthlies in 1904,[10] from which I conjecture that the thirty leading monthly magazines took in about $10 million. Magazine advertising was almost entirely for brand name products by the end of the century, so that these numbers give at least a rough idea how fast national advertising gained ground through the period.

In the absence of statistics on spending, there is nonetheless a quite direct and available expression of the change: look at the magazines. Sidney A. Sherman did that with *Harper's* for thirty-five years leading up to 1900, and tabulated the number of ad pages in each year's October issue. Here are averages drawn from this record:

1882–85	7 pages
1886–90	47 pages
1891–95	85 pages
1896–1900	92 pages[11]

Add to this the page tally of 181 for December, 1904, from Calkins and Holden and the trend is striking enough.[12] I can confirm it by counts from those magazines of which I own a representative sample, through the period in question,[13] augmented where helpful by Calkins and Holden's figures for December 1904:

Atlantic Monthly	November 1880	13 pages
	October 1885	20
	March 1890	28
	July 1896	34
	November 1900	83
	December 1904	121
Century	April 1895	86
	April 1900	98
	December 1904	150
Cosmopolitan	April 1888	43
	October 1892	61
	August 1896	71
	March 1900	95
	December 1904	90
Ladies' Home Journal[14]	August 1893	9¾
	February 1896	11¾
	December 1899	17¼
	January 1907	21½
Munsey's	September 1894	19
	May 1900	92
	June 1907	121

To generalize broadly over these crude sequences: advertising of brand products in the premier national medium seems to have doubled, roughly every decade, through this period. And since rates went up in proportion to circulations, the cost of magazine space was far more than doubling. Even this understates the pace of change, since of the six magazines surveyed here, three did not yet exist in 1880, and only one of those in existence (*Century*) ran any advertising to speak of.[15] There can be no doubt that an advertising explosion took place in magazines. And even though manufacturers had used other media to promote their products (newspapers, streetcar cards, billboards, trade cards, and so on), it seems fair to conclude that national brand advertising in general expanded vastly through the last years of the century.

Why Then?

I have already put forward a general answer to this question, and it is one of the central propositions of this book. Manufacturers turned to marketing and thus to promotion as a way of coping with crisis, making the environment less risky, and smoothing out the course of accumulation.[16] But it is important to try for more precision. For one thing, at this level of generality it is hard to tell which of many explanations is right – or which ones are central and which peripheral. Thus, standard works on the subject tend to produce lists of causes: urbanization, big investment in fixed capital, low marginal cost and a consequent incentive to mass production, specialized production and an increasing variety of products, better transportation systems, more distance between buyer and seller, social mobility, the new impersonality of social relations, and so on.[17] These are all genuine causes, but to marshal them in this way is virtually to say that national advertising throve because of the structure of modern societies. That structure included a position, as it were, for advertising. We need to know which manufacturers moved into that position, and why.

On this question, there has been an emerging consensus in recent years. John Philip Jones puts it in its plainest form: "the driving force in [the] first expansion of advertising was . . . the simple and pressing need to sell rapidly the burgeoning output of mechanized production."[18] A subtler version of this idea, one adopted by the two best scholars of early advertising, derives from Alfred Chandler's monumental study, *The Visible Hand*. It is that development of continuous-flow manufacturing processes, coordinated within one factory, to make low-priced consumer goods in profusion, led the producers to "integrate forward" – that is, to take on activities of distributing and selling, as well as extracting or purchasing, within the complex structure of the emerging, modern corporation.[19] A commitment to advertising was a natural part of this strategy.

I agree, but with reservations to be examined shortly. Some often-cited case histories of sudden and outstandingly successful advertising ventures dramatically instance the point. One is that of James Buchanan Duke and the cigarette, mentioned earlier. Before Duke turned to this line of production in the early 1880s, cigarette smoking was an unusual (and fairly expensive) practice. In fact, when Duke decided to install two of the new Bonsack machines, the 240,000 cigarettes they could produce each day were enough for the entire US market. To chase the large profits made possible by cheap mass production, Duke immediately began national advertising, and leased more of the machines. Within five years, national consumption of cigarettes had increased more than tenfold; Duke alone was producing and selling 2.3 million a day.[20] A less depressing and almost exactly parallel case, also mentioned in Chapter 5: at about the same time, two millers had developed machines in a continuous-flow arrangement that could produce twice as much oatmeal as Americans were eating; it was unknown as a breakfast food except in a few, mainly immigrant, communities. The two businessmen combined forces, and one of them – Henry P. Crowell – proved himself an advertising genius by spreading throughout the land images of a Quaker holding a box of oatmeal (see Figures 6 and 12), and persuading millions of Americans to change their breakfast habits from meat and potatoes to supposedly more healthy porridge.[21]

But it didn't always happen this way. Another familiar example is the National Biscuit Company's 1899 campaign for the first packaged and branded cracker – Uneeda Biscuit. I know of no innovation in cracker production that buried the company in excess biscuits and drove it to advertise. The "reel" oven had mechanized baking thirty years earlier; aside from cutting the cracker in an octagonal shape, the only novelty was sealing it in wax paper and cardboard, and although Nabisco patented an ingenious procedure, machines for making similar packages had been in use since the 1870s. I suppose one could save the hypothesis by saying that there can be long delays between the development of excess, high-speed, productive capacity and the inauguration of advanced marketing and advertising. That weakens the explanatory connection, however.

There are more drastic counterexamples. George Eastman set out to invent a new kind of camera and film for an as yet nonexistent mass market of amateurs; the idea of reaching that market, presumably through advertising, preceded the machinery to mass-produce the commodity, and in fact the commodity itself. Likewise, the safety razor. King C. Gillette did not even know at first what product he wanted to invent; he decided, on a friend's advice, to invent some kind of cheap throwaway item for daily use by millions of people. From the time he settled on a razor (in 1895) until the first razor hit the market, eight years passed, the delay owing in part to difficulties in designing machinery. It didn't work flawlessly in the first year of production; no flood of razors called national advertising to the rescue. Advertising came slightly *before* mass production. But really, the two were integral parts of Gillette's initial idea; from the start, he dedicated twenty-five cents per razor to promotion.[22]

Some much-advertised commodities for a huge market were not even mass-produced in the modern way: bicycles and pianos, for instance.[23] So

while this principle seems to explain many corporate decisions to advertise nationally on a large scale, it does not explain some at all; and
sometimes even when high-speed, continuous-flow production is an
important part of the picture, its introduction cannot have been the
main impetus toward advertising (Kodak, Gillette, Uneeda). We need
one or more additional causes; or we could settle for a looser theory with
many exceptions, suggesting a high degree of idiosyncrasy in choices to
advertise nationally.

I want to press for the first approach, though I cannot make more
than a plausible case for it, given the murkiness of details. Let us try to
scan, for a pattern, one group of such details: changes in the kinds of
products most advertised. For the period before national brand advertising began flourishing (about 1855 to 1875), I made an informal survey
of ads in magazines like *Harper's Weekly*, the *Nation*, and *Frank Leslie's
Illustrated Newspaper*, choosing weeklies because monthlies were neither
so popular nor so ad-laden at the time. The predictable conclusion:
patent medicines led, followed by ads for books and magazines. There
was a good deal of advertising for private schools and some for insurance. Nothing else stands out. Sewing machine ads appeared fairly often,
along with ads for other contraptions like scissors, sharpeners, skirt
shapers, lawn mowers, and watches. A very few manufacturers of small
products for daily use advertised them regularly by brand name: Baker's
(chocolate), Terrant's (seltzer), Sozodont (tooth powder), and virtually
no others.

For the transitional period of the 1880s, we can consult a list compiled
by Presbrey (pp. 338–9) of companies that advertised their brands widely
at the time. The medicine peddlers disappeared from the list – though
their absence owes partly to Presbrey's bias against that sort of advertising. He also ignores book publishers, and given his purposes that
omission seems proper, since publishers sell unique products, not a
brand name. Of primary interest, though, are the many new names –
Diamond Safety Razor, Hire's Root Beer, Kodak, Mellin's [baby] Food,
Pears' Soap, Williams' Shaving Stick, and so on – and the new *kinds* of
products some of these represent. Eleven brands of food appear on the
list, six of soap and cleaning products, four each of dentifrices and pens,
and five of pianos.

Presbrey's list for 1897 (pp. 361–2) shows an acceleration in some of
these trends. Twice as many soap-sellers appear, two and a half times as
many advertisers of recreational products (including ten of bicycles and
fourteen of pianos, these two leading all other commodities), and –
ahead of every other general product category – more than three times
as many food companies, a total of thirty-four. This last trend also stands
out in a comparison I made between the display ads in two *Ladies' Home
Journals* of 1893 and those in two issues of 1904. Makers of food products
were advertising 70 percent more in the latter year, the only group of

producers to show a significant increase. One final indicator of this change: in 1877–78, the N.W. Ayer agency (one of the two or three largest) derived just over 3 percent of its revenue from food advertisers; that percentage increased to 17.7 in the years 1900–01, when this kind of account far outstripped Ayer's second most lucrative (fuel and light- ing). By contrast, in the earlier pair of years 48.1 percent of Ayer's income came from makers of medicines (21.6 percent), books (10.2 percent), jewelry and silver (8.6 percent), chromos and greeting cards (7.7 percent). Taken all together, these product categories yielded only 13.2 percent of the firm's income in 1900–01.[24]

Evidently, increased promotion of food products led the surge of national brand advertising throughout this period. A closer look at these foods will point toward an insight into the general change. One survey analyzed by category all food advertising in the *Century* from its begin- ning in 1871, through 1903.[25] Through the first five years, there were very few ads for food, and the only products regularly advertised were starch and flavoring. By the middle years of the survey (1886–90), there was a sharp increase in food advertising generally, and a shift away from *ingredients*. Starch had disappeared; flavoring and baking powder received a modest amount of space; only cocoa and chocolate were among the leaders, and these were used for direct consumption as well as in cooking.[26] The other major campaigns were for teas – another dessert food – and for baby foods and soups. These last two indicate a clear tendency toward products sold in an advanced state of preparation: open the can or jar, heat, and serve.

The final years of the survey (1899–1903) show another huge increase in food advertising, and confirm the trend toward convenience prod- ucts. By a good margin, the most ad space went to a new group, makers of breakfast foods. Baby food remained a leader, joined by canned meats. There was also substantial advertising for five other ready-to-use staples – fresh and smoked meat, soup, canned fruits and vegetables, salad dressing, and cookies and crackers – as well as for coffee and candy. Only three products remained that suggest traditional work ("from scratch") in the kitchen: baking powder, gelatine, and the ambivalent chocolate. A new way of life takes on a shadowy form. One *could* breakfast on cereal and coffee, lunch on soup and tinned ham, snack on crackers, dine on a Swift roast with canned vegetables, and draw upon no skills beyond those required to open a can and light a stove. Not that a day of such convenience was the norm; but it beckoned, from the pages of the staid *Century* magazine.

From those of the *Ladies' Home Journal*, too, dedicated though they were to the sanctity of women's work. By 1904 (according to my count), display ads for convenience and dessert products outran those for ingre- dients by three to one; the ratio would be more lopsided if one measured advertising *space*, as makers of breakfast foods in particular boosted their wares in quarter- to full-page displays. In features and columns the *Journal* still offered recipes and techniques (as it does today); its food ads all but said, "Be quick, be modern, don't cook." The same message may be heard in its silences. For many mass-produced, branded, and packaged foodstuffs there was little or no magazine advertising: sugar, salt, oils, lard, starch, flavoring, noodles, rice, and so on; there was but a modest amount for flour. The ubiquitous Royal Baking Powder stands alone as an exception to this emerging rule: food manufacturers advertised broadly if, and only if, the use of their goods abbreviated traditional processes of readying food for the table. The advertised products were new in two related ways, aside from their being branded and packaged. First, they embodied more labor performed by factory workers and machines, which supplanted mundane tasks previously carried out by housewives or, to a lesser extent, by grocers or butchers; we could call them convenience foods.[27] Second, these repeat-purchase, packaged goods accommodated themselves to a new style of domestic life, one less dependent on the skills and work of servants or housewives, one in which many traditional kinds of home production had become – for those of at least moderate means – voluntary.

Let us follow this lead out of the pantry. The branded soaps that proclaimed their virtues in the magazines eliminated the chore of soap making. Washday had required the shaving of bar soap to make chips for tub or machine; now one could pour laundry soap from a package. Other branded home cleansers relieved women of similar tasks; likewise, dentifrices and shaving soaps. Certainly, Gillette's safety razor was a convenience good: "no stropping or honing," according to the slogan.[28] In clothing, ready-to-wear had been supplanting homespun since the Civil War, for men; suits, underwear, and accessories were widely advertised by 1900. This change happened more slowly with women's clothes, but by the 1890s makers of corsets and a few other basic garments had begun national ad campaigns. Finally, although the romance of large appliances was not scripted until the 1920s, gas ovens, ranges, refrigerators, and a few other modern devices did appear fairly often in ads of the 1890s.

Apart from these appliances, all the products just mentioned flowed from high-speed production lines; but that fact in itself does not explain the proliferation of ads for them. On one hand, many mass-produced commodities were advertised little or not at all. Thread, fabrics, dyes, matches, nails, tools, and paint come to mind; all belonged to home production tasks not much simplified during this period. On the other, one finds innumerable ads for bicycles in the 1890s, and for automobiles in the first decade of this century. These goods did not issue from continuous-flow processes of production, at that time. Nor, obviously, did they offer shortcuts in home production, but they did fit into the new style of life (what Raymond Williams called "mobile privatization," with reference to a later time), and served as accessories to the urban or suburban home. Significantly, too, bicycles and cars were new. Manufacturers could promote them under the sign of modernity, as well as that of efficiency. Somewhere in this same conceptual area belongs the camera, a staple of magazine advertising. Eastman much simplified the making of photos; but that activity did not replace or update some earlier home chore. The snapshot was an accessory of up-to-date family life, and a means of celebrating the new home. Meanwhile, as extended family networks grew more attenuated and communities more impersonal, that home and its breadwinner were increasingly protected by insurance, one of the few non-commodities extensively advertised in the 1890s; Prudential's symbol, Gibraltar, dates from this period.

Perhaps the ideal of the well-equipped, exemplary family home can help explain extensive advertising for three commodities that support neither Schudson's and Pope's emphasis on continuous-flow production nor mine on novelty and the short-circuiting of home production. These are pianos, china, and silver. For whatever reason, ownership of a piano seems to have become a cultural imperative for the family that could afford it, during this period. From 1870 to 1890, the number of pianos in use had increased only a bit faster than the size of the population, but from 1890 to 1910, it rose almost six times as fast. Thus, in the late 1880s there were an estimated 800,000 pianos in the country, or one for every 15 households; by 1910 the number was 4 million, one to every 5 households. Since the average piano cost about $200 at the beginning of this period, one-third of a working class annual income, one can confidently guess that these pianos were not evenly distributed through affluent and modest homes, even though second-hand instruments doubtless found their way into some of the latter.[29] So the great majority of middle and upper middle class families must have decided that their way of life entailed the possession, and doubtless use, of a piano.

Millions of people were taking up new standards of domestic culture previously restricted to the upper class. Visitors would be treated to music, or join in its making; they could also expect silverware and good china to appear on the dinner table. These were not new products or more efficient improvements on old ones, but traditional accoutrements of luxury and culture. It is as if, having eliminated much home production and streamlined the rest, these families were filling some of the newly available time and space with socially correct leisure activities and displays, drawn from the historical repertory of the class above them. Advertisers both fed and fed upon this aspiration, in an upscale movement characteristic of mass culture from its earliest phase.

To draw together the threads of this discussion: no single hypothesis quite explains all the categories of brand name advertising that supported this industry in its transformation at the end of the century, and that enabled the rise of the mass circulation magazine. But two, taken

together, make sense of the whole pattern. First, manufacturers advertised on a large scale when they saw a chance to situate their products
within a way of life that was becoming the norm for urban and suburban
people, mainly of the professional and managerial class.[30] I have called
some of these products new, or convenient, or efficient. The overarching
idea, though, is that they helped ease the transition from home as a site
of production to home as a site of consumption and leisure, and as a
badge of a new middle class, defining itself as both progressive and traditional, in ways to be explored later in this book. Needless to say,
national advertisers helped to *create* the new way of life, as well as seizing
the opportunity it offered them.[31] Second, most of the national advertisers were also motivated by the need to make full use of their machines,
avoid savage price competition, and extend corporate planning through
the sales process. But I hope to have shown that it would be wrong to
think of 1890s advertising as "producer-driven" in a simple sense. Those
who began and continued to advertise broadly were doing more than
trying to dump surplus product. They were looking for – and if successful, they found – a nexus between high-speed, continuous-flow
manufacturing and the reshaping of people's habits and lives. The hegemony of the integrated corporation reached out *beyond* final sales of
commodities, to a metamorphosis of aspirations and imaginations. In
this, corporations were no less powerful because those who took up
their messages *wanted* to be consumers. On the contrary, that is precisely why the rise of national advertising instances hegemony more
than it does manipulation.

The two explanations converge in a second way, one that responds –
finally – to the question that serves as the title of this section: Why then?
The nearly tautological answer is that in building the apparatus of mass
production, capitalists had brought millions of people together in cities
and towns, and so created the conditions that marginalized home production. (That many urban people tried at first to maintain rural ways is
clear from accounts of pigs, chickens, and backyard gardens in mid-
nineteenth-century cities and industrial towns.) In short, their reforming
of production made urgent a new kind of consumption, and they were
quick to shape needs that their own project had created. Thus it will not
do to invoke "expanding markets" alongside productive techniques as an
independent cause of the new social formation as Chandler does.[32]
Markets are shaped, not discovered. A transformation of home life and
hence of the market was inevitable at this time. The specific kind of privatization that in fact happened was not inevitable.[33] The sales effort of
integrated corporations, advertising included, helped make that solution
the dominant one, offering "an invitation and an injunction to partake
in a consumer society," as Pope puts it (p. 111).

Without saying so, I have implied through these pages that advertising
worked. Many analysts are skeptical. Julian Simon ends his careful book by

suggesting that the economic effects of advertising are murky, insub-
stantial, and not much worth studying. Michael Schudson, John Philip
Jones, and others cite evidence that sales cause ads, not the other way
around – so, to put it in more neutral terms, that the best predictor of a
company's advertising budget for the year n is its sales for the year $n-1$.
Paul Baran and Paul Sweezy advance a broader version of this thesis,
arguing that we should understand swollen ad expenditures not just as
a remedy for competitive pricing but as one of many strategies for
absorbing the surplus generated by monopoly capital, holding at bay the
system's tendency toward stagnation.[34]

Passing over the intricacies of this question, I suggest that the causes
and effects of a practice like advertising when first entered into the
social process may differ sharply from its dynamics in mature years.
Advertising may produce less than monumental results now, on average.
Then, it worked. Most immediately, it worked to establish brand names in
the minds of consumers and symbolically differentiate products that
were very similar. In the early 1920s, two professors of business conducted a survey of 9000 people that revealed the outcome of early
national advertising. In some product categories, the leading brand was
mentioned by more than half of those sampled, and more than twice as
many times as the second brand. Most are still familiar: Campbell's,
Arrow, Postum, Waterman, Wrigley, Uneeda, Welch's, Prophylactic
(toothbrush), 1847 Rogers Brothers, Royal (baking powder, not the
typewriter), Colt, Gillette, Ever Ready, Mennan, Williams (shaving soap),
Tiffany, Swift, Baker's: these names had been promoted vigorously from
the turn of the century or before. "Everybody" knew them, and they
claimed the lion's share of sales. In many product categories no brand
attained much recognition: umbrellas, leather goods, neckties, women's
clothing, raincoats, handkerchiefs, boys' clothing, rubber boots, flash-
lights, lamps, linen, curtains, ribbon, lace, yarn, silk, jewelry, fish, jelly,
and rice, for instance. Advertising pages in magazines of the 1890s are
silent, or nearly so, about most of these commodities.[35]

Let me emphasize, I do not claim that national ad campaigns for
yarn or umbrellas could have won universal recognition for leading
brands and laid the groundwork for corporate monopoly in these areas.
A quick scan of the two lists will show that almost all products on the first
meet my criteria of the "new," and that almost none on the second do so.
Manufacturers sensed or learned where advertising would work and
where it would not; after a period of some confusion, they learned to
advertise where old needs could be redirected or new ones created.

To underline that last point, consider the case of patent medicines,
branded products to whose manufacture continuous-process methods
could easily be adapted. Why did advertising for them decline from a
spate to a trickle, before the Pure Food and Drug Act of 1906 put many
of them out of business, and even before respectable magazines began

following the lead of the *Ladies' Home Journal* by refusing such business? To be sure, these concoctions did not deliver the cures they promised, but that had not discouraged their promoters or users during the middle decades of the century. My conjecture is that medicines fell out of favor mainly because they did not fit into the new domesticity that was emerging. The idea of modernity assigned some family concerns to experts outside the home, even as it brought corporate expertise into the home in areas like food preparation. Through the 1890s, MDs were vigorously asserting their claims to a monopoly of health care, pushing aside other practitioners, and stigmatizing home remedies.[36] A sign of this nascent profession's success was the increasing reliance upon it of modern families – the sort who read monthly magazines – for help with sickness and debility. Not only did makers of patent medicines gradually abandon their appeals to this audience; makers of some new products destined for market leadership dropped mention of supposed curative properties they had earlier stressed. Coca-Cola dissociated itself from medicines and became strictly a pleasure drink. Welch's and Postum did the same.[37] Cuticura stopped promoting itself as an ointment, and became a soap. Medicinal claims that had occasionally turned up in ads for cigarettes and gum disappeared. Advertisers were helping consumers to draw new conceptual boundary lines, where the actual qualities of their products were ambiguous.

Advertising worked, too, in brute, material terms. Among the corporations that had by 1913 consolidated their positions as leaders of the new economic order, nearly all those that made consumer goods had established brand leadership partly through advertising, during the period from 1890 to 1905 which is central to my study.[38] Of course that fact *could* express a law that bigness spawned advertising, rather than that advertising helped create bigness. That this was not the case is evidenced not only by the many success stories (Gillette, Kodak, Duke, and so on) in which advertising played a crucial role from the corporate beginnings on, but by the experience of new trusts during the most intense flood of corporate mergers in our history, from 1898 to 1900. Some of the new giants, like the National Biscuit Company, grasping that sales promotion was a safer course than cutting prices or buying out the competition, launched ad campaigns immediately, and were rewarded.[39] Others evidently assumed that their new monopoly status obviated the need for advertising: for instance, in the areas of bicycles, chewing gum, cigarettes, and baking powder. They were proved wrong, as smaller competitors began invading their markets (for example, Chiclets that of Wrigley's), and they quickly resumed advertising. Perhaps this explains why there was an estimated drop of 30 percent in the advertising trade in 1899, and why revenues then quickly rose to previous levels and above.[40] I am convinced that Frank Presbrey, Claude Hopkins, and the other chauvinists of early advertising were essentially correct. In the right circumstances, it contributed greatly to corporate success, as well as to the expansion of markets and consumption.

As it did that, it also constructed new social relations in and around the marketplace; to that subject I now turn.

The Rise of the Agency

The nexus of those relations was the ad agent, a shoestring entrepreneur in the 1850s, whose door-to-door efforts metamorphosed through fifty years into the complex but orderly work of the full-service agency. Shortly, I will simplify my task of exposition by writing as if, by 1900 or so, agencies were in sole command of the business of national advertising. That was not so. Sales departments of large corporations, and in some cases advertising departments, had much to say about the scale, placement, themes, and formats of ads.[41] To a lesser extent, advertising specialists working for magazines and other publications took a hand in this work. There were freelance copywriters and artists, too. Nonetheless, foregrounding the role of agencies will not distort the important truth. To wit, an extensive practice of advertising emerged, quite distinct from the efforts of the merchants and department stores that had earlier been the main advertisers; and that new practice was the professional work of specialists – in consciousness, I am tempted to say.

Nor will my simplification misrepresent the line of evolution in this field. Over time, all the major advertisers, even those with powerful sales departments, came to rely on the services of agencies.[42] Accordingly, agencies multiplied into the hundreds, even by 1890, and many became big businesses in their own right. J. Walter Thompson served 800 clients in 1901. Whereas the largest agency of the 1870s and 1880s had about 7 employees, N.W. Ayer had 164 in 1900, 298 in 1910. Its revenues rose from $1,380,181 in the former year to $5,464,655 in the latter.[43] I know of no figures for the growth of all agency business through this period, but there is no doubt that its share of total advertising revenues grew rapidly; if those did increase by more than 100 percent, during this decade, as the census figures assert, then the quadrupling of Ayer's business can probably be taken as representative of the whole industry. Calkins wrote in 1905 that not every national advertiser worked through an agency, "but the exceptions are rare, and are becoming rarer."[44] Agencies moved from the periphery to the center.

As they did so, their business also changed, slowly at first, and then dramatically just before and after the turn of the century. Through forty and more years after the founding of the first US agency in 1841, this business was a hodgepodge of contradictory and sharp practices. To summarize briefly a most confusing situation, there were four different business arrangements that linked agent, advertiser, and publisher: (1) the agent represented the newspaper publisher, as a seeker of business; (2) the agent sold space to the advertiser, then set out to buy it at the lowest price from the publisher; (3) the agent bought large blocks of space from publishers, then sold that space to advertisers at the highest possible price; (4) the agent undertook to manage, usually for a lump sum, the entire advertising space of one or more papers. In contrast with the structure that the ad business assumed in the 1890s and retains today, three features of early agency work stand out. First, it was unclear whom the agent represented: the advertiser of goods and services, or the publisher.[45] Second, and as a consequence, he was essentially a hustler, pressuring for rate cuts and rebates, trying to buy low and sell high, keeping his deals secret from publisher or advertiser or both. Third, he dealt mainly in space: so many column inches in so many papers for so much a week. Some agents did begin, in almost a random way, to provide advertisers some of the services that characterize the modern trade (more about that shortly), but it's a fair generalization that agencies did not yet think or act as buyers and sellers of audiences, or shapers of demand.

On the other hand, they opened up an economic space not previously demarcated, and put themselves solidly in it. Through their growing expertise in getting messages to potential customers, they made a claim to performing an indispensable function, a claim that manufacturers would have to take seriously when their great need arose toward the end of the century. Another crucial point about early agents: almost from the start their scope was regional, and soon national. Mason & Tuttle ran an ad in the New York *Herald* in 1844, which makes that clear:

ADVERTISING IN COUNTRY NEWSPAPERS.
Merchants, importers, and general dealers wishing to advertise in the principal cities and towns of the United States, are informed that an agency office has been opened at 128 Nassau Street, where files of all the principal newspapers are kept . . . . The benefits of advertising for country custom in the neighboring cities and towns, is [sic] too obvious to require comment . . . . [46]

By 1876, N.W. Ayer offered to get ads in *any* paper, American or Canadian. Agencies established national advertising as a possibility, well before there were many to seize it, other than medicine makers and publishers. A system of sorts was in place, when Quaker Oats, Procter and Gamble, and the rest made their moves.

What remained was for agencies to realize that their future lay in this trade, and to appeal for it more attractively than they had in the early days. That meant, above all, clarifying their allegiances, making it explicit that they would work for manufacturers and not for publications. Here, the decisive step was Ayer's invention of the "open contract" – open, mainly in the sense that the manufacturer agreed to pay Ayer a 12.5 or 15 percent commission on whatever space he bought, rather than buying from Ayer space in a specified "list" of papers. This meant that the agent could now work with the advertiser on a specially tailored campaign, unhampered by commitments to publishers. The contract was "open" in a second important way: Ayer undertook to give clients full information about rates he was paying for space, thus elimi-nating the incentive to play publisher off against advertiser. No longer would agents serve two masters. They were working for businessmen who wanted to sell their goods to consumers; they could focus exclusively on the needs of those firms, including the need to make ads *effective* as well as ubiquitous.

No great shift in capitalist social relations happens overnight. Ayer's commitment to the open contract did not prevent him from conducting some business in the old way for many years, when he could not persuade clients to accept the new. Other agencies were slower still. As late as 1887, J. Walter Thompson was presenting himself to clients as "exclusive agent" for "many of the best and largest magazines."[47] This underlines the uneven development of advertising relations, because from the 1870s on, Thompson led in the field of magazines, which were soon to become the main locus of modern, national advertising. Nor did agents make the change without some pressure from the more influential magazine pub-lishers, who also came to see the clarity of the new arrangements as in their interests. In 1901, Curtis, publisher of the *Ladies' Home Journal* and the *Saturday Evening Post*, issued an agency contract, binding them to stick to Curtis's announced rates and a fixed commission rate, on penalty of being denied access to these key magazines.[48] Nonetheless, by about that time the more successful agencies had accepted or welcomed the regularizing of their business practices, and through these new practices had placed themselves fully at the service of manufacturers, and so aligned their interests and outlook with those of big capital.

As they grew in size, changes in their internal structure showed how far they had come since the days of the door-to-door space salesman run-ning his business out of his coat pockets, or the one-room office stacked with ledgers and lists of newspapers. In 1900, Ayer's payroll classified employees in twelve departments. This specialization reflected the new functions the agency had undertaken, like copywriting (nine men), and the closer relationship with clients: the ten men in the "business getting" department not only sought new accounts, but served as continuing liaison people with old customers. Other agencies were moving farther in this direction. J. W. Thompson hit on the idea of the account execu-tive sometime in the 1890s: one person who would oversee the advertising campaigns of just a few clients; a bit later, Albert Lasker's bril-liance in this role helped make it an essential one for all agencies. Another trend confirmed that one: in 1891 the Batten agency was the first to adopt a policy of accepting only full-service accounts. That is, the agency would completely manage the client's advertising strategies – choice of media, copy, design, and so on. This bold move was a way of insisting that advertising was a specific business domain, best left to professionals.[49]

Indeed, agents began early to suggest, and then insist, that they *were* professionals. Making a plea for his open contract system in 1886, Ayer analogized his work to that of lawyers: when you want an attorney, you don't look for the lowest bidder; you look for one "whose skill, knowledge of the law, and personal character" ensure that he can best look out for your interests. Why not look for an ad agent with the same qualities? In 1887, Thompson was telling prospective clients that good agents were as skilled and as valuable as doctors and lawyers. In one of the earliest books on advertising, Calkins and Holden held that the agent is a "professional man" whose relation to clients is "similar to those of a lawyer, doctor, or architect." Neither publisher nor advertiser can understand the causes of advertising successes and failures; it's the professional's role to analyze the market, know media, write copy, create art, and plan campaigns using these skills and knowledges. Advertising should be a science, said a *Printers' Ink* writer in 1891; it *was* a "positive science," nine-tenths of the time, said Thompson in 1909.[50]

Thus, agents were formulating some of the standard claims that an occupational group makes when it wants to be regarded as a profession: it offers a service that no one else can perform well; its skill is grounded in a body of knowledge; a practitioner has no interest but that of his clients; he pursues that interest in a confidential and honorable relationship with those clients; and, of course, this arrangement is good for society as a whole. That some of these claims were, to put it politely, in advance of the fact is not really the point. True, there was nothing like a "positive science" of advertising at the turn of the century (nor is there now); there were no courses, no degrees, no academic study of the field; and many agents were charlatans. But the more reputable agencies were successfully making the case for their status as professionals to the audience that counted: makers of branded commodities. And agents were organizing themselves in the characteristic professional way. *Printers' Ink* began publishing in 1888; many other "journals" created a space for professional discourse in the decades that followed. Advertising "clubs" – local organizations where agents traded ideas and stories – sprang up in major cities in the 1890s. The International Advertising Association was founded in 1904.

More telling still, progressive ad men saw early on that they needed to regulate their own activities (like the more established professionals) and clean up their business, if they were to cast off their older reputation as unprincipled hucksters. Ayer's 1899 ad (Figure 1) strikes the professional note in several ways, especially his dissociating the agency from ads

Do You Know Uneeda Biscuit ?

The advertising success of the century is that of "Uneeda Biscuit" and "Uneeda Jinjer Wayfer."

The name "Uneeda" was coined by us. The name "Uneeda Jinjer Wayfer" was produced by us.

The popular catch phrases, "Do You Know Uneeda Biscuit", "Everybody Knows Uneeda Biscuit" and "Now Uneeda Jinjer Wayfer" were originated by us.

The advertising campaign was planned, and is being executed in all its branches by us.

We are not in the general scramble to get an advertising order regardless of the interest of the advertiser.

We do not accept advertisements relating to vile diseases, disreputable business or intoxicating drinks.

We are anxious for all the first-class advertising that can be made profitable to the advertiser and to ourselves— and only such.

Everybody Knows Uneeda Biscuit

Our long experience (thirty years) and our large business (the greatest in our line), should give us unequaled advantages and facilities for doing *good* advertising.

Advertising would open a profitable field to many a manufacturer who to-day is fretting over the evils of the old way of marketing goods, little dreaming of the opportunities that might be his. We are specially glad to talk to thinking men of this class.

NOW Uneeda Jinjer Wayfer !

N. W. AYER & SON,

Newspaper Advertising.
Magazine Advertising.   PHILADELPHIA.

Figure 1 Ad for N.W. Ayer & Son, *McClure's*, October 1899

"relating to vile diseases, disreputable business or intoxicating drinks." Refusing to promote wine and spirits was a matter of special principle for this teetotal family, but all the big agencies were shedding patent medicine contracts at this time, and stressing their affinities with reputable business. "I want only legitimate advertisers of the better class," said Thompson.[51] *Printers' Ink* in the 1890s was full of tut-tutting about the absurd promises of medicine proprietors, about "dead-beat" advertisers, "advertising cheats," scams of various sorts, supposedly "free" advertising, sales gimmicks, shady practices of discounting space rates, and so on. Advertising agents not only tried to discipline and rationalize their own practices, but made genuine and eventually successful efforts to force publishers to tell the truth about the circulations of their periodicals. This was critical, obviously, in order for the agents to deliver audiences of known dimensions to advertisers.

Agencies were clearing a messy terrain, straightening out troubled business relations, developing some real expertise as well as boasting of more than they had, setting down the rules of their own game, bringing publishers into line. They wanted corporations to believe in their services, and trust them as associates. It is interesting that they used the rhetoric and some of the practices of professionalism in trying to bring about that result, though the intuitive methods of the most notable early ad men made them unlikely professionals; and in the event, their work has never flowed into the channels of strict professionalism. They needed the confidence of those they served; they wanted respect and dignity; professional gestures helped. And ad men *were* like other members of the new middle class, in contributing to the rationalization and taming of competitive capitalism.

What Agencies Did

In 1904, the J. Walter Thompson Agency's *Blue Book* outlined to prospective clients "The Thompson Method," a very different bundle of services than the agency had offered ten or fifteen years earlier. Rather than just recommending space in one or another list of magazines, Thompson would study the prospects of the client's product line, check out the products and positioning of his rivals, advise on a selection of advertising media, prepare "new copy and new illustrations," and place them appropriately, with persistence and variation, over a period of time. Other house literature of the same period adds that Thompson's analysis included size, position, and cost of space, frequency of placement, forms of display, and style of type. Plans were detailed and comprehensive: an elegant one for the Pabst Brewing Company stretched out over thirty-six months.[52] Without question, the "Thompson Method" was that of the modern advertising *campaign*; the military term was already in common usage before 1900.

The "Thompson Method" was not his alone. Calkins and Holden reproduce a nineteen-page letter from "an agent" (presumably themselves) to a newly merged textile company, explaining in detail what kind of campaign they would run for $100,000 or more, and why the company needs to advertise in this broad way.[53] Nor was the concept of the campaign new in 1904. Presbrey says that agencies began to work toward it about 1890 (p. 524). Certainly some of them had fully achieved it before 1900. Adolphus Green of the newly formed National Biscuit Company decided to brand and package crackers in the summer of 1898, having had years of bitter experience with price wars, the alternative strategy. He consulted Henry N. McKinney of the Ayer agency, who worked with him to plan out the entire campaign: cutting the cracker in its distinctive octagonal shape, settling on a brand name ("Uneeda Biscuit," chosen with much care over alternatives like "Taka Cracker," "Hava Cracker," and "Wanta Cracker") and trademark, designing a package from the wax paper inside to the lettering on the cardboard box (Green, board chairman of a $55 million corporation, spent weeks on details of typography and design), writing slogans, planning ads for various media, and coordinating their placement very precisely with the sales efforts of the company – for example, by running "teaser" ads with just the name "Uneeda" in newspapers, on outdoor signs, and in streetcars of a city where distribution was about to begin.[54] The agency may also, as others did, have advised on samples, premiums, sales training, and approaches to retailers. The campaign began in January 1899, and a year later the company was selling 10 million packages a month, demand had outrun production, and profits were $3 million. Ayer did not wait that long to publicize its crucial role in advancing this modern method of salesmanship (see Figure 1): the agency knew by October that it had placed certain names in everyone's lexicon, and engineered "the advertising success of the century."

The campaign was the paradigmatic agency practice, even though its conception and execution were still erratic at the beginning of the century, because it gathered all the agency's capabilities into one intense, nationally coordinated effort to enter the minds and change the conduct of millions. For the first time, a particular institution offered to do that, and could. Naturally, it extended the offer to those who both needed and could afford to pay for such expertise: entrepreneurs and – mainly – corporations. I see nothing sinister in the motives of either party; packaged biscuits are fine with me, and I hope to achieve a nonconspiratorial tone in this discussion. But there is no neutral way to put the simple truth that a powerful business had grown up whose work was to alter consciousness and deliver customers, whose interests were structurally very close to those of still more powerful businesses, and not very close to those of other citizens – whatever one thinks of breakfast food and safety razors. The alignment of social forces changed.

The point becomes clearer if we look at some of the specific undertakings that ad agencies brought within their scope by 1905. A critical one was market research. Ayer evidently did the first serious market and media survey more or less inadvertently, when trying to woo a threshing machine manufacturer for its business in 1879. The company refused to tell Ayer's man in which papers it wanted to buy space, asking that the *agency* find out where and how best to advertise threshing machines. The Ayer partners decided to give it a try, and put the entire staff on the project for three days and nights: sending telegrams all over the US, gathering information on amounts and kinds of grain grown in every state and county, and finding out rates and circulations of newspapers in each district. The result of this crash program was a fat book of information, which the Ayer man offered to the threshing machine company only if it would give the account to Ayer. The company manager readily agreed, having tried for years to get such useful data. Gradually, Ayer came to understand that on the open contract system, it could and must compete for business by offering services like this. To do so was standard procedure for it and other agencies by 1900.[55]

Here, as so often in the genesis of mass culture, we have a practice that makes eminent sense for all concerned, within the rationale of the new system, yet that further tilts that system toward inequality. Why advertise threshing machines where no one grows grain? Why shouldn't agencies learn to study the nature and whereabouts of markets? Isn't it in the interest of farmers to know what kinds of machine are available? Yet down the slope of time from Ayer's 1879 survey we arrive – predictably – at eye-blink research in supermarkets, studies of galvanic skin responses to different TV weathercasters, brain-wave arousal studies, focus groups, and so on. A cadre of specialists finds more and more sophisticated ways to anatomize and predict the doings of non-specialists, and sells that knowledge to corporations that want to buy our attention and shape our needs. Market and audience research belong to the twentieth-century politics of knowing: who can look at whom with what instruments, who studies whom and with what ends, who becomes part of whose knowledge.

We can discover a similar politics of *discourse* in the new work of ad agencies. To begin at the beginning, they thought up thousands of brand names and trademarks. Sometimes a trademark is just the brand name given a pictorial representation; sometimes it is a separate icon, like Morton Salt's girl under the umbrella; but the two signs are functionally similar. Both also have a lineage that goes back well before the period of this study, and had the traditional function of preventing imitation and guaranteeing quality. But only toward the end of the nineteenth century did brands and trademarks become standard features of popular commodities. In 1870, 121 trademarks were registered with the US patent office, though many more were in use. In 1906 more than 10,000 were registered.[56] Presumably, brand names multiplied at a similar rate.

When the brand name is the name of the company, communication is direct enough. When it is a new coinage like "Uneeda," and especially when that coinage appropriates words or echoes from the common language,[57] we enter a new semantic space where proper names, established meanings, associations, and persuasion blur together. Agencies sought to help manufacturers achieve just that blur, and enter it into the linguistic stock of the culture. Similarly, trademarks blend the mnemonic, the representational, and the hortatory, and lay claim to a larger and larger place within our whole store of visual meanings. These things are obvious, and may seem inconsequential; but keep in mind that this infusion of muted commercial purposes into our repertory of meanings is a phenomenon of just the last hundred years. As Michael Schudson aptly asks: "Who does the naming in our society, who has the power of words, and how is that power used?" (p. 161).

John Philip Jones, the leading contemporary theorist of brands, offers this definition: "A brand is a product that provides functional benefits plus added values that some consumers value enough to buy." "Added values" include the "personality" of the brand, its association with certain sorts of people who supposedly use it, the belief (true or not) that it is effective, and its appearance or that of its package. Jones explicitly excludes the reputation of the manufacturer, because "consumers do not know who manufactures many of the brands they use."[58] In short, the values that accompany a product and make it a brand are psychological, and advertising is what adds them. The aura begins with naming and picturing; brands mystify from the outset.

I consider that more significant than the clutter of slogans turned out by agencies from the 1890s on ("99 44/100 pure," "It floats," "The Prudential has the strength of Gibraltar," and "The Beer that made Milwaukee famous" are some durable ones from that time), or the advertising jingles and songs that flourished at the same time, and have taken up unwelcome lodging in millions of minds right down through "If you've got the time, we've got the beer." Everyone recognizes these as language for hire, and their very dishonesty tends to call instant parody into play against them.[59] Also, in the 1890s most commercial verse was intentionally humorous, playfully mocking the serious purposes of advertising discourse. Nonetheless, it means something for a culture when so many of the formulaic epithets and verses that stand ready for use in any conversation were put on the tips of our tongues by ad men.

Most centrally, agencies came to produce millions of throwaway words daily – ad copy that did not (necessarily) repeat formulas from day to day or month to month, but flashed past the public eye and was gone for good. Of course copywriting had always been the heart of the trade. But until at least the 1850s, when a Boston agent named Pettingill began writing copy, the seller generally wrote his own text. A group of specialists in copy began to form in major cities through the next few decades, most of them freelancers, often journalists who wrote ads on the side. Their presence changed the conversation. Instead of a merchant or manufacturer speaking in his own voice to potential buyers, copywriters learned to speak for him, and to interest themselves in discussable qualities of a product in which they had no prior stake. Such ventriloquism made public discourse more oblique.

This development progressed slowly. A few copywriters gained major reputations (like John E. Powers, who worked for Wanamaker's in Philadelphia in the 1880s); and a few agencies began to offer copywriting as a regular service. H.P. Hubbard did so, but Charles E. Raymond, who worked for Hubbard, commented in a memoir that Hubbard's was "far in advance of the other agencies of his time."[60] Perhaps so, if he consciously sought to make production of copy a standard service. But other agencies were groping, or being pushed, toward the same practice, as somehow copywriting had come to seem a special technique rather than the natural act of one person sending an appeal to others. Thus Thompson's literature in the late 1880s often asks the advertiser to prepare his copy and send it in with his order; there is also this offer: "Advertisers who should desire to avail themselves of my services in preparing advertisements, and will send me all their data, circulars, etc., can have the same prepared without cost. Electrotypes only are charged for."[61] Clearly Thompson thought of copywriting and design as extras, and made no fuss about his skill in these matters. The N.W. Ayer agency also moved hesitantly; it offered preparation of copy as a service to clients sometime in the 1880s, hired a man in 1888 who gave much of his time to this activity, and hired another in 1892 to work full time writing copy. Yet in 1893 the agency still proclaimed that copywriting was a minor part of its work, done only for regular customers. This was a moment of uncertainty, when one famous ad man (Pettingill) could criticize another (George P. Rowell) in *Printers' Ink* for encouraging advertisers to write their own copy. (As late as 1891, Rowell found great difficulty in writing copy for a patent medicine he had bought: apparently he had no prior experience.) But as with so many of these practices, the confusion evaporated almost overnight. There were apparently only half a dozen or so full-time copywriters in New York in 1891, but hundreds by the middle of the decade; a *Printers' Ink* ad writing contest in 1896 drew 850 entrants. Ayer's new copy *department* had nine people in 1900.[62] At precisely the moment of fastest cultural change, "everyone" suddenly came somehow to agree that description and praise of commodities was a specialist job, one best performed in connection with increasingly schematic campaigns, and within the increasingly private and professional space enclosed by ad agency walls. Even as writing about national brands became ubiquitous, its production grew mysterious.

Much the same rapid transformation occurred a few years later in the making of visual imagery, which had figured little in magazine advertising before the 1880s, aside from small, stylized engravings that signified the genre of product or service being promoted. There was not even room for elaborate visuals in periodicals before that time, partly for technical reasons but mainly because publishers refused to let copy spill over the lines that divided one column from the next. Presbrey says that the first American full-page display ad appeared in 1879 (p. 247). Only when that kind of space was regularly available would it make sense to think of print ads as seriously representational, though agencies showed their interest in typography and design from an earlier time, by establishing their own print shops, as Ayer did in 1875. But they were slow to see the possibilities of a pictorial rhetoric. Some progressive magazine editors and design people, notably at the *Youth's Companion* (where the first full-color ad appeared in 1893) and at the *Ladies' Home Journal*, made those possibilities more evident, and agencies began to take heed. As with copywriting, they first hired freelance artists and (when the halftone process came into use around 1888) photographers. The Bates agency started an art department in 1896; Lord & Thomas had a commercial artist in its employ by 1898; by 1905 the big agencies took this function as an obligatory part of any campaign. I will consider the visual results later. Conceptually, the change meant harnessing art to the production of aura. Before the 1890s, visuals were sketchy and decontextualized for the most part. But by 1901, J. Walter Thompson was advising clients that pictures "should show the goods in actual use." Presbrey adds that the new practices "helped sell the product by showing it in use or in an atmosphere that made it a desirable acquisition."[63] Exactly: agencies brought illustration in to stimulate imagination and desire, and to spin webs of association around the product. For the first time an alternate visual world was given shape by artists in paid service to this ideal.

I have tried to show how intermediaries took up positions in previously simpler market relations, and added complexity or mystery to certain exchanges of meaning, as ad men – and especially agencies running campaigns – made their imperial move. Shortly I will discuss some of the ways they used their new powers of address. Before that, one last agency practice (out of many) deserves specific mention, because it helped to create the mass circulation magazine.

Since the beginning, agencies had advised clients where to place their ads, though such advice was sometimes hollow when an agent controlled only one particular list of publications. Gradually, agents took on the promotion of magazines as a medium, alongside others, as it became clear to what extent the future of advertising lay with national brands. J. Walter Thompson was the pioneer. Within ten years of his having chosen this specialization, he was explaining to clients that only magazines could offer a national audience, and that they "are read by thousands who are not regular readers of the papers, embracing the very best of the people," an "intelligent audience, who are of business habits and appreciate a business statement."[64] *Printers' Ink* endorsed the preference by running a piece by John Brisben Walker, praising the quality of writing and illustration in magazines, their national reach, their detachment from partisan politics, and the supposed fact that magazine ads "have absolutely no connection whatever with the editing of the magazine," so that the editor has "the good of the entire country at heart."[65] Less high-mindedly, but perhaps just as hyperbolically, Calkins and Holden advised their textile maker to use magazines ahead of other media, claiming that there were 5 readers of every magazine copy, so that a $100,000 invest-ment in space over a year's time in 25 magazines, with aggregate circulation of 9 million, would get the company's message to 45 million readers, half the people in the nation! (p. 211). Some agents were skep-tical about magazines for a while, but could not ignore the "revolution" of 1893 or the brisk trade at J. Walter Thompson. Ayer, who had stuck with newspapers, gave in and began pushing magazines in 1896.

Thus did agents help finance the rise of the monthlies. Perhaps more surprising, J. Walter Thompson and others also used their eloquence in urging magazine editors to take the leap toward dependence on adver-tising. Thompson argued that they could use ad income to pay writers and artists more money, improve the quality of their journals, expand sales, and continue around this expansive circle again. Resistance was at first high among the classier monthlies; when Thompson contracted with *Harper's* for just a hundred pages of ads per year, editor William Curtis threatened to resign, fearing that that staid publication would become a "cheap circus magazine."[66]

I don't want to claim too much for the ad men. Publishers like Frank Munsey and Cyrus Curtis needed no one to tell them that their enter-prise depended on advertising. Curtis, especially, was busy with schemes to make advertising more effective in the *Ladies' Home Journal*: inter-spersing advertising columns and pages with editorial material long before others stopped segregating the two, helping advertisers with typography and illustration, moving toward color, even, for a while, mail-ing out subscription copies with ad pages cut and "reading pages" uncut.[67] He shared with agents like Thompson an interest in the best positioning of ads vis-à-vis editorial matter. And Edward Bok, his great editor, kept right in step. Writing in *Printers' Ink*, he insisted that an edi-tor must be a businessman, must work with the magazine's business manager "like the blades of a pair of shears . . . ; sometimes, I may say, *sotto voce* – I think the business office is the biggest blade."[68] The felt com-mon interest between ad agents on the one side and publishers and editors on the other is nowhere more evident than in N.W. Ayer's advancing Curtis hundreds of thousands of dollars' worth of ad space and agency work to publicize the *Journal* itself, building its circulation toward the million mark at the end of the century. Curtis in turn used his pro-motional talents to address agents and manufacturers. After purchasing the moribund *Saturday Evening Post*, he invited them to get on board early: "You can buy space now for one dollar that later will cost you two dollars. The Saturday Evening Post is to be pushed into a circulation exceeding that of any weekly in the United States."[69] That's mass culture.

But, as I noted earlier on, the most telling expression of this common interest was the agencies' relentless promotion of advertising to manufacturers. Many needed persuasion. Even at Quaker Oats, for instance, where Henry P. Crowell was one of the first and most enthusiastic proponents of the national campaign, his partner Ferdinand Schumacher remained fixated on production, and thought Crowell's huge advertising budgets (for example, $500,000 in 1895) a foolish extravagance. Partly because of their different outlooks, the company was troubled by internal disputes culminating in the total war of a proxy fight before Schumacher was forced out in 1899.[70] To skeptics less intractable than he, the agencies drummed out an insistent message: What should one advertise? "ANYTHING AND EVERYTHING THAT IS GENERALLY PLACED ON SALE IN THE COUNTLESS STORES SCATTERED OVER THE COUNTRY. . . ."[71] One could think of publishers, editors, ad men, and progressive manufacturers as a vanguard, often collaborating, sometimes competing, to invent the consciousness industry. Manufacturers helped draw the boundaries of this new territory and without their needs it never could have been discovered; but ad men colonized it, and took over a choice plot for their own domain.

The New Social Relations: Of Trust and Concealment

"The purpose of advertising is to sell goods to people living at a distance." Putting the matter thus, as J. Walter Thompson did in reflecting on his work late in his career, raises issues of trust, as Thompson well understood. Advertisers must give the buyer a thousand miles away, "who has no redress, a square deal." Over distance, social relations attenuate. One cannot shake hands on a deal, look the other in the eye, and say, "My word is my bond." The seller is a stranger; buyers are masses; anonymity prevails. The city figures this kind of distance. Artemas Ward, one of the famous writers of copy, characterized the new situation thus: "With the growth of the cities new demands have arisen – new avenues of consumption have been opened." What the farmer produces, the townsman buys. "Artificial aids must support his artificial life. He must go to others for most of his supplies. He is urged forward by the high pressure of city life to such an extent that he welcomes the signposts of advertising which direct him to the satisfying of his needs."[72] Signposts key into a new map of society, point down "new avenues of consumption."

Not only distance and cities, but *corporations* obscure social links. It is interesting how rarely that thought turns up in the analyses of ad men like Thompson and Ward; perhaps it was too obvious to be remarked on.

A corporation has a name and an address; it has the legal status of a person; it acts as a person in the market; through advertising it speaks as a person. But it is not a person, nor is it the many persons who work for it, nor is it even the persons who own it. Corporations are peculiarly abstract social entities, with which, nonetheless, consumers enter into multiple, unequal relations every day of their lives. That fact, too, raised issues of trust a hundred years ago. In chapter 5, I touched on ways in which the new retailers dealt with those issues – fixed prices, money-back return policies, and so on. National brand advertisers also tried to give buyers a "square deal," or at least the appearance of one.

For advertising agents, the challenge of building trust was complicated. Distance, cities, and corporations were their métier. In addition, they had to overcome the prehistory of their own trade. It is probably no exaggeration to say that most ads for nationally sold, branded products before 1875 or so were dishonest, implicitly or openly making false claims. (The damage to public credibility was perhaps the more severe because at this time religious periodicals carried more national advertising than any other medium.) In particular, ads promised instant cures for every illness, not only through medicines but by the use of many elaborate devices. A steam bath cabinet "forces all impurities from the system" and guarantees successful treatment of rheumatism, neuralgia, grippe, gout, female complaints, insomnia, all blood, skin, nerve, and kidney diseases, obesity, the common cold, pimples, blemishes, asthma, and catarrh. (Why not tuberculosis and cancer too, one wonders, since those diseases were a pushover at the time?) And such ads appeared, not only in the 1870s, but in the late 1890s, even at that date casting doubt on the integrity of the cereal or garter modestly advertised in the adjacent column. In addition to cures, there was much early promotion of lotteries, land speculation, dubious securities, get-rich-quick schemes, spiritual panaceas, and the like. Wishful thinking was the coin of the realm.

Ad men in the 1890s and after understood that distrust of the manufacturer tainted their own legitimacy even when they were innocent, because "Advertising implies a contract between the maker and the public . . . ."[73] I have already mentioned two of their strategies, and very decent ones, for restoring confidence. One was to turn away ads "relating to vile diseases [and] disreputable business" (Ayer), and court only "legitimate advertisers of the better class" (Thompson). There was some backsliding, but over the long haul they dissociated themselves from crooks, even when it cost them substantial sums to do so. Another was to preach honesty to one another. As Pope notes in an excellent chapter on "The Ethics of Persuasion," "Homilies on the efficacy of truth may be located in almost all writings on advertising," and he quotes a number of them from *Printers' Ink* during the 1890s, to the effect that lying is not only bad in itself but bad for business, too.[74] Truth in advertising was and is a troubled ideal, but a necessary one for the enlistment of consumers' faith.

Two other strategies recast social relations less forthrightly, though I believe without cynical intent. Trademarks proved useful for more than a guarantee of unchanging quality and a bar to imitation: they could personify the company. Some did so naturally enough via the founder's image. The dour faces of W. L. Douglas (shoes), the Smith brothers (cough drops), and King C. Gillette (safety razors) soon came to represent corporations as well as products for millions of people. More confusing and much more common, later, was the use of a fictional character. Baker's Cocoa instituted the practice long before anyone else; the painting it adapted in the 1780s, "La Belle Chocolataire," has for two hundred years associated the company with tidiness and comfort. Cream of Wheat's smiling negro chef Rastus tied the inexpensive product to a style of life that included servants; the Campbell's Soup twins allied the company with health, mothering, and innocence. An inevitable next step occurred in the 1890s when the Quaker Oats figure began to vary in representation and setting from ad to ad, appearing in well regulated homes and speaking to "us" of ancient wisdom and modern eating habits. The company invented Aunt Jemima about the same time, then gave her embodiment in the person of Nancy Green, who debuted at the Chicago World's Fair, and for many years traveled around teaching housewives how to use the product. Betty Crocker, Captain Crunch, and Mr Goodwrench have added little other than sophistication to this root idea of equating impersonal corporation with old friend.

Undoubtedly the main movement toward this end, however, was the evolution of copy styles. Ad men and (a bit later) professors theorized endlessly about rhetoric, argumentation, and voice. How could you most effectively address the public? Methods like "reason why" and "talking style" gradually gained favor. Meanwhile the practice of leading copywriters like John E. Powers led theory in this same direction, replacing the bombast or frivolousness of much early copy with a blunt, honest style that projected reliability and neighborliness. I will be examining it in chapter 8. Here, the point is just that agents and writers gave the corporation a plain-folks voice, projecting an imaginary discourse among equals that obscured the nature of the company, the source of the speech acts, and the one-sidedness of the "conversation." Yet they achieved these mystifications through an earnest attempt to deal squarely with the consumer, not deceive her. They were reaching toward a democratic style, in a matrix of inherently unequal relations.[75]

This contradiction derived easily enough from the fact that agents put their talents and energies at the service of big capital, but in a project which (unlike the domination of factory and workforce) did not allow big capital to coerce and intimidate. The contradiction took root deep in the thoughts of advertising men. How do you get people to do something they did not intend to do, yet without exercising power over them? You change their intention. If the desired act is the purchase of a product, you change their felt needs. Advertising agents began to think in this way early. Presbrey says that by 1905, agents and manufacturers alike realized that progress lay not only in selling things "already established in the mass mind as wants"; it entailed "creating wide desire for articles of utility or pleasure which among the majority of people would not be regarded as needs until advertising pictured their desirability" (p. 526).

He is surely right. Simply note these typical, unabashed accounts of advertising's role:

- Advertising is a "powerful force whereby the advertiser creates a demand for a given article in the minds of a great many people or arouses the demand that is already there in latent form." (Calkins and Holden, p. 4)
- "Advertising aims to teach people that they have wants, which they did not realize before, and where such wants can be best supplied. If the merchant were to wait nowadays for people to find out for themselves that they needed his wares he would have plenty of leisure and plenty of nothing else." (*The Thompson Red Book on Advertising*, 1901, p. 12)
- The advertiser "takes the vague discontent or need of the public, changes it into want, and the want into effective desire" (Emerson P. Harris, 1893; quoted by Presbrey, p. 347).
- "[My aim in advertising] was to do educational and constructive work so as to awaken an interest in and create a demand for cereals where none existed." (Henry P. Crowell, on his success with Quaker Oats; quoted in Marquette, p. 67)
- "The modern advertisement is not intended for the man who wants the thing already. It is for the one who don't [sic] in order to make him." (Edwin G. Dexter, Professor of Education at the University of Illinois, in *Printers' Ink*, 1904; quoted by Pope, p. 68)
- Advertising is "literature which compels Action . . . [and] changes the mind of millions at will" (Lord & Thomas, Chicago ad agency, 1911; quoted by Pope, p. 13)
- "Advertising modifies the course of a people's daily wants" (N.A. Lindsey, *Printers' Ink*, 25 November 1891, p. 623).

Some of these writers qualified their claims in various ways, but evidently they all thought they could reach into the "mass mind," and alter its desires.

Could they? In certain circumstances they could and did, I have argued. But that is not the main issue, here; nor am I considering whether the wants they created were socially beneficial (breakfast cereal?) or deleterious (cigarettes?), by some transhistorical standard. The point is that ad men had entered into a new social relation with the public, one in which, with ever-growing resources, they bent their efforts to the creation of wants. The results of these efforts appeared insistently before the eyes of the public many times a day, so that thoughtful people *knew* they had entered the new relation: "Once we skipped [ads] unless some want compelled us to read, while now we read to find out what we really want."[76] This was a change in what it meant to be a person in society.

As that last quotation implies, if some found advertising a vulgar nuisance, many people welcomed the guidance of ads, not to mention the ever more engaging spectacle. Even complaisant addressees would have taken offence, however, had they known how ad men described them and this relationship to prospective clients. As usual, J. Walter Thompson's language was especially frank and vivid. He offered to "lead the willing customer and drag the unwilling" toward purchase. This adversarial impulse often flowed into military metaphors. "To hit the general public, aim at the Bull's Eye," he advised, speaking of "ammunition" and "scores." His methods were unequaled for "making successful attacks on the public," leading to "quick surrender" and "complete victory." To be sure, he alternated such bellicosity with more temperate maxims ("Always appeal to the common sense of the people by an argument to their judgment"), but mainly he offered to engage the public as quarry, opponent, object.[77] I readily acknowledge the bluff good humor in his tone. Still, the attitude that the metaphors exaggerate is genuine.

In a slightly different vein, Thompson likened advertisements to a salesman, "who accosts the lawyer in his office, the student in his study, the retired man of wealth at the family fireside . . . ."[78] To accost people effectively and change the structure of their desires, one must have an idea how they are constituted. Ad agents and theorists have carried on a discussion about that for a hundred years. It has been inconclusive. Merle Curti, in an oft-cited article, reported on "The Changing Concept of 'Human Nature' in the Literature of American Advertising."[79] Analyzing the language of *Printers' Ink* writers, he concluded that the majority of them took people to be rational and cost-efficient, from 1890 to 1910, and a minority saw people as irrational and subject to the creation of needs; the balance tilted the other way during the next two decades, and shifted again between 1930 and 1950. Without question, even while some turn-of-the-century participants were crediting the common sense of the audience, others spoke without embarrassment about the "credulity" or "gullibility" of the masses, conceptualized them as "grown-up children" or retrograde savages, and gave advice like "AIM LOW," and "you must write to impress fools." Pope (pp. 246–7) suggests that these opinions of the customer were prevalent. He is unquestionably right in attributing their increase to the new marketing situation, which "damaged, perhaps beyond repair, the approximate parity of buyers and sellers in American life" (p. 248). Face-to-face relations in more or less stable communities foster the premise of rationality on both sides; distant "masses" are more likely to seem childish and irrational.

From the perspective I am urging, it does not matter a lot whether most ad men read human nature as emotional or rational, or indeed, whether Schudson is right in arguing that advertising people's theories about human nature were and are inconsistent, pretentious, and only marginally related to the actual techniques used in ads (pp. 58–60). The important thing for social relations is that an intense discourse grew, in which those with access to the media theorized and constructed those on the receiving end, behind professional doors and without in any way consulting the latter. This was a top-down debate, like so many others joined at the time – about education, about literacy, about the dangerous classes, about urban misery, about crime, and so on and on. To these managers and professionals, the people were a problem to be analyzed and solved by specialists.[80]

To me, their analysis is most interesting when it drops from the heady sublime of "human nature" into the canny pragmatics of characterizing real social groups. What counted in daily business was to reach particular kinds of consumers, not abstract souls. For one obvious thing, ad men had to understand Americans, and they talked a good deal among themselves about our national characteristics, often in ways not especially flattering – Americans are speed-driven and spendthrift, have short attention spans, and so on. More specifically, ad men segmented the audience in various ways. "The census is the foundation stone of real advertising study," wrote Artemas Ward, noting that 25 percent of the people already lived in cities, with that proportion rising rapidly.[81] He pleaded for understanding of the urban ethos, but agents tried hard to enter the minds of farmers, too. Age, occupation, geographical region, ethnicity, all provided other ways of defining audiences. To illustrate the point, however, I will touch briefly on just the two most important dimensions of analysis: gender and class. (Race didn't count, since too few black people had the means to figure as a consumer group.)

Many have noted the feminization of the marketplace during the nineteenth century. Naturally, advertising people observed this change, and began to think about women as economic agents. Pope holds that "If humanity in general was rather weak and fallible, women in particular were, in the stereotypes of advertising men, irrational and subject to others' control" (p. 247). That such views received full articulation by the 1920s is certain.[82] Yet Pope offers only one citation from the 1890s to this effect, and my less extensive research hasn't turned up many. Pope infers from a statement by well-known ad man Nathaniel Fowler – "The woman who will not read advertisements is not a woman" – the trade's belief that "Ill-informed, emotional, and suggestible, women took special interest in advertisements" (p. 248). This was not Fowler's outlook. An admirer of advertising, he admired women for their responsiveness to it. He saw women as directing purchase "of everything from shoes to shingles," and thought them capable in this role: "The woman can buy better articles, from spool cotton to ulster overcoats, for less money than the average man can buy with more money."[83] Women displayed, precisely, a rationality in the marketplace.

J. Walter Thompson also considered women the family purchasing agents, to use a metaphor from a later time. "The women spend the money, and to reach the women, one must enter the family." He claimed to have set that as a goal in 1868, through ads in *Peterson's* magazine. Charles Raymond, who worked for Thompson, said Thompson's strategy was to "address your message to the intelligence, the curiosity, the love, and yes, the cupidity of the women, and the thing is done."[84] I don't believe Thompson thought cupidity all bad. Again, the main thing is that advertisers saw women as a primary audience early on, and began consciously to address them through ads. A survey of all the large display ads in three issues each of *Munsey's* and *McClure's* (two "general" magazines) between 1895 and 1907 bears this out: eighty-one ads indicate either through picture or through text that they speak to women in particular; only thirty-five single out men. Ad men thought they could reach an important audience of women, and communicate the right messages to them.

They thought rather more specifically about the public as divided into classes. I want to insist on this because others have not. Pope, the best historian of early national advertising, says that "campaigns rarely directed overt appeals to particular social classes or ethno-cultural groups, but admen were aware of social distinctions" (p. 13). I'm not sure what Pope means by "overt appeals"; certainly many ads traded on class aspirations and feelings, as I will show in chapter 8. And ad men were not just "aware of social distinctions": they made an understanding of those distinctions and of their economic importance a key part of the expertise they offered to manufacturers.

J. Walter Thompson, especially, insisted on the centrality of class, and that was natural since he trafficked in magazines, and magazines far more than newspapers or billboards aimed at particular social groups. You must "know how people live . . . . You must understand exactly how a man can support a family on ten dollars a week – and you must also know how a thousand-dollar-a-month family spends its income." Such claims made elementary business sense for an agency specializing in consumer groups. Thompson had to know which magazines reached people of each sort, in order to promise: "We can insure that automobiles shall not be extensively advertised to the working classes nor bargain jack-knives to the well-to-do" (this was in 1901). He used these kinds of knowledge early on to promote his lists of magazines. He divided farmers into "two classes – one a shiftless ne'er-do-well; the other the bright, sharp, shrewd, and intelligent man, who is wide awake to his own interests" (1888?). The latter, Thompson went on, bought the same manufactured goods as city people, and could be reached through the agricultural magazines to which he subscribed. For an affluent audience, Thompson recommended trade journals: "the combined wealth of the individual readers of Trade Journals exceeds that of [sic] the entire wealth of the balance of [the country's] population" (1889). He understood well the dollar value to advertisers of a class analysis: a circulation of a hundred thousand in a

> sensational, trashy weekly story paper is not worth, to a legitimate advertiser, one-tenth as much as an equal circulation in a journal of a high character, that has entrance into the *better class* of homes . . . . The great bulk of business, aside from the necessaries of life, comes from people of moderate or independent means associated with at least fair refinement and culture . . . . Hence, judicious advertisers seek to reach people having both TASTE for their goods and the MEANS to gratify it. (1887)

Could there be a clearer articulation of class consciousness right down to typographical emphasis, and precisely at the point where agents invited manufacturers to conceive and plan informed campaigns? [85]

Others in the trade wrote similarly. Calkins and Holden made a far more elaborate analysis of class and buying habits than Thompson, arguing, among other things, that it was pointless to aim ads at the Morgans, Astors, and Goulds, because their servants decided which soap and cereal to buy (pp. 286–305 make fascinating reading). These authors, too, connected the analysis to specific magazine audiences. They set off the *Ladies' Home Journal* against *Comfort*, for instance, as representing "two extreme types [of magazine] and their respective constituencies; the one, the highest type of an advertising medium, . . . reaching well-educated, well-to-do, intelligent American women; the other, poorly printed, . . . and reaching an uneducated and credulous class." The latter, nonetheless, was worth reaching: "Its readers buy only the most inexpensive things, but large numbers of them do buy, so that the space is worth what it costs the advertisers" (p. 73). Class was a matter of profitable knowledge, not high theory.

For magazine publishers, too: they collaborated with agents in this anatomy of the public along class lines. That Calkins and Holden should contrast the two magazines thus, in 1905, was no accident: Curtis fought a relentless battle from the 1880s on, both to secure for the *Journal* a toney readership and (doubtless with a good deal of hyperbole) to convince advertisers that he had it. He wrote to doubters that most *Journal* readers were suburbanites, churchgoers, professionals; among them were to be found no poor people nor – a fine gesture of

editorial omniscience – a single epileptic or tubercular.[86] Other publishers, some with an initial advantage over Curtis, also profiled their
readerships in class terms. The *Atlantic* claimed to reach "persons of
highest cultivation"; the *Forum*, readers of "culture, taste, enterprise,
and the means to gratify their many wants"; the *Illustrated Home Monthly*,
"intelligent, cultivated, and well-to-do families."[87] Later, some undertook research to back up such claims. *Ladies' World* photographed the
homes of all subscribers in a few towns, and showed the photos to advertisers. *McClure's* listed all its subscribers in Cleveland and found out
their occupations, to show "how many of the professional class, how
many of the leisure class and how many of the working class" read the
magazine.[88] Businessmen are marxists when it pays. Most publishers
identified their audience as "the professional class," for obvious reasons,
but not all did. *Frank Leslie's Popular Monthly* said it reached the "great
masses"; *Women's Argosy* may have been putting the same case more
politely in saying it entered "the homes of the people."[89]

There was of course some confusion, along with much puffery, in such
talk. Thompson held in 1909 both that the ten cent magazine appealed
to the masses and that it was "high class" (*Blue Book*, as reprinted in
Advertising Age, 7 December 1964, p. 20). But I hope to have shown (if
not over-shown) that an energetic discourse of social class developed
right along with modern advertising. Already in 1891, *Printers' Ink* ran articles with titles like "The Class of Readers Addressed" (15 April), and
stated in an editorial that agents could "cover almost any particular class
or locality" (25 November). This should not surprise anyone; consumption is class specific, and advertising had to be so, too. It had to know who
read what, who bought what, and how class figured in desire. (Scott
included the desire to be like more privileged people in his 1903 list of
ruling interests and motives, along with health, possessiveness, and so
on.) Ad men both took class as a given, and helped to construct it.[90]

A phrase crops up again and again in writing about this subject: "the
advertising controversy." The book that takes that phrase for its title in
fact engages in a number of disputes: How does advertising affect
demand? total consumption? brand loyalty? prices? profits? product
innovation? economic concentration? [91] More controversies than these
surround the practices of modern advertising. But three related ones
have claimed most attention: Is advertising wasteful or productive as a
whole, in economic terms? Is it an effective strategy for individual
companies, and if so, in what circumstances? And does it sell us things we
would not otherwise have bought, and perhaps do not need? Thoughtful
analysts like Simon, Schudson, and Albion and Farris tend toward mild
conclusions: advertising doesn't affect business cycles much, may or may
not increase total consumption, affects market shares but doesn't dramatically alter habits of consumption. Sometimes the analyst makes an
exception for advertising of new inventions or new genres of product.

Beyond noting that the exception covers many campaigns of the 1890s and 1900s, and repeating my earlier point that such campaigns definitely worked, I will not comment on these questions. They bear on advertising as an old institution, not a burgeoning new one. There is another controversy stirred by the assertion of many left wing cultural critics that advertising sells the existing social order as it sells products, and so works as a politically conservative force. Such thoughts as I have on the issue, I will save until I have examined the actual messages of 1890s ads. For now, I want to sum up the argument of this chapter by insisting that, apart from the ideological force of ads themselves, and in a way not captured by the debate over advertising's *effects*, the entrenchment of the new selling practices decisively changed the network of social relationships, changed the outlook for democracy, changed what it meant to be a person.

To start with what everyone then and now has observed, power relations shifted in the marketplace. In 1887, Thompson could already urge, to manufacturers, national advertising for any commodity "that you wish to compel retail dealers to keep in stock by inciting a demand therefor" (*Illustrated Catalogue*, p. 13). This idea won out. Recall how Gustav A. Berghoff, president of the Rub-No-More Co., described the change from a time (the 1880s) when the sales effort proceeded from manufacturer to jobber to retailer to consumer. Twenty-five years later,

> The manufacturer goes first to the consumer. By advertising he burns it into the consumer's mind that he [sic] wants a certain brand. Through premiums, gifts or bribes if you please, he induces her to try his brand. At tremendous expense the manufacturer educates her to ask for Fels Naphtha, Ivory, Rub-No-More, Arrow collars, etc., as the case may be. The demand created, the retailer goes to the jobber asking him to furnish the articles called for. Then the jobber goes to the manufacturer.
>
> Our company sells through the jobber, and we do the rest. We create the desire for our product through advertising.[92]

With his usual acuity, Thompson made clear the importance of this change for the manufacturer. The Industrial Revolution, he remarked, had "solved the vast economic problem of production," but left distribution as a continuing challenge. The manufacturer "had to depend on the country storekeeper and the equally uninterested proprietor of the city shop. His name did not reach the consumer; he was always in danger of losing his entire trade in a single year; he lived in the shadow of the nightmare of cut-throat competition" (*Advertising as a Selling Force*, 1909). He needed a way to revolutionize selling, and ease this crisis of competitive capitalism; Thompson understandably credits advertising with having supplied the remedy. Through it, indeed, manufacturers gained power over small shopkeepers, intervening from afar in face-to-face relations between the latter and the customer. They also gained power over jobbers and wholesalers. Ad men and agencies did not accomplish this change singlehanded, but they facilitated it, and themselves occupied a new position of some strength in the emerging social order.

I have argued that their new relation to the public was in some ways mysterious. They gave the corporation a disembodied and confusingly personalized voice. They also represented it in public spaces with signs and images that obscured its nature and economic role. Similarly, they established an inherently mystifying discourse about products. Even as they seemed to bring commodities into clear focus, with names, trade-marks, distinctive packages, and so on, they created around them a non-material aura, the "added value" necessary to differentiate goods of similar price and material features, and thus build brand loyalty. As Raymond Williams says, the "crucial cultural quality" of advertising is this addition of "magic,"[93] even when it also presents true information. Perhaps it is worth troubling the reader one last time with a reminder that at this level of analysis it does not matter much how successful ad men were or are in finding the right magic to affect consumers' pur-chases or transform their social outlooks. Even if advertising is as unscientific or random as Simon, Schudson, and Marchand sometimes imply, it makes a difference that very large sums are spent with the *inten-tion* of filling our minds with magic, and with the undeniable result of crowding the channels of public discourse and representation with such messages.

In carrying out this project, naturally, advertising men undertook to conceptualize the cognitive and emotional make-up, the life situations, the social aspirations, the capabilities, and the inadequacies of citizens, the better to create needs among them. They carried on an increas-ingly sophisticated conversation about these matters, in professional and business venues to which citizens had no access, not even, at this time, through legislative constraints on advertising claims. The flourish-ing of that private discourse in the twentieth century, backed by billions of dollars, has itself encroached on democracy. It makes "us" unwitting objects of "their" talk and actions. Of course it is also true, as all apolo-gists for advertising and some nonpartisan commentators say, that advertising "made businesspeople interested in what the consumer had to say" (Leiss, Kline, and Jhally, p. 103). Putting it like that is fairer than speaking of the sovereign consumer; still, there is no parity of means or intent between what we "say" to business people through our purchases or as participants in market research, and what they say and think about us. Agency practices have helped remove important areas of concern, such as what our society will produce, from public discussion.

In these ways, the developments I narrated earlier in this chapter have changed the structure of our society, our real relations to one another. Those relations constitute us as agents, define our scope, set the terms of our daily conduct. Of course advertising does not by itself constitute our humanity. As both proponents and critics agree, "Advertising is part and parcel of a highly industrialized, market-oriented society."[94] J. Walter Thompson, who understood many things early and well that others have labored to rediscover, noted in 1909 that advertising was "part of the existing commercial universe. It could not be abolished or reduced to any noticeable degree without changing the entire economic aspect of life" (*The J. Walter Thompson Book*). The thought offers little consolation, though, like most who share it, I have no wish to give up washing machines and cornflakes. The embeddedness of advertising in "the entire economic aspect of life" has since 1909 made some bad social relations, as well as some good products, seem normal and inevitable.

To conclude on a main theme of this chapter: consolidation of the advertising business strengthened – and helped *make* – the corporate ruling class, stabilizing its mastery of production, extending its reach into the consumer market, pacifying the environment within which it accumulated capital, and increasing while obscuring its power to intervene in the daily lives of citizens. Some capitalists consciously undertook parts of this project, though on behalf of their own interests, not those of their whole class. Others stumbled into the new arrangements, or failed to adjust and so lost out. What I have stressed here is the role of ad men in articulating goals and formulating strategies that served the purpose of the big bourgeoisie – the agency of agencies, if you will. The latter took on the management of consciousness to advance their own interests. But the opportunity for doing so in this way was created largely by the inchoate interests and needs of capital. Thus does power often flow through indirect channels, and the mediated processes of hegemony.

7

Readers, Consumers:
The Professional-Managerial Class

That said, I want now to shift the narrative focus. Every historical script is a collaboration, whoever outlines the plot. Some of the collaborators demand a different story altogether, as did Populists, the strikers of Homestead, Nationalist followers of Edward Bellamy, and many others in the 1890s. Some write stories of their own, adapting motifs of the main plot for their own purposes or concentrating on subplots, as did magazine publishers, advertising agents, and department store owners. Still others – most people, with at least part of their conscious effort – try to shape the stories of their own lives, paying little mind to the script of the more powerful, though of course enacting and contesting it. People make history but not within circumstances of their own choosing, in Marx's tidier formulation.[1]

I have devoted much of this book to the movers and subplotters of the magazine revolution, stressing the gravity of their needs and the efficacy of their projects. Along the way magazine readers – consumers – have faded in and out of view mainly as a social group whose needs could be understood and reconfigured in service to the corporate sales effort. From here on I will concentrate more on the way they experienced the transformation of American society, steered a course within it, and in no small measure helped bring it about. Having figured in the last chapter as people who were studied and targeted by others so that their attention might be bought and shaped, they now emerge as people creating their own lives and consciousness. In the three chapters that follow, I will examine advertisements and the editorial contents of the magazines as responding – successfully, on the evidence of circulation and profits – to the desires and aspirations of this newly assembled readership. Here, my intention is to reflect on the changing situation in which they found themselves during the post-Civil War decades, and on some of the strategies they pursued to negotiate it. I refer to the making of a professional-managerial class (PMC) and the validation of its outlook and aims.

I take this class to have included professional workers themselves, those who did similar mental work but without benefit of formal professionalization (including writers, editors, advertising men, and others who figure centrally in this study), mid- and upper-level corporate managers, their counterparts in government and other institutions, and highly skilled people who worked with numbers and technical processes. This aggregate amounted to somewhat over 1 million people, or one-fifteenth of the workforce, in 1880 and about 3.5 million, or one-tenth of the workforce, in 1910. Since fewer family members worked for pay in the PMC than in the working class, I conjecture that people in PMC families made up perhaps 7 or 8 percent of the population in 1880 and maybe 12 percent in 1910. I conjoin the 1880 and 1910 figures to suggest the growth of this group through the period of my main concern. But to do so immediately discloses the near irrelevance of census figures to inquiries like this one, since I posit that the PMC did not exist as a recognizable or conscious formation in 1880, but was well organized and purposeful in 1910. Census categories don't express deeper social realities. Nor do they even correspond to shallower distinctions that matter for purposes such as mine, as anyone knows who has dived into the *Historical Statistics of the United States* in search of class lines, and realized that not long before 1900 a "clerk" could be a third-in-command in a manufacturing firm, whereas by 1910 the designation included almost nobody but ill paid, subordinate, and often female workers. Add the further difficulty of blurry boundaries between the PMC and other groups such as small businessmen, sales representatives, prosperous farmers, and so on, and I hope it is clear why I do not wish to take the class as empirically defined. Rather, I hope that this chapter and the next three will gradually bring a picture of these people into focus and make it seem plausible and useful to regard them as a social class.

City and Suburb

The city was their soil. North American cities mushroomed in this period: most of the major ones more than doubled in size between 1865 and 1900; a hundred US communities doubled in the 1880s alone; many small towns became small cities. One should not overemphasize the shift: even in 1900 fewer than half of the people in the US lived in places the census classified as urban (though well over half in the central Atlantic and Northeast states did), and in spite of the evident depopulation of older rural areas, the number of people farming also rose substantially through 1900, and improved acreage more than doubled.[2] Still, in important ways this was an urban society by the end of the century. The city was the main locus of production and power; it figured centrally in the people's understanding of what their world had become. I will not rehearse the familiar statistics, celebrations, and laments, but will just mention a few salient features that defined a new environment for millions of middle class people, by the 1890s.

How would such people have perceived the others whose migration swelled the population of cities? Very many of the latter were native farmers. Rural New England had of course been emptying out since the 1820s, as the Erie Canal and then the railroads opened up better land and brought the older districts into competition with western farms. The exodus continued through the century; in the 1880s two-thirds of New England's 1500 "towns" lost population, as did two-fifths of Pennsylvania and almost five-sixths of New York. Nor, by this time, was this mainly a migration from the poorer Atlantic seaboard farms to richer land in the West. In the same decade, more than half the townships in Ohio, Illinois, and other Midwestern states lost population,[3] and in fifty plains counties (mainly in Kansas and Nebraska) nearly a third of the people left – about half for the Far West and half for cities (Kolko, p. 28). By 1900 the city had become the main destination for departing farmers, and this was a one-way migration: twenty farmers came to the city for every city person who went the other way.

Stephen Thernstrom sums up this shift by saying that the main source of urban growth, and of total population growth in the US, was the "high fertility of natives living outside the city."[4] To be sure, when a family of eight or nine children was commonplace, the family farm could not practically be divided up among sons, generation after generation. But rural fertility would not have swelled the cities had the end of the century not been a time of agricultural crisis: a crisis of overexpansion, compounded by the rising value of land, high interest rates, erratic prices for farm produce, and the eternal vicissitudes of the weather. Farm income in western Kansas, for one dramatic instance, fell by 59 percent in 1893 (Kolko, p. 25). Such disasters turn farmers into tenants, or farm laborers, or refugees. Those who poured into the cities came with few resources beyond the sale of their labor power. They were mainly "unskilled" from the standpoint of the urban job market, richly skilled though they had been in agriculture.

Alongside these new proletarians, the older middle class saw another mass of rural people: immigrants. Thirty-four million of the more than fifty million poor Europeans dislocated by industrialization, harsh national policies, and famine in the nineteenth and early twentieth centuries came to the US. Most of these people had little choice but to take city jobs in manufacturing, construction, and service. They became an urban majority: by 1880, more than 70 percent of residents in New York, Chicago, Cleveland, Detroit, St Louis, Milwaukee, San Francisco, and many other large and small cities were immigrants or children of immigrants.[5] Most of these people came from northern and western Europe and Canada; as the flow continued and increased through the last two decades of the century it drew in millions from eastern and southern Europe. With little English and little experience of city life, they seemed even more alien to the native-born middle class. In addition, a large

majority of all but the Jews came with the intention of returning to
Europe, and something like a third of them actually did; they saved
money, sent it home, declined to "Americanize" (Kolko, pp. 69–71).
Needless to say, their perceived strangeness, poverty, and isolation fed
the discourse of "dangerous classes" and of the city as a place of disease,
vice, and crime.

    Its mystery had deepened in part, too, just because of its new size and
complexity. The walking city of the early Republic was familiar terrain to
all its residents. They knew its neighborhoods, and neighborhoods were
themselves mixed: commerce, artisanal production, residence; people of
various ranks and conditions. Wealthy people tended to live near the
center, but with humbler residents in alleys nearby. Necessary transactions of daily life brought one face-to-face with fellow townspeople of all
sorts. The "sorts" themselves were easily comprehensible on a grid of
known hierarchies and affiliations, within familiar patterns of deference
and obligation. The city was compact, and densely settled, sharply
demarcated against the countryside that began abruptly at its edges.

    The larger urban places had long ceased to be walking cities at the
end of the nineteenth century. As late as 1850, a circle with a two mile
radius encompassed the settled area of Boston and contiguous suburbs.
Philadelphia's built-up area amounted to about ten square miles, most of
it between the Delaware and the Schuylkill, easily traversed on foot in an
hour or so. New York was scarcely larger. By 1900, metropolitan Boston
had a ten mile radius. A decade later, Philadelphia comprehended 130
square miles; Chicago, now the second largest city, 185 square miles;
New York 299.[6] And their built-up areas, including haloes of suburbs,
were far larger. No one ranged on foot over such spaces. The horsecar,
the railroad, and the streetcar carried people on regular paths from
home to work or to shop. Lawyers commuted about six miles to their
offices, on average, in New York and Boston (Jackson, p. 315); laborers
and clerks traveled to workplaces by public conveyance, too, though not
usually that far. The separation of work from leisure, production from
consumption, could be plotted on the map of the functionally segregated city; and residential neighborhoods themselves were far more
segregated by wealth and style. A resident who moved about in the
course of daily life saw thousands of strangers to whom he or she had no
known connection. Social relationships went in disguise now, except at
work and in the neighborhood. No one had a personal, sensuous grasp
of the city's physical precincts, its processes, its peoples.

    Nor was it easy to understand and adapt to the most obvious thing
about cities: the rapidity of their growth and change. No central authority – governmental or financial – planned expansion through the
century, in cities any more than in the nation as a whole. Hartford instituted the first city planning commission in 1907; Los Angeles passed the
first major zoning law in 1909.[7] Some older cities like Philadelphia

established the familiar gridiron plan for streets almost from the beginning (1682) or, like New York, added it on later (1811).[8] Beginning in 1785, territory west of the Ohio River was plotted on a checkerboard grid, and many cities that grew up in this area filled up mile-square sections with streets laid out on the same pattern. But grids were plans for streets and for real estate exchanges, not for cities as working social systems.[9] What planning city people did to make things work, they did piecemeal through water and sewer commissions and the like, delegated to utilities (gas and electric companies), or franchised out to private enterprise, as with streetcar lines.

Cities grew according to the dictates of the profit motive and individual choice, regulated only by market forces, political jockeying, and bribery. Even big developers took a *relatively* small part in expanding the city. For instance, as the newly annexed towns of Roxbury, West Roxbury, and Dorchester quadrupled in population from 1870 to 1900 to over 250,000 (40 percent of all Boston), no one company or person built more than 3 percent of the 23,000 new homes, and large-scale builders (20 or more homes) built fewer than a quarter of them. A total of 9000 people made the decision to build.[10] Land speculators and subdividers made fortunes in city real estate, from John Jacob Astor on down, but they didn't plan cities or even neighborhoods. Neither did the banks, large and small, that made loans to developers and private builders, or the building and loan associations that numbered in the thousands by 1900. If anyone fixed the course of growth it was the moguls of the street railway lines, who often built out beyond the threshold of immediate profitability; but they planned only where the city would next expand, not what it would be like.

The same point could be spelled out for industrial and commercial development; I have emphasized the disorder of residential expansion because my interest is in the circumstances of the mainly native born, non-manual workers who were in cities before the flood of newcomers arrived, who were borne aloft precisely by that flood, as well as by their own prudence and industry, and who had begun making themselves into a kind of middle class as early as the 1830s. Think of them as shopkeepers, successful artisans turned businessmen, an emergent group of managers and other office workers, ministers, doctors, and so on. They and their families had income roughly from two to ten times the $500 a year that was common among skilled workers in 1890. They had options beyond scrambling for subsistence. They had aspirations. They had status to create and protect, in an urban world very different from the walking city with its clear social ranks and face-to-face relations. They were committed to urban areas by the men's occupations; they valued the city's improving amenities and the life chances it offered their children. At the same time, they could see it filling up with people from whom they felt themselves quite distinct; they experienced its rapid and chaotic growth; they saw neighborhoods in decline even as real estate prices rose. I want to consider how such people met these challenges and used the economic advantage they had.

In pursuing this inquiry, I will give a good deal of emphasis to the ways they negotiated, appropriated, created, were shaped by, and gave meaning to social space in these new urban matrices. My premise is that "classes are necessarily constituted in and through the use of space,"[11] though of course not only in that way. Space, in this sense, is both a social product and a powerful determinant of social process; it is "the outcome of past actions," and "what permits fresh actions to occur," or prohibits them. This is obvious in the case of, for instance, a factory or a school; but everywhere, social space "implies, contains and dissimulates social relations"; or, as another writer puts it, everywhere "relations of power. . . are inscribed into the apparently innocent spatiality of social life,"[12] just as people use the power they have to shape spatiality and conform it to their needs. I will be concerned with various settings of interaction – locales – from individual rooms to suburban homes, to the suburbs themselves and on "out" to other urban and more distant sites frequented and made significant by PMC people. I suggest thinking of the ensemble of such locales, the ways they are articulated into regions and zoned for social practices, their social definitions, their valuations, and their uses as a complex PMC social space, within the far more complex social space of whole cities, the nation, and the world.[13]

A first step is to look at where these people chose to live. Even the mixed cities of the early nineteenth century included small areas where wealthy or "middling" people clustered together. These patterns of segregation became more distinct by mid century, when not only prosperous merchants but many former artisans who now supervised the manual work of others had residences apart from office or shop – the famed rift between work and leisure was widening. Addresses made a difference. But the geography of social distinction was finely etched, especially in cities like Philadelphia that expanded on a grid of main commercial arteries, broad cross streets, and interior alleys (mews). Stuart Blumin analyzed the households in five small segments of the city in 1860. A typical conjunction: a block of Pine Street contained the substantial homes of three prosperous merchants, a physician, a clerk, a clothier, and two partners in a large furniture business, all men of property. Stampers Street, the alley behind it, included households headed almost entirely by propertyless artisans and unskilled workers. A medium-width street in a similar area split the difference, with two jewelers, a silversmith, a tailor, a bricklayer, and a machinist, all reporting to the census taker property worth over $1000, suggesting a transition from artisan to businessman; and others who certainly did not work with their hands: bookkeepers, clerks, small retailers, and schoolteachers.[14] These people mingled in the same markets and lived less than a stone's throw from each other, but each block of homes constituted a mini neighbor-hood organized by occupation and signaling a particular social level.

By 1880 these areas had become more homogeneous neighborhoods, some commercial, some working class, some solidly middle class. Segregation proceeded similarly in other cities. By the 1870s well-to-do residents of Providence were moving out from downtown along Broadway and Elmwood, while the wealthy expanded with the "aristo-cratic East Side" along Waterman and Angell Streets. Immigrants, now almost half the population, lived near the wharves and factories and on the western edge of the city.[15] In New York, the well-to-do moved up the avenues from Washington Square, while the Bowery and the Five Points became poor immigrant districts. People sorted themselves out by resi-dential area in smaller cities, too. In Utica, with a population of 22,000 in 1860, "the modest but comfortable homes of the middle classes were concentrated in the fourth ward of the city, just to the east of the com-mercial hub and across town from the major factories and their immigrant workers"; most of these artisans and shopkeepers owned homes worth from $1000 to $2000.[16]

Segregation by street and block shaded into segregation by neigh-borhood, and a still broader pattern emerged in many cities, with manual workers near the downtown district, middle class people two to five miles out, and the wealthy in enclaves on the periphery. An excep-tion to the rule: some old elites and other wealthy people could afford to maintain elegant homes at the best addresses – the Beacon Hills and Gramercy Parks and Rittenhouse Squares – of the old city, in spite of increasing land values. This pattern was established among bankers in Boston by the 1850s, before the development of affluent outer suburbs: presidents and cashiers stayed in the prestigious spots of the inner city; porters and messengers could afford only crowded housing nearby; mid-dling bank workers – tellers, bookkeepers, and clerks – moved out to modest gentility in the pre-annexation suburbs.[17] Similarly, in Chicago, an observer of 1874 noted that "Professional men, clerks, and others of moderate income but whose tastes rise above rows of cheap cottages, have been attracted in great numbers" to the fringe areas of the city and its new suburbs.[18] Sam Bass Warner, historian of sorting by distance in Boston, summarized thus: middle class families "clustered together by their income capabilities and transportation needs so that the class divi-sions of the society came to be represented in large areas of similarly priced homes." Residential differentiation of this sort was probably an inevitable sequel to the elaboration of social strata attendant on capital-ism's specialization of the labor process.[19]

Middle class people, just by virtue of their incomes, had choices avail-able that most manual workers did not. They could afford more spacious lots and homes; they could afford the expense of streetcar or train fares in the daily commute to work for men, frequent shopping trips for women, and excursions for families. The city gave them their living and access to urban styles of consumption and culture, but urban forces pushed them away from its center, too – set limits to their choices. They could *not* afford genteel addresses and homes in the center, and what they could afford nearby became less desirable through the century because the space of the old city was increasingly given over to commerce, manufacturing, and the tenements and cheap houses of the poor and of the broad, now mainly immigrant, working class. City neighborhoods deteriorated, except for those that were posh and too expensive. By the second half of the century it was a commonplace, though certainly an exaggeration, that no one lived in Manhattan except the rich and the poor; a similar division held in other cities, old and new. Economic circumstances pressed middle class people to migrate outward. The borderland also attracted them, with its physical blend of country and city, and with its promise that one could dwell among people of like means, like values, like social standing. Moving there was one of the many choices that enacted and formed a class.

Suburb: the concept would seem to promise more precision than "borderland," "fringe," or "periphery," since it suggests a named place housing people, many of whom commute to work in a nearby city. Working from this definition, one can trace the evolution of suburbs through the nineteenth century, beginning from a surprisingly early date. A regular steam ferry service linked Brooklyn to Manhattan in 1814, and thousands were commuting by the 1830s. A similar service began across the Hudson in 1821; by the 1850s, ferries crossed between Jersey City and New York every fifteen minutes, and affluent people were commuting by rail and ferry from the planned villa community of Llewellyn Park twelve miles into New Jersey. Rail service came to Westchester County villages in 1844; by the end of the century eighteen of them had incorporated and trains brought more than a hundred thousand people to Manhattan daily. Similar growth occurred in the villages that later became the Bronx and Queens. One-third as many people – over a million – lived in New York's suburbs as lived in the city by 1900.

Boston began suburbanizing a bit later but did so more thoroughly. A few hundred crossed the Charles daily from Cambridge to Boston in the 1840s, fifteen hundred in the late 1850s, with parallel developments in Charlestown, Dorchester, Roxbury, Brookline, Newton, and dozens of other streetcar and railroad suburbs. Resistance to annexation hardened earlier around Boston than elsewhere, so that metropolitan growth after 1880 was almost entirely suburban, and by 1900 more people lived in suburbs than in the hub itself. Philadelphia and Cincinnati sprouted suburbs at about the same time. Land in Germantown, near the former city, rose to $5000 an acre by 1860 and to $3000 in Clifton, near Cincinnati, later the same decade. Newer cities like Detroit and Chicago that grew up with the railroad had suburbs almost from the start – a hundred of them existed around Chicago in 1873 and they were home to three hundred thousand people in 1890.[20] The figures tell a clear enough story of irreversible growth in suburbs, from erratic beginnings in the 1820s to something like a dominant middle class institution around 1900.

It is not, however – told this simply and empirically – the story that will explain how middle class people sought to locate themselves geographically and symbolically in exploding cities over the course of the century. For one thing, while the commonsense definition of the suburb on which I have based this sketch of linear growth precisely describes a relation in space and a practice of commuting, it ignores changes in the social meaning of suburban space. Early commuters were not adopting a pattern of life already mapped onto class coordinates; the first suburbs were not suburbs at first, in a socially intelligible sense. The village of New Hartford, two and a half miles from Utica, fit the definition; but it is unlikely that Lavinia Johnson's son-in-law thought of himself as a suburbanite when in 1859 he went by stage coach to his business in town each day and was met on his return by his wife Mary.[21] They were living in the country. Germantown, half an hour from Philadelphia by railroad in 1839, was not yet a suburb, even if some of the gentlemen with summer homes there sometimes commuted to work. But soon after that date, when many shopkeepers and manufacturers had cottages or villas there and made the daily trip to town, an architect described a Germantown house as "a suburban residence" – though also suitable as "a country residence" or a "farmhouse," suggesting the conceptual uncertainty that clouded the meaning of such places.[22] Those who commuted to Boston, though numerous, were a minority of Cambridge residents at mid century, and the old town never became a suburb in the usual sense, but a semi-autonomous city.[23] Roxbury was first a village, then a suburb, then a deteriorating section of Boston.

Not just the shifting character of such localities made any unified comprehension of them impossible before the last third of the century; the outskirts of cities also embraced contradictions. There was the village that retained its pre-industrial aspect and routines even as a few commuters settled in. There were the great estates along the Hudson River by the 1840s, the country seats of prominent families on the English model, the homes of gentlemen farmers, the summer retreats of the moderately prosperous, all creating an association between the near countryside and gentility. But in sharp contrast, during their first big enlargement, the new cities of the United States, like many in the Old World, also overflowed into miscellaneous and disreputable precincts around the edges. Slaughterhouses and tanneries deterred residents who had a choice. In the last years of the walking city, laborers who could not afford midtown homes walked farthest, from the outskirts. Prostitution flourished there in some cities. The "living out" system in the South meant that slaves, then free black people, lived in peripheral slums; the black districts of New Orleans were called "suburb sheds." A Philadelphia observer at mid century held that nine-tenths of the city's rascals lived in "the dens and shanties of the suburbs." Preparing to lay out Central Park at the edge of New York in 1857, "Frederick Law Olmsted and Calvert Vaux had to order the eviction of hundreds of rag-pickers, junkmen, and drivers who had established squatter settlements there."[24] Suburbs housed the poor, the rich, rural folk, and not many of the urban middle class.

As that changed, it did so unevenly. Lots of middle class commuters lived in Cambridge by 1860, in part to get away from Boston's new Irish proletariat; but by that time Cambridge too had a population nearly half foreign born, mainly Irish, who worked in local brickyards, tube works, a bleachery, meat packing houses, and so on. In Westchester County at mid century there were "miles upon miles of unmitigated prosperity" near the railroad, with "lawns and parkgates, groves and verandahs, ornamental woods and neat walls, trim edges and well-placed shrubberies, fine houses and large stables"; but behind this strip of wealth was a desolate country-side filled with ramshackle farms and the rural poor. Hamtramck developed as a suburban center of vice on the edge of Detroit. Adjacent to well-to-do, Protestant, dry Oak Park, Cicero, Illinois filled up with Slavs and saloons. Chicago threw off working class suburbs along with its Wilmettes and Winnetkas.[25] The urban gridiron street plan spilled out into nearby suburbs and, along with a lack of trees, made some of them hard to distinguish from the city proper, visually and symbolically.

No single form of the suburb was available for middle class people to adopt as an ideal or migrate to when means permitted. The suburb as a place of residence in a commuting relationship to the city did not trans-late immediately or automatically into a site with evident class meaning on the blurred map of new urban space. That kind of specificity required five or six decades of a complex enough social process, in which the individual choices of middle class people played only one part. Those choices took place on a terrain already defined by capitalism itself, which had largely overridden traditional meanings of spatiality, including that of place, by rendering space a commodity to be bought and sold in the market. This arrangement brought "all space under the single measuring rod of money value," not only effecting its homogene-ity as "freely alienable parcels of private property," but putting it into equivalence at this level of abstraction with *all* marketable goods. Disruption of an older spatiality left PMC people, like everyone else, to seek identity and distinction by using whatever resources they possessed in market transactions. The purchase or rental of suburban space was one available strategy, but it was a choice whose class meaning did not exist in advance, and had to be wrested from the blank abstractness of the land market.[26]

Further encumbering the freedom of middling people to make autonomous choices was the presence in an ostensibly democratic market of actors with far greater resources, far greater power to shape social space. As with all the transformative changes of the nineteenth century, big capital took decisive though erratic steps in suburban development – more formative than in the earlier building of cities – following the urgencies of its own project. Broadly speaking, it sought not only to create the conditions of industrial and urban expansion, but to profit by creating those conditions.[27] I will mention just two of its closely related ventures.

First, land speculators and developers bought, divided, and sold enormous tracts of farmland on outskirts throughout the century, anticipating where the city would expand and land values would increase, and pushing it in those directions. Some speculators took their profits and moved on, leaving development to others. Some developers paid little attention to the kinds of neighborhoods they were opening up, and some built promiscuously, without regard to promoting social distinction. Samuel Eberly Gross developed 16 towns and 150 subdivisions around Chicago from 1880 to 1882; some of the 7000 houses he built and sold cost less than $1000 and none of them cost more than $5000. Depending on location and need, profits could be made by planning dense neighborhoods of single- and two-family houses as much as from subdividing for the wealthy or middle class.

But from early on, *some* speculators and developers sought to increase land values by attracting the affluent. Samuel Ruggles set aside nearly 40 percent of the Manhattan farm he bought in 1831 for an "ornamental" private park, and by 1845 Gramercy Park was a highly fashionable neighborhood. Likewise, in the 1850s Llewellyn S. Haskell reserved fifty acres out of the four hundred that made up Llewellyn Park as a "ramble"; chose architect Alexander Jackson Davis to design a picturesque landscape with winding and undulating roads; built romantic cottages and villas on lots averaging three acres; emphasized privacy and punctuated the idea with a gatehouse. He sold to whoever would pay, and the planned community filled up with businessmen, professionals, and well-to-do bohemians. Backed by a group of eastern investors, Frederick Law Olmsted and Calvert Vaux designed Riverside, near Chicago, on a similar plan, beginning in 1868; its financial success was uneven, its influence great – as was that of other suburbs laid out by Olmsted and Vaux such as Brookline and Chestnut Hill near Boston and Yonkers and Tarrytown Heights in Westchester County. Nearby Bronxville, a project of millionaire William Lawrence, was another prototype. Creating these Edens mainly for the wealthy, developers etched a residential pattern that was widely celebrated in magazines and available for imitation on a more modest scale by the 1890s.

Rich investors colonized the periphery in a second way. They sent railroad and streetcar lines out in spokes from every city, thus encouraging commuter settlements near village train stations and along streetcar routes, which often stretched out into undeveloped land with the speculator and the developer not far behind. These roles were hardly separate. Landowners pressured and bribed transportation companies to build tracks in their direction. Many wealthy men were both speculators in land and investors in rail and streetcar lines. Streetcar magnate Henry M. Whitney bought farms along a country drive in Brookline and built his West End line solely to promote development there. Nevada Senator Francis G. Newlands and other investors formed the Chevy Chase Land Company and in 1888 got a charter for a streetcar line out Connecticut Avenue from Washington into Maryland, after they had systematically bought farmland along the proposed route. They planned a wide, commerce-free avenue and began selling large lots just across the line in Chevy Chase with the understanding that houses on the avenue would cost more than $5000, those on side streets over $3000. The Pennsylvania Railroad planned a new route for its trains out of Philadelphia towards Pittsburgh about 1870, bought the farms that sat on the proposed right of way, then began selling land to developers and developing some areas itself, the result being the affluent new Main Line suburbs. A bit later, Pennsylvania Railroad executive Henry Howard Houston turned 3000 acres of his land in Chestnut Hill, Pennysylvania into a planned suburb, to his great enrichment, partly by influencing the railroad to build a branch line, with stops on his property.[28] Such alliances and collusions created dozens of suburbs, both wealthy and not-so-wealthy, in the last quarter of the century. Though working class suburbs remained, and borderland squalor too, these hustlers and visionaries helped stabilize a class ideal of socially homogeneous, respectable communities with good transport to the city – the suburb as a sign of distinction.

Of course the symbolism of distinction would count for little without the material advantage from which it springs. Those choosing suburban life wanted not just attractive homes and respectable neighbors, but comfort: good streets (eventually, paved streets), schools, and so on. Whatever the admixture of rural nostalgia in this middle class exodus, most joining it were unwilling to give up city services for the actual conditions of farmhouse life. Suburbs had to be modern. Developers understood that need, and jockeyed to have new streets declared public ways. Utility companies understood it, and, like streetcar companies, spread their networks out in advance of city expansion. In this area the new commuters also took bold initiatives of their own. Kenneth Jackson points out that until the 1860s, when perhaps three-fourths of the property owners wanted streets paved in an outlying area they petitioned the city to do the job, and paid extra assessments to cover the cost. But in the ensuing decades it became more common for cities, under pressure from middle class commuters, to pave streets at public expense. "The centralization of street administration meant that all city dwellers subsidized those who moved to the edges."[29] The latter had influence and political skills to seek and obtain the advantage of urban services, and to help create metropolitan water, sewer, health, and police authorities. These strategies gained city comforts for suburbanites fleeing from city perils and costs.

The desires of middle and upper class people for distinction and comfort came together in two kinds of legal moves – often battles – that occurred repeatedly throughout the second half of the century and after: incorporation and annexation. In most of the US outside New England, which had always been divided into towns, states made it easy for people in a locality to incorporate as a town once there were a few hundred who wanted to. Tens of thousands did so, often in hopes that their crossroads would become a metropolis of the booming West. Near the towns that did burgeon into cities, incorporation became the instrument of advancing other hopes. Native Protestants incorporated their suburban tracts to be separate from Catholic immigrants in the cities or in working class suburbs nearby. People cherishing respectability incorporated to keep out saloons and gambling. They incorporated to improve services when cities were unable or unwilling to provide them. They incorporated to take advantage of high tax revenues from industries, or to keep industries out. Above all – and this motive ties in with the others – middle class and affluent people on the outskirts incorporated to create autonomous, socially homogeneous towns and exclude those with meaner homes paying lower taxes. Incorporation was a guarantor of local class autonomy.

Annexation of peripheral towns and rural land by cities was a contrary project, though in the earlier years of suburbanization there was a good deal of uncertainty about the interests of both cities and suburbs in the matter. Some suburbs, lacking good water or unable to finance other services, petitioned for annexation. City people and governments, seeing the costs, sometimes refused. For the most part, as wealth moved outwards after 1850, cities favored annexation, and the disputes took place within suburbs themselves. Annexation would improve services, strengthen the metropolitan economy, give suburban interests a decisive role in city governance, promote reform. Or, annexation would raise suburban taxes, reduce autonomy and community, permit a flow of immigrant workers into or near exclusive neighborhoods, and enmesh commuters in the pathology and corruption of the metropolis. Those who held the second of these positions gradually won their case. Beginning with Boston after the 1870s, city after city found itself landlocked by its resistant suburbs and left to steer its own course. The shift in interests was especially clear when commuters used incorporation as a tactic to protect themselves against annexation: after New York City swallowed up part of what is now the Bronx in 1874 a number of Westchester villages incorporated, and the same thing happened again in the 1890s.[30] An important social boundary was drawn. Following the path of the affluent, middle class people were devising ways to use the city's resources while preserving domestic independence. Suburbanization gave a particular class inflection to the famed separation of work from leisure: distances between the two activities gradually took on a class coding that was further clarified as incorporation and the refusal of annexation gave legal boundaries to the space of residence, domesticity, and leisure.

In this uneven process of augmenting and recoding urban space, distancing and the achievement of legal autonomy were strategies in service to a drive for distinction as well as comfort. By the end of the century, broad peripheral zones of social homogeneity and exclusiveness had given physical embodiment to the ideal, realizing more fully the block-by-block stratification of housing begun in urban neighborhoods well before the Civil War. In the 1880s a guidebook to the Boston area recorded that "Professional men abound" in Jamaica Plain; "this seems to be a favorite suburb for their residence." A Unitarian minister who had lived there for ten years called it "the best that suburban Boston could give," though he worried in a common late-century way that "the well-to-do folk were beginning to follow a rather perilous modern fashion of clustering away from their unprosperous fellows." The widespread concern did not prevent the clustering. In Overbrook Farms near Philadelphia, rapidly built up during the 1890s, by 1900 51 percent of the householders were executives and financiers, 24 percent professionals, 10 percent managers, 7 percent builders, 8 percent retired people and others without occupations, and none were working class people. Residents were overwhelmingly white, native-born, and Protestant, except for live-in servants.[31] The latter, along with others who supplied goods and services to the affluent, did live separately in modest enclaves within some wealthy suburbs like Chestnut Hill near Boston, where a quarter of the residents were laborers, gardeners, and domestics in 1890. This figure was 50 percent or more in some railroad suburbs, but such pockets of poverty, far from tainting the exclusivity of these places, signified the ability of suburbanites to maintain a wholly dependent workforce conveniently close at hand.[32] More obvious signs of prestige were aristocratic gatehouses or ornate railroad stations and "village" squares that marked the passage from areas of less prestige to some of the planned suburbs; the parkland settings and curved streets of many others; the large lots, lush plantings, and stylish houses of almost all. The well-to-do suburb visually proclaimed the distinction of its "real" residents even if it housed subordinate others in their midst.

To use this language of signification and presentation might seem to miss a simpler and deeper point: that suburban homes *embodied* the wealth of their owners. Indeed, ownership seems to have been a main cultural ideal through much of the nineteenth century, to judge from a profuse literature on homes that identifies building and owning one's house with achievement, independence, security, status, and moral soundness. But it is important to keep in mind, since my subject is the formation of a new class and its way of living, that home ownership was an *old* social ideal, and a social fact for most white Americans. In the early days of the Republic most people were farmers and most farmers owned their land and the buildings thereon. (In discussing this question, I ignore the difference between owning outright and borrowing to own; the pertinent distinction here is between owning and renting.) The rhetorical valorization of ownership may best be understood as a holding operation with a nostalgic political force, in a period when industrialization displaced and disrupted old relations of home, land, and work. The many advocates of ownership from mid century on linked it to a healthy polity with prosperity for all, a society in which class distinction had little force. Thus, articulations of the ideal commonly stressed its universality. Andrew Jackson Downing, one of its most influential early spokesmen, hoped to spread high standards of domestic taste "in a country where the ease of obtaining a house and land, and the ability of almost every industrious citizen to build his own house, constitute a distinctive feature of national prosperity." These thoughts of 1850 echoed on through later decades, as in architect Bruce Price's 1890 identification of "that American trait which inspires every man, no matter how subordinate his position in the business world, to assert his individuality and independence by owning a home which is the outgrowth of his special tastes and needs."[33]

Usually, phrases like "every man" and "every industrious citizen" in such ideological discourse can be read as referring to the middle and upper classes; yet the ideal was in fact widely diffused, if sometimes shorn of its old republican connotations, and attached to different systems of value. Stephen Thernstrom's well known study of Newburyport, Massachusetts revealed that a majority of the working men who remained there for two or three decades did come to own real property by 1880.[34] Ten years later, in Boston, 40 percent of the mainly working class families in the old, inner suburbs owned their homes.[35] Contemporary studies of working class life suggest that ownership was a common goal, and the success of builders of cheap houses like S.E. Gross in Chicago shows that many achieved it. Immigrants more than native-born workers were inclined to make significant sacrifices in order to own homes.[36] In the great internationalization of labor through the nineteenth century, home was a destination; the solidity of ownership compensated for cultural uprooting and offset the alienation of labor.

Furthermore, middle class people in and around cities seem not to have made ownership a main goal. In the wealthy Philadelphia suburb of Overbrook Farms, mentioned earlier, only about three-fifths of householders were homeowners, and in other Philadelphia suburbs the ratio varied from about 40 to about 55 percent. In Detroit, at the turn of the century, the rate of ownership was higher among immigrant workers than among native, middle class whites, and in one new, affluent suburb 60 percent of the families rented. In the nation as a whole, just over one-third of non-farm families owned homes in 1900; the ownership rate in suburban Boston was less than that.[37] Evidently, having the title to one's house did not clearly differentiate middle class suburbanites and the increasingly immigrant working class from whom they were trying to distance themselves; or if it did, it signalled a *lower* standing. To the extent that distinction is visible in self presentation, obviously ownership is irrelevant. One doesn't post the deed on one's front door.

Home ownership could not be the mark of middle class respectability for a family. Residence in a single, detached dwelling had old social meaning, but was not a badge of class. Detached homes stood in opposition to seedy tenements, but also to the elegant row houses of the old city. The ideal of a family domicile separate from other homes was all but universal, except in a few Eastern cities, and widely realized. In smaller cities like Muncie (the Lynds' "Middletown"), detached homes were from the beginning the preferred form of housing for all classes; a large majority of working class people managed to rent or buy them.[38] And of course millions of far from affluent farmers did, too. If a single home were to proclaim class distinction, it had to do so by its location and by its particular features. In the prized locations – suburb and fine city neighborhood – not only were houses larger than in working class districts, they configured their separateness in a particular style, neither urban or rural.

How it was set off against the urban, both in concept and by half a century of uneven yet directed practice, I have already indicated. It is important to see also how the suburban idea opposed itself to the rural, or else it can seem a purely nostalgic idea, a blinkered refusal of the industrial and commercial project of development that after all had created social space for the PMC. John Stilgoe is doubtless right in saying that "In 1840 the national imagination accepted the farm as the perfect objectification of the perfect life and declared the most beautiful country to be that composed of beautiful farms and a few crossroads churches and schoolhouses, all in equilibrium with one another, with time, and with nature," and perhaps right that such images were "the standard that impelled the first would-be suburbanites to live away from cities on two- or three-acre 'cottage farms.'"[39] This standard may even have persisted deep in the imagination of 1890s commuters, but only with such graftings of other standards and social purposes as to make it almost unrecognizable.

Take the use and presentation of land around the suburban house – what became the "yard." Its very size marked it off from cramped and cluttered spaces behind, and sometimes beside, urban houses. Lots in cities were often 25 feet wide; the suburban lot spread to at least 50 feet with a depth of 100 or more; 75 by 200 was a common size. Unlike city houses or old farm houses, suburban ones were built a distance from the road, sometimes by regulations such as that in Olmsted's Riverside that required a 30 foot setback. What to do with this space? By 1870 a rich literature had begun to address the question, in books and magazines. One strategy reproduced the farm standard in miniature: the suburban grounds would contain fruit trees, berry bushes, a vegetable garden, beehives, a chicken house. A strand of home improvement writing well into our own century stressed the economic advantages of home agriculture: the commuter's wife and children could help offset the cost of suburban life by reducing food bills; a number of magazine articles even instructed suburbanites how to make supplementary incomes by marketing eggs or honey.[40]

But alongside this ideal from the outset, and prevailing over it in the long run, was another that distinguished sharply between yard and farm. The first book – and an influential one – entirely about suburban grounds, Frank J. Scott's *The Art of Beautifying the Home Grounds* (1870), disparaged home gardening as retrograde, in conflict with urbane enjoyments. He, like many later authorities, saw the yard not as a place of fecundity and enterprise, but as a decoration. Arranging it was "the art of picture making and picture framing, by means of the varied forms of vegetable growth."[41] There might be fruit trees, but food was not the point, and any agriculture was gradually relegated to the back yard, where privacy allowed expression to many individual tastes.

The evolution of the *front* yard best reveals the core ideology of suburban grounds. After some controversy as early as Scott's time about whether the front yard should be a hedged-in family enclave or part of an harmonious cityscape, the latter idea won out. The yard was to offer an open sightline to the house; only unobtrusive boundary plantings should mark it off from the neighbor's yard. People came almost universally to achieve this effect by having lawns, with a few trees and plantings located for visual effect. The neatly trimmed lawn is crucial. In this form, grass is patently divorced from agricultural purpose, and from any use at all other than recreational (for example, croquet). It is, precisely, part of a framed picture, a view, both from the street and from the house. Its closest affinity is not to the messy, utilitarian farmyard but to the grounds of the English country house, accommodated over two centuries to an ideal of landscape that expressed wealth, ownership, leisure, and elevated sensibility. The "elevation" derived from the owner's ability to separate consumption from production, and conceal the latter. As Raymond Williams puts it, the eighteenth-century seat was surrounded with

> a rural landscape emptied of rural labour and of labourers; a sylvan and
> watery prospect, with a hundred analogies in neo-pastoral painting and

poetry, from which the facts of production had been banished: . . . the expression of control and command.[42]

The American yard of the 1880s or 1890s could hardly realize such aristocratic detachment and mastery. The suburban front lawn was no English greensward, nor could it suggest the army of gardeners that groomed the great American estates. Indeed, part of the idea was that the commuter would benefit from the healthy exercise of mowing his own lawn (reel mowers became widely available in the late 1860s). But the closely cropped, neatly bordered, and quite useless grass enacted in miniature the same kind of conspicuous consumption, as well as conformity to a PMC esthetic of the parklike community.[43] The yard revealed the attentiveness (or slovenliness) of its *own* production, but denied any suggestion of production for markets or for domestic subsistence. And of course rows of tidy front lawns said nothing about their owners' relations to the system of industrial production that made these suburbs possible and necessary. They were zones of leisure and consumption, mediating between public street and private house, and announcing that the latter, too, was a place of respectable leisure and consumption.[44]

I have emphasized a structure of class feeling that both drove and flowed from suburbanization; I have made central the erasure of production and the achievement of social identity around consumption, location, homogeneity of family presentation, autonomy. Many other aspirations and longings fused, or jostled uneasily against one another, in the suburb. There was of course the idea of a retreat from the city, seen as tainted by commerce, overcrowded with undesirable neighbors, dirty, unsanitary, vicious; and simultaneously as fashionable, progressive, full of necessary goods and services, home of cultural institutions, site of improving work, source of income – so that one would not want to retreat *too* far from it. There were various ideals of the country: the farm of personal or collective memory, the country seat, the vacation spot, the park, the cottage hideaway – all at play in the suburban imagination in spite of the historical disparity or discord among them. There was a class-specific ideal of domesticity that held together (uneasily) both privacy and community, the family refuge and the proud public evidence it gave of taste, achievement, and status. There was the increasingly strong, partly tacit understanding of how PMC people should be like one another, and the contrary impulse toward individuality, defined against the perception of lesser folk as homogeneous masses. What held this bundle of contradictions together, I think, was class confidence and the separation of consumption from production, both geographically and symbolically.

To press this point I have of course made simplifications. Middle class people did not just pursue an emergent class ideal; they took practical steps to improve their lives. They negotiated the maze of urban real estate values to their best advantage. They sought more room and better services. They moved where friends were moving. Furthermore, many did not go at all, preferring houses in genteel city neighborhoods when affordable, or even, in some cities, apartment living. Many PMC people lived in small towns, where the issues discussed in this section arose much less insistently. Finally, suburban life had different meanings for husbands and wives, meanings often in conflict, according to Margaret Marsh:

> The ideology of domesticity in its earliest incarnation was primarily woman-defined, and it had at its center a cultural institution, the family. The suburban ideal of the same era was largely male-defined, and had at its center a physical space, the residential suburb. Middle-class women embraced urban life in the second third of the nineteenth century . . . . [E]arly suburban life was created by . . . a particular kind of man – one with a vision of American life touched by nostalgia and connected to the rural origins of the United States.[45]

These visions were partially but precariously reconciled by the end of the century, in her view. Certainly the man who commuted daily to the city center to do law or business and the woman who sometimes shopped there stood in permanently different relations to suburban domesticity.

For all that, I suggest that the evolution of the suburb and its mores had a central importance in the formation and the self-concept of the PMC. This new social location augmented personal appearance as a way of coding identity in the murky space of the industrial city, a "world of strangers."[46]

House and Home

Seeing the country as an actual or utopian alternative to the cities capitalism made is a historical illusion: capitalism is "the basic process" in the history of both, as we know and remember them. So argues Raymond Williams in *The Country and the City*. In part, the suburb expressed the same utopian hope of a space outside our mode of production as had inspired early critics of the industrial city. Yet obviously the suburb, too, owes its existence to capitalism's wholesale reorganization of space, its reshaping of nature, its reconfiguring of human relations. I have made that argument with emphasis on the formation of a new class, and on the efforts of people in that class to negotiate the opportunities and dangers put in their path by industrial capitalism,[47] to use as advantageously as possible their small share of the social surplus. I would have given more emphasis to the efforts of certain capitalists themselves to seize opportunities for accumulation – land speculators, developers, railroad corporations, streetcar entrepreneurs, and so on – had my purpose been to tell this part of the story from the perspective of production rather than consumption, of capital rather than of PMC magazine readers. The two stories always go forward together, separable only for analysis.

As I turn now from suburbs as social space to the houses in which people lived, I will hold to the same emphasis. But I begin with a reminder of capital's agency, which grew enormously during the nineteenth century in the area of house-making. One has only to look from this angle at the most familiar historical processes, to appreciate the change. In the early Republic almost everyone lived on farms and in relatively isolated villages. They built their own houses with the help of neighbors and sometimes of paid local artisans. They built with locally available materials and in regional vernacular styles. They had, and needed, little capital beyond their own resources and what they could borrow locally. In the last quarter of the nineteenth century most home building took place in cities and suburbs, and was done by people other than those who would occupy the houses. Realtors and builders often paid for construction, then lent money to buyers; the building and loan associations that multiplied rapidly after the Civil War were another source of capital. But mainly, urban people rented: 77 percent in cities over 100,000, in 1890. Annual returns on investment in rental property ran about 10–12 percent, and capital poured into this attractive venture.[48]

Housing became an industry in this sense, and also in other familiar ways. Planning and execution moved apart, the former into the offices of builders, developers, architects, manufacturers, and so on; the latter into the hands of construction workers. More and more parts of the house were made in factories: first, in the eighteenth century, the lumber itself, cut and planed in sawmills rather than hand hewn. The major changes came after 1850, with mass produced moldings, window sashes and glass, doors, shingles, roofing, architectural detailing from plain to gingerbread and beyond, columns and capitals, bricks of various strengths and colors, tiles, interior panelling and wainscotting, balustrades and railings, wire-lath, chemical plasters, and so on and on, not to mention heating and plumbing. From the prefabrication of stock doors and window sashes to mass production of whole houses to be shipped by rail and assembled on site was not a long step, though only a few entrepreneurs took it in the 1890s.[49] Well before then, new houses were assemblages of machine-made commodities, with little craft involved.

For all the sentiment that gathered through the century around family, domesticity, and the Christian home, as an enclave of private virtue, housing itself had become big business. It had to. The forces that made the city required building on a previously unimaginable scale. The urban population quadrupled from 1860 to 1890, while family units contracted. Whole metropolises rose up in a few decades: Chicago, from 30,000 in 1830 to 300,000 in 1870 to 1 million in 1890, was only the most spectacular example. One million people needed 200,000 houses and apartments. Construction on this scale, around the country, required a colossal movement of capital, not just for the buildings themselves but for roads, water systems, sewers and other necessary services. Taken together, the costs of housing were the largest category of national expenditure through the century.[50] Add on investment in city and suburban land, and the agency of capital is plain enough. In combination with other agencies it built more houses in the three postwar decades than had been built in the prior 250 years of European settlement, radically transforming American domestic space before the eyes of a generation.

But it did not determine the outcome of that transformation with the precision and power it used to reshape the labor process or construct the railroad system. Industrializing the production of housing components did not settle the actual forms of the houses that would be built. It opened up some possibilities and closed off others (for all but the wealthy who could import Italian marble if they wished); but for the builders of middle and working class houses it created many more choices than had been available. So did the practice of balloon framing as it quickly displaced mortise and tenon construction from the 1830s on and eliminated the craft of joinery. Balloon framing not only made houses stronger, cheaper, and easier to build; it gave almost free rein to the imagination of the designer, as one can see in a glance at any high Victorian home. In effect, what industrialization offered to builders and owners was a vastly enlarged realm of individual and social choice in making and elaborating shelter. What middle class people did with the expanded range of practical and semiotic possibilities thus opened up to them is the subject of the next few pages.

It is a subject that has drawn attention from many scholars, especially in the last two decades – the moment of the "new social history." I will make no effort to repeat or even summarize the story they have told with satisfying richness of detail and with an unusual degree of consensus. Instead, with indebtedness to their work, I offer a meditation on three topoi and three stages in the evolution of home design that seem to me crucial in understanding the outlook, aspirations, and needs of the people who welcomed mass circulation magazines into their houses at the end of the century.

1. Exterior form: from morality to style

As people were freed from dependence on vernacular traditions and artisanal skills in close relation to local materials, an energetic discourse of architectural choice rose up. What should a house be like? What values should it express? Around mid century a number of writers such as Andrew Jackson Downing, Calvert Vaux, Lewis F. Allen, and O.W. Fowler theorized domestic architecture and influentially published hundreds of model home designs. These pattern books proliferated as a genre, along-side similar articles in magazines: *Godey's Lady's Book* alone printed 450 house plans; the *Ladies' Home Journal* took up the task of improving taste in home design during the 1890s and after, as *Godey's* declined and disappeared. Pattern books shaded over into mail order catalogs for house plans, with entrepreneurs like Henry Hudson Holly and George Palliser, who sold blueprints inexpensively and corresponded with customers about specifications and about peculiarities of homesites. Holly, Palliser, and others mass-marketed the architect's services, making custom design available to people of modest means. All the theorists, publicists, and marketers taken together circulated thousands of images of houses and made the vocabulary of home design familiar to millions of people thinking about how to organize their material lives and build their cultural capital. An area of choice previously open only to the wealthy was by the 1880s common for everyone with savings or good credit.[51]

The proliferation of treatises, the intensifying debates, the cornucopia of images, gave expression to a variety of often conflicting ideals, with perhaps no universal theme other than what a weighty matter home design was, how consequential for family and society. It is possible, however, to identify in this noisy conversation and in the actual building of houses a progression through three stages, from the 1840s through the end of the century. They overlap and clash, but I propose this simplification.

In the early period designers and polemicists framed the discussion in moral terms, with strong emphasis on the symbolism of design. Some saw the house as a character builder, a producer of American leaders; volumes such as *Homes of American Authors* and *Homes of American Statesmen* praised the humble farmhouse (Handlin, p. 21). A related school of thought argued for simplicity in the pursuit of republican virtue and rough equality among Americans. The Greek revival was promoted partly in terms of democratic affinities between ancient Greece and nineteenth-century American society, and also as a declaration of architectural independence from English styles, especially Georgian. Christian renewal movements stimulated a lively discourse of home religion and of the home as both a Christian influence and a symbol: the vertical reach of Gothic revival houses was promoted in these terms, as was the cross-shaped house. Many writers and builders made paramount the home's harmony with its natural setting, in ornate line and variety of materials; the picturesque style was one expression of this ideal. Homes were imaged and built to make statements about nation, family, democracy, faith, nature, character.[52]

These urgencies gradually yielded to a new dominant ideal after the Civil War: individuality. Architects, social critics, and theorists of domesticity increasingly conceived of the house as a projection of its owner's taste, and urged creativity in the elaboration of forms. Art of this kind took its models from a dozen international and historical styles, mixing and modifying them with abandon. Porches, verandahs, towers, turrets, porte-cocheres, ornamental chimneys, railings, irregular roof lines, could turn basic structures into imaginative creations. Balloon frame construction made such complexities easy to realize, and steam powered milling produced an endless variety of ornamental details. The eclecticism and visual extravagance of the high Victorian house is familiar to all; its main justification was an ideology of personal expression.

By 1890, a critique of Victorian elaboration had begun to gain force, and the outlines of a third home ideal to emerge. Its framers included architects who stigmatized the Victorian house as artistically unprincipled; domestic reformers who advocated a healthy and efficient home; and tastemakers of the Arts and Crafts (or Craftsman) school, who promoted simplicity of forms and honesty of materials. Many of these people were professionals – PMC people – as were those moving to suburbs and buying or renting new homes. Increasingly they inhabited and articulated a structure of feeling that was reformist, progressive, modern. They valued practicality and problem solving; they were impatient of formality and excess. Although high modernist ideas such as "less is more" and the house as a "machine for living" were still decades away, similar sentiments collected into an articulate credo. Theorists promoted clean lines, austere detail, plain materials. No single building style realized these ideals, but all those that came into favor in the fifteen or so years after 1890 represented a retreat from or revulsion against the eclectic and picturesque. Georgian and colonial revivals found models for simplicity in earlier traditions; the foursquare and homestead temple styles gained popularity; Craftsman homes and bungalows appeared; the prairie style was on the architectural horizon. This tempering of elaborate individuality in home design did not, of course, signal the end of proud display. Rather, it made display a more collective act than before. The suburban street with each house different yet all in tacit agreement about comfort, modesty, and practicality effected a harmonious architectural presentation of PMC ease, confidence, and prosperity, while PMC reformers broadcast an ideology of the rational home.[53]

2. Elaboration and simplification of interior space

The inside of the middle class home evolved in three parallel stages of conception, feeling, and design. Early in the century, post and beam construction made for plain room shapes, repeated downstairs and up. There might be a small sewing room or birthing room to vary the pattern; only the kitchen – often more or less tacked on at the back of the house – differed from the others in form because of its function and technical requirements. Aside from the "best room," with its fancy mantel and extra moldings, most interior spaces were easily adaptable to new purposes as families grew or shrank and circumstances changed.

The second-stage ideal of individuality that multiplied exterior styles called for specialization of inside spaces, too, and balloon frame construction permitted almost any arrangement. This was partly a matter of using design to segregate the three main categories of domestic event (socializing, private family activities, and work), and of further adapting space to particular functions such as receiving guests, entertaining them, breakfasting, dining, reading, playing, cooking, caring for infants, sleeping, and bathing, as well as accommodating servants, in the grander houses. The respectable home expressed and facilitated the varied fullness of high Victorian domesticity. As Gwendolyn Wright puts it,

> The irregular outline of Victorian houses revealed the occupants' search for individuality and their interest in functional design. Each bay window, porch, and other protrusion was considered evidence of some particular activity taking place within; it made the space exactly right for playing the piano, sewing, reading, or tending a hot stove.[54]

A closely related goal was for *each* family member to have private spaces for self-expression, development, and rest. Articulation and specialization of household space would foster the valued interior depth of each person, while proclaiming the status and social development of the whole family.

When the theory and construction of exterior shapes turned away from the extravagantly personal, toward the end of the century, new middle class people also reconceived living space within the home. The third-stage tendency here was toward openness, flexibility, and simplicity. It had begun earlier, when people deviated from the older plan of insular rooms with small doors leading to hallways. They separated downstairs rooms from each other with portières, folding doors, or doors that slid back inside walls leaving an arch that united two rooms more than it divided them. In the 1890s, builders went farther, opening up much of the ground floor. The entry hall disappeared or shrank into a small vestibule with a closet. Parlor and sitting room fused into one large living area, perhaps divided only by a broad arch from the dining area. Margaret Marsh's survey of pattern books found that around 1870 over 80 percent of the designs for middle class homes included two or more living areas; just after 1900, 63 percent called for just one. Upstairs, bedrooms of course remained separate, but there were fewer of them: 84 percent of the later designs called for four or fewer, compared to 39 percent in the 1870s.[55] Architects like Frank Lloyd Wright talked of spaciousness and freedom; domestic reformers talked of efficiency and health; theorists of the family home talked of common space and shared activities – the ethos that the 1950s would call "togetherness." The severe line between private and public space within the home eroded, and the middle class family became less insular, more contiguous with its suburban neighbors, more visibly like them.

Only one specialization continued apace: that of the bathroom, with its new industrial technology and sanitary surfaces. The necessary infra-structure developed only after the Civil War: at that time just over 100 municipalities had water systems, and many of those served only a few people, but by 1900 3000 towns and cities provided water, and about half the population had access to it. Sewers came more slowly: one-third of Boston's city budget went for sanitary projects during the same period. Advances in plumbing equipment and bathroom fixtures allayed fears of malfunctioning and of deadly sewer gas. Average expenditures for plumbing a middle class house tripled between 1860 and 1890. Owners and renters of such homes began to take this convenience for granted, and indeed it marked a clear divide between them and the working class, as well as between urban sophistication and small town or rural backwardness. In 1893, from 53 to 88 percent of families in New York, Philadelphia, Chicago, and Baltimore used outside privies. In 1890, there were only twenty-four complete bathrooms in Muncie, a town of 6000, and one family in six or eight had running water of any sort in the house. Such amenities were all but unknown on farms.[56]

Electrification of homes and the installation of central heating pro-ceeded along the same lines of class differentiation. The PMC's pursuit of modernity called for more dependence on technical systems in base-ments and within walls, even as it argued for simplification and openness of room space. The two aspirations worked harmoniously together: indoor plumbing permitted the concentration of bathing, washing up, and eliminating human waste in one efficient room; while open down-stairs floor plans became practical only with central heating. The simpler home was also more practical, efficient, and comfortable. It allowed the PMC family to relish these advances, and put them on display for visitors.

3. Reflections on the parlor

When the second-stage, middle class hall and parlor dissolved into a more open, ground-floor space, the change signaled a major shift in cul-ture and feeling. If the interior of the nineteenth-century home was, in Henry Ward Beecher's words, "the measure of [a man's] social and domestic nature," the parlor was the place where that measure could be offered and taken. Decorator Ella Rodman Church, writing in *Godey's Lady's Book*, called it "the *face* of a house – the most noticeable part – and that from which visitors take their impressions of the whole."[57] The entry hall mediated for visitors between outside and inside, public and private; it was "neither wholly interior nor exterior, but a sheltered testing zone which some passed through with ease and others never went beyond,"[58] having left their calling cards for scrutiny and a later decision. Those who survived the social test were admitted to the parlor, where they saw manifest the character of the family and its understanding of culture.

There are two ways to understand the Victorian parlor (or "best room" in humble parlance, or "sitting room," or occasionally "drawing room," a term of English connotation). First, its furnishings revealed the family's taste in design and art, by alluding to prestigious styles. In the parlor, too, artifacts that told something of the specific family's history and place in society were displayed: portraits, photographs, cameos, locks of hair, mementos, samplers, small meaningful items of all sorts arrayed on walls, mantels, cases, *étagères*, and whatnot shelves. These gave the parlor the character of a record and a shrine. Second, the parlor was a "theater of culture."[59] Through the objects they arranged there, people showed not only the level of their own cultivation but their knowing participation in an evolving national culture of respectability, piety, and refinement. In that august room they enacted with friends the ritual of the formal call, which played its part in establishing and reproducing the networks of proper society. There, too, with friends and relatives and clergy, they enacted the rituals of marriage and funeral service; there, some of them carried out the evening rituals of Christian domesticity – prayers, reading, music, serious and intimate family talk. (Others did those things in a back parlor or sitting room, keeping the front parlor shut up in its own solemnity except for visits.)

In these ceremonies they performed culture; through the room's furnishings they spoke its conventional language. Ideally (and very commonly in fact) the parlor contained a sofa and formally arranged chairs, often a matched parlor suite; a piano that indicated the women's accomplishments; a fireplace with mantel and mirror; a wall-to-wall carpet and the best drapery; shelves and cabinets for memorabilia; pictures on the walls; decorative lamps and a chandelier; and, under the latter, the ubiquitous center table. It was a kind of altar, formally draped and bearing a figurine or other signifier of art; a Bible representing membership of the Christian community; and an album of photos and other relics unique to the particular family. This parlor vocabulary conveyed the domestication of religion and the religion of domesticity.[60] At the same time it expressed an understanding about the past and the future of American culture. In displaying the signs of their own refinement and propriety, middle class families also enlisted in the broad civilizing project of the nineteenth century. Showing off their own treasures, they showed how far they and their like had progressed from the rudeness of colonial and early republican home life, with its visual reminders of rural necessity and home production, toward cosmopolitan leisure and controlled beauty. Quoting historical styles – "empire," "Queen Anne," and so on – however inaccurately, such families aligned themselves with international high culture. And as they diligently pursued this ideal through the decades after the Civil War, they gradually changed the "face" of the house from its aspect of standardized gentility to one of gorgeously eclectic abundance.

This movement, and the complex aspirations that joined in articulating the Victorian parlor, came under increasingly severe criticism toward the end of the century. The use of a best room and of the family's resources just for special occasions struck many as wasteful. The formality of the room began to seem inflexible and forbidding as the strict rituals enacted there fell out of fashion. Designers attacked the riot of styles that clashed together in the more and more elaborate parlor; moralists attacked the ostentation; the new advocates of home efficiency attacked the overstuffed clutter as unhealthy and hard to keep clean. A class coming to see itself as modern, practical, rational in arrangements, and direct in manners, rejected the old parlor as artificial, unauthentic, a facade.

They could appreciate it with tolerant condescension toward those still living on the periphery of modern life and preserving through necessity or ignorance or loyalty to the past the ways of their hardy ancestors. Sarah Orne Jewett gives classic expression to this feeling. In *The Country of the Pointed Firs* the rusticating narrator and her summer landlady, Mrs Todd, make a day trip to a remote island off the Maine coast, to call on Mrs Todd's aged mother. There they are shown into Mrs Blackett's

> little old-fashioned best room, with its few pieces of good furniture and pictures of national interest. The green paper curtains were stamped with conventional landscapes of a foreign order, – castles on inaccessible crags, and lovely lakes with steep wooded shores; under-foot the treasured carpet was covered thick with home-made rugs. There were empty glass lamps and crystallized bouquets of grass and some fine shells on the narrow mantelpiece.

The room is "suggestive of serious occasions"; Mrs Todd was married in it.

> It was indeed a tribute to Society to find a room set apart for her behests out there on so apparently neighborless and remote an island . . . . Mrs. Blackett was of those who do not live to themselves, and who have long since passed the line that divides mere self-concern from a valued share in whatever Society can give and take . . . . Mrs. Blackett was one who knew the uses of a parlor.[61]

The narrator is sophisticated, urban, a writer. She appreciates the parlor from a great cultural distance, as standing for an irretrievably past "Society."

Fiction of the period written by PMC writers for similar readers often measures cultural distance in this way. In Howells's *The Landlord at Lion's Head*, Westover (the focalizing character) is a painter, boarding with an ill-fated family on a poor New England farm while he paints the famous mountain profile named in the novel's title. Mrs Durgin shows him the parlor, holding up the lamp so that Westover can note "the appointments of the room." What we see through *his* eyes are "the drab wallpaper, the stiff chairs, the long, hard sofa in haircloth, the high bureau of mahogany veneer." Later, she hangs a photograph of his painting "over the mantel-piece, in what he felt to be the place of the greatest honor in the whole house": he understands the parlor's historical meaning, the more so because Mrs Durgin has kept it "much in its former state" even after succeeding commercially with a hotel on the old farmstead.

In Mary E. Wilkins's (Freeman's) "A New England Nun," the perfect order of Louisa's "delicately sweet" sitting room signifies her irrevocable spinsterhood; we know she can not marry her worthy but rough fiancé when he makes her uneasy by rearranging the autograph album and the "Lady's Gift-Book which had belonged to Louisa's mother," on the center table. The room is a shrine to past domesticity, not a place of transition to the future. In Wilkins's "The Revolt of 'Mother,'" Sarah Penn's main charge against her oppressive, taciturn husband is that he will build a new barn rather than the long-promised house with a parlor. Their daughter will have to be married in the drab kitchen:

> What would you have thought, father, if we had had our weddin' in a room no better than this? I was married in my mother's parlor, with a carpet on the floor, an' stuffed furniture, an' a mahogany card-table.

Sarah's "revolt" is to move the household goods into the just-completed barn while her husband is away: "The great middle space would make a parlor, by-and-by, fit for a palace." Our sympathies are all with her, but like the educated narrator, we smilingly condescend to these marginal people and the antique semiosis of their gender war.[62]

PMC readers could cherish their honorable lineage as figured in the old best room, but could not see their new progressive identities in the late Victorian parlor – stuffy, ornate, strewn with knick-knacks, pretentious, artificial. Many commentators gave voice to these objections. Another objection was never put, in the way I believe it to have been felt: working class people, many of them, now had parlors and were decking them out in cheaper imitation of the high Victorian, middle class parlor. Some immigrant traditions favored the kitchen as a gathering place for family and visitors, but other immigrant groups and native workers aspired to the dignity of the parlor, and invested resources in it as soon as they could manage.

Mary Antin speaks nicely of her family having "achieved a carpet" in their parlor, though living poorly in Boston's lower South End. Neighbors on Wheeler Street had "miserable" three- or four-room flats, and the parlors were mean: "The centre table in the 'parlor' was not loaded with books. It held, invariably, a photograph album and an ornamental lamp with a paper shade; and the lamp was usually out of order." But parlors there were, even if they had to double as bedrooms. On the lower West Side of New York, just after 1900, a survey found that in the "typical home" of a wage earner,

> The "parlor" is usually gaudy with plush furniture . . . , carpet on the floor, cheap lace-curtains at the windows, crayon portraits of the family on the walls, and usually religious pictures of saints, the Virgin Mary, or "The Sacred Heart," sometimes a couch, and the ubiquitous folding bed.

But in the better working class apartments of this district, the parlor contained

> a leather couch, a bookcase and desk with a few good books, frequently a piano, a pier-glass (bought second hand), a carpet or Wilton rug (usually with brilliant coloring and glaring patterns), the usual family portraits and bric-a-brac, red-plush albums, "tidies" on the chairs . . . .

And in the workers' free-standing houses of Homestead, the steel town near Pittsburgh, "even the six [English-speaking] families each of whom lived in three rooms attempted to have at least the semblance of a room devoted to sociability" – a parlor:

> The furniture, though sometimes of the green plush variety, often displays simplicity and taste. A center table, a few chairs, a couch, and frequently either an organ or piano complete the furnishings. Usually there are pictures – the family portraits or some colored lithographs – and almost always that constant friend of the family, the brilliantly colored insurance calendar.[63]

There is irony enough in these cultural shifts. Social workers, domestic theorists, and urban improvers – that wing of the PMC newly and actively concerned with the conditions of working class life – welcomed the humble tenement parlor as a space dedicated to civility and middle class family values, an investment in the social system, a bulwark against the dark forces of revolution or anarchy. But they imagined a scheme of furnishing and decor organized around PMC ideals of hygiene and efficient care. They urged painted walls, stained floors without carpeting, unupholstered furniture, plain shelves instead of sideboards, modest arrays of pictures and mementos, a general neatness and simplicity. Workers' ideas often ran counter to each point in this catechism. *They* wanted the abundance and refinement they rightly understood as evidence of middle class respectability, though this understanding was half a generation out of step by the 1890s. Makers of furniture, carpeting, upholstery, and bric-a-brac both met and stirred desire by offering more and more inexpensive, mass-produced imitations of styles the PMC now found vulgar. A settlement worker explained to a young woman about to be married how unhygienic plush was, and the woman seemed convinced; but a later visit to the new home discovered a parlor "overfilled by the inevitable 'parlor set,' while plush curtains hung at the windows and on either side of the door." Anticipating disapproval, the bride welcomed her visitor with, "you must remember you have had your plush days."[64] (Compare Margaret Byington, sadly noting the green plush of Homestead, above.)

Such an articulate awareness was probably rare; when working class housewives "achieved" carpets, plush, and clutter, I imagine they did so in proud emulation more than in resistance. Either way, the middle class esthetic was under pressure from "below." Perfected through several decades, it was what Katherine C. Grier calls an esthetic of "refinement":

The standards of the aesthetic of refinement employed sets of sophisticated analogies between realms of human activity, as between behavior and the appearance of objects. The "softening of the world" of refined behavior could be symbolically rendered through upholstery and drapery in the parlor. "Refinement" could be rendered visually as attention to and appreciation of detail. Social "polish" was manifested through competence in the use of specialized artifacts and also through ownership of objects that displayed high "finish." "Finish" incorporated the characteristics of smoothness, shine, and ornament, which were expressive of increasing control over materials, just as "finished" or "polished" manners indicated perfect self-control. Finally, all these valued characteristics in the material world and in social behavior were demonstrations of artifice, the techniques of improving natural materials with human skill; thus refinement also implied the treasured and enlightened ideal of progress.[65]

The final sentence of this admirable analysis brings out the contradiction latent in the esthetic and in its social meanings. Moderately well-to-do middle class people had appropriated and adapted an upper class standard of self-presentation; they were *able* to do so because machine production allowed the paraphrasing of aristocratic styles at lower and lower cost, in a wide commercialization of gentility.[66] It became more than acceptable to fill the parlor with machine-made goods: so long as they were tastefully arranged and interspersed with objects unique to the family, their display sounded the harmony of individual and national improvement. But there was no check to this diffusion of taste. If the middle class parlor-maker could allude to a commissioned portrait or an old master by purchasing a gilt-framed print from a catalog, the steelworker or shop girl could allude to middle class iconography with a ten cent chromolithograph or a free insurance calendar. The hand-crafted empire furniture of the wealthy

modulated into the Grand Rapids parlor suite of the respectable and
then into the $23, four-piece parlor "suit" offered in the 1897 Sears
catalog. Cheap pianos assembled from machine-produced parts allowed
a music historian to write in 1904, "Almost every [American] home,
even among the humble, possesses its instrument and some amount of
piano music."[67] If industrial progress admitted those at the end of the
chain to the esthetics of refinement, what was left in it of distinction?

Perhaps this puzzle explains the frenzied efforts of some families to
individualize taste and blend styles cacaphonically from one room to
another, or in esthetically specialized corners of a single room: Japanese,
Moorish, Turkish, French, and Eastlake, jostled together. The chorus of
protest against Victorian eclecticism rose in volume, sometimes joining
with a moral critique of ostentation. Two plainer fashions gained in
popularity among the discerning, at the end of the century. Craftsman
or "Arts and Crafts" woodwork and furniture, with its plain lines, dark
colors, and sturdy mass enacted a revulsion against finicky detail and
plush surfaces. It also suggested a return to more honest, pre-industrial
times, though of course most of it was machine made. Both points hold,
as well, for the second fresh style, colonial revival, which alluded to a
more specific, reassuring American past. As William Seale notes, the
colonial revival was taken "most seriously by upper middle-class suburban families and the minor rich; . . . and became entwined with the
genealogical interests of its prime supporters."[68] Beneficiaries of industrial capitalism distanced themselves symbolically from its real practices.
Craftsman and colonial revival styles used a vocabulary that also – conveniently – repudiated both upper class decadence and working class
vulgarity. One can observe a gradual transition in the language used to
promote household goods: McClure's ads of 1896 deploy the older lexicon (see Grier) of rich, polished, soft, elegant, comfortable, and so on,
in the interstices of the new: efficient, clean, healthy, useful, durable,
new, improved. "Beautiful" and "cheap" sound uneasily together.

The uneven tendency toward decorative restraint accorded well with
emergent ideals of practicality, ease, and systematic living. It blended
with the simplification of exterior design and reconfiguration of down-
stairs home space according to the open plan. Taken together, these
changes meant the end of the parlor itself as an apt expression of PMC
identity and aspiration. It gave way around 1900 to the "living room," a
very different organization of space, possessions, and cultural meanings. The living room declared a family's independence from the need
for self-presentation along the lines of old formality. It offered to erase
the boundary between the way a family acted privately and the way it was
at home to visitors. It would be "the room without facade,"[69] though of
course there can be no escape from facade, from culture, into the purely
natural. The new mode of presentation relaxed the need for best behavior; a new class was at home with itself.

The changes I have described were carried forward mainly through the use of commodities, and in the language of what Jean-Christophe Agnew calls "a commodity aesthetic . . . a way of seeing the world in general, and the self and society in particular, as so much raw space to be furnished with mobile, detachable, and transactionable goods."[70] But of course such an esthetic is a field of contestation, not a unified understanding shared by all classes, or by all within a single class. As early as the 1850s some middle class people felt quite at home – literally – with such an esthetic. Later, as cheaper production and gradually rising incomes permitted, immigrants and native born working class families cheerfully paraphrased it in their home lives. Partly in recoil, many of the new middle class ceased to "celebrate" an identity between themselves and the commodities in their front rooms. Furnishings were not to stand directly for their selves and their place in the respectable world, but for a rational, easy, practical way of life. That way of life readily admitted the newer mass-produced, brand named commodities whose advertising representations filled, and supported, the popular magazines of the 1890s and after – instrumental products like soap, cereal, and canned food, that enabled purchasers to get on smartly but quietly with their efficient lives. I suggest that the use of mass-produced goods for tasteful display in parlors established habits and feelings that transferred over time to the new commodity esthetic of sensible living, which required no formal display for its justification.

Reconfiguring Decorum

The middle class model of conduct changed toward the end of the century, along with the changes in home design and decorative practice that I have surveyed. Something more abstract changed, too: the way people in an emergent class understood their relation to one another and to other classes. Simply put, as the PMC shaped and enlarged a comfortable social space of its own, it gradually relaxed the demanding code of manners its predecessor class had elaborated to govern social intercourse.

For a glimpse of the older code, I offer a sampling from the observations of scholars who have studied nineteenth-century rituals of visiting – the activity that staged, with high contrivance and at the same time quite nakedly, social relations of equality and invidiousness. Here is Kenneth L. Ames on the use of calling cards in "ceremonial calls," between noon and five o'clock:

> Since husbands did not normally accompany their wives when they paid calls, the wife could leave her husband's card where she visited. If the lady

of the house being visited was at home, the lady visitor could leave two of her husband's cards, one for the lady and the other for her husband. To leave her own card would have been redundant . . . .

If . . . the woman she intended to visit was not at home, she might leave three cards, one of her own and two of her husband's. The latter two were to be distributed as before, but her card would be left for the mistress of the house; "a lady leaves a card for a lady only." This cult of protecting the virtue of matrons extended to that of maidens as well, for in some circles it was not considered appropriate for a young lady to have visiting cards of her own. Her name was printed beneath that of her mother on the latter's card . . .

If a woman of higher social position returned a card with a call, it was considered a compliment. If the roles were reversed and a woman of lower social status returned a card with the more intimate, more familiar call instead of just a card, the gesture could be interpreted as brash or presumptuous.[71]

Other categories of calls – condolence, congratulation, friendship – had their own rules, beginning with the symbolism of folding cards to place in the silver card receiver:

Each corner of the card assumed a distinct meaning when turned down: the upper right-hand corner signified a personal visit; the upper left, congratulations; the lower right, a formal leave-taking when departing the community for some time; the lower left, condolence. Bending the entire left-side end of the card denoted a call upon the family at large.[72]

Then there were subcodes, such as that for initiating courtship: a man might ask a female friend to leave his card at the home of a young woman he hoped to meet; she could cut off the relationship before it began by ignoring the card. Card rituals served to regulate acquaintance and intimacy within a social group, and to define its boundaries. Not to take part in them, Ames writes, "was to risk being categorized as ill bred, the Victorian euphemism for lower class."[73]

When the lady of the house or her servant admitted a guest, another set of rules came into effect. Karen Halttunen and her sources describe it thus:

The moment when a caller first entered the parlor was a critical point of the genteel performance: "Coming into a room and presenting yourself to a company should be also attended to, as this always gives the first impression, which is often indelible." Upon entering the parlor, the visitor was to proceed immediately to the mistress of the house and greet her first. The polite visitor's physical carriage and facial expression conformed perfectly to bourgeois demands for self-restraint:

Her face should wear a smile; she should not rush in head-foremost; a graceful bearing, a light step, an elegant bend to common acquaintance, a cordial pressure, *not shaking*, of the hand extended to her, are all requisite to a lady. Let her sink gently into a chair, and, on formal occasions, retain her upright position; neither lounge nor sit timorously on the edge of her seat. Her feet should scarcely be shown, and not crossed.

Such careful self-control was never to betray, however, any stiltedness: "She must avoid sitting stiffly, as if a ramrod were introduced within the dress behind, or stooping." After successfully accomplishing her entrance, the polite visitor remained in the parlor for the proper interval – ten to twenty minutes for ceremonial calls. A well-bred lady signaled her intention to leave soon by leaving her parasol in the hall, and wearing her bonnet and shawl throughout the visit; a gentleman carried his hat and cane into the parlor for the same purpose. At the end of the call, the visitor made some final comments, bowed gracefully, and maneuvered out of the parlor without turning his or her back on the hostess.[74]

A different script governed teas. "Hostesses were to send invitations, either engraved or hand-written, on stationery that was folded into a square shape, and worded according to the specific conventions of the etiquette arbiters." Guests

followed explicit rules from the moment they entered the house. They were to "meet informally," Agnes Morten advised in her 1894 volume, *Etiquette*, "chatting for a while over a sociable cup of tea, each group giving place to others, none crowding, all at ease, every one the recipient of a gracious welcome from the hostess . . ." One was to talk to relative strangers "in a chatty, agreeable way," but not to introduce oneself . . . .

One must drink noiselessly, leave the spoon in the saucer, hold the cup by the handle. The hostess must arrange settings in a rigidly prescribed way, with silver implements and porcelain cups, accompanied by light and graceful food.[75]

For all this regulation of body and speech, the etiquette books insisted that the rules governing teas were delightfully relaxed by contrast to those governing the conduct of hosts and guests at a dinner party, the supreme occasion of nineteenth-century gentility – as might be expected, given the contradictory demands, at table, of basic physiological processes and civility's injunction to refine the body out of existence.[76] But I will not take this discussion through the draped archway that led from parlor to dining room. Nor will I stop to observe other rituals, besides calls and teas, typically enacted in the middle class parlor: musical evenings, theatricals, whist parties, weddings, funerals, and so on.[77] Instead, after a brief sortie outside the home, I will reflect on the

class meaning of genteel performance, and on the obsolescence of the
ideal in the moment when the PMC constructed its social space.

A look at advice given to would-be genteel folk for conduct in the
streets may help contextualize the rules of calling and parlor etiquette.
Ladies and gentlemen out walking could not determine who they would
and would not see, who might try to catch their eye, who might
approach or address them, who might pass within inches or brush
against their clothing. These forms of encounter would signify intimacy
or acquaintance among equals in the parlor; such meanings had to be
refused in the streets. Respectable people were to walk purposefully but
without haste, avoid looking directly at others, talk softly, laugh modestly
if at all, glide through crowds as if invisible. They must not audibly
address each other by name or make introductions. They must maintain
exact control of social distance.

> A welcome social acquaintance was to be greeted with a cordial bow or a
> graceful wave of the hand; a more distant acquaintance, with a brief touch
> of the hat; an unwelcome acquaintance, with a cold bow or, in extreme
> cases, a cold stare of nonrecognition . . . . Ladies were to be greeted with
> great deference, but only when they first registered recognition; no true
> gentlemen was to greet a lady who appeared unconscious of him.[78]

Street decorum mirrored the etiquette of calling in that it neatly cali-
brated degrees of acquaintance and respectability, so defining intended
social affinities and discriminations. For us, it clarifies the context of
such a need. In smaller, older communities, most residents were known
to one another, and known within established relations of rank and
obligation. If not, clothing and demeanor might reliably substitute for
personal knowledge. But many towns and cities grew too large for frequent recognition of passers-by, and new strangers crowded in each year.
Furthermore, as historians like Halttunen and Kasson have shown, the
new conditions of relative anonymity, along with the premium on competitive striving, encouraged urban people to put on fronts, to make
self-presentation their first line of battle for the spoils of the market.
There may actually have been more impostors and hustlers per city
block in 1850 than in 1800; certainly the new lore of the city held that to
be so, and advice abounded for preserving aloofness and fending off
deception or indignity. Even more important, I think, in understanding
mid-nineteenth-century domestic and social ritual, is to see it as a middle *class* strategy for drawing social boundaries in new conditions – fluid
populations, the competitive market – that obliterated old hierarchies
and broke old social bonds.

Granted, etiquette books may be a genre of utopian dreaming more
than of ethnography. One can wonder if more than a few fanatics of propriety enacted all the ritual there scripted; and one can be sure that even

in the heyday of Victorian formality some people of unimpeachable standing took pleasure in and won admiration for abridging the rules: informed deviation can usually trump slavish observance.[79] Granted also that the purveyors of etiquette were translating upper class codes for middle class imitation, and that those codes ultimately derived from courtly European models. What richer lode to mine, for a middle class in formation seeking to distinguish its conduct from those it saw as inferiors? Still, the very profusion of etiquette books, their large sales, and the insistent flow of collateral advice in periodicals suggests a demand for and preoccupation with gentility among middle class people. Were that not enough, there is also the hard, corroborating evidence of Victorian domestic facades; of rooms specialized to divide genteel performance from the instrumentalities of shelter and nurture; and of the paraphernalia of culture – hall stand, parlor table, *étagère*, upholstery, carpeting, tea settings, sideboard, and so on – housed now in museums and lovingly described by cultural historians. Together, manners and material culture partially unveil for our contemplation a style and an ethos well suited to the aspirations of middle class people in growing industrial and commercial cities.

In the course of its move to the suburbs the PMC simplified home design, opened up interior space, and turned against the semiology of the formal parlor, as I have already suggested. They also abandoned or relaxed many of the canons of genteel performance here described. How, and why? In answering, I will steer the discussion back toward my main subject.

Modernizing, middle class people gradually came to see the highly scripted performance of respectability as confining and unnecessary. "From the 1880s on, the central ceremonial ritual of the Victorian parlor – the formal call – was coming under increasing attack; by 1895, according to the *Ladies' Home Journal*, it survived only in the visit of congratulation or condolence."[80] Formal dinners became less fashionable, among the same sort of people, as did the grand sideboards and their cheaper imitations, along with what Kenneth Ames calls "the courtly paradigm" of conduct.[81] Magazines and advice books came to favor informal teas, ladies' luncheons, stand-up suppers, and evening parties. Some of the ceremonies usually enacted in middle class parlors through the 1870s became commercialized: weddings and of course funerals, translated to *funeral* "parlors" beginning in the next decade.[82] And in general, visiting among professional and business people seems to have declined from the 1890s on. "Business class" women in the Lynds' "Middletown," for instance, testified that "the old-time call with cards and white kid gloves has completely gone out. No one ever comes to call." And that "clubs have done away with calling . . . . People used to call on a bride just after she was married and she would go promptly with her mother to return the calls." And, "I never see [my friends] unless I run into them somewhere occasionally or they come over to dinner. It was different with my mother. She and her friends were always in each other's homes."[83] I believe that this change in the forms of sociability in Muncie from the 1890s to the 1920s took place somewhat earlier in major cities and their suburbs.

In fact, the segregation of classes in urban neighborhoods and especially through the suburbanization that proceeded apace from the 1870s on is one obvious condition of possibility for the way the PMC departed from earlier middle class manners, esthetics, and arrangements of domestic space. Genteel performance regulated acquaintance and social standing – patrolled the boundaries a middle class was trying to draw for itself. This strategy made a lot of sense in the early industrial city, the "world of strangers" one would encounter on every sortie outside the home. To enforce rules of physical restraint and of polite social intercourse was to create distinction in that world's public spaces. Parlor culture and ceremonial calls linked the private spaces of middle class people in each city or large town. These practices not only served as rites of admission and exclusion; they built class consciousness, both in the rudimentary sense of knowing who belonged, and in the more abstract sense of knowing what standards and customs made people of the class worthy of their social position.

Moving to a suburb was a different kind of strategy. Not everyone in these economically homogeneous neighborhoods knew everyone else; on the contrary, the new suburbs were often weakly organized as communities. But there, personal strangers were not class strangers. A home in a good suburb automatically signaled respectability and protected one from random encounters with the socially inferior, except of course for the delivery men and servants whose deferential presence further underwrote the gentility of suburban space. In this setting, strict rituals of recognition and distancing became redundant. They persisted for a while, then gave way to easier forms of sociability that PMC families could permit themselves when surrounded by the more or less like-minded and like-incomed.[84] Lowering the pressure in this way on demeanor, carriage, speech, and gesture, in the streets and around the borders of parlor and dining room, was in itself a significant change in class consciousness, especially for women, as will become evident in my discussion of magazine fiction and controversies over the "New Woman."

Other arrangements and activities confirmed the geographical meaning of suburban space. The final decades of the century saw mandatory public schooling become nearly universal except in the South. As the mere fact of having some education ceased to confer distinction, suburban parents recreated it by ensuring that their children went to well-funded elementary and high schools with suitable classmates. In these years, too, the high school grew into a major institution; the student population quadrupled between 1890 and 1910.[85] And although high schools came to exist in every town and city, the suburban high school had a special PMC character, with its green campus, its social life outside of classes, and its college-oriented curriculum. The National Educational Association appointed its Committee of Ten in 1892, with Harvard's President Eliot as chair, to standardize secondary education; the College Entrance Examination Board began testing students in 1901. In the early 1890s most college students had first attended private schools. That quickly changed as high schools expanded, and as suburban high schools became equivalent in function, if not in prestige, to Eastern preparatory schools. Obviously, suburban education counted not just for social distinction, but toward class reproduction, tied as it was to that key PMC institution, the university, and to the PMC project of legitimation through specialized knowledge.

Leisure activities cemented the class solidarity of the suburbs. Almost as soon as Overbrook Farms was founded on the Main Line near Philadelphia, in the early 1890s, its people started a tennis club, then made an athletic field, then a golf club. Most of the men and many of the women belonged to the Wheel Club in 1900. Families went sledding and skating together in winter.[86] Suburban streets, parks, and school grounds allowed easy mingling of equals, without the formalities of club membership and certainly without the need for elaborate rituals to police the borders of acquaintanceship. Going to church also meant congregating with respectable neighbors. While theological differences and denominational snobberies no doubt survived the move to the suburbs, they lost some of their social force in a place where everyone had good incomes, and almost all were Protestants of native birth. The high seriousness of nineteenth-century, middle class Christianity deflated somewhat. Piety in itself was no longer a main class marker, though membership in one church rather than another came to be one.[87] Churches grew more like other social organizations.

Of these, there were very many. One of the Lynds' informants, quoted above, said that "clubs have done away with calling." That may have happened later in Muncie (a boom town in the 1890s) than elsewhere, but I believe the speaker grasped an important relationship. Famously, middle class people entered into thousands of voluntary associations well before the Civil War; doing so was one strategy in their project of class formation. Those organizations often had broad improving aims: abolition, temperance, religious renewal, moral reform, benevolence, charity. After the war, business and professional associations sprang up in cities, as did lodges and their female auxiliaries. The 1870s and 1880s brought an explosion of women's clubs, many devoted to self-improvement – reading clubs, literary societies, cultural groups – along with sewing circles and purely social clubs. In the 1890s, women's clubs dedicated themselves to community improvement, park development, recreational reform, the quality of schools, and so on.[88]

I connect this movement in several ways to PMC class formation. First, like the other activities mentioned above, club and association meetings enlarged and changed the meaning of homogeneous domestic space. When small, they took place in homes, but apart from and, to an extent, in substitution for the bonding rituals of calling and formal dining.[89] Otherwise, such groups met in venues like church parlors and club houses, an expanded middle class terrain. Second, in their dedication to solving problems and improving communities, many women's clubs paralleled the mainly male professional organizations, trade associations, and municipal reform groups that were the vanguard of the PMC, as well as the somewhat less prestigious lodges.[90] Such work created a class style and expressed a solidarity of purpose. Third, from 1890 on, clubwomen, like male professionals and reformers, pressed their issues through a national organization: the General Federation of Women's Clubs. Furthermore, national groups often collaborated locally:

> Joining doctors in the public-health campaigns, for example, were social workers, women's clubs, and teachers who specialized in the problems of youth; lawyers who drafted the highly technical bills; chambers of commerce that publicized and financed pilot projects; and new economists . . . .[91]

Such alliances united consciousness as they won authority and power. And fourth, all these groups – even the literary societies – built a bridge of social and self improvement across the gap between work and leisure, public and private, so that the PMC vision of progress through expertise and planning illuminated both spheres. This perspective helps explain why ostentatiously ceremonial etiquette lost its urgency and its appeal.

Shopping was another activity that shaded the border between work and leisure, and between consumption and production, more than is perhaps usually recognized. Through the nineteenth century, women increasingly took on the task of making purchases, as an adjunct to and substitute for home production.[92] This shift accompanied the spread of neighborhood food stores, more gentrified than large public markets. Shops for clothes and other articles also became more class-segregated, so that there were many stores in a city where a middle class woman could encounter mainly others like her – another extension of respectable space outside the home. But perhaps the main change was the emergence of the modern department store in the 1890s. As noted in chapter 5, these palaces of consumption catered to people of various classes, but enticed well-to-do women not only through attractive goods and stunning architecture and decor, but by the inclusion of elegant spaces and services: lunchrooms, tearooms, waiting rooms, art galleries, and so on. Some of the services offered at the Emporium in San Francisco in 1899 were obviously meant as enticements to educated and stylish women: the parlor with magazines and writing materials, the telegraph office, the theater ticket office, the manicuring and hair-dressing parlor, the art rooms. Susan Porter Benson suggests that the better stores "created the women's equivalent of the men's downtown club," and, indeed, some of them made rooms available, free, for club meetings. Crowded displays of cheap goods on the ground floors, and by the turn of the century in bargain basements, helped divide stores into elegant and vulgar sectors. Managers sometimes explicitly drew class lines: one New York store banned unruly East Side children from the lounge, and another gave free tickets for afternoon tea to regular customers and those who looked prosperous. Stores made charge accounts available only to wives of "substantial citizens." Going downtown to shop was another way for women to travel along what Stuart Blumin nicely calls an "axis of respectability," and at the same time exercise their domestic competence.[93]

As middle class spaces like these proliferated in cities and suburbs, the axis of respectability lengthened. Travel had been an upper class prerogative and mark of distinction as late as the 1870s. After the Civil War, less affluent people began following the wealthy to elegant resorts like Newport, Saratoga Springs, Long Branch, and St Augustine, as affordable hotels went up there. Resorts with a middle class base grew up at Asbury Park and Atlantic City, on Block Island and Martha's Vineyard, in the Adirondacks, White Mountains, and Catskills. A dozen railroads advertised in *McClure's* through the summer of 1896, promoting such destinations as the Berkshires, Cape Cod and the islands, the Sierras and California, the resorts of Wisconsin and Minnesota, Denver and Colorado Springs, and Chautauqua, as well as the speed and luxury of the trains themselves. Yellowstone and Yosemite, with their culturally produced natural beauty, attracted thousands from the 1880s on. New York, Philadelphia, Chicago (especially during and after the 1893 World's Fair), and other cities became middle class tourist destinations. Europe, once reserved for those who could afford six months on the Grand Tour, drew 100,000 Americans a year around 1900.

Material conditions of travel (along with rising incomes) helped make this expansion of middle class space possible toward the end of the century. A ticket from New York to Chicago cost more than $20.00 before the Civil War, $15.00 in the 1870s, $5.00 in the 1880s. Steamship fares dropped proportionately, reaching $30.00 to $50.00 for a second class cabin to Europe in the same decade. Thomas Cook brought his business to New York, then to other US cities, after the war, and other travel agencies began competing with Cook in the 1880s: they made travel expertise available to novices, and offered tours and excursions with all expenses included for those who had to be concerned about budgets (this of course rendered them déclassé in the eyes of the elite). Guidebooks began appearing to help organize travel, enumerate the obligatory sights, and teach middle class people how to take them in.

Fred Harvey's restaurants and hotels lined American railroads by the 1890s, dependable stopoffs comparable to the Howard Johnson chain in the automobile era.[94] Big city hotels multiplied, as did restaurants; both provided stunning appointments, flattering service, and an enlarged public space for PMC people.

Vacationing grew cheaper and more regimented, but maintained upper class connotations. Advertising aimed at PMC tourists emphasized luxury and exclusiveness. Guidebooks retained an upscale perspective; whether describing Paris shops or the Chicago World's Fair, they directed tourists to safe and respectable locations and instructed them in proper conduct. Pictures of steamship and railroad passengers show them stylishly dressed and decorously behaved. They learned to avoid déclassé attractions like Niagara Falls, and to choose the White City over the Midway Plaisance at the Chicago Fair. PMC vacationers went where they would see and be seen by others of their own class, or better. In addition to expanding middle class space, the new tourism helped foster PMC consciousness by flattering its consumers that they had the emotional depth required for the quasi-religious experience of what John Sears calls "sacred places"; by giving them authentic, visual experience of sites already marked in advertising and travel literature as culturally significant; and by affording them cognitive and esthetic familiarity with a world in which only those with decent incomes and educations freely moved.[95]

As the PMC created a habitus in these ways and others, it tapped into and benefitted from a process of cultural definition and classification that had gained momentum through the second half of the nineteenth century. This was the making of high culture, its institutions, its refined spaces, its practices of reception. Scholars like Lawrence Levine, Paul DiMaggio, and Alan Trachtenberg have made the case well and decisively; I will simply connect the story they tell to my argument.[96]

Before the Civil War, public staging of the "arts" was highly promiscuous by later standards. Museums exhibited waxworks, relics, exotica, rare plants, fossils, and monstrosities, along with paintings, prints, and sculpture. Concerts included polkas and negro melodies alongside the works of Handel and Haydn. Operas were interlaced with popular songs. Stage companies presented Shakespeare's plays, or scenes from them, along with farces, minstrelsy, singing, and so on. Little value was placed upon the integrity of the artwork; scenes and arias might be repeated or omitted according to the tastes of the producers or the demands of the audiences. The latter were insistent and interventionist, cheering and booing, shouting down actors, joining in musical performances. And they were socially mixed to a degree unthinkable in later years. Ladies and gentlemen attended the same events as industrial workers; both groups appreciated Shakespeare and Stephen Foster; there were no special qualifications for viewing old masters or listening to Mozart.

By the end of the century sorting and segregation marked off the arts (no quotation marks needed, now, to signal anachronism) from popular entertainment, "legitimate" theater from vaudeville, grand opera from lesser forms, symphonic music from the vernacular, fine arts from Barnum's curiosities, and of course literature from trash. Audiences at highbrow performances became restrained; visitors to the new museums kept a reverent silence, and no longer spat on the floor or brought dogs and small children. A sharp divide separated artists from amateurs, performers from audiences. Art had acquired its aura. Its appreciation required long apprenticeship, in college or from instructive magazines, for those not born into upper class homes. Urban elites encouraged these divisions by founding and supporting the great symphony orchestras and museums of fine arts, and by regulating both the kinds of cultural production that could appear there and the ways culture was to be received. Critics policed the boundaries of art. The Arnoldian project for Culture metamorphosed into class distinction.

It will be obvious how these developments contributed to the elaboration of PMC space and awareness I have been describing. The theaters, opera houses, concert halls, and museums that became hallowed sites of art lay along the axis of respectability that reached out from middle class homes. Professionalization of performance and criticism accorded with the value set on expertise and knowledge by PMC people. The idea that art represented the highest reach of human evolution, and that only the most refined sensibilities were capable of experiencing it fully, fed PMC aspirations to psychological depth and complexity. Doubtless its relation to high culture, so constituted, carried with it some anxiety and ambivalence. The PMC commitment to practical knowledge and action did not harmonize fully with a commitment to esthetic detachment; the PMC derived its authority from building bridges and reforming social arrangements, not from burning with a pure and gemlike flame. And entering the new temples of art and music meant encountering, not quite as equals, the upper class people who had built the temples, and whose ease there expressed a birthright. Still, the encounter was flattering as well as intimidating. The PMC established an enduring relation to high culture, one that the new mass circulation magazines nourished, if somewhat more self-consciously than the old monthlies.

Which brings me back for a moment to the central topic of this study. The mass circulation magazines that sprang up in the 1890s gained admission into a way of life already coherent and intelligible to those pursuing it. They had ceased to rely as much as the mid-nineteenth-century middle class had on the rituals of purity, the semiotics of gentility, and a sealed-off Christian domesticity for their sense of who they were and what standing they deserved in US society. Closely monitored circles of local acquaintance had given way to metropolitan and national affinities, to a greatly extended axis of respectability. I have plotted this change of class feeling and orientation onto public and semi-public spaces. In so doing I have used the concept of space for the most part literally: houses, stores, streets, parks, resorts, hotels, restaurants, theaters, museums, and so on. But I have also tried to keep in mind representations of space – the maps people carry in their minds of the places they go to or might go to (or would scrupulously avoid) – and the meanings they attach to these places, including the value set on real and imagined relations to the people who frequent them. Magazines, I will argue, helped chart PMC social space; their representations of it afforded compelling guidance.[97] They also constituted a figurative yet very real cultural space homologous to the literal spaces that came more and more to define the PMC's understanding of itself and its world. Magazines circulated nationally to people with common values and interests; they entered similar homes everywhere, and were part of what made those homes similar. And of course magazines helped shape the values and interests of PMC people, including an interest in the brand named commodities advertised there. In the next three chapters I will try to make good on this claim.

Reproduction

This term has several related meanings that I want to encompass: biological, familial, social. When couples make and rear children, in capitalist societies organized around nuclear families, they endow those children from birth with entitlements, disabilities, and expectations, by virtue of the parents' social location. The family thus conjoins biology and society, and makes ideological sense of that nexus. Married couples try to ensure that their children maintain or improve upon the social standing the parents have achieved; the family reproduces itself through the children's lives. Obviously this process extends beyond individual families; the couple came from two different birth families, and if the children marry they join *their* birth family to others. Reproduction of a family, in the social sense, is always reproduction of families, and so outward to reproduction of all the families whose suitable connection can be imagined, that is, of a class.[98] How families and classes deal with *un*suitable connections is an interesting matter, and a famous subject of the novel.

I have been describing the formation of a class in spatial terms; to speak of reproduction is to add a temporal dimension, one that plays an important part in individual, family, and class consciousness. People's efforts to understand and manage their lives include envisioning, desiring, and shaping a future. It should be easy to see how the spatial reconfiguration I have sketched in this chapter to distinguish the newer middle class of the century's end from its mid-century antecedent implied a different strategy of reproduction as well.

Beginning well before the Civil War, middle class couples began limiting the number of their children, prolonging their childhoods, and setting a high priority on their nurture and education. One can see this emphasis in the responsibility laid upon mothers for the moral development of children, in the literature of Christian domesticity. From the point of view adopted here, these injunctions and practices can be grasped in part as a recipe for family and class distinction through the enactment of gentility. Children would learn the elaborate conventions of self-control and social mingling that I have described, along with proper standards of dress and speech, the accomplishments and range of reference that constituted a polite education, and the values and attitudes that accompanied and justified this kind of respectability. Internalizing these norms counted as building *character*, highly prized in itself and also invaluable as a transgenerational expression of family worth.

Character, so fashioned, also qualified the young man for middle class work. In that arena, his carefully tutored restraint guaranteed punctuality, sober habits, prudence, honesty, respectfulness toward employers and clients, and other qualities that, more than his formal education, would set him apart from his working class counterpart, who had only labor power – skilled or unskilled – to sell in the marketplace. Cultural capital translated into earning power, and thus amounted to a plan for the economic reproduction of family and class over time, as well as for recognition at any present moment.

The remapping of social space along an extended axis of respectability eased the pressure on new middle class families to foster such tight discipline of conduct and emotion in their young. Suburbs and homogeneous city neighborhoods were safe zones within which it was less urgent for children to internalize, and parents to monitor, social boundaries. The new arrangement permitted a transvaluation of character into personality, as it rendered the parlor and the formal call obsolete. PMC children played in the same streets and parks, went to the same schools and Sunday schools, had their own social affiliations and organizations, grew into common habits of consumption and entertainment, went with parents to class-approved vacation sites, attended the same colleges. In this elaborated space they met many who would be socially plausible mates, and few who would not. The nuclear family delegated some of its authority and some of its responsibility for the future to external networks and institutions. As Stephanie Coontz puts it, "Now class differences were reproduced by families doing *similar* things," and, I would add, in similar places across the land.[99]

High school and college were probably the most important such places. Public secondary school enrollment nearly quintupled, from 110,000 in 1880 to 519,000 in 1900, while the national population rose 50 percent. This figure tells us that the high school was beginning to play a significant role in American education, but tells little about its class meaning.[100] A conjecture is possible: since in 1900 nearly all children received some elementary schooling, while only about 10 percent of the age group were in high school, it makes sense to see the latter as primarily an upper middle class institution, and to understand attendance there as an advantage offered to PMC children, who did not need to leave school in order to contribute to the family income. For this reason, keeping a boy in school to the age of eighteen was a particular mark of class, and indeed well more than half of high school students were girls.

As with the earlier, nineteenth-century middle class, a strategy that funded distinction also funded economic achievement for the next generation, more and more often in the characteristic PMC form of the career. In 1880 a high school diploma was a rare achievement. By 1900, parents thought of high school in the way older elites had thought of private schools: as preparation for college. There, young people would qualify themselves through knowledge and skills for advancement in business or – after graduate study – in the professions. The latter were no longer casually open to gentlemen, but only to men and sometimes women of ability who went through regimented programs of study, apprenticeship, and initiation into the routines and values of the various guilds. No such rite of passage led young men into the rapidly growing managerial ranks of business yet, but neither was admission limited to those with capital or family connections, or to scrambling entrepreneurs. In 1900, 20 percent of those graduating from "leading American colleges and universities" went into business, and 30 percent of those graduating from the most prestigious private universities.[101] College brought together, at one stage of their careers, those who would become executives in business, those headed for the professions, and those who would marry members of both sets. In this way it helped forge national bonds of experience and ideology throughout the class, as well as preparing its youth for advancement and authority. Not incidentally, some colleges and universities also brought them into the proximity, if not exactly the company, of upper class youth, thus allowing those who would be both rivals and allies to know something of one another. Some fraternities and sororities straddled this boundary; all guarded against the intrusion of the déclassé, nourished intense bonding among elites, cleared avenues of sociability and marriage, and reproduced networks of advancement and authority.

Distinction and advancement were complementary processes carried forward in the university, prime locus for the organization of professions. Its role in reproduction makes sense, too, in that the PMC grounded its self-definition and the idea of its historical agency in a particular relation to knowledge. It thought of its initiates as possessing a broad capability for development, to be specialized and deepened through mastery of a discipline. So educated, the individual could claim certain privileges – control over work, limited autonomy from market forces and bosses, affluence, respect – guaranteed formally in the most successful professions, informally

in the ranks of specialized management and the new government bureau-
cracies. In exchange, the PMC offered to "society" (in its view) expertise,
efficiency, the ability to regulate and rationalize capitalist development, dis-
interested leadership into modernity. On another analysis, it offered to the
dominant class scientific management, conversion of knowledge into
profit, and moderation of open class conflict; to the working class, schooling, sanitation, better housing, city planning, social work, endless advice on
how to be more like the middle class, and in all these ways a modest bulwark against capital's unlimited drive toward exploitation.[102]

So the PMC's way of investing in the future, its strategies of reproduction, traded on the fungible resources it brought to this moment of
capitalist development: not significant capital, not just abstract labor
power, but a capacity and a particular relation to useful knowledge – a
capacity not mysteriously inborn but inseparable, of course, from a family income in excess of (say) $1500 a year, from the privileges of
suburban life or its equivalent, from the ability to delay children's entry
into the workforce, from the command of educational resources, from
the kinds of cultural capital discussed above, and so on. Let me pause at
this level of theory to make four related observations.

First, it was possible for a group of people so positioned to organize
themselves into a class only because a shift from competitive to monopoly capital opened up the possibility. That change encompassed not
just the rise of the big corporation, with its ever more articulated
internal structure, its "rationalization" of the labor process, its turn to
quasi-professional management, its assumption of control over the sales
effort, and its reliance on the consciousness industry that accompanied
that new project; but also new kinds of response to social disorganization
and struggle, the professionalization of government and social services,
the effort to manage the working class in its leisure as well as at work, the
ambitious new project of understanding and mastering society as a
whole system. A class cannot invent itself apart from deep strains and
shifts in the relations of production and of social reproduction.

Second, for all its sense of inevitable progress and historical mission,
and in spite of its happy exemption from bloody battles at factory gates,
the PMC took strong initiatives on its own behalf and against other classes
and groups. These initiatives ranged from the struggles of physicians,
architects, and other would-be professionals to disqualify competing practitioners and control areas of work for their own benefit, through the
efforts of scientific managers to deskill and control labor, to the supervi-
sion of working class life against considerable resistance, to assaults on the
untrammeled power of capital through dozens of regulatory reforms. A
class can make itself only through conflict with other classes.

Third, the PMC acted vigorously to *shape* the new social formation,
even as it took up the opportunity presented by capital to shape itself.
On the theory adopted in this study there can be no question whose

initiatives had most historical force. The bourgeoisie led in recreating capitalism. But other classes were not (never are) passive recipients of ruling class direction. Through the whole period of transition the US working class acted on its own behalf with unusual militancy; so, at times (including the 1890s), did farmers. But that is another part of the story, and here I want to emphasize merely that the emergent PMC strove purposefully if not militantly to effect its own design for the future, and that part of its design was precisely to temper the militance of class conflict through reform and rationalization. Though of course neither the PMC nor big capitalists could have understood their relations in this way, the PMC offered to moderate coercion into hegemony.

And fourth, the decisive role of the dominant class in revamping capitalist production and distribution meant a decisive role, too, in reorganizing social space. It built the factories, assembled the workers, made the systems of transport and communication, shaped the cities. The PMC negotiated its own social space within limits set by bourgeois command. Characteristically, that social space was at a distance from physical production; in-plant managers and some engineers went to work where the machines were, but most PMC men commuted to professional offices, commercial sites, corporate headquarters, cultural institutions, and the like. In fact the PMC distinguished its enlarged social space in part by erasing reminders of physical production, as from the decorative home grounds in the obviously non-productive suburb. Thus it makes sense to view this class as producing itself, to a considerable extent, in the spheres of home life, community, and culture. Yet as social practices in those areas advanced reproduction, they turned back inevitably toward production, and the PMC's complex relation – part facilitator, part adversary – to capital's project of making and selling things for profit and of marshaling the labor of millions toward that end. Perhaps these observations will help explain some of the gaps, distortions, and mystifications in PMC consciousness, and in the magazines' representation of social process and social space, to be discussed in future chapters.

It may seem a long stretch from the rituals and artifacts of suburban culture to this totalizing conspectus on historical transformation; but what my analysis of domesticity, leisure, and reproduction has driven toward is just this insistence on the dynamic presence of the whole social system in the interstices of everyday life, and, to complete the dialectical maneuver, on the consequentiality of small domestic initiatives in refashioning a social order.

Work/Consumption

Thus far, leisure and reproduction have served as loose categories in my inspection of how middle class people came to live away from paid work, at the end of the century. Now I turn to production, last in the familiar triad. Home production, by contrast to factory production; but the opposition holds still only for a moment of abstraction and analysis. Making and maintaining things at home increasingly meant using things made in factories; producing was consuming. Hence the form of title I have given this section. Needless to say, consumption was (is) thoroughly entangled with the activities of leisure and family reproduction; the three basic categories are not at all discrete. When a housewife frosts a birthday cake for her six-year-old, she is simultaneously producing and consuming (sugar, vanilla, and so on); the birthday party is work, and yet a leisure activity in that it is voluntary and festive; it contributes to both material and psychic reproduction. Having noted the blurriness of the concepts, however, I will return to my heuristic use of them, trying to problematize as well as clarify them along the way. I will also revisit the subject, introduced in the previous chapter, of the sorts of commodities newly and widely advertised in the 1890s, and of how they entered into home production – this time with the emphasis on class distinction.

It is a commonplace of social history and a premise of this study that capitalist production for the market gradually displaced home production, in at least three ways. Capitalist manufacture drove out cottage industry; it produced many commodities, from soap to furniture, that had previously been made at home for use at home; and it drew and forced millions into wage labor who, in the older system, would have been working domestically. In doing that, it also took rural recruits into cities where lack of space and legal restrictions made it difficult, then impossible, to keep pigs and chickens or to grow the staples of home production. Through such processes, capital both created new needs and met them through the making and selling of commodities.

Many of these, ready for final use, slowly eliminated or at least made optional whole spheres of domestic work. Ready-made clothing and shoes, candles and lamps, rugs and carpets, breakfast cereals and crackers in boxes, dishes and flatware, medicines and toothpaste: these and dozens of others let money and a trip to the store or a mail order from Sears replace long and complex labor. Other new products of industry, also ready for use, had never been produced at home, but neither did they enter into or change housework: cameras, chromolithographs, gramophones, bicycles.

To think only of innovations like these would be to imagine the steady abbreviation and cancellation of home labor – in effect, its transfer to factories. But of course nineteenth-century factories also made thousands of commodities for use *in* home production. Prototypes of what we now call "major appliances" began to appear early in the century, and evolved throughout – none of them was a sudden invention: the ice box, the cast iron range and oven, the water heater, the furnace for central heating, the sewing machine, the first crude washing machines. All these were in fairly widespread use by 1900, and advertised copiously to readers of the *Ladies' Home Journal, McClure's,* and so on. Add the availability of indoor plumbing, city water, gas, and electricity, and it is clear that the technical basis for cooking, heating, clothes making and repair, cleaning, and sanitation had changed entirely since colonial days.[103]

Then there were the lesser devices for housework: jars and later cans for preserving food, from well before mid century; ironing boards from the same period; the carpet sweeper from the 1880s, the electric iron from the 1890s, enameled and aluminum cookware from the same decade. Manufacturers offered a cornucopia of small utensils to speed the cook's work, including egg beaters, apple parers, cherry stoners, sandwich cutters, meat grinders, a pie lifter and turner (so that the housewife would not have to reach into the hot oven with her hands). Food molds came into fashion; one catalog offered over a thousand designs, and each well-equipped kitchen was to have a variety in stock. Innovations became urgencies; an 1881 cookbook specified 139 necessary implements; an 1894 article by Mary J. Lincoln, head of the Boston Cooking School, asked the housewife to own 373.[104] Cleaning tools and preparations also flooded the market, along with small accessories for making and mending garments.

One can wonder how much this plethora of aids to housekeeping actually lightened or shortened domestic labor. Clearly, iron ranges made cooking easier and cleaner than it had been in open hearths, indoor running water hugely simplified laundering and dish washing, gas and electricity sped many tasks. But the elaboration of tools and accessories for cooking surely tempted housewives to elaborate their cooking as well, especially when accompanied by the blandishments of advertisers and the ever more detailed advice of cookbook writers, both pressing the values of efficiency, method, sanitation, and modernity. The astonishing proliferation of machine-made bric-a-brac, architectural detail, ornamentation, and elegant touches like silver napkin rings must have added more to the burden of dusting, cleaning, and polishing than was subtracted by Sapolio and Gold Dust. Certainly there was a chorus of laments around the end of the century that, compared to the tremendous advances of mechanization and the division of labor in most areas of production, housework remained primitive, arduous, and isolated.[105] And what could one expect other than a very mixed picture of "progress," when it was driven more by the need of manufacturers to multiply individual requirements and desires and to sell commodities than by any movement to change the politics of domesticity?

That question can serve as a reminder of how misleading any inventory of products, along with a chronology of their introduction, is bound to be if taken as a measure of historical process. Not only does it leave out the social relations of making and selling, in which capitalists' needs shape and limit those of consumers, it passes over the complex imbrication of work and consumption, suggesting instead a simple narrative of advancement from the arduous primitive to the streamlined modern. And it obscures class relations that pervade the sphere of consumption itself. With that issue in view, the story looks quite different, as will be obvious in a return to the main question of this chapter: How did the PMC organize its daily life? More specifically, how did PMC women work and consume, compared to the women of other classes?

Susan Strasser rightly emphasizes, in *Never Done*, the slow and uneven diffusion of domestic technologies. A look at the dates of various innovations might suggest that before the Civil War many homes had central heating, indoor plumbing, efficient iron stoves, gas lighting, refrigerators, sewing machines, washing machines, and the like. In fact, a tiny affluent minority lived with such advantages then, and even in the 1890s most working class homes lacked them. For one basic example, recall the figures noted earlier (p. 142) on urban residences without indoor toilets in 1893. A house with modern conveniences was a distinguishing mark of class. Much the same appears to have been true for the regular use of the brand name products so broadly advertised in the new magazines. Packaged cereals and crackers, canned vegetables and fish, packed meat, ketchup, soft drinks, and so on show up rarely in the itemized budgets of working class people, so assiduously tracked by PMC reformers in the early 1900s.[106] In spite of their modest prices, these were dietary staples only for well-to-do people before 1900. Those who had to practice thrift made most meals from raw and bulk ingredients, with kitchen labor standing in for factory production. Washdays were not replaced, for them, by the use of commercial laundries. Again, PMC women, and not their working class counterparts, were able to slough off the work of clothes making, as men's wear, and by 1900 much women's wear, was commodified – though the stylish would continue to do some fancy work at home or hire seamstresses to individuate their fashions.

That last point signals another distinction: those who could afford to delegated household work not just to machines and their operatives, but to individuals paid directly for their services. Although the proportion of the labor force in domestic service declined steadily through the second half of the nineteenth century, while complaints circulated endlessly about the "servant problem," the truth seems to be that most middle class families had servants around 1900. The Lynds' interviews suggest that two-thirds of "business class" families in Muncie employed full-time working girls in 1890. Martha and Robert Bruère's informal study of middle class budgets found that of sixty-two families with earnings of $1200 to $5000 around 1908, only eight spent nothing for "service," and twenty-six paid more than $100 a year, suggesting at least a half-time employee. Census figures for 1900 show that in the larger cities there were on average close to 150 servants per 1000 families, with higher figures in the South and lower in the West. That does not mean that 15 percent of families hired help, of course; Lucy Salmon's survey of Vassar graduates in 1890 discovered 2545 servants in 1025 households. Assuming that most of her respondents were *upper* class women, I offer a rough estimate that about 10 percent of non-upper class families had servants in the 1890s, with on average one per family, and that those families included most of the PMC. In spite of fifty years of laments like the Bruères' – "The middle-class servant is obsolescent" – it would seem that for professionals, "petty proprietors," managers, and officials, the servant problem had not changed much since 1860, when 85 percent of such people in Milwaukee had servants.[107] The PMC held onto this distinction, and this easement of household labor, thus in a small way aligning their lives with those of the wealthy.

This supposition makes sense in other ways of how PMC families shaped their lives. Domestic help allowed them to preserve a traditional form of gentility while also enabling wives to move out along the newer axis of respectability, to shop, meet with women's groups, attend plays and concerts, travel, and so on. Less obviously, this arrangement placed the lady of the house in a direct relation to an African American woman or a woman of the mainly immigrant working class, at home, that paralleled the PMC's broad supervisory connection to the working class through management, professional efforts at social improvement, and "expert" advice. The mistress of a servant gave instructions and exercised authority as part of home administration, itself ideologically represented as a profession.

That understanding, pressed upon middle class women from mid century by domestic feminists like Catherine Beecher and Sarah Josepha Hale, and taken up in a different form by the proponents of domestic science before and after 1900, is the third distinction I wish to note, in the area of home production. Even as PMC women freed themselves from the lofty ideology and impossible daily requirements imposed upon their work by the doctrine of separate spheres, many of them adopted the successor ideology of the home as a professionally managed system. Although some language carried over from the older doctrine – "science," "laboratory," "economy," "efficiency" – it entered into a different practical context and structure of feeling. At the end of the century those terms were supported by the presence of home economics programs in universities; cooking schools and cooking textbooks and cookbooks that substituted exact measures for the old "pinch of salt" and "great lard"; emergent sciences of nutrition and sanitation, with their admonitory bulletins to the modern housewife; professional medicine and architecture, each with its freely given domestic advice; psychologists and child-rearing specialists bringing method to motherhood; and advertising's sensible voice, attaching these bodies of expert knowledge to factory-made commodities for use in rational housekeeping.[108]

Understandably, some historians have described this process as

thrusting upon the housewife an even greater burden of warnings, prescriptions, and anxieties than did the older ideal of angel in the house.
True, doubtless, for many hopeful aspirants to middle class decency,
whether fresh from the farm or at the upper edge of the urban working
class. But I suggest that PMC women – armed with labor-saving appliances, ready-to-use commodities, domestic help, simplified home
design, and the esthetic of moderation in furnishing and decor – were
able to adopt the ideology of domesticity as a profession, preside over
many of its routines, and yet exempt themselves from the redoubled
efforts it called for and the worries it promoted. Indeed, as they supervised the work of their maids at home and, through charitable and
reformist club work, enlisted in the project of instructing the less fortunate, they positioned themselves more as expert advisors with
authority, drawn from their own class, than as those offered the advice.
I do not wish to belittle the quantity of unpaid and undervalued labor
such women did and continue to do, or to attribute to them the free-
doms of leisure class wives. But it is important to see that they had
choices available to them very different from those facing women of
smaller means.

The fact of choice stands out in the earliest studies of middle class
budgets around 1900, decades after social workers and reformers began
peering into the domestic accounts and practices of working class people
(and of course that delay in itself says much about the social relations of
knowledge that obtained between the two classes). Ellen Richards noted
that "very little variation is allowable until the lower limit of choice is
reached," at an income level of at least $600, but that great "variety of
choice" appeared in the expenditures of middle class families. "One
family economizes on rent, another on clothes, another on other
expenses," but nearly all used around 25 percent of their incomes for
what Richards called "Higher Life": savings, charity, travel, church,
books, insurance.[109] Middle class budgets reported in the Bruères'
Increasing Home Efficiency show expenditures for "advancement" rising
from 23 percent in the $1000–$2000 bracket to 45 percent between
$3000 and $4000; their category includes the items Richards listed, plus
health, entertainment, education, recreation, postage, telegrams, "and
other things not absolutely necessary to the continuance of the family" –
or, as one might put it, those things that constitute a realm of freedom.
These average figures understate the variety of choices actually made; for
just one instance, a number of families set aside nothing for savings,
while quite a few saved more than 20 percent of their incomes.[110] The
categories of "higher life" and "advancement" themselves reveal how
contemporary students of family life understood the possibility of indi-
viduation and refinement as a blunt material fact, while urging it as a
class ideal.[111]

To look at these budgets another way, the one-fourth of income, or more, reserved for advancement meant that an individual PMC family could call on its own resources to support the fulfillment of desire, beyond necessity. Or again: there was a class-specific, historically produced need for such elaboration of desire, of choice, of autonomy in leisure and reproduction. Homes were more private and families more separate than in working class life, which spilled out into the communal space of the streets, and thence into neighborhood saloons, arcades, dance halls, vaudeville houses, amusement parks, and (after 1900) nickelodeons.[112] PMC families distinguished themselves by using their means to pursue depth and culture rather than "cheap amusements," and often adopted a critical posture toward the banality and promiscuity of working class leisure, though an occasional theorist like Simon Patten hailed "the communal life" of these pastimes as a stimulant to docile wage labor and a basis for what we now call consumer society.[113]

In sum: it is an error to mark off consumption as a separate activity in the circuit of work, reproduction, and leisure. Better to see the use of commodities as a series of moments in the whole process. Shopping for the beef is work; so are cutting it into stewing pieces, browning it, adding the vegetables, keeping the range fired up, serving the stew, washing the pot and the dishes. More true for the pot, which has no end use at all except in labor; less true for three yards of calico, which will see many end uses after its fabrication into a dress, punctuated with laundering and mending. A second and related error is to grasp consumption as the same activity, with the same meanings, across class lines. For a millworker's family around 1900, wages of $500 a year paid for consumption that belonged mainly to the realm of necessity: the work of home production and reproduction. An engineer's salary of $2000 supported much consumption in the realm of "higher life" as well as much that was needed but also respectable (the fashionable gown as against the homemade dress), and in which end use was interspersed with the paid labor of people other than the housewife, or with her labor eased and made reputable in ways described earlier. To the first family consumption meant little more than survival, and a hard won decency. To the second it enacted and signified distinction. For the capitalist with an income of $30,000, perhaps augmented by a salary, consumption took place almost entirely in the realm of choice, and could be conspicuous, in Veblen's sense – a form of distinction often stigmatized as wasteful and anti-social.

In arguing thus for the mutual embeddedness of consumption and the work of social reproduction, I have had in mind the five "areas of personal and social experience – work, consumption, residential location, formal and informal voluntary association, and family organization and strategy" that Stuart M. Blumin sees as rather fully defining an emergent middle class "way of life" in the mid nineteenth century.[114] The second of the two categories under scrutiny in this section corresponds roughly to his "family organization and strategy." I hope to have suggested along the way that "residential location" and "voluntary association" are separable only for analysis from consumption and reproduction. Rent and mortgage payments *are* consumption; the location of a residence – a family strategy for reproduction – entails a certain level of expenditure on these items, as well as on decor, furnishings, maintenance, plantings, and so on. Voluntary association will follow different patterns when 25 percent of the family budget is available for "higher life" than when nearly all of it must go for necessities.

I mean to have suggested, too, that PMC work implies certain kinds of activity in these other areas, and *requires* some (education the crucial one) so that the next generation can engage in similar lines of privileged work. The critical kind of work that partially delimited a middle class at mid century, Blumin argues, was mind work, in opposition to manual work, as white collar to blue collar in later terminology. Already in the 1880s that distinction had begun to lose its class significance, as low paying jobs for clerks and other mind workers proliferated, as more and more clerks were women, and as such jobs ceased to carry with them reasonable hopes of advancement.[115] By 1902, male clerks in Boston mercantile establishments earned about $500 annually, on average – less than skilled manual workers – while traveling salesmen and managers made about $1500.[116] An old boundary was fading, a new one being drawn in the larger companies with their many layers of white collar work and through the successful efforts of some groups to organize their mental labor along professional lines. The PMC took advantage of the historical chance to differentiate its work from that of the older middle class, and of course from that of the industrial working class, as it differentiated its consumption, family strategies, residential choices, and networks of association. I hope to have shown to what extent the change was an integrated process.

As has been implicit throughout the discussion, and sometimes explicit, the PMC way of life emerged with, fostered, and was sustained by a fairly coherent set of values and attitudes. They amounted to class awareness, if not to class consciousness in the marxian sense. Class awareness, as Anthony Giddens puts it, "does *not* involve a recognition that these attitudes and beliefs signify a particular class affiliation, or the recognition that there exist other classes, characterised by different attitudes, beliefs, and styles of life . . ." or that the class in question might be in an antagonistic relation to those other classes. He argues that because middle classes set a high value on individual merit and initiative as means to upward movement in social hierarchies, they tend not to develop militant class consciousness, and in fact tend to deny the reality of class altogether.[117] I think the American PMC at the end of the nineteenth century was somewhat more conscious of its identity and common purpose than Giddens's distinction implies, but that it did think more in terms of mobility and merit than in terms of fixed lines and antagonisms. Indeed, many PMC people saw their historical task as one of mediating and softening antagonisms between capital and labor, and perhaps as bringing into existence a relatively equal social order within which everyone would enjoy the influential vision of Bellamy's *Looking Backward*. Of course, the PMC saw itself as *different from* (and superior to) the working class, but in a tutelary relation to it that might lead eventually to greater likeness. It goes without saying that the PMC experienced other differences – black/white, native/immigrant, normal/deviant – as vividly as those of class, and to the detriment of any coherent class understanding. More about this and about the troubled matter of ideology in chapters 10 and 11.

Now, I want to conclude with some thoughts about how nationally advertised commodities entered into PMC class awareness, thus preparing for an examination in the next chapter of how advertisers addressed and sought to manage that awareness. First, in the spatial terms I have been using, brand name commodities lay along the new axis of respectability that helped unite PMC awareness. This was literally so, in that one's peers visibly sported Waltham watches, Kodak cameras, and Remington bicycles in respectable places; they, too, showed off Higgins & Seiter china and silver, Bradley & Hubbard lamps, Seth Thomas mantel clocks, or the equivalent, in their living rooms; one could assume that Rubifoam dentifrice, Ivory Soap, Gold Dust Washing Powder, and Quaker Oats would be found in the back regions of their homes. Also on the axis were the nationally circulated magazines in which ads commended these products for beauty, efficiency, durability, and cleanliness, and the stores that displayed and sold the commodities. Ad images and copy built commonalities of meaning and affect in *conceptual* space among PMC people around the country. In short, these products and their auras resided not only in proper social space but in the system of symbols through which PMC people understood their affinities, their place in the world, and their historical agency.

For all the artificiality and simplification implied by reifying the PMC as a homogeneous and well-defined group, and by saying that "it" did this or felt that, as I have throughout this chapter, the usage is valuable in its insistence on common experience and outlook. It also has the value, at this point in the argument, of questioning one familiar critique of consumer society: that it dissolves not just traditional systems of meaning but all "symbolic structures outside the self," and erodes "meaning in general." In this view, the self now must locate identity in consumption, as the "boundaries between the self and the commodity world collapse in the act of purchase," and the self is reconstituted as "an assemblage of commodities."[118] Any inhabitant-observer of an advanced capitalist society can see the element of truth here; yet it is misleading to think of commodification as an exchange of meanings primarily between their commercial producers and consuming individuals or families. Classes use commodities to think collaboratively about a society and their locations in it, as did the PMC around 1900. This is not just a matter of "People in the new mobile, urban world of the late nineteenth century" requiring "new symbol systems" to "locate and identify themselves,"[119] though it is partly that. The PMC created and understood social space in a variety of ways like those described here; they located themselves quite literally in suburbs and colleges and vacation places; they identified themselves to one another through manners, culture, and energetic activity at work and in leisure. Brand name products entered, and took on meaning within, a confident way of life already defining itself. Advertising took up the words and other symbols of a consolidating class awareness and linked them to commodities. It responded to a need for social belonging that the PMC was deftly meeting in other, more direct ways, and that is not well understood by imagining a lone and confused urban recruit in a world of strangers, however well such an image fits Dreiser's Carrie Meeber.

Nor should the class-wide purchase and use of similar commodities like brand name cameras, watches, and breakfast cereals lead us to think of the PMC as a Weberian "consumption class," though shared habits of consumption did help to forge bonds among people who had many other affinities and common projects, and etch their difference from other groups, a fact they and the ad agencies well understood. I think the PMC experienced different chiefly as better. Michael Schudson writes that people "seek not social superiority, as a rule, but social *membership*."[120] This is a false opposition: membership in the PMC meant superiority to most other classes and groups; for that matter, PMC envy of upper class privilege mixed with feelings of intellectual and moral superiority. Such feelings have much to do with the way commodities give satisfaction. As is famous among critics of mass culture, they do not satisfy, at all or for long, many of the needs to which advertising connects them: needs for friendship, achievement, family cohesion, independence, freedom from anxiety. Yet material advantage – the ability to consume at a *relatively* high level – correlates well with satisfaction, in most societies, whether the general "standard of living" is low or high.[121] The PMC consumed at a relatively high level, in the time of its emergence, and that expression of superiority fortified other complacencies.

This helps explain what otherwise might be a mystery: why class distinction seems to have been linked to the use of so many inexpensive and banal commodities for household use: cereals, cleaning powders, tooth care products, canned vegetables, soaps, kitchen implements, and so on. Mary Douglas and Baron Isherwood note that acts necessarily performed with high frequency signal low rank, both in the general and the household division of labor.[122] Goods like those just mentioned are used in high-frequency tasks, and based on that fact alone their use should rank low among consumption events. But in the 1890s PMC people could buy them much more readily than could working class people, and such commodities also helped reduce the repetitive drudgery of domestic work. In addition, the meanings added to such goods by advertising helped locate them on the axis of respectability and mark their use as prestige consumption rather than subsistence consumption. The very fact of a brand name helped confer such distinction, along with the assurance of consistent quality, purity, and safety – themselves a mark of distinction for the middle class home.

The magazines that came into such a home were of course commodities with brand names; their consumption, too, conferred distinction. An etiquette manual of the 1890s instructed the couple of "small means" how to give "a perfect little dinner," with claret, champagne, "a neat maid-servant in cap and apron," a house "neatly and quietly furnished," and "the late magazines on the table."[123] The maid and the wines suggest the contextual meaning of "small means" and the referent of this proper couple's emulation. The display of magazines signaled the couple's attainments and aspirations, and its affinities with other PMC families – including, surely, the dinner guests – who participated in the same culture. The late magazines would not have appeared on working class parlor tables. The studies of working class life after 1900 show little expenditure for reading material of any sort: less than $5 a year, on average, in New York families with incomes of $800 went for "books and papers," a category that includes magazines but appropriately leaves them unmentioned, since few were bought. The other study of New York workers indicates that 266 out of 318 families took newspapers, but only 3 purchased magazines. (Both studies mention *Munsey's* as one of the few read; the others from my referent group were the *Ladies' Home Journal, Everybody's,* and *Collier's.*) In Homestead, steelworkers apparently took no magazines but could read them at the free library.[124] In spite of the big circulations attained by the new, cheap monthlies, their consumption was highly class-specific, as was the more general pattern of consumption and awareness they promoted.

How they did that is the subject of my next three chapters; how advertisers addressed and created that awareness is the subject to which I turn first. I hope that as I reassert an emphasis on the selling and shaping of consumers, my readers can hold that emphasis in tension with the very different emphasis in the present chapter on the way a class made its own consciousness and way of life.

8

The Discourse of Advertising

In chapter 6 I excavated the social relations "behind" advertising. Now I will consider those relations as manifested in the ads themselves.

At the outset, I acknowledge the problem of sampling. Millions of ads appeared in monthly magazines between 1890 and 1905, the focal years of this study. Indeed, a main theme of my argument is the saturation of public spaces with commercial messages and images. I have looked at some thousands of these advertisements, in about thirty magazines of the period: a lot, but a tiny fraction of the whole. In this chapter I refer at times to broad surveys of that fraction. For the most part, though, I direct the reader's attention to exemplary ads, reducing the thousands to about twenty against which he or she may test my observations. Furthermore, I have chosen for reproduction ads that, by turn-of-the-century standards, are relatively advanced, in the sense that their premises and techniques became more common in later decades.

Leiss, Kline, and Jhally criticize "semiological" analysts for this kind of selectivity; they achieve "a richness of detail with respect to only a few 'ideal types' of ads."[1] I offer a limited defense of the procedure. First, the ads I have rescued from obscure decay were by no means unusual; every issue of every magazine from 1895 on included at least a few such and sometimes many. Second, even if, in spite of that, one were to call them "ideal types," they demonstrate a point of great importance: that the codes upon which they depend *were available* for use. Readers knew their conventions; the language they used was embedded in consciousness. To think otherwise is to believe that advertisers spent millions of dollars sending consumers unintelligible messages, or messages that, if intelligible, seemed outlandish to their audience. The effectiveness of the advanced ads, measured in sales, make that unlikely.

Appearance and Image

Figures 2, 3 and 4 will clarify what is at stake here. The page from the *Atlantic Monthly* shows characteristic styles of advertising in 1880. Display is minimal, visual representation almost absent. Lines of agate type

speak in mainly sedate, declarative sentences or fragments about qualities of the product. Reading the ads, except for their abbreviations
and ellipses and the strain on one's eyes, is much like reading any other
text in the magazine. Of the products themselves, only four (Colton's,
Victor Baby Food, Hanford's Baking Powder, and Mason & Hamlin) are
branded, household goods of the sort most advertised twenty years
later, by which time the cures and chromos that were staples of 1880
advertising had nearly disappeared from magazines.

Figure 3 instances the kind of ad on which I will be concentrating.
Display is compelling; visual representation is photographically exact
though surrealistic. Three different type sizes and two different faces
render a slogan, an imperative, and a terse bundle of information about
the camera, its price, and its availability; in spite of the text's brevity, it
manages to name Kodak four times and Eastman twice. There is plenty
of blank space on the page; composition is elegant. An interaction of
text, image, design, product, and reader takes place that calls for the
bridging of lacunae. What does the slogan in the upper left hand corner
mean? Why need it be said? Who is saying it? To whom? What *is* a Kodak?
Why would one want it in one's pocket? Why is the man dressed that
way? Why do we see only this portion of him? Advertising had constituted readers for whom, presumably, these things caused no more
puzzlement than they do for us, today. We, too, are literate in this code;
presumably, readers of 1880 were not.

I include Figure 4 to illustrate the sorts of ads, more common around
1900, that I will be overlooking. I'll not comment on these, beyond suggesting that in every way except their less spectacular use of imagery, they
resemble the Kodak ad much more than they resemble the ads of 1880 – in
typography, in design, in presentation of brand names, in address to the
reader. Squint a bit, and you might almost imagine the Van Camp's or
Libby's ad in a periodical of the 1950s; nothing like them appeared in 1880.

In fact, the look of advertisements changed radically just in the two
decades on either side of 1900. Large ads proliferated. An early survey
found that in 1892, 18 percent of those in the *Century* were full-page ads:
in 1908 that figure reached 43 percent.[2] The ratio of half-page to full-page
ads, 2.5 to 1 in the 1880s, reached 1 to 3 in 1920.[3] Individual copies I have
of *Munsey's* contain the following numbers of full-page ads: 1895, 14; 1900,
35; 1907, 44. In issues of the *Ladies' Home Journal*, ads of a quarter-page or
larger went from 4 in 1893 to 16 in 1899 to 25 in 1907. (A quarter-page in
the *Ladies' Home Journal* is as large as a full page in *Munsey's*.)

As sheer size increased, so did the ratio of picture to printed text. For
Munsey's in the years mentioned above, the number of large ads in which
text occupied less than half the space rose from 8 to 18 to 19; for the
Ladies' Home Journal, from 2 to 8 to 12. Illustrations became standard features of ads; Daniel Pope reports a survey of four publications showing
that in 1894, 30 percent of their ads included pictures, while in 1919 the

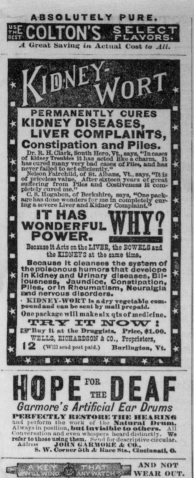

Figure 2 Assorted ads from the *Atlantic Monthly*, November 1880

Figure 3 Kodak ad, *Century*, April 1900

Figure 4 Assorted ads from *Munsey's*, March 1900

percentage had risen to 90 (p. 235). Even these numbers understate the change, since texts themselves took on an artistic appearance: more blank space, larger type, and varied fonts highlighted the physical appearance of words, in counterpoint to their discursive meanings. The Libby's ad in Figure 4, for example, uses graphic appeal far more effectively than do even those ads in Figure 1 that contain pictures.

The conclusion seems inescapable: just when ad agencies gained control over communication from producers to consumers, they restructured that communication to privilege visual impressions and play down discursive appeals. I do not read this as in any simple way a shift from rational to emotional. I'm not even sure it signals a reduction in the informative content of ads, though one study has shown a marked tendency in this direction through the first eighty years of this century.[4] Information can come in small packages; and one must recall how much *false* information was circulated in earlier advertising. Without doubt, however, these changes in design amounted to a new mode of address to consumers, and new meanings for material goods, to be explored later in this chapter. These took shape as the industry itself did.[5]

Needless to say, the industry pondered and promoted this encroachment of the visual. *Printers' Ink* carried many discussions of typography, signs and emblems, borders, engraving, uses of the photograph, and so forth. Early on, some theorists began arguing that design was as important as content (for example, Theo L. DeVinne, in an article from 7 January 1891). They assigned it such importance because they thought visual form made direct claims on attention and feeling. J. Walter Thompson held that ads should include a "terse" statement of facts, "so cleverly displayed and illustrated as to be quickly noticed and held in the memory"; an ad that is "neat, attractive, bold, . . . fixes the eye, commands attention and unloosens the strings of the pocketbook." Pictures, especially, were seen as short cuts to persuasion: Thompson thought them "more than half the battle," because the wish to see pictures is "human nature"; "human nature . . . will continue to be moved by pictures," wrote another expert. This privileging of the visual is evident in an offhand list Thomson made of the "essentials of good advertising": "speaking type, clever designs, plenty of daylight, forceful argument, simple straightforward wording and an attractive appearance." Verbal content does seem less than half the battle, by its relative importance in a series like this.[6] Older advertising assumed a reader wanting a product and willing to search through dense columns of type to find news about it. The newer visual advertising set out to ambush the reader's attention, produce affect quickly, and lodge in the memory.

Sometimes it did so through decontextualized images of the product itself. In Figure 5, the photo has been clipped to let the auto proclaim its own quiddity against a void of blank page. The *icon* itself is utterly concrete, its place in the social and natural world utterly abstract; no suggestion of

THE COSMOPOLITAN

Any Pope-Toledo Car sold by any Dealer will run at a Mile-a-Minute Clip

TYPE IX—45 H.-P.

Price, $6,000.00, Fully Equipped. F. O. B. Toledo. Extension Cape Cart, Victoria, or Canopy Top, $250.00 extra.

PLEASE read the headline again. Note the emphasis we put upon the word "any POPE-TOLEDO Car sold by any dealer." That's the point for you to take into consideration—the performance of any POPE-TOLEDO Stock Car—not the performances of the POPE-TOLEDO Racer, or any other racer. POPE-TOLEDO Racers have won triumph after triumph. POPE-TOLEDO Cars will represent America in the world's great Gordon-Bennett Cup Race. But that is not specially important to you. What you want to know is, "Will I get the same sort of a car when I go to my dealer to buy a POPE-TOLEDO that has won every notable speed, hill-climbing and endurance contest that has occurred in the past two years?" The answer, the plain and emphatic—"You Will." You will get an exact duplicate of the same car that won at Boston, Minneapolis, Indianapolis, Cincinnati, Pittsburg, Dayton, Buffalo, Cleveland, Delmonte, St. Louis, Detroit, Denver, Milwaukee, Albany, Yonkers, Chicago, Philadelphia, Garden City (H. H. Lytle, in regular stock model POPE-TOLEDO defeated everything in Vanderbilt Cup Race, excepting only 90 h.-p. Pandhard and 80 h.-p. Clement-Bayard, making 300 miles at an average speed of 46 miles per hour), Rockford, Ills., Omaha, Nashville, Tenn., Peoria, Grand Rapids, Los Angeles. 100-mile world's track record in Texas on January 3rd, everything in its class and in the class cars costing $4,000 to $6,000 at Ormond Daytona in February. A significant fact about all these races is that the time has not varied over 2 seconds to the mile.

Get a copy of our 1905 Catalogue, which contains most of the records of these races, gives all details of construction and describes

30 h.-p., front entrance	· · · · ·	$3,200.00
20 h.-p., side entrance	· · · ·	2,800.00
30 h.-p., side entrance	· · · ·	3,500.00
45 h.-p., side entrance	· ·	6,000.00

Canopy or Victoria Top, $250.00 extra.

POPE MOTOR CAR CO.
Desk 4, TOLEDO, OHIO

Members Association Licensed Automobile Manufacturers.

When you write, please mention "The Cosmopolitan"

Figure 5 Pope-Toledo Motor Car ad, *Cosmopolitan,* June 1905

who might drive such a vehicle, through what landscape, on what errand of business or pleasure. Many early car ads used this technique, in common with ads for other machinery or commodities of intricate design: watches, stoves, organs, and so on. In particular, the magazines displayed page after page of typewriters, abstracted from office or home.

A different kind of abstraction takes place when an ad presents just the product's *symbol*, usually its trademark, as in Figure 6.[7] The Quaker stands for this brand of cereal; his image is familiar through countless appearances in various media, as well as on packages in the store. While icons refer us to the product, symbols are more like reminders of their own incessant repetition in public spaces. They convey little or nothing about the product except its arbitrary signifier. (I will return later to the texts of these ads, and their connections to the images.)

The third major kind of abstraction is the *index*, an image of people, places, or occasions to be somehow associated with the product and its use. Neither icon nor symbol appears in the Ivory Soap ad (Figure 7); the

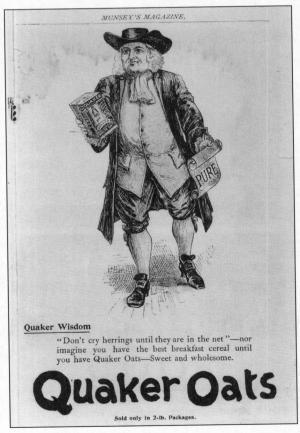

Figure 6 Quaker Oats ad, *Munsey's*, October 1895

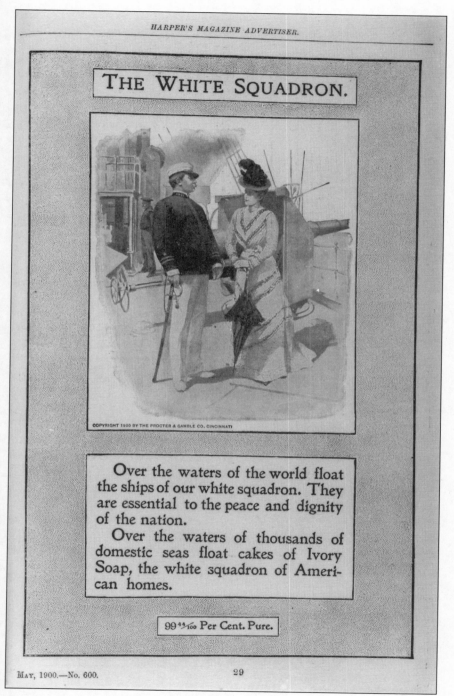

Figure 7 Ivory Soap ad, *Harper's,* May 1900

reader must consult the text to find out what is being advertised, and
indeed will discover the answer only at the end. The index stands in the
foreground, promoting curiosity about its metonymic link to some product. Soap ads tended to rely heavily on index and aura, for obvious reasons.

Many ads combine two, or even three, of these modes of reference, as
does the one for Vitos (Figure 8). The product is there in pan and on plat-
ter. The trademark is on the package; I'm not sure if the domestic servant
was registered as a trademark for Vitos, but she appeared in many ads for
the cereal, and thus functioned as a symbol. The tidy kitchen, glimpse of
back yard, and maid herself render the desired social index about which,
more later. Yet even with all three kinds of reference at work the ad remains
fairly abstract as to place, time, specifics about the family who are going to
breakfast on fried mush, and so on. Schudson marks such abstraction as
characteristic of contemporary advertising, too, whose mode he calls "capitalist realism." Ads referred, and refer, to demographic categories and

An Autumn Morning Dish.

Pillsbury's VITOS, the ideal Wheat Food, can be prepared in
the form of fried mush, but fried mush of unusual delicacy
and ease of digestion. Fried mush made of Pillsbury's
VITOS is neither greasy nor heavy. Served with maple
syrup it is an ideal breakfast dish for cool autumn mornings

PILLSBURY-WASHBURN FLOUR MILLS CO., LTD., MINNEAPOLIS, MINN.
MAKERS OF PILLSBURY'S BEST FLOUR.
Please mention McClure's when you write to advertisers
138

Figure 8 Vitos ad, *McClure's*, October 1899

social types, he says (p. 212), leaving the viewer to connect, through a fantasy of choice, to his or her own circumstances.

Images like those in Figures 7 and 8 present what Roland Marchand calls "social tableaux," "advertisements in which persons are depicted in such a way as to suggest their relationships to each other or to a larger social structure."[8] The woman serving Vitos works for a sensible, modern, reasonably affluent family. The man on shipboard is an officer, the lady has enough social standing to earn deference during her tour, both are Americans, the task of the navy is to defend and honor such exemplars of American womanhood, and so on. Such tableaux were extremely rare before 1890, when most graphics were crude engravings or woodcuts; they proliferated during the 1890s and after, and are of course the heart of contemporary advertising, especially on television. In their configurations, products began to take on ranges of social meaning hard to imagine before.

One curious fact, now, before moving on to the verbal part of advertising messages. Ad men virtually never used halftones in the composition of social tableaux, though reproductions of photographs appeared more and more in other kinds of display. (From the mid 1890s to the mid 1900s, the number of full-size ads using photographs went from 1 to 8 in *Munsey's*, 0 to 6 in the *Ladies' Home Journal*, and 6 to 18 in *McClure's*.) As noted, there were photos of products in large numbers, and also of decontextualized individuals (or parts of individuals, as in the Kodak ad), as well as some photos of landscapes, houses, and so on. But line drawings, paintings, and engravings were the preferred methods for representing people in recognizable social contexts and relationships. Conceivably, this means only that agencies had not the means, yet (studios, models, roving cameramen), to produce tableaux photographically. I suspect, though, that they stayed away from such images more because the camera would lessen the abstractness and idealization of which Schudson speaks, and because "art" seemed a better stimulus for the social imagination.

Voice and Address

I turn now to the words in advertisements, before discussing the relations between verbal and visual.

In early ads, a person addressed whoever might be interested in his offer. The merchant announced a new supply of linens for instance; if one went to the premises, one might not only examine the linens but discuss them with the person who had placed his words in the newspaper. As advertising went national, the possibility of such a follow-up diminished – though in an effort to preserve the feel of it, some companies, like Sears, invited customers to visit the plant or warehouse when traveling. Through a hundred years, as distant corporations joined local sellers in

the ad pages, they kept open a channel of response: the mail. In Figure
2, all but the Colton's ad included an address. Most were strictly mail
order ads: send 50 cents and get the chromos; write to John Garmore &
Co. at the southwest corner of 5th and Race Streets in Cincinnati, and
get the circular on artificial ear drums. Even non-mail order ads invited
interaction. Mason & Hamlin gave the locations of its Boston, New York,
and Chicago stores, as well as offering free catalogs and price lists by
mail. The makers of Kidney Wort said, "Buy it at the Druggists" but also
offered to send the cure by mail, post paid. Hanford's offered a free sample of its pure powder; Victor offered a free treatise on "the Proper
Nourishment of Infants."

All these practices continued into the present century, but the proportions among them changed sharply through the critical years of this
study. For instance, display ads for home products (including food)
broke down this way, in the proffered means of sale:

	Only through stores	Only by mail
Munsey's		
October 1895	31	33
June 1907	32	10
Ladies' Home Journal		
April 1893	36	41
January 1907	46	12

There were also moderate numbers of ads in all four issues that both
indicated the availability of the product in stores and also offered to send
it by mail. Still, the overwhelming tendency was toward elimination of
mail order advertising.

It is interesting that even as manufacturers stopped selling their goods
by mail, they often kept open a line of communication with the customer,
as in the Hanford's and Victor ads in Figure 2. Thus, in the 1907 issues of
both the *Ladies' Home Journal* and *Munsey's*, well over one-third of the
advertisers selling only through retailers invited readers to send in for a
premium, a sample, a catalog, an instructional booklet, or the like. Many,
perhaps most, of the others made the same sort of offer via the package.
Seemingly, it was important to keep open the possibility of a personal
exchange, even as corporations grew massive, concentrated, and distant.

I believe that these things can help toward an understanding of verbal
rhetoric in ads. As Judith Williamson notes, "advertising has no 'subject.'
Obviously people invent and produce adverts, but apart from the fact that
they are unknown and faceless, the ad in any case does not claim to
speak from them, it is not their speech."[9] It is speech on behalf of the
company; the company stands behind it – even legally, in latter days. Yet
a company cannot speak. "Its" words in an ad require that the reader constitute an imaginary speaker. Ad men understood that challenge, at some

level, and created styles that would guide the reader in this task. They wanted to preserve the *feeling* of personal communication. They did so sometimes through the vestigial exchanges by mail to which I have alluded. Mainly they did so by trying to achieve a personal voice. Calkins described this insight, referring to a time (1898–99?) when he "had not yet learned the important truth that an advertisement addressed to five hundred thousand women at a cost of four thousand dollars does not differ in any material way from one addressed to one woman at a cost of a one-cent postage stamp."[10] Writing style could represent one-to-one communication.

For that to occur required abandoning the formal tone of most earlier advertising, or at least reserving it for promotion of distinctly highbrow commodities:

> Those who are acquainted only with the lower-priced Cabinet or Parlor Organs cannot realize the capacity, variety and rare excellence now attained in the finer styles of these instruments manufactured by the *Mason & Hamlin Organ Co.* (Figure 2)

Ad men twenty years later occasionally echoed such an aristocratic sentence, with its third-person address, personal distance, leisurely subordination, formal diction, and sheer length, when selling a luxury few could afford, and one associated with high culture. But they never would have used this style, except in irony, to sell baby food, as the copy writer did without irony in the Victor ad of 1880 (Figure 2):

> This invaluable and strictly American Food prepared from the recipe of one of N.Y. City's most eminent physicians, may be implicitly relied on as the best known substitute for mother's milk. As a diet for the aged, the sick or convalescent, it is unapproached.

Those who wrote copy in 1880 did often personalize in one way: they included testimony from named individuals. "Dr. R.H. Clark, South Hero, Vt., says, 'In cases of Kidney Troubles it has acted like a charm. It has cured many very bad cases of Piles, and has never failed to act efficiently.'" So reports the Kidney Wort ad (Figure 2). Such endorsements from the unknown and the great (see Liszt's kind words about Mason & Hamlin) punctuated early advertising. Perhaps as much because they tied the product to the voice of a named person as because they conveyed authority, testimonials persisted with some frequency in ads of the 1890s and 1900s, and, indeed, are common today. Henry Ward Beecher's praise of Pears' Soap boomed out from ad pages for two decades (one historian says that it first appeared in the *Ladies' Home Journal* in 1889,[11] but I have it in the October 1885 *Atlantic*).

Pears' varied the context, adding testimony from Sarah Bernhardt

Figure 9 Pears' Soap ad, *Harper's*, May 1900

and attributing a preference for the soap to "professional people" in general – their images ranged around a bar – in an ad of 1900 (Figure 9). The images further personalized the product, and some ad men carried this practice to an extreme, as in the Packer's Tar Soap ad (Figure 10). The photo did not call to readers' minds the appearance of an already famous endorser, whose authority was marshalled behind the product, usually quite inappropriately (James Garfield for oatmeal, Beecher for soap, golfer Harry Vardon for tobacco, and so on). This picture brought Nurse Curtis out of obscurity in Chicago, and displayed her previously unknown hair to perhaps two million viewers, as living, personal proof of Packer's Tar Soap's effectiveness. If this ordinary woman can achieve glamour, so can you.

Mrs Curtis's *sentence*, however, recreates a social distance that the photograph is trying to bridge. Her syntax ("but five years, that you may see") strives for the register used by Henry Ward Beecher and by the

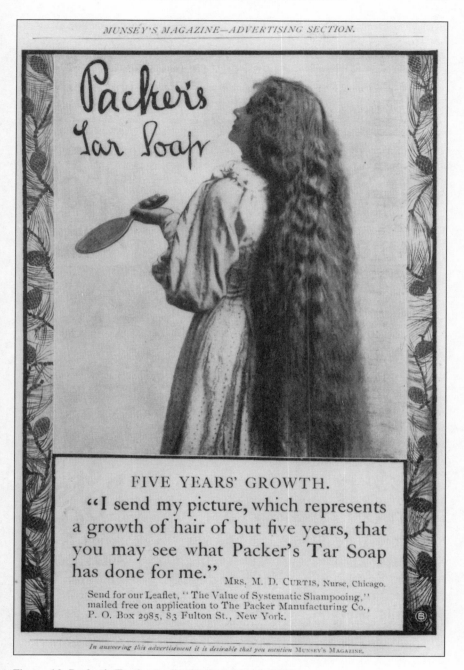

Figure 10 Packer's Tar Soap ad, *Munsey's*, March 1900

copywriters of 1880, rather than for the more homey resonance of Bernhardt's message, or that from Dr Clark of South Hero, Vermont. Pears's copywriter may have felt the social and stylistic tension. Certainly his sentences align themselves with Bernhardt's in both form and content, not with Beecher's: "All sorts of stores sell it – all sorts of people use it." Better, perhaps, not to count on endorsers for the right tone. When released from any such obligation, ad men gave the company an easy manner. Elizabeth Brock (see Figure 11) speaks only through her countenance; her proud mother has no voice (hundreds of mothers did speak, in earlier Mellin's ads). The copywriter preempts conversational space, and tries to constitute the manufacturer as a cheerful, wise, helpful, certainly female *neighbor*.

Figure 11 Mellin's Food ad, *McClure's*, August 1905

One can generalize that point: the new voice of advertising positioned the company close to the reader in concern, familiarity, and social standing. Of course the neighborly person claims the right to *advise* the reader, a right grounded in expertise and worldliness. She knows how Mellin's Food will interact with milk in the summer, even when travel necessitates a change in the milk; he or she knows that fried mush made with Vitos will digest easily (Figure 8); he knows about achromatic lenses and automatic shutters (Figure 3). The neighbor is more expert than the reader. But even when he parades special knowledge, as in the Pope-Toledo ad (Figure 5), he does so in a manner that levels and ingratiates. He does not presume upon his insider's familiarity with road races, speed records, and horsepower to talk down to the reader. Rather, he lets the reader in on his knowledge, crediting him with good sense and practicality: "that is not specially important to you. What you want to know is . . . ." Advertising for many new devices undertook to explain their qualities, sometimes in technical detail; but syntax and tone invited the layperson in, mediating between science and daily life. "This is a new kind of razor. The piece of steel that does the work is two edged and is about as thin as this piece of paper." So ran the first ad for King C. Gillette's wonderful contraption,[12] in 1903, and as the company explained, month after month, about tempering and grinding, and helped initiate the audience through diagrams and microscopic photos of razor edges, it kept the friendly, man-to-sensible-man voice.

The savvy neighbor could sometimes urge, exhort, even needle the reader, as in Figure 12: "How foolish to keep on eating meat . . . . Why then?" Even in doing so, however, he credits the reader with already knowing that Quaker Oats is economical and tasty, and that "dietary experts" endorse it as an alternative to meat. He maintains an intimacy of tone, and helps cement the implied bond through the pun on "Reflection" in the headline, for jokes and puns (already common in advertising) imply an audience that will know how to interpret them, and share the fun. In these and many other ways did ad men create a persona for the distant corporation.[13] As they did so, they personalized the reader, too. The Quaker looks out of the mirror at *you*, serving – weirdly enough – as your reflection, and thus inviting you to think of the sideboard, crystal, silver and china as yours. Already, in 1900, a fair number of ads made a place for the viewer in their imaginary spaces, requiring her presence there to complete the scene. More common was use of the second-person pronoun itself: "Put a Kodak in *Your* Pocket"; "What you want to know is . . ."; "Mellin's Food will make milk agree with *your* baby"; "nor imagine that you have the best breakfast cereal until you have Quaker Oats." Not one of the 1880 ads (Figure 2) ventures such an address. Williamson points out that "The 'you' in ads is always transmitted plural, but we receive it as singular" (p. 51); here in the very mode of interpellation rests the premise of individualism.

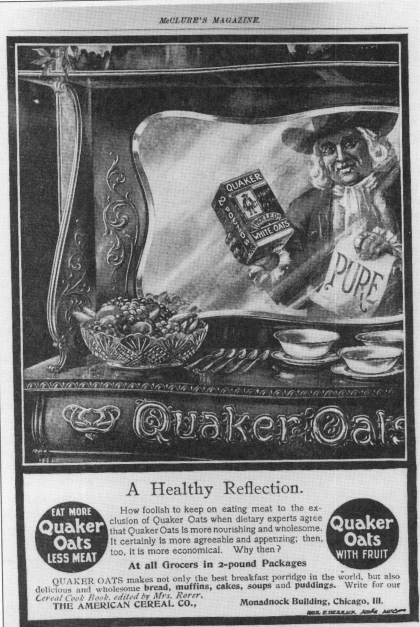

Figure 12 Quaker Oats ad, *McClure's*, October 1899

Ads "gave the appearance and feel of a personal relationship," as Marchand says of the 1920s (p. xxi). I have remarked what kind of a "person" occupied the speaker's role in that quasi-relationship. Through the rest of this chapter I will be circling around the more difficult question of who occupied the other role, of how ads constitute "you." As an individual, for certain; and as one with freedom to act decisively to better the terms of his or her life. What else can one say about the construction of this reader? I approach the question, first, by considering what she or he was expected to understand.

For, as Williamson notes, ads "enclose us . . . in a world that has to be interpreted" (p. 71). That requirement is far more demanding today than in 1900, to be sure; yet I believe that it increased more dramatically between 1880 and 1900 than in the ninety years since, or, to put it more specifically, that a greater discontinuity separated the meaning system of the Mason & Hamlin ad (Figure 2) from that of the Quaker Oats ads (Figures 6 and 12) just a few years later, than separates the meaning system of the latter from that of the Maidenform ads or Lite beer commercials of our own time. Many turn-of-the-century ads placed the reader in a bewildering matrix of signs, and assumed that he or she already had the knowledge to decipher them.

Nor was that an unreasonable assumption, partly because the producers of advertising pulled meanings into their discourse that had already existed in other areas of life, partly – and this is the last point I will make about the rhetoric of address – because advertising was preeminently a discourse of repetition, funding comprehension over months and years of insistence. Long before the 1890s, ad men understood that "desultory advertising" made little impression; and some of the early display ads, like those for Royal Baking Powder, ran in the same format for years or even decades, in dozens of periodicals. But the critical method of the 1890s and after was *incremental* repetition. "Always keep in each and every *Ad.* [sic], no matter what the size may be, one leading Idea, Trademark or Design," wrote Thompson in 1895; but also, "Tell your story over and over, with all its *variations*, in a series of ads . . . ."[14] Those variations were critical. They allowed the Quaker, for example, to step off the package and into magazine advertisements, becoming more than a trademark by his association with "Quaker Wisdom," and then to emerge as a flexible character looking out of the mirror at you, entering your kitchen to offer advice, dandling a baby, and so on through endless small innovations. (The trademark Aunt Jemima actually became a real-life person, going around the country and giving demonstrations.) Of course agencies imitated one another, too, cribbing, varying, and developing methods of signification. As they constructed the language of advertising over time, so could regular readers gradually take in its principles and join in the production of its meanings.

Connections

Analysts of contemporary advertisements point to subtle features of design and signification that one might not have noticed without help – or, as in the case of Wilson Brian Key, that are mainly products of the analyst's fantasy life.[15] My task is partly the opposite one of showing that what seems obvious now was not necessarily obvious then. Ways of connecting image, text, and product that have become second nature over the decades are nonetheless not natural or inevitable, and might have required some getting used to when they were new.

To ground the discussion, I begin with an ad that did *not* bring new ways of decoding into play, that for the Pope-Toledo car (Figure 5). A reader had to know what a car was; beyond that, the icon required no inferences (though a reader might of course make some). It was there, on display, unrelated to any landscape or social tableau. The headline names the icon as a particular brand of car; the caption tells which model it is; the text presents some information about it and other models, letting the reader connect the icon to real-world events, and to his own future life. Text annotates icon.

Now consider Figure 13. The image is an *index*, linking the icon – Londonderry – to table, linen, place settings, fruit bowl, vase, roses, and electric lamp. Read literally, the image "says" only that these things are

Figure 13 Londonderry ad, *Harper's*, May 1900

all on a table. Much more needs to be understood. The headline specifies a focal point in the image: the picture is *about* the bottle, in a way that it is not about plums or roses. As headline descends into caption, the resulting sentence tells how china, roses, and the rest inflect the meaning of the bottle: they don't just happen to be there together; they *belong* together as realizations of the idea, "well appointed." Of course the reader is expected to know already that the unnamed objects on the table connote respectable elegance; indeed, the composition of the image places the reader in a sitting position at the table, or a bit back from it. It is her table, or that of someone in her social circle. They know what kinds of things belong on it – except perhaps for the spring water. In case of any doubt, the caption insists that Londonderry belongs there, and on every such table. (That it does so via a transparent falsehood is also something the reader is presumed to understand: this is an innocuous lie, part of the accepted language of advertising.) Text explains how the image should be generalized, something the image cannot say by itself. I note, however, that ads like this represent a stage in the evolution of a code. Later there would be no need for such a caption, as readers learned the principle of generalization. Perhaps the caption was redundant for most readers even in 1900.

Less so the text of Figure 14. The Kelly-Springfield index is harder to resolve. Clearly the reader is to make some connection between the photograph of elegant carriages and the superimposed drawing of half a wheel and tire, through which we see the rich on parade. Read literally, the surreal image says: on the other side of a half wheel, fashionable people are out for a drive. Since that makes no sense, the picture calls for some association between humble tire and elegant parade, other than that carriages have tires. The text makes the link very explicit. Not all carriages have Kelly-Springfield tires; the smarter the rig, the more likely it is to be so equipped. Why? Because the tire *represents* "good form." The text adds the needed social connotation to the product – a necessary bit of instruction, since "all tires look alike." In making certain that the reader gets it right, the text is also teaching him to read other magical juxtapositions in other ads, initiating him further into the language of advertising.

The Ivory ad (Figure 7) takes the need for annotation to an extreme. Here, as noted earlier, the reader cannot even tell what product the picture indexes without consulting the text, which establishes a relation between image and product that no one would have suspected. It is an absurd one, to be sure, and the reader can hardly be expected to take the analogy literally, believing that a bar of Ivory in the bathtub guarantees the peace or dignity of the household. Teased in this way, however, she can register the more telling – and by now familiar – association posed between a mundane commodity and a high social tone, while accepting or rejecting the more problematic one between soap and chauvinism.

Figure 14 Kelly-Springfield Tire ad, *Cosmopolitan*, June 1905

Figure 15 Coca-Cola ad, *McClure's*, August 1905

With the Ivory ad we reach the limits of what I have called annotation: comment on or explanation of the picture. Many ads of the period crossed that boundary into a different relation of text to picture. In Figure 15, one of the rare ads that present a social tableau photographically, the text does not imply that the athletic couple are about to have a Coke, or that elegant people do, or that Coke is as healthy as exercise, or any such thing. It offers its simple advice with no reference to the picture, other than the weak link of "After Exercise" – and the young people look remarkably *un*exercised. The ad counts on the reader to supply the appropriate connotations – modernity, fashion, youth, nature, and so forth – on his or her own.

The Cream of Wheat ad (Figure 16) extends a similar vote of confidence in its reader. That the product is "dainty" bears no relation to the picture, but resonates instead against twenty years' worth of cereal ads urging Americans to forgo meat at the breakfast table (see Figure 12). The only relation of text to picture (another learned one) is between the

Figure 16 Cream of Wheat ad, *Munsey's*,
June 1907

product's name and its symbol, the negro chef, who, like the Quaker before him, had emerged from the fixity of his trademark appearance to become a mobile character in ads. The reader needs no prompting to make the right connections. Invited by the chef's eye contact and proffered service through the windowlike frame of the ad, she can both see what style of life Cream of Wheat connotes, and imagine herself into it.

Finally, an ad that counts upon the reader to grasp the main meaning of an image over "noise" from a text that virtually contradicts it. The text of the R & G Corsets ad (Figure 17) speaks of productive technique and machinery in authoritative detail – iron forms, stitching, stretching, pressure, steam. Such practical and rather violent methods naturally create "permanence of shape," in a "sensible corset." Could this text have been attached to this image through a mix-up? The picture shows no factory, no machines, no labor. Only in the phrase "comfortable and shapely" does the text come within light years of the dreamy undress, the seductive languor, the elegant, leisured sexuality, that call out from the image. Presumably the reader was by this time well schooled in the double consciousness required by such an ad, and indeed by consumer culture in general.

I have focused on relations between image and text, and in particular on gaps in meaning. My claim is that readers had learned how to supply connections, fill gaps, participate in the construction of meaning. Older advertising practices had, to be sure, helped clear the semiotic way: outdoor display paintings, posters, and trade cards. The latter came closest to the aims and formats of 1890s magazine ads. Although in the ante-bellum period these small illustrated cards chiefly promoted the wares and services of local merchants, after the war manufacturers circulated millions of them to advertise branded products: patent medicines and threads above all, but, increasingly, soaps, canned meats, flour, cereals, clothing, small appliances, and other such commodities. From the 1870s on, with the perfection of chromolithography, most cards were in color, and more elaborate in design than any magazine ads of the period, or for that matter of the 1890s. They often imaged the product, its package, its symbol, or its use. They linked it semi-arbitrarily to people (comic negroes, Uncle Sam, children, handsome women) and scenes (pastoral landscapes, the Brooklyn Bridge). Most pertinently, they joined images to texts.[16]

But the way they did that signals a major difference between trade cards and magazine ads. The bulk of the copy was on the back of the card. Released from direct confrontation with the image, and thus from the spatially implied need to annotate it, copy could and did speak at length about the uses and virtues of the product, where to buy it, where to write for catalogs and premiums. (In this respect the trade card worked like the R & G Corsets ad, whose image in fact resembles those on many a corset trade card.) To put this the other way around, separation from practical text freed up the image to be mythic, playful,

Figure 17 R & G Corsets ad, *Munsey's*, March 1900

primitive, nostalgic, artistic, patriotic, humorous, erotic, or various combinations of these. Although some images did make direct, utilitarian
appeals, and a very few linked the product to tableaux of middle class
domesticity,[17] for the most part, trade card iconography belonged to an
older advertising tradition of the fantastic and carnivalesque, well analyzed by Jackson Lears in *Fables of Abundance.*[18] The extent to which these
images acted as floating signifiers is suggested by the means of their distribution – passed out by storekeepers to customers after a purchase or
included in the manufacturer's package as a kind of bonus – and by the
ultimate uses to which millions were put – collected as curiosities in
albums or posted as art on people's walls: either way, with pragmatic
copy hidden from view, and utilitarian aim deflected.

The kinds of signification examined in this chapter built on earlier,
eclectic practices of advertising, but I believe that readers of magazine
ads learned to construct their meaning chiefly through the tutelage of
the new ad men themselves, who sometimes explained anomalies, sometimes alluded suggestively to them, sometimes ignored them. Both
parties to this exchange were learning a kind of language.[19] To learn a
language is to become a particular kind of person, one who knows that
syntax, those logical relations, that lexicon, those concepts. (I speak
metaphorically; advertising is not literally a language.) Perforce, the
audience absorbed a semantics of commodities as it learned to read
ads, since ads are about commodities. This is not to say that everyone
internalized these ways of making meaning, passively and uncritically.
Then as now, some "saw through" ads, scorned them, took offense,
resisted their premises. Even such folk learned the system, if they read
ads at all. To just that extent, they became the "you" invoked by the
voice from nowhere.

Advertisers aimed at a result more specific than that, of course. They
wanted the real person out there to see herself or himself in a compelling relation to *a* product, not just to *all* products. Inevitably, while
discussing the reader's decoding of the advertisement, I have also
touched upon this subject – speaking, for instance, of how some pictures
have a place in them for the viewer to occupy. Accept the visual invitation, and "you" are in a relation to the product as well. I now offer some
thoughts that bear directly on this relation.

It had (and has), really, just one general form: if you used X, you
would become Y, or like Y, or your life would be changed in way Z.
Sometimes the promise is explicit: "Mellin's Food will make milk agree
with *your* baby . . . ." Sometimes it works through a surrogate for "you":
Packer's Tar Soap made Nurse Curtis's hair long and lovely; therefore
(the unstated inference) it will do the same for yours. Sometimes it
mutes or fudges causation: "Professional people prefer Pears' Soap"
(if you prefer it, you will be like them). And sometimes the promise
is neither stated nor implied, except through the reader's ability to

understand the magical language of ads: "Drink Coca-Cola" (and you will be like that sophisticated, young, affluent, and rather sexy couple). "Put a Kodak in *Your* Pocket" (and be like that impeccably dressed gentleman). This is the logic – the "imagery" – of "self-transformation through purchase," in Lears's nice phrase (p. 42). Yet accompanying the magical promise, sometimes overshadowing it, is an implied statement: you *already are* like the right people. (Therefore buy the product they buy.) The general form is unvarying and unsurprising. All interest resides in whatever substance ads give to the idea of "like."

My reader already has a fair idea what connections were salient, and I will pass over most, concentrating on just four of them. A plethora of ads, for instance, assumed the reader to value health, youth, and good looks. The Coke ad combines these appeals; singly or in various combinations, they grounded very many ads of the period, more than indicated by the ones reproduced here. Good looks in particular were posed as an ideal; youth had not yet been valorized to the degree that happened later. My tally of appeals made by ads that explicitly addressed women gives beauty first place. Even in the *Ladies' Home Journal*, with its emphasis on family values, beauty ranks third out of the seven appeals I identified as dominant, led only by nurture and social emulation.[20] Nor did advertisers expect only women to seek good looks through purchases; appearance runs ahead of success as the leading value in ads addressed to men. The magazines presented hundreds of images encouraging the reader's wish to be attractive. The only significant gender difference: then as now, the erotic was primarily a feminine category. (There were ads for men's underwear, but none remotely so evocative as the one for R & G corsets.) That, for both sexes, the purchase of commodities available everywhere was offered as the avenue to outstanding good looks, is a tension inherent in the promotion of mass-produced goods, and in the discourse of advertising, with its plural address and individual reception.

That tension exists in another very large group of ads, linking reader to product through celebrations of family and home. Many of the products were for home care and improvement, and the magazines themselves were a kind of home product, for family consumption. Naturally, then, sellers of shingles, heating systems, paint, furniture, tableware, cleaning powders, and so on would press these commodities upon readers as means toward beautification and elaboration of the home. More noteworthy was the imaging of a desirable home setting around simple, inexpensive consumables like breakfast foods, as in Figures 8, 12, and 16. Oatmeal contributes nothing to the appearance of one's house, and may be eaten in a tenement or a rural shack. The association of such foods with elegant suburban homes was as arbitrary as it was common. At this period, too, ads began to appear that tied such products to domestic warmth and care; many envisioned the feeding of

The first step towards lightening

The White Man's Burden

is through teaching the virtues of cleanliness.

Pears' Soap

is a potent factor in brightening the dark corners of the earth as civilization advances, while amongst the cultured of all nations it holds the highest place—it is the ideal toilet soap.

Figure 18 Pears' Soap ad, *McClure's*, October 1899

people as an act of loving nurture, rewarded by love. Especially common
were ads featuring small children, their welfare dependent upon the
choice of the right baking powder or laundry soap. Nothing more typi-
fies advertising today than the invitation to prove one's worthiness as
wife and mother, express one's affection, and hold one's family together,
by acting correctly in the market, buying a commodity mass-produced by
strangers. That contradictory appeal has its roots in the first epoch of
national brand advertising.

I want to linger a bit on the other two appeals, central to turn-of-the-
century advertising, which imply and sometimes exploit such
contradictions. One is the exaltation of the historically new, a value that
became almost universal in ads of the period. One might dismiss this
appeal as intrinsic to advertising, in that sellers must encourage the
reader to abandon a familiar product, or to try a genre of product she
has never used before. Besides, many consumer goods of the 1890s and
1900s *were* innovations: pocket cameras, safety razors with disposable
blades, horseless carriages, and such; while many others – breakfast
cereal, bar soap, tinned meat – were produced and packaged in historically new ways. But inspection of the ads of 1880 (Figure 2) reveals that
not a single one pressed the claim of newness, unless it is there in Mason
& Hamlin's phrase, "rare excellence now attained." Several of the products could easily have been promoted for their advance over earlier
brands or earlier kinds of consumption: Victor Baby Food, Hanford's
Baking Powder, Hop Bitters, Kidney Wort, Garmore's Artificial Ear
Drum, Birch's watch key, even the cheap chromos whose profusion at
this time was a triumph of productive technique. But the copywriters
were silent on this theme, while, two decades later, ad after ad sought to
link products to innovation or modernity. Kodak listed high tech features; Kelly-Springfield aligned itself with the invention of the rubber
tire; Pope-Toledo glorified unheard-of rates of speed; R & G promoted
its "new number 397" and its advanced methods of production; Quaker
Oats advised readers to give up the old custom of eating meat at breakfast; Coca-Cola associated its drink with two newly modish sports; Ivory
stretched for affinities with the modern navy; and so on.

Time had become progressive, overwhelming readers with novelty,
and generating a wish to be in the vanguard of history. A few advertisers
sought connections between their products and incidents on the grand
stage of historical event: any reader in 1900 would have understood
Ivory's allusion to the great victory at Manila Bay. Through a representation of Admiral Dewey himself, and through its connection between soap
and imperial destiny, Pears also joined in the forward march of history
(Figure 18). A few ads began to appear, too, that tied products to notori-
ous cultural movements. From Rubifoam's appropriation of 1890s
feminism (Figure 19) to Virginia Slims' appropriation of the 1970s brand
is not a very long way at all (baby). But mainly, advertisers stayed within

Figure 19 Rubifoam ad, *Cosmopolitan*, August 1896

the spheres of production and consumption, as they imaged modernity. And surely the changes they had wrought in production explain why an ideology of newness permeated the language of advertising after 1890. It hailed readers as smart, up-to-date, venturesome, PMC people precisely because advertisers had to foster a new way of life that depended on their commodities, and help the audience feel good about the new terms of existence, as if those terms were both inevitable and intelligently chosen. Ad men were "missionaries of modernity."[21] I have no doubt that PMC readers did welcome the new way of life and many of the new commodities. At the same time, major shifts in material and moral culture are always in part disquieting to all but the most blinkered of yuppies. The shift through the end of the nineteenth century had been abrupt. Middle aged people could remember a time when Manhattan was mainly farmland, when there were no large corporations outside of the railroad business, when most communities were largely self sufficient, when most families grew what they ate and made what they wore, when markets were small and local, when industrial capitalism had yet to win its hegemony on the field of battle. As they ceded large areas of material life to distant corporations, middle class people gained healthier food, warmer houses, ease of movement, sanitary plumbing, a host of benefits; but they lost much that had made for continuity, community, and manageable scale. Advertisers, for all their boosterism, could not ignore the reality of these dislocations, nor the practical necessity of building trust.

A common strategy for doing so led to a conflation of modernity and tradition that still pervades mass culture. The Quaker Oats ad of 1895 (Figure 6) is an example. The new figures here as the product itself, in its specific and novel use as a breakfast food; as the motto *"Pure,"* suggesting advanced methods of production; as the manufactured package, in silent opposition to the unbranded barrel of oats; in the legend at the bottom of the page, with its insistence on a new way of buying things, and in the absence of the corporation's name and address – the brand, already known to the instructed audience, can stand by itself. But the weight of symbolism in the ad tilts the other way. A seventeenth-century Quaker, with his intimations of solidity, thrift, and old-fashioned good sense, arbitrarily represents the new product. The text – again, arbitrarily – links it to a proverb, with its wisdom from time out of mind, from an oral tradition largely banished by the industrial and commercial relations that actually surround the ad. Modernity encompasses the traditional and comforting, we are to think. The new builds on the old, without rupture. Quaker Oats pressed this contradiction remorselessly.

We can see it elsewhere. Rubifoam is "up-to-date," but like the New Woman, it respects those things that never go out of fashion. Kelly-Springfield's modern product fits easily into the culture of an old upper class (driving carriages not cars, in 1905). Ditto for Londonderry. An old-fashioned baby validates what the experts at Mellin's know about nutrition. Henry Ward Beecher speaks from the grave, and with ancestral authority, about the virtues of Pears' Soap. The contradiction in the R & G ad, already noted, is a variation: the most advanced methods of production yield a product that releases an erotic, private selfhood now made elusive by industrial rhythms and demands. Similarily, many ads hinted that machinery's triumph over nature had preserved or even restored an organic human connection to it: the glimpse of yard from the Vitos kitchen, the window opening the Cream of Wheat dining room into a garden, the rubber tire as means of access to park preserve, the association of Coca-Cola with pastoral golf links. Some ads did more than hint. Nature and industrial product seamlessly join in another Cream of Wheat ad (Figure 20), while the traditional way of life depicted easily accommodates scientific expertise about "gluten, phosphates, nitrates." Marchand says of interwar advertising that "techniques for empathizing with the public's imperfect acceptance of modernity" were what made it modern (p. 13). The point is apt, and for the period of my concern, too.

Even more common and more straightforward than the appeal to modernity was the final appeal I will consider. Ads consistently addressed readers as belonging to one of the two highest social classes, or as aspiring to be like such people. All but three or four of the ads reproduced here do so, directly or obliquely, through text or through image. Surveying appeals to women in nine issues of *McClure's, Munsey's,* and the *Ladies' Home Journal,* I found slightly more in this category than in any other. (I grouped appeals to propriety, respectability, and stylishness together

Figure 20 Cream of Wheat ad, *Century*, April 1900

with those relating the product to a high social position.) These were ten cent magazines read by broad audiences, though of course not by "everybody." One might construe an "upscale" ad in *Atlantic, Harper's* or *Century* as addressing people who had already achieved affluence and social standing, and as confirming their sense of superiority while showing it to be compatible with the use of common, branded goods. In the cheaper magazines, such an ad assumed the wish to emulate, and to rise. Either way, it took the social hierarchy for granted, constituting its audience as as one that valued prestige. The point is evident, in all those well-appointed tables, elegant sideboards, respectable professionals, happy servants, leisured ladies, and well-dressed men. I will not belabor it.

I simply want to suggest that in this appeal, too, resides one of the central contradictions of consumer culture. "Put a Kodak in *Your* Pocket" was the paradigmatic message, with its implication that if you do, you will join the social community of others who do, and with the further implication that your enlistment in it will represent either a step up in the social scale or the conservation of your already achieved position. Advertisements showed no Kodaks sliding into patched or ragged pockets. No bottles of Londonderry spring water appeared on makeshift tables made out of crates. No hod carriers drank Coca-Cola while eating their lunches from pails, "after exercise." When the lower orders did (rarely) appear in ads, in other than famulary roles, their presence generally connoted *failure* to use the product, as in Figure 21;[22] and even here, the lower caption holds out a possibility that the black girl *could* be "like" the white girl. Ad men linked even cheap products to envied social status, inviting consumers to rise through their purchase and use.

This was not and is not a hollow promise; by using certain goods in certain ways, people do signal and in part create their class positions. But the "you" of advertising reached many people then, and many more now, for whom the promise was chimerical. You could join one or more consumer groups (Williamson nicely calls them "totemic") by using Cream of Wheat, Coca-Cola, and so on, and not alter your class standing a whit. In fact, since marketing sought to get these products into everybody's hands and mouths, to the extent that it succeeded it canceled its promise to mark the buyer as superior. Invidious consumption feeds on itself like a mythical snake. Marchand calls such advertising a "Parable of the Democracy of Goods":

> By implicitly defining "democracy" in terms of equal access to consumer products, and then by depicting the everyday functioning of that "democracy" with regard to one product at a time, [advertising] tableaux offered Americans an inviting vision of their society as one of incontestable equality" (p. 218).

Already in the 1890s, this conflicted ideology had lodged itself in the

Figure 21 Pears' Soap ad, *Ladies' Home Journal,*
December 1899

center of advertising practice. Its entrenchment has not, in my view,
done much for the understanding of social process or for political
democracy itself.

By the beginning of the twentieth century, ad men had developed a
language that spoke through connections between image and text, and
connections among product, index, reader, and disembodied corporate
voice. As they engaged real readers in this discourse, they presumed
tacit knowledge of its principles of meaning, and acceptance of its taken-
for-granted values. Thus they constituted readers in ways I have tried to
describe here, ways that involved naturalizing deep contradictions and
magical systems of meaning. Let me repeat two disclaimers. First, many
ads of the period were less mystifying than those on which I have concentrated. Second, many readers remained skeptical or scornful. But all
readers *could* participate in the most magical idioms of advertising, and
it was hard for any but the poor, rural, or illiterate not to be readers of
at least some ads, not to take part in this new literacy of goods.

On the Ethos of Consumption

I have stressed contradictions, impossibilities, obfuscations. If in doing so, I have implied that the universe of advertising's discourse was a troubled one, the ads themselves, looking out from my pages, refute any such idea. This was a cheerful world. As a *New York Evening Post* editorialist commented in 1909, newspaper ads stood in sharp contrast to the dire news they accompanied:

> What a reconstructed world of heart's desire begins with the first-page advertisement. Here no breakfast food fails to build up a man's brain and muscle. No phono records fail to amuse. No roof pane cracks under cold or melts under the sun. No razor cuts the face or leaves it sore. Illness and death are banished by patent medicines and hygienic shoes. Worry flies before the model fountain pen. Employers shower wealth upon efficient employees. Insurance companies pay what they promise. Trains always get to Chicago on time. Babies never cry; whether it's soap or cereal, or camera or talcum, babies always laugh in the advertising supplement. A happy world indeed, my masters![23]

Even aside from the efficacy of products and services, the represented world of magazine advertising was heartening. Smart, handsome people; impeccable homes; elegant social panoramas; an easy relationship to nature; uncontested well being.

Along the way, I have more than once paused to insist that some technique was not, as one or another scholar had thought, an innovation of the 1920s or after; in the postscript to this chapter I will elaborate on that claim. It is interesting to note, however, two common tactics of 1920s advertising that are indeed hard to find in the earlier period. One is the negative appeal, or "scare copy." As Marchand, Stuart Ewen,[24] and others have shown, terrors lurked in 1920s ads. Halitosis, scummy teeth, "ashtray breath," premature wrinkles, dull fingernails, and a host of other deficiencies constantly threatened to exile the reader from reputable company or even spousal affection. A woman's home was a nest of pitfalls; guests might judge her socially unfit should they spy an old-fashioned toilet seat in her bathroom. A man's career might stall or end if he failed to use the right soap or razor blade before an interview. As the Lynds said, ads "aiming to make the reader emotionally uneasy, to bludgeon him with the fact that decent people don't live the way *he* does," were common in the 1920s; they were unusual a generation earlier.[25]

To be sure, a few patent medicine ads continued to mention "vile diseases" around 1900, but always instantly curable. A soap ad warned mothers that failure to use the product on babies might lead to pimples later. Cuticura announced that "March Winds Chap Tender Skins," but the text moved on immediately to the remedy. An ad for the Brunswick-

Balke-Collender pool table urged, "Mothers – Keep Your Boys at Home"; but the accompanying picture showed the boys happily shooting pool with the rest of the family, not slouching into degeneracy at the local pool hall. One handgun ad showed a terrified couple discovering a burglar; more showed armed citizens *confounding* criminals. Even life insurance ads rarely asked the husband to imagine his wife and children left destitute, as was common in the 1920s. Scanning the ads I have reproduced, you can see that they are almost entirely silent on the dangers of *not* using a product. Life is not disastrous without it, only better with it.

Commentators on the 1920s have also remarked that ads frequently offered products as antidotes to ills or malaise brought on by industrial life itself. Demanding competition, the fast pace of work, decline of parental authority, challenges to autonomy and individuality, redefinition of gender roles, and so on, all made it urgent for people to seek remedy in the consumer marketplace. Not so around 1900. Nary an ad I've found suggested that economic and social change – surely as rapid at the time as during the 1920s – had imperiled health, family, or personal identity. Progress was unequivocal. Advertised goods did not defend one against its cruel undercurrents: they praised and manifested it. Cultural historians and critics who see life with commodities as rather pathetic "compensatory fulfillment" for the loss of traditional meanings now banished by capitalist social relations misread, I think, not just the ethos of early national advertising, but the PMC's active construction of new meanings and historical agency that I traced in chapter 7.[26] To derive a critique of industrialism and urbanization from these ads, one has to study absences, rifts, and contradictions, for explicit content presents no such critique.

The *Post* editorialist was right; this was a sunny moment in the ad world. Taken as a whole, these commercial images and advisements exuded confidence about the present and optimism about the future. They admitted no doubts about the social system. Schudson's just aphorism, "Advertising is capitalism's way of saying 'I love you' to itself" (p. 232), was more apt then than it is now. Then, no insecurity prompted manufacturers to shine their corporate images or explain to audiences the superiority of free enterprise and the American way of life. Social tableaux conveyed that message without words. Pleasure and self-satisfaction abounded, conferring their blessings on products. Jackson Lears holds that from the 1890s to the 1920s, the "most persistent theme in all national advertising was the promise that the commodity would provide the purchaser with the fun of living."[27] Again, truer of the first date than the second. Romance surrounded products, from the sturdy and practical to the rare and elegant.

And one should not overlook what is most obvious in thumbing through any of these magazines: the advertisements themselves were a

spectacle, a cornucopia, a gallery of popular art. The Sears catalog let
products stand for themselves in crude icons, dazzling only by profusion.
Magazine advertising invented, celebrated, played, fantasized, deco-
rated. Frank Munsey claimed in 1895 that the ad pages of his magazine
had as much appeal for readers as did the editorial pages;[28] such modesty on the editor's part was probably not totally disingenuous. Ads
entertained, even as they smiled on the world of products, and on the
reader for having chosen well, or being about to choose well, from
among those products.

    Advertising instructs us in seeing and understanding the made
objects that surround us, which is to say, most of the perceived and
touched world that most people inhabit most of the time. (Those
"mosts" are there to allow that a forest ranger or vacationing backpacker
in the Sierras moves among un-made things, but even those fleeing the
made world take along ingenious arrays of commodities, and stumble
over discarded soft drink cans.) In re-presenting objects, ads connect
them to one another, to situations, to social processes, to us and our
desires. They teach us the "communicative function of goods,"[29] and
the place of goods in "our" way of living and imagining. If a large number of people take in ad messages, advertisements enter significantly
into the fabric of meanings that constitutes culture.

    By glossing these meanings, ads also explain how to participate in soci-
ety. They tell what meanings commodities have for other people,
whether just for the ad writer, for the celebrity endorser, for the average
user like Nurse Curtis, or for the imaginary people in ad images. So they
gesture toward courses of action by which "you" might become like those
exemplary people, join their company: to be modern like the owners of
those fine homes in the cereal ads, buy and use Cream of Wheat, Vitos,
and Quaker Oats. More broadly, as analysts have been saying for
decades, and as industry people were saying before 1900, an ad for any
product tends to promote *all* products except its direct competitors, in
that it speaks well of consumption as a means of participation in the
desired society. Plumping for modernity, 1890s ads identified it with the
use of branded commodities in general; no ad implied (absurdly) that a
dirt farmer or sweated seamstress could be modern by introducing just
one advanced product into his or her milieu. Participation meant organizing one's activities around many of the new branded commodities.

    These analyses apply with special force to turn-of-the-century adver-
tising. Its ebullience, optimism, and neighborly good sense flowed
together in an untroubled stream. As it assigned new meanings to goods,
it showed little awareness of conflicts among those meanings, and anticipated little resistance. There was, apparently, no need for ad men to
acknowledge a tension between work and leisure, or to offer products as
defenses against the system that produced them (as is the case now
whenever an advertiser insists that a product is "natural"), or to coopt

themes from oppositional movements (for example, the use of black professionals and liberated women in TV commercials). Needs are always social, consumption is always social, as Schudson and others have well said. Advertising has not corrupted some golden age culture in which people satisfied only "real" needs. But through most of its history, national advertising, taken as a totality of messages, has in one way or another acknowledged that the social comprehends processes and needs that are at odds with one another. It barely did so in the moment of its first flowering – though this was a time of labor battles, Jim Crow repression, populist resistance, suffragism, temperance crusades, and so on. "Advertising, in its modern forms, . . . operates to preserve the consumption ideal from the criticism inexorably made of it by experience," says Raymond Williams.[30] Just so. What needs commentary is why at its inception modern advertising took so little cognizance of that critique.

I suggest two answers, one obvious and one less so. First, there was no need to *preserve* this particular consumption ideal because it had not previously existed. This is not to say, of course, that Gilded Age Americans abstained from purchase and use of material goods. Famously, they bought chromolithographs by the millions, roamed the department store palaces, added filigree detail to furniture and houses, and filled the latter with bric-a-brac. Decoration was not the principle of the new brand name commodities, however. Mainly utilitarian items, they bespoke uniformity and a streamlined home life. Advertisers glorified that new ideal without much check from "experience," which had not yet brought round the revenges of consumerist modernity. Who expected, for instance, that Gillette blades and Coke bottles would pave a garden path toward global trash glut? The consumption ideal struck some as vulgar, but such feelings did not impede the vision of simple, sanitary, efficient, economical progress.

The less obvious reason for turn-of-the-century advertising's untroubled buoyancy is that it carried on a conversation among the like-minded. Its upscale inflection expressed a wide agreement that the audience could and should mark its respectability by adopting – and leading others into – the new style of living. The other themes I have stressed harmonize with this one. The pursuit of commodified good looks, the vision of the peaceful and well-appointed family home, and the affiliation with modernity joined together to form an ideal well within reach of the PMC, and partially achievable by millions of others who aspired to membership in that class. The structure of feeling organized by these ads flattered such people, addressed them as the bearers of enlightened progress, equated their well being with the well being of the whole society, as ideology always does. Ad men, themselves professional aspirants and, by income, equals of the audience, were experiencing a tonic rush of success. There is no reason to suspect them of cynically promoting a social ideal they saw as hollow. The unreal "you" of their discourse was also, for them, a "we." Through it they said "I love you" to their own class.

How could advertising's love song muffle dissonant noises from other social quarters? No mystery surrounds ad men's relation to the industrial ruling class. It paid the tab for their new enterprise. They had to take on its project as their own, in the sphere of marketing and consumption, and they did so with conviction. This was a matter of genuine common interest. Nor did corporate interests collide with those of the audience in this sphere. Mass producers wanted millions to buy convenience goods, and millions welcomed those goods as aids to sensible living. That it should be *admirable* living as well was a nice side benefit. Across the market, relations between the PMC and the ruling class were unproblematic.

More conjecturally, in the spheres of work and social control latent tensions had not yet become acute. True, even before S.S. McClure gave Ida Tarbell the go-ahead to write about Standard Oil, in 1901, one wing of the PMC had identified itself with a critique of the corporate order. But that critique was mainly reformist, and in any case it had already found mild expression in central projects of the PMC: rationalizing production, bringing science into technique, regulating trade, professionalizing government, ameliorating the lot of the poor, and so on. The PMC could deplore arrogant trusts and robber barons, yet see the former as deviant and the latter as vestigial, while seeing most of the new corporations as dynamic, efficient, and progressive allies in the making of a beneficent social order. Nor was such a perception inaccurate, as business shaped "Progressive Age" reforms to its own ends. So advertising's sunny view of the corporate world probably raised few hackles.

As for small farmers, industrial workers, and the immigrant poor: ad men would not have thought it advantageous to remind readers of their needs and struggles. I don't think it was necessary, either, in the way that it became necessary around 1970, for advertisers to allude (reassuringly) to social movements. Populism weakened as an independent movement after 1892; frightening strikes became fewer after 1894; imperialism presented itself as in the interests of all (see Figure 18); a string of prosperous years from 1896 on nourished the hope that a new corporate order could gradually bring the masses into the scope of its benign gaze. PMC activists were working toward that end; others could easily ignore disagreeable events and dangerous classes during leisure hours, when ads spoke to them of reputable homes and modern products. So national advertising burgeoned as an optimistic discourse outside the arena of class conflict, even as one offering to *resolve* class conflict through the democracy of goods.

For a while in the early days of its eminence, national brand advertising did that without much check from reality. It opened vistas of free choice and self improvement; it outlined personal and class identities for readers to step into through purchases; it spoke of social advancement

both accompanied and facilitated by consumer comforts. In the intervening hundred years, it has continued to put forward all these
enticements. But at the beginning, within the safe confines of a middle
class medium, the contradictions of individuality and mass, invidiousness
and democracy, were less nagging than they have since become. People
had not been consuming in this new way long enough to suspect that its
satisfactions would always germinate the seeds of new anxieties, or that
the prophets of consumption were building a case for it that went
beyond any reasonable expectation. The only vehement resistance to
advertising expressed feelings that it was too strident, too insistent a
presence, too vulgar. Ad men combatted that resistance by improving
their skills, making the images more polished, perfecting techniques of
ingratiation, being reasonable, not lying so much. They accommodated
their discourse to the manners and expectations of decent people.

As they naturalized it in this way, they also inevitably changed those
manners and expectations. Does advertising shape values, or just reflect
them? Of course it does both. If it did not reflect and flatter the audience's values, the audience would slam the door on its foot. The
question of whether advertising is conservative or trend-setting seems to
me similarly miscast. It *must* offer both to conserve what people want
conserved (home, family, and so on) and to keep them in step with the
march of fashion, indeed of history. It must say both "you can be the
same you" and "you can be a new you." That follows from advertising's
most rudimentary aim: to get people to admit new objects and habits
into their old lives.

Recognizing these banal truths leads some to conclude that advertising really doesn't matter much, or even that things could not be
otherwise than the way they are. Such views issue from a kind of solip-
sism of the present century. Once the consumer culture built its
momentum up, advertising could not be held accountable for the way
we were, or are. And as J. Walter Thompson already saw in 1909, one
could not have deleted advertising from the social process without
changing everything else. But there was a moment when "everything
else" was not yet in place. I have lingered for a long time on that
moment, trying to recreate the sense of history as a field of possibilities,
even if also powerfully driven toward some and away from others.
Advertising made a difference then, not just by opening the gates of
vision onto a new way of life and helping bring it about, but by engaging
millions of people in a previously unknown discourse about objects, persons, and social relations. The discourse itself, I have insisted, was a
social relation of world historical consequence.

It was a discourse of power, speaking in an amiable voice to those who
had no answering voice, and whose desires and ideas were persuasively
conceptualized where the amiable voice originated – in ad agencies.
Agents looked after their own interests, but could hope to succeed only

by taking on the projects and the interests of still more powerful men. Those men needed a particular kind of social order, peopled by consumers rather than by citizens or by workers. Of course we are all three. To address us as only the first was a pivotal act of mystification, taking the fetishism of commodities well beyond the stage it had reached when Marx made his brilliant observations.[31]

Stuart Ewen has received a good deal of criticism for seeing 1920s advertising as part of a conscious plan to buy off resistance to capitalism and create a docile social order beyond the workplace (in *Captains of Consciousness*). It was not a conscious plan for most businessmen who adopted this strategy; the criticism is partially just. But I hope to have shown the intricate ways in which it *was* a plan of sorts, incrementally shaped by generals, captains, and corporals of consciousness,[32] as well as by the quartermasters of consumption – the people who read the ads and bought the goods. Ewen deserves credit for having restored politics and broad social power to the story of advertising's growth. Corporate leaders around 1900 did not know just what story they were writing or how it would turn out, but they knew who would draft its plot and with what general ends in mind. It was in many ways a happy plot, as the typewriter, lamp, and radio that enable and ease my work of criticism assure me. Yet the social relations of its writing foreclosed any chance of its being a democratic story.

Postscript

The reader will have noticed in my text and notes an intermittent dispute with other scholars over the dating of trends and practices, perhaps amounting to a kind of 1890s chauvinism on my part. I do consider the question important, but on the assumption that only specialist readers will be as taken by it as I am, I have relegated a fuller discussion to these paragraphs.

Beginning with Ewen's *Captains of Consciousness* (1976), there has been an extraordinary revival of interest in the history of advertising. I have profited immensely from Ewen's work and that of Pope, Lears, Schudson, Marchand, Fox, and Leiss, Kline, and Jhally, to mention just a few. Not only have some of them opened up new veins of material; all of them (except Fox, whose purpose is different) have brought a sophistication and depth to this inquiry that distinguishes them from earlier historians like Presbrey, Hower, Wood, and Turner. (Raymond Williams pointed the way with a 1960 study, later included in *Problems in Materialism and Culture*, but he concentrated on British advertising.) I am indebted to them all.

So it is in the spirit of collaboration rather than rebuke that I want to correct an impression given by many of these studies: that advertising took on its characteristically modern forms only in the 1920s and after. Some of these scholars do not deal with earlier periods; those who do, like Pope and Fox, do not discuss older advertisements themselves in detail, or reproduce them. Merely *by* reproducing a selection of them here, I hope to have demonstrated that for all its crudeness in comparison to later advertising, that of the decade around 1900 established themes, techniques, ideologies, and ways of generating sense that most scholars assign to later periods. I am not speaking of "firsts" – the first full-page display ad, the first use of photography, the first color ad, the first use of a famous painting, and so on – but of the time by which certain styles became common enough for us to assume that the audience saw them as routine, and understood their language as part of its tacit knowledge. I will mention just four main points.

First, to repeat myself, some scholars say or imply that extravagant use of visuals was rare in early national advertising, and that lengthy texts generally carried the burden of persuasion. I have already presented my case for a different view. On a similar theme, Marchand says that "In the early 1920s the photograph was still the exception in advertising art" (p. 149). Perhaps he means "art" in an honorific sense. Photographs invaded ad sections quickly during the late 1890s. There were 20 photos in *McClure's*, December 1895; 61 in October 1899; 11 in *Munsey's*, October 1895; 36 in May 1900. Much of this photography was not artful at all, but purely iconic. Still, its popularity shows how eagerly ad men seized upon a new visual possibility. More important than that, for my case, is the fact that already by 1900 many ads relied on readers to understand cryptic or contradictory relations between visual and text, a development that Leiss, Kline, and Jhally associate with the post-World War II period (p. 151). Mystification and magic came in with national advertising itself.

Second, Marchand (pp. 15–16), Leiss, Kline, and Jhally (second edition, pp. 63, 231, 279–81, 330–44) and others suggest that the foregrounding of *people* (rather than products) was a late development, as was the personalizing of voice and address. Again, I have already shown this process at work in the 1890s. It virtually had to happen then, since that was when ad men undertook to mediate between corporations and individual readers. The personalized text was an inevitable strategy.

Third, some scholars imply that only gradually, through the twentieth century, did advertisers realize the "communicative function of goods" for marking "distinctions – honor, prestige, power, rank – in social groups" (Leiss, Kline, and Jhally, pp. 46–7). Turn-of-the-century advertising offered an intensive course of instruction in just this kind of communication, as it invited readers to signal prestige and rank through the use of unlikely commodities like soap, cereal, and spring water. No theme was more insistent.

Fourth, and most generally, there seems to be wide agreement that advertising in its early national phase concentrated on describing the product and its functioning (or even the processes of its making – see Ewen, p. 80), and later shifted to more and more indirect benefits accruing from use of the product, as well as to emotional appeals, symbolism, totemism, and so on. Leiss, Kline, and Jhally offer a four-stage schema for the historical evolution of the trade which makes this assumption about early advertising (pp. 189–215, 23–36, 277–97). The schema is certainly helpful in thinking about statistical trends, but it should not be understood as tracing the emergence of themes and communicative methods. All the techniques these authors associate with later periods were in prolific use by 1900. To be sure, very many ads also lingered on qualities of the product, but even in these the description was often less "informative," and the information less central to the ad's purpose, than the schema implies (for example, Figures 3, 5, 8, 11, 12, 14). Early on, advertisers moved away from informative copy, and the more expensive the ad, the more likely it was to emphasize other values. That, too, strikes me as inevitable: most individual ads, by 1900, were installments in extended campaigns, and one could hardly expect many new buyers to be won by explaining for the 387th time what ingredients a breakfast food contained and how they facilitated digestion. A discourse of repetition quickly uses up facts, makes them stale, drives ad makers toward less concrete meanings.

Advertising of the 1920s looks and sounds quite a bit different from turn-of-the-century advertising, but these four claims do not capture the differences. As noted, scare copy and the promotion of anxiety took off in the 1920s. So did narrative and dramatic advertising rendering social crises and happy solutions. (Interestingly, many ads of the period told their stories at leisurely length, asking several minutes' worth of the reader's attention – a less common demand in 1900, I believe.) Social tableaux became more elaborate and cleverly mimetic. A comparative study would reveal much more, and might suggest important principles of cultural change. But visual extravagance, personalization, social status, and communicative magic, called into play by corporate needs and the peculiar relations of the discourse, permeated brand advertising at the outset.

9

Charting Social Space

Advertising pages brought news of useful and reputable goods; they taught readers a symbolism of commodities and social life; they flattered a new class for its values while elaborating and clarifying those values – in ways advantageous to corporations, certainly; but still, ads met recognizable needs even as they shaped them. Who knows how many readers turned to the ad pages first, or tarried there longest? But in theory, audiences came for the journalism, fiction, and visual displays framed by (or in the *Ladies' Home Journal*'s case, mingled with) the ad pages. That cultural fare had to meet other kinds of need, had to give satisfactions that readers knew they wanted or at least should want. So it makes sense to approach the editorial content of the magazines by asking how it did that, how the newly successful editorial formulas were able to form a large group of people into an audience. Unfortunately, I cannot put that question to a sampling of readers, but must infer needs from the journalistic practices that apparently met them, as well as (the circularity is not complete) from additional information about those people and how they lived.

In chapter 7 I tried to synthesize a good deal of such information around the idea of social space, following the transformation of the old, walking city with its close juxtaposition of home and workplace and intermingling of social ranks into a conurbation far more segregated by types of activity (production, commerce, domesticity, culture) and by residential affinities. In the 1890s these two patterns coexisted and overlapped, with transition from the first to the second proceeding apace. The change, well underway in the 1870s, stirred both pride and anxiety, as many novels recall for us: Booth Tarkington's Ambersons creating their own fashionable fortress of a neighborhood in a fictionalized Indianapolis (*The Magnificent Ambersons*); Howells's Lapham family, realizing that Nankeen Square in the South End of Boston is not the place to live if their daughters are to prosper socially, and inaugurating their social climb with an architect-designed house on the New Land of Back Bay (*The Rise of Silas Lapham*); Wharton's Countess Olenska, courting the displeasure of Old New York by renting in a dowdy block of West 23rd Street, far over toward the river (*The Age of Innocence*).

Spatial distinctions like these had power for every urban family aspiring to respectability in the 1890s.

I believe that a central need of people who became readers of *Cosmopolitan*, the *Ladies' Home Journal*, and the rest was to fix their bearings in the fluid social space of that moment, and do so to their social advantage. Magazines that came into homes helped establish and announce the social level of those homes. They also provided their readers with a range of information and interests that linked them conversationally to other readers in the same circle of acquaintance, and culturally to like-minded readers across the nation. In this they collaborated with the reconfiguration of social space and with the new styles and meanings of consumption described in the last two chapters.

A main project of readers was to orient themselves, to be literally at home, on the new social terrain. It was an urgent task for editors and publishers to further that project, whether they understood it that way or not. It is my hypothesis that the magazines upon which I concentrate my attention helped stake out and survey the cultural ground being settled by the professional-managerial class, even as they made themselves a class.

To summarize earlier discussions: the PMC stood in a special relation to the means of production and to other classes; increasingly it felt and acted as a class, too. Engineers sensed a kinship not just with other engineers, but with urban administrators, lawyers, managers, health workers. Most subscribed to an ideal of the efficient, rational, planned society, in partial opposition to the untrammeled energies of capital. Most shared an allegiance to organized knowledge, with science itself as a kind of ideal, which the new university physically embodied, as well as giving a home to the multiplying "schools" that guarded and enlarged professional knowledge and credentialed new aspirants, and serving as a key institution of class reproduction. The youth of various PMC groups mingled in schools and colleges, intermarried, made homes in the suburbs and the "right" urban neighborhoods, ran those homes according to often tacit but well understood principles, raised children with suitable manners and ambitions, and associated with one another in an endless variety of clubs, churches, school boards, civic organizations, and so on. Such practices add up to a way of life, the culture of a class.

Culture in the *narrower* sense also plays an important part in the building of class identity. It cements affinities and quietly performs exclusions. Taste in music, dramatic performance, visual art, and home decoration cannot be reduced to class feeling, but is clearly much influenced by social peers. As noted in chapter 7, through the second half of the nineteenth century a process of cultural distinction and elaboration went forward in the United States, drawing class lines around spaces and activities perceived as cultural. Urban elites made decisive moves, founding museums, opera companies, and symphony orchestras under upper class trusteeship in the 1870s and 1880s, but admitting somewhat wider publics into these precincts of high culture. They fixed boundaries between art and entertainment, culture and spectacle, philanthropy and commerce, mapping a previously inchoate landscape along class-based coordinates. Elites carried forth the "sacralization" of art and culture: purging it of amateurism, widening the separation between creators and audiences, framing art as difficult and pure, divesting it of more accessible, popular elements. Barnum-like exhibits were distinguished from art museums; ragtime from the symphony. Vaudeville, dime novels, comics, the saloon and the dance hall, Coney Island and the nickelodeon, the ethnic club and the sports park drew more uniformly working class participants. Culture became a system that clearly signaled and manifested social class: refined and sacralized at the top of the hierarchy, pleasure-seeking and openly commercial at the bottom.

A more specifically middle class culture had also been developing through the century. Resolutely self-improving, it resided in proliferating Chautauquas, reading circles, lending libraries, correspondence schools, informative books, Protestant churches. Especially, it resided in the home: home conceived as refining and elevating, sealed off from corrupt politics and brutal marketplace, and redeemed by the ministrations of women. This culture valued information, enlightenment, and elevation of the spirit, whether found in *Godey's Lady's Book*, in domestic advice books, in sentimental fiction, in improving tracts, or (for children) in the pages of *St. Nicholas* and the *Youth's Companion*. It celebrated individual achievement, tempered with gentility and the domestic virtues.

The PMC-in-formation found in this inherited culture something to sustain it: especially the impulse toward self-improvement and the premium on information. But the new professionals, managers, and reformers, as they broadened the horizon of their life chances and claimed a share in national leadership, also experienced much in this older middle class culture as restrictive, perhaps enfeebling. Its construction of "a privileged domain of refinement, aesthetic sensibility, and higher learning" set too wide a gap between culture and world-changing activity.[1] Likewise, identification of culture with the feminine and the private sphere ill served the ambition of the new class to make its ideas, values, and tastes prevail in the world. Again, it wanted a culture more secular than that ruled by Protestant clergymen and disseminated through religious periodicals and books of sermons. After all, it grounded its social authority in science and expertise; its rectitude derived from certified knowledge rather than from piety. The PMC identified itself with the new, with progress, with the modern; it wanted a culture that privileged these ideals rather than looking to old verities.

It will be helpful to think about the new mass magazines as responding to such cultural needs and aspirations, as staking out a cultural middle ground. Not that the editors envisioned the audience they thought they were reaching in explicit terms of social class. McClure persistently spoke of his magazine as combining "the first excellence" and "the widest interest," with no contradiction "between popularity in a magazine and worth." He attributed his success to the realization that a large audience wanted the kinds of literature and illustration found in the elite magazines, but that the prices of those magazines made their "circle of readers . . . comparatively limited."[2] Responding to a slur in the *Independent* – that 10-cent magazines couldn't reach the "only audience worth addressing, . . . thinking people" – he made his defense simply by enumerating the fine writers published in *McClure's*.[3] Apparently he thought that perhaps half a million Americans wanted "the best" culture, and could afford it for a dime, but not for a quarter. If so, he saw his audience more in terms of taste than of class, since tens of millions could have afforded a dollar a year for *McClure's*, had they coveted it.

That is evident from a brief article in the *Ladies' Home Journal* by a Wisconsin school teacher, who, with his wife and two children, lived on an income of $200 a year, much less than the annual wages of a skilled factory worker. In analyzing his budget he explained, "since good reading matter should be in every home, we buy the *Ladies' Home Journal* and another dollar magazine, besides subscribing to an educational journal and two weekly papers."[4] In spite of this implied appeal to those on the lower fringe of decency, Curtis told advertisers none of the *Journal's* readers were poor; in fact, he claimed they had "the means to gratify luxurious tastes," and he sought the subscriptions of social register families.[5] Within the magazine, one could read knowledgeable talk about high culture, yet also learn the right way to wash underwear. The contradictory tugs were amusingly at work in a feature on how to serve terrapin cheaply.[6] The more realistic Bok knew that the magazine's readers were generally of the middle class (which he saw as a stabilizing influence between the dangerous lower class and the rotten upper class [Steinberg, p. 44]). Should this seem a stable enough boundary, however, one might note that Henry Mills Alden, for many years editor of the elite *Harper's*, held that "the main audience for the best literature" was "the great middle class."[7] Editors were less accustomed than advertising agents to think specifically about the class of their readerships, and I have found no evidence that McClure, Bok, Walker, or Munsey intended a role for their magazines in the construction of PMC identity.

But conscious intent is one thing, intuitive practice another. The very logic of the publishers' economic project drove them to take part in PMC class formation. They needed large circulations, in order to justify high advertising rates, and rely on ad revenues rather than magazine sales for profitability. But not any large circulation would do, as Frank Munsey had painfully learned when his schemes to promote circulation of the *Golden Argosy* succeeded brilliantly, but brought commercial failure because its youthful readership, having little money to spend, was not worth much to advertisers.[8] The large, potential audience that did have money to spend was the PMC and its older middle class fringes. How to reach that group? The 10-cent price surely helped, by taking the new magazines out of the realm of luxury consumption. But more critical was the cultural mix that differentiated these magazines from *Harper's*, *Atlantic*, and *Century*, with their presumptions of leisure and of high refinement already attained.[9] That cultural mix will be my subject through this chapter and the next. For now, it will be enough to repeat that the editorial contents of the magazines had to attract a PMC audience, for reasons grounded in the economics of the enterprise and, most deeply, in capital's need for wider and more reliable circulation of commodities. An opportune confluence of historical currents made that audience ready both for a national culture that would strengthen its class identity, and for brand name commodities themselves, presented by advertisers as invaluable to the creation of the modern, progressive, respectable self. Unlike the readership of a newspaper, clustered by locality and often by political allegiance, the readership of a national magazine was from the perspective of advertisers a group that consumed at a particular level, and from at least the intuitive perspective of editors, a social class.[10]

Magazine/*Magasin*

When one thinks of the mass circulation magazine as a physical object, and of how it mediated the world for its possessor, the resort to etymology is irresistible. Much more than earlier magazines, these were indeed like warehouses, profusely and quite miscellaneously stocked. What connects a French painting of Esther before King Ahasuerus, a profile and photograph of Mark Hanna, a genealogical account of the Carroll family of Maryland, a novel about "Carpathia," eight photographs of beautiful European and American women, a photographic essay on modern warships, sheet music for a song called "Plain Little Ann," commentary on the stage and its stars, a review of *Poker Stories*, a mocking survey of recent fads, a dozen or so short stories, and a handful of poems? Nothing obvious, but they all came bundled together in the October 1896 issue of *Munsey's Magazine*. Like museums of a slightly earlier time, these magazines were storehouses of the odd and the notable, but also of the commonplace.

They were also like *stores*, to pick up another etymological thread. The colored cover was an enticement to buy the magazine, seconded, often, by the editor's plugs and promotions; and something like half the pages were given over to images and descriptions of commodities for sale. What connects Mark Hanna to Quaker Oats? Or either of them to

Prudential insurance? We have become used to discontinuous forms, from vaudeville to the flow of TV entertainment and news and commercials, so that such juxtapositions seem normal. The nineteenth century had already made them familiar to city people, in public spaces like the exhibit hall and the department store. Magazines brought them into the home, into the hands, before the eyes.

That is important. Magazines had long been illustrated, but the new ones greatly increased visual display, and – *Munsey's* in particular – made halftone photoengravings a staple. To flip through the pages of one of these magazines was to have the eye pictorially arrested dozens of times, hundreds if the advertising pages are included. The initial impression, and perhaps the appeal, was as much of pictures accompanied by print as vice versa. That impression was partially borne out by the internal relations of photographs to print. Illustrations had been just that: pictures that illustrated something in the text; and whereas the new editors sometimes used photographs that way, often the photographs were the point of an article, with text demoted to commentary. To be sure, these magazines were drab in comparison to the ones we see now, but they made a sharp break with the greater plainness of earlier magazines.

The visual presentation of the magazine announced its own status as an elegantly made commodity that would grace a modern parlor, and the editors did not subdue its materiality. Nor its commercial project: they gave editorial space to accounts of its rising circulation, and boasted about price cuts, in 1893 and after, stressing the union of cheapness and quality. In other words, they addressed the reader as party to a novel business enterprise, customer hitched to an exciting trend. Further, they called attention to the actual process of making their commodity. In his famous ad in the *Sun* and in his magazine itself, Munsey spoke of the low price of paper and the modern printing machinery that made possible his 10-cent price. McClure expatiated on his new offices, near Madison Square, occupying "an entire floor . . . two-thirds of an acre . . . more than twenty windows at either end . . . three swift elevators to convey passengers, and two to convey freight." And he wrote in detail about his rotary presses, binding "appliances," and modern typesetting machines (*McClure's*, June 1896, p. 97). Walker, too, bragged about his (Hoe) presses, ran a history of the Hoe family and its printing achievements, and evoked *Cosmopolitan's* physical production graphically by running pictures of his new plant on the Hudson. Readers were invited to regard the magazine they held in their hands as a full realization of nineteenth-century business and industrial genius.

Paul DiMaggio traces the division of cultural experience into high and popular, with the former framed, sacralized, and distanced from its refined audience, and the latter frankly presented as commercial entertainment (see note 95, chapter 7). Against this dichotomy, the mass magazines were a hybrid. They offered their contents as surrounded by the aura of elite culture, yet simultaneously proclaimed their commodity status. This ambivalent appeal offended some, but was suited reasonably well to a PMC readership that wanted a distinguished culture yet also prided itself on its vigorous activity in the public sphere and its alignment with modern industry, science, and technique.

The kinship of "magazine" to "*magasin*", then, was more than etymological. To pursue it one step further, consider that three of the four leaders – all except *McClure's* – sorted much of their fare into *departments*, small sections that appeared month after month under the same title, so that a reader might regularly visit her favorite displays. In 1896–97, *Munsey's* featured "Artists and Their Work," "In the Public Eye," "Types of Fair Women," The World of Music," "The Stage," "Storiettes" (very brief stories), "Literary Chat," and "Etchings" (poetry). At the same time, *Cosmopolitan* had similar cultural departments as well as "The Progress of Science" and "The Month in England." The *Ladies' Home Journal* bred departments like rabbits. Regulars through the period were Bok's "Editorial Page," "Side Talks With Girls," "The Open Congress" (answers to miscellaneous questions), "Literary Queries," and "The King's Daughters" (social and moral advice for women). Finally, although McClure did not segment editorial contents in this way, his magazine presented its *advertisements* by category of merchandise: bicycles, jewelry, proprietary articles, typewriters, and so on, with a large "miscellaneous" section, thus evoking in print the experience of the department store.

In addition to named departments, the magazines further subdivided writing into unnamed but familiar genres. The policy was quite conscious at *Cosmopolitan*, where, according to one former editor, Walker classified the "products of the pen" roughly into groups, "as fiction, travel, sport and adventure, natural science, history, etc.," and held that every issue should have one of each group, so as "to attract the greatest possible number of readers."[11] The rationale for this scheme was apparently precise: Walker contended, for example, "that every magazine that went into the household should publish verse, since so many women keep scrapbooks filled, not with prose, but with lyrics and sonnets and ballads."[12] In short, the magazines included an astonishing potpourri of material, but organized explicitly and tacitly into categories that implied the diversity and individuality of taste among the readership, offering each member of the family something for his or her special pleasure or need. (This held for the *Ladies' Home Journal* as well, incidentally: it included a fair number of pieces addressed to men, and Bok considered it a magazine for the whole family, although its domestic advice was mainly for women.)

This positioning of the reader as free-choosing, individual consumer gains definition from his or her location as prospective buyer of any number of different magazines, perhaps as many as a hundred "general" monthlies, many of them in visible competition on newsstands as well as through self-advertisement. Even if one excluded the cheap "story papers" and the highbrow magazines, there was a wide range of middling fare to chose from. Nor, by any means, did the four 10-cent, mass circulation magazines under consideration here present identical profiles. A family might subscribe to all of them, and have the satisfaction of owning four distinct cultural products.

The distinction of the *Ladies' Home Journal* is of course plainest, against this comparison group. The others had nothing to set beside its advice columns, and its format called to mind the actual home with a specificity answering fully to its name. A single issue (February 1896) included two articles on kitchen affairs and dining; one on nursery furnishings; three on musical practices, plus a new song, evoking the music room; one on lingerie (the bedroom); one on repair of clothing (sewing room); a feature on parties (living room or parlor); two on gardens; and one on the whole house, "A $5000 Colonial Home" (with plans and drawings by the author, architect Ralph Adams Cram). Even aside from thematizing the home, the *Journal* was distinct in its patently instructional aims, which extended well beyond the regular columns. This issue contained a factual article on the presidency by Benjamin Harrison, an inspirational profile of the young queen of Holland, a confidential account for girls of "Womanliness" (by "Ruth Ashmore"), one on "Young Manhood" (by the Rev. Charles H. Parkhurst), an editorial by Bok urging young women to try domestic service rather than factory work, and a second endorsing the simplification of mourning customs. The *Journal* was moral, as well as domestic, and unembarrassed about it.

Munsey's resembled the *Journal* in its explicit pedagogy – telling the reader how to rate authors, critics, fashions – but in little else. It was ostentatiously worldly. If the *Journal* can be read as a moralized tour of the home, *Munsey's* in 1896 took its reader through the city and the precincts of culture, to European spas and courts, to country houses and the Yale game. As noted above, its departments constituted painting, theater, opera, literature, and so on, as spheres of regular interest. The *Journal's* visuals looked into home and garden (though it did run an illustrated series on the actress Mary Anderson); *Munsey's* put female pulchritude forward for the male gaze: actresses, singers, princesses, society women – all gorgeous, and thinly clad if their station permitted. Above all, *Munsey's* filled its pages with people, celebrities great and small, briefing its readers on who was or was about to be "In the Public Eye."

Cosmopolitan also made the contemporary world its concern, but a world whose contemporaneity was represented less through celebrity gossip and an insider's briefing on culture, and more through the "Progress of Science," the perfection of social technique (automobiles, identification of criminals, removal of the police from politics), political and economic developments worldwide, warfare and empire. The magazine offered to make readers savvy about where the world was headed, about the "real" forces of history – as one might expect from an editor who had made modest fortunes both in iron and in real estate, who owned the Stanley Automobile Company, and who was inspired by Bellamy's *Looking Backward*. Each issue carried the motto, on its title page, "From every man according to his ability: to every one according to his need," so directing the reader's imagination toward a more rational future.

McClure's would adopt a similar orientation after the turn of the century, but at the moment of my first sampling (1895–97), its worldliness was of still another kind. In a promotion for the coming year's issues ("The Edge of the Future," October 1896), the editors sought the reader's interest mainly in the writers who were to appear: Kipling, Stevenson, Ian Maclaren, Conan Doyle, Crane, Harte, Huxley, and a dozen others. Even in touting the monumental series on Lincoln that McClure had orchestrated, he made as much of Ida Tarbell's authorship as of the subject, boasting that her first installment of Lincoln's life had added a hundred thousand new subscribers within two weeks of its appearance. The famous people given prominence in the magazine belonged to history and literature: Lincoln, Napoleon, Gladstone, Longfellow, Twain. The ones offered as celebrities of the moment were those who wrote about the illustrious dead and elders, and above all the novelists and story writers whose recruitment was a main occupation of the peripatetic S.S. McClure.

Each magazine, through its contents, placed the reader differently, and articulated this difference through its characteristic address to that reader. The editorial voice rang clearest in the *Journal*, where Bok allotted a (folio) page in each issue to his own editorials, saturated with earnest authority. "For too long a time has the American girl been criticized as being a hothouse plant, while her English sister has been lauded to the skies for her greater love of outdoor sports." "An insult to a woman is usually invited." "But to the man who dulls his mind, deadens his intellect, saps his vitality and dwarfs his self-respect by overindulgence in wines or alcoholic stimulants of any kind the race is hopeless, – and irrevocably so." "But this is the sort of intelligence [i.e., domestic] that the woman of the future must have, and, all the bosh and balderdash to the contrary, the home is and will remain woman's distinctive sphere" (May 1898, p. 14). Bok set the tone as no other editor did. There were a dozen or so other named writers of "editorial contributions," which made up about half the magazine every month, as well as more shadowy figures: "the musical editors," "the literary editor," "the *Journal's* architect." All these played variations on Bok's confident wholesomeness. Furthermore, the *Journal* was easily the most intimate of the magazines, inviting and responding to hundreds of queries from readers every month, in anticipation of the "Dear Abby" format. Bok meant his magazine to serve as a personal friend to the audience, and a most tute-lary friend it was.

None of the other editors or magazines hailed readers so intrusively; but again, *Munsey's* was in some ways closest. Needless to say, it offered no domestic advice and little moral delicacy. But judgment in the magazine was insistent, guiding and sometimes badgering the reader with supposedly urbane cultural and social evaluations. Some were favorable, but the ones that probably gave most satisfaction were put-downs. A new play is "quite the baldest specimen of dramatic construction that ever saw the footlights in a reputable theater," and "a frigid farrago of impossibilities" (October 1896, p. 97). Brander Matthews is "wasting precious time upon fiction that is not even second class . . . . Such is the fatuity of cultivated minds" (November 1896, p. 211). Of Maeterlinck: "His first book . . . naturally found no publisher" (November 1896, p. 213). Judgment may be offhand, as in asides about "the dreary waste of latter day American fiction" or the "Yellow Book menagerie" and its "monstrosities" (November 1896, pp. 114–15). Or it may be forthright: "A sad token of the utter degeneracy of our modern maidens, as well as of the corrupted morals of our youths, is to be found in the poker chip fad" (October 1896, p. 122). (Men gave the chips, signed, to women, as tokens of admiration.) As *Munsey's* literary editor put it, "A critic is no critic at all if he forswears discrimination and devotes himself to eulogy . . . . Judgment is infinitely more important than praise . . . ." (October 1896, p. 115). Praise, or at least wide-eyed admiration, was accorded in plenty to the socially elevated, and Munsey's commentary relayed to his audience the down-the-nose view toward culture of just that social group.

Unlike Bok, Frank Munsey did not render judgment in his own, attributed voice, though in the early, precarious days of the magazine he did write a good deal of unsigned material. He reserved his own voice (and, again, it's hard to guess who wrote what in *Munsey's* columns) for huffy or boastful comments on the magazine itself. From the same volume: "*Munsey's* has no party bias"; "Gladly then does *Munsey's* show . . . virtue rewarded"; "*Munsey's* never offers premiums"; "*Munsey's* is not of this class" (that is, the sort of magazine that charges female beauties to print their photographs); "*Munsey's* is stronger than ever before . . . . No intelligent reader can afford to do without it," and so on. In short, *Munsey's* addressed the reader with an authority felt as contested, under fire, having always to be truculently asserted and defended. That authority was in fact claiming a new, urban position, with its acceptance of bohemian life, its boulevardier's knowingness about new social tendencies, its open-mindedness toward Jews, Ethical Culturists, even divorce. But without traditional pieties to authorize its stance, it adopted a far more hectoring and scrappy tone than the *Journal.*

In *Munsey's* this tone dominated or framed the individuality of particular writers: in addition to the unsigned columns, many articles and short stories carried the authors' names only at the end. In this, *McClure's* represents an opposite extreme. It included no unsigned material except the occasional comment from "the editors," and always placed authors' names at the beginnings of stories and articles. Beyond that, it insisted on the fame or past achievements of contributors: "author of . . . ," "editor of . . . ," and so on; and as I mentioned earlier, it pinned the appeal of future issues to the repute of the writers whose work would be published there. Apart from McClure's pride in that, the magazine implied almost no editorial voice. S.S. McClure was an impresario who organized the show but only rarely stepped before the curtain to praise it, and *then* his praise was for excellence without respect to prior canons or genres or respectabilities – for pure talent and quality. The magazine's address privileged the individuality of genius.

Cosmopolitan also foregrounded the writer, but as an insider or eyewitness, not a genius. Sarah Bernhardt wrote about "The Art of Making Up." Major E.G. Féchet, who was there, told for the first time "The True Story of the Death of Sitting Bull." A member of Grant's staff, now a general, purported to solve the "mystery" of the great man's career (why he had failed at everything until he succeeded in war). The insider might be famous – Theodore Roosevelt on the New York police – or not: "The Story of the Samoan Disaster" as "Told by an Eye-Witness," whose name appeared only at the end of the article. John Brisben Walker based his editorial authority on the marshaling of such experts, not chiefly on his own assorted opinions, the public expression of which he would have thought amateurish. When he did write for the magazine, it was as an expert among experts, as with an article on the horseless carriage, "Some Speculations Regarding Rapid Transit." Through its address, *Cosmopolitan* constructed an active and practical reader who needed reliable information on and expert analysis of the present moment, of the formative past, and of what was coming next.

In this survey I have meant both to convey a sense of the plenitude – the sheer display – that filled the pages of these magazines in the mid and late 1890s, and to argue that the four leaders positioned themselves as sharply distinct products in spite of their patent similarities. Taken as a group, they implied a reader who was an ardent and skilled consumer of cultural fare, a reader capable of negotiating a near infinity of choices, secure in his or her individual taste. Edward Bok, looking back on his achievement, articulated the simile on which I have based this section: "A successful magazine is exactly like a successful store: it must keep its wares constantly fresh and varied to attract the eye and hold the patronage of its customers." But he also knew that the "wares" needed a personal intermediary, like the proprietor of a small shop, and he set out "to convince the public that he was not an oracle removed from the people, but a real human being who could talk and not merely write on paper."[13] Here are the two principles I have conjoined: plenitude, and the feeling of personal guidance. In different words, McClure made the same connection, offering his magazine as "a moving, living transcript of the intelligent, interesting, human endeavor of the time," but monitoring that "transcript" with the same "responsibility" to readers he would feel if it were for "ourselves and our own kin."[14] The magazines both filled this new media space with "wares" and, in ways I have tried to illustrate, projected a singular human presence into the potentially overwhelming, commodified array.

Personality integrated; it also individuated. The editor or his implied persona did not – with the possible exception of Bok – hold phenomena together in an explanatory framework or a holistic understanding. Rather, he was like a tour guide, pointing to this thing as notable, that as interesting, another as worrisome, still another as curious. The magazine itself was a discontinuous form, and most of the favored genres other than fiction reinforced discontinuity and discreetness. Narratives of the Samoan disaster or Sitting Bull's death let events themselves supply a beginning and an end point. The memoir – Elizabeth Stuart Phelps on Harriet Beecher Stowe and numerous others – assembled anecdotes and scraps of conversation around the already constituted allure of a famous person. The vicarious tour (a woman climbs the Matterhorn; hunting walrus in the Arctic) put remote places and strenuous activities on view. The survey of new contrivances (warships, automobiles, submarines) simply cataloged. The celebrity article collected memorable facts into an illusion of intimacy with the great man or woman. The "visit" admitted readers to the home or country retreat of painter, writer, or statesman, and documented what would now be called his "life style." The cultural departments were handy annotated catalogs of new plays, new novels, recent paintings, great singers. Pointing, describing, and enumerating were the characteristic gestures of these articles; taken as a whole they enacted a rhetoric of taxonomy and accumulation. One thing that strikes this modern reader is the virtual absence of argument as a genre in the buoyant, early years of the mass circulation magazines. Argument seeks finality, closure.[15]

Toward the beginning of this chapter I suggested that the new magazines helped readers to "fix their bearings in the fluid social space of that moment." The point of this section has been to urge that they did so in the first instance by positioning the reader as a consumer surrounded by cultural "wares,"[16] and becoming qualified to choose among them. But that kind of location is by itself quite anonymous, really a form of social *dis*location. Clearly the group I am positioning as the principal audience wanted a more precise and honorable placement than that, and I now turn to ways in which the magazines addressed readers as more than cultural consumers.

A Social Place

Begin by considering "place" literally. People read the magazines in homes all around the nation, but the magazines did not consider all parts of the nation as places worth representing. The *Journal* ran a series (in 1897–98) of photographs taking readers "Inside of a Hundred Homes," in "all parts of the country." The May 1898 installment depicted twenty rooms, porches, and terraces. Seventeen were in the metropolitan East and its suburban penumbra, or in California. One of the others was a vacation cottage. That left just two homes from the rest of the country, one in Michigan and one in Hamilton, Ohio, the latter standing as the lone representative of the small-town heartland. A similar selectivity pervaded all the magazines. Iowa was not a visible place, Arkansas was not a place, Montana was not a place, though one of them might momentarily and as it were accidentally come into view, as when an article on amateur photography included three scenes from Minneapolis (*Cosmopolitan*, January 1896). For most part, the contemporary US appeared in these magazines as the eastern seaboard from Washington to Boston, with less frequent glimpses of California, Chicago, the aristocratic South, the scenic or untamed West.

One can be more specific. For *Munsey's* and, to a lesser extent, *Cosmopolitan, the* place was New York City. They drew the reader's knowing (or envious, or naive, or wondering) gaze to its theaters and concert halls, its performers and millionaires, its police and politicians. But almost never, in the 1890s, to its slums: the view of the metropolis was that of an insider or a sophisticated visitor seeking what was celebrated, and of course making it celebrated by so identifying it. These magazines assumed and helped promote an interest in New York as a cultural magnetic field, influential throughout American society. By placing the reader there, and by furnishing monthly bulletins on the city's events and "seasons," *Munsey's* especially made him or her a canny participant in its social flow.

The significance of this emphasis becomes clearer when one surrounds imagined New York with places to which it was linked socially by a similar kind of attention. There were London and Paris, Bayreuth and Russian palaces, Venice and the Rhine: a vicarious reconstruction of the Grand Tour for those not entitled to it by birth and wealth. (The *Journal* offered "Ten Weeks in Europe for $200," by "two girls" who executed the thrifty vacation.) Within the US, the magazines toured country homes and cottages, Sag Harbor and Buzzard's Bay, Yale and Princeton. These were understood as already established places in a known social geography. Another genre of article took readers to St Andrews, the Arctic, Catalina Island, Mount Hood: places to pursue sport, risk, and natural splendor; *Cosmopolitan* specialized in such fare. To bring these exotic spots into imaginative existence was to imply that the reader might, having learned about them, actually follow the author's adventuresome footsteps.[17] Finally, *McClure's* and the *Journal*, especially, constructed Boston and rural New England as significant because they offered glimpses of a residual culture seen as "our" heritage.

Place was (and is) social. The magazines invited PMC readers to know vicariously a circuit of places – an upscale "axis of respectability" – of which a full and "natural" experience was available only to the wealthy. That was changing, as accounts of the $200 European vacation and the $300 forest cabin make evident. Yet the predominant mode of geographical presentation here wavered between vicarious and anticipatory experience. You might go "there" but if not, you would at least have socially valued knowledge of what "there" was like – even if you lived in Iowa, Arkansas, or Montana. Where most readers actually lived is a matter for conjecture, but the *Journal*, the only one of these magazines to focus on the home, made it clear that its presumed readers lived in suburbs and in good urban neighborhoods, where entertainment of social equals was a frequent and easy practice. At such parties, knowing talk about Sag Harbor and Venice could help fix the range of social reference that would be part of a new class's cultural capital.

Its gaze was directed upward. European royalty were a dependable attraction in all the magazines. Munsey made a concerted attempt to promote their counterparts in American society, with articles on the lineage of "Prominent American Families" (Carrolls, Danas, Washingtons, Polks), on the Daughters of the American Revolution, and on "Some Colonial Dames." Profiles of politicians in *Munsey's* department, "In the Public Eye," sounded a similar tone, at once bluff and fawning. McClure favored the New England literary aristocracy as personally remembered by its survivors. Bok gave prominence to high church clergymen, senior statesmen, and the wives of both. Only Walker abstained on the whole from adulation of older elites, giving more attention to the energetic doings of people closer to the middle class readership: businessmen, scientists, inventors, bureaucrats, planners.[18] Chiefly, the editors supposed their readers to want mediated intimacy with a loosely defined, traditional upper class.

Much of the cultural chatter in the magazines assisted readers in imitating – if they wished – the supposed attitudes and knowledge of that class. *Munsey's* was most explicit in its aim of communicating such a point of view to its audience, as I have already mentioned with reference to its promotions and put-downs. A typical sentence like "It will be curious to see what the New York opera goer is going to find to grumble about next winter" (October 1896, p. 80) places the reader inside a circle of the initiated. Profiles of singers, actresses, writers, and painters in all the magazines had a similar function: enabling readers to strike cultivated attitudes toward their work, even if not schooled to such attitudes from childhood. In fact, it is hard to imagine actual members of the upper class accepting such instruction as dignified or appropriate. They probably would have agreed with *Munsey's* "Literary Chat" editor, in reviewing an etiquette book:

> We can hardly believe there are club members who need to be told that one does not bow to a woman from the club window or mention her name in the billiard room. And surely there can be no need of stating that a gentlemen does not dance without gloves! (February 1897, p. 632)

Yet social and cultural knowledge equivalent to those rules was a staple, in *Munsey's* and the *Journal* most frankly.

Better to perceive the social coordinates that located the implied reader, glance in the opposite direction: downward. There almost nothing meets the eye.[19] True, Bok gave advice to impoverished young women and discoursed on servants, but abstracted from any context. The magazines were virtually mute on the subject of workers, in the 1890s. Immigrants received only the occasional sidelong remark, as in a profile of Detroit Mayor Pingree, exploring narrow streets, "surrounded by a crowd of Poles or Bohemians" (*Munsey's*, December 1896, p. 325). Of the polite silence surrounding African Americans, I will speak at a later point. One can read more about all these groups in the elite magazines; perhaps the upper class audience, more secure in its social position, could more comfortably and charitably read about the dispossessed. Many PMC readers had daily contact with working class people. They chose suburban homes to avoid such contact in leisure time. The magazines respected that impulse, creating their version of segregated cultural space.

They also located readers in historical time: at the moving edge of the present. *McClure's* invited its audience to feast on the work of new writers and the newest work of famous writers, a harvest reaped by the editor in his regular expeditions to the cultural frontier. To read the magazine would be to gain a step on others aspiring to literary savoir-faire. *Munsey's* offered its chaperonage to a somewhat different frontier: the newest novel, the upcoming opera season, the plans of theatrical producers, the fad of animated scarf pins just now sweeping New York. The reader would consume, not the new cultural gleanings themselves (except for reproductions of paintings), but the most advanced and urbane talk *about* them.[20] *Cosmopolitan* admitted readers to temporal privilege of the same sort, but promised them also an unparalleled view of technical, scientific, and social innovations: X-rays, electroplating, identification of criminals. In fact it opened a window onto the future. In his November 1895 "Speculations Regarding Rapid Transit," Walker told readers they could "expect to see" millions spent on the macadamizing of country roads and even on asphalt highways, that business would fan out from city centers, that the horse would soon be "relegated to an inferior position," that the aeroplane was just over the horizon.[21] (He also depicted a monorail system, but for freight rather than passengers.) The temporal position of the *Journal's* reader was more ambiguous, because of the strong emphasis on residual values. But Bok kept readers posted on modern household practices and on changes in custom, in a generally approving tone.

Each magazine pressed upon readers its guidance in keeping them *au courant*, and contemporary observers theorized this development. For instance, in the *Atlantic Monthly* of July,1900, Arthur Reed Kimball wrote that the "office" of the magazine was "to interpret the significance of life as it is being lived, after it is mirrored, *en passant*, in the press, but before its perpetuation in the book" (p. 122). But he was making a partisan distinction, on behalf of the older magazines; his title was "The Invasion of Journalism," and he deplored the trend among the *Atlantic's* racier competitors toward up-to-the-minute news and entertainment. Similarly, an editorial in *Harper's* sternly proclaimed a policy of excluding the "timely" from its pages, and, like the university, emphasizing the "most essential interests" of our "culture" (September 1902, p. 647); it was the only magazine, the editors suggested, lately to have ignored volcanoes and Edward VII. In this gesture of the elite magazines, one can see class distinction in process: what *Munsey's* and the rest proffered as new and timely, *Harper's* dismissed as faintly vulgar. An upper class can rest its cultural legitimacy on tradition; the PMC audience valued tradition of a sort, but sensed its affinities with the new, and saw its mission as forward looking. That, at least, was the vantage point assigned it by the most successful 10-cent magazines.

I want now to extend this metaphor of location and vantage point by bringing into its domain one of the most striking features of the new magazines, their visual content. Every commentator on the magazine revolution mentions the halftone process, whose development made it possible to print reproductions of photographs quite cheaply, and on type-compatible paper. Some even suggest that this technology helped *cause* the "revolution," and there are comments by its leaders to encourage such a view. When McClure began to dream of a "cheap popular magazine," he considered that the halftone "made such a publication then more possible . . . . Not only was the new process vastly cheaper in itself, but it enabled a publisher to make pictures directly from photographs, which were cheap, instead of from drawings, which were expensive."[22] Munsey loved pictures, considered them essential, and chose them himself long after he relegated other editorial tasks to subordinates;[23] Bok paid close attention to the visual appeal of photographs in advertisements.

The halftone did not create the mass circulation magazine, but all the editors used it copiously to offer a spectacle they thought would help attract a broad public. In a single issue during 1896, *Munsey's* printed 61 halftones (October), *Cosmopolitan* 39 (April), and *McClure's* 33 (June). The *Journal* lagged behind with 11 (February), though it soon took steps to catch up. But this does not tell the whole story of the magazines' visual presentations: the photographs they printed were augmented by hand-made pictures, in roughly inverse proportions. Thus, in the same issues there were 30 drawings and other such illustrations in the *Journal*, 24 in *McClure's*, 15 in *Cosmopolitan*, and 9 in *Munsey's*. The situation was still more complex: a number of the photographs, especially in *Munsey's* and *Cosmopolitan*, were of paintings, monuments, or other art works. Also, many tailor-made illustrations were photographically reproduced. Some pastiches of drawing and photo were then reproduced by the halftone process. Some negatives were touched up with acid to sharpen the contrast of light and dark. Furthermore, some halftone plates were retouched by engravers. A still more complex interaction between hand and mechanical production, and a fairly common one, began with a photograph, from which an artist made a drawing, which was itself photographed, and then reproduced by the halftone process.[24] It is too simple to suggest that photographs made the magazines. Rather, pictures of various and mixed provenance came before the reader's eye, inviting him or her to adopt the position of a viewer.

Photography had been around for nearly sixty years before the moment of the mass circulation magazines, and of course it was much celebrated as a great invention of the century. From the beginning, there were efforts not only to make multiple copies of photographs, but to find ways of reproducing them in books. In fact, the very first gropings toward photography in the 1820s, by Joseph Nicéphore Niepce, were aimed at bypassing the human artist through the use of a recently invented process of mechanical reproduction, lithography.[25] Photography and art were entangled in other ways: early on, inventors looked for ways of photographing and then reproducing paintings, and books of such copies began appearing around mid century. Techniques also proliferated for working from photograph to engraving, especially by transferring the former to the block on which an engraver would work. In short, long before the 1880s, when the halftone gradually emerged as a technical and commercial possibility, a mutual implication had deepened among photography, the graphic arts, and the fine arts – quite apart from the interminable debate as to whether photography *was* an art.[26]

In this context, the explosion of halftone images in the 10-cent magazines meant far more than just visual enrichment, which was understood by many contemporaries as a degenerate appeal to weakened intellects and shortened attention spans. And it certainly did not, for readers of the late 1890s, mean satisfaction of an appetite for journalistic timeliness. Until the 1898 war, little in the magazines even approached the newspaper ideal of giving readers visual access to the immediate event. On the contrary, even when photographs brought images of men and women "In the Public Eye," they virtually always adopted the portrait code: a formal picture, usually of head and shoulders (like a sculpted bust), sometimes of the seated or standing dignitary, but always posed, usually posed in a studio, and usually attributed to that studio or to a particular photographer. Similarly, actresses and singers appeared "as" one character or another, though not actually on stage; even a rarity like "Mme. Bernhardt in Street Costume" (*Cosmopolitan*, March 1896, p. 531) is a studio portrait, duly attributed to Reutlinger of Paris. Then there were prolific photos, especially in *McClure's*, from the past: Lincoln, Twain, Gladstone, Stowe, Longfellow, Holmes, and so on. They, too, were of course portraits rather than snapshots, and often identified as to provenance: "This portrait of Dr. Holmes has a special value in that it is from an unpublished photograph which was possibly the last taken of him before his death" (July 1896, p. 119). Or, "From the last original unretouched negative of the martyred President, made by Alexander Gardner, photographer to the Army of the Potomac, the Sunday before the assassination . . ." (p. 173). Pictures of the famous living and dead were monumental, stylized, and offered as significant *re*presentations of already significant pictures, via the professional camera and a new technology.[27]

This holds true still more obviously for halftone reproductions of paintings, bas reliefs, sculptures, and famous buildings. The content of these pictures was marked as art; the reproductions (often full-page and on special, high-finish paper) were usually arranged in gallery-like portfolios; and the photographer or studio normally received credit along with the painter. To this list one may add most illustrations drawn to accompany specific texts: these were often signed by the artist, sometimes captioned with the artist's name, and (in *McClure's* and the *Journal*) listed in the table of contents. That is, they were treated as new art works, much as illustrations had been treated in the elite magazines of the 1880s, but with the important difference that now most of them were photographically reproduced rather than engraved. The photographer remained anonymous, as for that matter the engraver generally had. (That parallel gains force when we recall that halftone plates of illustrations dense in texture were often touched up for emphasis *by* engravers – a sad decline in the use made of these master craftsmen's skills.)

To be sure, the magazines contained numerous halftones – of horseless carriages, climbers on Mt Rainier, a village in Venezuela – that elude the generalization I nonetheless put forth: that in the early years, mass circulation magazines used photography and the halftone process mainly to circulate images *already endowed* with esthetic value or formal propriety. This is not to deny William Ivins's and Estelle Jussim's claim that in this period photographic reproduction clarified for the public a distinction heretofore obscure: one between pictorial creation or expression (art) and communication of visual information (fact). I believe that distinction was becoming clear, but it would be a mistake to think that in the magazines of 1895–97 it segregated halftone pictures into two neat groups, with the Venezuelan village on one side and the recent painting by Burne-Jones on the other. And the mistake would not just be one of seeing a messy terrain as too well-ordered. It would be of misunderstanding what kind of privilege the supposedly neutral camera extended to readers.

Certainly it did afford images of China and South Africa and Catalina Island, and this function became more salient after 1900. At the earlier moment, though, most of the pictures offered the reader a visual experience coded as in itself memorable, almost as would be the case in an art gallery or historical museum. Furthermore, although these views of people and art came at readers with the implied warranty of absolute truth, since they were (supposedly) unmediated by the work of the engraver, the magazines did *not* present the views as unmediated, period. As I have said, they called attention to the photograph, the photographer, the studio. In addition, art editors (or their prototypes) arranged halftones on the page to suggest their quality as an expression, not just as a supplement to the information given in the printed text. Halftones appeared as full-page, half-page, or smaller illustrations, and in various placements on the page – in a corner, across top or bottom, right in the middle where they would push aside both columns of type, and so on. Halftones of both original photographs and drawings might also be framed with black lines, given no frame but the straight edge of the picture, clipped so that part of a significant object ran beyond the frame, or cut back so that they met the white space on the page in an irregular pattern. In other words, formatting tended to refuse any distinction between the informative and the artistic functions, since all the pictures were displayed esthetically.

What magazines offered readers through visual spectacle was something like Malraux' "museum without walls," but the sense of his metaphor needs broadening. Looking at a reproduction of an Old Master was "like" being in a museum, with the camera guaranteeing that likeness (except that these were black and white pictures). But seeing the work of the Pre-Raphaelites was more like being in a gallery: and seeing "Some Examples of Recent Art" in *Cosmopolitan* or "Artists and Their Work" in *Munsey's* was perhaps more like being admitted to the artist's studio or the home of a wealthy collector who kept up with the current work of practicing artists. Old portraits of Lincoln or Mark Twain or the Carroll family gave viewers surrogate access to family or official archives. Photos of German princesses took one inside palace grounds. Glamorous shots of actresses transported one to theater lobby or Broadway restaurant. The camera promised accuracy, but a good deal more than that: it placed the looking subject in a variety of imagined sites, bodily entry to which would have required affluence, social standing, know-how, and good taste, in some combination. The same holds true for many of the halftones that functioned more purely as factual channels: for example, those of golfing in Scotland and deep sea fishing off California.

In sum, photographs in the magazines located the reader socially much as articles and departments did. Unsurprisingly, pictures also carried out the same sorts of exclusions. My sample volumes and issues from 1895-97 contain well over a thousand halftones, perhaps six or seven hundred of which began with photographs "from nature," as the old phrase went. Among the later ones are a few that showed poor foreigners from a tourist's perspective, but virtually none that represented the US working class or underclass: the one significant exception was a photo-essay in *Cosmopolitan* (November 1895, pp 34–9) on the identification of criminals, which showed two unfortunates being immobilized by force to be photographed, and photos of several others from police files. (Needless to say, the point of view here was that of the police and the law-abiding public.) Hand-made illustrations for stories and articles included a rich iconography of the poor and unfortunate, as of course did paintings. But the magazines did not subpoena the camera as witness to poverty, degradation, vice, or struggle; they declined to take the looking subject where he or she would have had imaginatively to go in order to view such scenes.

Remember, this was half a dozen years after the tremendous stir made by Jacob Riis's tenement photos in *How the Other Half Lives* (1890); photos of the down-and-out had long been circulated, and photography as stimulus to social reform was a familiar practice. You might expect an audience identified with reform to have wanted and been given such pictures. These magazines excluded them: possibly on a tacit principle of what was permissible in a family medium, possibly because magazine reading was a leisure activity not to be spoiled by reminders of workaday problems; but possibly also because something like the sense of social location I have been describing was at work, a feeling that to look with the camera man inside tenements and factories would be to contaminate the flattering placement of readers in sites of beauty and dignity that was effected by the great majority of photographs.

True, the privilege of looking at the unfortunate is a manifestation of power, of PMC power in particular. With the right to manage goes the right to see. But with such seeing goes, also, an unsettling relation of inequality and the sense of the viewer's perhaps unjust *economic* privilege.[28] So the magazines stayed away from the documentary mode, from both written and visual exploration of the lower depths. They did not contribute directly to surveillance or to the progressive "regime of truth" (Foucault's phrase) which was already in formation elsewhere in American society. They were teaching their audience to want "its information pure, uncontaminated by artistic inconveniences,"[29] and to think of the camera as a guarantor of pure information. But that information was about elevated and elevating things, from Gladstone's appearance to that of Pre-Raphaelite paintings or English silver. John Tagg speaks of a moment in the development of Courbet's "realism" when "technique, forms and styles of the past . . . serve as models but are far from neutral mediators since they *retain and connote* the residues of older contents."[30] The magazines of the 1890s effected a similar process. The halftone was of course a "new" technique, and highly regarded as such; but its novel powers of authenticity were mobilized, paradoxically, to recapitulate the "techniques, forms and styles of the past," and thus "retain and connote" far more than bare "residues of older contents." Tagg argues that any realism is historically specific, and the photographic displays in these magazines strikingly exemplify the point.

Editors gave readers older visual contents, and evidently readers wanted them. Why? I'd say, to participate vicariously in old, upper class cultural experience, mediated by the most modern PMC technology. Victor Burgin explains that "the neutrality of the objects before the camera" is an "illusion."[31] The objects already carried meaning, authority, and implicit social structure; the new technique democratized an old way of fixing the gaze on them. Both the objects and the technique helped construct the ideology of PMC social placement in close proximity to the upper class yet more modern, and even egalitarian, in cultural means. If I am right, this confirms once again the truth that no medium or technique of representation has a single meaning, apart from the circumstances of its use.

Chief among the "objects" already endowed with social meaning were human forms and faces. I want to comment briefly now on the omnipresence in these magazines of the individual person, taken as more than a visual phenomenon. Photographs helped place the reader in a close though formal relation with important people, but not only pictures did that. Text accompanied the great majority of them, sometimes just as annotation, more often as the main channel of information, to which the pictures were ancillary. My sample includes articles and briefer notes on hundreds of individuals, framed as separate subjects of interest by title and typography. In addition, hundreds more received attention in groups ("Unknown Wives of Well-Known Men"; "Three Women Painters") or in paragraphs within the cultural departments. *Munsey's* was most prolific in this genre, but all the magazines made profiles, biographical sketches, memoirs, and celebrity news staples of their monthly offerings.

The word "celebrity" may seem an anachronism in this context, but by 1850 it had acquired its modern sense; in fact, McClure took the idea of his "Human Documents" series, one of the magazine's early successes, from a series called "Portraits of Celebrities" in the English magazine, the *Strand*.[32] A celebrity is someone known for being well known, as Daniel

Boorstin commented, while pondering why we have only celebrities now, and no heroes.[33] If that is so, the shift in outlook was well underway by the 1890s. The magazines endlessly told about people conceived as *already* famous, taking it for granted that readers would want to know more. And they also (especially *Munsey's*) gave advance notice of people likely to *become* celebrities. Apparently cultural capital, for this audience, consisted partly in a storehouse of shared knowledge about individuals who had attained standing as cynosures, or were on the way to it.

"Cynosures"; "celebrities": the terms I am using urge a particular way of thinking about the representation of notable individuals that in some ways conflicts with that of Theodore P. Greene, in *America's Heroes: The Changing Models of Success in American Magazines*. Since Greene's is one of the few comprehensive and serious analyses of the material with which I am working, I will summarize his findings and try to explain the differences between his understanding and mine. Greene seeks evidence of changing values in US society, by examining biographical articles in popular magazines of several different periods.[34] As his title indicates, he assumes that the subjects of such articles can stand as exemplars, models, heroes: "these magazine biographies can lay some claim to represent those figures in which the men of their time were most interested and those standards of success which were most approved" (p. 9). His chapter on turn-of-the-century "heroes" identifies "fame" as the leading standard of success, followed by "social contribution," "achievement in field," and "monetary standard." The qualities to which the articles attribute the "hero's" success are fierce individuality, indomitable will, mastery of "the human and material environment," and the perseverance to overcome "obstacles and adversity" (p. 164). To signal this configuration, Greene titles his chapter, "The Hero as Napoleon" – and indeed, Napoleon was a favorite subject in the magazines, rivaled only by Lincoln.

To mention just those two names is to suggest the pertinence of Greene's ideas, which also serve well enough for some other figures covered in my sampling from the mid to late 1890s: Richelieu, the German Emperor William II, Grant, Gladstone, Chinese statesman and military man Li Hung Chang. Others who are less obviously "heroes" – Harriet Beecher Stowe, Charles H. Taylor (editor of the Boston *Globe*), Kipling – are held up for admiration in similar terms. Greene notes the preeminence of artists and writers among those profiled, and explains it by calling creative artists "perfect examples of the hero-type honored at this peak of individualism," with "the inner-directed pattern of determination, perseverance, and hard work" (pp. 152–3). Yet sketches of Joshua Reynolds, his near contemporary Thomas Lawrence, Whistler, and others in my sample do not emphasize the hard struggle for "success," but rather the artist's unusual characteristics and quirks, and his conduct after having achieved fame. Then there are lives that can hardly be understood as successes in the usual way: Don Carlos, pretender to the throne of Spain, Queen Wilhemina of the Netherlands, Mesmer – this last represented, in a history of hypnotism, as a confused, pre-scientific publicist.

It is hard to wrap the term "success" around some of the people favored with portraits and biographies. But that is not the main reservation I have about Greene's analysis. What it misses, by concentrating on admirable qualities and narratives of achievement, is a rhetorical strategy I find central: the reduction of distance between reader and biographical subject. Take Lincoln, whose "Life" by Ida Tarbell ran through a number of issues of *McClure's* in my sample volume (summer and fall 1896), and, according to McClure, "told on our circulation as nothing ever had before."[35] The July installment, "Lincoln as a Lawyer" (pp. 171–81), promises through its subtitles the kind of familiarizing I have in mind: "Reminiscences and Anecdotes From Men Who Practised With Him At the Bar; His Humor and Persuasiveness; His Manner of Preparing Cases, Examining Witnesses, and Addressing Juries." Presumably Tarbell did not write these subheads, but she begins her account in the same spirit: "One of the first books which interested Abraham Lincoln as a boy was a treatise on law . . .," and continues with his memory of reading Blackstone's *Commentaries*: "'Never in my whole life,' said he afterwards, 'was my mind so thoroughly absorbed. I read until I devoured them.'" The strategy initiated here persists through the installment; Tarbell assumes the reader's admiration of Lincoln, and rather than arguing the case for his greatness, she personalizes it. Examples:

- Lincoln's horse was "described as 'poky' and the buggy as 'rattling.'"

- "He found humor and human interest on the route where his companions saw nothing but commonplaces. 'He saw the ludicrous in an assemblage of fowls, in a man spading his garden, in a clothes-line full of clothes . . . .'"

- "generally he took part in all the frolicking which went on, joining in practical jokes, singing noisily with the rest, sometimes even playing a Jew's-harp."

- "Unless [Lincoln] joined the circle which the judge formed in his room after supper, his honor was impatient and distraught, interrupting the conversation constantly by demanding:
    'Where's Lincoln?' 'Why don't Lincoln come?'"

- Judge Lawrence Weldon: "I can see him now, . . . standing in the corner of the old court-room; and as I approached him with a paper I did not understand, he said, 'Wait until I fix this plug for my "gallis" and I will pitch into that like a dog at a root.'"

- Lincoln, to a prospective client: "You must remember that some things legally right are not morally right. We shall not take your case but will give you a little advice for which we will charge you nothing. You seem to be a sprightly, energetic man; we would advise you to try your hand at making six hundred dollars in some other way."

And so the highly episodic narrative continues, right to its concluding anecdote of Lincoln inadvertently reading in court an opinion unfavorable to his client, saying, "May it please the court, I reckon I've scratched up a snake," and going on to win the case anyhow.

This casual intimacy, this offer of vicarious, affectionate, personal memory is evidently the telos of the portrait. It was McClure's originating intent, too, according to his biographer. In giving Ida Tarbell her assignment, he told her to follow Lincoln's footsteps, talk to his surviving acquaintances, borrow their old photos of him, "bringing to life again the man McClure described as 'the noblest character of our history' . . . . "[36] The narrative act of "bringing to life," needless to say, was augmented by reproductions of photographs, not just of Lincoln but of his bookcase, chair, and ink stand, of a courthouse where he practiced, of a building in which he had an office, of a label he wrote for a packet of miscellaneous letters and clippings: "When you can't find *it* anywhere else look into this." The whole presentation moves, not to heroize a mortal, but to humanize a hero. Tarbell's representation of Lincoln should be understood, I think, as continuous in its rhetoric with the graphics I discussed earlier and with its own accompanying graphics. It re-places the reader, and in a privileged spot.

Such is the dominant spirit of most biographies of 1896–97: they do of course reproduce a kind of hero-hood, and sometimes the rhetoric of canonization is intense. A portrait in *Munsey's* begins, "Emma Eames Story, the great prima donna, perhaps the most beautiful woman on the stage, the wife of a celebrated painter, is a figure for all time, one of the women whom this decade will put in fame's gallery . . ." (February 1897, p. 522). But a sentence later the register shifts – "She is the American girl" – and before long we are within the "American atmosphere" of the Storys' Parisian home, including the mantels and bathtubs from Chicago. The main gesture in most of these biographies is one of approach across barriers of fame and social distinction, with these attributes more often assumed than argued. An article on Kaiser William II begins, "In the year 1862, in the most beautiful part of a country famed for its beauty, there was played a political drama with but two characters and no audience save the birds, the fishes, and the tame deer of the royal park near Berlin" (*Cosmopolitan*, November 1895, p. 17), then proceeds to a zoom shot of this private talk between Bismarck and the Emperor's father, adding the reader to the "audience." *McClure's* portrait of Gladstone begins, "As the westering sun sinks to its setting, a white-haired old man comes out from his library and seats himself on the stone steps that lead from the castle front to the lawn" (August 1896, p. 197), and the facing photo shows the great man resting in his shirtsleeves, with an ax and surrounded by wood chips. One of the more monumental profiles, on Richelieu, nonetheless establishes the personal approach with an opening quotation: "When I have once made up my mind, I go straight to the point. I mow down everything that stands in my way, and then I cover it all with my red cassock" (*Munsey's*, February 1897, p. 609). To move the reader in close is nearly always a tacit or explicit offer.

If it is so in representations of the acknowledged great, it is even more evidently the point in portraits of those we might call the obscurely famous: shadowy figures like princesses of Romania, "Royal Children," actresses who have married titles, reclusive artists and writers, Daughters of the American Revolution, and so on. These people have names or named positions in the historical and social world, but barely exist for the reader as individuals before the journalist and the camera bring them into focus. Other subgenres purvey intimacy by taking readers vicariously into the company of the cynosure: interviews, visits, reminiscences (of Harriet Beecher Stowe by Elizabeth Stuart Phelps; of W.T.G. Morton, discoverer of anesthesia, by his widow). These last bring the reader close through the mediation of an actual intimate, often herself a celebrity, so that the reader's privilege is doubled.

From these familiarizing genres it is not a great distance to the unashamed celebrity gossip of *Munsey's*, which carries us into the social orbits not only of singers and painters, but of politicians and businessmen, with knowing if anonymous chaperonage. Roger Wolcott, governor of Massachusetts, "has often been called the handsomest man in Boston. He is a little more than six feet tall, with a ruddy complexion and grayish hair and mustache." "At Washington [Charles Henry Grosvenor, a Republican party leader] is familiarly known as 'Santa Claus,' for reasons that will be revealed by a glance at his portrait." Llewellyn Powers, candidate for governor in Maine, "is both tall and broad shouldered, and his massive head, covered with a sweeping growth of long black hair, gives evidence of mental and physical strength. Though rich beyond his boyhood dreams, he holds to the most democratic simplicity of living. Everybody in Houlton knows and likes him." These gleanings from the department "In the Public Eye" (October 1896, pp. 19–21) convey the knowing tone and easy familiarity that were a staple of *Munsey's*. The other magazines were a bit less smug, but a copy of any would give the reader a lot of insider's knowledge for his or her 10 cents.

More than knowledge, though: they passed on attitudes toward and judgments of the famous and not-so-famous, judgments rendered in an authoritative tone and with little nuance or contestation, judgments and attitudes ready for instant adoption or adaptation by the reader less secure in his or her own urbanity. Anonymous editorial staffers wrote with the same confidence as known authors, locating the characters and deeds of celebrities on an implicit scale of propriety and worth, and locating *readers* by admitting them to this circle of shared values. Most comments were laudatory, but scandal and failure received enough mention to make it clear that a rating system was at work. The magazines offered to their dispersed audience something like the shared knowledge and shared values of a community – indeed, a class.

Why does my reading differ significantly from that of Theodore Greene? Partly, I think, because he takes a preponderance of his examples from the years 1899 to 1903, and by then the heroizing impulse had strengthened, driven by the jingoistic fervor of Manila Bay and San Juan Hill. (Admiral Dewey became an instant hero, not just a celebrity, after 1898.) But the main reason for the difference may be that Greene conceives of the magazines' readership as "Americans," seeking models of national and personal identity and taking nostalgic comfort in the idealization of the achieving individual against a backdrop of new corporate power. I am supposing, by contrast, that readers were Americans of a particular if fairly broad social group; that they were not seeking remedies for doubt and alienation in the face of corporate capital, but were quite comfortable on the new terrain and thought of themselves as succeeding or at least likely to succeed there; and that they wanted in their homes and in their conversational repertory the cultural capital that would signify and project their class standing. The relation to fame that these magazines offered them was cultural capital in a neat package.

If I am right, this exchange between producers and consumers helps explain two related contradictions in the phenomenon of the celebrity, both then and now. As with the reproduced work of art, the celebrity must have what Walter Benjamin called an aura, precisely to serve *as* cultural capital; yet the reduction of social distance, the insider's view, threatens always to disperse that aura. Again, the reader is proffered intimacy, special access; yet that access comes through a mass medium, on sale everywhere. These contradictions derive from the very situation of a new middle class audience, buying its culture in the market and consolidating itself not through family ties and old privileges but through participation at a greater distance in more public institutions and practices, including that of the new magazine.

In charting the social space illuminated by these magazines and locating the implied reader's position within it, I have emphasized the spatial and social relations of the visual and the viewer, and the dynamics of approach to distant and distinguished persons, alive and dead. These are slightly oblique ways, though I hope useful ones, of addressing the main – and fairly obvious – point about social placement: seen globally, the magazines located their readers in a kind of cultural center, a Chautauqua without walls and with a good deal less moral earnestness than the real thing. What replaced that earnestness was a more forgiving kind of urgency, that of keeping up. The implicit offer the magazines made to their readers was of socially correct participation – reading the right fiction, seeing the new paintings, knowing who counted as a celebrity, having sophisticated (if second-hand) views on the current theatrical season, and so on.

Editors mediated Culture in different ways. McClure put "the best" on display; its very appearance in his magazine was to constitute a seal of approval. Bok did the same, but also certified its propriety, its gentility. Munsey and his anonymous commentators struck far more urbane postures, defending the nude in art and praising Zola, yet still setting limits, beyond which fell the profanity in Crane's *Maggie* and the decadence of *The Yellow Book*. Whereas Munsey projected cultural authority through a bluff, savvy, rib-nudging tone, Walker claimed it through his stable of named and respected correspondents. All four acted as cultural gatekeepers and tutors – two rather different roles that blur and overlap here, indicating a cultural ambivalence in the audience, which wanted both to be taught and to be addressed as already knowing. This was a class feeling its way into Culture, not fully settled there.

The magazines gave guidance through a myriad of nuanced appraisals, and perhaps more tellingly through implied and sometimes explicit classifications: what was and wasn't (really) Art or Literature. They helped define or create the aura, and instructed readers in the etiquette of reception, much as did the Boston Symphony Orchestra and Museum of Fine Arts for an older and more secure upper class. That the venue of mass culture stood in a vexed relationship to such a project of cultural distinction barely received notice, apart from a few cluckings of the tongue over the ascendancy of the commercial motive in drama and fiction. The salient perception was surely that of McClure, boasting about his democratization of Culture, or of Munsey defending the press against charges of sensationalism: "To a very large class of our people the newspaper and the magazine stand in place of a complete education, and there is no denying that each of them is able to accomplish wonders" (January 1897, p. 512).

These pages give few hints of the anxiety that Theodore Greene hypothesizes about the eclipse of the individual by corporate capital and technology. One might imagine that since the magazines themselves were rapidly becoming a major industry, their publishers might wish to conceal the new mass relations of cultural production they were creating. Not at all. As noted earlier, Munsey, Walker, and McClure all boasted descriptively to readers about advanced techniques and unprecedented circulations. McClure argued what the others took for granted: that fine culture and large scale went harmoniously together. To quote more fully a passage mentioned earlier:

> The founders of *McClure's* saw no reason why a magazine of the first excellence should not also be a magazine of the widest interest. They saw no necessary conflict between popularity in a magazine and worth. They believed that if a magazine written by the best writers, illustrated by the best artists and processes, and treating of themes attractive to the largest number of people were produced at the right price, it must inevitably have a large circulation. (June 1896, p. 97)

The rhetoric congratulates the founders while flattering their mass audience, conjoining distinction and popularity in a way that has since characterized the self-promotions of the media, but with more confidence then and fewer doubts.[37]

In general, the magazines aligned themselves and their readers with new technology, running up-to-the minute accounts of electric power generation, submarines, medical science, the chances for air navigation, and so on. *McClure's*, announced its editor in the same blurb quoted above, "has given the first authoritative account of the most important new devices and discoveries made since it began publication," and Walker had a still better right to this boast. No one fretted about antagonisms between the machine and the individual. On the contrary, the machine – above all the automobile – was to guarantee liberty. The horseless carriage, says Walker, will bring to those in "moderate circumstances" the freedom previously accorded only to the rich, of "transporting themselves at will over the country." No more the "inconvenient country boarding-house" as holiday destination; rather, for the middle class it will be a matter "of buying a horseless van [imagined to house a "dining-room, a bath-room, a kitchen, and six or eight sleeping bunks"], fitting it up with bedding and cooking utensils, and camping at night in the most delightful retreats, by the clearest springs, alongside the most musical brooks, under the broadest spreading birch tree." Perhaps when that utopian moment heals the rift between country and city, the urban visionary will learn to know a birch from a beech. Be that as it may, he is confident that "simple and inexpensive devices within the reach of all will render humanity independent of the aggregations of capital" ("Some Speculations Regarding Rapid Transit," *Cosmopolitan*, November 1895, p. 33). For Walker and for his readers as he understood them, the dream of autonomy through science and technology precluded nightmares of homogenized consumerism and corporate control.

This is to restate with a different inflection my earlier point that the magazines situated their readers on the crest of progress, and in partnership with liberating time. Science and technology, but also the new institutions and practices of social management, helped define that location. Urban planning, financial institutions like the New York Clearing House, the postal service, universities, and more came in for untroubled celebration. The police as well: with new methods of identification, "a man, once a criminal, is always a criminal, and remains to his dying day under the watchful eye of the police," wrote A.F.B. Crofton in a *Cosmopolitan* article interlarded with mug shots (November 1895, pp. 38–9). Obviously Crofton did not expect his readers to worry that *they* might be under surveillance until their dying days. The "regime of truth" was their regime.

Of course my point about social class was not the overt concern of magazine writers and editors. They, like the ad men, cast US society as progressive in an undifferentiated way, good for all its members. A sunny patriotism bathed the reader in its warmth. Although it sometimes took on the voice of a rather strident boosterism, as in *Munsey's* championing of American artists and public men, for the most part it seemed not to require assertion, certainly not belligerence. It nestled comfortably in the grooves of the writing, with easy references to the American girl, the typical American family, the American traveler, American capability and energy, American indifference to rank, and so on. McClure advertised Tarkington's *The Gentleman from Indiana* as "A clean, wholesome, American love story." A vague racialism surrounded these complacencies, but American "blood" was acknowledged to include "a strong infusion of Celtic and Teutonic" (*Munsey's*, December 1896, p. 312), and Anglo-Saxon superiority was more a given than an occasion for chest-thumping or for eugenic alarm. Patriotic feeling had not yet swelled into jingoism. There was a good deal of animosity toward the deeds of the European powers in Africa and South America; as for American imperialism, John Brisben Walker argued that "we" should help Cuba become a republic, not by fighting Spain, but by giving or lending it $200 million (August 1895, pp. 470–71).

The US was a benign society moving toward peaceful leadership by means of its industry and culture. The magazines celebrated its achievements in the present and worked to construct a proud past for it – through portraits of Grant and Lincoln, through memoirs of writers and sages (Boston was "the American Athens"), through the romanticization of the Civil War, and (in *Munsey's* and the *Ladies' Home Journal* especially) through a rather contradictory effort to provide for the nation an aristocracy of "Prominent American Families," "Colonial Dames," and the like. "We are creating our history, and we want it to be as great and good as the history of famous nations that are, or have been," a writer on American artists in Paris could unselfconsciously assert (E.H. Wuerpel, "American Artists' Association of Paris," *Cosmopolitan*, February 1896, p. 409). There was little doubt of "our" reaching that goal. The most general message sent out by these magazines was, "you can feel good about your country and your agency in its

history." Among the social "places" assigned to readers, a reliably grati-
fying one was that of Americans.

No Social Process

This America, this catbird seat for the PMC, was often vaguely evoked as
an immaterial unity. When given body, it configured itself around repetitive themes. To review: there were its privileged spots, with New York at
the center; there were its people, paraded past the reader as celebrities;
there was its history, also instanced by striking individuals, and offered as
a credentialing system for its bright destiny; there was its progressive
"now," propelled by public men, business leaders, innovators, scientists;
there was its rather separate, leisured "now," a panorama of cultural
artifact and event. Around it lay the rest of the world with *its* personages
and notable places and culture, arrayed for the vicarious enjoyment and
untroubled judgment of the domestic reader. I simplify, but not a lot, to
emphasize that in proffering this selective representation the magazines
not only flattered the reader, but flattered him or her as a specific kind
of person. They were among many speakers that hailed the reader
(Louis Althusser's term is "interpellated") with unvoiced names that
carried ideology at a level below that of statement or argument.

The self so hailed was an individual – that almost goes without saying –
in spite of the mass production and circulation of the message, and in
spite of its conformity to the interests of a whole class. Indeed, the PMC
may be defined partly by its members' understanding of themselves as
free individuals. What were the terms of that freedom? It resided first in
the ability to become what one wants to become. To be sure, magazine
biographies laid stress on early nurture, especially parental inculcation
of firm moral principles and purposefulness. However, the assumption
was not that children reared in this way were extraordinarily fortunate,
but that naturally the right sort of parents would transmit such values.
Parenting was not seen as problematic, and in fact was hardly constituted
as a subject of instruction at all, except in the *Journal*. And there, despite
the earnest morality that saturated those pages, instruction given both to
parents and to youthful readers had far more to do with social conduct
and manners than with the inner core of selfhood that would enable a
child to determine its own future.

That is to say, the *Journal* openly taught the internalizing and presentation of social identities – *class* identities – as did the other magazines
more indirectly. It is interesting to set this observation alongside the
thesis of T.J. Jackson Lears, in his classic study of the "therapeutic worldview" that took shape during this period, responding to a widespread
sense of "unreality" and "weightlessness." Lears associates this malaise
with the transition from entrepreneurial to corporate capitalism, with

markets, with the anonymity of city life – just the changes that are the subject of this book.[38] There is no question that many felt unmoored from an older ethic of self control, autonomy, and restraint; or that mind cures, mysticism, nostalgia, rural retreats, a turn toward the medieval or the primitive, and the other remedies Lears documents, gained many adherents. But the therapeutic worldview is barely discernible in the mass circulation magazines of the late 1890s. Moreover, the feeling that selfhood is accomplished partly or largely through the perfection of social roles, far from promoting anxiety and neurasthenia, is here a source of confidence, as in a shared project of development. This optimism comes through even more decisively in magazine fiction, I will argue in the next chapter.

The seeming contradiction has force only if one expects culture to speak in a single voice, contemporaries all to share the same outlook, and individuals to be monochromatic. These magazines could hardly have attracted hundreds of thousands of readers, and presented them to advertisers in the right mood of openness to purposeful consuming, had the editors presented a steady diet of neurasthenia. Nor would *these* PMC readers have been much taken with the "anti-modernism" Lears finds in other venues. Finally, it is easy to imagine a single reader welcoming the buoyant PMC modernism of Walker or Munsey for one evening's reading, and nursing private anxieties about decadence and weightlessness the next evening through a reading of Max Nordau.

The magazines spoke to their audience in a cheerful, daytime voice. They proclaimed a self grounded in solid, middle class nurture and strengthened by class identity. They helped readers achieve it. Autonomy was not a hard-won struggle over corporate odds nor a losing struggle against them, but the natural prerogative of people making their way quite nicely in city and suburb, and at home with modernism because they were helping create it. Life was possibilities. The social, as represented in the magazines, was the arena of readers' exploits, not a field of limiting forces or of determinations.

Needless to say, in order so to enable the uncaused self, that representation of the social had to be carefully drawn. It had to exclude, for certain, just those forces and determinations that might render suspect the autonomy of the PMC self. Or better: since magazine journalism could hardly claim reference to the contemporary world *without* noting forces of production, their rapid transformation, changing class relations, the shaping of people into consumers, the reconstruction of the family and of patriarchal relations, and so on, it had to reference these in ways that would neutralize them *as* determinations. Business, of course; but not the capitalist class. New techniques of production explained, but not as expressions of capital or means to subject and degrade labor. Progress, but not the massing of corporate control. Manliness and womanhood, but not gender as script or prison. The proliferation of new commodities (in the ad pages), but not the selling of the consumer; art and literature, but not culture as distinction and class formation. To put it this way is banal enough: who imagines that editors of mass publications would press a marxist account of the world on readers?

Yet it should not be imagined, on the other side, that the editors themselves were ignorant of historical forces or neutral toward them. Munsey considered businessmen the proper leaders of American society and lionized J.P. Morgan in particular. Bok thought success the inevitable reward of honesty and hard work, poverty a temporary accident. He believed change in society possible only through the moral improvement of individuals, and in a rare political editorial, he dismissed the misery and unrest of 1894 as "anarchy . . . the poisonous product of discontent" (November 1894, p. 14). McClure, the least politically oriented of the four, nonetheless was capable of editorializing (well after the moment of 1895–97), on the social transformation of the US: "Today we are a nation of corporation employees: directly or indirectly the corporation controls our living. And, as the corporations grow greater and greater, fewer and fewer men control them, and our individual lives with them" (September 1910; quoted by Lyon, p. 326). Walker, the *most* political of the four, much influenced by Edward Bellamy, wrote a piece for the September 1892 *Cosmopolitan* called "The 'Homestead' Object Lesson," in which his analysis was even more pointed than McClure's: "In fifty years the creation of wealth has become prodigious; the distribution of wealth has become frightful in its inequalities" (p. 572). He compared the Carnegies and Fricks to slave owners who thought they had the right to control the earth; capitalists, though kindly men at home, became "fierce, determined, grasping" at work, because of "our peculiar institutions" (p. 575). Workers would organize militarily, in time: Walker appealed to men of "my own class" to "regulate this one-sided distribution of wealth, lest it should be regulated by bloodshed" (p. 574). No shrinking from the historical process there.

But from 1895 to 1897 – in the wake of Homestead (1892), the panic of 1893, the Pullman strike and depression of 1894, and the rise of populism and Bryan culminating in the election of 1896 – those who read the volumes in my present sample found virtually no mention of national crisis and no analysis of the society's transformation in terms comparable to those Walker had used in 1892. Indeed, the magazines kept silent on many subjects that would have been essential to any such analysis: immigrants, industrial workers, poor people, as mentioned earlier; and also work itself, unionization, strikes, race, markets, consumer culture, the degradation of much city life, socialist and anarchist ideas, and free market ideas themselves, as an articulated system. How to explain these representational gaps? And how to understand the political homogeneity of the four magazines, given the rather striking differences in outlook among their proprietors?

A tempting answer would be the influence of advertisers, that is to say the very corporations that were forging the new social order. But I have come across no accounts of blackmail or direct suasion by manufacturers, not even *un*successful attempts to censor editorial content. And while it is a platitude of media criticism that cultural producers dependent on advertising internalize the values of their customers and exhibit a docility beyond any that is enjoined upon them, there are reasons to doubt that this dynamic was much at work in the early days of the mass circulation magazine. For one, much the same ads appeared in all the magazines, mass and elite, despite their differences in outlook and emphasis, and this pattern continued when some of the periodicals turned to their "muckraking" critique of big business. For another, as ad agencies took over more and more of the negotiating with periodicals for space and rates, they became a buffer between publishers and manufacturers, and their task was to secure market shares, not to bully successful editors. What little evidence I've run across suggests that it was policy at the magazines to keep editorial and advertising departments at arm's length; certainly this was so at the *Journal*, the most clear-sighted business operation of the four, where it was clear to Cyrus Curtis from the outset who paid the piper. He didn't let them call the tune.[39]

Anterior to these reasons, and explaining them, is the one big reason: advertisers urgently needed to reach large and nationally distributed groups of consumers with the right incomes and attitudes, and the new magazines appeared to be the best conduit to that audience. As soon as the new methods of selling took root, every manufacturer in certain lines of consumer goods had to have space in the magazines or cede his competitors an enormous advantage. By 1893 the *Journal* had more advertisers knocking at the door than it had room for (Steinberg, p. 28), and by 1896 the other three magazines (and many with smaller circulations) were bulging with ads. In the nascent consciousness industry, it was a seller's market, much as for network TV in the 1960s, and those buying the attention of consumers in order to praise soap and cereal did not insist on praise for the corporate order in the medium that had that attention to sell. Of course they didn't need to insist, and that fact leaves my question about political homogeneity unanswered.

The most persuasive answer, I believe, gives only a small and unconscious role to ideological manipulation, and a veiled role to the interests of advertisers. In terms current at the time, it had to do with the intersecting ideals of the "general" magazine and of the "family" magazine. The former term distinguished these monthlies not only from agricultural, technical, domestic, and professional journals, but also from religious periodicals and from partisan or socially committed ones. "General," despite its apparent inclusiveness, was a term of limitation, of negation. It erased, from its conception of the audience, their existence as farmers, as engineers, as housewives, Methodists, Democrats, and so on. The "general" magazine addressed readers around or above categories of occupation, party, religious faith, and gender. (The *Journal* was not a "general" magazine; apart from gender, the point applies to it as well.) The idea served three aims: to reach the largest possible audience by setting aside many of its divisions; to position it in the spheres of leisure and culture; and to put it at ease by disengaging its occupational and sectarian commitments. Clearly, all three aims were those of advertisers too; and as clearly, all three authorized a sunny and conflict-free representation of the social world. That representation took its lineaments from the similar market interests of publishers and manufacturers, not from the ideological goals of either.

As the idea of the "general" blurred social coordinates, the idea of the "family" magazine restored them, but deceptively. Its main force was not to exclude those cut adrift from nuclear or extended families. Doubtless it did banish the interests of drummers, shop girls alone in the city, migrant laborers, and prostitutes, but not because they lived independently of parents and spouses. It disregarded them along with *married* drummers, shopgirls, laborers, and prostitutes because they were all the wrong class. "Family" was code for "respectable." The paradigmatic scene it called to mind was of the magazine on the parlor table, where it might be picked up by the young lady of the genteel family. What was too crude for her sensibilities, as conceived by her parents and by the clergy and by all the ghosts of nineteenth-century moralists, had no place in a family magazine.

The conjunction of these two ideals was nothing new. *Godey's Lady's Book*, the premier magazine of mid century, had enacted them with its polite domesticity and its non-partisanship. (It even declined to take sides in the Civil War, an overextension of neutrality that lost it many subscribers.) The *Century*, leader in the 1880s, was known among writers as a magazine whose "contents were limited to matter which would not offend any one – a policy that is better for the counting house than for the making of good literature."[40] The monthlies of the 1890s filled their pages with new "contents" but preserved those old taboos that still made the "counting house" prosper, including those against recognition of social conflict. Editors thoroughly internalized these taboos. Howells wrote that when he took a job at *Harper's* he asked the publisher about the limits of the acceptable; "there appeared to be very few things" one could not say, but approach to some would cause the house to sound "a little bell." "I tried to catch the tinkle of the little bell when it was not actually sounded."[41]

These conceptions of the audience and the accompanying taboos dictated many editorial policies. Most obviously, the "little bell" tinkled in the ear of an editor at a whisper of sexual impropriety. And if it didn't, the boss was there to ring it loudly. Charles Hanson Towne recalled that although Walker generally allowed him to select poetry for *Cosmopolitan*, when Richard Le Gallienne submitted his translation of the *Rubaiyat*, Walker intervened. He prefaced it with an editorial note defending it as "real literature," but printed only parts of it. "Then he proceeded to eliminate whole lines, printing asterisks in their stead; for he claimed that as *Cosmopolitan* was a family magazine, which was placed on the library table, it was not fitting that the youth of the land should be familiar with certain passages . . . ." He broke off serial publication of Tolstoy's *Resurrection* midway, because he thought the later installments "strong meat" (Towne, pp. 39–40). Similarly, Bok instructed an essayist on modern fiction to avoid discussing Tolstoy and Zola (Steinberg, p. 54). Victorian mores held, in this cultural site.

On the other hand, it would be a mistake to read the taboo as foreclosing on sex in some purely biological definition. Munsey continually ran sexy photos of actresses and singers; Munsey and Walker reproduced paintings of nudes and semi-nudes; articles in their two magazines spoke indulgently of Joshua Reynolds's rakishness and of actresses in the same period who were mistresses of their social betters. Munsey defended Zola. Walker printed James Lane Allen's *Butterflies*, whose realism extended to sexual passion and illegitimacy. Sex could be thematized in these magazines if (a) it was framed as Art; (b) it was a vice of the lower orders; or (c) it was brought under moral censure.[42] A statue of a bacchante, representing "a woman in an advanced state of exhilaration, and innocent of clothes," is technically well done and "realistic," but not suitable as centerpiece of the fountain at the Boston Public Library, an "educational" institution (*Munsey's*, December 1896, pp. 261, 264). The realism of Hardy and George Moore is acceptable because of its truth and quality, though it "deals with questionable things," while D'Annunzio's "revolting" new novel, lacking art, is "unpardonable" (*Munsey's*, January 1897, p. 631). Art and truth redeem sexuality for the proper, sophisticated audience, if not for the general throng that might pass by the Boston Public Library. It is interesting, too, to note the terms of moral reproof. Kipling shows "bad taste" (*Munsey's*, December 1896, p. 504); D'Annunzio "the manners and morals of the poultry yard" (p. 631); a new English play is "unfit for polite ears" and hence for "New York's select audiences" (*Cosmopolitan*, February 1896, p. 444). Manners and taste are on the line in these border patrollings of sexual morality: the taboo manifests itself as one of class sensibility.

The quest for the polite, "general," "family" readership also laid strict constraints on the treatment of religion. It had little place in the four leading magazines, as a subject of discussion. Only the *Journal* permitted direct presentation of religious ideas, as in Margaret Bottome's folksy meditation on "I am the resurrection and the life" (February 1896, p. 26), in columns of advice from ministers, and in Bok's own generalized piety – and the *Journal's* ambience was no more than vaguely Protestant. In fiction it was permissible for characters to advance doctrine, less so for narrators. Writers speaking in their own voices revealed few commitments beyond a Christian faith evacuated of most content. They wrote *about* famous clergymen and notable churches; they wrote about Glastonbury and Richelieu and the Christian past; they wrote about the secure religious beliefs or simple piety of great men and women in an approving tone. But they did not advance or defend doctrine and they stayed miles away from religious controversy. The lore and history and institutions and leaders of Christianity appeared as furnishings of proper culture, represented in a quiet, neutral voice, harmonizing easily with the secular urbanity that was the magazines' home register.

The ban on engaged religion was well understood, and coupled with one on "politics." "Magazines intended for general circulation must, of course, exclude politics and theology," wrote Henry Mills Alden (*Magazine Writing and the New Literature*, p. 78). An editorial in *Harper's* insisted that the magazine had always "excluded partisan politics and all subjects upon which readers were divided on sectarian lines in religious thought and feeling" (September 1902, pp. 646–8). I think this coupling of routine exclusions with the unstated taboo on rude sex puts us in a better position to understand the political silences with which this discussion began. Partisanship would "of course" preclude "general circulation." In a long article on "The Making of an Illustrated Magazine," Walker explained that "To be successful, *Cosmopolitan* must draw its circulation from the entire people of the country"; to that end, it "does not enter the field of politics, and can afford to have the interest of the entire people at heart" (January 1893, pp. 260, 272). "*Munsey's* has no party bias," said the columnist of "In the Public Eye"; this parenthetical remark occurred in the midst of a calm, even-handed, and broadly admiring rundown on main figures, Republican and Democratic, in the pivotal election of 1896 (October 1896, p. 15). Bok, though a lifelong Republican, kept the *Journal* detached from electoral politics (Steinberg, p. 48). Not only would partisanship damage circulation; I conjecture that it would also violate the class-coded decorum of a family magazine. Just as politics and religion were off limits for conversation at a dinner party (at least until the men retired with cigars and brandy), their contestation had no place on the living room or library table. Party politics, in any case, were a mug's game, associated with Tammany Hall and unscrupulous lowlifes. The PMC identified itself with rational reform and good management, not the hurly-burly of rounding up votes.

All four magazines held aloof from the electoral fray. *Munsey's* came closest to it, with photos and brief biographies of Bryan, McKinley, Mark Hanna, governors and senators, "A Famous 'Reform Mayor'" (Hazen S. Pingree, of Detroit). But as that title suggests, the magazine represented politicians strictly within the celebrity genre: fame is fame. At the same time the *Journal* ran a series explaining various branches and departments of government, "This Country of Ours," by Benjamin Harrison – the political celebrity as author, definitely not as Republican advocate. (Later, Bok signed up Theodore Roosevelt as a writer on manly and civic duties.) *McClure's* drew no closer to the savage politics of 1896 than by printing articles on Lincoln, Grant, and Gladstone. *Cosmopolitan*, the same – though it did offer its readers a serialized Bellamy-like, utopian narrative of "Altruria" (sequel to Howells's 1892–93 *Traveller from Altruria)*, thematizing at that imaginative distance the great issues of wealth and power.

Aside from the Altruria tale, the exclusion of electoral politics held as rigorously for less mediated social conflicts like that between capital and labor, and for understandings of US history that would oppose the two terms in that way. It's not that there was at that moment a truce in the class struggle or a nationwide vow of silence upon it. Intellectual journals like the *Arena*, the *Forum*, the *North American Review*, and the *Nation* observed no such ban. One could sometimes read about deep conflict and crisis in old, upper-class monthlies like the *Atlantic*. Working class periodicals like the "story papers," not to mention dime novels, richly represented the militancy and dignity of labor.[43] But as the mass magazines assembled their middle class audience ("general," "family"), they projected a social space in which readers could understand themselves as autonomous, historically favored individuals. This was a space unvexed by conflict, a space where change was smoothed out and universalized as *progress.* Behind it, history stood as Culture and as selective, legitimizing *tradition.* The implicit ideology held sway, I am arguing, not because it expressed the editors' own beliefs and not because advertisers demanded it, but because it was what would sell magazines at this particular time to the audience advertisers most valued, and stroke them into the kind of expansive mood most hospitable to dreams of modern consumption.

I have described the mood in ways that suggest the term "escapist," but that won't quite do. The magazines spoke to their readers as smart, capable, energetic, confident people who could survey the world around them, see where it was going, and help it get there. Some subjects and issues were closed off to them, in this medium, but much fell within their purview, demanding their involvement or their informed and critical observation. Better to understand this irregular escapism, I want now to look more carefully at one invisible and one quite visible subject: race and gender.

The Place of African Americans

Where were black people on this beachhead of mass culture? The short answer is, outside the arena of public discourse organized by the new cultural producers. Race was not exactly unmentionable, and black people were not literally invisible; but race – what was elsewhere called "the Negro problem" – made no appearance as a constituted issue in the magazines that make up my sample. That is to say, they included no article on it, nor did columnists or writers allude to controversy or debate around it, nor did they assume any shared "position" on it; it was too much a part of common sense to *require* debate. They simply did not place it on the agenda.

The sole exception was half a column on limitation of the franchise in Mississippi and South Carolina by means of literacy tests, in *Munsey's*. Its take on the issue is interesting. The anonymous writer makes clear that the laws aim "to prevent the domination of the negroes," a majority in these states, but neither approves nor condemns that goal. Instead, he frames the question as "a curious problem" for Congress in that the Constitution would require the two states to lose representation in the House proportionate to the number of its citizens denied the vote for reasons other than rebellion or crime. "What is the duty of Congress in the matter? The question is an awkward one," because it would "be a misfortune" to allow open disregard for the Constitution. But "who will arise to cast the first stone?" So ends the discussion (January 1897, p. 511); and so much for the Negro question. Why its exclusion? Here is my conjectural reply, beginning with a glance backward.

After the war, radical Reconstruction had brought southern blacks into public life very quickly, but not on the basis of any social contract likely to endure. I agree with those historians who hold that the enfranchisement and (within limits) empowerment of black Americans responded chiefly to motives quite distinct from a commitment to racial equality. One motive was of course vengefulness against the Confederacy. The two decisive ones, however, were the determination of Republicans to maintain political dominance and the determination of northern business leaders to preserve their ascendancy, given momentum through the Civil War boom. Southern whites opposed both projects; a congressional delegation from the states of the Confederacy, enlarged by reapportionment and elected only by whites, would have impeded both Republican political control and the project of industrial capitalists. That spectre, more than anything, brought enough powerful northerners in line to accomplish radical Reconstruction, but did not guarantee political support that would last once those two aims could be achieved by other means, and once the impulse toward national reconciliation overcame the impulse toward punishment of southern whites.

Thus, disenfranchisement of black people followed directly if unevenly upon the election of 1876 and the Compromise of 1877. In consequence, blacks virtually disappeared from public office by the early 1880s, and, equally important, ceased to exist as a political bloc that could demand attention from white politicians to black aspirations and resistance. Upon the withdrawal of northern concern (not to mention federal troops), southern whites gradually eliminated black influence in public affairs, and enforced a sharper and sharper division of public spaces into black and white. Trains and streetcars, courts and jails, schools, eating places, city and county offices, all underwent gradual segregation through custom and coercion, before Jim Crow laws formalized these arrangements in the 1890s and after. Black poverty and local vigilantism ensured the division of black from white living quarters, so that when laws segregating neighborhoods came on the books after 1900, they were scarcely needed.[44]

For northerners, this was all a remote and not very troubling process. Virtually the only racial oppression that held the attention of northern liberals was lynching, and even about that there was relatively little outcry through the 1890s, when that form of repression was at its height. Meanwhile, migration did bring increasing numbers of black people into the proximity of northern whites: the flow rose from about 40,000 per decade through the 1870s and 1880s to about 110,000 in the 1890s. But – still a tiny minority – they, too, came into mainly segregated jobs and living patterns. By and large young and untrained, as well as uprooted, these newcomers did not for many years constitute an economic or political threat to white complacency.

In the journals that aired and formed influential northern opinion, political discussion of race thinned out. The Civil War was there, steadily depoliticized and rendered as a field of heroism (on both sides) and romance. The South was there, as a quaint and rather backward section, gradually rehabilitating itself.[45] Reconstruction was there, for a while, increasingly rewritten as a chaotic and ludicrous detour from the road to progressive, white nationhood. And in time Booker T. Washington was there, as virtually the only black voice granted an audience by white editors. I condense, of course, but the point is that a shroud of forgetfulness and ignorance fell over hegemonic northern discourse.

In the South, meanwhile, a lively discourse grew up, explaining and justifying the oppression of blacks. The main rationale came out of Darwinism, which in the North had been fused with the doctrines of Smith and Ricardo to generate a parallel theory of economic progress, in which race figured little. Influential works like Frederick Hoffman's *Race Traits and Tendencies of the American Negro* (1896) argued that blacks were a genetically inferior people who had been temporarily and artificially preserved, even improved, by slavery, but who, released into the free competition of American society, had already degenerated and would continue to do so until the race disappeared. Thus was racism warranted, as biological destiny: to educate and otherwise coddle a doomed race was to impede the natural process of evolution and the inevitable triumph of whites. The even more vicious argument that negroes were in fact dangerous beasts, another species, also resurfaced at this time. On the other side were, at best, conservative paternalistic southerners who cast the negro as a child, needing protection in a permanent lesser status. For the most part, northerners averted their ears from this debate, regarding it as unseemly, and in any case, not their problem.

The most dynamic and powerful groups in American society had, by the time of the magazine revolution of 1893, accepted the "common sense" of white supremacy and lost interest in debate over race relations, seeing them as increasingly irrelevant to the social project of industrial capitalism and to the PMC vision of modernity, in particular. Nor did editors of the new monthlies want to cloud the sunny optimism of readers about their favored status and social mission, and about the new social order that had cast them as the bearers of rationality and progress. To bring forward the intractable disgrace of the negro question would have been to undermine the complacency of the audience and disturb its receptivity to commercial messages, as well. In brief, I suggest that shifts in the perceived national agenda after the Civil War conspired with the particular interests of the new cultural producers to make race a non-subject in their magazines through the late 1890s.

It did maintain a shadowy presence in the *elite* magazines. As early as 1890 the *Arena* printed an article by Professor N.S. Shaler prefiguring Hoffman's influential thesis that American negroes came from an African stock just one "step above the lowest savagery" which had improved through the opportunity for blacks to "ape" their white "social superiors" during slavery. Shaler saw no subsequent deterioration of the race, but held that negroes still lacked any business, political, and family sense, and should not have the vote ("The Nature of the Negro, December 1890, pp. 26, 28). On the other side, readers of such magazines could encounter racial uplift arguments like those of Booker T. Washington. For instance, in "The Awakening of the Negro" he forecast that "the industrial progress of the negro" would bring about "right relations between the two races," and that "whether he will or not, a white man respects a negro who owns a two-story brick house" (*Atlantic*, September 896, pp. 322–8). An occasional voice favored higher education and voting rights for African Americans.

To anticipate for a moment the subject of my next chapter: the elite magazines also included fictional representations of black people, for the most part sanitized by conventions of the plantation tale, a subgenre of the dialect sketch that shared the unifying ideology of regionalism ("local color") and joined it to the literature of reconciliation between North and South. The Uncle Remus tales, printed in the *Century* from 1883 on, were but the most famous instance. By ostensibly honoring while slyly contesting those conventions, Charles Chesnutt was able to publish several of his conjure stories in the *Atlantic* and *Overland* monthlies during the late 1880s. The fact that the editors of those pages refused to publish the openly contestatory fiction he went on to write, and the requirement laid upon him by Houghton Mifflin (the *Atlantic*'s book publishing partner) to write more conjure tales (a decade after he had left the form behind) in order to have a book of stories accepted, show the pressure of ideology on generic conventions and vice versa, and how limited were the possibilities of challenging racism, even in sites of high culture where abolitionism had flourished a few decades earlier.[46]

In the cheap monthlies, as I have said, those possibilities were virtually nonexistent, and the deepening American racial crisis was kept at or beyond the horizon. One horizon was temporal. Ida Tarbell could assume that readers of her biography of Lincoln would approve of his anti-slavery positions,[47] and both in her series and elsewhere abolitionists received approval. Triumph over cruelty and injustice fit snugly into myths of progress. Another horizon was geographical: references to race as controversial in Africa occasionally occurred. Culture may have been still another, to judge from a brief, commendatory paragraph in "Literary Chat" on Paul Lawrence Dunbar, "one of the very few men of his race who have won a genuine reputation in literature" (*Munsey's*, February 1897, p. 635).

Lending plausibility to that hypothesis is the fact that black figures sometimes appear marginally in *fiction*, almost as part of the scenery: a wagon rattling by, driven by "a little bare-headed negro with a pea-stick for a whip" (*Cosmopolitan*, December 1895, p. 167); a ship's fireman with a "woolly head," speaking a few lines in funny dialect and requiring to be choked into action (*McClure's*, September 1896, pp. 367–8); families on the platform at a train station, kissing promiscuously and sending out "peals of that indescribable negro laughter" (*Munsey's*, October 1896, p. 109). Or a white character might signal his provinciality by saying something like, "I always did like pop-eyed niggers. They look so Godforsaken an' ugly" (*Ladies' Home Journal*, December 1897, p. 13). Rarely is a black character given a name or a role in the plot. A major exception is instructive: in a rustic, neighborhood dispute, the "colonel" orders the ex-slave Scipio to shoot two antagonists. Scipio executes the command, but with "the negro irresponsibility that leaves 'consequences' to higher natures," and convinced that the colonel had actually done it: even in murder, the negro is denied agency (Mrs F. W. Dawson, "A Tragedy of South Carolina," *Cosmopolitan*, November 1895, p. 56).[48] Black people figured only as minor characters, servants usually, adjuncts to white people's affairs, denied the power to act independently, and thus utterly unthreatening.[49] No truly disturbing image of a black person troubled my reading of about a hundred stories from this period; and *without* exception, no image of blacks as a rebellious social force, or as full participants in human relations. Their presence was marginal, and without reproach because impotent.[50]

The disappearance of race from social critique or analysis and the recasting of negroes as contented buffoons in fiction made their image available for easy appropriation into one of the new mass culture's key

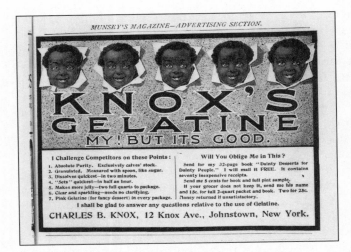

Figure 22 Knox's Gelatine ad, *Munsey's*,
March 1900

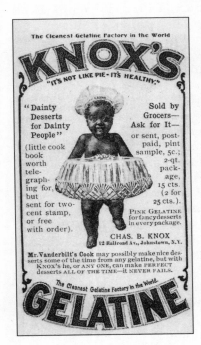

Figure 23 Knox's Gelatine ad,
Ladies' Home Journal, December 1899

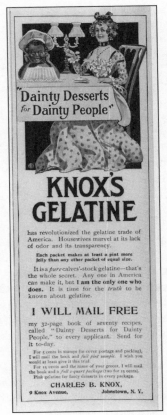

Figure 24 Knox's Gelatine ad,
Harper's, May 1900

Figure 25 "Onyx" Black Hosiery ad,
Ladies' Home Journal,
February 1896

Figure 26 Ayer's Cherry Pectoral
Plaster ad, *Ladies' Home Journal,*
February 1899

systems of meaning. So I conclude from the relative abundance of images in advertising, by comparison with editorial contents. They were not so abundant as is perhaps implied by the gathering of examples reproduced here (see Figures 16, 18, and 21–9),[51] but common enough to prompt the question, Why did advertisers often choose to remind readers of a subject virtually banned from articles and relegated to the margins in fiction? Why did they assimilate these images into their system of meaning? One answer is obvious: advertising had to be happy talk, and the magazines had drained from the subject of race nearly all upsetting connotations, making it part of a stylized social backdrop, meant to reassure middle class whites about their place in the world. Further, the reservoir of culturally available images included two black stereotypes tailor-made for reinforcement of complacent good cheer:

Figure 27 Hinds' Honey and Almond Cream ad, *Munsey's*, June 1907

malted corn-flakes ready to serve

Kornelia Kinks

"W'en I show gran'pappy da lil' box what have Ko'n Kinks, he say, 'Go 'long, chile, dat ain't no mo' co'n dan it is goobers;' but I say, 'Yo' jes' tas' it.' An' he tas' an' tas' an' tas', an' bimeby he et de whole box up, an' he say, 'It am suttenly wunnerful how w'ite folks kin mek jes' co'n tas' so good.'"—*Kornelia Kinks.*

5c. Korn-Kinks, the new food, corn and malt, to be eaten cold or hot, for breakfast and all meals. For sale at all grocery stores. 5c. a package.

The H-O Company, Buffalo, N. Y.

Three Minutes

Only required to take, develop, and finish the above picture with the

NODARK
CAMERA

Size of camera, 3½ in. wide, 4½ in. high, 12 in. long.
Size of pictures, 2½ in. x 3½ in.

With this camera the entire tedious and difficult science of photography is reduced to such simplicity that any child can use it.

NO DARK ROOM.
No Costly Chemicals.
No Printing Frames.
No Blurs or Hazy Results.

The process is so perfect that every plate comes out right. There is no secret about the Nodark Camera—simply a new dry-plate tintype is used instead of glass plates or films. Every Nodark Camera is complete and perfect. **Also includes 26 plates, 1 developing chamber, 2 bottles of solution, and instructions how to operate and make the pictures.**

Price $6.00.
Express prepaid.
Buy from your dealer. If he won't supply you, write us.
Free booklet sent on request.

POPULAR PHOTOGRAPH COMPANY,
112 Bleecker Street, New York.

Figure 28 Korn Kinks ad,
Ladies' Home Journal, January 1907

Figure 29 Nodark Camera ad,
Harper's, May 1900

the happy servant and the pickaninny. If we associate the young black man in the Nodark camera ad with servants (he has complaisantly agreed to pose for the up-to-date tourist and amateur photographer), all these images but one allude to one or the other of these stereotypes.[52]

But a satisfying answer must do more; it must explain why, given an infinite number of possible, soothing images, a fair number of advertisers chose these. To approach that kind of answer, consider the visual language of advertising and commodities that developed in the 1890s. As I showed in chapter 8, it is a language that exploits gaps, constituting the reader as one who can bridge them. Notice that of all the ads that picture black people, only one offers in its verbal text any explanation of the image, or any specific connection between product and race. That is the one for Pears' Soap in Figure 18, with Admiral Dewey in the center, and the native in the lower right hand corner, gratefully receiving soap from the missionary. Here, the text ventures to gloss the image, partly I think because the latter is so far-fetched, and partly just because the image does *not* evoke one of the two standard stereotypes. The other ads offer no bridge; the reader is supposed to make sense out of the arbitrary connection between black person and product. How?

With three of the products, the black figure is a trademark image: Cream of Wheat, Korn Kinks, and Knox's Gelatine. I include three Knox ads to suggest how advertisers repeated and varied these images, month after month and year after year, so that the trademark figure came, magically, to stand for the brand. I suspect that this practice helped clear the semiotic way for other ads that made incidental use of black figures (and of course for all ads that left readers to make sense of gaps). The "you" constituted by ads is, among other things, one who can read across fissures and discontinuities in the semantic field.

Be that as it may, without question the "you" of these ads *could* read the images; if not, advertisers were paying for indecipherable communications, and provoking, surely, great confusion and resentment among readers. What did readers understand from these juxtapositions of brand and black persons, beyond the ideology of a trouble-free social space? I think they read them mainly under the signs of modernity and class. The entire universe of ads proclaimed a new way of living that involved brand name commodities available everywhere on store shelves, to be used in much-simplified routines of daily domesticity and leisure. But modernity is never felt *just* as progress, and turn-of-the century advertising, like advertising today, often reassured its audience that old values and social relations were still somehow present and dependable, among the new. Images of servant and pickaninny, marginal to the new market system but still happily attendant upon its masters, helped enact this nostalgic gesture. The gesture had power, especially when the black people were *children* – "natural" and pleasure loving.

As for class: the ads clearly situated the implied "you" in opposition to a black person either outside the circle of the genteel – and outside the commodity world itself – or as a compliant subordinate in the rituals of genteel life, like golf, photography, or an elegant breakfast. But there may be a subtler process of meaning, here. If I'm right, a deeper form of class flattery derived from a tacit opposition: that of sophisticated, confident, urban, northern person to an unnamed *white* other – southern cracker or industrial working class immigrant, say – who would *not* be at home and at ease among images of harmless negroes and racial harmony, even between children. In other words, precisely the new middle class's distance from and invulnerability to racial conflict made it possible for such people to read links between household products and black people as a compliment to their social poise and liberal views. Likewise, as Claire Potter argues, the racial ideologies advanced by such imagery and by the mechanisms of segregation structured "the ways in which all citizens encountered new processes of class formation," and "collaborated in producing the nation itself as a 'cultural artifact' which was contained and constituted by whiteness."[53]

These last thoughts are speculative, and certainly open to dispute. In indirect support of my general proposition, though, consider one contrasting use of ideology. The Rubifoam ad (Figure 19) shows that advertisers were quite capable of appropriating social conflict to their ends, when they perceived it as relevant to their audience. The New Woman was the middle class feminist of the 1890s, a perplexing creature who went about in public on her own, took up tennis and golf (like the lady in the Hinds ad), adopted sensible dress, and generally asserted herself against many traditional restrictions of gender. This rebellion disturbed most men and some women, and very much did constitute a subject for debate in the 10-cent magazines (see the next section). Rubifoam chose to disarm this conflict and bring it within the discourse of modernity, reducing female assertiveness to a matter of "costume" and "fashion," and linking it to an "up-to-date" dentifrice – exactly the same move toward recuperation executed with such persistence and skill by Virginia Slims in recent years, with their "You've come a long way, baby"[54] campaign. The Pears' Soap ad featuring Admiral Dewey performs a similar gesture with respect to imperialism; but, with the possible exception of the one for Ayer's Plaster, I have not found a single ad that adopts race in the US as a political challenge, even to the extent of trivializing and recuperating it.

Editorial silence, fictional marginalization, and advertising appropriation add up to a consistent policy of representing the social order as white and right, with black people smilingly present but not really part of it, certainly not problematized as giving the lie to its claims of rationality and decency. I say a policy; yet there is little evidence of conscious intent. One of Bok's editors cited the racial policy of the *Journal* in rejecting an article on southern life because it touched on "several matters which are of really no value whatever to us, such as the Crackers and Negroes. If any references at all were to be made to these two classes, we should consider it worthwhile to have only the slightest references."[55] For the most part, the tinkle of the little bell did the job. Race was "of really no value whatever" in furthering the project of these magazines, and black people waited politely at the edge of white social space.

In 1904, with the muckraking movement well underway, *McClure's* ended the long moratorium on debate about race in the mass circulation monthlies. It published an article by Carl Schurz, expert in the condition of blacks since Andrew Johnson had sent him south to study it after the War. Schurz argued for negro suffrage, predicted higher levels of achievement for blacks, and called on "high-minded and enlightened Southerners" to spread a spirit of "chivalry" toward blacks among their more "prejudiced" compatriots. But he felt constrained to limit the reach of his argument by disassociating it from "the preposterous bugbear of 'social equality'" ("Can the South Solve the Negro Problem?," January 1904, pp. 274–5). And McClure felt constrained to commission a balancing response from Thomas Nelson Page, famous for his plantation tales of "old time darkies." In three articles titled "The Negro: The Southerner's Problem" (later published in a book by the same name), Page presented a version of Frederick Hoffman's Darwinian argument: nine-tenths of the race had, in the new conditions of freedom, "either stood stagnant or retrograded"; "lazy, thriftless, intemperate, insolent, dishonest, and without the most rudimentary elements of morality," they constituted "a vast sluggish mass of uncooled lava over a large section of the country" (May 1904, pp. 100, 101, 98). I wonder if these two positions would have marked the new boundaries of discussion when it erupted in the national arena after 1900, had commercial and political forces not conspired to deny a presence for black people other than as stick figures, in the first site of national, mass cultural production. And I wonder what the consequences have been since, of representing black people to this upscale and in many ways progressive white audience mainly in condescending and reassuring images, as adjuncts to consumer culture.[56]

A New Woman's Place

In the same sampling of monthlies from 1895–97[57] appear nearly fifty articles and columns signed by women writers; about twenty articles and short pieces mainly about women (among them George Eliot, Russian mathematician Sonya Kovalesky, Harriet Beecher Stowe, orator Mary Ellen Lease, many Daughters of the American Revolution, and in the *Journal* "Unknown Wives of Well-Known Men"); nine articles about activities of women (from lace making to mountain climbing); dozens of stories by or about women; and innumerable photographs and paintings of women. In some of these categories the *Journal* leads, but in all four magazines women figure very prominently.

This will probably surprise my reader no more than it does me; for a number of obvious reasons there could be no exclusion of women like the exclusion of black people just considered. Probably most readers of the magazines were women; at least that seems to have been a common opinion. Male readers were also interested in women. The class whose social space the magazines entered and helped define was half female, and its gendering had much to do with its self-image. For fifty years women had been at least grudgingly accepted as writers; thousands of them worked in journalism by the late 1890s, so that they had an established voice in the public arena.

These banalities ensured attention to women and their "interests," as well as to men's interests in women, but not to more than traditional conceptions of those interests, which were indeed a staple of the magazines: from the practical domesticity featured in the *Journal* to fictional narratives of romance and marriage to profiles of famous women to the halftones of actresses and "Fair Women" in *Munsey's*. It was quite consistent with the principle of unvexed social space developed earlier in this chapter for the magazines to have displayed women as quietly or even brilliantly being their immutable selves and so exemplifying the naturalness of the social order. Such an appearance would correspond – with obvious differences – to that of marginal, happy "darkies." But gender was not so tidily packaged or so easily written off as a non-issue. Where no one posed the "negro question," there was distinctly a woman question, for a few years indexed as that of the "New Woman."

Even as middle class doctrines of separate spheres, the vocation of domesticity, and the angel in the house had hardened through the middle decades of the century, many women and some men had challenged them, from before Seneca Falls onward. Suffrage was their most forward cause, but they also called for liberalization of divorce laws, changes in the oppressive property relations of marriage, access to education, and other reforms. By the 1890s, more radical feminists like Charlotte Perkins Gilman had articulated a deeper critique of gender roles, women's domestic subordination, and even the bourgeois family and the ideal of motherhood. These ideas were in the air, and the New Woman was associated with them. But those women who seemed most provocatively new did not join movements or agitate in the streets. They never organized as a group. There were no women's charters or founding conventions. In fact, few of those labeled New Women even designated themselves that way. Rather, one may best understand the phrase in its journalistic currency as a handy means of referring to, and often stigmatizing, a loose cluster of projects, goals, and styles.

These were among the most salient: belonging to clubs, doing social work, living apart from parents or husband, moving about in public alone, working for a living or on principle, seeking wide and worldly knowledge through formal education or otherwise, thinking for oneself, speaking assertively about public issues in mixed company, giving speeches, taking part in sports (cycling, swimming, golfing), smoking, wearing or agitating for rational dress, seeking equal marriage, disavowing marriage altogether, caring little for love, denying the obligation of motherhood. If a single adjective can characterize all this, it is probably "independent," and it was often so used. The New Woman was or wanted to be free in important areas of her life: work, social activities, self development, self presentation, affection, relationship.

These aspirations came forward intermittently through the 1880s and more persistently in the early 1890s, stirring a fair amount of debate. In the March 1894 issue of the *North American Review*, novelist Sarah Grand sympathetically voiced some of them and, apparently for the first time, called their bearer "the new woman."[58] Another well known novelist, "Ouida" (Marie Louise de la Ramée), responded in the May issue, where she castigated the "New Woman," capital *N* and capital *W*. The name stuck, and circulated rapidly through much heated discussion in magazine articles, satire, cartoons, novels, and plays, both in Britain and in the US. Some installments were long and searching, most notably a series of six articles in the *Saturday Review* elaborating and defending the New Woman's positions, along with some rebuttals from [Mary], Lady Jeune. Already in May 1895 the proponent "A Woman of the Day" (Mrs Roy Devereux) could say that the New Woman was seen as "an excrescence on the face of society," and was "the jest of every fool and the *bête noire* of every philosopher" – an indication of how quickly the New Woman had been framed as a subject of controversy.[59]

To be sure, much of that controversy played itself out as, precisely, jest. This Patricia Marks richly demonstrates in her study of British and American satirical magazines; the 10-cent monthlies, too, occasionally adopted this strategy of light dismissal. An article in *Cosmopolitan* on amateur photography included as an example a posed shot of a tug of war, men against women, all fully braced and nearly supine on the grass, with the caption, "The New Woman Taking Her Position" (January 1896, p. 258). In the column "Impressions by the Way," as early as November 1895, *Munsey's* commented: "today, we are told, one of the cherished tokens of the New Woman's emancipation is her cigarette" (p. 220). Later, the same department ran a paragraph about a Chicago woman's "triumphant success in a field hitherto monopolized by tyrant man – that of burglary." It titled the piece, "Woman in Another New Role," referred to the burglar as "this eminently new woman," and concluded, "let us hear no more of the exploded myth of 'woman's' weakness'" (December 1896, p. 384). The Rubiform ad (Figure 19) mines the same vein. Even an article sympathetic to the New Woman could remain on the same level of triviality, though without the jest. There was one such outside my sample, "The New Woman and Golf Playing" (*Cosmopolitan*, August 1896, pp. 352–61). After beginning, "What the bicycle has left undone toward the transformation of the life of American women, the game of golf bids fair to complete," the article ran through a history of golf and mentioned a number of male and female players. It entered the debate only in the mildest terms, praising the healthfulness of the game for women and approving of ankle-length skirts and loose clothing with no stays, but leaving such choices to "taste." The phrase "new woman" appeared only in the title, apparently as a serviceable hook for the reader's attention.

Most casual references had more of an edge, came closer to the raw nerve. A celebrity profile on the secretary of state and his wife praised her charm and modesty, and revealed that she opposed women's suffrage, thought women could "find sufficient work in their own homes," approved of their athletics "in moderation," and thought herself "not a 'new woman'" (*Munsey's*, March 1897, p. 699) – in case anyone missed the point. Her opposite, Kansas Democrat Mary E. Lease, received credit for political achievement but in a tone that bristled with defensiveness and hostility: "the feminist Boanerges of Kansas"; "she is certainly a type"; "her oratory might evoke smiles in the classic halls of Congress"; her husband (a druggist) "may be classed among the 'unknown husbands of famous wives'" (*Munsey's*, January 1897, pp. 457–8 – note the mocking reference to the *Journal's* "Unknown Wives" feature). The brief profile of Sonya Kovalesky concluded its account of her tragic conflict between "femininity" and professional distinction, "As a type of the restless, aspiring, modern woman who ignores the limitations of her sex, she is both interesting and instructive" (*Cosmopolitan*, November 1895, p. 99). More portentously still: "I am not going to say anything about or against the 'New Woman' or the 'New Man' . . . but I do say that the thing that women and girls want most of all things, is a character like Jesus Christ's, and that can be made in a house with very humdrum work to do, or out of it if necessary" – this from Margaret Bottome's religious column in the *Journal* (February 1896, p. 26). "If necessary" captures the grudging acceptance in these magazines of a woman's working for wages. If *not* "necessary," her ventures into the economic and political spheres broke rules and caused frowns.

But that isn't quite the whole story. There were, after all, those divas and first ladies of the stage, glowing at the dazzled reader from the pages of *Munsey's* and sometimes honored even in the *Journal*. They did not bear the stigma of the advanced woman, nor did the many women who wrote for the magazines, nor those whose novels were reviewed there, nor the artists and illustrators. Was this an indulgence granted to "artists," assumed to be of lower classes? I don't think so, because many women from fine families (for example, Emma Eames, the singer) were featured, and others might join such families by marriage, without censure. Women in the arts did not sin against womanliness, unless by voluntary indecorum or principled feminism. Even George Eliot's personal life won a stout defense in *Cosmopolitan* against attacks by two well known antagonists of the New Woman, "Ouida" and Mrs Lynn Linton (January 1896, pp. 312–16; to be sure, the author did apply to Eliot the adjective conventional in such circumstances: "tragic"). The arts and letters were a safe arena for women's achievement.

Elsewhere, achievement might need legitimation. The woman who wrote for *McClure's* of climbing the Matterhorn reported and brushed off male skepticism about her unladylike determination (July 1896, pp. 127–35). The author of a *Journal* article giving advice on learning to play the violin felt the need to justify women's becoming as proficient as men, by an appeal to intuitive and sympathetic female "nature." Since their natures were also "maternal," it was all right for them to become *teachers* of violin (February 1896, p. 12). The *Journal* also advocated careers in nursing, sympathetically dealt with the Sisters of Charity, and had a word of retrospective praise for Mary Astell's eighteenth-century project of founding a women's college, a project unfairly terminated by Swift's mockery. *Cosmopolitan's* discussion of the "tragic" Sonya Kovalevsky granted her "genius" and considerable "scientific attainments": perhaps if her "femininity" had not been so "intense," and especially if she had not professed platonic marriage, she would have been permitted her masculine accomplishments without scandal.

Here was the nub of contestation. A woman was unsettlingly "new" if she disrupted old understandings of the feminine. Then the rhetoric of limit-setting grew stern, particularly in the *Journal*, which, as the only "ladies'" magazine of my four was also the only one to address the question directly in its columns, before and after the moment of the New Woman. Bok, writing in 1893, favored easing the way for women who "must . . . go out and battle with the world" in business,

> [b]ut there is increasing among us constantly a type of woman who is an unfortunate outcome of this over-discussion of the woman in business, and upon her mind it is having a disastrous effect. It is the young woman – for she is usually young, often very young, more's the pity, who seeks a business career, so that she may be what she calls "independent." . . . Believe me, my young woman, when I say that there is no independence in the business world for any living woman . . . . The poorest, hardest-working woman in her home is a queen of independence compared to the woman in business, whether she be employé or employer. (April 1893, p. 18)

Ruth Ashmore, during the New Woman fray, wrote:

> I do not encourage ignorance. The more a woman knows the better companion is she for her father, her brother, her sweetheart, her husband or

her son. But she must know the proper things . . . . She was made to be his friend and adviser; she was not made to imitate him either bodily or mentally. The conservative woman has been a power all through the centuries . . . only just now there is a fear of her being terrified out of existence by the loud screaming of those sisters of hers who, in their desire to repudiate their womanhood, become sexless." (February 1896, p. 16)

Bok, two years later, welcomed athletics for women "within proper bounds," but primarily defined those boundaries:

> It is bad enough when a women chooses to make an exhibition of herself in scant skirts when she is riding on her wheel in the public highway, but no possible excuse has she for parading herself in abbreviated skirts either in or around a public hotel. When she does so she violates every grace of womanhood . . . . A woman's bathing-dress was never intended to be used as a lounging-robe on a public beach. It is a singular fact how heedlessly women unsex themselves in these things . . . . No kind of dress need ever rob a woman of her femininity so long as she conforms to rules of modesty and propriety . . . . It is woman's mission to make life gentler and more beautiful, to make the world a better place to live in, to elevate mankind . . . . she has a mission to protect her birthright of deferential regard . . . . (May 1898, p. 14)

These judgments were of course commonplace. What bears notice is how, in seeking to contain women's movement into careers, education, and athletics, the *Journal*'s moralists continued stridently to deploy traditional concepts of woman's essence without acknowledging the widespread challenge to just that concept, and even while allowing or encouraging its modification.

The policing effort had to be energetic, in fact, precisely because some of what the New Woman wanted also served less articulate and surely less conscious purposes of the new man, the new class, and the new cultural entrepreneurs. The PMC distinguished itself from the old upper class partly through the greater freedom of "its" women and the greater openness of its gender relations. I defer an elaboration of the point until the next chapter, when I look at the accommodation and management of New Women's aspirations as erotic attractions, in narratives about courtship. In the present context it will be enough to note that the 10-cent monthlies hailed their female readers (along with the men) as people actively engaged in the class project of modernity; as people knowledgeable about the public sphere and invested in its rational progress; as people making a new way of life; not as ladies decoratively exercising the static privileges of a gentry, and certainly not as homebound angels softly guarding a haven from the heartless marketplace.

To stand by the genteel ideology would have been to disavow the one essential – if unstated – premise of the magazines' economic practice: that their readers and especially their women readers were eager and adventurous consumers. As consumers they had to go out into the world, had to be active in it in that way, whether they tended home and family or sought "independence" in working for a living, or did both. The New Woman's assertive reformism did much more than just reflect this economic imperative, needless to say. But the two were roughly harmonious, and both stood in contradiction to the ideal of woman secluded in a domestic and moral femininity. Hence the nervous rhetoric of the *Journal* as it struggled to adapt that ideal of woman's mission to her necessary role in its own commercial mission. Its construction of the feminine creaked and groaned from the strain.

The other monthlies, not defining their readers by gender, could afford to omit the contradiction from their editorial agendas. But it remained problematic for them, too, as the worried discourse of the advanced woman shows. All the magazines labored uneasily with the received idea of the feminine. All felt free to constitute or allude to it as a puzzle, a difficulty, a subject. The masculine posed no such challenge, and was almost never addressed, even in *Journal* articles giving advice to young men or to male lovers. The existence of the masculine as "unmarked" pole in the opposition of genders is of course a very old story, but strikingly retold in this moment of the New Woman. It was woman's essence that the new circumstances had thrown into doubt, and that had to be arduously reshaped and patrolled.[60] The principle of unvexed social space could not override that need, because the white, PMC woman's place was a critical dimension of that space.

No such urgency pressed upon editors the adjudication of racial essences, for the great northward migration of black people and their visibility as consumers were still in the future, along with the rise of the New Negro.

1902–03: Place Achieved

In surveying magazines of 1895–97, I have given analytic priority to class, trying to understand how a rather large and scattered group of people might have come to see itself as unified in outlook, feeling, conduct and interest. I have supposed that the most rapidly growing magazines achieved their success as business enterprises in part by contributing to this process of class formation. Along the way, I have articulated an idea of social space that, I hope, has been helpful in seeing how the magazines positioned their readers geographically, rhetorically, and in relation to other social groups. And I have argued that the social space so charted was on the whole a tranquil one, imagined to be free from conflict and uncertainty, except for an internal challenge to older, middle class gender arrangements. But my second chronological sampling of these magazines takes me to the moment when some of them began to make their most indelible mark on historical memory through the activity Theodore Roosevelt labeled "muckraking."[61] It will be my goal in this section to consider how that kind of reformist critique entered and changed the comfortable social space delineated in the late 1890s, and in so considering, to offer a brief overview of the magazines once they had consolidated and stabilized their own commercial space.

McClure's for January 1903 included the third installment of Ida Tarbell's critical history of the Standard Oil Company; Ray Stannard Baker's indictment of the United Mine Workers ("The Right to Work"); and Lincoln Steffens's exposé of city government in Minneapolis, the first in a series later published as *The Shame of the Cities*. McClure took note of this memorable conjunction in an editorial: all three articles, he said, might have been entitled "The American Contempt of Law." He concluded that "we" all would pay for the costs of corruption: "And in the end the sum total of the debt will be our liberty" (p. 336). The term "muckraking" did not come into currency until 1906, but the activity accelerated rapidly after 1902. *McClure's* led the march, followed by *Everybody's* and *Collier's*, which joined the circulation leaders by mid decade. *Cosmopolitan* came aboard (for example, David Graham Phillips's "The Treason of the Senate"); and even the *Ladies' Home Journal* followed up on its long-standing opposition to patent medicines by agitating for the Pure Food and Drug Bill. Among the magazines under scrutiny here, only *Munsey's* generally abstained; "prosperity rests on upbuilding, not in destruction," the editor said.[62]

How did cultural producers who had built thriving businesses on PMC contentment and a cynosural regard for the eminent come to turn scandalized attention toward the wielders of economic and state power? I mean this as a question not about particular editorial decisions – it's clear enough that investigative journalism paid off for a while, by the usual calculus – but about belief and feeling and perhaps need, as they shaped relations between producers and audiences.

Consider first that muckraking coexisted with celebration.[63] One might, for instance, set the first installment of Tarbell's Standard Oil series alongside *Cosmopolitan's* lead article in the same month: November 1902. "One Hundred Years After" (pp. 3–11), by former Nebraska Senator John M. Thurston, was a preview of the Louisiana Purchase Exposition, with sixteen etchings of the "temples" and "palaces" that would, according to Thurston, surpass those of Chicago's 1893 White City. The article's first sentence gives a fair idea of the senator's tone: "The world's fair to be held in St. Louis in 1904, promises to eclipse in magnificence and grandeur all expositions heretofore held." Superlatives pile up through his account of the huge sum of money appropriated for the fair, the splendor-to-be of the exhibits, the "architectural plan more beautiful in its completeness than anything heretofore known," the size of the grounds, the modernity of the technologies to be used, and so on.

Thurston's wide-eyed enthusiasm for the fair serves a broader purpose: triumphant praise for US society itself. The Louisiana Purchase was, along with the events commemorated at Philadelphia in 1876 and Chicago in 1893, one of "the three great landmarks of American achievement and development." Not only did it double the size of the country and incorporate vast agricultural and mineral resources;

> far greater in importance . . . was the extension of the boundaries of the United States to the Pacific Coast, thereby giving to the new republic a continental domain extending from ocean to ocean, and making it thereafter impossible for any other nation to obtain a dangerous foothold on the continent, or to menace the growing dominion of our country in the new world.

Although Thurston asserts that but for the Louisiana Purchase the US "might to-day have been hemmed in by European powers" or "in all probability . . . eliminated," the embattled stance of his prose clearly responds not to the dangers and menaces of 1803, but to the successful military adventure of 1898. The government's exhibit will include a "proper presentation of what we have so splendidly accomplished on land and sea, in bringing free government to Cuba," and will commemorate "work already accomplished in the Hawaiian Islands, Porto Rico and the Philippines, and the splendid part played by our Government in China . . . ." He speaks of "our impregnable position on this continent," our new "foothold in the Orient," our "commanding position" in Asia, "our power and prestige recognized by every nation of the earth," and so on and on.

This "power and prestige" is inseparable from "our marvelous capacity for invention and manufacture," which has "aroused" the world "to the fact that the United States is an active competitor in every corner of the globe." Inseparable, too, is the triumph of democracy: "above all things, this Exposition should be the great object-lesson of what a free people can accomplish under a republican form of government," a lesson equally for "the monarchist and the anarchist." Thurston seals up this ideological package of industrial power, imperial glory, and state legitimacy with the dependable ribbons and bows of modernity. The Exposition will feature "an air-ship tournament, with a prize of one hundred dollars for the winner"; in St Louis, "for the first time, fleets of soaring yachts will beat the air with untrammeled wings." This will be "distinctly a twentieth-century affair," heralding "the most important epoch of modern times," "a new century of such magnificent possibilities as were not dreamed of by the fathers." The fair will be a beacon for "the millions who are struggling onward and upward toward the ideal," in the article's words.

The senatorial afflatus,[64] though consonant with the self-congratulatory journalism of 1895–97, seems quite at odds with Tarbell's revelations about the vicious and illegal methods used to build Standard Oil, and certainly with McClure's description of his January 1903 issue as "an arraignment of American character." Yet the writers themselves take no notice of dissonance. Thurston's "we" purports to embrace everyone between the monarchist and the anarchist. McClure acknowledges no smug, Thurston-like reading of the American future, in contrast to his own. His "we" incorporates everyone, too, when not acting through interest groups: "We forget that we all are the people . . . ." Tarbell repeated the inclusive gesture – "We, the people of the United States" – at the end of her *History* (October 1904, p. 671).

Writers at the inception of muckraking expressed contradictory outlooks but did not admit antagonists into their rhetorically constructed worlds, at least not by name or by political label. Nor did the several magazines stake out editorial positions that would politically define their journalism, differentiate them from one another, and perhaps segment their readerships politically. No visible polarization took place around the "arraignment of American character" or the legitimacy of corporate and governmental power. Editorials in one magazine did not attack the complacency or subversiveness of another. Munsey and McClure had contrary views, but in conversation each called the other "great" if "a bit crazy" (Britt, pp. 94–5). Decorum and the self-definition of magazines as "general" and nonpartisan forbade open scrapping among them. McClure, at the height of muckraking, scotched ads for his magazine that linked it to reform, and urged his staff not to pursue a "mission," but just to print the best reading possible (Lyon, pp. 266–7). But beyond that, I see them as in fact sharing a common project, one quite in keeping with Thurston's triumphalism.

All shared his confidence in the harnessing of nature through ever-advancing technique. Two of the three heralded progress toward wireless communication; the generation of power ("Niagarics") and electricity's uses in medicine, lighting, and transportation drew excited comment. *McClure's* praised the work of the Pasteur Institutes, and *Cosmopolitan* eulogized Adolf Lorenz for his innovations in surgery. *Munsey's* ran five articles on the automobile and the happy future it would engender, including suburbs and the installment plan. Turbine-powered yachts, a new ocean liner, and the Hoe press made the blood race. *McClure's* celebrated the draining of the Zuyder Zee and *Cosmopolitan* printed "Romances of the World's Great Mines."

Unsurprisingly, the magazines did not trouble the reader's vision with warnings about social or environmental difficulties that might arise in the course of technological development. Nor did they make any distinction between discovery and use. In fact *science* had little place in their pages, apart from its applications. "Science is truth. It is the Divine breath," wrote Walker; yet he had by this time eliminated the "Progress of Science" department that had earlier been a trademark of *Cosmopolitan*, and instead was running a series on "Captains of Industry" (not much different in tone from *Munsey's* articles on millionaires), where science was but an enabling tool in corporate development. Although the occasional article appeared on a lone inventive genius, the construction of knowledge and technique was mainly a corporate affair, with no questions raised about the assumption that knowledge made and deployed by a few, knowledge turned into capital and sold in markets, would work for the common benefit. Likewise, the human transformation of nature was a simple good, whatever social relations might lie behind the word "human."

Nor did the magazines' faith in progress discriminate much between the application of technique to nature and its application to social relations themselves. Societies were malleable, as muckraking itself implies. Whether attacking Rockefeller's corporate practices (as did Tarbell) or praising the Morgan and Rockefeller organizations (as did Walker); whether deploring corruption in Philadelphia or holding up police work in London and Paris as a model for New York; whether laying bare the social pathology exemplified by "street waifs" or looking toward the perfection of child rearing and education (as in a long series in *Cosmopolitan* by H.G. Wells on "Mankind in the Making"); writers and editors by now took it for granted that the application of reason and science to social arrangements was improving them, or would improve them if not impeded by lawlessness in high places and ignorance in low. Seen this way, the muckraking mood was an angry awareness that known and tried principles were in some sectors being ignored or set aside, in "these days of rapid progress toward correct methods of thought in every field of activity" (*Cosmopolitan*, December 1902, p. 123 – this from an article on training wild animals!). Walker, especially, was confident in the spread of correct thought:

> Education is so rapidly developing the American mind that ideals are every day becoming higher. No man or set of men may stand in the path of this progress toward the highest form of republican institutions. There will be at all times enough men ready to step to the front, and say "No," in words that will carry across the continent. (January 1903, p. 246)

Who were these men? To take another lead from *Cosmopolitan*, which was most forthright in articulating the vision of progress shared more or less by all the magazines: the men of the future were specialists, whose training was "absolutely essential" but who knew far more than "their own calling" and who saw "changes coming in time to prepare in advance for the next event." These PMC characteristics – discovered in James Dill, a corporation lawyer – were the engine of "twentieth-century progress" (March 1903, p. 589). Progress was the mission all took for granted. The magazines celebrated it *and* sought to correct its errant passages. Both ways, they asserted a managerial confidence I have associated with class.

It also attached itself to nation, as in Senator Thurston's sea-to-shining-sea effusions. What I called the "sunny patriotism" of 1895–97, that of pride in native American decency and nation-building heroes of the past, swelled by 1902–03 into a more boastful and combative mood. No decorum restrained the expanding chest and jutting chin. "The Greatest Republic in the World," casually runs a subhead for an article on the White House (*Munsey's*, April 1903, p. 65). "Not a Nation of Fools," says another, in an article on how foreigners who tried to "humbug" Americans met their comeuppance (*Munsey's*, June 1903, p. 414). Writing on the electrical inventor Peter Cooper Hewitt, Ray Stannard Baker shifted easily out of his muckraking voice to note that Hewitt won success in "the American way," and to comment, even more flatteringly, that "As a people we like to see a man deserve his success!" (*McClure's*, June 1903, p. 174). The lead-in to a profile on industrialist Henry M. Whitney could assume that "as good Americans, we are triumphing with an honest, loud noise over the victories of American industries abroad" (*Cosmopolitan*, February 1903, p. 470). Writers counted on readers to have a simple pride in nationality: against the charge that his series on Standard Oil and city government promoted despair, McClure replied editorially that the cure for corruption was not socialism but "*Patriotism*" (July 1903, p. 336).

Patriotism had a military edge, in this imperial moment. *Munsey's* especially took the might of the US as a dependable interest of its readers. It ran an article on the establishment of Fort Riley as a training school, in answer to an "urgent military need" to realize the nation's "potentially vast" "fighting strength," and another on naval training at Culver (in Indiana!) to strengthen the navy's ability to defend "the interests of the United States as a world power"; a third article explained and praised the newly created general staff ("The Brain of the Army") as furthering the "one great task of preparing the nation's forces for war"; a fourth clucked at Congress for financing a new harbor defense "monitor," obsolete in view of the new awareness that "the best way to defend our own shores is to threaten those of the enemy"; a fifth celebrated the organization of Spanish War veterans (pp. 131, 423, 900, 41, 676–78). *Cosmopolitan* joined in a bit less fervently; only *McClure's* took its "Patriotism" without guns.

That the complacent nationalism of 1895–97 had given way to a more bristling jingoism in 1902–03 is in part due, of course, to the Spanish War, and to the way that magazines had seized on war feeling to build circulation. (*McClure's*, no abstainer then, printed twenty-eight war-related articles in a year, and editorially announced its readiness to meet the large new demand for its coverage ["McClure's Magazine in War Times," June 1898, p. 206].) The ego expanded globally. The rest of the world came to exist not just as a field for tourism and adventure, but as an imagined stage for American prowess. The Philippines, inhabited mainly by "Mohammedan fanatics and savage tribesmen," would be transformed "into a model tropical dependency" (*Munsey's*, July, 1903, p. 526). *Cosmopolitan* foresaw the annexation of Canada ("The Americanization of the Canadian Northwest," April 1903). *McClure's* ran an O. Henry tale in which six Americans drunkenly celebrating the Fourth of July in El Salvador inadvertently become heroes of a revolution: they are marginal dropouts from US society, but, even so, far more competent than the natives (pp. 328–34). The structure of feeling within which muckraking emerged was one that valorized great power for the nation and for a forthright style of action felt to be typically American.

It probably goes without saying – and I will say it briefly – that this power was unambiguously male and Anglo-Saxon. The dismissive tone of the above reference to Filipinos and of O. Henry's rendering of Salvadoreans finds echoes in the offhand, uncontested denigration of lesser US groups. A footnote mentions among undesirable nurses for children the black mammy, "kind, slavish, and picturesque" (*Cosmopolitan*, December 1902, p. 203). An article on women's lack of objectivity cites as an example the failure of women who had wept over *Uncle Tom's Cabin* to show similar concern for "the gross injustice wrought by negro-domination during the years of carpet-baggery which by comparison made slavery seem innocent and wholesome" (*Cosmopolitan*, November 1902, p. 36). In fiction, blacks show their "usual laziness" and are unapologetically called "darky," "nigger," "buck coon," and so on; a Mexican is a "greaser"; Chinese are quite without honor; Indians are dirty and dull-witted. In an article on Oklahoma, people of foreign birth are a "worthless element" who quickly lost out to "energetic and enterprising Americans" in pioneering the Territory (*Munsey's*, May 1903, p. 226). Women are often fickle, irrational, contradictory, domestic, insincere, weak. They are sometimes more flatteringly represented, but a striking feature in most discussions of women is the liberty and ease men feel in saying what women are, what they want, how they should be. The New Woman has disappeared almost without a trace. The white, male claim to be the nation, its power, and its future meets no resistance, and so is felt not to be a claim at all, just truth.

Two of the three magazines gazed admiringly at that power where it was most plainly concentrated: in the persons of rich men. *Cosmopolitan* profiled nineteen "Captains of Industry" during the six months of my survey, in addition to Walker's own article on J.P. Morgan. Whether the subject of attention was a sugar monopolist (Henry Osborne Havemeyer), a stock manipulator (James Robert Keene), or a street railway magnate become reform mayor of Cleveland (Tom Loftin Johnson), writers analyzed rich men's techniques of control and accumulation with hardly a ripple in the prevailing tone of wonder and praise. *Munsey's*, always given to making celebrities of the rich, continued to feature them in gossip columns, and ran articles on "The Equipage of the Millionaire" and "The Gardens of the Rich." It argued for the social value of ostentatious display as an incentive to hard work, and (in "The Richest Americans") held that millions came only to those who met public needs, and that God's hand was at work in the creation of monopolies.

Wealth, progress, nation: these ideological beacons guided the journalism of 1902–03 when it looked up from its routine cultural explorations and charted the movement of history. The same beacons fixed the gaze of readers, inviting them to place themselves in the vanguard of twentieth-century progress and the expanding global space of US capitalism. To return then to the question that opened this section: Where did the social critique of muckraking fit in? I have written enough to show that it coexisted with celebration, but was that coexistence just an unresolved contradiction, with critics and celebrants blind to each other's disclosures?

I want to suggest, rather, that despite an occasional cry of alarm, like McClure's editorial, little in the early months of muckraking provoked concern about the basic soundness of the American system of power, or positioned readers as dissenters from it.[65] A look at Ida Tarbell's accomplishment in the first major exposé of the period will help clarify the point. Her *History of the Standard Oil Company* comprised a first part in nine installments from November 1902 through July 1903 and a second part from December 1903 through October 1904. I will concentrate on the first part, some of which appeared in the volume in my sample.

It follows the fortunes of the company and of John D. Rockefeller up to 1882, when the Standard Oil Trust was formed with capitalization of $70 million, and with a virtual monopoly on refining. Tarbell, who spent five years in research, organizes her material around episodes of conflict, related with much drama of personality and high suspense. Because Rockefeller is the one central agent throughout these episodes, he is formally the hero of the story, with a hold on the reader's powers of identification in spite of a running ethical critique – much as one identifies with Dillinger or Bonnie and Clyde. Generically, the narrative is a success story, resonating even with the Alger formula in marking Rockefeller's humble origins and inflexible moral character, though also indexing the story of the world conqueror, explicitly in several analogies between Rockefeller and Napoleon. Thus the implicit question of the narrative, given by its form, is: How did Rockefeller manage to attain wealth and power? Not: What were the social conditions of his being able to do so? Or: How is the economic system changing? Or: Do we want what it is bringing us?

To be sure, the answer to the first question is in part such as to scandalize. He schemed, deceived, bullied, manipulated, coerced, and so on; he violated principles of fair play and open competition; he left a trail of victims, including a poor widow or two; he maintained a posture of rectitude in family and religious life that ill comported with his merciless conduct in business. But if moral judgment of Rockefeller's career is a central issue, that judgment is at least clouded, and perhaps turned away from the implied condemnation, by two steady themes in Tarbell's carefully balanced reckoning.

First, sharp and often illegal business practices were widespread; Rockefeller may have excelled in dirty play, but he only beat others at a cutthroat game already in progress, whose rules he didn't write. Of the South Improvement Company cabal: "It was, of course, a direct violation of [the railroads'] charters as public carriers, but such violations had been in practice for at least four years in the oil business, and for a longer period in other industries" (December 1902, pp. 123–4). Again:

> Mr. Rockefeller knew that if he did not get rebates somebody else would . . . . If somebody was to get rebates, why not he? This point of view was no uncommon one. Many men held it and felt a sort of scorn, as practical men always do for theorists . . . . Those theories which the body of oil men held as vital and fundamental Mr. Rockefeller and his associates either did not comprehend or were deaf to. This lack of comprehension by many men of what seems [sic] to other men to be the most obvious principles of justice is not rare. (January 1903, pp. 259–60)

From this lofty viewpoint, "justice" and "good" are merely labels businessmen apply to their own differing interests. And in any case, the oil men, Rockefeller's main antagonists through most of the story, are represented as greedy brawlers with "an exaggerated sense of personal independence" (p. 259), and worse, short-sighted and inept.

By contrast – and this is the second exonerating theme – Rockefeller is "no ordinary man." He has "powerful imagination," "the intelligence to analyze the problem into its elements and to find the key to control," and "the essential element to all great achievement, a steadfastness to a purpose once conceived which nothing can crush" (p. 259). He is "endowed with far vision" and "indomitable purpose" (February 1903, p. 392). His "genius" is recognizing "the critical moment for action in complicated situations" (p. 399). No wonder the ghost of Napoleon haunts the margins of Tarbell's history. Business *is* like war. Rockefeller is the consummate general, and not only in his will and his power of action: analytic intelligence, vision, and control figure critically in the admiring portrait. Through Rockefeller, "A great idea was at work in the commercial world" (p. 392).

Tarbell devoted the final installment of Part I to that idea and to its realization in the Standard Oil Trust – to the "Legitimate Greatness of Mr. Rockefeller and his creation" (June 1903, p. 215). These promotional words were followed in July by an analysis, not a narrative, and of the company rather than of the man. It was altogether laudatory. The Trust "was centralized in 1882 as perfectly as the Catholic Church or the Napoleonic Government" (p. 312). With "a marvelous genius in organization Mr. Rockefeller had devised a machine with a head whose thinking was felt from the seat of power in New York City to the humblest pipe-line patrol on Oil Creek. This head controlled each one of his scattered plants with absolute precision" (p. 313), bringing into rational harmony "everything from making barrel bungs to making treaties with foreign governments" (p. 312). Every component of the company was strategically placed, exquisitely geared to others, its production controlled with exactitude, its minutest operations tracked by the keen eye of the accountant. The company's "revolutionary management" (p. 315) made efficiency a god, rationalized production, cleansed all traces of sentimentality from the making of choices. And these principles beautifully integrated the extraction of oil, its transportation, its refinement, its packaging, its sales: the Trust had realized Rockefeller's "vision of controlling the petroleum of America from the time it leaves the ground until it is put into the lamp of the consumer" (p. 323).

Just four years after the most intense spasm of mergers in US history, Tarbell writes in celebration of their best paradigm. What she hails is precisely the huge, vertically integrated corporation reigning with its visible hand over an entire sector of production and coordinating the efforts of thousands. She does not so name it, of course; nor does she see it as ushering in a historically new organization of human society, though in her running contrast between its coordinated planning and the chaotic, speculative, short-sighted ventures of the oil drillers one may now discern a clear preference for monopoly over entrepreneurial capitalism. She voices a conventional nostalgia toward those obsolete men and their passion for "personal independence," but resolutely sets that emotion aside when she turns to the perfection in Standard Oil of tendencies seen as already strong in social life – centralization, control, rationality, efficiency – and favored by the progressive logic of human development. The Trust was built through conspiracy and crime, but the final installment of Tarbell's history encourages the reader to leave behind (pointless) indignation at the story related in earlier chapters and instead feel pride in this instance of American dynamism and expansion. Her language, less inflated than that of Senator Thurston, takes part in the same rite of national self-praise.

I have focused on Tarbell's *History* not only because it was arguably the first and certainly the most probing work of investigative journalism in the muckraking period, but also because it scrutinized what was most profoundly modern, in a society whose elites so valued the new. Vice and graft had lodged in the cities for half a century; the buying of Senate seats and the buying of senators were time-honored practices; unsanitary meat and worthless proprietary medicines were already on the way out; workers had taken rough measures against those who refused to strike since the early days of the union movement; the power and lawlessness of the railroads was the main scandal of nineteenth-century capitalism in the US. But Standard Oil instanced a major historical development, and Tarbell admired precisely what was new in it, reserving opprobrium for its use along the way of ruthless tactics already commonplace in the time of the robber barons.

I don't mean to suggest that muckraking had no critical edge or that it merely replayed existing formulas of mass culture. In the mid and late 1890s, none of the popular magazines had printed exposés of people like Rockefeller. Political scoundrels like Ames of Minneapolis, Clark of Montana, or Aldrich of Rhode Island would have been profiled euphemistically as men in the "public eye" or – more likely – overlooked as a potential offense to the eye of the delicate reader. The work of Steffens, Phillips, Baker, and Sinclair sounded a note of populist rage not heard previously in these magazines, though strident in other venues. What I want to urge is that it be heard not as a questioning of deep social structures or an act of resistance to the gathering of corporate and state power, but as a cry of "foul play" against familiar kinds of infraction. Infraction of what? Of the equally traditional principles of individual freedom, open competition, lawfulness, and honorable conduct by those with high standing and social power. In that sense McClure spoke well enough for his angry authors in saying that the cure for corruption was patriotism, since their exposés appealed to middle class readers' most conventional feelings about American forthrightness and decency.

But why, then, did journalistic practice in 1903 and after break the cheerful silence about social pathology that had been a rule of magazining in the 1890s? Here are my speculative answers. First, the magazine makers had gained confidence as they mastered the new commercial principles and stabilized their business. They felt less hemmed in by the rule of respectability, less restricted by proven formulas, bolder in imagining journalism that would challenge and surprise readers. Second, a closely related point: although they persisted in regarding their magazines as non-political, they were readier to exercise the influence they sensed was now theirs, readier to push American society a bit in the direction they favored. McClure could press his reformism, Walker his increasingly corporate version of Bellamyism, Munsey his faith in upper class rule. (Bok had *never* been reticent about using his magazine as a pulpit, and he was less so now.) Editors began to think of themselves as agents of history, not suppliers of an unmet cultural need: they hired writers who shared that conception. Third, also closely related, and most speculative: the class coherence and privilege explored in this chapter came to support a kind of proprietary feeling by 1902. PMC editors, writers, and by presumption readers thought themselves legitimate claimants to stewardship of the rapidly transforming society, with a stake in its achievements, responsibility for its course, and ideas that would make its project of development a success. No longer satisfied to wait expectantly in the anterooms of upper class culture and admire celebrity from a distance, they were ready to share power.

Not *contest* for it: nowhere in the pages of these magazines can be found a call for expropriating the expropriators, needless to say, nor for challenging their ultimate control over resources, labor, and the social surplus. *Munsey's* adulation of millionaires and *Cosmopolitan's* of "Captains of Industry" met no opposition among muckrakers to the continuing rule of the capitalist class, only objections to the business practices of some within it, to their buyouts of legislators, and to monopoly. In fact, capitalists received credit, as in Tarbell's paean to the organization of Standard Oil and Walker's to J.P. Morgan, for inventing the most rational ways yet of coordinating human knowledge and effort. PMC writers did not want to end corporate leadership, only steer it along the course it had itself set toward centralization and efficiency.

To do that – to regulate – was a congenial undertaking for the PMC. The journalists did not make prescriptions or suggest legislation; they assumed that their counterparts in government could carry the mission forward. Regulate the railroads, break up monopolies, pass the Pure Food and Drug Act, enact health and housing laws, take city government away from Tammany Hall and put it in the hands of professionals, elect senators directly, and so on. Such proposals were nothing more than an extension of the managerial ideal into the sphere of politics. With knowledge and expertise it was possible to "cure whatever is wrong in the industrial situation," as Tarbell put it in the penultimate paragraph of her *History* (October 1904, p. 671).

The subject of her verb "cure" is "We, the people of the United States," and as noted earlier, such populist rhetoric often came forward in muckraking perorations. In his January 1903 editorial McClure asked who might stem the tide of lawlessness and answered, "There is no one left; none but all of us . . . we are all the people . . . ." Winding up his first article on a city that had managed partial reform, Steffens attributed the success to "an intelligent, determined people," to "the citizens of Chicago" (*McClure's*, October 1903, p. 577). But if an awakened public was the imagined source of reformist energy, the execution of reform would surely be the task of those with credentials. What they envisioned was not so much the rule of experts as an edgy partnership of driving, progressive industrialists and knowledgeable regulators: between business and government, to put it another way. Many of the biggest businessmen wanted that too, wanted what Gabriel Kolko calls "political capitalism," to temper the warfare of competition now that they had won hegemony through it.[66] And through the legislation of the Progressive period they largely achieved such stability. The journalists of 1903 could not foresee that outcome, and some of the more populist among them would not have liked it. But they knew there were ills to "cure" in the economic and political "situation," problems to solve: it is that attitude that joined with the self interest of large capitalists and the ambition of leaders like Roosevelt to create political capitalism.

The PMC journalists saw it as capitalism with its irrationalities set right. Even on the rare occasions when they looked at core contradictions they reshaped these as problems to be solved. In his long series, "Mankind in the Making," H.G. Wells took on inequality and, to cure poverty, pre-scribed such measures as ending "reckless parentage" (that is, forbidding the poor to have children), taking children away from parents who failed to provide for them, and incarcerating those parents in "celibate-labor establishments" until they had paid off their child care debt to the state (*Cosmopolitan*, November 1902, p. 81). Robert A. Woods (a prominent Boston social worker) took on the antagonism between big capital and labor. In an article that begins, "If the total number of contests now going on between employer and workmen in the United States were massed together into a single great struggle, it would appear as if the country were in the midst of an industrial revolution," he goes on to recommend profit sharing, model towns for workers, and other ventures in "progres-sive management" to restore a "friendly feeling" and prevent strikes ("The Human Touch in Industry," *Munsey's*, June 1903, pp. 321–8). John Brisben Walker took on the central contradiction itself in an editorial of 1901, heralding the formation of US Steel as "the beginning of the most wonderful revolution in the world's history," claiming that Morgan, Rockefeller, and the rest have solved the problem of production, and urg-ing that they now solve "the greater and vastly more complex problem of distribution" by assuring that workers receive the product of their labor (*Cosmopolitan*, April 1901, p. 680). In adopting the problem-solution for-mat that has been a staple in magazines since then, turn-of-the-century journalists placed themselves imaginatively in the centers of power.

Of course the great majority of articles in these magazines addressed, not the labor question or inequality or corporate power or municipal corruption, but cozier subjects like the Americas Cup races, memoirs of theatrical agents, the life of Tolstoy, what women like in men, travels in Switzerland, the Barbizon school of painters, animal trainers and magi-cians, singers and actresses. Such topics had already been naturalized in the 1895–97 period. But the imaginative identification with power I have found in a few articles that considered basic social arrangements and a few more that critically investigated the workings of business and gov-ernment also pervades the rhetoric of many less engaged articles. An assertiveness runs through these volumes that differs markedly from the untroubled *gemütlichkeit* of the earlier moment.

It is evident in the lifting of taboos, the greater willingness to ignore the sound of Howells's "little bell": not just the transgressions of muck-raking, but lesser articles on street waifs, Riis's dark explorations, New York beggars, the underlife of Park Row, an evening at a gambling house, the lives of jockeys. Editors now posited readers bold and urbane enough to look into the social abyss or at its shabby margins. Hardly "fearless," journalism nonetheless presented itself as ready to uncover the distasteful and shocking. Readers would want to see, to know, to judge, to imagine remedies. Magazines hailed them as so entitled. Investigative articles were in this way analogous to social workers' and bureaucrats' invasions of the home lives of the poor. But editors and writers also felt empowered to do what social workers never did, spy out the practices of businessmen and public leaders – indeed, of everyone *but* PMC reformers, who occupied the unmarked position and spoke the clear, neutral language of reason. They assumed the professional's right to peer into dark precincts of society. Violation of that natural right by inside deals, collusion, private arrangements, and cabals generated much of the indignation of the muckrakers.

They wrote, of course, in the name of "the public" and "the people," but the people they wrote to and for were a class asserting its particular right to know, a class of influentials. Walker, who was given to brief anno-tations on articles in *Cosmopolitan*, made it clear that this was his understanding. In reaching "the million and a half readers of *The Cosmopolitan*," an essay by Elbert Hubbard calling for a new Peracles will reach Pericles' contemporary equivalent, "a hundred thousand earnest men and women moving in the direction of higher ideals" and "hourly building higher and more perfect the social system" (November 1902, p. 114). In a note to an article on road improvement he reminded read-ers of his crusade for better highways, claimed that "men of influence" understood the need, and commented that "the modern magazine is, after all, the forum in which even a measure before Congress must be discussed" (January 1903, p. 355).

Magazines at this moment claimed a new authority, and expressed it in a rhetoric more decisive than that of half a dozen years earlier. Senator Thurston's tone, sampled at the outset of this discussion, is at an extreme but by no means off the scale. More significant than tone, I think, is the way writers constructed authority. Rather than claiming it by reputation or simply by having been "there" as tourists and observers, many of them now earned it by systematically gathering evidence. (George W. Alger praised Tarbell's *History*, for its "enormous" research, for giving "all the facts" "from such a multitude of obscure sources"[*McClure's*, December 1904, p. 223].) Evidence pertains to argu-ments: magazines in 1903 ran far more to argument as a form than did those of 1895–97, which were mainly content with description and cele-bration. Even *Munsey's*, earlier the home of the offhand judgment and exercise of taste, presented in 1903 arguments for ritual in the church, for wealth as a social good, for the automobile, for better roads, for paternalism in industry, for water conservation and irrigation in the West, for art in public libraries, against the jury system. Articles pressed claims and came to rhetorical closure, rather than just stopping, as so many had done before. The magazines bristled with purpose. They addressed readers not as aspirants to culture and authority, but as possessing them. They spoke as if to a class that needed little help in knowing its social place, one that had achieved historical agency.

10

Fiction's Inadvertent Love Song

Journalism mapped the social world, situated readers in it, instructed a new class in its navigation. Fiction worked within much the same coordinates and traced similar ideological motifs: modernity, class confidence, the absence of social conflict. But fiction dreams and plays, and does not need to argue or present evidence. It gives satisfactions other than purported correspondence to reality. And it made its way into the mass magazines through a somewhat different process of cultural production.

S.S. McClure's enlistment of Ida Tarbell foretold much about the development of "magazining" in the next two decades. He first saw her name on the proofs of an article for his syndicate, about paving the streets of Paris, shortly before *McClure's* began publishing. He read it, and said to his colleague John S. Phillips, "This girl can write. I want to get her to do some work for the magazine." He visited her in Paris, signed her on for some articles, continued to like what she wrote, and soon hired her as a staff writer. Just before her arrival, McClure determined to publish, in his "Human Documents" series, a fine collection of portraits of Napoleon with a brief accompanying text; but the writer he commissioned didn't satisfy him, and he telegraphed Tarbell to ask if she would write a "Life of Napoleon." She did, and during its publication, beginning in November 1894, the circulation of the magazine doubled. He decided to put her on the "Life of Lincoln" the next year, and circulation doubled again.[1] Small wonder that he later set her to work on the Standard Oil Company, resulting in another journalistic coup.

Napoleon, as a subject, was somewhat outside Tarbell's previous competence and interests, Lincoln more so, and Standard Oil remote indeed from the direction she had set for herself before McClure turned up at her apartment in 1893. But he had gained confidence in his ideas for articles; he knew from first reading Tarbell's prose that she had "exactly the qualities" he "wanted for *McClure's*." This yoking of a writer's "qualities" to an editor's conception – hallmark of magazine publishing in the present century – was largely an innovation of McClure's restless and fertile brain. There were a few instances of this practice before his telegram hurried Ida Tarbell from her vacation with family in

Pennsylvania to the collection of Napoleon engravings and the Library of Congress in Washington, but McClure was the first to build a magazine around this relationship of editor to author, as boss to worker.

Traditionally, editors had of course encouraged regular submissions from some writers, but had not generally told them what to write. For the most part, the traditional editor sifted through manuscripts voluntarily submitted, and chose the ones that seemed best, by culturally given standards. McClure disdained this passive role. "Anybody could make a magazine," he said, by buying a mix of history, fiction, travel articles, and so on, "but it would not make a good magazine . . . ." A magazine should instead "represent the ideas and principles of one man or a group of like-minded men," and "have a single purpose all through." Those "men" (McClure, it should be noted, was among the first editors of a "general" magazine to hire women as editors) would supervise "the treatment of a topic to make it just right for our use . . . . That is the reason why I or some of my assistants always collaborate with the author of a great feature . . . ."[2] Such collaboration, McClure called "magazining."

It changed the nature of literary work, as Christopher P. Wilson has shown, reducing the writer's autonomy even as in some ways it professionalized the job of authorship.[3] By the end of the period discussed in this book, the change was apparent to all. The *Independent* noted in an editorial that "The modern editor does not sit in his easy chair, writing essays and sorting over the manuscripts that are sent in by contributors. He goes hunting for things. The magazine staff is coming to be a group of specialists . . . who are assigned to work up a particular subject perhaps a year or two before anything is published . . . ."[4] A bit later, George Jean Nathan concurred that magazines, like newspapers, were using the "staff system," and that major articles were "almost always born in the editorial office rather than out of it." He tied this development to the necessity for mass cultural producers to know in advance "the pleasure of the present reading generation" and satisfy it.[5] Editing is a "creative job, a looking-ahead profession, . . . a constant feeling of the public pulse," wrote Charles Hanson Towne, who was Walker's secretary at *Cosmopolitan* around 1900. Walker would "dictate ideas for future articles" while working in bed early in the morning, or while shaving. He took pains "to extract ideas" even from famous authors.[6] Bok and others did the same: they sought to define and direct culture, to set agendas, to constitute the discussable, rather than just weigh and rank essays germinated independently, in the known matrix of class and culture. The generic and thematic results of this understanding were my main subject in the last chapter.

With fiction, the case was different. To be sure, editors sometimes discovered new fiction writers and made their reputations; but an incident parallel to McClure's ambush of Ida Tarbell also contrasts sharply with it in important respects. Booth Tarkington had been struggling unsuccessfully for several years to establish himself as a writer when, in 1899, his manuscript of *The Gentleman from Indiana* found its way to *McClure's*. (His sister sent it in.) Viola Roseboro', who had quickly become the keenest arbiter of fiction in the business after McClure hired her in 1896, read the manuscript, came into the boss's office with tears in her eyes, and said, "Here is a serial sent by God Almighty for *McClure's Magazine*." McClure, inclined to agree, asked another of his editors, Hamlin Garland, to give a second opinion. In a letter to Tarkington, Garland pronounced his verdict: "You are a novelist." McClure summoned Tarkington to New York for a triumphal welcome, promising the young man, "We are going to push you and make you known everywhere – you are to be the greatest of the new generation, and we'll help you to be." He undertook to serialize *The Gentleman from Indiana*, postponing a novel by Anthony Hope (famous for *The Prisoner of Zenda*) to make room for it, and putting Tarkington in company with Kipling. He personally supervised and encouraged Tarkington through weeks of revision, much of it done at McClure's home on Long Island. An advertising campaign followed, which flabbergasted the author: he wrote that but for the curvature of the earth, McClure would be able to see the billboards in Indianapolis from his office in New York. In effect, McClure *made* Tarkington "the greatest of the new generation," as he had done for Tarbell in her journalistic sphere.

But he did not try to channel Tarkington's "qualities" into novel-writing projects conceived in New York. The farthest he went in that direction, after serializing Tarkington's second novel, was to advise him not to publish his third (*Cherry*), as Tarkington moved away from the material so favored by God Almighty. One might put an investigative journalist on assignment, but not a novelist. Nor did *The Gentleman from Indiana* measure up to an articulate, preconceived standard for fiction, so far as I can tell. In any case, neither Roseboro' nor Garland nor McClure himself has left testimony as to just what God Almighty found so compelling in the new novel. They simply proclaimed its excellence.[7]

It will be worthwhile to stick with McClure as impresario for a bit, since of all the new editors he was the most indefatigable hustler of writing, since through his syndicate he assumed an influential role as promoter of fiction several years before the others, and since *McClure's* is linked to a number of fiction writers who stand out in cultural memory from hundreds of others well known at the time: Crane, Kipling, Cather, Conrad, London, Stevenson, Doyle, Dreiser, Garland, O. Henry, and more. Without question, McClure ranks well ahead of his competitors (of genteel magazines as well as cheap ones) in mediating the work of young writers, who later became well known to a wide public. But for my purposes this observation needs to be qualified in two ways.

First, McClure and his staff "discovered" only a few of these, in any significant sense; perhaps Tarkington is the one pure instance of his finding an unknown novelist and securely establishing his reputation. Early on, he recognized the value (ambiguity intended) of fiction by Cather, London, Dreiser, and O. Henry, but for one reason or another failed to make his magazine the main channel of their valorization. Crane, his most tantalizing near miss, handed McClure a manuscript of *The Red Badge of Courage* in early 1894, but although McClure urgently wanted to print it, he had no money to buy it with, and by the time he had the money, Crane had given up and sold the novel to another syndicate for an incredible $75 (Lyon, p. 129). Afterward, McClure paid more than that for individual short stories by Crane, but he had missed the moment. In any case, over the twenty years of his greatest influence, McClure generally sought to corral fiction writers already winning fame rather than to discover the unheralded. He went after Stevenson upon hearing from others that the latter represented "the new movement" in English fiction, and listened eagerly to reports that Kipling or Barrie might be "the coming man" (*Autobiography*, pp. 179, 206). When starting his syndicate, in 1884, he lined up well-established writers, and promoted them as such to the newspaper editors who were his prospective clients: "the best story-writers," "a number of our most popular authors," "well-known authors," "leading writers," "every first-class writer in the United States whose literary engagements will give him time to accept additional commissions from me." The accompanying lists supported these boasts: Harriet P. Spofford, W.D. Howells, E.P. Roe, H.H. Boyesen, Sarah Orne Jewett, Helen Jackson, and so on and on (*Autobiography*, p. 168; Lyon, pp. 57–9). In short, with only a few exceptions, McClure either sought leads from the *au courant* or just accepted the valuations of the cultural marketplace, rather than trying to set a new course of his own, when he bought fiction for syndicate or magazine.

Second, although he did read mountains of fiction, and chose for publication stories and novels that met his own standards, he left no articulate account of those standards. When he started the magazine, he "meant to reprint only the best" of the two thousand stories acquired for the syndicate; in context, "best" seems to mean the same thing as "most successful." He summed up his excited first response to Anthony Hope's work in the phrase "real stories." Kipling's early stories were "wonderful." He first read Meredith (quite late in the latter's career) with "the most intense interest" (*Autobiography*, pp. 209, 228, 231). "Interest" and "interesting" are the key words. McClure did not care to be much more specific in the only statement I have seen of his criteria, and a brief one at that:

> I had but one test for a story, and that was a wholly personal one – simply how much the story interested me. I always felt that I judged a story with my solar plexus rather than my brain; my only measure of it was the pull it exerted upon something inside me. (*Autobiography*, p. 204)

McClure has been credited with a major assist in realism's displacement of sentimental fiction. If so (and I think the claim is exaggerated), he took the initiative from his solar plexus and from the air he breathed on his transatlantic celebrity visits; he never articulated a credo of realism, or seemed aware that others were doing so.

On the other side of a certain line, Edward Bok of the *Ladies' Home Journal* primly opposed what he took to be the impropriety of realism and naturalism, and fussed with writers over unsuitable subjects like the stage, suicide, and the consumption of alcohol. He asked them to temper criticism with hope, sadness with humor, near disaster with happy endings,[8] demands that the urbane McClure would never have made, though he often edited for brevity and style. But Bok's interventions sought to insure that the fiction pages of the *Journal* would not unsettle the complacency of its readers or grate against the high moral tone of its advice and crusades; he was not pursuing an esthetic or a program for literature. When he gave a public account of his editorship, in his autobiography, he sounded much like McClure: in the mid nineties he set out to raise the cultural level of the magazine; he noted that Howells and Kipling "commanded more attention than" any other novelists of the day, and would "give to his magazine the literary quality that it needed, and so he laid them both under contribution," thus setting his course along "more permanent lines" than in the past. A few years later he again "devoted his attention to strengthening the fiction in his magazine," and quickly "ran the gamut of the best fiction writers of the day." That category was instanced by Twain, Harte, Doyle, Jewett, Garland, Hope, Marion Crawford, John Kendrick Bangs, Kate Douglas Wiggin, Mrs Burton Harrison, Elizabeth Stuart Phelps, Mary E. Wilkins, Jerome K. Jerome, and Joel Chandler Harris.[9] In the vagueness of his evaluative language, Bok sounds much like McClure; and indeed the results were not much different, for McClure published most of these same authors at one time or another. For both, "best" decisively meant known and successful, and was otherwise virtually devoid of meaning.

If there was an apostle of the real among the great editors, it was doubtless John Brisben Walker of *Cosmopolitan*. In a remarkable short essay called "The Novels of 1950" (December 1902, pp. 236–7), Walker complained that the novel had come to seem "either silly or tame," and that soon "the sort of fiction we are now receiving will be deemed as unentertaining as some of the novels which had vogue forty years ago, but which are to-day interesting only as curiosities of public taste." The reason: "real lives as they are lived to-day" are "vastly more interesting than the conceptions of the most alert novelists," who have "merely a suspicion of the events which crowd thick and fast into the larger spheres of action." This was not a plea for fictional realism, however, which by 1950 would have used up its material other than real lives; and "It will be considered an impertinence to work out the details of a life which the writer never knew and at best but vaguely guesses at." Instead, demand will arise for "stories of real lives, told by men transacting real affairs," and will translate into fees of half a million dollars for such books. The novel will yield to them: "Science is taking possession of her realm. Science means truth. Fiction must give way to truth."

As this suggests, Walker cared less for fiction than the other editors; he printed less of it, and strained against the confines of familiar genres, especially by publishing some utopian narratives and what we would now call science fiction. But in spite of his predilections, he paid tribute to the expectations of readers, with many stories by the usual authors, and with running commentary on literature of the day by Andrew Lang and Israel Zangwill. For the most part, the fiction that actually appeared in *Cosmopolitan* validated the same externally given "best" as did the stories in *McClure's* and the *Ladies' Home Journal.*

Among those who created the mass circulation monthly, the only one who publicly announced a program for fiction was Frank Munsey:

> We want stories. That is what we mean – stories, not dialect sketches, not washed out studies of effete human nature, not weak tales of sickly sentimentality, not "pretty" writing. This sort of thing in all its varieties comes by the car load every mail. It is not what we want, but we do want fiction in which there is a story, force, a tale that means something – in short, a story. Good writing is common as clam shells, while good stories are as rare as statesmanship.[10]

With appropriate discount made for Munsey's incessant, self-promoting bluster, the manifesto did have more substance than anything McClure, Bok, and Walker wrote, at least in its negation. Munsey was sharply distinguishing his project from – while caricaturing – that of the Gilded Age editors. Fiction in his magazine would outface the genteel culture of *Harper's*, the *Atlantic Monthly*, and the *Century*. Instead, apparently, it would offer more eventful plots and blunter emotions.

And Munsey did present an array of stories somewhat different from those published by his competitors. He soon established a department of "Storiettes"; brisk tales of a thousand or two thousand words, implying a reader who wanted to *consume* fiction in batches, rather than savor it as part of a leisurely, cultural banquet. In addition, few of the standard writers from the other magazines wrote for *Munsey's*, especially in the early years. Their absence, however, probably owes more to the fact of Munsey's notoriously low rates than to any principled refusal on his part to print conventional magazine fiction. (An extreme example: he paid thirty-five dollars for his first O. Henry story, in 1901, though four years later he saluted the writer's fame with a ten-cent-a-word contract.) In any case, while fiction in *Munsey's* around the turn of the century did differ markedly from that in the class magazines, it belonged to roughly the same cultural range as that in *McClure's*, *Cosmopolitan*, and the *Journal*.

There is a ready explanation. Although Munsey edited the magazine almost single-handedly before his great success of the mid nineties (and even churned out fiction for it himself), once it was making large profits he distanced himself from its contents, reading almost none of the material submitted and little of the magazine itself. A story told by one of his editors describes his editorial method. The editor brought into Munsey's office a romance by a writer previously published in the magazine, saying it was long enough for about eight installments.

"Let me see it," says Munsey, running his fingers through the pages, lifting it, gazing off into space. "You've read it?"

"Oh yes. It is a very fine story. All about the time of the Huguenots in France, wonderful historical period, colorful background, great action in it."

Munsey hefted the manuscript again, asked about the heroine and the story's likely cost, and said, "Very well. We'll accept it" (Britt, pp. 96–7). Historical romances were perfectly standard fare in the mass magazines. Since there is no evidence that Munsey hired editors of any special discrimination, one may assume that they acted on pretty much the same appraisal of popular taste, announced by the market and by the whole network of cultural producers, as did competing editors elsewhere. Certainly there was nothing in *Munsey's* book-talk department – "Literary Chat" – to indicate other than conventional judgment at work, apart from some surprisingly kind words about Zola.

My aim so far has been to suggest that at the inception of the modern culture industry its most influential managers entered into a relationship with fiction and fiction writers quite different from the one they developed with article writers, and for that matter with illustrators, columnists, photographers, and staff. Between about 1890 and 1905 they and their subordinates came more and more to plan the contents of the magazines in advance: to conceive ideas for articles or series, assign them to writers, support and direct research when necessary, and revise and edit what the writers produced. Not so with fiction. The editors did go out after it, rather than just waiting for it to come in; and they tried to bring some writers into contractual arrangements, as had their predecessors. With rare exceptions, however, they refrained from assigning writers preconceived ideas for stories, or instructing them to write in particular genres. They did not spell out clear directives for would-be contributors of fiction, or even (with the exception of Munsey) make public their preferences. Rather, each of them appropriated some of what was out there in the amorphous flow of story, mainly accepting previously established literary valuations.

Their respect for the creative autonomy of story writers stood in tacit opposition not only to the editorial intrusiveness with which they carried out their plans for nonfiction, but also to a practice of fiction making widespread in other venues. One example will clarify the point. In 1894 a young writer of dime novels named William Gilbert Patten came into the office of the publisher Street & Smith and presented himself to one of its editors, Edward Stratemeyer. Patten was dissatisfied with the sharp practices of his previous publisher, and wanted Street & Smith to try out his talents. Stratemeyer assigned Patten a title, *The Boy from the West*, and in two weeks Patten produced a sixty-thousand-word story to match it. Stratemeyer liked the story, and the two men struck a bargain.

The character of Street & Smith's relationship with its writers is manifest in a letter Patten received from the head of the firm after a year or so. Ormond Smith sent him a packet of stories about British school life from various publications, and proposed a new "series of stories covering this class of incident, in all of which will appear one prominent character surrounded by suitable satellites." That hero "should have a catchy name . . . as upon this name will depend the title for the library." Then Smith got specific:

> The essential idea of this series is to interest young readers in the career of a young man at a boarding school, preferably a military or a naval academy. The stories should differ from the Jack Harkaways in being American and thoroughly up to date. Our idea is to issue, say, twelve stories, each complete in itself, but like the links in a chain, all dealing with life at the academy. By this time the readers will have become sufficiently well acquainted with the hero, and the author will also no doubt have exhausted most of the pranks and escapades that might naturally occur.
>
> After the first twelve numbers, the hero is obliged to leave the academy, or takes it upon himself to leave. It is essential that he should come into a considerable amount of money at this period . . . .
>
> When the hero is once projected on his travels there is an infinite variety of incident to choose from. In the Island School Series, published by one of our London connections, you will find scenes of foreign travel, with color. This material you are at liberty to use freely, with our hero as the central character, of course, and up-to-date dialogue.
>
> After we run through twenty or thirty numbers of this, we would bring the hero back and have him go to college – say, Yale University; thence we could take him on his travels again to the South Seas or anywhere.[11]

Patten thought hard about the name, came up with "Frank Merriwell," and set out to execute Smith's plan, with some negotiated changes along the way. The instant success of the Frank Merriwell stories propelled Patten and his boy hero through two decades of adventures and profits, until Merriwell, by then a businessman, began to lose his mass appeal.

This was not only fiction to order; it was formula fiction. In each story some crisis tested and confirmed a known hero's qualities in predictably satisfying ways. By the 1890s, repeat experiences like this had been cheaply available for nearly half a century. Street & Smith popularized them through their *New York Weekly* and a host of other papers and (later) magazines; Beadle and Adams rendered them in the form of the dime novel from 1860 on; each publishing firm crossed over into the other's territory, and they had many competitors. Among them, they gave the public heroes ("real" and invented) whose names have outlasted particular stories: Buffalo Bill, Kit Carson, Nick Carter, Diamond Dick, Deadwood Dick, Calamity Jane, and so on. In addition, there were series like that of Horatio Alger, endlessly retelling the rags-to-riches story but with different heroes, at least in name.

There were many other formulas, blends, and transformations. The domestic novels so condemned by Hawthorne, and by canon-makers ever since, related stories of female self-abnegation, suffering, and discipline under the tutelage of a mentor, ending in spiritual redemption. There was what Mary Noel calls the Grand Reunion plot, with abduction, false imprisonment, lost identity, and other complications, happily resolved by a sorting-out of couples and families at the end; this one was salient in story papers like the *New York Ledger*. There was the instructive "ordeal" formula of the politer children's magazines, a plot that severed the child from caring adults, presented him or her with a challenge at least partly moral, and rewarded the good child by reuniting it with its family. There was the seduction-rape plot most insistently worked out in George Lippard's dime novels of the mysterious city. [12]

About these and other kinds of popular fiction, many of them made to editorial specifications, and all of them formulaic, the pertinent generalization for my purposes is that the audiences they aimed at and satisfied lacked power and cultural authority. These stories targeted adolescents or women or uneducated people or people with little cash or audiences combining two or more of these attributes. Formula fiction offered entertainment, instruction, consolation, and pride to people whose lives were relatively limited. Perhaps mainly for that reason, this literature (except for the genteel children's stories, which were tolerated) drew condescension and scorn from arbiters of culture. It was escapist, it was immoral, it was trash, it was in a word not *literature* at all. In declining to spell out rules and criteria for fiction, then, McClure and the others were distancing themselves from kinds of cultural production seen as cheap and vulgar, and from unattractive audiences.

Now turn the matter around and look at it from the other side. To print only the (undefined) best fiction available, and not tailor it to standard patterns, was to imply three things. First, that those pages of the magazine charted a space of individual creativity and imagination, free from rules and prescriptions; *there* might be found autonomous literature.

Second, that the audience was a discriminating one, able to form its own judgments, sensitive to nuance and variety, and ready to experience new styles.[13] And third, that writers, editors, and audiences were participating in a discourse of high culture, associated with education, money, leisure, and social respectability. In these ways, magazine fiction nicely complemented the articles' mix of cultural commentary, praise for men and women of distinction, presentation of new trends and ideas, and instruction in social protocol, even though fiction and articles came to the reader through sharply different processes.

To put it in still another way, while the new magazines diverged sharply in journalistic content from the *Atlantic, Harper's*, and the *Century*, and while the new editors tended to think of the fiction in that prestigious threesome as effete, they maintained some of the practices and premises that framed stories in the older, upper class magazines. They implicitly assured readers that the fiction selected and presented in their pages stood in candidacy for admission to the category of literature. In both cases, this was a reasonable claim, though time and the processes of canon formation have obscured its plausibility. *Harper's* or the *Atlantic Monthly* might, in the 1880s, present the fiction of Henry James next to that of Constance Fenimore Woolson, the one a major figure today and the other remembered only in comprehensive histories. But as Jane Tompkins points out, both held roughly equal status in American literature through the early decades of this century. The same relationship holds between Mark Twain and Mary Wilkins Freeman, both featured in the *Ladies' Home Journal* around 1900, or between Stephen Crane and Elizabeth Stuart Phelps in *McClure's*.

Phelps, who wrote stories for McClure's syndicate, appeared in his magazine primarily as a memoirist, calling up reminiscences of Stowe, Holmes, Whittier, and so on. This was a common sort of mediation, the well-known writer giving readers an insider's report on literary life. Similarly, each of the new mass magazines except the *Ladies' Home Journal* maintained a regular column of literary notes, rendering judgments on contemporary work and keeping tabs on the doings of authors, some of whom were represented by fiction elsewhere in the magazine. In short, the editors constructed a complex literary milieu, interweaving criticism, gossip, memoir, biography, and fiction itself, offering to put the reader in contact with literature both as an experience and as a process of cultural discrimination. They planned and managed the latter, even as they implied that literary production itself was beyond management, flowing from springs of talent and genius that could only be discovered.

In articulating, and doubtless somewhat exaggerating, these distinctions, I have tried to explain why the failure of the main editors to regiment fiction as they regimented nonfiction was no real anomaly. To have arranged for stories that endlessly played variations on recognized themes, and that appealed to readers as addicts of stylized fantasy, would have cast readers, editors, and writers in unflattering social roles. Contrariwise, to offer readers the unfettered "best" fiction was to address them as culturally advanced individuals. More concretely, it was to imply that through consumption of a 10-cent magazine they could enter into much the same discourse of and about literature as had previously been monopolized by the elite monthlies.

But literature, with a small or capital *L*, comes out of other literature and out of socially constituted needs. Whether consciously understood and promoted as generic or not, a story resonates against previous stories, and against socially produced expectations and aspirations of audiences. It does its "cultural work" (Jane Tompkins) even when its conventionality is unannounced, largely unperceived, disguised as individual genius. I hold that to be true of much fiction in the mass circulation monthlies before and around 1900, and will now argue the claim.

Courtship and Ideology

First, a note on my method, if it deserves such a name. I began by reading fiction of this period unsystematically. Once I had some hunches about its structural principles, thematics, and styles, I read all the stories in the same volumes (from 1895–97 and 1902–03) of *McClure's*, *Munsey's*, and *Cosmopolitan* that grounded my analysis of articles, features, departments, and so on in the last chapter. (I did not zero in on the *Ladies' Home Journal* in the same way, because I had less steady access to bound volumes of that magazine.) I strengthened some hypotheses, dropped others, and made sure that my characterizations would answer to a large and semi-random sampling of this fiction, not just to my own wish for tidiness and friendly evidence. Nonetheless, I will not try to categorize – much less individually discuss! – all of the nearly two hundred stories. Instead, I will concentrate on the two most common types I found, glance briefly at a few others, and ignore a good bit of peripheral static. In doing so I will overlook a few extraordinary fictions, such as the one in my sample by Kipling, but hope in compensation to achieve some economy in describing the broad mainstream.

With that much said as preface, and leaving blank for now what I mean by "type," I offer for delight and instruction a paradigmatic story of courtship, by Juliet Wilbor Tompkins, from the October 1895 issue of *Munsey's Magazine.*

"On the Way North"
The train strolled along as only a Southern train can, stopping to pick flowers and admire views and take an unnecessary number of drinks. Why should you hurry when you have barely a dozen people in your

three cars, and the down train will keep you waiting anywhere from half an hour to half a day at the switch? Everybody in the three cars would have taken the same view, except the young man from the North, who was trying to get back there again. He read his paper down to the last "Wanted," and calculated on its margin how much it must cost the company to run a car for one commercial traveler, very sleepy, one old man near enough to his second childhood to claim half fare, a negro nurse with a white baby that wasn't big enough to have any fare at all, and himself, Gardiner Forrest – of New York City, thank goodness!

If only things were different and she were on this train! He had heard her tell Douglas that she expected to go North about the twenty-seventh, though she hadn't taken the trouble to mention it to him. If she had chanced to take this train and things had been different, they could have disposed of her aunt some way. Perhaps fate would have sent her one of her numerous headaches. Amy never had things the matter with her, which was one reason you liked to travel with her; and she was the nicest, jolliest girl in the world, which was the other reason.

Was there ever such a slowcoach of a train, or such a stupid journey? It was a relief when the conductor banged the door, and, coming down the aisle with a step that was almost hurried, stopped at the opposite section to speak to the negro nurse.

"There's a lady fainted in the forward car, and there don't nobody seem to know what to do with her," he said. "There's nothing but men in there, and they ain't much good at nursing. Can't you come in and lend a hand?"

"Course I can," she said with only a slight negro accent, rising in evident enjoyment of the situation. "I'm a fust rate nurse. I'll drap the baby right here, sir, if you'll just see he don't fall off. He won't trouble you a mite." And to Forrest's dismay, she plumped the child down on the seat facing him, and bustled off after the conductor.

The two eyed each other in silence a few minutes, each measuring his man. Forrest decided to begin with a high hand, and let the other see who was master.

"Young man," he said, "if you dare to yell or wiggle or do anything unusual, I'll lick you!"

The nurse had said "he," and he took her word for it. If it should turn out to be a lady, he would apologize and retract. The baby leaned towards him and said distinctly, "Papa!"

"Good heavens!" ejaculated Forrest. "Do you want to start a scandal? I'm not your papa. You have made a mistake."

"Papa," repeated the baby, breaking into a gummy smile with two absurd teeth in the middle of it.

"Don't say it so loud," implored Forrest. "Really you're all off. We're not related at all. You can't bunco me, my friend."

This evidently reminded the baby of something funny, for he burst into a hic-coughing little giggle that made his temporary guardian roar with laughter.

"Papa, take baby," he shouted.

"Oh, I can't possibly. I don't know how. I'd lose your head off or something," remonstrated the other. The baby still held out eager arms, crying,

"Take him, take him!" and a warning change began to come over his face. Even Forrest knew what that meant.

"Say, drop that," he exclaimed. "You mustn't cry, you know. Nobody does now, it's bad form. Here, I'll come over beside you and you can get in my lap if you know how to work it. Steady there, general. I suppose the proper way was to grip you around the waist, only you don't seem to have any. What a lot of clothes you do wear!"

He was so absorbed in getting the baby safely settled that he did not notice that the train had stopped at a wayside station, and that a tall girl, evidently of the North, was staring at him in utter amazement from the door of the car.

"There you are, Napoleon Bonaparte," he was beginning triumphantly, when a girl's voice with a suspicion of laughter in it said, close beside him,

"You seem to have a new business, Mr. Forrest."

Forrest started to spring to his feet, but remembered the baby just in time.

"Miss Baramore!" he said. "I never was so glad to see any one in my life, but I can't get up very well. Do sit and tell me if I'm holding the little beggar all right."

Amy Baramore laughed outright as she dropped into the opposite seat.

"Did you steal it?" she asked.

"No; it is a ward in chancery. I am to manage its affairs till its nurse comes back from the forward car, where someone is ill. What good luck brings you here – without your aunt," he was going to say, but changed it to a rather lame "anyway?"

"My aunt is going to join me at Ross. She went on there while I stayed over night with the Carters," she said, answering the unspoken question with calm mind and directness. It was much better to say a thing right out than to have it in your mind and try to hide it, when you were talking with Amy Baramore.

"Papa!" broke in a little voice.

"There he goes again," Forrest exclaimed. "It is a clear case of blackmail, Miss Baramore. I offered to compromise on 'uncle' and a gold watch, but he wouldn't even consider it. I'll smash him if he doesn't give it up before your aunt comes. She doesn't like me any too well as it is."

Miss Baramore leaned forward and held out a gloved finger to the baby, without noticing the last remark.

"I never knew a baby intimately," she said. "We haven't had any in the family for years, except some little cousins that were too far off to count. I didn't know how dear they were," she added, as the baby's hand curled around her finger and tried to put it in his mouth.

"Mama?" suggested the baby, evidently not very sure on that point.

"That will do," said Forrest severely. "This has got to be stopped. He'll be setting up some little brothers and sisters next. I suppose the first duty of a nurse is to tap on the window and point out objects of interest."

"Pretty horsies and baa lambs and choo-choos," added Amy. Forrest looked dismayed.

"Say, I don't really have to talk that rot, do I?" he broke out. "It won't injure his brains or anything to hear straight ahead English for a little while? I'll stick to words of one syllable, if necessary, but I can't do baby talk, and I won't."

"I'll interpret for him," she answered. "I can do it fairly well. I used to practise it on my dog."

Forrest laughed a little to himself.

"I'll tell him a story, and you translate it for him," he said. "Nurses always tell stories. Well, once upon a time there was a poor little boy who played all day in a shabby back yard; and right next door there lived a beautiful little girl who had everything she wanted, including a stunning back yard to play in. The little boy loved her so much that he couldn't keep away from the fence that divided them; but when the little girl saw him she always nodded pleasantly, but coolly, and strolled away to another part of the garden, sometimes with another little boy. He was miserably conscious that his little coat was disgracefully patched and his little trousers disgracefully unpatched, and that his back yard was no place for such a beautiful little girl, but still he went on – why don't you interpret?"

"It isn't very much of a story, baby," said Amy, "but of course if you want to hear it, you shall. It's about a little boy who was poor and loved a little girl who had lots of pretty toys, and he wouldn't come near her because he hadn't so much as she had. And when she looked over and smiled at him, he was always looking down at his poor patches, so he didn't see it. Wasn't that silly?"

"She is not a literal translator, baby," said Forrest, "but she improves on the original. I advise you to keep to her version. Do you think he could have induced that beautiful little girl to play in his dingy back yard, Miss Baramore?"

"Perhaps it only needed some straightening to be a very attractive little back yard," she answered, looking out of the window. "Girls are rather clever at that." Her lips twitched a little, then their eyes met, and they both laughed.

"I wonder – " he began.

"Kid all right?" asked the conductor, pausing at their section. "Nurse says she'll stay in there a spell longer, if he isn't troublesome. The lady is sort of nervous, and don't want to be left alone."

"He's all right now," said Forrest. "We'll send for her if there are any complications."

"Yes. Well, we may stop on this switch a considerable time if you want to get down. The other train's generally pretty late."

"Shall we?" Forrest asked his companion.

"I'd like the air, but I am afraid the baby would be in the way."

"We'll go and sit on the back platform, then," he said, shouldering the baby and leading the way through an empty car that was behind theirs to the rear platform.

"Give me little Napoleon," she said, seating herself on the steps. "He is going to take a nap right here. What a delicious day it is!" Forrest dropped down on the step below, leaning his back against the car that he might face her.

"When did you leave St. Augustine?" he asked presently.

"About a week ago. We have been making two or three necessary visits."

"I suppose you left Mr. Douglas in tears?"

Miss Baramore laughed.

"It is very humiliating," she said; "but an awfully pretty Southern girl, a Miss Potter, turned up the day you left, and she utterly cut me out in twenty-four hours. Mr. Douglas and his yacht and his millions were entirely at her service all the rest of the time. Aunt Emma was horribly disappointed. I was sorry not to see more of you, but you only stayed such a minute."

"I was glad to get away," he said frankly. "It's dismal to be at a place like that on business when every one else is there for pleasure. You were the only person there I cared anything about, and I saw so little of you."

"You didn't try very hard to see more."

"No, I didn't care to compete with Croesus, Jr., and his yacht. A rising young lawyer, who hasn't risen yet, wouldn't stand much of a chance."

Miss Baramore gave him an inscrutable look, and turned her attention to the baby.

"I had quite a long talk with your aunt one day while I was at St. Augustine," he said, after the rickety little down train had scrambled past them. "She gave me some of her views on matrimony."

Amy looked a little annoyed, but only said, "Yes; she has a great many of them."

"I didn't know but what some of them were yours, too," he went on. "She dwelt particularly on how unhappy a girl was when she gave up the things she had always been accustomed to."

"Oh, if she loves her brougham and her maid better than she does her husband, I suppose she is," Amy answered, bending over the sleeping baby, who would have seen something if he had been awake. "I wonder why we don't start? The train passed some time ago."

Forrest leaned out to see the reason, then jumped to his feet with an exclamation of dismay. Neither engine nor train was in front of them. The little way car stood all alone in state upon the switch. Over the tops of the trees several miles below them, lay a vanishing trail of smoke.

"What on earth shall we do?" she asked, after a bewildered silence.

"We might walk on to the next station and telegraph to your aunt," he suggested.

"She wouldn't get it in time. The train must be half way to Ross now. I'm not worrying about Aunt Emma. It's the baby."

"Confound it! I never once thought of him."

"His poor nurse will be simply crazy. Oh, we must catch the train!"

"The last station was behind that ridge, wasn't it?"

"The one ahead may be just as far off, and you never can carry this heavy baby. He weighs a ton."

"Isn't it just like this lazy, slipshod, good for nothing country, leaving cars around on switches! Oh, I wonder – wait here a minute."

It was fully fifteen before Forrest came back and seated himself on the step.

"You know we're in a hole," he began seriously. "If it were just for ourselves, I should propose walking, but we've got to get that baby back as soon as possible, or the nurse will be wild. We have passed the morning train, and there won't be another along till three thirty. Now, we are on a down grade, it looks like an easy slope for several miles. What do you say to coasting as far as we can in this car?"

They looked at each other in silence a minute.

"What do you think?" she said at last.

"I think there is a certain risk in it. We may strike a bad grade or jump the track, though I don't think it is at all likely if we are careful. Moreover, Ross is in a valley, I know, and we may coast almost to the town, where the baby's nurse will probably get off to look for us, poor woman. I think we ought to try it, but I will do just what you say."

She looked off at the blue outlines of the hills, rising above the thick tangle of woods in which they stood; then down at the baby in her lap.

"I'll take little Napoleon in before we start," she said. They laid the sleepy little passenger on a seat near the front door; then Forrest started the car, and they began to roll slowly towards the North.

"Isn't this delicious?" Amy cried, leaning against the rail of the front platform while Forrest kept his hands on the brake and watchful eyes on the track, which wound easily down through the dense woods. "Why don't people always travel this way? You are spared all the noise and dirt of the engine."

"It might be awkward when you wanted to go up hill," he answered.

"Oh, you wouldn't. You would start at the North Pole and coast down to the South. I never get over the feeling that you go up hill to go north."

"It's lucky for us you don't," he was beginning, when the car rounded a curve and, without a second's warning, plunged down a sudden grade. Forrest's heart leaped as he looked first at the descent before him and then at Amy beside him, for there was real danger.

"Hold that!" he shouted, giving the brake a vigorous turn and dashing through the car to set the one at the rear. When he came back, they were still traveling along uncomfortably fast, bumping and jerking on the uneven track. Gripping the brake with one hand, he flung his arm around her to steady her. Their eyes met, and it was all said without words. At last the track began to stretch out level before them, and even a little up hill, and the tension relaxed. Forrest drew a long breath, and, without preface or apology, stooped and kissed her.

"You're dead game, Amy," he said. He might have added more, for he had taken his other hand from the brake, but a long wail came through the open door of the car.

"That poor kid!" he exclaimed remorsefully. "If I didn't forget his little existence. There, old man, it's all right. Here's your friend. Do you think it's too cold for him out here?"

"Not a bit. Give him to me and I'll fasten his cloak. What do you say to getting off the car now and walking the rest of the way? I don't care for any more tobogganing, myself."

"I don't believe there are any more bad grades," he answered, sitting down on the step beside her. "You can see that we are nearly at the bottom of the valley." He did not add that as both brakes were set, and the car was still running along at a pretty good rate, he saw no way of getting off with her and the baby. "Well, little Napoleon Bonaparte," he went on, "have you heard about the latest engagement?"

"It isn't announced yet, baby, so you mustn't breathe a word about it to any one," she added.

"Tell me, Amy," he said presently, "did you care for me down at St. Augustine? You took a funny way of showing it, if you did."

"I wondered if I didn't, but I wasn't sure. I'll tell you something if you'll promise never to breathe it to Aunt Emma."

"I'm not likely to."

"Well, then, Mr. Douglas asked me to marry him the day you left, and I refused."

"Because of – somebody else?"

"I suppose so, though I didn't acknowledge it till I saw you in the car with the baby. You were so dear with him! Then – "

"Then?"

"I knew I wanted to play in your back yard."

They were at the bottom of the valley now, and the car was moving very slowly. Forrest had taken off the brakes, but it was evident that their ride was nearly at an end. As the car came to a standstill near a bend in the track, a sharp whistle close in front of them make his heart contract with fear that was not for himself. Was it a belated freight train? Had the time table been wrong? Before Amy could get her breath, he had swung her and the child down to the ground with a command to "Run!" and was dashing down the track, pulling off his coat to wave as a signal.

At the bend she saw him stop suddenly, lean against a tree for a minute, then put on his coat and turn back again. Around the corner stood the little station of Ross, and in front of it lay their own train, whistling signals to its scattered passengers. Buckets and a hose near one of the wheels, at which men were still tinkering, showed that the daily hot box had not been omitted.

They mounted the rear platform, and sank down with a sudden feeling of exhaustion.

"Poor child, you look all done up," said Forrest. "We must go and pacify the baby's nurse, and then you shall rest."

"Oh, here you is," said a cheerful negro voice behind them. "Hope the baby ain't troubled you. You've been right kind to him. I stayed till the lady dropped off. She hadn't no business to be on the road at such a time. There, honey, come back to your mammy."

They stared at each other blankly after she had left them, then Amy began to laugh hysterically.

"They never knew it," she exclaimed.

"Conductor!" shouted Forrest.

"Oh, you're back, are you?" he returned, pausing at the steps. "I was whistling for you. Thought you might have walked farther than you meant. Most ready to start."

"Yes, we are back," said Forrest. "I think that car you left on the switch must have followed us. I saw one like it around the bend there. You couldn't have been very careful about the brakes!"

"Them brakes are no good," said the conductor calmly. "She's done that several times before. Lucky she didn't smash into us. I was going to pick her up on the return trip, but we might as well take her along, now as she's come so far."

He disappeared, and Forrest was bending over Amy for a little private communion when a somewhat acid voice remarked from the doorway of the car,

"When you are at liberty, Amy, perhaps you will come and speak to me."

"Oh! Aunt Emma," Amy explained, "I'm so sorry. I quite forgot you."

"And yourself too, apparently," returned Aunt Emma, inspecting Forrest through her lorgnon. "I should think you might have waited to speak to me before plunging off into the woods with a casual acquaintance."

"But, Aunt Emma, you don't understand," began Amy.

"And I don't wish to," said Aunt Emma severely, leading the way back into the car. "You are under my chaperonage at present. When you are home again, you may do as you please. I shall wash my hands of you."

They followed her lingeringly, not as abashed as they ought to have been, and stopped to look at the baby, now lying at happy ease on his nurse's broad lap.

"We ought to do something handsome for him, Amy," Forrest said.

"Yes, indeed," she answered. "Dear little man! But for him it might never have happened. What shall we give him?"

"Dindin!" suggested the little Napoleon.

The story is slight, and may not seem worth taking seriously. I do; but there will surely be readers whose understandable instinct is to brush it aside as a piece of fluff, a transitory entertainment, and I ask them to give it sustained attention – intermittently through the following pages, in fact – for two reasons: first, understanding its appeal will unlock some important meanings of a very large body of magazine fiction; and second, in a study like this one, "entertainment" is not a term of dismissal, but shorthand for exactly the kernel of experience from which the entire social process of mass culture grows. To ground the discussion of these larger matters, however, it will help to begin with a few critical comments of a traditional sort, usually reserved for more enduring works of literature.

I note, then, that the plot moves Gardiner Forrest and Amy Baramore from unspoken longing, to veiled declarations of interest in one another, to a wordless embrace, to an understanding then briefly realized in fuller verbal intimacy. The Aristotelian "action" (or motive) of the story is, roughly, "To give words to the heart's desire, and fulfill it in marriage." That can happen only after Forrest shows himself to be amateurishly tender with the baby as well as resourceful in a crisis, and after Amy shows herself to be "dead game" in the face of physical danger. Character, so revealed and enacted, manifests their rightness for each other. I would tie the story to the structure of literature through Northrop Frye's scheme, remarking that we have here in nearly perfect miniature the mythos of comedy, complete with tyrannical old order, blocking characters, even the green world and the city. In that context I would mark how the couple are stranded in an asocial space, almost a wilderness – "blue outlines of the hills, rising above the thick tangle of woods in which they stood" – and how, passing the test of character there, they return deservedly to the social world and to the socially defined relation of betrothal. And I would situate the story in American literary history by setting its breezy dialogue and chatty, confident, socially relaxed narrative style against the formality of a genteel narrative voice, now falling into disuse.

Except for the last point, these observations reference the story to literature and myth as a transhistorical whole; the point about narrative style invokes a hermetically sealed history of literature. I now want to anchor the critical points to a reading of history, not as "background," but as what Fredric Jameson calls "an ultimate *semantic* precondition for the intelligibility of literary and cultural texts."[14]

In the first instance, I refer the story to the history emphasized earlier in this book: in particular, the emergence of large, bureaucratically organized corporations to supervise industrial production; the attenuation of previously personal relations through national transport and communication networks and through urbanization; and, urgently propelling those changes, the chaotic scramble of competitive capitalism, of cyclical calamities, and of warfare between workers and owners. These are big abstractions. But a real-life counterpart of Gardiner Forrest would have had the Pullman strike of 1894 fresh in his memory, along with the panic and depression that began in 1893. He would have had to imagine his life chances as more hopefully lodged in advancement through a corporate career than in individual enterprise or in the shaping of materials by hand. And he would have known that such a career entailed relating to other people – strangers – more through railroad travel and newspapers than through community and extended family ties already given by birth. (An Amy Baramore would have known these same things, less directly, and sensed, too, the increasing remoteness of her family's old money and strict manners from the dynamism of the new corporate order; but this story is not mainly "about" Amy, as its narrative point of view shows.)

Against the historical emergence of monopoly capital, the Aristotelian action of the story – to give words to the heart's desire, and fulfill it in marriage – has a specific force and appeal. For instance, it validates the personal, internal self, by confirming its feelings through the preverbal understanding of another person ("it was all said without words"), then by making those feelings at home in the social medium of language, and finally by projecting them toward a marriage that will keep the private self intact even while institutionally binding it. Such epiphanies of mutual, intuitive knowing have had great power, of course, since well before Jane Austen's Emma realized that she and no one else must marry Mr Knightley, or the longings of Elizabeth Bennett and Fitzwilliam Darcy broke through past errors and misunderstandings into words that healed and united. But the utopian bourgeois impulse toward selfhood grounded in feeling had taken on a different kind of urgency in the context, not of a Hampshire village, but of impersonal corporations, the managed society, great cities, a new social space.

Perhaps that explains why the test that proves affection and equality occurs in a natural setting away from other people, certainly away from economic life, yet in an archetypal product of the industrial system, the railroad car, cut loose from the control of its inept corporate master, and tamed by individual courage and cunning. That the dual test of worth moves toward obliterating the differences between the sexes – *he* holds the baby; *she* joins in a bold adventure – seems to me to contest the separation of spheres and of gender roles, and to affirm the ideal of the New Woman, as described in the last chapter. Likewise, I see the offhand, colloquial style of the story as eradicating the distance that print interposes, and proclaiming a kind of generalized neighborliness and affability that weighs in against both the traditional manners that forestall intimacy and the impersonality of corporate relations, not to mention the thoroughly commercial transaction in which Tompkins's reader was a participant. (Compare the voice of advertising – see chapters 6 and 8.)

As for the comic plot, which organizes the whole narrative, it is of course unabashedly traditional, hardly a feature out of place. (That's one reason the story can be told so brusquely: we all know it already.) Yet this rendering of the myth also strains *against* tradition, by highlighting and historically referencing that part of the mythos that identifies the marriage feast at the end with a freer social order. Aunt Emma is not just Holdfast, *the* tyrant; she figures a particular nineteenth-century generation seen as checking social mobility, enforcing antique rituals of gentility, and forbidding evolution of the New Woman – a girl "you [like] to travel with," who can handle herself outside the home and away from chaperonage, being a good sport and making alliances on her own. The shadowy Mr Douglas, the other blocking character, is not just a seemingly advantaged rival in love; he represents a retrograde upper class, out of touch with *work*. Forrest was in St Augustine on "business"; Douglas was there to play on his yacht. To Amy he represents a brougham and a maid, not a person active in the world. Forrest – a "rising young lawyer, who hasn't risen yet" – is obviously putting a lot of distance between himself and that dingy back yard, by strenuous effort, and a technical rationality that comes forward right at the beginning of the story, when the impatient young man reads "his paper down to the last 'Wanted,' and calculate[s] in the margin" how much money the railroad is losing on the nearly empty car. This technical rationality, of course, is what later conquers the runaway car and wins Amy's kiss. Forrest is the mobile individual, whose power and ambition have affinities with and a clear place in the new corporate order.

In short, Tompkins harmoniously adapts the age-old myth of comedy to problematic changes linked to the ascendancy of monopoly capital. Needless to say, a harmony so effortlessly achieved must override, exclude, displace, and contain much that threatens it. Override: the hero exhibits a power of action in this isolated setting that could hardly find much expression in his New York office; his mastery of the railroad car conceals the fact that he must harness his abilities to imperatives of the system that produced it, if he is to continue "rising." Exclude: some threats to Forrest's project of autonomy, like those instanced in the

panic of 1893 and the labor wars of 1892 and 1894, lie far beyond the
horizon of this sunny tale. Displace: big capital appears in the story as a
sleepy, southern railway, as Mr Douglas's yacht and brougham, and as
Amy's family wealth. In these static or impotent forms, it is a patsy before
the hero's will and resourcefulness. Contain: the tender, personal feelings, to which Tompkins assigns primacy in her conception of how we
might be fully human, will be (happily) quarantined within the domestic sphere toward which the story gestures through the yearning couple,
private understanding, kiss, and baby.

This is just to say, not that "On the Way North" is deceptive or stupid,
but that like all narratives it is "a symbolic act, whereby real social contradictions, insurmountable in their own terms, find a purely formal
resolution in the aesthetic realm" (Jameson, p. 79). At this level of analysis, what the story is "trying" to do is extol a particular kind of modernity,
make a secure place within it for two autonomous selves, each confirming the other, and avert the eyes from barriers thrown up by just that
modernity to realization of the selfhood it idealizes. Perhaps it will help
clarify the point if I list a few other ways in which I see the story performing this kind of symbolic work. (1) It writes a happy ending to the
Civil War, portraying the South as content in its subordination to northern capital, refractory only in impeding northern efficiency – "this lazy,
slipshod, good for nothing country." (2) Likewise, it rewrites the after-
math of Reconstruction, nullifying racial conflict through the
complaisance of the nurse, who, with "only a slight negro accent," is
clearly on the way toward unproblematic integration – and this in the vir-
ulent early days of Jim Crow. (3) As already mentioned, the story
pointedly aligns itself with the New Woman, and yet envisions no less-
ening of her independence, only the fruition of it, in marriage. (4) It
exalts the new urban or suburban nuclear family which will embody
Amy's and Gardiner's hopes: neither partner has mentionable parents,
and Aunt Emma will surely be no more than an occasional intruder, not
an enforcer of family customs and upper class morality. The extended
family, it seems, has nothing to offer but repression of desire.

That is enough to suggest how the story intervenes in history on the
side of progress, even while incorporating a good deal of nostalgic material for reassurance. Now I will move into a second framework of
interpretation, no longer viewing the text as an individual symbolic act
responding to historical events and crises, but seeing it instead as participating in a continuing dialogue of class. I have argued throughout
this book that the new monthlies were an important laboratory for developing images, ideas, practices, and myths that advanced the solidarity
and confidence of the professional-managerial class and helped define
its relations to both capital and labor. The contributions of "On the Way
North" to this project are plain.

Not only is the admirable hero oriented toward the dynamic and progressive future, but he is moving into it as a young professional, a lawyer. He comes from humble origins, and is entering the business world, evidently with some university education in his background. He is sharply differentiated from Mr Douglas ("Croesus, Jr., and his yacht") by having to work for a living; from Aunt Emma by the stiffness of her exclusionary manners and by her class-bound views on matrimony; and from Amy herself by the contrast between their childhood back yards and between their present circumstances. Clearly the comic resolution of the story spreads its utopian good will not only over modernity and the free bourgeois self, but over the future of Forrest's class as well. And it does so mainly through an unequivocal triumph of the middle class hero's values and capabilities over those of the upper class. Forrest takes "the jolliest girl in the world" away from her socially natural mate, and from his inherited money. Amy herself, free spirit and New Woman, defects from her class in favor of a husband who can both dandle a child and stop a runaway coach: the domestic and heroic virtues seem a manifestation of the same abilities that enable him to rise through law and business. Aunt Emma shrinks into powerlessness.

In short, a second historical reading of the comic plot, this time situating it within the dynamics of class, suggests that the aura of its benign fulfillment confers ideological blessings not only on a vague doctrine of progress and a new economic order, but more specifically on the project and prospects of an emergent class. "They lived happily ever after," the unwritten final sentence in every story of this kind, refers to more than the fortunate couple; it applies also to the future of the lawyers, businessmen, planners, and mediators for whom Gardiner Forrest stands, and whose values bask in the glow of requited love.

Let me briefly annotate the other literary features of "On the Way North," against this second interpretive grid. Evidently the "motive" of the story gains much of its appeal from the fact that when desire breaks into speech, the words overcome a silence enjoined partly by upper class defenses on the one side (Aunt Emma would condemn any relation more intimate than "casual acquaintance" between Gardiner and Amy), and by middle class timidity on the other (he "wouldn't stand much of a chance"). That the forbidden words issue first in the oblique mode of baby talk, and with reference to a childhood misunderstanding, signifies that this particular class boundary is an artifact of the adult social world and of its unfair distinctions, which the forthcoming marriage will annul.

The test of character occurs in a space and a situation where such distinctions have no power, and where timeless virtues like boldness and ingenuity take precedence. That Forrest should turn out to possess those traits, along with class-specific ones like pragmatism and technical rationality, conforms the latter with the hero myth, and so *naturalizes* them. (I would note in passing that the hero's name, while impeccably Anglo-Saxon and indeed highbrow, blatantly asserts his affinity with the natural; while the heroine's first name, by invoking the classless feminine role of beloved, negates her uncompromisingly aristocratic surname.)

The narrative voice of the story, too, naturalizes the outlook of the PMC. It is a knowing, confident voice that takes its values as unproblematic and uncontested. Thus the narrator and the reader strike an amused alliance with northern, technical superiority, in a clause like "the daily hot box had not been omitted." Mock heroic prose ("The two eyed each other in silence a few minutes, each measuring his man") glides effortlessly into the genuine heroic ("Forrest's heart leaped," "there was a real danger," "a sharp whistle . . . made his heart contract with a fear that was not for himself"), with no self-consciousness of how the first tone might imply a critique of the second. Nor is there any felt contradiction between tacit praise for Amy's masculine "calm directness" of speech, and the narrator's coy conspiracy in Amy's feminine *in*directness, as she bends over "the sleeping baby, who would have seen something if he had been awake." The narration effortlessly draws upon a variety of registers, as a social group might do that felt itself liberated, by success and growing authority, from any rigid, single class code.

Understood as taking part in a discourse of class, the story manages to announce on behalf of the PMC its transformation into the darling of history, yet also to banish any thought of irreconcilable conflict. True, Forrest defeats Aunt Emma and Mr Douglas, but that Amy should marry him shows the class rivalry to be bridgeable; that she should *love* him discloses that PMC charms can win over progressive members of the upper class – just as in fact the PMC was making itself indispensable to the new historical project of capital.

It would be convenient for my argument if Gardiner Forrest had managed along the way North to stave off a rebellion of railroad workers, and earn their gratitude and respect. Failing such aid to the critic from Tompkins, I must be satisfied that the ineffectual workers ("one of the wheels, at which men were still tinkering") blend in harmlessly with the backward, pastoral scene; that the conductor – a labor aristocrat – is suitably inept and properly ingratiating toward Forrest; and that the black nurse is neither oppressed nor resentful. Forrest's managerial talents hold center stage; were *he* to run the railroad, defective brakes would not stay long unrepaired, and there would be no daily hot boxes. But mainly, the working class is absent, offering no impediment in fact or imagination to the PMC thrust. Just one year after the Pullman strike and three years after Homestead, this happy PMC dream pushes class conflict beyond the horizon of concern, where it hid from journalism as well.

How to explain this easy serenity? Biographical conjecture is a start. Juliet Wilbor Tompkins was born in 1871 into a California ranching family. Though her father had died, there was enough wealth for the mother and three children to maintain ownership of the fruit farm near San Leandro, with excursions into San Francisco society. The children rode horses; wrote verse, fiction, and light opera. Tompkins and her sister went to Vassar. After Juliet graduated in 1891, she chose to try making a career out of her writing – something of a New Woman herself. She worked on the *San Francisco Examiner*, and by the mid 1890s was regularly published in *Munsey's*; the "Literary Chat" editor described her in 1896 as "a young writer who has become one of our popular contributors." In 1897, Munsey "sent for her," and she became an associate editor at his magazine.[15] Evidently she found a PMC life attractive, and succeeded easily in it.

Frank Munsey had arrived in the PMC context of New York cultural production from the opposite direction, literally and figuratively. His was a poor farm family in Maine, where he was inspired by the cheap story papers of Augusta to try for a publishing career. His ambition had carried him through several triumphs and flops by the time he or his assistants discovered how well Tompkins's work met his red-blooded criteria for fiction. With the magazine's success as a base, he went on to make a fortune in publishing, retailing, and real estate; but in 1895 (age forty-one), he was a rising young editor who hadn't risen very far yet. Having barely evaded bankruptcy at the beginning of 1894, he had reason for exhilaration as his 1895 earnings pushed past $150,000 (Britt, pp. 86–8). Like Tompkins, he could feel buoyant about the projects and outlook of the PMC at this moment, especially about the mobility of the male and female individual and about careers open to talents.

That sort of consideration may explain why Tompkins wrote and Munsey liked such a story as "On the Way North." Beyond individual need and intent, there is a sense in which if they hadn't brought this story forward, someone else would have. Plainly, although not "factory" fiction, it instanced a simple formula, which, as I will soon show, was in demand. The formulas of mass culture work as smoothly as they do in part precisely because they reduce complex historical needs and conflicts to comfortable ideology. They offer up possibilities of meaning that seem untroubled, uncontested. And they must do so because their producers are constrained by their position between advertisers and audiences. To advertisers they must deliver not just the attention of many readers, but attention of a certain quality. Readers must feel broadly content with their place in the world, so that the drift of their anxieties may be channeled into smaller concerns like the need for a healthy breakfast or for a laundry soap that won't shrink clothes. Finally, to close the argument at this level, recall that the audience in question consisted mainly of PMC members and aspirants; theirs was the satisfaction Munsey had to cultivate. (Imagine how little appeal this story would have had for a populist farmer, a millworker, a negro nurse – or for that matter, a Vanderbilt or Baramore.)

I want to gesture, now, toward a third kind of explanation before moving on to other courtship narratives. The exigencies of mass cultural production favored happy endings; when the plot drew its energy from romantic attraction between the sexes, the happy ending toward which it strove was necessarily marriage. Ergo: the myth of comedy. Given the generally realistic premises of this fiction, that meant writing the end of the comic plot as a union of people like the audience's "us," pointing toward the sort of home and family that was comprehensible because normative in their social surroundings: that is, a privatized home, a refuge from the public sphere of competitive striving. But the comic plot, like any myth carried over from one social formation to another, "continue[d] to emit its ideological message" even after new social content had replaced the old, as Jameson puts it (p. 151). Thus the plot formula tended to carry trace elements of the wider social reconciliations that were ideologically crucial in other epochs. For example, we might think of how Austen's comedies, already mentioned, drew all the classes visible to her into a village harmony conferring its blessings upon the assimilation of capitalist farmer or city merchant into the old rural gentry. Farther back, we could recall the rectification of false identities and shedding of disguises at the end of a Shakespearian comedy, answering to anxieties about noble family lines and legitimacy that characterized a society in transition from feudalism. Perhaps the plot even carried faint memories from its Western origins in Roman comedy and Athenian new comedy, in which an "impulse to marry outside the group . . . threatened to dissolve the boundary that separated citizens from strangers," but was contained within "the fundamental bond of kinship," thus reaffirming "the integrity of the citizen group," and "a natural harmony in the society."[16]

The happy resolution of Amy and Gardiner's story strictly required no more than their agreement to form one household in an anonymous cityscape. But for historical reasons the plot easily reaches out to hint at more inclusive unities. The baby is any baby. The archetypal servant recognizes Forrest as suitable patriarch; the conductor, a sort of inadvertent tricky slave, attends to his comfort. Amy steps out from her well guarded fortress, showing by her jolliness and gameness that class was only a disguise of her real self. And the train carries the rightful heirs of a new social order out of this provincial backwater and to the metropolitan center where they will be at the heart of the citizens' group. Sunny comedy adds archaic ideological reassurances to more timely compliments, casting hero, heroine, and audience as bearers of ancient legitimacy.

Variations

Now, having lingered for many pages over one tidy fiction, I want to suggest the variations to be found among the nearly one hundred stories of courtship and marriage in my sample. But before doing so, let me address the latent circularity in this way of putting it. There is no way to identify a particular story as the paradigm and others as variants. Nor did

any editor lay down ground rules for "the" marriage story, as Ormond
Smith did for the stories he wanted Patten to write about school life. Nor
did writers assemble and reassemble the same fixed set of elements and
techniques: on the contrary, given that there was a premium, in these
magazines, on freshness and originality, a writer would presumably try to
write each new tale of marriage in a way that would surprise. Then in
what sense can the group be "variations" on a plot instanced by "On the
Way North"? Couldn't I have chosen any of a hundred other stories as my
model, no more and no less arbitrarily? I think that the answer is: almost.
Clearly, talk of paradigm and variations is the critic's invention. Beyond
pleading the necessity of some such analytic convenience, I would also ask
the reader to accept provisionally my judgment that Tompkins's story is
especially complete, in the sense that a tally of repeated events, character
systems, narrative strategies, and so on, in *all* the stories about marriage,
would yield a list of most common elements, and more of these are present in "On the Way North" than in most of the other stories.

But raising this question of method opens up a potentially more devastating one: What reason is there to take a hundred or so stories about
courtship and/or marriage as forming a "type" at all, especially since, as
will shortly appear, no single element or structure other than the narrative interest of marital union is present in all the stories? Does the type
reduce to amorphous "matter of marriage," comparable to Matter of
Britain in medieval romance? Conceptually, an adequate reply, after
Wittgenstein, is that the stories bear a family resemblance, beyond their
common subject matter. At least I came gradually to believe that I could
spot a courtship or marriage story (as opposed to one in which courtship
or marriage played an incidental part), and I reckon that readers and
writers around 1900 had a similar concept. If this be allowed, it does
make sense to speak of variations, though not in the sense of departures
from a fixed paradigm. Rather, the situation is like that described by
Michael Denning with respect to dime novels, which he imagines as "a
stage on which contradictory stories were produced, with new characters
in old costumes, morals that were undermined by the tale, and words that
could be spoken in different accents." The "figures and characters" in
those novels were "a body of representations . . . alternately claimed,
rejected, and fought over."[17] Denning's "fought over" is perhaps too
rough for the polite arena of domestic fiction: otherwise, his formulation
applies well. Courtship stories around 1900 were in dialogue with one
another, registering through character and event a kind of statement
and counterstatement about gender, conduct, feeling, social rank, and
other important matters.

Thus – to settle for a while on issues of class and modernity – occasionally the hero's PMC work comes forward as itself a narrative interest:
a doctor's nurturing care for a poor patient gradually enhances his attrac-
tiveness to the richer heroine (a, b[18]); a professor's weekly lectures at "the

fashionable Wednesday Club" document his growing confidence, as he
wins away the affections of his earnest young lady from a richer suitor (c);
the vigorous but poor Dick Rudder has won Bonny's heart, but can't win
her mother's approval – since his rival is a "splendid match" – until he
rather desperately succeeds in marketing a patent inhaler, which turns
out to be more than the placebo he initially thought it was (d). More
commonly, though, the hero's PMC competence, like that of Gardiner
Forrest, shows in something he does *away* from work. A novice broker,
son of a poor farmer, accepts a wager, from his gentleman-farmer-broker
boss, that he cannot scythe a field of wheat in a day; he wins the wager
and, in the process, the heart of the boss's daughter who "delighted in
the swift, undeviating toil of the young giant . . . " (e). An engineer
impresses a neighboring millionaire's daughter by "devotion to his little
house" and four acres, and then by his take-charge manliness when the
millionaire loses his fortune and dies of apoplexy (f). Job and career des-
ignations act as social locaters, little more. Class flattery fixes upon
qualities mysteriously associated with the hero's economic standing and
promise, not revealed through patient detailing of challenges met in
work. In fact, my sample includes but one story that is purely "about"
business or professional achievement, with no love interest (g).

Most courtship stories take the negotiating of class in the public
sphere as beyond need of representation; they project it into character,
where it then expresses itself as moral and erotic power. Often it is lightly
indexed indeed. As Ellen itemizes the features of two candidates for her
hand, she does note that one is "very wealthy" while the other is "by
inheritance, poor; by profession, a lawyer." But the narrative interest in
this brief story derives entirely from a series of visits Ellen receives just
after she has determined in private colloquy to marry the rich man – "a
great catch," and "more acceptable to my relatives and friends." In turn,
her mother, a friend, Ellen's aunt, and her younger brother all advise
her to marry the rich man, or take it for granted that she will do so (a
minister, interestingly enough, remains neutral: "Both are excellent
young men"). Then, at the very end of the story, the lawyer shows up to
renounce his claim: he, too, assumes that she will choose his rival. But
she is "amazed at her own gladness" to see him, and instantly reverses
her earlier decision. We get only a glimpse of him (all we see is that he
has strong feelings), and clearly neither his career nor his PMC qualities
count for much. The point is that Ellen chooses against the regnant
social logic, perversely chooses as much *because* social logic dictates otherwise as because her heart speaks a different argument. In fact, in this
as in many stories the two reasons merge: feeling stands in conventional
opposition to class and family expectations, and the PMC hero becomes
the beneficiary of the opposition, sometimes quite effortlessly. Very
often a young woman functions as arbiter of that ancient conflict, and as
little else. This story is significantly titled "A Girl's Way" (h).

So far I have tracked stories that place love in alliance with PMC values and virtues through the heroine's correct choice of the poorer (but rising) suitor. "We" know she will not endure a lifetime of penury, because the hero's qualities will translate into success after a while, but her choice postpones affluence, as it defies the practical wisdom of class hierarchies. The story need not turn out this way. Scrutiny of another common ending will hint at the suppleness of ideology. Martin Page has made a success with his first novel. He loves the actress Jeannette Curtis, and in fact has modeled his heroine on her. She wants the dramatic rights to his novel. So does "the most powerful theatrical manager in the country," who surely will make Page a wealthy man. Page forgoes that prospect in order to advance Jeannette's career. She grasps what he has done ("Good gracious! Martin's fortune is made – and he loves me enough to unmake it"), and instantly renounces her own claim. Their eyes meet. As she rushes out to tell the producer he may have the dramatic rights, she bumps into that very person, on his way to tell Martin that *he* intends to star Jeannette in his production. Both lovers have made the right gesture, but with no sacrificial consequences (i).

Follow this lead, and we arrive at fictions in which sacrifice is no more than an abstract principle, an aspect of character. Remsen's New York cab collides with another, containing a girl of "the right sort." Her dropped card tells him she is Susanna Forrester from Monterey, Ohio. By chance – the story is called "A Hint from Fate" – Remsen's banker asks him to recommend a man for an electrician's job ($1200 a year) in Monterey; by further chance, the wealthy Remsen is a qualified electrician, and he heads for Ohio in this disguise. Things go well with the unconventional Miss Forrester until Remsen reveals his wealth in an effort to detach her from his rival, a bank cashier she intends to marry: "I'm rich, very rich. I can give you everything." She is disgusted; he apologizes; she follows the cashier to Colorado; he turns out to be a fortune hunter who marries a rich widow; Remsen chases Susanna down in Boston, showing love by his persistence though she is now a "jilted lady"; they look "each into the other's eyes"; they love, they will marry (j). Money has been an obstacle and a source of confusion, but since it is irrelevant to both lovers at the deepest level of character, they may have both it and each other.

In another revealing instance the author provides alternative stories for her heroine: one if Katherine Lewis crosses to the west side of Fifth Avenue, a second if she stays on the east side. The trivial decision would lead to either of two completely different romances for the wealthy young woman, yet with similar outcomes and identical meanings. The west side brings her a struggling young businessman who at first is interested in Katherine's $30,000 a year, but soon comes to love her purely – then loses her when he (honorably) tells her of his original motive – then *wins* her again when, falsely informed that she has lost all her money, he remains faithful. The east side brings her an English heir far wealthier than even she is, but: (1) she doesn't know that; (2) he doesn't know or care about her wealth; and (3) she rejects him when falsely told that he is after it. Once the confusion is sorted out, she can obey her feelings and join the two fortunes without a moral descent. The stated point of this mildly philosophical double story: "environment, that shapes personality, is ruled by it" (k). In fact, though, only two features of Katherine's personality count here: her quintessential feminine appeal, and her aversion to being wooed for her money. The latter eradicates the difference between struggling businessman and British heir, and suggests that we can read the valorization of PMC character even in stories, like the three just discussed, which reconcile love and money with no poignant delay. If an upper class person doesn't care about money in affairs of the heart, he or she symbolically joins the PMC elect, freed from stiff old upper class imperatives.

I use that phrase to press a connection between all the stories discussed up to now and some that do not identify wealth or walk of life as an issue, even in passing. A formulaic element I have not emphasized is that PMC heroes almost always exhibit at some point a frankness or even a kind of blurting clumsiness, when feeling breaks through decorum. Many of the heroines do, too, and if not, they respond to directness or informality as a token of genuineness. Recall Gardiner Forrest's verbal and non-verbal sallies across the class barrier, and Amy's conspiracy in chaperonless intimacy. Sometimes that dynamic stands as sole indicator of a challenge to rigid class relations and old customs. In one of *Munsey's* storiettes, two lovers have quarrelled, and the woman declares that she will never marry: "Marriage . . . is a thing for weak minded women to embrace as a last resort . . . ," she says to her uncle. She storms out for a drive on the boulevard, where she predictably runs into her estranged suitor. He boldly joins her, uninvited, in her cart. "Mr. Russell!," she says. "I don't answer to that name, from you," he responds, giving back her first name in defiance. Quickly he overrides every formality she throws up as a barrier; his intrusive declaration of love puts her "in a thrilled turbulence of joy" and wins the day (l). We know nothing of either person's qualifications for the match, except that both seem to have plenty of leisure time; but we can tell that their betrothal is a triumph of youthful unconventionality.

Here is a scene from another story, apparently featuring two upper class people, since nothing presses either to end longish stays at a fashionable Swiss resort. Bessie Durand has been eliciting and then refusing proposals from eligible young men; she is in fact taking notes on the proposals in hopes of gathering material for a novel, but each swain disappoints by his conventionality, as he shifts from "Miss Durand" to "Bessie" with a soulful look in his eyes. Archie Severance, however, already marked as almost insultingly unconventional, has not only attracted her interest, but also discovered what she is up to, by reading her notebook. Thus, at a romantic, high waterfall:

"Miss Durand," he said [not "Bessie"], "I love you. I ask you to be my wife."

"Oh, Mr. Severance," replied Bessie without lifting her eyes from the foaming chasm, "I hope that nothing in my actions has led you to –"

"Am I to understand that you are about to refuse me?" cried Archie above the roar of the falling waters. Bessie looked quickly up at him, and seeing a dark frown on his brow, drew slightly away from him.

"Certainly I am going to refuse you. I have known you only a few weeks."

"That has nothing to do with it. I tell you, girl, that I love you. Don't you understand what I say?"

Her alarm grows, as he accuses her of trifling:

" . . . have you gone suddenly mad? How dare you speak to me in this fashion?"

He grabs her wrist and intensifies the assault. She:

"Now that I see you are a ruffian, I hate you . . . ."

He seizes her around the waist and breaks the guard rail.

"What are you going to do?" cried the girl, her eyes wide with terror.

"I intend to leap with you into this abyss; then we shall be united forever."

"Oh Archie, Archie, I love you," sobbed Bessie, throwing her arms around the neck of the astonished young man . . . .

In the rapid denouement she confesses, "I don't believe I would ever have accepted you if you hadn't forced me to. I have become so wearied with the conventional form of proposal" (m).

Of course both are play acting at the beginning of the scene, but that in itself credits them with disrespect for high serious courtship protocol; and the passion that forces its way through the charade is real. They deserve each other because they are (almost) equally unconventional, breezy, even naughty, or, in the word I have been using, *modern*. The apparently endless fascination that attaches in these stories, both light and serious, to blunt words and deeds at tender moments seems best understood as encoding a cultural revolution of sorts. To us, turn-of-the-century boldness looks pale indeed, as it already did by 1916, if one believes Fitzgerald's *This Side of Paradise*. But in the 1890s it seemed fresh, and the titillation it provoked, I conjecture, derived from PMC expansiveness more than from intrinsically erotic content, if there is such a thing. Men and women whose vitality rushes through seams in the tight structure of "old" manners find each other with great regularity in these stories. Their unions allude both to the victory of the new social arrangements in new social space, and to the class justice that removes impediments to PMC advancement, even when both parties are fortified by old money.

All that seems necessary to stir these feelings and their attendant ideology is *some* social rule perceived as old-fashioned. The etiquette of first-name usage will do, in a pinch. So, for a final example, will age. An unstated rule says that the groom should be a few years older than the bride. "Perhaps, if it had not been for the stupid accident of years, she might have loved Bobby as he demanded, instead of in a maternal, protective way; but her milestones outnumbered Bobby's, and no amount of arithmetic would set it right" (n). Bobby sets it right within a page by letting her think he is about to marry someone else. "Arithmetic . . . be hanged," she sobs to herself after he has left, and when he sneaks back to observe the effects of his ruse, the usual epiphany of lips and eyes instantly occurs. She is only two years older than he.

Five years separate another lady from her young suitor; she refuses him because she fears "the speech of people," imagines gossips saying, "Isn't it nice dear Kitty is going to be married," and suppressing the thought, "at last." The couple are out riding in a carriage; an accident that could have been fatal threatens (a car startles their horse); the prospect of death and her suitor's resourcefulness during the crisis show her that "what other people say doesn't count in comparison . . . " (o). A slight economic gap divides both pairs of lovers, but the age taboo provides the main social resistance to love. When the heroines reassess this restriction, and realize that it is artificial and silly, they perform the appropriate gesture of modernity.

I could go on, but will spare my reader. Age, manners, money, class: all these, I have tried to suggest, have a certain kind of equivalence in the courtship story. It is not just that any one of them (or two or more) may occupy the same structural position, that of a socially posed barrier to the marriage of people who by a higher logic *should* be married. They also cluster together ideologically, representing potential barriers to accomplishment of the PMC's historical project. Successful completion of the formula asserts (again and again and again) that the project is both historically unstoppable and morally right – right, because the formula identifies it with the marriage of true minds, given as a timeless, universal good.

Some courtship stories do *not* arrive at the desired conclusion; these carry much the same ideological force. Very rarely an Aunt Emma figure has her repressive way. The one pure instance of this variation in my sample demonstrates the wickedness of such class and generational power by having both young lovers die as a consequence of it (p). Another rarity is the love plot aborted by the one *legitimate* social obstacle. Two of "nature's elect" discover their "mysterious bond" when thrown together by a train collision. Both act nobly; they deserve each other. But he is on the way to his wedding (his bride a clearly inferior "moneyed maid") and she too is engaged. They can only say "I'm sorry," and part (q). Their epiphany retains its glory, but (I infer) to let it override their prior commitments would disrupt the sustaining ideology by declaring the marriage bond itself to be less than eternal. It would take a few decades for PMC ideology to accommodate that idea.[19] Usually, when courtship ends in separation the fault is in one of the lovers: either failing to assign love its proper weight (s), or – the other side of the coin – setting too high a value on decorum (she won't apologize for an indiscretion [t]) or on etiquette (he uses common speech to test her; she turns it and him away, with her upper class facade [u]). These stories tend to be didactic in tone, admonishing women, especially, not to get out of line. When love misfires, the writer brings ideology forward to draw the moral. In any case, failed courtships confirm the pattern through the causes of their unhappy endings. What would defeat my claim would be stories ending unhappily in betrothal or happily in separation.

There are a very few that verge on the second of those possibilities, and I will mention two of them in order to help fix another boundary of the genre. One (by Juliet Wilbor Tompkins) features a lady's maid of sterling character, which she exhibits by loyally serving, loving, and enduring the unjust tirades of her difficult mistress. When the young heir of the family, who has been apprenticing as a rancher in the West, returns for a visit, he quickly falls for Lizzie and proposes to her. After her initial shock and anger, she feels for an instant "a tumult of hope and fear and wonder," then recalls her bond to her mistress and the pain such a union would cause. "No, Mr. Ralph, it's impossible," she says, and he passes on easily to a woman of his own class; while she weeps in her room over the sacrifice she has made (v). The other story (w) is virtually identical in the ways I want to foreground except that it takes place on a Western ranch rather than in the East, whence the hero has fled to escape ruined finances and a botched romance. In his loneliness he invites a café waitress to a dance, is charmed by her honesty and good heart, and confirmed in this downward movement of his affections by the angry eyes of the lady from back East, who has turned up in Queen City for the Wild West show, and seen him with "Dimple." The hero proposes to Dimple, whose face shows "pure joy and adoration" as she accepts. He then performs splendidly on a bronco, securing victory for his ranch, but is knocked out in a freak accident. Both women are by his bedside, the lady from the East having been reminded by his heroism that she loves him. Each is willing to sacrifice, but Dimple is the one who does so, returning sadly to the precincts of her own class.

The courtship story confers its ideological blessings on socially disparate couples only if both partners belong or are about to belong or have the right to belong to one of the reputable classes. A hero may *love* a waitress or servant: that he spies nobility of character in her humble person may even redound to his credit, as in these two tales. To *marry* her, however, would be to break an unwritten rule of the genre, that both lovers must have fine (refined?) sensibilities, of a sort found only among people who come from good families or have lived in the right circles. To be sure, many a hero or heroine is described as "poor," but such a person has either fallen from wealth while retaining gentility, or is well launched in a PMC career, like Gardiner Forrest. The two rancher heroes might get away with it if permanently exiled from Eastern society and wealth, but not if readers are to perceive them as "like us."[20] People "like us" are not snobs; they treat working class characters decently. But their managerial, paternal relation to that class would collapse into serious ideological confusion if they married into it.

Two wealthy characters do fall in love with poor immigrants and eventually marry them; a look at what makes the ending acceptable will confirm the general rule. Elinor Atwater has settled in the "Sicilian quarter" of New York to teach kindergarten, abandoning the privileges conferred on her as the daughter of a rich banker, and leaving behind the highly suitable man who wants to marry her, though she agrees to do so if he will wait until she has satisfied "her New England conscience." She becomes fond of the Sicilian street musician who lives in the next apartment. Three things permit them to marry. In reverse narrative order, but ascending order of importance, (1) her betrothed releases her from her promise because he has found a less reluctant bride; (2) Elinor and Gervaso begin successfully collaborating in a PMC career – he writes sketches of immigrant life in Italian, which she translates and sells to metropolitan newspapers; (3) he came from a distinguished family in Sicily, and had been to university and taken the Grand Tour before his father's extravagance blew away the family fortune and sent Gervaso to the Lower East Side (x). So he is in effect only temporarily disguised as an impossible husband; were it not for that premise of the story, I doubt that any amount of journalistic success could have sanctioned the marriage.[21]

Kathleen Reilly is a seven-year-old urchin with a brogue when she stirs an apparently enduring affection in an aristocratic boy by knocking him cold with a stone after he insults and dares her. Fortunately, when after eighteen years they meet again (in conflict once more – he is the attorney for a railroad that is trying to destroy Kathleen's father's road house business and buy the property), Kathleen has been transformed in speech, manners, appearance, and mind by four years of college on a scholarship, though she still lives with her immigrant family. She's "a good fighter" and a keen businesswoman, too, in the enchanted eyes of the lawyer, who braves his mother's "hysterics" to tell her his resolve (y). Like Gardiner Forrest, Kathleen hasn't risen yet, but a PMC education and acquired gentility make a rift in the class barrier, through which upper class love may flow. Thus even those courtship stories that propel a working class person into the sphere of narrative interest manage to stick to what I consider the real subject of this genre: affinities and relations within and between the two main higher classes, and especially the rosy prospects of the PMC at this fluid moment in its history.

To repeat: I am trying to map a boundary of the genre, along dimensions of class. What lies across the boundary? In the first place, the trail of courtship nearly peters out, there. My sample includes no stories that mate urban working class couples, only a handful whose main narrative interest is the wooing of farmers or small town folk with no claim even to middle class standing. These differ in critical ways from the stories I have been exploring. Disparities of class and wealth do not define barriers to be surmounted, though family prejudice may. There is no triumph of modern ways over rigid old customs. In fact, both parties usually seem caged in traditional cultures, with no opening of vision onto wider prospects, freer choices. And that, I think, is at the generic nub.

Courtship stories tell of a choice freely made, one that often results in dramatically improved social circumstances for one partner, and that always results in emotional transcendence for both, because after all each has found in the other a soul mate. Uncontrolled feeling may initially propel a lover, but mind and will augment emotion in effecting the happy union. The pair wins a victory over something in the environment and something in the self that previously stood in the way of felicity. When we cross the class line I have described, however, the premises of individual choice and power become invalid. Environment, broadly understood, makes the decision. And since a determined marriage (I exaggerate only a bit) does not evoke the new social order of the comic plot, the happiness of the ending is much diminished, weighed down by fate.

For example, in a novella plainly influenced by Hardy's *Tess of the d'Urbervilles*, a Kentucky farm boy and girl are drawn closer and closer by physical desire, until, at the climax of the story, "the betrayal of [her] self-control" and his "helpless sense of surrender" force them to do what lovers in the courtship story *never* do: lie in each other's embrace, with a polite trio of asterisks inviting the reader to supply the unspeakable details. (The narrator interpolates a passage on how young people are defenseless against the "low storm" of "Nature, who cares only for life and nothing for the higher things that make life worth the living.") The lad wants to do the right thing; the girl, recognizing his unreliability, makes him swear to be true; and they run furtively off at night to be secretly married, across the river in Ohio. "At last she was happy and at peace. But there was a pitiful fear of him in her eyes, . . . " on their way up to bed in the strange hotel. Nature has determined their attraction, and produced these mixed feelings. That she and he are neither free nor progressive is emphasized when they see on the desk of the marrying official dozens of sheets of paper covered with names – "the rolls of the secret marriages of the people of Kentucky" – including, unbeknownst to the couple, "the names of her own father and mother" on one of the old, yellowed sheets (z). Heredity, hormones, and social milieu conspire to determine this marriage.

Readers familiar with Northrop Frye's categories will recognize that in his terms the boundary just crossed is one of *mode*, not myth. We have followed the comic plot into different conditions for human action. In the courtship story proper, hero and heroine have at least as much power to act freely as does the implied reader, when confronted with social or environmental challenges. In stories like the one just described, the characters have less power.[22] They fall away from free agency, toward victimization. As this happens, omniscient narrators change their position vis-à-vis characters, mobilizing sociological, or even biological, kinds of explanation. All those names on the register of Kentucky's secret marriages show that our heroine and hero fall short of complete individuality: they act in predictable ways, given a set of circumstances; and the narrator speaks to his readers over the heads of the lovers, explaining lovers to readers in language that the lovers would not themselves be able to use or understand. He looks down, into their lives.

To pause a bit longer with the distinction: narrators of courtship stories may place characters and events in frameworks of psychological explanation (c, r); doing so modulates down from a key of full freedom, but preserves the individuality of the character and, in fact, tends to validate his or her unique selfhood, so long as psychology adds depth but doesn't decide the outcome of events. More often, narrators connect philosophical questions to the story, such as that of fate versus individual will (k), or that of charitable ethics (b), or those of "pessimism" and "realism" (a). When this happens, the story offers itself as an instance or test of a hypothesis, but that in no way reduces the stature of the characters. Writers bring philosophy or psychology to bear in explaining the conduct of people "like us"; they often shift to a *sociological* understanding when representing uneducated rural or provincial or immigrant folk. That nullifies the interest of the courtship story, as is easy to see if one imagines what would happen to "On the Way North" if rewritten as the story of a Gardiner Forrest who could enact only the shabby culture of his upbringing.

I want to say, then, that when fiction in the 10-cent monthlies casts its eye on the doings of people across a certain class line, it also enters another generic venue. At the deepest level, that traversal concerns relations of author, characters, and readers. In courtship stories, very much need not be explained or even narrated because the characters are "like us." In the other genre, the author is like a tour guide, mediating previously hidden lives to a readership of social voyeurs. I don't plan to discuss this genre in detail, and will give it only the nonce label, "elsewhere."[23] As that name suggests, this genre does not take shape around a particular plot line, but around the act of social exploration. It does include a few stories about getting married, but subsumes that plot within a much broader interest: roughly, why people in other cultures or subcultures do what they do.

Thus, whereas courtship stories are about Americans or occasionally Britons,[24] it doesn't matter in "elsewhere" stories whether the sweethearts work out their narrow life chances in a New England fishing village (aa) or preparing to emigrate to the US from a village in Donegal (bb). Again, the courtship story ends before marriage, and virtually no stories about "us" explore the emotional dynamics of married life except to comment on the courtship that preceded it. "Elsewhere" stories accord poor people no such privacy, whether outlaw distillers in the hollows of Appalachia (cc), French peasants on a day trip in Paris (dd), or Jewish sweatshop workers on the lower East Side (ee). (Speaking of "elsewhere," this bit of narration is characteristic: "Such men [as the hero] do not formulate thoughts in words: they feel dumbly, like dogs and horses.") Most "elsewhere" stories, in any case, do not mainly concern either courtship or marriage. They document (a word one could never use of stories about "us") events in the lives of people seen as driven by obsessions or controlled by forces they cannot comprehend – though "we" can, with the writer's help. French Canadians feud over practically worthless fishing rights (ff); a Chippewa family is destroyed by a lumberman's ruthlessness (gg); a southerner, brought low by the Civil War, forces his black servant to shoot his neighbors because their hogs keep wandering into his cotton patch (hh); poverty leads an Italian peasant girl to theft (ii); and so on through the simple annals of the poor.

The post-Civil War story bears the title, "A Tragedy of South Carolina"; it proceeds from the murder to the southerner's suicide and then to the death of his beloved daughter, last surviving member of the family. The stories about the Chippewa family and the sweatshop workers also take the form of tragedy, as do a number of others in this genre. That narrative possibility also marks it off from courtship stories (whose saddest ending is, with rare exceptions, loneliness), and from stories about "us" in general. This makes sense, for one reason internal to the fiction and one external. The first is that PMC free-choosers control the circumstances of their lives, apart from an occasional death by accident or disease; "elsewhere"-people do not. The second reason is that, presumably, PMC readers could feel detachment about the collapse of poor people's hopes and lives that would have been harder to attain when imagining people "like us" sinking into catastrophe. I doubt that fictional fare of the latter sort would have done much to sell magazines.

Here we encounter ideology in one of its most transparent forms. Tragic or not, "elsewhere" stories are, precisely, about people *not like us,* whose lives help define by negation "our" special position in the social order. Any one of several techniques may effect the necessary distancing. An omniscient narrator may stipulate "our" relation to "them": "A pair of suspenders was never owned in its entirety by any one of his caste" (hh); "It is an old story in the Ghetto . . . " (ee); "They were dressed in their holiday clothes, shabby enough to all except the wearers" (dd). Often the story is humorous in the way of ethnic jokes, making harmless fun of, say, the speech and manners of "fifty-six little children of Israel" in "an East Side school-room," while belittling their tribulations (jj). Occasionally the story is heart-warming, projecting generous feelings into social regions thought to exclude them. Sometimes a first person speaker brings back to hearers "like us" a story from elsewhere. Sometimes the story is narrated in dialect by one of "them." And nearly always the characters speak in dialect: Irish (a favorite), Jewish, southern, mountain, New England rural, Negro, German, French, Italian, and more. In this, "elsewhere" stories recall the "dialect sketch" that Frank Munsey scorned, and now it is easier to understand why he felt that way: dialect stories tend to represent human possibility trapped in provinciality, at best quaint and at worst doomed. Munsey wanted energy, plots that went somewhere, and usually an upbeat moral.[25] With some justification, he linked the dialect sketch to "washed out studies of effete human nature," but the other editors had no such scruples, understanding, perhaps, that the devices of class distancing protected the PMC audience from reading powerlessness into their own lives.

I hope this brief trespass into what I am calling "elsewhere" has helped clarify, by opposition, the principles of the courtship story, as well as its ideological force. Now I will return to its safe premises, and add some final interpretive thoughts. In "On the Way North," the adventure in the severed railway car is pivotal, but my inventory of other courtship stories may have made it seem eccentric. Indeed, not many of them depend on brushes with danger; yet such intrusions occur often enough to warrant inquiry, even if they are not essential to the formula. Most dramatic is the train wreck in (q) that literally throws together the ideally suited couple, each of whom, alas, is pledged to another. Also catalytic is the carriage accident in (o), which, by confronting the heroine with "desperate danger," puts the fear of gossip in perspective for her, and allows her love to override the social custom that had blocked it. In four other stories already discussed (f, j, l, w), mishaps with horse or carriage anticipate and promote the recognition of love.

Many other couples are brought together by peril or courageous action or both. Consider some variations on this motif. Two lovers have parted because of what she takes to be "barriers of impossibility" between them. Years later, after training as a nurse, she goes west to forget him. He is in the same area, by chance, on a "capitalist" mining venture, and suffers a near-fatal gunshot wound and fall on Bald Knob. Brought, delirious, to the ranch where she is staying with her brother, he takes her presence there to mean reconciliation. The doctor forbids her to undeceive him while his life is in danger, she cares for him through the dangerous period, and – well, you get the idea (kk). In another story, Marjorie has rejected John because she sees his wish to marry her as a selfish preoccupation with his own happiness. His brother Alfred also loves her; that he has *not* declared his love, Marjorie reads as unselfish restraint. John is Captain Ovington, and is to test a new military balloon the next day. Alfred joins him in its basket; an accident tears the balloon from its mooring and they are carried out over the ocean. Alfred faints with fear as they descend, and John leaps into the sea, lightening the load enough to keep the balloon aloft. Both are rescued. The conviction that John is dead has made Marjorie realize her (equally selfish) love for him, and she embraces him even before learning of his sacrifice for Alfred (ll).

These stories call upon readers to take the hero's ordeal seriously. Others make light of the adventure, especially when both lovers find themselves in the same fix: menaced by comic burglars in a seaside house (mm); trapped on a beam in a barn by a ferocious bulldog (nn); stranded and late for dinner when their boat slips its mooring at a small island on a resort lake (oo).[26] Although the hero gets credit for bravery and resourcefulness, it is not of the sort that in itself wins a Desdemona's love; no more does Gardiner Forrest win Amy Baramore's heart through heroism alone. Rather, the functions of danger are, first, to precipitate a man and woman from the polite social space of courtship into a different order of action, opening up vistas of risk that reduce the hazards of PMC or upper class intercourse to modest proportions by contrast; second, to reveal an integrity of being, usually in both man and woman, not previously known; and third, to brush aside whatever false barriers had separated the lovers, and unite them at an emotional level felt to be more authentic. In short, these are liminal experiences. They take the protagonists across a threshold that divides mundane relations from a higher rapport.

Understood in this way, the optional adventure brings about a crux in the formula that is all but mandatory. That is the moment when "it" is all said without words, to evoke the language of "On the Way North" once more. Of course there are nearly always words, but the lovers' rapport transcends words, and normally finds its initial expression in more intuitive and immediate ways. Bodies rush to embrace, or hearts threaten to burst through the chest, or hands lock, or heads rest softly on shoulders, or lips strain toward lips, or all of the above. And eyes, brimming eyes, wet eyes, eyes with a great light in them, smiling eyes, hurt eyes, stabbing eyes, adoring eyes, wavering eyes, lifted eyes, honest eyes, kind eyes, dancing eyes, big brown eyes, liquid eyes, and a hundred other kinds of eye give delectable access to feelings previously denied or withheld. (One pair of versatile eyes show – all at once – boldness, infinite admiration, infinite delight, desire, angry helplessness, and bitter amusement.) At the liminal moment, souls meet on a new plane. Needless to say, these meetings of flesh and eyebeams signal an erotic connection whose more explicit description is impossible, given the mores of the day. More critical, though, is the fact that sexual, spiritual, intellectual, and moral attraction gather into a transcendent wholeness, in the moment when social impediments fall away.

That moment puts lovers beyond categories of social difference; it also projects them outside of time. A fair number of courtship stories allude to that idea in the same way "On the Way North" does, by joining two adults who had first been attracted to one another as children. One might almost infer that perfect matches are hereditary. Certainly they are perdurable. Another group of stories defer betrothal or marriage for ten, twenty, even in one case fifty years (pp), while one partner or the other holds to a (foolish) vow or obeys a parent's (tyrannical) wish or serves out a prison term for a crime someone else committed, or just stubbornly resists acknowledging the other person as a soul mate. The passage of time does not weaken and may strengthen the bond, once it is fused in a liminal instant. (This premise also lies behind the expectation, in courtship stories though not necessarily in other genres, that a marriage of the right people will stay happy while life lasts.)

That a particular body of fiction represents love as a condition of transcendence carries little surprise. What I want to bring out, as I approach the end of this section, are the *contradictions* latent in the particular structure of feeling I have charted. The liminal experience is in effect the stories' reason for being; it is what makes them tellable. They begin with socially rooted circumstances, including the obstacles of family, class, wealth, opinion, and so on, that stand in the way of union. The moment when feeling pours out through eyes and lips cancels the power of social difference, transporting the lovers into a space where they are just two selves. Yet, as I argued earlier, the stories also align themselves with a specific class project and destiny, one that calls for activism in the social process. They try simultaneously to celebrate a social identity and deny the force of social roles in general.

Likewise, they place themselves in the camp of modernity, positing a forward momentum of history and imagining a vanguard of young people who will guide it where it is going. The stories make much of bold social gestures, fresh speech, no-nonsense manners, and release from the weight of a static past. Yet the liminal experience stops time; it foretells a stasis of the two selves, in harmony just as they are in their eternal now. No suspicion intrudes that the progressive movement of history which enabled their union will continue, and that they must change with it or be rendered old fashioned in their turn. Perhaps these contradictions always lie beneath the sweet assurances of the comic plot, but they seem especially taut in these turn-of-the-century fictions – though of course never acknowledged on the surface of the narration itself.

These abstract thoughts will take on sharper definition, I think, if followed into one thematic region where courtship stories do wear their contradictions more or less openly. That is in the construction of female gender. As so often, that lovely schmoo of a story, "On the Way North," can serve to launch the discussion.[27] It was Amy Baramore's spirited independence that won Gardiner Forrest's affections. Companionable, at ease without a chaperon, advanced in her ideas about marriage, adventuresome, a good sport: these are attributes that make for competence out in the world. They do not suggest an easy fit with the requirements of domesticity, yet they earn Amy a wife's role. Perhaps she, like female readers commended for their liberation from old confines of gender, will learn to enact her modernity in an efficient household full of nationally advertised goods.

Many courtship stories would prompt such doubts, were the reader to breach fictional decorum by trying to imagine the married life that must follow the end of the tale; for women often bewitch suitors with their unconventional, even manly, conduct. The couple trapped on the beam by the bulldog (nn) have never met before, but she laughs with him at their predicament, allows him to comfort her with a clasp of the hand, shares in the dangerous adventure of a night escape, invites him to dinner, and asks if he is married. No wonder he tells her "what a genuine brick" she is. Independent women romp through these stories, intensifying their desirability by outrageous frankness, strong ideas, mettle in tight spots, and so on, as if in defiant response to Henry Higgins's question, "Why can't a woman be more like a man?"

Now and then an actual reversal takes place. Mr Dayton falls through thin ice while skating; he is at the end of his endurance when Miss Lane appears, sizes up the situation, and with "a quick, sure motion" throws him an end of her long fur boa. As he repeatedly says, "You have saved my life." Their hostess, aware of the couple's fondness for each other, notes how romantic this is. Miss Lane is not so sure: "in romance the man saves the girl." This turns out to raise a serious difficulty. When he proposes to her, she angrily turns him down, thinking he acts only out of gratitude. He takes counsel with the host, who goes to the heart of the issue: "It's extremely awkward . . . for a man to have his life saved by a woman. It's all wrong, and only the kind of thing that could happen in these days of 'bachelor girls' and emancipation." Through much pained discussion, she holds to her emancipated scruples, and is about to leave when her gown catches fire and *he* saves *her* life. "It's all right now," she says. "We're on equal terms" (qq).

Although this story does not reveal what "equal terms" will be after marriage, it does locate the gender question historically. The courtship story was straining to accommodate the New Woman. Generally it did so by representing her as non-ideological, enchanting because of her emancipated spirit, and a suitable bride for the modern male. Many of the stories made heroines of actual "bachelor girls" – a somewhat later term

for women making their way in careers or doing good works, unchaper-
oned in the city: writing women, painting women, teachers, business
women, social workers, philanthropists, even (at the margins of
respectability) an actress or two. Often their stories arrived at the standard ending with no anxiety on display.[28] But anxiety was in the air, as is
evident in the huffy quotation about bachelor girls and emancipation.

Taken as a group, the stories carried on a debate about the New
Woman, even "fought over" her portrayal (Denning's phrase). Consider
the three stories in my sample with "New Woman" in their titles. One
narrates a brief scene between a self-styled "really new woman" and the
suitor she refuses because marriage is "medieval." He quickly wins her
away from the "ridiculous notion" (and "fad") of "perfect equality" by
talking coarsely to her, as men do at their clubs. She weeps, he puts an
arm around her: "I love you far too much to treat you as an equal"; and
"I had to give you back the pedestal you had thrown away" (rr). The second story, ironically titled "The Sad Fate of a New Woman," begins with
the thunderous news that Mildred Starke is married – thunderous
because she has been famous as a slum crusader, sportswoman, and
preacher against marriage (a "double misery"). But yes, she has suc-
cumbed to a man "carried away by love," and all her "new woman"
energies have turned into wifely sparkle and dependency (ss). These two
stories rebuke the would-be New Woman with what, I suppose, was
meant as good humor. The third ("A New Woman") is far from light.
The heroine has torn loose from her family and headed for "the freedom, the independence, and the many sidedness of a bohemian
existence as she pictured it . . . ." At age twenty-seven she has struggled
through to success as an illustrator, and is content, until an apparent
suitor disrupts her emotional calm. Convinced that he will propose, she
debates long with herself and decides to refuse. But as it turns out, he
loves another woman. Looking out her window at day's end, the heroine
sees two children waiting for their father's return; when he appears,

> there was a shout and a rush, and both had to be kissed and tossed high
> in the air before the three went up the steps and the door closed behind
> them. No one, Miss Humphreys remembered, was waiting for her, or
> coming to her. She was free to come or go as she chose – free as the air
> or the mist outside.

Ritualistically, she repeats, "I am glad . . . that I decided as I did," then
bursts into tears as the story ends (s).

Now, at least two and probably all three of these stories were written by
men, and they all date from 1896–97, when the question of the New
Woman burned. But after she had turned into the less threatening "bachelor girl," there were still plenty of stories that problematized her
independence. Many written by women and some by men allowed her in

both periods a happy betrothal, envisioning no loss of her vitality and spunk. A smaller number by both men and women had her abandon her "ridiculous notions" about marriage, and accept the firm but gentle rule of a mate. And a very few stories by both men and women left her isolated and regretful. Clearly, a range of possibilities existed within this hegemonic discourse; the question remained open. But one possibility was not realized in my sample: that of a liberated woman who chooses to remain single and is happy. The limits of fictional "debate" did not stretch so far.

It would be easy to read these stories as forecasting a time when many PMC women would remain single by choice, when a kiss would not be an eternal pledge, when divorce would be common. Of course the stories do not "want" any such historical outcome; indeed, they seal it off, occasionally by rejecting it in horror, but normally by rewarding the modern woman with a happy marriage. Unwanted contradictions remain, however. The liminal experience freezes modernity into a cold pastoral like the one on Keats's urn: "For ever wilt thou love, and she be fair!" And as she crosses the threshold of release from old social confinements, the new woman rushes into the oldest of all. The gesture of modernity and the ideology of class liberation in courtship stories meet little resistance in the imagined public sphere. But the blithe reconciliations of the comic plot can't quite put to rest all concern about domesticity and woman's nature. I think this strain inevitable in a body of fiction that calls on love and marriage to effect so much ideological and cultural work.

Out West

What about *man's* nature? Courtship stories do not often bring it forward for interrogation; they assume that men want to get married and will be able to do so without loss of the qualities that define them. If a story makes gentleness a requirement, as does "On the Way North," the hero easily achieves it. If the plot confronts a suitor with the hurdle of danger or adventure, he easily vaults it. Hardly ever do stories open up the possibility that a man might not be manly; the one about the brave and cowardly brothers in the runaway balloon (ll) is an exception. PMC and upper class heroes do what the situation demands. When they enter the relation of betrothal, they need not undergo any conversion; no suspicion arises that marriage could limit their power of action or check their buoyant modernity.

When a man "like us" leaves the *here* of this fiction, though, tests of his nature may become the main subject of the story. (*Here* is both a geographical and a social concept; see chapters 8 and 9: it includes respectable circles in the present day Northeast, the older Midwest, and, by courtesy of Anglo-Saxon affinities, Britain.) Some of the serialized novels in my sample take the hero and heroine through amazing

intrigues and dangers in South America, Greece, Italy, "Carpathia."
Occasionally, the past is the arena of adventure – though I was surprised
to find few historical romances in these particular magazines. Mainly, the
West serves as testing ground for the hero's elemental qualities.

In one story already discussed (w), Herrold has gone west to start
over, after disgracing himself through gambling, and losing his money
and his beloved in the process. There he shows his gentlemanliness with
Dimple the waitress, as I recounted earlier. For my present purpose,
however, the point is that he also regains full integrity as a male by riding
a bronco to victory for his ranch, in the rodeo. Another story trans-
plants a "scion of Beacon Hill" to North Dakota after the ruin of his
family's fortune has led to his social ostracism and thus revealed the
decadence of aristocratic Boston (tt). He displays his deeper worth by
defeating a corrupt political machine in a campaign for sheriff and then
riding through prairie fire to rescue his loved one. In tales like these, the
easterner's authentic manhood is proved by ordeal in a place where
social credentials don't count, only steadfastness and daring. His victory may rehabilitate him after a deserved fall back East, or simply bring
out a manliness that the East had devalued. Either way, these stories of
the triumphant tenderfoot constitute the West as a place that screens out
superficialities and identifies real men.

Before turning to a type of Western story more common than this
one, let me clarify my generic hypothesis. It might seem logical to have
included stories of darkest Europe and of the American West in my category, "elsewhere," mainly as *social* regions, the first occupied by people
"like us," and the second a place where common people negotiate lives
held in by sociological limits and dull determination. But in these terms,
the West stands in opposition to both locations. It differs from "elsewhere" in being a place where people, but almost always men, can do
things decisively, heroically, existentially, enacting or creating their moral
natures often with a single deed. Unlike "elsewhere" people, they can do
this even if, until the critical moment, their lives have been unfree. The
West differs from "here" in being a place where social traditions and
hierarchies are nearly irrelevant.

Not that it is the territory beyond the frontier, site of many earlier and
later Westerns, where a Gary Cooper or John Wayne figure helps a frag-
ile civilization establish itself against the surrounding forces of
lawlessness, in endless reenactment of the social compact. These turn-of-
the-century magazines have acknowledged the closing of the frontier,
and their fictional West is a part of American society. Trains go there,
economic enterprise is underway, there are schools and courts of law.[29]
This is not the wilderness of Leatherstocking or Boone nor the bar-
barous outland of many dime novel Westerns. But relations of people to
nature and to one another are more rudimentary in this newly tamed
West than back East. Class counts for little, and tests of character do not

generally pivot on money, manners, or public opinion. A story of the West may incorporate a courtship plot, but if so, more seems to be at stake than marriage – more, that is, within the value scheme of the genre.

Now, consider a Western plot as clichéd as that of the tenderfoot: the story of the crook with a heart of gold. The sheriff is bringing in Bill Anstey, killer of at least two lawmen. Crossing the desert at night, they find two children, stranded beside a dry spring. They give the kids their water and take them along. One of the horses dies; there will be no chance for all four people to reach civilization. A bond has grown between Anstey and the sheriff through their common concern for the children. The sheriff grows slack in his watchfulness; Anstey passes up a chance to escape. At the end Anstey makes the noble choice. A doomed man anyhow, he insists that the sheriff kill him in summary justice, and go for safety with the children (uu).

Terse Western dialogue that masks feeling in toughness or humor serves as the medium of exchange between sheriff and condemned murderer in another story. Jim Cumso at first objects to being hung next to a "Dago" laborer, but yields to the friendly sheriff's appeal: a double hanging will put the town of Oxide on the map, and guarantee the sheriff reelection. The night before the execution, Jim befriends the laborer, and comes to believe his claim that another man committed the crime for which the Italian has been sentenced. Jim uses his credit with the sheriff to demand speaking time at the gallows. As he proclaims Giuseppe's innocence, the *guilty* Italian ("Dagoes look so much alike," says Jim) tries to flee and is captured. Justice will be done, and not an eye remains dry in the tough crowd as the sheriff binds Jim's hands and feet for his own hanging (vv). In a third story, a rancher hires a laconic Indian named Shauk, who has been condemned to death for murder, to work for the last few weeks of his life – there is no jail in town, and Indians never "skip out" in such circumstances. Through daring and consummate skill, Shauk saves the rancher and his young bride from a stampede; but the rancher's efforts to get a reprieve fail, even though the Indian Shauk had killed "warn't worth the powder it took to shoot him." Shauk goes stoically to the scaffold (ww).

Each murderer performs a compassionate act that makes his death sentence seem petty and that forges a mutuality-beyond-law between him and sheriff or rancher. That last element is important. Sometimes the mutuality turns into a neat reciprocity: the "bad" man risks his life to save somebody good, and the lawful man breaks the law to let the bad man escape. A deputy sheriff, on the trail of a killer who has been in hiding for eight years, gets lost and happens on a remote homestead where abide (you guessed it) the killer and his little family. The sheriff gets the drop on the reformed killer, but when the latter hands over his gun the sheriff recognizes it as the mate to his own: he had given it to a man who saved his life in a shoot-out years before. The sheriff lets the killer resume his peaceful life, and forgoes a thousand-dollar reward (xx). In another story a fleeing bank robber ("a fresh and livid scar marred and distorted the once handsome face") happens in on the *sheriff's* family while the sheriff is pursuing him elsewhere. The robber holds off a band of Apaches to save mother and son, receiving a bad wound in the fray. When he comes to, the sheriff is back. Instead of taking the robber in and claiming the reward, he tells the bad man of "the blamedest, queerest dream" he has just had: that, left for dead, the bad man has stolen a horse from "down yonder – in that clump of chaparral" and lit out "for the Blue Pass, the only one that hain't guarded jest now . . . ." The man with the scar accepts the oblique offer, and vanishes into the clump of chaparral (yy). Criminals and lawmen achieve justice on a higher plane than that of legality, certainly higher than that of cash rewards. Usually, in fact, there is a hovering sense that the bad man's crime wasn't really so bad, and that the law is a faulty arbiter of men's deepest moral natures.

It should be noted that in all these stories the criminal either has a family, or is about to be married (Giuseppe the "Dago"), or saves part or all of a family. That motif of the Western tends to persist in a variant of the story that lacks the noble criminal: a lawful man deviates from strict legality for a cause. Long Jim, a cowboy whose sole dream is to buy the Dawson ranch, has won almost enough to do that in a poker game. His luck holds up through the final pot; the no-good loser falsely accuses him of cheating, and draws a gun. Jim shoots the man dead, in self defense, but relinquishes all his winnings for the little son of the man he has shot, a child who has stirred wistful feelings in the tough old cowhand (zz). A district attorney declines to prosecute a Mexican counterfeiter, ostensibly because he has made a slug out of the evidence (a soft dollar containing mostly lead) in order to defend himself and his fiancée against a vengeful convict, but really because his fiancée has sentimentally pleaded the case of the Mexican (called "Mr. Greaser" by the D.A.) after the Mexican's sweetheart has passionately intervened (aaa). Not only love or parental feeling can prompt a transgression: friendship will suffice, as when another D.A. joins with a gang of bank robbers. His friend the sheriff catches them in the act and kills three, including the D.A. But he tells the town of Lodge Pole that the D.A. died fighting the thieves: "he was my friend, after all," he explains to his wife (bbb). This genre places some personal tie or sentiment above the law.

Transgression of the law is the key, even when writers mine the West for humorous narrative and thus lower the moral stakes. An Englishman has bought a worthless mine in Colorado from its crooked owners. His lawyer, the story's hero, knows there is no remedy at law; instead, he breaks a dam to flood the crooks' working mine below, then sells the spent mine back to them at an exorbitant price as the water rises toward their machinery (ccc). Or, a Mormon who has run away from his eighty wives in Utah gets into a predicament with still another woman, through droll events too complicated to summarize here. The minister, "a cheerful, practical sort of lad, ready to indorse anything that would smooth the rugged road of life," solves the problem by having the Mormon renounce his religion "and all its works," so that he can begin with a clean slate (ddd). Both these stories appeared in *McClure's*, which did not draw upon the formula Western favored by *Munsey's*. Nonetheless, for *McClure's* writers too, Western material seems to dictate plot resolution through breaking the law, or looking the other way as someone else breaks it.

Given this pattern, I am inclined to see a few other stories as extensions of the Western. Some transport to countries like Ecuador or El Salvador the tenderfoot who repairs through high deeds the disgrace he has suffered back home, or the lawless adventurer who does something that is right by a higher standard. Others relate the tale of the good-hearted criminal, but in some non-Western venue. For instance, Jimmy Valentine, a safe-cracker released from prison, goes back to his trade, with his nemesis, the cop Ben Price, on his trail. In a small Arkansas town Jimmy falls in love with the banker's daughter, gives up crime, opens a shoe store. Shortly before he is to marry, his fiancée's little niece gets herself locked in the bank vault. Nothing for Jimmy to do but roll up his sleeves, get out his expensive tools, and reveal to all what he really is. The girl saved, Jimmy heads for the door, a criminal once more. There Ben Price is waiting for him, and Jimmy says, "Well, let's go. I don't know that it makes much difference now." But Ben gives him his straight identity back: "Guess you're mistaken, Mr. Spencer . . . . Don't believe I recognize you" (eee; this story, like aaa, is by O. Henry, a master of the formula). Stories of crime tend to gravitate toward the Western, as transgression opens up possibilities of reform and justification by a higher law, dear to the genre.

I could pursue this theme through other variations, but after consuming more than two alphabets' worth of stories, this chapter owes the reader some conclusions. I have included Westerns for two reasons. First, there are more of them in my sample than of any other genre, aside from courtship stories and "elsewhere" stories; those three types, taken together, make up more than half of all the stories in my sample, and well more than half of those that strike me as formulaic, or at least generic.[30] The second reason is strategic. Westerns stand in opposition to courtship stories in important ways, as already noted. It is interesting to ask, therefore, how the two genres connect on the level of ideology, whether they solve analogous "social equations" (Jane Tompkins, *Sentimental Designs*, p. xvi).

Start with an obvious difference – not to say incompatibility – between the two genres. Westerns of the main type smile on lawbreakers, lawbreaking, or non-enforcement of laws. Courtship stories, while they savor breaches of decorum and trespass of class lines, never present heroes who break or ignore laws. PMC and upper class characters are by definition respectable people of the sort laws are made to protect. Moreover, the end of the courtship story projects the couple toward the relationship of marriage, a legal confirmation and sanction of their love. They achieve their justice through the law, not beyond it. (Unthinkable, too, that justice should entail one or more violent deaths, as is generally the case in serious Westerns.)

Two considerations bridge this ideological chasm. I have mentioned that Westerns usually justify transgressions by good works that benefit children, women, families, or lovers who want to start families. In this tough world, recognition of a moral order higher than the law looks through the violent affairs of men into a sentimentalized domestic sphere, the same privileged space that courtship stories gaze into from a different standpoint – except, of course, that Westerns abstract the domestic away from its familiar PMC coordinates and locate it in a realm felt as archetypal. That ties in with the second consideration: Westerns take place "out there" on a margin of US society. The same laws govern conduct but are more permeable, more tentative, requiring constant reaffirmation and also adjustment to individual circumstances. As that suggests, out there one's relation to law is more immediate. Almost every man carries a six-shooter, even lawyers. (Courtship stories abound with lawyers, but they are apparently administrators, bureaucrats; we never hear about criminal cases, much less guns.) Justice regularly demands that individuals humanize the law and so renew the social compact. This puts men to moral tests unthinkable back East. Western transgression is not really about overriding the stable laws in which the older society nestles, but about defining manliness, in a what-if setting that lets readers imagine their way "back" from eastern amenities to more elemental conditions.

The most obvious thing to say about the ideological work so performed is this: Westerns assure readers whose life chances depend irrevocably on the urban, corporate order, that individual action and character still count. In this, they reduplicate the function of great-man profiles and biographies, but in the shadowy domain of fantasy. Captains-of-industry articles present actual examples of consequential action (for that matter, so do shame-of-the-cities articles); Westerns transport the reader to an imaginary place where such action is the norm. Both offer to reconcile individuality with the faceless order individualism has created.

Something more subtle also happens. Transgression is a liminal experience like the exchange of gazes in courtship stories, when "it" is all said without words. Remember the sheriff's "dream" (yy): through the relation of it he communicates a different message to the man with the scar, namely, that he will look away while the robber escapes. When Ben Price says to Jimmy the safe-cracker, "Don't believe I recognize you," he conveys the same message. When the sheriff who is bringing in Bill Anstey regains consciousness after a fall, he sees his gun lying on the ground, where Anstey could easily have picked it up and made a getaway; the two men's eyes meet, "soul to soul." The sheriff simply utters his stock expletive "God A'mighty!" – but he and Anstey both understand the compact beyond law that now binds them. Nearly always, laconic or oblique or ironic speech of this sort accompanies transgression; no one, lawman or criminal or reader, ever fails to grasp the richer meaning that is unexpressed.

Situations like these place the two men beyond language as well as beyond law. They achieve a mutuality grounded in a tacit code of decency and honor, and in complete integrity of being. Sometimes God makes one of His rare appearances at these moments,[31] to signal transcendence. Law declines into a system of regulations adequate for daily life but unable to express the deepest moral imperatives. Society itself falls away. Men, it would seem, can reach full selfhood only in a space apart from social codification.

Here, I suggest, Westerns and courtship stories meet on a particular ideological terrain. I read the liminal experiences in both as articulating a dream of untrammeled individuality, confirmed in the mirror of another free soul's recognition. In a peculiarly American way, many of these stories wish society out of existence, or at least posit a trans-social realm where the most intense realizations of being occur. In Westerns, especially, this movement of thought is a nostalgic one, evoking a more primitive social formation than that of actual readers. In both kinds of fiction, though, the consolations of the liminal repress similar anxieties. These magazines speak to an audience firmly allied with modernity, yet apparently concerned that monopoly capital, while creating the very conditions of the audience's prosperity, also threatens it in the vulnerable area of autonomy and wholeness. The stories ease that contradiction.

How do Westerns contribute to the dialogue of class? As I said earlier, eastern social distinctions don't count in the fictional West, and the delicate negotiations of PMC and upper class do not constitute a theme of these stories. If an aristocrat or lawyer goes west, he must stand judgment by the same criteria that apply to sheriff and cowboy; he usually does well, but not because of his eastern credentials. Rather, he, like westerners, earns credit by demonstrating the kind of integrity I have described, meeting ultimate tests of selfhood, and intuiting the right thing to do in moral situations where mere legality is no guide. Any Western hero, at least at the critical moment, will be forthright but restrained, value justice, practice at least rough courtesy, and in general show in his conduct "the perfect, organic expression of disciplined being." A natural gentleman, he is "in truth, what he present[s] himself to be."[32] This is very much the PMC ideal of conduct, transplanted to harsher and more archetypal circumstances than those of Fifth Avenue.

But why, then, the apparent classlessness of the West? Doesn't that deflect any gesture of flattery to the audience? I would tentatively respond in this way. First, the outlook of Westerns does not completely deny social hierarchy. Look outside the circle of characters worth the reader's interest, and one finds "Dagoes," "Greasers," a few black people, a frighteningly strange Chinese cook. These are beyond narrative interest, except as they stir the feelings of main characters. Nor do proletarians stand in candidacy for heroism; they are absent or, like the "Dago" railroad workers, discounted as individual agents. Although cowboys were, historically, proletarians,[33] the stories do not present them that way. In short, the people who matter are, first, economically free agents and, second, almost universally Anglo-Saxon. (Most of the few exceptions are Native Americans.) Within those confines, society is indeed a kind of protoplasm from which anyone may emerge as an individual through distinguished conduct. To put it that way is to read these stories as *naturalizing* the idea of activist gentlemen, identifying those qualities the audience saw in itself with a trans-social and timeless code of honor that would display its superiority in any environment.

Westerns complement courtship stories in this way, and also through a kind of oblique commentary on the worrisome matters of gender, class, and modernity. Back East, we admire the gentlewoman's unconventionality or forwardness, yet the accrediting of those qualities raises a concern that the courtship genre contains only with some uneasiness, as noted at the end of the last section. Westerns contain it very easily indeed. Most women are steadfast, loyal, and plucky, regardless of class; to that extent the genre naturalizes an ideal of female gentility, too. But the assumptions about significant action relegate woman to the role of the protected. Not only can she not fight Apaches or rob a bank; she cannot even join in the liminal experience that these stories prize. Honor-beyond-law is for men to achieve, on *behalf* of women and children. I don't know how or if the readership divided by sex, with respect to these two genres; people who did read both would learn that women are as fine as men, but that male excellence is more adaptable, more universal. Women readers who relished the sort of compliment extended by courtship stories, however, might well have found Westerns thin gruel.

Westerns also teach, in a way not possible for stories about the contracting of marriages, that gender is both an unequal opposition and yet one that implies no antagonisms. Men simply worship and define women; women (and their children) need to be defended. Bad men exist, who terrorize women, but their wickedness does not express an inherent conflict between the sexes. This point generalizes easily: there are no social conflicts at all, of a structural sort. No class antagonisms, no rebellious cowboys, no uprising of "Greasers" (except for bandits from across the border), not even – in these stories – traditional struggles between cowmen and homesteaders. Westerns draw just one line of social embattlement, with criminals on one side and law-abiding citizens on the other, and this is distinctly not conceptualized as a class line. Some outlaws are crude and ignorant, some wily and humorous, some elegant and well-spoken; we find the same sorts of men on the right side of the law. The stories offer no genetic hypothesis to explain why some break laws and others obey and enforce them; the difference is a mysterious one of character. Furthermore, it is not ineradicable. Bad men can ennoble themselves when morally challenged; good men can break or obstruct the law. Such crossovers are the point of the genre. Seen this way, it envisions a United States with no socially constructed antagonisms or irreconcilable interests. A change of heart or a generous deed can heal any rift.

Westerns sound an ideological theme that runs through the discourse of class in just about all the stories, of whatever genre, in my sample. The fictional society has classes, but no deep conflicts of interest or need dictate that classes must contend with one another, or that issues must be settled to the advantage of one and the distress of another. Strikes and labor organization are virtually absent from the social scene. Rich people do not exploit workers; they simply have money. Black people have no complaints. The Civil War, a living memory for many around 1900, and for all Americans the bitterest class conflict of the nation's history and the most open clash between modes of production, has in fictional representation lost political meaning. It is a backdrop against which family dramas and romances are played out; or warriors show themselves to be brave or cowardly in the test of battle; or Yankee and Rebel shout friendly insults to each other across no man's land, and perhaps share a meal or bury a comrade before resuming hostilities.[34]

These exclusions and mutings of conflict answered well to the PMC wish to understand society as an arena of individual endeavor, and a network of problems that PMC rationality could solve or ameliorate. The fiction did much more than that, of course, and I hope my selective treatment has hinted at the richness of even the most formulaic stories, while passing over Kipling, Stevenson, Crane, and so on. At the same time, my main aim has been to show how ideologically structured and *interested* this body of popular fiction was. That conclusion, if true, strikes me as the more significant because the editors had no articulate or even discernable program for ideological instruction through stories. They just printed the "best" of what was available in this inviolate realm of individual creation. Their mediation of the cultural process drew upon initiatives from elsewhere, or maybe *no*where identifiable. It would not distort the picture too much to think of a whole class and cultural moment as authoring these stories. Hegemony works rather differently in the production of "art" than in the marshalling of direct discourse, or the densely coded language of advertising. But I hope to have shown how these three discourses, which arrived in the pages of the magazines by distinct routes and there executed different practical tasks, collaborated almost seamlessly in their ideological work.

Appendix

C   = *Cosmopolitan*
LHJ   = *Ladies' Home Journal*
M   = *Munsey's Magazine*
Mc   = *McClure's Magazine*

a.   "The Doctor," Hamlin Garland, *LHJ*, December 1897
b.   "One Woman's Story – A Study," Margaret Deland, *C*, February 1896
c.   "A Shy Man's Wooing," Margaret L. Knapp, *LHJ*, January 1898
d.   "A Bird's Eye View of Heaven," Phillip Verrill Michels, *Mc*, July 1903
e.   "The Mower from Wall Street," Lynn Roby Meekins, *M*, April 1903
f.   "Be It Ever So Humble," Lynn Roby Meekins, *M*, July 1903
g.   "Bullock, Jr. and the Octopus," William Hamilton Osborne, *Mc*, October 1903
h.   "A Girl's Way," Lulu Judson, *M*, November 1896
i.   "The Dramatic Rights to 'Laurel Crowns,'" Elizabeth McCracken, *C*, December 1902
j.   "A Hint from Fate," David Graham Phillips, *C*, March 1903
k.   "Two Sides of a Street," Mary Raymond Shipman Andrews, *Mc*, August 1903
l.   "On the Boulevard," Emma A. Opper, *M*, March 1897
m.   "Out of Thun," Robert Barr, *Mc*, July 1896
n.   "The House That Bobby Built," Mary Lindsay, *M*, July 1903
o.   "The Speech of People," Mary R. Drury, *M*, August 1903
p.   "Betty Maria's Guard," Laura Spencer Proctor, *LHJ*, June 1903
q.   "In Collision: Two of a Kind," James Edward Dunning, *C*, February 1903
r.   "Alcyone – A Breeze from the West," Catherine Frances Cavanagh, *M*, October 1896
s.   "A New Woman," M. K. Conyngton, *M*, March 1897
t.   "A Momentary Indiscretion," Sarah Grand, *C*, December 1895
u.   "A Broken Lorgnette," Joseph Sebastian Rogers, *M*, October 1896
v.   "For Faithful Service," Juliet Wilbor Tompkins, *M*, July 1903
w.   "Young Herrold's Good Angel," Anne O'Hagan, *M*, April 1903
x.   "An Episode in Elinor's Life," Minnie J. Reynolds, *M*, August 1903
y.   "The Great Northeastern and the Cow Girl," Anne O'Hagan, *M*, September 1903
z.   *Butterflies: A Tale of Nature,* James Lane Allen, *C*, December 1895
aa.   "In the Time of the Sweetbrier," Harriet Prescott Spofford, *Mc*, September 1896
bb.   "Judy," M.G. Sampson, *Mc*, July 1903

cc.   "Mandy's Raid," Grace MacGowan Cooke, *M*, May 1903
dd.   "The Happy Day," Mary E. Wilkins, *Mc*, May 1903
ee.   "The End of the Task," Bruno Lessing, *Mc*, October 1903
ff.   "Old Man Savarin," Edward William Thompson, *Mc*, August 1896
gg.   "Dead and Down," John R. Gill, *Mc*, May 1903
hh.   "A Tragedy of South Carolina," Mrs. F.W. Dawson, *C*, November 1895
ii.   "Tonia: A Story of Crime from Poverty," Ouida, *C*, December 1895
jj.   "A Little Matter of Real Estate," Myra Kelly, *Mc*, June 1903
kk.   "Luck on Bald Knob," Mabel Earle, *M*, August 1903
ll.   "The Selfishness of John," Marvin Dana, *M*, June 1903
mm.   "The Robbery of Oldport," Anne O'Hagan, *M*, May 1903
nn   "The Day of the Dog," George Barr McCutcheon, *Mc*, August 1903
oo.   "Lovers on an Island," Barry Pain, *C*, December 1902
pp.   "After Fifty Years," Anne Warner, *M*, September 1903
qq.   "The Requirements of the Situation," George Hibbard, *Mc*, August 1903
rr.   "One New Woman," Percival Pollard, *M*, November 1896
ss.   "The Sad Fate of a New Woman," Julian Ralph, *C*, March 1896
tt.   "The Man for Sheriff: A Dakota Story," Frank Tracy, *Mc*, October 1899
uu.   "Breed of the West," Charles Tenney Jackson, *C*, March 1903
vv.   "In the Other Cell," L.H. Bickford, *M*, November 1896
ww.   "Shauk," Will T. Whitlock, *M*, December 1896
xx.   "The Call of the Quail," Frank Nielson, *M*, May 1903
yy.   "The Sheriff's Dream," Frank N. Stratton, *M*, September 1903
zz.   "A Silhouette of the Seventies," Frances Weston, *M*, November 1896
aaa.   "One Dollar's Worth," Sydney Porter [O. Henry], *M*, April 1903
bbb.   "The Redemption of Joel Prentiss," Oscar King Davies, *C*, November 1902
ccc.   "Ruggles' First Case," Chauncey Thomas, *Mc*, July 1903
ddd.   "By Proxy," Henry Wallace Phillips, *Mc*, October 1903
eee.   "A Retrieved Reform," O. Henry, *C*, April., 1903

11

Considerations

I began this study with the claim that something of unusual interest happened about a hundred years ago: a "magazine revolution" established in the United States a new kind of cultural production – one of major historical consequence whether or not we call it "mass culture" – and change came about very rapidly, as such things go. After pausing to ask what kind of explanation could best account for such an upheaval in the field of culture, I proceeded to work through the one I find most helpful and inclusive, beginning with a systemic crisis for industrial capital, and marching through the reinvention of corporate structure and purpose, the new effort to expand and control sales, the institutions that facilitated that effort, the practices of advertising in particular, the changes in social structure that brought forward an apt audience (the PMC) for advertising and for the new monthly magazines, the ads that represented and praised commodities to that audience, the journalism that attracted its attention and helped orient it, and the fiction that fed and flattered its imagination.

The sequence of steps in an argument of this sort cannot be innocent. In the sequence adopted here I recognize at least two implications. One, the real causes come first, while later chapters descend toward contingent causes, then mere effects. Two, the real causes have to do with big capital, factories, machines, products, and profits; secondary causes include the labors of middlemen to move products about and win over consumers; farther downstream are the projects of writers and editors, then those of the new middle class that bought magazines and the commodities advertised there; and at the end of the causal flow come representations, meanings, ideology. Change the spatial metaphor, and one could track my argument as moving from economic base steadily "up" into the airiest regions of superstructure. These implications of the book's organization are not far from my intent, yet they misrepresent it somewhat.

Do economic forces ("in the last instance") write the script of history? Well, yes, if the answer must be yes or no. I prefer that other marxist way of putting it: that people make history, but not in circumstances they have created or chosen. That holds even for the powerful manufacturers of the last century, *driven* to transform the system they had so chaotically built, by intolerable contradictions within it, not least the resistance of workers. More restricted, it seems plain, was the agency of other actors in the story I tell here. To put the generalization in a rough-and-ready hypothetical form: if ad men and mass marketers and magazine entrepreneurs had not stepped forward to perform their roles, capital would (short of revolution) have found other means to run its show; but if the aspirations of ad men and the others had not responded to a need of capital, their efforts would have come to naught.

It should be clear that agency occupies a central spot in the version of economic determinism to which I subscribe. I know that the idea of agency has been under critique for twenty-five years, with some post-structuralists wanting to eliminate it altogether. In their way of thinking, the decentered subject dissolves into structures and circuits of meaning; agency looks like a residue of humanism (a pejorative) and metaphysics; and causality disappears. There are ways to write history within such a framework: Foucault's is one from which I have learned. And I have paid a good deal of attention to ways in which structures speak through subjects, as in the discourse of advertising. But a thoroughgoing poststructuralism will not allow the sort of explanation I attempt in this book, grounded as it is in reasonable choices made by individuals and groups aware to different degrees of their historical agency and with very different abilities to get what they want. Further, some poststructuralisms would dismiss as phantasmal the historical transformation I am trying to explain, or attribute it to chance, in what Perry Anderson calls "the randomization of history."[1] I choose not to enter these debates, which in any case will not make the need for historical explanation go away by branding it chimerical. Rather, I locate my work in the tension – present in marxism from the beginning – between structural or "capitalogical" accounts of change, and accounts based in class struggle. The whole inquiry is my response to this conundrum, with these reflections on agency standing as an effort to sum up.

I understand agency and determination not quite as the metaphors of causal magnitude and serial transmission implied by my sequence of chapters would have it. In many specific instances, to be sure, a manufacturing corporation with large resources, following a conscious design, directly enlisted the services – caused the actions – of a lesser firm. Just so, the National Biscuit Company prompted the advertising activities of N. W. Ayer in the "Uneeda Biscuit" campaign of 1899. But the plenitude of such transactions by no means warrants a general description such as this: manufacturers had needs, framed intentions, then put advertising agencies to work, and so on down the causal chain to actual ads and the consciousness of viewers. No: the agencies were pursuing their own designs, adjusting them as changing circumstances allowed or demanded. They vigorously competed with one another.

Beyond that, they effectively promoted the new way of doing business; they badgered recalcitrant manufacturers; they often reinvigorated the businesses of those they won over, and helped put other, more backward manufacturers *out* of business. Only by standing far back from this busy, interactive process can the observer grasp it analytically, abstractly, and I think accurately, as a movement initiated and orchestrated by capital.

The kind of cultural history I fantasize would be multi-dimensional, multi-perspectival, non-linear. One might enter a story at any point and reassemble its parts, to achieve a different emphasis. The story I have attempted here could have ad men as its protagonists, or merchandisers, or commodities themselves, or magazine editors, or writers, or texts, or readers. In fact, over the years of my work on this study, readers – decked out as a new social class – elbowed their way in from the distant margins to the center of my attention, pressing me to reconceive this as their story, a story of class formation. No doubt the finished text bears disruptive traces of that shift in understanding and emphasis. Not to fuss too much about challenges posed me by the complexity of my subject, and certainly not about tactics of chapter arrangement. The point is, any supple account of historical process needs to hold two principles in tension with each other: the decisive power of economic forces and of those actors best located to harness them; and the equally crucial, if less decisive, agency of many others seeking their own ends with smaller means.

This dual focus matters especially in thinking about cultural production as part of production in general, lest one fall into the old (marxist) habit of seeing culture as derivative and somehow separate. Not only – a familiar point by now – is cultural production quite as material as the making of soap or shoes. It has over the last few centuries followed soap and shoes into the increasingly universal market, with the 1890s a pivotal moment in that long revolution. Indeed, a main theme of my story has been the market initiatives taken by small cultural producers, not big capital. The sale of creative ad making to soap makers, the sale of audiences' attention to advertisers, and publishers' assembly of large audiences for this purpose by selling *them* a new kind of cultural fare, are critical instances of such leadership, no less momentous than – and plainly inseparable from – the selling of brand name soaps to consumers at the grocery store by Procter & Gamble. More: as the example shows, entrepreneurs of culture led in vastly enlarging the market, making it more nearly universal. The selling of consciousness is but the most telling innovation here, a critical instance of how, in advanced capitalism, "the dominant culture reaches much further than ever before in capitalist society into hitherto 'reserved' or 'resigned' areas of experience and practice and meaning," as Raymond Williams wrote.[2] One gloss to be put on the story of magazines is precisely the extended reach of commodification into previously reserved areas of "private" life.

If the analysis I have elaborated in this book is more or less right, cultural actors on the periphery of big capital with modest resources played a significant role in bringing about this major historical transformation, and not on marching orders from big capital. In the fluid medium of the rapidly expanding market, many and various agents pursued many and various projects, the articulation of which into a new hegemonic system few of them envisioned. Often, for that matter, they worked at cross purposes with one another and with capital itself: McClure's muckraking and Walker's flirtation with a Bellamy-style socialism are obvious examples. Each seeking his own advantage, the closest they came to a unified vision was in understanding the opportunity afforded by manufacturers' need to sell products in a more disciplined way; or even more vaguely, they caught the momentum of the broad social change we call commodification, sensed the appeal of products and imagined the reorganization of daily life around them and their meanings.

That last thought brings the motives and actions of consumers, of the magazines' readers, squarely into the realm of historical agency. Placing them there, I allow some weight to the premises of neo-classical, supply-and-demand economics. Small choices to buy something rather than nothing, one thing and not another, do accumulate and register. Granting that obvious truth, however, concedes little force to the ideology of market democracy and sovereign consumer. It's not just that the analysis offered here posits the sovereignty of capital, mediated through the vice-regency of others with more market power than consumers; and not just that certain kinds of purchase were pretty well determined by earlier movements of capital that brought people to cities and pushed home production to the margins. I have also tried to show, in my narrative of PMC formation (chapter 7), that we can best understand that class's daily purchases not as atomized free choices but as a patterned activity inseparable from, and consequent upon, a decades-long effort to establish certain kinds of social presence, authority, privilege, comfort, and meaning. I locate the agency of the PMC in that broad project, not in its capacity to influence production through its choices from among the wares on grocers' shelves.

That can serve as a reminder that for all the importance I assign to markets in the launching of mass culture – which is, after all, commercial culture – the negotiations that culminated in monopoly capitalism went ahead vigorously in other sites as well. Recall the self-organization of PMC people in professional groups, trade associations, women's clubs, civic organizations, cultural networks; their attachment to colleges and universities; their activism in reform politics; their aggregation in suburbs and consolidation of a broader social space: all the formal and casual affinities that shaped them as a class and gave force to their class interests, more consciously, I would think, than styles of consumption. The point holds for the capitalist class as well. I have put emphasis on

their generally successful efforts to predict and regulate the sale of commodities; but alongside that project, and at greater distance from the
market, capitalists also sought advantage through corporate mergers
and vertical integration, their decisive strategy of social transformation –
not to mention such routine practices as commercial banking, stock
manipulation, the making of cartels, the purchase of senators, the
attempt to guide business-friendly legislation, and so on. Agency in the
market is central to my analysis, but it always articulates with hegemonic
work in other arenas.

To juxtapose the projects of big capital and the PMC as I have just
done is to rephrase the question of agency, and to pose more abstract difficulties than that of locating the opportunistic successes of ad men and
magazine publishers in conditions of possibility laid down by the needs
and activities of manufacturers. McClure and the others would have
failed, no matter how large the circulations they built, had advertisers not
wanted to reach big national audiences in order to rationalize the sales
effort; McClure's efforts on his own behalf assisted capital, in a small way,
in extricating itself from crisis and transforming the economic order. So
much is clear, if not uncontestable. But what sense does it make to say
that a whole subordinate class, pursuing its own interests, found openings
to do so in the interstices of capital's project, and thereby contributed to
it? Can such a claim capture the enormously variable activities of PMC
people, even as roughly as do most statements about class? Can one class
act as the *agent* of another while also acting for itself? Can the activities of
the PMC be understood that way, though it understood them rather differently, and for that matter saw itself as an antagonist of capital in areas
such as reform politics and critical investigation? Finally, since many
PMC people had jobs in corporations, and thus, like laborers, both
directly served capital and were exploited by it, why rope them off conceptually from the working class, and pen them in with free
professionals, bureaucrats, cultural entrepreneurs, and the like?

I am tempted to leave those questions and move on; my study gives
them sharpness, but does not resolve them, and I do not want to leap
into the conceptual briar patch that has grown up around the heuristi-
cally invaluable hypothesis of a class "between labor and capital."[3] A few
provisional comments, however, before seeking more open ground: the
PMC both assisted and rationalized capital's reassertion of dominance
around the turn of this century. It did so through foundational work in
the culture industry, my main subject, as well as by exercising managerial skill in corporations, bringing applied science and engineering to
bear on production, doing the legal work required for mergers, and so
on. Other PMC activities looked and felt more like opposition to the
untrammeled workings of big business: social work, urban reform, muckraking, the regulatory legislation of the 1900s. Yet in none of these
projects did the anti-union, anti-populist PMC support working class

self-organization; indeed, in retrospect, all of them tended to strengthen the rule of capital by making it less abrasive and coercive, more reasonable, more "natural," more hegemonic.

Might we then think of the PMC and the capitalist class as an historic "bloc" in Gramsci's sense: a political alliance built around harmonious interests and a common conception of the world?[4] At occasional moments such as the election of 1904 and the second Roosevelt administration, something of the sort may have crystallized. Prominent reformers (mayors, governors, and their allies) included some from wealthy families among their predominantly PMC, college educated numbers;[5] legislation such as the Hepburn and Pure Food and Drug acts could certainly not have passed without at least reluctant support from congressmen indebted to big business. But the bullying it took for Roosevelt to bring the latter in line, as had been required to weld progressives and Republican conservatives together in the winning coalition of 1904, suggests an unstable arrangement not voluntarily sought or based on a perceived harmony of aims. The articulation of those aims happened far less in the public arena of politics than in the labyrinth of economic relations like those described in the early chapters of this study.

And perhaps in ideology. Although no common conception of the world united business leaders and reforming professionals on matters of corporate power and the free market (between which, business leaders tended to see no conflict), on loftier planes of ideology the PMC intellectuals who edited and wrote for mass circulation magazines served not just as organic intellectuals for their own class, but as promoters of a world view hospitable enough to the work of the bourgeoisie. Think back over the reassuring beliefs I read from texts of ad, essay, and story. The celebration of modernity, the idea of rational progress, the erasure of social conflict, the privileging of individuality, the cult of the great man, the dream of the nation as essentially Anglo-Saxon and called to imperial power, the deference toward high culture: none of these challenged upper class complacency or capital's project of accumulation. On the contrary, inflected just a bit differently, each could carry forward the main task of ideology: to represent the interests and outlook of a dominant group as universal common sense.

To ask why this confluence should have occurred in the pages of magazines produced by the PMC for the PMC is to pose, in an historically specific context, the question that rises from or hides unasked in so much critical analysis of mass culture, and one of the main questions that led me to this study: How does it so often and so persistently happen that commercial culture, made to earn a profit by pleasing large audiences, rather than to propagandize on behalf of capitalists – including those who own the means of its production – nonetheless looks and sounds a lot like propaganda for capitalist social arrangements? The literature on American mass culture offers many complex, empirically grounded answers, some of which (by Edward Jay Epstein, Herbert Gans, Gaye Tuchman, Todd Gitlin, Noam Chomsky and Edward Herman, and others) have influenced my inquiry.

Reflection on the PMC and the ruling class around 1900 points to a more general answer: the common sense of an hegemonic class is likely to seem commonsensical, also, to a subordinate class helping to administer and renew hegemony and well positioned within it to achieve success, comfort, and dignity. This answer goes much farther toward explaining ideological convergence in the mass circulation magazines of 1900 than toward explaining similar convergences in network television circa 2000. But it will be worth keeping in mind when I come to speculate on continuities across that hundred-year period.

Such an explanation of convergence gains force from a truism anterior to this whole inquiry: the making of culture has become capitalist production, with a momentum that picked up smartly through the success of the mass circulation magazine. More truisms: behind the frenzied clatter of the editorial office, its urgent labor on the written word and exchanges of managerial speech, was the still noisier industrial space of the printing plant, integrated into the business at the outset or as soon as capitalization allowed. Publishers mass-produced a physical product, which they sold at a loss, and used it to mass-produce an immaterial product, the attention of readers, which they sold at a profit. Like makers of bicycles or razors, they appropriated surplus value extracted from the work of employees at all levels, who sold their labor power as a commodity. Foremen and middle managers and business managers organized the labor process, monitored the flow of materials into the factory and through production out to final sales, tallying costs and revenues, cutting the former as necessary. Magazine companies borrowed from banks, sold stock, reinvested profits, copiously advertised their products. If we think mainly of their transactions in cultural talent, we lose sight of the fact that the magazine entrepreneurs, their staffs, and, at a somewhat greater remove, their writers and illustrators, lived daily in the same relations of production as did people in the bicycle and razor businesses. Like relations at work may be expected to foster like ideologies.

To put it that way, however, is again to imply an understanding of ideology as endpoint in a chain of causes, or in the other metaphor, sitting atop a superstructure. These metaphors do not capture the force of ideology as itself a cause, turned back on action, which any but the most rigid materialism would allow; otherwise, they are roughly adequate, if we take ideology to be an assemblage of tacit or explicit beliefs, as I have done here for a few paragraphs and as most theorists always did in earlier stages of the marxist tradition. But I mean to be working with a greatly enriched notion of ideology in the more recent tradition drawn out of Gramsci and Althusser, and associated these days especially with cultural studies.

In that concept, ideology is the whole of consciousness as it arises from and interacts with material and social life. Thus it includes the values, attitudes, expectations, and habituations that permeate and guide daily experience, along with the meanings people make out of material life, the way meanings speak through us, and the very processes of signification. Ideology does not stand above or apart from social relations, institutions, practices, social space, the built world, and so on, but constantly makes sense of and indeed reproduces them – except of course when and where hegemony is not working smoothly, as in the late 1960s generally, and in many sites of contestation since then.[6] This conception is rather imperialistic, to be sure, and I have no wish to polemicize on its behalf, or to censure more restricted uses of the term. The point is to achieve a perspicuous understanding of historical process, and, right now, to sort out the consequences of a major cultural change.

With those preliminaries, I suggest that ideology in the narrower sense, as spun out in the pages of the magazines, was of less moment than ideology in the expanded sense, as embedded in the production and consumption of the magazines. I grant that beliefs propounded, or held as unchallengeable assumptions, in main cultural venues can help set the agenda for public policy, or set limits to it. There can be little doubt, for instance, that the complacent chauvinism of the leading monthlies collaborated (on a different social plane) with the jingoism of the yellow press to make the Spanish War politically acceptable, not to say wildly popular. But in reestablishing the social order on a somewhat different basis, ideology at other levels seems to me to have done more decisive political work. One example is the incorporation of culture. I mentioned it as a reason that magaziners produced ideology (narrow sense) compatible with the project of big business. More important, I think, is that the change *naturalized* cultural production as itself big business, with the usual relations and practices thereof. Without this assimilation (carried forward also by newspaper publishers), would it have seemed natural or even tolerable, thirty years later, to set aside the air waves as a medium for corporate cultivation and the sale of consciousness?

Along the path of this study, I have paused to remark a number of more particular innovations in social life, all connected one way or another to this large one. To recall, quickly: advertising agencies brought together expert knowledge about citizens, now seen as groups of consumers. On behalf of manufacturers, ad men paid by the head for the attention of such groups, who were drawn to the cultural fare magazine editors solicited and shaped and put between covers. Another group of hired writers and artists at ad agencies stirred desire in the audience and organized it around household products, now given added meaning through brand names, trademarks, packaging, slogans, and social tableaux. Audiences learned these new configurations of signs, and reimagined their identities in terms of such signs – doubtless at times with reservations, resistance, or irony, rather than bland acceptance; but still, the new discourse, made by unseen experts without the consent of the audience, lodged itself in the latter's semiotic world. The wise and friendly voice of the ad man hailed (*interpellated*, in Althusser's term) the reader as a person in whose life consumption played a main role. Displays of products in markets and department stores and mail order catalogs did the same. As the scale of marketing enlarged, purchases became transactions among strangers; the buyer confronted goods with less mediation by familiar neighborhood merchants, and more by anonymous corporate voices. As a strategy for negotiating the increasingly mysterious relations of urban life, middle class people took part in rearranging the city and carving out a PMC social space. On a conceptual plane, magazines helped create and map that space, punctually entering its domestic quarters with cultural flattery and instruction. These and other new relations, institutions, and practices were – and are – saturated with ideology in the broad sense, a reasonably coherent ideology we might for shorthand call "commodification."

For several reasons, I think it more consequential than ideology in the narrow sense, which for purposes of this comparison I will now simply refer to as Ideology. Ideology varies across texts and speakers. For instance, McClure, Munsey, Walker, and Bok inflected it quite differently, but they all (perforce) joined in the same practices of commodification. Ideology, though it lives between lines and behind frames as much as in direct statement, is nonetheless more out in the open and so more contestable than commodification. In fact it always *is* contested, if not on different pages of the same magazine then in other magazines and papers on offer at the same newsstand and through the same postal system.

You may resent commodification, but you can't argue with it, and you can't help practicing it, short of heroic abstentions or retreats. Indeed, few people, and certainly not I, can help *liking* many of its ingenious pleasures and routines, even while despairing of its politics. Ideology tends to be shallow: human nature is always and everywhere the same; but then those South Sea islanders really are different from "us." Our nation stands at the pinnacle of progress; but oh, for the good old days. We are all united as Americans, but watch out for those bankers/immigrants/New Women/free silver nuts . . . . It's every man for himself; but we Christians love our neighbors. And so on. Commodification lodges deep in the psyche, reinforced there by myriad quotidian acts and encounters that hum, "This is how things are, this is natural." Finally, because Ideology is shallow, contestable, and variable across texts, it bends rather easily over time, as well, under the pressure of events and contestation. Tycoon worship eases into muckraking, patriotic belligerence into isolationism, the great society into the sick society, the war on poverty into the welfare mess. Commodification took root a hundred and more years ago, spread out from its PMC origins like kudzu, choked off alternatives. To uproot or transcend it would take a profounder revolution than just(!) expropriating the expropriators.

Its stability, along with its many easements and its near transparency, made commodification a strong force for equilibrium in the whole hegemonic process, stronger I contend than Ideology – or for that matter, than the state apparatuses of regulation and repression and schooling, or certainly, now, than the hotly controverted institutions of church and family. Commodification hides, even as it collaborates with, the exploitation behind the market, the always-more-social nature of production, our interdependence and paradoxical disconnectedness.[7] It does this silently, beyond comment and almost beyond notice.

When I began studying these magazines I imagined that their editorial contents might cheerlead for the brand name commodities on display in their advertising sections and for a way of life organized around products. Not at all.[8] Commodities of the soap and cereal variety stay politely behind the scenes, even in the *Ladies' Home Journal* with its abundant domestic advice; and commodification draws neither celebration nor analysis nor critique. In the fiction, where dreams of happiness thrive, the featured commodities range "upward" from the omnipresent piano and faddish bicycle to fur boas, brilliant gowns, tapestries, carriages, the occasional yacht, soon automobiles: the furnishings of wealth. And while ostentation may come under PMC censure, there is virtually no critique of middle class commodification, such as that already launched in novels by Howells and Dreiser, and salient in magazine fiction of the 1920s. In the jubilant youth of commodification, magazine Ideology took no notice, limning instead vistas of freedom and advancement. Perhaps by the time critique arrived in this venue, commodification was unassailable, except in the commonplace mode of contempt for excess and vulgarity – for those *arrivistes*, in other words, who haven't got it right.

Whatever the worth of that conjecture, it seems clear that commodification stirred little resistance among PMC people to the new social order, and may have helped win their consent. I introduce the word "consent," here, because of the place it has in hegemony theory: not referring, as in pluralistic thought, to the formal "consent of the governed," but evoking the enlistment of subordinate groups in the project of the ruling class through the suasion of ideology (in the broader meaning), which naturalizes domination as "common sense" and thus reduces the necessity of force to an undercurrent of routine policing, and, always, to an ultimate threat held in reserve should rebellion erupt. It will be obvious that my inquiry contributes little to the elaboration of this idea. For all the reformist enthusiasm of the PMC, there was no remote chance of its organizing to challenge capital's rule, though a handful of defectors to socialism would do that. PMC consent was easily won through its ties to business and government, through its material well-being, through the respect and standing it achieved. For professionals and managers, the yoke of commodification was as light as the inducements were sweet.

And no one should take from this study the inference that workers were lining up behind the PMC to offer their consent. The gradual improvement in wages from 1880 to 1900 brought the working class only to the distant borders of commodification; they would not migrate into its heartland for another half century. Nor did their antagonism to capital dissolve into its common sense. Labor regrouped quickly after its defeats by military force at Homestead and in the Pullman strike. The American Federation of Labor sextupled in size. By 1904 the number of strikes annually reached the same level (about 4000) as in the early 1890s. Some of these were big and militant. Labor ran San Francisco for a while in the general strike of 1901. Roosevelt threatened use of federal troops in the Pennsylvania coal strike of 1902 before the intransigent owners would even talk to the successful strikers, through federal mediation. The governor of Colorado imposed bloody martial law to put down strikers there in 1904. Through those years hundreds of unionists were killed and thousands injured: clearly, the mergers and consolidations that brought the modern corporation into existence failed – did not intend – to enlist workers in a new hegemonic equilibrium. Consent remained precarious; force was a daily fact of relations between capital and labor.

By and large the PMC, through its activist wing in the Progressive movement, abstained from these struggles or obliquely sided with business; in going after the Tammany Halls of the big cities, reformers were, after all, seeking to replace (corrupt) working class organizations with rational management by businessmen and their PMC allies, even if their plans called for some gas-and-sewer socialism. Progressives had sympathy for workers as residents of the city, looking after them with sanitary measures and settlement houses, but no solidarity with workers at work. Their contribution in that sphere was scientific management. They saw in organized labor at least as dangerous a threat as in organized capital; they lamented, and had since before Bellamy, American society's unfortunate tendency to divide into antagonistic classes.

These points taken together suggest a relatively anemic hegemony around 1900, in which the new middle class consented to comfortable subordination, workers experienced coercion and fought back, and farmers continued to languish in the ruins of populism. What do the magazine revolution and attendant changes tell us, then, about the history of commodification and consent? Only this: that capital discovered, partly by inadvertence and the agency of another class, a method of incorporation that could, and in the event did, serve as a pattern for a wider hegemony over time, once expanded powers of production and workers' claims to a decent share enabled tens of millions to choose and be chosen by commodification. Even this modest claim, if allowed, makes the initial moment of our national mass culture a watershed. A well-oiled cultural apparatus was then in place whose aggrandizement, replication, and refinement could proceed without let.

"The initial moment of our national mass culture": how much depends on the chronological exactness of my claim? One could argue for the 1830s and 1840s as pivotal, given the rapid expansion then of manufacturing, the wide distribution of machine-made fabrics and ornaments, the emergence of a new middle class domesticity, the appearance of large city stores, and the explosion of the penny press, which in part mediated these other developments with its copious local advertising. The 1920s have been another favorite choice, and with good reason, if one privileges the maturity and synergy of the culture industries: movies, popular music, radio, and sports, along with a much enlarged periodical press. Some would delay the moment until the 1950s, when finally most of the working class was cut in on commodified abundance, and television projected the same images, dramas, and celebrities into almost every home. All critical moments, certainly; and I am well aware of the scholar's temptation, after many years' work on a project, to proclaim the astonishing significance of his or her findings. Not everything that made us who we are happened between 1890 and 1905.

Still, the periodization I am recommending has conceptual plausibility and, I think, explanatory power. Let me remind the reader that in my view no form of cultural production before the mass circulation magazine fully instanced mass culture as I defined it in Chapter 2: "voluntary experiences, produced by a relatively small number of specialists, for millions across the nation to share, in similar or identical form, either simultaneously or nearly so, with dependable frequency; mass culture shapes habitual audiences, around common needs or interests, and it is made for profit." Critically, that profit came for the first time from selling the attention of the audience to advertisers, a transaction embedded in many forms of cultural production since, along with the new social relations of marketing and advertising upon which I have dwelt. So the events of the 1890s were both fresh and historically decisive. Beyond that, I have linked them – as effect to cause, but I hope more dialectically than that – to a major crisis in capitalist development, to capital's internal transformation, and to a new hegemonic system that evolved out of that crisis. It is the compression and heated interaction of all these processes that most strongly supports a before-and-after conceptualization, with the break point around 1900. To repeat: What's at stake here? Well, how we explain the movement of history, and how we understand modernity.[9]

A final question, before I turn to some remarks on modernity and mass culture after 1900: Is the story told here one specifically about

modernity in the United States, yet another tale of American excep-
tionalism? I believe not. Take the case of Britain, the only other one
about which I know enough to comment. Capitalist development began
there, and ran through many of its phases, well in advance of its progress
in the US: not just industrialization and the commodification of labor
power but, by the end of the eighteenth century, a proliferation of newspapers, magazines, advertising strategies, and consumer goods not to be
matched in the US until at least the 1850s. McKendrick, Brewer, and
Plumb argue persuasively for a "consumer revolution" in Britain from
1750 on, in which many "necessities, decencies, luxuries" previously
owned by the rich came "within the legitimate aspirations of almost
all . . . ."[10] Discount the conventional hard-hearted obtuseness of that
"almost all," and one can still allow that an ethos of spending and a
logic of material emulation and display spread through a broad middle
class with income enough to act out such desires.[11] Furthermore,
because Britain was so much smaller than the US, its infrastructure of
railroads made possible the quick circulation of periodicals and ads by
the 1840s; and indeed, there soon were, in effect, national *newspapers* of
a kind not realized in this country until the *New York Times* and *Wall Street
Journal* vastly enlarged their distribution and *USA Today* appeared on the
scene. Partly for this geographical and genetic reason, the magazine
has not been so important in Britain as it has in the US.

For all these early, major differences between histories and
economies, a convergence occurred at the end of the nineteenth century that would seem remarkable, apart from the framework of analysis
I have proposed. Let me quote Raymond Williams at some length, on
economic changes that lay behind the appearance of display ads in
British newspapers around 1890:

> The great bulk of products of the early stages of the factory system had
> been sold without extensive advertising, which had grown up mainly in
> relation to novelties and fringe products. Such advertising as there was, of
> basic articles, was mainly by shopkeepers: the classified advertisements
> which the newspapers had always carried. In this comparatively simple
> phase, large-scale advertising and the brand-naming of goods were neces-
> sary only at the margin, or in genuinely new things. In the second half of
> the century, the range widened (branding is especially notable in the new
> patent foods) but it was not until the 1890s that the emphasis deeply
> changed. The Great Depression which in general dominated the period
> from 1873 to the middle 1890s (though broken by occasional recoveries
> and local strengths) marks the turning point between two moods, two
> kinds of industrial organization, and two basically different approaches to
> distribution. After the Depression, and its big falls in prices, there was a
> more general and growing fear of productive capacity, a marked ten-
> dency to reorganize industrial ownership into larger units and combines,

and a growing desire to organize and where possible control the market. Advertising then took on a new importance, and was applied to an increasing range of products, as part of the system of market control which, at full development, included tariffs and preference areas, cartel quotas, trade campaigns, price fixing by manufacturers, and economic imperialism . . . . The system of selling space changed, from the old eighteenth-century shops which 'took in' newspaper announcements, through systems of agents and brokers, to the establishment of full-scale independent advertising agencies, and, in the newspapers, full-time advertising managers who advanced very rapidly from junior to senior status. Pressure was brought on the newspapers, by advertising agents, to publish their sales figures. Northcliffe, after initial hesitations about advertising . . . was the first to realize its possibilities as a new basis for newspaper finance. He published his own sales figures, challenged his rivals to do the same, and in effect created the modern structure of the press as an industry and an expression of market relationships with the 'mass reading public'. . . .

By tying the policy of newspapers to large circulation, Northcliffe found the formula and the revenue from the new advertising situation. He was then able to make quite rapid technical advances in journalism itself. He started the half-penny *Daily Mail* in 1896 with new and expensive machinery . . . , and also with new arrangements for rapid sale . . . . The improvements meant a considerable cut in the price of a single copy, if a large circulation could be achieved, and the new scale of advertising revenue was a capital factor in the necessary investment. The true 'Northcliffe Revolution' is less an innovation in actual journalism than a radical change in the economic basis of newspapers, tied to the new kind of advertising.[12]

During the same period, illustrated magazines evolved: less suddenly than in the US and in the shadow of newspapers, but with the same economic foundation, the same social relations, the same miscellaneous format, the same practices of iconography and display, roughly the same class-based segmentation of audiences and cultural fare, and against the same background of dynamic change in the marketing of commodities. If the parallels don't quite add up to a triumphant Q.E.D., they do strongly support the now familiar idea that modernity and mass culture were thrown up, not by unique contingencies in one society, but by a (necessary?) process of crisis and reconfiguration in world capitalism.

The Sequel: Magazines

Bok kept the *Journal* preeminent for another two decades; it flourishes today. Profits from it, augmented by loans from the N.W. Ayer agency, enabled Curtis to put a million dollars into promotion of the moribund *Saturday Evening Post*, which he bought for $1000 in 1897; the *Post* became the nation's leading magazine, and around it Curtis built a publishing empire.[13] Munsey also reinvested his magazine profits, but mainly in newspapers, which he bought and sold with a ruthless eye on the bottom line. He lost interest in *Munsey's*, which declined toward its extinction not long after Munsey's own death in 1925. So did *McClure's*, after its irrepressible founder attempted and mainly failed in one grand scheme after another. Walker sold *Cosmopolitan* to Hearst in 1905; its fortunes rose and fell and rose again through various incarnations, the last as the women's magazine revived by Helen Gurley Brown in the 1960s. The founders modernized cultural production, but that did not guarantee continuity or even survival for the magazines they made.

It did ensure continuity and growth for the *kind* of magazine that reached a large audience and thrived on advertising. Some nineteenth-century magazines adapted to that principle and are still doing well: *McCall's, Popular Science, Woman's Home Companion, Good Housekeeping*, along with others founded later, such as *Time*, the *New Yorker*, and *Newsweek*. The *Reader's Digest*, like the first two of those three a product of the 1920s, flourished without advertising until the 1950s, and with it after that, when it became the most widely circulated magazine in the world, and was surpassed in the US only by *TV Guide* (founded in 1948).

On the other side of the ledger, a host of pre-1900 leaders in addition to *McClure's* and *Munsey's* eventually died, most before World War II; they include the *Delineator*, the *Literary Digest*, *Peterson's*, *Everybody's*, *Collier's*, *Leslie's*, and the *American Magazine*. Perhaps more surprisingly, some magazines founded or built into leaders after 1900 and still giants in the postwar period collapsed in the different environment of the 1960s and 1970s, though some were later revived on far more modest terms. In fact, 60 percent of the magazines with one-million-plus circulations in 1930 and 30 percent of that size in 1950 perished by 1974.[14] Thousands of lesser magazines have come and gone since 1893, and as this mortality bill shows, even spectacular success is no guarantee of longevity.

On the other hand, the field of magazines has always been wide open to new entrants. Some made it with the backing of well-heeled publishers. Curtis added the *Post, Country Gentlemen*, and much later *Holiday* to its portfolio; Time, Inc. branched out with *Fortune, Life, Sports Illustrated*, then *People*. (Both companies had failures, too.) But many more magazines began with virtually no capital, and claimed places in the market through the entrepreneurial and editorial heroics of their founders, as was the case with *McClure's* and *Munsey's* in the 1890s, *Time*, the *Reader's Digest*, and the *New Yorker* in the 1920s, and in the postwar period *TV Guide* (pre-Annenberg), *Hot Rod, Playboy, Rolling Stone*, and so on and on.

Across the spectrum of mass culture, in no other medium have economic fortunes been so volatile, continuity so precarious. Indeed, I can think of no parallel in other areas of production, though of course many brands have come and gone. It is ironic that having been instrumental in stabilizing sales for makers of other commodities, those who made the early mass circulation magazines and their successors so often failed to stabilize the sales of their own products. Facilitating the arrival of monopoly capital, magazine companies came to occupy only a small place in the new system. For a while things looked set to turn out otherwise. In 1918 Curtis had become a giant, with 43 percent of all national advertising revenue from consumer and farm magazines; Hearst, Crowell-Collier, and a few others claimed most of the rest. The ten leading magazines accounted for 70 percent, the five leaders for 56 percent, of advertising dollars.[15] This is just the pattern of concentration – both corporations and "brands" – we expect to find in most areas of production, under monopoly capital. By the late 1970s, however, the largest publisher (Time, Inc.) brought in just 12.7 percent of all magazine advertising revenue, and the top five magazines 28 percent.[16]

What explains this dramatic decline in centralization? The instability of individual magazine enterprises is itself an explanation on one level; publishers have had difficulty controlling large market shares partly because some of their products tend to decline and become unprofitable, in spite of efforts at renewal and "repositioning" – what the *New Yorker* is attempting now, with Tina Brown as editor. But what explains the instability? One cause is a general property of the magazine as brand name product: it is an assembly of miscellaneous bits that changes each week or month, and changes more over longer stretches of time, sometimes disruptively, as when a new editor takes over with a mandate to shake up the mix. The same holds for the miscellany that is a radio station's weekly schedule or a TV network's programming, but with the important difference that magazine readers either buy the whole package or don't buy any of it, rather than sampling (for free) as broadcasting audiences do. Fickleness ruins magazines. Nor does a magazine meet daily, specific, local needs in the way a newspaper does. Its hold is more tenuous, more dependent on the talents and interests of the editor and on his or her responsiveness to shifting tastes.

Mention of other media heavily dependent on advertising points toward another, more obvious explanation. Until radio became a vehicle for national advertising of brand name products toward the end of the 1920s, magazines took in the lion's share of that trade. Radio won a good deal of it (15 percent by 1945), television much more. In 1945, consumer magazines still accounted for 13 percent of all advertising (including newspaper ads, direct mail, billboards, and so on). By the end of the 1970s, that share had dropped below 6 percent.[17] An even more telling shift accompanied this change in proportion. In the first decades of this century many magazines could claim to be "general" – that is, for everybody. I have noted the mystification latent in that category:

Cosmopolitan and the others reached few working class people. (Nor were "women's magazines" like the *Ladies' Home Journal* for all or even most women.) The major magazines of the 1890s specialized by social class, as did their successors of the 1920s, whose far larger circulations still included few outside the broad middle class. Nonetheless, the category "general" did stand in reasonable contrast to specializations of other sorts: the religious papers, farm magazines, children's magazines, story papers, trade papers, political journals, and so on.

Broadcasting assembled truly general audiences, and national ones as well. Network radio pushed magazines aside in the 1930s and 1940s as the best channel for commercial messages about inexpensive brand name products, until radio was supplanted by network TV and became a local (though general) medium. Against this competition, the most nearly general magazines either failed by the 1970s (*Life* and other giants), sharpened their class definition (*Time* and *Newsweek*), succeeded in a parasitic relation to TV and other media (*TV Guide, People,* the supermarket tabloids), or – well, what *is* one to say of the *Reader's Digest*'s durable formula?[18] The great majority of profitable consumer magazines now make no claim, either to readers or to advertisers, of generality. They have specialized their appeals to readers by interest: home improvement, cooking, beauty, sex, child rearing, computers, cars, money making, popular music, and of course those older special interests in religion, politics, farming, and so on. The specialization has proceeded farther than this list suggests; to take just one example, we have not only magazines that cover sports in general, but magazines about each individual, major spectator sport, and also about cycling, skiing, canoeing, sailing, scuba diving, hunting, fishing, running, camping, backpacking, snowmobiling, weightlifting, body building, riding, tennis, golf, auto racing, flying, karate, shooting, and more.[19] The magazine business offers to organize groups around highly specific categories of consumption, and also around styles and scales of consumption. That is, from the advertiser's point of view a given magazine is desirable not just as a medium for the promotion of beauty aids, but as an avenue to the commodifiable desires, of say, single, white, working women, age twenty to thirty-five, with incomes of $15,000 to $30,000.

Another development has accompanied this specialization. After decades of adherence to the formula of 1893 – sell the magazine for almost nothing, build a large circulation, and profit from the sale of readers' attention – in the 1950s and after, subscription and single-copy rates began a steady rise in constant dollars, as did the portion of income derived from those sources, which in the 1970s actually passed income from ads. Needless to say, this does not mean that the magazine industry has reverted to its pre-1893 basis. Then, there were few special interest magazines of the contemporary sort, and advertising was a sideline for them. Nineteenth-century magazines did not bring readerships together as groups of consumers. Few of today's consumer magazines could survive without their ad revenue.

But they also differ strikingly from the lineage of *McClure's* and *Munsey's* and the *Post*. They occupy niches in an enormously complex market, and they serve their readers as accessories to particular interests and activities, chiefly grounded in leisure and consumption. One could conceptualize them as belonging to ensembles of commodities. A serious skier will want one or more ski magazines in complementarity to the right skis, boots, togs, and so on. Such a function is very far from that of the old "general interest" magazine.

I have gradually strayed from the question that led me to these reflections: Why has the magazine business been so volatile? We are scanning, it would seem, not a well-demarcated field of capitalist production like furniture making that has always been risky and unstable, but a business that has in effect changed what it makes, twice in a hundred years. The mass circulation, "general" magazine did famously if mercurially for seventy years or so, selling consciousness. Then it ran into devastating competition from a more powerful seller of mass consciousness, and modulated into a specialized product that made money in a new way, did not depend on enormous circulation (though even highly specialized magazines have audiences that would have been enviable in 1893), and in fact regained a certain stability by meeting very specific needs of both readers and advertisers. Thus, although the magazine industry did not for long configure itself in the oligopolistic pattern that is the signature of twentieth-century capitalism, and, as noted earlier, came to play a more modest role in the new system than the successes of 1890 to 1930 seemed to foretell, that role is neither marginal nor, I think, evanescent.

Consider it again. Big capital turned its energies to rationalizing sales, in order to control the exchange value of the goods pouring out from factories, and thus (within limits) ensure profitability. Its early successes in this endeavor were largely with inexpensive commodities given identity and meaning through the practices of brand naming and publicity that have been a main subject of this study. By the 1920s it greatly extended the reach of this project, enlisting many more consumers of the cheaper goods and, with the aid of a dramatic expansion in consumer credit, establishing mass markets for more costly products like cars and appliances. In the postwar boom this process again went briskly forward, nearly saturating the whole potential market for the older products and for newer ones like television and stereo.

During this period, capital also reached out to cultivate special tastes of the more affluent, then the broad middle class and, as they shared really for the first time in national prosperity, the working class. So proceeded not only a sharp increase in the number and kinds of goods felt to be necessities and decencies, but a colonization of leisure with thousands more individualized wants and products – as is reflected, for

instance, in the long list of specialized sports and outdoor activities a few
paragraphs back, each of which constitutes a magazine readership. Thus,
while television became the premier channel for reaching a general
(though still of course demographically segmented) audience of consumers, capital was busy elaborating consumption and audiences into
new markets. Magazines in their new incarnation have proven essential
to the formation and exploitation of those markets, and so to monopoly
capital's project of accumulation.[20] An indication of their serviceability in
it may be the fact that the corporate structure behind magazine publishing is now typically the modern conglomerate that integrates and
synergizes a variety of media enterprises, rather than the big magazine
company, or even the big publishing company that manages some combination of books, magazines, and newspapers.

Another take is possible on the transformation of the magazine business since the 1960s. Many analysts now see a break at about that time in
the evolution of capitalism. What I call monopoly capitalism and some
call Fordism ran into serious trouble, marked in the US by a host of
familiar symptoms, from a steady decline in real wages to the negative
and worsening balance of trade and the great expansion of public and
private debt. Fordism, on this view, has given way to a "regime of flexible
accumulation."[21]

Production becomes highly mobile, leaping oceans to where conditions are most favorable, quickly establishing new centers like Silicon
Valley and the various *maquiladoras*. Exotic new financial instruments
turn the globe into a single, endlessly ramifying system; movements of capital blur boundaries and the contours of national economies. The old,
stable, well-paid, core labor force shrinks, and around it grows a vast,
international periphery of ill-paid part-time and occasional workers. New
techniques and products proliferate. Markets and consumption styles are
constantly refashioned. Is it helpful to see the refoundation of the magazine industry as a small part of this large shift, and to periodize its history
in conformity with this more encompassing one: from entrepreneurial to
monopoly capitalism around 1900, and from the latter to a regime of
flexible accumulation around 1970? I have made a case for pinning the
emergence of mass circulation, consumer magazines to the first change.
Perhaps the rise of niche or boutique magazining from the 1960s on correlates by more than chance with the second modulation of capital. To
argue that is outside the scope of my study and beyond my competence. I
leave the idea as a conjecture, and stimulus to further work.

As for the contents of magazines, their cultural intervention across all
these decades: it is interesting how much of what Theodore Peterson
wrote forty years ago in his reasonable "Assessment" seems right and
germane still.[22] Magazines served the important function of introducing
new ideas, perspectives, attitudes, styles. "Their recognition invested a
subject with importance" (p. 388). In more modern lingo, they exercised

a framing, agenda setting, gatekeeping role. But because of their tight interdependence with advertising, they did this with a generally conservative bias; advertising "gravitated toward the publications which did not offend the majority and which were not inimical to the conditions under which business operated" (p. 389). Ads themselves, in "playing on existing drives and attitudes," reinforced such values as "material success" and "social conformity." Editorial contents tended "to perpetuate the ideological status quo" (p. 390), both because magazines were themselves businesses "with a vested interest in the maintenance of the existing economic system" and because publishers that needed to attract large readerships had to observe invisible, majoritarian limits on the sayable. These same constraints made for relatively docile fiction and art in the main consumer magazines, which managed talent in more or less the same way they helped constitute celebrities.

Apparently without benefit of Frankfurt School guidance, Peterson continued:

> Magazines must also share blame with the other mass media for creating a pseudo-world, a picture out of focus which readers sometimes confused with the real thing. The world was spun of both articles and fiction. [And of ads, I'm sure Peterson would have agreed.] It was a world of optimism and good works in which science worked only beneficent miracles, in which poverty was at worst a nuisance, in which anyone could do anything if he persevered, in which the most ill-matched couples could find marital happiness if they really tried, in which evil was justly punished, in which virtue and talent were inevitably recognized and reaped their due rewards, a world of golden light and few shadows. (p. 392)

Articles and stories bent content to formula (especially, I would say, that of problem/solution). Journalism was weak on explanation, often assuming that "any subject could be discussed in terms of personalities and anecdotes" (p. 393). The imperative of brevity made for fragmentation and superficiality, and "made it impossible for magazines to treat certain subjects at all."

For all that, Peterson wound up his assessment cheerfully enough. Although serious political and economic critique diminished in mainstream magazines after the muckraking period, it persisted in journals of opinion. Ease of entry into magazine publishing meant that smaller publics could be organized around dissident or radical views. Magazines put issues in a "national perspective," and fostered "a sense of national community" (p. 394). They supplied cheap entertainment and gratification, instructed millions in strategies of daily living, and disseminated high culture inexpensively. "Finally, one of the most reassuring strengths of magazines was their variety"; in the aggregate, they "represented a wide range of tastes and opinions" (p. 396). So, Peterson.[23]

I would turn a colder eye on the variety of magazines, seeing it as in part reinforcing the ideology of individual choice in style against a neutral backdrop of the social, of freedom in the construction of identity, and of happy pluralism in politics. The great successes of women's magazines, for instance, offered little challenge to male domination until a strong political movement arose in the 1960s, after which things changed, but not in altogether pretty ways: think of strenuous efforts in the venue of women's magazines to recuperate feminism, as in the figure of the "Cosmo Girl." In general, have these magazines done more to liberate women as a group or to assist them in negotiating subordination through an endless array of personal choices? Set the new *Cosmopolitan* alongside *Playboy* for a disheartening look at "variety" that leaves power relations in place. The same point holds, though more ambiguously, for *Ebony*, *Essence*, and the other negro consumer magazines that grew up after the war.

I have devoted many pages to the question, and will merely repeat my opinion, here, that commodification is not good for democracy, however compatible with certain kinds of diversity. Another obvious limit on the democratic potential of variety in consumer magazines is that they reflect and reproduce inequality. Advertisers in 1895 needed to reach a large group of people with significant purchasing power, so *McClure's* and the *Ladies' Home Journal* and other PMC-based magazines won influence for the ideas of big business with relatively small readerships because those readers were especially valuable to advertisers. A magazine called *Euromoney* does nicely, I'm told, with just a few thousand subscribers who tend to be ministers of finance, commercial bankers, and the like.[24] The dazzling variety of magazines for skiers, golfers, stereo aficionados, gourmet cooks, and so on is not fertile soil for dissident ideas – with exceptions, of course: for example, magazines for skiers, backpackers, and the like will often express concern about environmental threats to the pastimes of their readers.

That observation points toward magazines for subcultures, groups of consumers that do want rebel or outlaw ideas, such as rap and heavy metal fans, bikers, gay men (*Details*[?]), artists, hot rodders, and on to the margin where *Soldier of Fortune* peddles its murderous wares and messages. This partial list doesn't encourage optimism about the liberatory politics of variety, as played out in the market for specialized consumer tastes.

Progressive politics, on the other hand, is a social commitment not easily mobilized to boost the sale of commodities other than progressive books, Guatemalan crafts, and the like. So even though there are numerous lefties, feminists, gay rights activists, and so on with disposable income, our magazines tend to be bare of display ads. They cost a lot, depend on volunteer labor, survive on the beneficence of angels, or some combination of those strategies. I subscribe, now or sometimes, to the *Nation*, *NACLA Report*, *Z*, *Off Our Backs*, *In These Times*, *New Left Review*,

Socialist Review, Radical Teacher, Extra!, Cuba Update, and who knows what else. I bet the median income of their aggregate readership exceeds the national average, but few indeed are the national advertisers reaching out for our patronage via their pages. *Ms. Magazine* gave up on advertising after twenty years and only then became profitable. *Mother Jones* has aggressively sought advertising recently, as its editorial content has veered toward the trendy and sentimental (whether this is cause and effect, I don't know). Still more obviously, there can be no profit-making consumer magazines for groups whose attention is of little or no value to advertisers: welfare mothers, the homeless, people with Downs' syndrome, illegal immigrants, patients in state mental hospitals, prisoners. The organizing potential of such groups will not be catalyzed by circulation and development of their ideas in commercial magazines. All this points to the stunted meaning of "variety" in the magazine market, not to mention "democracy" and "free speech." Which is not of course to say that stunted free speech has no value; only that democratic change will not be propelled by forces set loose in the magazine revolution of 1893.

The Sequel: Mass Culture

This book is about magazines but also, I claim, about the establishment of mass culture in the United States. If the preceding three hundred or so pages have not made the claim plausible, no last-minute heroics can save it. Nor do I want to promote a myth of origins: that the meaning and shape a set of practices had at its inception determined its trajectory forever after; or, in this special case, that the fusion of marketing practices and cultural production in the first mass circulation magazines set the direction for all future development of mass entertainment. So I will settle here for a few summary thoughts and conjectures.

For one thing, only some culture industries that have come to maturity since 1900 have built on the principle more or less accidentally discovered by 1890s magazine entrepreneurs: charge almost nothing for the cultural experience and profit by selling the audience's attention. Broadcasting did, very consequentially indeed, and I have expressed my doubt that it would have done so – taking over the public air waves for private gain – had advertising not naturalized itself as support for and parasite upon entertainment, through the precedent of magazines and newspapers. Movies expanded on a different basis, as did mass market paperback books, spectator sports, and popular music, for all of which audiences pay directly and substantially. The neatness of the distinction is only apparent, to be sure. Much of the income from movies and major sporting events derives from their presentation on TV, and hence from advertising; radio and the record industry are hardly separable for analytic purposes these past four decades; best-selling books make money through film and TV; and I have noted how magazines backed off from the formula of 1893 during the same period. The best generalization, surely, is that all major media twine together now in a lucrative net of relations in which the sale of audiences is salient but far from exclusive. We pay for culture and so do advertisers. Or, from another angle, we pay for culture both directly and by buying other commodities. The magazine revolution dimly foreshadowed but neither determined nor drafted a blueprint of the globally integrated, late-twentieth-century culture industry.

Nonetheless, origins count for something, especially when they set vigorous practices, relations, and institutions in place. I conclude, then, with three comments on momentum and continuity. First is just to emphasize that the events of the 1890s located advertising – a new kind of advertising organized by new kinds of practitioners – in the center of American cultural production, and that it has remained there since, with effects too familiar to require elaboration. I wrote earlier about the instability of the magazine business, the disappearance of one successful magazine after another and the proliferation of new ones. Advertising agencies merge and sometimes divide but rarely go under. A magazine gathers its audience around mutable interests, and the value of the audience to advertisers changes – most notably as it ages and dies (compare the *New Yorker's* current effort to attract young readers, even if that means antagonizing old habitués like me). An ad agency has know-how, resources, and connections that can easily be redeployed. It offers to sell consciousness in general. How reliably advertising can do that is a vexed question, but its having done so with astonishing effectiveness when it was new addicted capital to its ministrations. The addiction has lasted.

Second, its work in tandem with that of the magazine entrepreneurs did much to accelerate a process already underway that most observers (and participants!) agree has deeply marked life in our century: the tight linkage of social identity with the purchase and use of commodities, including cultural products. The point has often been exaggerated. We do not understand our own or other people's identities solely through the medium and meanings of goods or even, I think, primarily that way. Nor have consumer identities erased older ones, as wider and wider segments of the population entered into consumer culture. Rather, old identities have been reconfigured around, articulated with, consumption: mother, worker, Christian, American, and so on.[25] Still, it is incontestable that consumption-based or consumption-enhanced identities loom large in most people's understandings of themselves and their world, to the disadvantage of clear thought and (in my view) sensible politics. Commodification is a strong ally of hegemony. The magazine revolution gave impetus to this change, the more so if one includes the new social relations it naturalized, and that I have sufficiently remarked earlier in this chapter and throughout the book.

Third, it seems to me historically reverberant that the engine of our national mass culture was ignited among and by the new professional-managerial class. Again, caution is in order: there was no direct line of advance from the beachhead of PMC mass culture around 1900 to its colonization of all classes by the 1950s. Working class people vigorously took part in commercial entertainments at the same time PMC people were taking up *McClure's* and Quaker Oats: Coney Island, vaudeville, the dance halls, minstrelsy, the foreign language press, and so on. At least one main culture industry, cinema, began as a working class amusement and slowly spread to more genteel venues. All these strands and more were woven into the tapestry of the mass culture we have now.

But perhaps significantly, working class people did not enter much into the nexus of advertising and culture until its middle class foundation was solid, and for the obvious reason that working class people had too little spare cash to draw the attention of advertisers. That began to change in the 1920s. The first really profitable working class magazines – confession and detective story magazines, movie fan magazines – sprang up then, and more working class readers took up "general" magazines like the *Post* as income met aspiration. (More than two-thirds of the population were regular magazine readers in the immediate postwar years.[26]) By the end of the 1920s, radio advertising entered millions of working class homes. Radio segued into television, the universal medium of advertising-based culture. To tell the story this way is to see it as a process of diffusion from the PMC to the working class, or, from advertising's point of view, as one of expansion and absorption.[27]

What has it meant that commercial practices honed on the PMC were then extrapolated to other audiences, other consumers? That seems to me an extremely interesting question for another book, another author. Here are some further questions he or she might entertain: How did the sturdy PMC values of modernity and upscale emulation fare when transported to a wider population? What consequences did the happy erasure of class, race, and social conflict in the PMC magazines have later? Did the ideology of classlessness survive to help produce a nation in which most people consider themselves middle class? Did the logic of commodification proceed inexorably to create an imaginary in which, for many, our society seems equivalent to a style of consumption? And if so, what is to be done?

Notes

1. The Experience

1. Thompson Products Company was founded in 1901, I find, but a small anachronism is permitted in my fictional account.

2. Nor would there be in 1895; *Harper's* remained more conservative, graphically, than the cheaper monthlies, which sported color on their covers in the late 1890s.

3. Louise Hale Johnson, *History of the Town of Hawley, Franklin County, Massachusetts, 1771–1951, With Genealogies,* (Mystic, Conn.: Charter Oak House, 1953), p. 182.

4. Stuart Ewen, *Captains of Consciousness; Advertising and the Social Roots of the Consumer Culture* (New York: McGraw-Hill, 1976), p. 114.

5. My can also reads, "*Absolutely Pure,*" but, conforming to a law that did not yet exist in the Johnsons' time, goes on to explain that in addition to cream of tartar the powder contains starch, bicarbonate of soda, and tartaric acid. I wonder what the Johnsons understood by the word "pure" in this ad, or by "99 44/100 Pure" (sic) in the Ivory Soap ad next to it.

2. The Origins of Mass Culture

1. Michael Denning writes, "All culture is mass culture under capitalism," and argues further that debates like the one I summarize here "have been superseded. There is no mass culture *out there*; it is the very element we all breathe"; "The End of Mass Culture," in James Naremore and Patrick Brantlinger, eds, *Modernity and Mass Culture* (Bloomington, Ind.: Indiana University Press, 1991), pp. 258, 267. Superseded or not, the debate goes on.

2. Even the economic function, it may be. At the end of *Issues in the Economics of Advertising* (Urbana, Ill.: University of Illinois Press, 1970), Julian L. Simon concludes that local and industrial advertising is important economically, but goes on to say: "those branches of advertising which are most in dispute – advertising for such products as beer, autos, soap, and aspirin – do not seem to have much effect upon the economy in any way, direct or indirect, and hence from an economic point of view it is immaterial whether they are present or absent . . . . All this implies that the economic study of advertising is not deserving of great attention except for special problems . . . . (As the reader may realize, this is not a congenial point at which to arrive after spending several years working on the subject.)" (pp. 284–5). I might add that anyone who has spent several years working on a subject must read this conclusion with a mixture of admiration and discomfort.

3. James Playsted Wood, *The Story of Advertising* (New York: Ronald Press, 1958), p. 18.

4. Frank Presbrey, *The History and Development of Advertising* (Garden City, N.Y.: Doubleday, Doran & Company, 1929), pp. 3, 16.

5. I take this account, and what follows, mainly from Foster Rhea Dulles, *America Learns to Play; A History of Popular Recreation, 1607–1940* (New York: Peter Smith, 1952), chapters II and III. Astonishingly, this seems to be the most recent general history of its subject.

6. Let me enter a disclaimer, here, which I will repeat at intervals through this study. I mean to be descriptive, not judgmental, in putting forth such claims. Farm and village life expressed some values that I endorse, and that were eroded or destroyed by capitalism and urbanization. It also was a hard, narrow life, and in some ways a mean one. Although I do not accept Marx's phrase, "the idiocy of rural life," as accurate for these people at this time, neither would I choose that life for myself, were it available to be lived. And a return to it, or something like it, is not what I wish for our society. I will try to grasp the feelings of Americans as they both welcomed and resisted a new social order through the course of the nineteenth century. In this task, nostalgia is as much a hindrance as the triumphalism of Whig history.

7. Robert A. Gross, "Comments on Ohmann," *Berkshire Review*, vol. 16, no. 106, 1981. The article on which he comments is "Where Did Mass Culture Come From? The Case of Magazines" (pp. 85–101). It contains some material I adapt for this and the next three chapters.

8. Frank Luther Mott, *A History of American Magazines, 1741–1850* (New York: Appleton, 1930), p. 29.

9. Dulles, *America Learns to Play*, pp. 140, 142–3.

10. Ibid, p. 127.

11. For the best account see "William Shakespeare in America," in Lawrence W. Levine, *Highbrow/Lowbrow; The Emergence of Cultural Hierarchy in America* (Cambridge, Mass.: Harvard University Press, 1988).

12. Robert A. Gross, "Comments on Ohmann," p. 106.

13. Michael Schudson, *Discovering the News; A Social History of American Newspapers* (New York: Basic Books, 1978), p. 18.

14. The situation was quite different in France and Britain, of course, where daily papers became national media by mid century. Correspondingly, magazines have never been quite so important there as in the US. Mass culture is everywhere alike, but geography can affect the balance of the media that carry it.

15. That is, the rule that no headline or graphic could be wider than one column, since that would require cutting through the bars within whose margins the typesetter worked.

16. There were obvious limits to this last change: national advertisers had other choices available to them; local advertisers had to rely mainly on newspapers. By 1919, national advertising amounted to only about 30 percent of what appeared in the papers (Presbrey, *The History and Development of Advertising*, pp. 591, 595), and I imagine that the proportion is smaller today.

17. I take this account from John Tebbel, *A History of Book Publishing in the United States*, vol. 1 (New York: R.R. Bowker, 1972), pp. 243–5, and from C. Hugh Holman, "'Cheap Books' and the Public Interest," in Ray B. Browne, Richard H. Crowder, Virgil L. Lokke, and William T. Stafford, eds, *Frontiers of American Culture* (Lafayette, Ind.: Purdue University Studies, 1968), pp. 26–30.

18. Tebbel, *History of Book Publishing*, vol. 1, p. 221.

19. John Tebbel, *The Media in America* (New York: Thomas Y. Crowell, 1974), p. 250.

20. Tebbel, *History of Book Publishing*, vol. 1, pp. 206, 222, 247.

21. Paperbacks were a very minor part of the scene from 1900 to 1939, when

Pocket Books launched the third paperback "revolution"; only after World War II did paperback publishing become the heart of the industry – along with other "subsidiary" ventures such as movie and TV adaptation.

22. John Tebbel, *A History of Book Publishing in the United States*, vol. 2 (New York: R.R. Bowker, 1975), p. 12.

23. Ibid., pp. 123–6.

24. Frank Luther Mott, *A History of American Magazines, 1885–1905*, vol. IV (Cambridge, Mass.: Harvard University Press, 1957), p. 6; Theodore Peterson, *Magazines in the Twentieth Century* (Urbana, Ill.: University of Illinois Press, 1956), p. 7.

25. Presbrey, *The History and Development of Advertising*, p. 471. Jackson Lears quotes from testimony by advertising executive James Collins to Congress in 1907: "A magazine is simply a device to induce people to read advertising . . . . The entertainment department finds stories, pictures, verses, etc. to interest the public. The business department makes the money": Jackson Lears, *Fables of Abundance; A Cultural History of Advertising in America* (New York: Basic Books, 1994), p. 201.

26. Quoted in Presbrey, *The History and Development of Advertising*, p. 468.

27. Ibid, pp. 469–70; Wood, *The Story of Advertising*, p. 198.

28. Presbrey, *The History and Development of Advertising*, p. 471. That a magazine staff should have assumed this function shows how fluid the ad business still was.

29. Mott, *The History of Amerian Magazines*, vol. IV, pp. 364–5.

30. The post office cracked down on this practice in 1907, holding that these were mail order catalogs rather than magazines, and denying them the cent-a-pound rate unless they collected subscription money in advance. Almost all of them collapsed at that time.

31. For a full, if rather chatty, account, see Ruth E. Finley, *The Lady of Godey's* (Philadelphia: J.B. Lippincott, 1931).

32. A brilliant idea, which would have been obvious to any publisher except for the widespread contempt of advertising. I don't know if the *Journal* was the first to mix ads and articles in this way; I do know that the standard monthlies preserved the separation for years after it was clear who buttered their bread. Since librarians apparently shared the publishers' view of advertising, they removed it when binding the monthlies. As a result, one must find individual copies of unbound magazines in order to study the ads of this period.

33. Other women's magazines were not far behind: especially the *Delineator*, but soon afterward, *McCall's*, the *Woman's Home Companion*, and *Vogue*. (*Cosmopolitan* did not become a women's magazine until much later.) Mott, *History of American Magazines*, vol. IV, gives a good sketch of the *Journal's* early years, pp. 536–45. See also Edward Bok, *The Americanization of Edward Bok; The Autobiography of a Dutch Boy Fifty Years After* (New York: Charles Scribner's Sons, 1921); Edward Bok, *A Man From Maine* (New York: Charles Scribner's Sons, 1923); and Salme Harju Steinberg, *Reformer in the Marketplace; Edward W. Bok and The Ladies' Home Journal* (Baton Rouge, La.: Louisiana State University Press, 1979).

34. Presbrey, *The History and Development of Advertising*, p. 488.

35. Not for *all* of them, of course: more about that in chapter 7.

3. Explaining Things

1. John Tebbel, *The Media in America* (New York: Thomas Y. Crowell, 1974), p. 279.

2. James Playsted Wood also cites the need, recognized by Congress, for wide circulation of ideas, in the interest of "national unity"; *Magazines in the United States*, 2nd edn (New York: Ronald Press, 1956), p. 99.

3. S.S. McClure, *My Autobiography* (London: John Murray, 1914), pp. 130–31.

4. Edward Bok, *The Americanization of Edward Bok; The Autobiography of a Dutch Boy Fifty Years After* (New York: Charles Scribner's Sons, 1921), p. 163.

5. Algernon Tassin, *The Magazine in America* (New York: Dodd, Mead and Company: 1916), pp. 354, 360.

6. Frank Luther Mott, "The Magazine Revolution and Popular Ideas in the Nineties," *Proceedings of the American Antiquarian Society*, vol. 64, p. 195, 1954.

7. Carl F. Kaestle, Helen Damon-Moore, Lawrence C. Stedman, Katherine Tinsley, and William Vance Trollinger, Jr, *Literacy in the United States; Readers and Reading Since 1880* (New Haven, Conn.: Yale University Press, 1991), p. 25. To the high rate of literacy, James D. Norris adds rapid population growth and rising personal income as causes: *Advertising and the Transformation of American Society, 1865–1920* (Westport, Conn.: Greenwood Press, 1990), p. 31. None of the three showed a spurt in growth in the years leading up to 1893.

8. Robert A. Gross, "Comments on Ohmann," *Berkshire Review*, vol. 16, no. 106, 1981.

9. Michael Schudson neatly disposes of the appeal to literacy as an explanation even for this earlier cultural shift, in *Discovering the News; A Social History of American Newspapers* (New York: Basic Books, 1978), pp. 35–9.

10. Theodore P. Greene, *America's Heroes; The Changing Models of Success in American Magazines* (New York: Oxford University Press, 1970), p. 70. See also Wood, *Magazines in the United States*, p. 103.

11. That is why Third World literacy campaigns have generally done well only in revolutionary societies like Cuba and Nicaragua, or when conducted as part of a process of empowerment, as with Paulo Freire's work in Brazil and elsewhere.

12. Anyone interested in a rich discussion of these issues with reference to England should consult Raymond Williams, "The Growth of the Popular Press," in his *The Long Revolution* (New York: Columbia Press, 1961), pp. 173–213. Williams contests the standard view that the Education Act of 1870 established the basis for national, mass circulation newspapers.

13. Frank Luther Mott, *A History of American Magazines, 1885–1905*, vol. IV (Cambridge, Mass.: Harvard University Press, 1957), p. 4. Mott goes on to note that new magazines have often flourished during depressions; *Life, Coronet*, and *Newsweek* made quick starts during the 1930s, for instance.

14. Theodore Peterson, *Magazines in the Twentieth Century* (Urbana, Ill.: University of Illinois Press, 1956), p. 42.

15. See, for instance, Peterson, *Magazines in the Twentieth Century*, pp. 41–2; Tassin, *Magazine in America*, p. 308; Greene, *America's Heroes*, p. 68; Peter Lyon, *Success Story; The Life and Times of S.S. McClure* (New York: Charles Scribner's Sons, 1963), p. 114; Salme Harju Steinberg, *Reformer in the Marketplace; Edward W. Bok and The Ladies' Home Journal* (Baton Rouge, La.: Louisiana State University Press, 1979), pp. xi–xiii.

16. In addition to those mentioned so far, Wood, *Magazines in the United States*; George Britt, *Forty Years – Forty Millions; The Career of Frank A. Munsey* (New York: Farrar & Rinehart, 1935); and Larzer Ziff, *The American 1890s; Life and Times of a Lost Generation* (New York: Viking Press, 1966), in his chapter on magazines.

17. Britt, *Forty Years – Forty Millions*, p. 81.

18. McClure, *My Autobiography*, p. 207.

19. For an excellent analysis, which influenced my perspective, see chapter 1, "The Technology and the Society," in Raymond Williams, *Television: Technology and Cultural Form* (New York: Schocken Books, 1975), pp. 9–31.

20. Ibid, pp. 13–19.

21. See Schudson's discussion of these issues, with respect to the penny press of the 1830s: *Discovering the News*, pp. 31–5.

22. For a philosophical treatment of these questions that has helped me, see

Christopher Lloyd, *Explanation in Social History* (Oxford: Basil Blackwell, 1986), especially the introduction and chapter 8.

23. Richard D. Brown, *Modernization; The Transformation of American Life, 1600–1865* (New York: Hill and Wang, 1976), p. 19.

24. Daniel Lerner, *The Passing of Traditional Society; Modernizing the Middle East* (Glencoe, Ill.: Free Press, 1958).

25. For a summary of these controversies and a bibliography, see Richard A. Higgott, "Competing Theoretical Perspectives on Development and Underdevelopment: A Recent Intellectual History," *Politics*, vol. 13, May 1978, pp. 26–41.

26. Two of the classic studies are Paul F. Lazarsfeld, Bernard Berelson, and Hazel Gaudet, *The People's Choice*, 3rd edn (New York: Columbia University Press, 1968), and Elihu Katz and Paul F. Lazarsfeld, *Personal Influence: The Part Played by People in the Flow of Mass Communications* (New York: Free Press, 1955). A summary and critique of the Lazarsfeld tradition is Todd Gitlin's "Media Sociology: The Dominant Paradigm," *Theory and Society*, vol. 6, 1978, pp. 205–53. A much more sympathetic application of this work to ideas about mass culture is Herbert J. Gans, *Popular Culture and High Culture; An Analysis and Evaluation of Taste* (New York: Basic Books, 1974).

27. *A Contribution to the Critique of Political Economy*, in Eugene Kamenka, ed., *The Portable Karl Marx* (London: Penguin, 1983), 159–60.

28. Marx and Engels, *The German Ideology*, in Robert C. Tucker, ed., *The Marx–Engels Reader*, 2nd edn (New York: W.W. Norton, 1978), p. 172, emphases in original.

29. For a helpful analysis and extension of their ideas on communication, see Armand Mattelart, "Introduction", Armand Mattelart and Seth Siegelaub, *Communication and Class Struggle; 1. Capitalism, Imperialism* (New York: International General, 1979), especially pp. 36–53.

30. I take this way of putting it from Perry Anderson, *Considerations on Western Marxism* (London: Verso, 1979). Of course there were other important thinkers about culture in this generation; some, like Lukács, were close in spirit to Frankfurt School thought; others, like Benjamin, Brecht, and Gramsci, were very different. I chose the Frankfurt School to achieve a simplification whose purpose will be obvious.

31. Some in the Frankfurt tradition have worked to fill the gaping hole in the theory where one would expect an account of ownership *and control* of the media; the work of Herbert Schiller stands out, as in *The Mind Managers* (Boston, Mass.: Beacon, 1973), and *Mass Communications and American Empire* (Boston, Mass.: Beacon, 1971); also Benjamin M. Compaine, with Christopher H. Sterling, Thomas Guback, and J. Kendrick Noble, Jr, *Who Owns the Media?; Concentration of Ownership in the Mass Communications Industry* (White Plains, N.Y.: Knowledge Industry Publications, 1979). Others have enriched the essentially static theory by reintroducing the facts of opposition and crisis; for instance, Hans Magnus Enzensberger, *The Consciousness Industry; On Literature, Politics and the Media* (New York: Seabury, 1974). It is also my impression that very many particular discussions of mass cultural forms and the ideology behind them adopt the Frankfurt School perspective, even when they proclaim no theory. That perspective spread throughout left movements of the 1960s in the United States, and remains an idiom and habit of thought taken for granted by critics and journalists who have no wish to engage questions of the sort I am raising here.

32. Antonio Gramsci, *Selections from the Prison Notebooks*, trans. Quintin Hoare and Geoffrey Nowell Smith, eds, (New York: International Publishers, 1971). Gramsci, a founder of the Italian Communist Party, was imprisoned by Mussolini in 1926 and released as he was dying, in 1937. The *Notebooks* are episodic, unsystematic, and couched in a cryptic vocabulary designed to baffle the censors. Hence, later commentators have in effect put Gramsci's thought back together – possibly with more coherence than Gramsci would have achieved, or even wanted. For one helpful

guide among many, see Carl Boggs, *Gramsci's Marxism* (London: Plato Press, 1976). A more theoretical and historical account is that of Ernesto Laclau and Chantal Mouffe, *Hegemony and Socialist Strategy; Towards a Radical Democratic Politics*, trans. Winston Moore and Paul Commack (London: Verso, 1985).

33. A number of studies have now appeared that do trace the process with subtlety and power. Todd Gitlin's work stands out; see *The Whole World is Watching; Mass Media in the Making and Unmaking of the New Left* (Berkeley, Calif.: University of California Press, 1980), and *Inside Prime Time* (New York: Pantheon, 1985). I have drawn on Gitlin's analysis of hegemony in *The Whole World Is Watching*; see especially p. 3–13 and pp. 252–8. In a more general way, I have also been greatly influenced by Raymond Williams, through such writings as "Base and Superstructure in Marxist Cultural Theory," *New Left Review*, no. 82, 1973, and *Marxism and Literature* (New York: Oxford University Press, 1977); and by Stuart Hall's many discussions: see, for instance, "The Rediscovery of 'Ideology': Return of the Repressed in Media Studies," in Michael Gurevitch, Tony Bennett, James Curran, and Janet Woollacott, eds, *Culture, Society and the Media* (London and New York: Methuen, 1982).

34. Thanks to Richard Vann for helping me clarify this difference.

35. There are traces in my exposition, here, of arguments about history and theory in E.P. Thompson, *The Poverty of Theory and Other Essays* (New York: Monthly Review Press, 1978), and of David Harvey's account of accumulation and contradiction in *The Urbanization of Capital; Studies in the History and Theory of Capitalist Urbanization* (Baltimore, Md.: Johns Hopkins University Press, 1985).

36. Shortly before sending the manuscript of this book to Verso, I received Matthew Schneirov's *The Dream of a New Social Order; Popular Magazines in America, 1893–1914* (New York: Columbia University Press, 1994). Schneirov is critical of the way I articulated the idea of hegemony and applied it to the "magazine revolution" in my first article on the subject, "Where Did Mass Culture Come From? The Case of Magazines," *Berkshire Review*, vol. 16, 1981, pp. 85–101, later reprinted with minor changes in my *Politics of Letters* (Middletown, Conn.: Wesleyan University Press, 1987). He finds that after distinguishing the idea of hegemony from that of direct bourgeois control over consciousness, I folded it back into the classical marxist and Frankfurt School position by equating hegemony with ideological domination, treating economic change as separate from and causative of cultural change, and taking the hegemony of corporate capitalism to have been an accomplished fact by around 1900 rather than an active and contested process (Schneirov, pp. 9–11, 255–7).

I believe that Schneirov mistakes, somewhat, my 1981 argument, but I certainly left it open to such a critique by compressing it almost to vanishing point and stripping it of nuance. I largely share his understanding of hegemony, and imagine he will object less to my present argument in this chapter and throughout the book. We will doubtless continue to disagree, however, on the matter of economic causation. While I, like him, take economic and cultural processes to be always in interaction, I do assign priority (non-temporal) to the economic. This is not a matter – as Schneirov seems to think – of asserting that big capital governed magazine culture through the intermediate practices of advertising. See my discussion of this matter in chapter 6 and, especially, chapter 11.

Schneirov's study is ample and textured, a welcome addition to the scholarship on early popular magazines and mass culture. I wish it had been available to me earlier in these labors. My main criticism is that Schneirov barely touches on the commercial universe (including advertising) within which the magazine revolution took place, and so restricts his analysis of cultural process mainly to explicit projects and ideas of editors and writers. My review of *The Dream of a New Social Order* will appear (or will have appeared) in *Reviews in American History*.

4. What Capitalists Needed

1. Charles H. Hession and Hyman Sardy, *Ascent to Affluence: A History of American Economic Development* (Boston: Allyn and Bacon, 1969), p. 412. For roughly corresponding years, Simon Kuznets fixes the national income at $215 per capita and $401 per capita, in *National Income: A Summary of Findings* (New York: National Bureau of Economic Research, 1946), p. 32. Perhaps this is the place to tell some and remind others that simple numbers like these are in fact highly complex artifacts (Kuznets received a Nobel Prize for his work in developing them). They hide hundreds of assumptions, inferences, guesses, and approximations, especially for the years before the 1920s, when Herbert Hoover made it his project to meter our national life in exact and consistent numbers. Anyone who has worked with different (authoritative) sources will have often come across puzzling disagreements, well beyond those explained by minor differences between concepts such as GNP and national income. In addition to the opacity of the historical record, keep in mind the abstraction of statistics from the activities of human beings, and in particular the nearly exclusive attention given by mainstream economists to markets, and regard all the numbers I cite with appropriate skepticism, even though I will now continue to cite them as if they were bedrock.

2. Hession and Sardy, *Ascent to Affluence,* pp. 422, 424; their source is the Census Bureau's *Historical Statistics of the United States.*

3. Hession and Sardy, *Ascent to Affluence,* p. 417.

4. Alex Groner and the editors of *American Heritage* and *Business Week, The American Heritage History of American Business and Industry* (New York: American Heritage, 1972), p. 157.

5. Robert L. Heilbroner and Aaron Singer, *The Economic Transformation of America* (New York: Harcourt Brace Jovanovich, 1977), p. 59.

6. Alfred D. Chandler, Jr, *The Visible Hand; The Managerial Revolution in American Business* (Cambridge, Mass.: Harvard University Press, 1977), p. 193.

7. Simon Kuznets, *Capital in the American Economy: Its Formation and Financing* (Princeton, N.J.: Princeton University Press, 1961), pp. 64–5.

8. Paul A. Baran and Paul M. Sweezy, *Monopoly Capital: An Essay on the American Economic and Social Order* (New York: Monthly Review Press, 1966), p. 226.

9. I derive this inference from the moving averages of gross capital formation in Kuznets's table, *Capital in the American Economy,* pp. 572–4.

10. I am drawing on two of Kuznets's tables (*National Income,* p. 53; and *Capital in the American Economy,* p. 96), in order to focus on the period of my main interest, and also to extend the comparison into the mid twentieth century. The tables report slightly different data, but both get at the ratio of capital formation to total product.

11. Kuznets, *National Income,* p. 67.

12. Hession and Sardy, *Ascent to Affluence,* p. 424. From 1879 to 1899, manufacturing capital rose from $2.8 billion to $9.8 billion.

13. Kuznets puts it at 55 percent for non-financial corporations, and at 70 percent for large manufacturing corporations, from 1901 to 1912 (*Capital in the American Economy,* pp. 248, 253). Gabriel Kolko, working from several sources, says that the manufacturing sector generated 70 percent of its capital internally from 1900 to 1910 (*Main Currents in Modern American History* [New York: Harper & Row, 1976], p. 2). In addition to the softness of data I mentioned in note 1, refractory problems of analysis make these figures even more dubious than most – see Kuznets's remarks, *Capital in the American Economy,* pp. 220–27. Still, it is clear that industry was expanding mainly out of its profits, during this decade.

14. Hession and Sardy, *Ascent to Affluence,* p. 428.

15. Kolko, *Main Currents,* p. 35.

16. Thomas C. Cochran, *Business in American Life: A History* (New York: McGraw-Hill, 1972), p. 213.

17. Miriam Beard, *History of Business*, vol. II, *From the Monopolists to the Organization Man* (Ann Arbor, Mich.: University of Michigan Press, 1963), p. 160.

18. Hession and Sardy, *Ascent to Affluence*, pp. 429–30.

19. Groner, *American Heritage History*, p. 216.

20. Hession and Sardy, *Ascent to Affluence*, pp. 414; based on a study by Kuznets.

21. The militance of American workers in this period is well documented, though often forgotten. I have taken some of the information in this section from Jeremy Brecher's *Strike!* (Greenwich, Conn.: Fawcett, 1974), a good general history sympathetic to workers.

22. Quoted by Heilbroner and Singer, *Economic Transformation of America*, p. 106.

23. All quoted in Thomas C. Cochran and William Miller, *The Age of Enterprise: A Social History of Industrial America* (New York: Macmillan, 1951), pp. 139–40.

24. Most of these numbers come from Hession and Sardy, *Ascent to Affluence*, pp. 456–9; the one about railroad track is from Kolko, *Main Currents*, p. 7.

25. Heilbroner and Singer, *Economic Transformation of America*, p. 106.

26. William Appleman Williams, *The Contours of American History* (Chicago: Quadrangle, 1966), p. 363.

27. Hession and Sardy, *Ascent to Affluence*, p. 443. Kolko (*Main Currents*, p. 35) gives a different rate (4.2 percent) for the last decade, but agrees that profits were lowest then.

28. At least that is how I read Louis Galambos, *The Public Image of Big Business in America, 1880–1940: A Quantitative Study in Social Change* (Baltimore, Md.: Johns Hopkins University Press, 1975).

29. Robert H. Wiebe, *The Search for Order: 1877–1920* (New York: Hill and Wang, 1967). I have drawn on his synthesis, along with Kolko's, for many of the ideas that underpin my argument.

30. See Michel Aglietta, *A Theory of Capitalist Regulation; The US Experience*, trans. David Fernbach (London: NLB, 1979). Aglietta's theory elides the moment of historical change on which I am focusing, and the centrality then of PMC initiatives; he sees the Fordist arrangements of the 1920s and the even later saturation of working class life by commodification as implicit in corporate crisis and restructuring around 1900. Also, note that the concept of the sales effort upon which I draw comes from Baran and Sweezy's largely incompatible theory of monopoly capitalism. I believe there is a wide enough area of congruence between the two theories to warrant my amalgamating them in this ad hoc way. To adjudicate the theoretical dispute is beyond my scope and ability.

31. In the last two paragraphs and the next one, I draw heavily on the argument of Martin J. Sklar's *The Corporate Reconstruction of American Capitalism, 1890–1916; The Market, the Law, and Politics* (Cambridge: Cambridge University Press, 1988). See pp. 47–52 for his discussion of corporate property and law.

5. Moving the Goods

1. This chapter is a summary of and meditation upon standard secondary works. I suggest that anyone interested in studying the history of corporate integration and the sales effort consult Alfred D. Chandler, Jr, *The Visible Hand: The Managerial Revolution in American Business* (Cambridge, Mass.: Harvard University Press, 1977), Chandler's references, and other more or less standard works cited here. Chandler is such a giant among scholars in the field that I want to add a few comments on my use of his work. I have learned a great deal from *The Visible Hand*, and this whole chapter is heavily indebted to it. I have accepted Chandler's account of particular changes rather uncritically, in part because of his reputation among other scholars

and in part because in the areas where I *have* read fairly widely (mass retailing and advertising), I have found Chandler accurate, fair, and astute. His general thesis – "that modern business enterprise took the place of market mechanisms in coordinating the activities of the economy and allocating its resources" (p. 1), internalizing a variety of functions previously carried on by discrete companies – seems to me important and right.

At the same time, my perspective is quite different from Chandler's. Those who know his work will recognize the critique inherent in some of my arguments. Chandler explains the rise of integrated corporations mainly by reference to technological change: in transportation (the railroads) and communication, and in production itself (continuous process machinery, etc.). My readers know why I find such explanations unhelpful. Chandler offers the market for goods itself, and the huge increase in demand, as a secondary explanation. This abstraction ignores a profound change of life. "Demand" can't be understood as a force mysteriously appearing from nowhere, or as the natural effect of more people and more income; it expresses, in the late nineteenth century, the new way of living with and by commodities which the corporations themselves helped to create. They did so in part by changing the very terms of survival, by making wage labor a necessary condition for most people. Chandler says nothing of this.

Also, in deciding to ignore "the labor force" (p. 6), he omits what I take to be a major project *and cause* of the managerial revolution: the control and deskilling of workers (see Harry Braverman, *Labor and Monopoly Capital* [New York: Monthly Review Press, 1974]). Chandler says nothing of economic crises, bankruptcies, the boom and bust cycle: his index is innocent of entries under "depression" and "recession" for the period from 1870 to 1900, the key moment for integration and oligopoly. He holds that the first corporations to integrate did so because "existing markets were unable to sell and distribute products in the volume they were produced" (p. 287), as if that condition was an evenly developing problem to be solved rather than a crisis that appeared and disappeared, threatening the very existence of businesses in depression years. Chandler even omits the Civil War as a factor in corporate development (the index entry refers readers to four brief mentions). In short, *The Visible Hand* is history without conflict.

2. See Chandler, *The Visible Hand*, pp. 17–19; Glenn Porter and Harold C. Livesay, *Merchants and Manufacturers: Studies in the Changing Structure of Nineteenth-Century Marketing* (Baltimore, Md.: Johns Hopkins University Press, 1971), pp. 5–7.

3. Chandler, *The Visible Hand*, p. 18.

4. Porter and Livesay, *Merchants and Manufacturers*, p. 65.

5. Chandler, *The Visible Hand*, p. 224; Chandler, *The Visible Hand*, pp. 213–24, is my main source for the preceding paragraph.

6. By "wholesaling," I mean selling in quantity to retailers. From another point of view, all department stores internalized the function of wholesaling, in that they bought goods directly from manufacturers.

7. Ralph M. Hower, *History of Macy's of New York, 1858–1919; Chapters in the Evolution of the Department Store* (Cambridge, Mass.: Harvard University Press, 1943), p. 46. His initial line of goods also included handkerchiefs, hosiery, and gloves.

8. For an account of the resistance to department stores, see William Leach, *Land of Desire; Merchants, Power, and the Rise of a New American Culture* (New York: Pantheon, 1993), pp. 26–30.

9. Robert W. Twyman, *History of Marshall Field & Co., 1852-1906* (Philadelphia: University of Pennsylvania Press, 1954), pp. 122–6.

10. Hower, *History of Macy's*, p. 167. All of my information on Macy's comes from this valuable history.

11. Boris Emmet and John E. Jeuck, *Catalogues and Counters; A History of Sears, Roebuck and Company* (Chicago: University of Chicago Press, 1950), pp. 15–18.

12. Ibid. pp. 174–5.

13. Ibid. p. 100.

14. *Sears, Roebuck and Co. Incorporated, Consumers Guide, Fall 1900*, edited and abridged by Joseph J. Schroeder, Jr (Northfield, Ill.: DBI Books, 1970), pp. 590–91.

15. Chandler, *The Visible Hand*, pp. 233–5; Godfrey M. Lebhar, *Chain Stores in America, 1859–1959* (New York: Chain Store Publishing Corporation, 1959).

16. The "structure" I speak of here comprises the institutions and processes that deliver products to families and individuals. To be sure, the revolution in sales extended beyond that part of the economy, for manufacturers were themselves customers. About the ways they supplied their needs, a similar story might be told. Modern commodity dealers arose, simplifying and commanding the movement of grain, cotton, and other agricultural products to food processors and textile mills. Many producers of iron, steel, and other metals followed Carnegie's lead by building their own sales organizations to reach their market of small and large factories. Makers of industrial machinery and electrical equipment did the same. Some extracting companies integrated "forward," and some refiners, smelters, and metal producers integrated "backward," internalizing in both cases the movement of materials from under the ground to factory receiving docks. Everywhere, the role of small middlemen was taken over by large ones, or by sales forces or middle managers within integrated corporations. So this part of the marketing revolution exactly paralleled the one I have been discussing; but because it had little direct impact on the making of consumers and mass culture, I will leave it behind with this footnote – to the great relief of readers who may have begun to fear that this study would have no limits whatever.

17. Chandler, *The Visible Hand*, pp. 289–99. He makes high volume, continuous process production the main cause of the move toward marketing. But there are too many other causes (see below) and too many counter examples (he mentions many in his chapter on mergers) to support this form of technological determinism.

18. Porter and Livesay, *Merchants and Manufacturing*, pp. 157–62.

19. See Chandler, *The Visible Hand*, pp. 320–44.

20. Porter and Livesay, *Merchants and Manufacturing*, pp. 215–22.

21. Gustav A. Berghoff, president of the Rub-No-More Company. Quoted from the Bureau of Corporation Records (File #7222-30-1) by Porter and Livesay, *Merchants and Manufacturing*, p. 225.

22. A further symmetry reveals itself in this new set of arrangements: big producers tended to distribute through small, scattered outlets (soap, cereal, oil, typewriters, cameras, etc.), while big retailers marketed the products of small factories which they both served and dominated. This pattern led to symmetries in advertising, too, about which more later.

23. Paul A. Baran and Paul M. Sweezy, *Monopoly Capital: An Essay on the American Economic and Social Order* (New York: Modern Reader Paperbacks, 1966), p. 130.

24. Following Barbara and John Ehrenreich, "The Professional-Managerial Class," in Pat Walker, ed., *Between Labor and Capital* (Boston, Mass.: South End Press, 1979), pp. 5–45.

25. John William Ferry, *A History of the Department Store* (New York: Macmillan, 1960), p. 4.

26. Returns amounted to 12 percent of sales at Marshall Field in 1890, to cite an extreme example: Susan Porter Benson, *Counter Cultures; Saleswomen, Managers, and Customers in American Department Stores, 1890–1940* (Urbana, Ill.: University of Illinois Press, 1986), p. 98. Department stores were more or less forced to adopt some of these policies by the nature and size of their businesses. Most notably, a store owner could not count on hundreds or thousands of sales clerks to bargain in his best interests: H. Pasdermadjian, *The Department Store; Its Origins, Evolution and Economics* (London: Newman Books, 1954), p. 23.

27. Susan Strasser, *Satisfaction Guaranteed; The Making of the American Mass Market* (New York: Pantheon, 1989), p. 28. Strasser offers a wealth of helpful analysis of the new commodity relations.

28. Hower, *History of Macy's*, pp. 61, 63. These ads appeared in 1858 and 1860, when most advertising was dull by comparison.

29. *Consumers Guide, Fall, 1900*, from the prefatory letter headed "KIND FRIEND" and signed "SEARS, ROEBUCK & CO. (INC.)," and from p. 1.

30. Emmet and Jeuck, *Catalogues and Counters*, p. 86.

31. I take that formulation and some of these ideas from Richard Terdiman, *Discourse/Counter-Discourse; The Theory and Practice of Symbolic Resistance in Nineteenth-Century France* (Ithaca, N.Y.: Cornell University Press, 1985).

32. The phrase is from Leach, *Land of Desire*, p. 41. His treatment of these matters is full and enlightening, especially in chapter 2, "Facades of Color, Glass, and Light," and chapter 3, "Interiors."

33. Theodore Dreiser, *Sister Carrie* (New York: Bantam, 1982), p. 18.

34. Hower, *History of Macy's*, opposite p. 335.

35. Twyman, *History of Marshall Field*, p. 29.

36. James Brough, *The Woolworths* (New York: McGraw-Hill, 1982), p. 100.

6. Advertising: New Practices, New Relations

1. This page of ads is reprinted in Frank Presbrey, *The History and Development of Advertising* (New York: Doubleday, Doran & Company, 1929), p. 162. A general note about Presbrey's book: it is not a scholarly history in the academic sense; Presbrey has no footnotes, and rarely indicates his sources. Yet he was an avid collector of historical material; the book is rich in detail, especially for the period that is my main concern. Presbrey was himself an agency president, beginning in 1896, and knew the terrain first hand. Recent historians of advertising have accepted him as reliable, on the whole. I do, too, but want to give warning that my many references to Presbrey lack the authority of scripture.

2. Presbrey, *The History and Development of Advertising*, p. 396.

3. P.H. Erbes, *Fifty Years; 1888–1938*, a special issue of *Printers' Ink*, vol. 184, no. 88 (28 July 1938), p. 88.

4. Quoted by Presbrey, *The History and Development of Advertising*, p. 350.

5. Earnest Elmo Calkins and Ralph Holden, *Modern Advertising* (New York: D. Appleton and Company, 1912), p. 1. Calkins actually wrote the book, but added Holden's name to publicize their agency. The book was first printed in 1905.

6. Julian L. Simon, *Issues in the Economics of Advertising* (Urbana, Ill.: University of Illinois Press, 1970), table opposite p. 188. Otis Pease puts the share even higher, at 4 percent for 1910, and according to his figures, that share has not been exceeded since: *The Responsibilities of American Advertising; Private Control and Public Influence, 1920–1940* (New Haven, Conn.: Yale University Press, 1958), p. 13.

7. Daniel Pope, *The Making of Modern Advertising* (New York, Basic Books, 1983), pp. 21–7. I don't find Pope's argument for his numbers especially convincing; a dubious assumption is that advertising in newspapers and magazines remained constant as a proportion of *all* advertising from 1880 to 1935. Given the tremendous increase in magazine advertising, that seems unlikely. But Pope does show the impossibility of tracing advertising's progess in reliable numbers through the period in question.

8. For per capita figures see Neil H. Borden, *The Economic Effects of Advertising* (Chicago: Richard D. Irwin, 1942), p. 48.

9. Ibid; see the table on p. 48.

10. See Calkins and Holden, *Modern Advertising*, pp. 120–21, 76.

11. Sidney A. Sherman, "Advertising in the United States," *Journal of the American Statistical Association*, vol. 7, no. 4, December 1900.

12. One must discount somewhat the numbers for the early 1880s, when *Harper's* was pursuing a genteel, anti-ad policy; even in 1904, *Harper's* was still running many pages of ads for its own books. Still, the numbers suggest the pace at which national brand advertising was expanding.

13. One must consult the original issues. Except for the *Ladies' Home Journal*, all the monthlies listed here rigidly segregated ad pages from editorial pages, and librarians almost universally lopped off the ad pages before binding periodicals. Maybe they shared the feeling of genteel editors that advertising was an unsightly intrusion into cultural space, and should be kept on or beyond the margins. Yet as early as 1887, exhortations to save this historically valuable material began to appear. Thus Norman C. Perkins, in the *Library Journal*, vol. 12, p. 355: "the unconsidered trifles of to-day become the history of tomorrow"; and more specifically, "almost any magazine advertisement will become interesting within 10 years, and curious within 20, and likely enough important within 50." This, from an article called "How to Bind Periodicals," by Norman C. Perkins.

14. *LHJ's* quarto pages were about four times as large as those of the other magazines. Its advertising rates were also far higher: $4000 per page in 1904, compared to $500 for *Munsey's*, according to Calkins and Holden, *Modern Advertising*.

15. Its early acceptance and solicitation of display ads helped break down the wall between literary culture and commerce, and overcome the strangeness attendant on pairing sonnets and soap. See Presbrey, *The History and Development of Advertising*, pp. 469–70.

16. This development occurred at about the same time and for the same reasons in England, but with newspapers rather than magazines leading the way. See Raymond Williams, *The Long Revolution* (New York: Columbia University Press, 1961), especially pp. 200–201.

17. For example, see Pope, *Making of Modern Advertising*, pp. 31–7; Simon, *Issues*, pp. 173–87; Borden, *Economic Effects*, pp. 24–9, 49–51. Simon, with his customary lack of pretense, says his discussion of causes "takes the uninspiring form of a laundry list," as well as itemizing forces that "seem obvious to the reader" (pp. 173–4).

18. John Philip Jones, *What's in a Name? Advertising and the Concept of Brands* (Lexington, Mass.: D.C. Heath, 1986), p. 23.

19. See Pope, *Making of Modern Advertising*, p. 63, and Michael Schudson, *Advertising, the Uneasy Persuasion; Its Dubious Impact on American Society* (New York: Basic Books, 1984), p. 164.

20. Alfred D. Chandler, Jr, *The Visible Hand; The Managerial Revolution in American Business* (Cambridge, Mass.: Harvard University Press, 1977), pp. 291–3.

21. The principal source is Arthur F. Marquette, *Brands, Trademarks, and Good Will; The Story of the Quaker Oats Company* (New York: McGraw-Hill, 1967). Understandably, Chandler, Schudson, and Pope use both of these examples in support of their arguments.

22. Russell B. Adams, Jr, *King C. Gillette; The Man and His Wonderful Shaving Device* (Boston: Little, Brown, 1978), pp. 19-22, 51, 56.

23. Since no big integrated corporations emerged in these areas, they are not exceptions to Chandler's thesis; but they challenge Pope and Schudson's use of that thesis to account for advertising.

24. Ralph M. Hower, *The History of an Advertising Agency; N.W. Ayer and Son at Work, 1869–1939* (Cambridge, Mass.: Harvard University Press, 1939), pp. 214, 217.

25. Calkins and Holden, *Modern Advertising*, opposite p. 302. The survey was done by Thomas Balmer, an ad man for the *Ladies' Home Journal* at the time.

26. So, in making tallies I will arbitrarily assign half of the cocoa/chocolate ads to the ingredient category, and half to "dessert" foods.

27. Pope stresses newness and convenience (*Making of Modern Advertising*, pp. 47–8), but sees these as disjunct qualities, not as joined in an unfolding way of life.

28. In Britain, George Packwood had nationally advertised and distributed an improved strop and sharpening paste in the 1790s, an instance of the much earlier emergence in that country of some marketing practices. See Neil McKendrick, "George Packwood and the Commercialization of Shaving," in McKendrick, John Brewer, and J. H. Plumb, *The Birth of a Consumer Society; The Commercialization of Eighteenth-Century England* (Oxford: Basil Blackwell, 1982).

29. I base these figures on estimates from Arthur Loesser, *Men, Women and Pianos* (New York: Simon & Schuster, 1954), pp. 549, 552–3. Loesser says that fast production of pianos did lead makers to advertise, but since he has in mind forty per week as very high output for a factory, clearly we are not concerned with high-speed, continuous-process manufacture or large fixed capital.

30. That the city was the privileged locus of ad campaigns is indicated by the choice of many manufacturers – e.g., Campbell's, Arrow (shirt collars), Wrigley, and the National Biscuit Company – to use streetcar advertising along with, or in place of, magazine advertising. See note 35 for my source. The same changes in products advertised took place in Britain. See Raymond Williams, *Problems in Materialism and Culture*, (London: NLB, 1980), pp. 174–6.

31. This was for many a conscious historical strategy. For just one example, an early statement of the National Biscuit Company urged that too many women "still cling to the task of spending hours beating batters and watching them in the oven, when they might buy cakes and cookies that rival their own. Every woman's baking day can now be banished in the limbo of tallow dips and home spinning"; quoted in William Cahn, *Out of the Cracker Barrel; The Nabisco Story From Animal Crackers to Zuzus* (New York: Simon & Schuster, 1969), p. 67.

32. Chandler, *The Visible Hand*, p. 8.

33. Many contested it, and advanced other visions. See Delores Hayden, *The Grand Domestic Revolution; A History of Feminist Design for American Homes, Neighborhoods, and Cities* (Cambridge, Mass.: MIT Press, 1981), for a valuable account of historically real alternatives.

34. Schudson, *Advertising*, p. 17; Jones, *What's in a Name?*, p. 24; Paul A. Baran and Paul M. Sweezy, *Monopoly Capital; An Essay on the American Economics and Social Order* (New York: Monthly Review Press, 1966), pp. 116–17, 125–6. But since stagnation and growing surplus were not a deep structural problem for capitalism until after 1907, according to Baran and Sweezy, one cannot cite this problem as a cause of national advertising's first large growth in the 1890s.

35. George Burton Hotchkiss and Richard B. Franken, *The Leadership of Advertised Brands* (Garden City, N.J.: Doubleday, Page and Co., 1923).

36. See, for example, Barbara Ehrenreich and Deirdre English, *For Her Own Good; 150 Years of the Experts' Advice to Women* (Garden City, N.J.: Anchor Books, 1979), especially chapters 2 and 3.

37. Pope, *Making of Modern Advertising*, p. 60

38. Pope's table of the largest magazine advertisers of 1913–15 (*Making of Modern Advertising*, pp. 43–5) is, as he notes, essentially a list of the leading firms in the various industries. From the other side, Chandler's list of the country's largest corporations in 1917 includes, among those that made goods for sale to consumers, virtually all the largest advertisers of the preceding twenty years (*The Visible Hand*, pp. 503–12).

39. See Chandler, *The Visible Hand*, p. 335.

40. Erbes, *Fifty Years*, pp. 89–94.

41. In 1889, for instance, 45 percent of *LHJ* ads were still placed directly by manufacturers; see Salme Harju Steinberg, *Reformer in the Marketplace; Edward W. Bok and The Ladies' Home Journal* (Baton Rouge, La.: Louisiana State University Press, 1979), p. 26. But note that at the same time N.W. Ayer's clientele consisted mainly of manufacturers (Hower, *N.W. Ayer and Son*, p. 211).

42. Pope, *Making of Modern Advertising*, pp. 147–8.

43. Hower, *N.W. Ayer and Son*, pp. 494, 577; Pope, *Making of Modern Advertising*, pp. 20, 176.

44. Calkins and Holden, *Modern Advertising*, p. 134.

45. Hower's account of the various business arrangements (*N.W. Ayer and Son*, pp. 16–24) is lucid; Pope's is rich in detail (*Making of Modern Advertising*, pp. 112–26). George P. Rowell, an important early agent, had been in business several years when a man at the *Chicago Tribune* surprised him by asking whom an agent represented. Rowell replied to this "conundrum" by saying that he represented himself. *Forty Years an Advertising Agent: 1865–1905* (New York: Printers' Ink, 1906), p. 98.

46. Presbrey reproduces this ad, *The History and Development of Advertising*, p. 263.

47. *J. Walter Thompson's Illustrated Catalogue of Magazines*, 1887, p. 14. For access to this and all other in-house publications, I am indebted to Cynthia G. Swank, archivist at the J. Walter Thompson Company. These documents are now in the J. Walter Thompson Company Archives at the John W. Hartman Center for Sales, Advertising and Marketing History, Special Collections Library, Duke University, Durham, N.C. Research Archivist Marion Hirsch has most helpfully checked my references.

48. James Playsted Wood, *The Story of Advertising* (New York: Ronald Press, 1958), pp. 338–9.

49. Hower, *N.W. Ayer and Son*, p. 494; Stephen Fox, *The Mirror Makers; A History of American Advertising and Its Creators* (New York: William Morrow and Co., 1984), pp. 31, 40; William Leiss, Stephen Kline, and Sut Jhally, *Social Communication in Advertising; Persons, Products, and Images of Well-Being* (Toronto: Methuen, 1986), p. 109.

50. Hower, *N.W. Ayer and* Son, p. 110; *J. Walter Thompson's Illustrated Catalogue*, 1887, p. 5; Calkins and Holden, *Modern Advertising*, p. 4, 31, 174; Thompson's booklet, *Advertising as a Selling Force*, 1909.

51. *Illustrated Catalogue*, 1887, p. 14. Rowell, looking back from 1905, *wished* he had had the "manliness" to refuse scam ads, but told frankly of charlatans whose copy he placed (*Forty Years an Advertising Agent*, p. 395).

52. *The Thompson Blue Book on Advertising*, 1904, pp. 7–8; *Where Good Advertising Is the Constant Product*, 1905?; *J. Walter Thompson/Advertising*, 1897, p. 20. (A *Printers' Ink* article, as early as 1891, advised taking a year to plan a camapaign for a new product.)

53. Calkins and Holden, *Modern Advertising*, pp. 201–19. The letter advises that the campaign stress the quality and value of American fabrics and feature patriotic motifs, in order to take business away from imported woolens. The agency advertised its services in these terms, about 1900: "We are something more than mere agents for the advertiser. It is our business to study the conditions of his business, to make an advertising plan for the promotion of the sale of his goods, to place his advertising in the desirable publications to reach the kind of people he desires to interest, to attend to all the details of this work – in a word, to become his advertising department"; Earnest Elmo Calkins, *"and hearing not –" Annals of an Adman* (New York: Charles Scribner's Sons, 1946), p. 210. He says that such propositions were novel, around 1900.

54. Hower, *N.W. Ayer and Son*, pp. 115–16; Cahn, *Out of the Cracker Barrel*, pp. 65–98.

55. Hower, *N.W. Ayer and Son*, pp. 88–93.

56. Alex Groner and the editors of *American Heritage* and *Business Week*, *The American Heritage History of American Business and Industry* (New York: American Heritage, 1972), p. 250.

57. Adolphus Green, chairman of Nabisco, called McKinney's coinage the "most valuable [word] in the English language" (Cahn, *Out of the Cracker Barrel*, p. 72).

58. Jones, *What's in a Name?*, pp. 7, 29–31.

59. Children, supposedly vulnerable to sales pitches, delight in such parody. I can't resist quoting from memory this take-off of the "Pepsi Cola hits the spot" song, which inspired hilarity among ten-year-olds in the early 1940s:

> Pepsi Cola sure does stink,
> Pour it down the kitchen sink,
> Tastes like vinegar, looks like ink,
> Pepsi Cola is a stinky drink.

This was our way of reclaiming meter and rhyme from the ad man.

60. Charles E. Raymond, *Getting on in Advertising*, typescript in Company History and Reminiscences Collection (1932), J. Walter Thompson Archives, p. 7.

61. *The Red Ear* (1888?), p. 62.

62. Hower, *N.W. Ayer and Son*, pp. 96–7; Rowell, *Forty Years an Advertising Agent*, p. 376; Pope, *Making of Modern Advertising*, p. 138; *Printers' Ink*, 1891; Erbes, *Fifty Years*, p. 67.

63. *The Thompson Red Book on Advertising*, 1900, p. 11; Presbrey, *The History and Development of Advertising*, p. 527.

64. *Illustrated Catalogue*, 1887, pp. 1, 5, 6.

65. John Brisben Walker, "The Modern Magazine," *Printers' Ink*, 13 April 1892, p. 476.

66. Raymond, *Getting on in Advertising*, p. 45. Leiss, Kline, and Jhally rightly insist that agencies "never responded just passively to changes in media, but in many cases became an active force in their development" (*Social Communications*, p. 123). Their discussion of this complex interaction is excellent.

67. Steinberg, *Reformer in the Marketplace*, pp. 19–28.

68. "Editors as Business Men," *Printers' Ink*, 7 January, 1891, p. 4.

69. *Printers' Ink*, 6 December 1899; quoted by Presbrey, *The History and Development of Advertising*, p. 483.

70. Marquette, *Brands, Trademarks and Good Will*, p. 68. E.S. Turner notes that in England, many manufacturers thought advertising ungentlemanly; the "way to do business was to surround oneself with a circle of customers and to cultivate personal relations with them." *The Shocking History of Advertising!* (New York: Dutton, 1953), p. 101.

71. *Illustrated Catalogue*, 1887, p. 13.

72. *The J. Walter Thompson Book; A Series of Talks on Advertising*, 1909, pp. 27, 63; Artemas Ward, "Urban Versus Rural Advertising," *Printers' Ink*, 7 January 1891, p. 17.

73. Calkins and Holden, *Modern Advertising*, p. 9

74. See also T. J. Jackson Lears's discussion in "Some Versions of Fantasy: Toward a Cultural History of American Advertising," *Prospects*, vol. 9, 1984, pp. 365–8.

75. Lears mentions "advertising's role in obscuring and blurring authority relations," "Some Versions of Fantasy," p. 397.

76. From an 1897 article in *Harper's Weekly*, quoted by Pope, *Making of Modern Advertising*, p. 5.

77. The first of these quotations is from *The Thompson Red Book on Advertising*, 1900, p. 9; the last is from *J. Walter Thompson/Advertising*, 1895, p. 7; the others are from *Thompson's Battery*, 1889 – an aptly named brochure. I speak as if Thompson himself wrote these words; though he surely relied on employees' promotional skills as the agency grew, the first person singular suggests his close identification with this literature.

78. *Thompson's Battery*, 1889, p. 9.

79. *Business History Review,* vol. 41, Winter 1967.

80. Inevitably, they soon enlisted the aid of another nascent profession, psychology. In the 1890s, Thomas Balmer, an agent in Chicago, sought advice from Professor Walter Dill Scott of Northwestern, later its president. In 1903, Scott published *The Theory of Advertising,* and in 1908 *The Psychology of Advertising,* a spate of similar treatises followed. Scott's psychology tended toward the obvious (appeal directly to the senses, etc.), but he understood that attenuated relations between buyer and seller had opened the space for advertising, which must try to "preserve as many as possible of the good features of the old institutions" ("The Psychology of Advertising," *Atlantic Monthly,* vol. 93, no. 33, January 1904). Advertising uses of psychology became quite sophisticated in the 1920s; around 1900, agents served as their own amateur psychologists.

81. *Printers' Ink,* 7 January 1891, p. 16.

82. See, for instance, Roland Marchand, *Advertising the American Dream; Making Way for Modernity, 1920–1940* (Berkeley, Calif.: University of California Press, 1985), pp. 66–9.

83. Pope cites *Fowler's Publicity,* 1897; I quote from Presbrey, *The History and Development of Advertising,* pp. 317–18, who gives a slightly different wording to Fowler's text; perhaps he had a different source.

84. "Reaching the Millions," in the *Thompson Blue Book on Advertising,* 1909–10, p. 18, as reprinted in *Advertising Age,* 7 December 1964, p. 28; Raymond, *Getting on in Advertising,* p. 49.

85. *The J. Walter Thompson Book,* 1909, p. 43; *The Thompson Blue Book on Advertising,* 1901, p. 8; *The Red Ear* (1888?), p. 4; *Direct Acting * High Pressure* (1889); *Illustrated Catalogue,* 1887, p. 12, emphases in original.

86. Steinberg, *Reformer in the Marketplace,* pp. 3–5. Bok supported this effort by always trying to edit the magazine "on a slightly higher plane" than his estimate of readers' actual class and culture. See *The Americanization of Edward Bok; The Autobiography of a Dutch Boy Fifty Years After* (New York: Charles Scribner's Sons, 1921), p. 165. In 1915 he spoke quite precisely of his target audiences: first, families with incomes between $1200 and $2500; second, those between $3000 and $5000 (Steinberg, *Reformer in the Marketplace,* pp. 6–7).

87. Ads in *Illustrated Catalogue,* 1887, pp. 40, 48, 56.

88. Calkins and Holden, *Modern Advertising,* p. 291. This survey had to have been done before 1905; I don't know if the report survives; it is not in the McClure archive at Indiana University; and McClure's biographer, Peter Lyon, has not heard of it (personal conversation).

89. Ads in *Illustrated Catalogue,* 1887, pp. 38, 64.

90. They did so from a vantage point in the professional-managerial class. In time, of course, some became wealthy, but of the dozen or so whose origins I know, only Thompson and Albert Lasker came from moderate affluence, and none was a college graduate. Most came from farms or small towns in New England, New York, or the Midwest; several had very religious backgrounds. By the time directories of advertising people came into existence in the 1910s and 1920s, the profile was quite different: ad men (and a few women) tended to be college graduates from well-to-do families, who liked golf and classical music and were themselves paid at three times the national average (see Pope, *Making of Modern Advertising,* pp. 177–9, and Marchand, *Advertising the American Dream,* pp. 32–8). Salaries around 1900 varied bizarrely. In 1903, Lasker was earning $52,000 as a 23-year-old, while Earnest Elmo Calkins was about to quit his $35-a-week job with the Bates agency. Still, even his was a middle class salary. Ad men could identify with the upscale audience and look down on the farming and industrial lives they had escaped.

91. Mark S. Albion and Paul W. Farris, *The Advertising Controversy; Evidence of the Economic Effects of Advertising* (Boston, Mass.: Auburn House, 1981).

92. Quoted by Glenn Porter and Harold C. Livesay, in *Merchants and Manufacturers; Studies in the Changing Structure of Nineteenth-Century Marketing* (Baltimore, Md.: Johns Hopkins University Press, 1971), p. 225; see the whole quotation in chapter 5, p. 72.

93. Williams, "Advertising: The Magic System," in *Problems in Materialism and Culture*, p. 185.

94. Leiss, Kline, and Jhally, *Social Communication*, p. 42. But it is a different matter to go on and say, as they do, "there is nothing special about advertising." I hope to have identified some special features of it. One may concede the impossibility of abstracting it from a whole social process, and yet resist the blurring entailed by seeing it as "only one ingredient in the mix" of communications as Leiss, Kline and Jhally do. Other scholars who believe that advertising has transformed our society have tended to stress its efficacy in establishing "a consumption ethic," teaching that the "good society" is achieved "largely through consumption": James D. Norris, *Advertising and the Transformation of American Society, 1865–1920* (Westport, Conn.: Greenwood Press, 1990), p. xviii. This indisputable judgment tends, as in Norris's informative study, to minimize the deeper agency of corporations, as well as the transformation of social relations I have emphasized.

7. Readers, Consumers: The Professional-Managerial Class

1. Opening of *The Eighteenth Brumaire of Louis Bonaparte*. Readers attuned to debates about the writing of history will observe for the nth time that I posit a "master narrative," however nuanced and qualified. The nuance matters most to me in this study, but without something to *be* nuanced, nuance is a mouthful of air. So I acknowledge the rebuke of those who think master narratives untenable; perhaps they will find uses for much of this story within interpretive matrices of their own.

2. Gabriel Kolko, *Main Currents in Modern American History* (New York: Harper, 1976), p. 24.

3. Arthur Meier Schlesinger, *The Rise of the City, 1878–1898* (New York: Macmillan, 1933), pp. 67–9.

4. Stephen Thernstrom, "Urbanization, Migration, and Social Mobility in Late Nineteenth-Century America," in Herbert G. Gutman and Gregory S. Kealey, eds, *Many Pasts: Readings in American Social History*, vol. 2 / 1865–the present (Englewood Cliffs, N.J.: Prentice-Hall, 1973), p. 112.

5. Herbert G. Gutman, *Work, Culture, and Society in Industrializing America; Essays in American Working-Class and Social History* (New York: Knopf, 1976), p. 40. Gutman notes that less than 2 percent of Londoners had come from outside the British Isles, in the same year.

6. Kenneth T. Jackson, *Crabgrass Frontier; The Suburbanization of the United States* (New York: Oxford University Press, 1985), pp. 23, 140; Sam Bass Warner, Jr, *Streetcar Suburbs; The Process of Growth in Boston, 1870–1900* (Cambridge, Mass.: Harvard, 1962) p. 2.

7. David P. Handlin, *The American Home; Architecture and Society, 1815–1915* (Boston: Little, Brown, 1979), pp. 152, 154.

8. Jackson, *Crabgrass Frontier*, p. 74.

9. For an account of the grid pattern, the real estate market, and social disutility in Berkeley, California, see Lars Lerup, *Building the Unfinished; Architecture and Human Action* (Beverly Hills, Calif.: Sage, 1977), pp. 80–88.

10. Warner, *Streetcar Suburbs*, pp. 181, 184.

11. Richard A. Walker, "Class, Division of Labour and Employment in Space," in Derek Gregory and John Urry, eds, *Social Relations and Spatial Structures* (New York: St Martin's Press, 1985), p. 186.

12. Henri Lefebvre, *The Production of Space*, trans. Donald Nicholson-Smith (Oxford: Basil Blackwell, 1991), pp. 73, 82–3; Edward W. Soja, *Postmodern Geographies: The Reassertion of Space in Critical Social Theory* (London: Verso, 1989), pp. 6–7.

13. I take the notions of locale, region, and zoning from Anthony Giddens, "Time, Space and Regionalisation," in Gregory and Urry, *Social Relations*, but this is perhaps the place to say that I wrote this chapter and the one entitled "Charting Social Space" before I knew the work of Lefebvre, Giddens, Soja, Walker, David Harvey, and other geographers and spatially oriented sociologists. When I began the study I had no commitment to spatiality as a concept, central or otherwise, but it inserted itself and began to seem necessary. Perhaps in a very small way this supports the claim of Soja and others that space, though long exiled from marxist thought, is a generative principle in historical materialism. If my work has contributed to marxist geography, however inadvertently, it has done so by proposing a considerably more textured spatiality than others have charted, and for a class other than the bourgeoisie or the proletariat. Pierre Bourdieu does theorize social space with respect to professionals and managers, and makes central the element of value and social distinction that runs through my exposition; but his concept of social space is a good deal less literal than mine: it refers to the relative positioning of classes and class fractions within something like a space of social cognition and evaluation. He is closer to the concept I want when he writes of a "socially ranked geographical space," but here his idea is limited to the distance from or proximity to cultural centers and resources of a group's area of residence. See Pierre Bourdieu, *Distinction; A Social Critique of the Judgement of Taste*, trans. Richard Nice (Cambridge, Mass.: Harvard University Press, 1984), p. 124. This is a small part of what I hope to capture.

14. Stuart M. Blumin, *The Emergence of the Middle Class; Social Experience in the American City, 1760–1900* (Cambridge: Cambridge University Press, 1989), pp. 170, 175.

15. John S. Gilkeson, Jr, *Middle-Class Providence, 1820–1940* (Princeton, N.J.: Princeton University Press, 1986), pp. 137–8.

16. Mary P. Ryan, *Cradle of the Middle Class; The Family in Oneida County, New York, 1790–1865* (Cambridge: Cambridge University Press, 1981), pp. 181–2.

17. Henry C. Binford, *The First Suburbs; Residential Communities on the Boston Periphery, 1815–1860* (Chicago: University of Chicago Press, 1985), p. 134.

18. Everett Chamberlin, *Chicago and its Suburbs* (Chicago: Hungerford, 1874); quoted by John R. Stilgoe, *Borderland; Origins of the American Suburb, 1820–1939* (New Haven, Conn.: Yale University Press, 1988), p. 145.

19. Warner, *Streetcar Suburbs*, p. 66; see also the map on p. 63. Ira Katznelson notes that as this process of differentiation separated middle class and working class neighborhoods, it also "came to divide the working class into distinguishable subgroups that occupied quite different parts of the city," with different principles of cohesion by race, ethnicity, and so on; *Marxism and the City* (Oxford: Clarendon Press, 1992), pp. 276–7. Reconfiguration of the city thus made for fragmentation of the working class, even as it helped unify the PMC. David Harvey argues for the inevitability of residential differentiation and, indeed, of suburbanization, in *The Urbanization of Capital; Studies in the History and Theory of Capitalist Urbanization* (Baltimore, Md.: Johns Hopkins University Press, 1985); see especially pp. 117–24.

20. Jackson, *Crabgrass Frontier University Press*, pp. 27, 33, 36–8, 93, 95, 97; Stilgoe, *Borderland*, p. 52, 60, 133; Schlesinger, *The Rise of the City*, p. 108.

21. Ryan, *Cradle of the Middle Class*, p. 147.

22. Stilgoe, *Borderland*, pp. 132–4.

23. Binford uses the term "suburb" for Cambridge and like communities, but the

burden of his argument in *The First Suburbs* is that their history can not be grasped in terms of commuting and dependence.

24. Jackson, *Crabgrass Frontier*, pp. 16–8.

25. Binford, *The First Suburbs*, pp. 162–3; Stilgoe, *Borderland*, pp. 68–70, 148; John C. Teaford, *City and Suburb; The Political Fragmentation of Metropolitan America, 1850–1970* (Baltimore, Md.: Johns Hopkins University Press, 1979), pp. 18–20.

26. David Harvey, *Consciousness and the Urban Experience; Studies in the History and Theory of Capitalist Urbanization* (Baltimore, Md.: Johns Hopkins University Press, 1985), pp. 11–14; the phrases quoted are on p. 13.

27. See Harvey, *The Urbanization of Capital*, pp. 156–7, and all of chapter 6.

28. Warner, *Streetcar Suburbs*, pp. 60, 125; Jackson, *Crabgrass Frontier*, pp. 91, 123; Robert Fishman, *Bourgeois Utopias; The Rise and Fall of Suburbia* (New York: Basic Books, 1987), pp. 142–4. Not all these projects succeeded. Alexander Stewart, New York's first department store magnate, built fine homes in his planned community at Garden City, L.I., many of which found no takers. Olmsted's Riverside Improvement Company went bankrupt in the panic of 1873. This was a story of uneven development (Jackson, *Crabgrass Frontier*, pp. 8, 84–5).

29. Jackson, *Crabgrass Frontier*, p. 131.

30. Jackson, *Crabgrass Frontier*, p. 152. I have drawn most of the information in these two paragraphs from Teaford, *City and Suburb*, and Warner, *Streetcar Suburbs*, ruthlessly simplifying the intricate story they tell.

31. Margaret Marsh, *Suburban Lives* (New Brunswick, N.J.: Rutgers University Press, 1990), pp. 50–51, 97, 99.

32. Jackson, *Crabgrass Frontier*, pp. 99–100.

33. These quotations, along with many similar ones, are from Jan Cohn, *The Palace or the Poorhouse: The American House as a Cultural Symbol* (East Lansing, Mich.: Michigan State University Press, 1979), pp. 69, 93.

34. Stephen Thernstrom, *Poverty and Progress: Social Mobility in a Nineteenth Century City* (Cambridge, Mass.: Harvard University Press, 1964), especially pp. 116–22.

35. Matthew Edel, Elliott D. Sclar, and Daniel Luria, *Shaky Palaces; Homeownership and Social Mobility in Boston's Suburbanization* (New York: Columbia University Press, 1984), p. 141.

36. Kolko, *Main Currents*, p. 87. There is a good deal of anecdotal evidence to the same effect in contemporary studies. See also Daniel Horowitz, *The Morality of Spending; Attitudes Toward the Consumer Society in America, 1875–1940* (Baltimore, Md.: Johns Hopkins University Press, 1985).

37. Margaret Marsh, *Suburban Lives*, p. 99; Olivier Zunz, *The Changing Face of Inequality; Urbanization, Industrial Development, and Immigrants in Detroit, 1880–1920* (Chicago: University of Chicago Press, 1982), pp. 152–61; Edel et al., *Shaky Palaces*, p. 291; Warner, *Streetcar Suburbs*, p. 26.

38. Robert S. Lynd and Helen Merrell Lynd, *Middletown; A Study in American Culture* (New York: Harcourt, Brace & World, 1929), pp. 93–109.

39. John Stilgoe, *Common Landscape of America, 1580 to 1845* (New Haven, Conn.: Yale University Press, 1982), pp. 206–7.

40. John Stilgoe, *Metropolitan Corridor; Railroads and the American Scene* (New Haven, Conn.: Yale University Press, 1983), pp. 272–7; Fishman, *Bourgeois Utopias*, pp. 146, 148.

41. Quoted by Handlin, *American Home*, p. 175. See his whole account of Scott, pp. 171–83.

42. Raymond Williams, *The Country and the City* (New York: Oxford University Press, 1973), p. 125.

43. Thorstein Veblen gives critical attention to the "pecuniary beauty" sought in grounds and lawns; *The Theory of the Leisure Class* (New York: Modern Library, 1934), pp. 133–9. Fishman points out the implied ideal of community (*Bourgeois Utopia*,

pp. 146–7). The contradiction partly resolves itself in the ability of one family to borrow distinction from the conspicuous consumption of its neighbors.

44. Jackson's discussion of the yard (*Crabgrass Frontier,* pp. 54–61) has helped me here.

45. Marsh, *Suburban Lives,* p. xiii; see also p. 41.

46. Karen Halttunen makes this point and uses this phrase in *Confidence Men and Painted Women; A Study of Middle-Class Culture in America, 1830–1870* (New Haven, Conn.: Yale University Press, 1982), pp. 37–9.

47. The suburb was not the only possible resolution for capitalist middle classes: things happened differently in France. But neither was the suburb a uniquely American resolution: in fact suburban development here partially followed models already established in England. See Fishman, *Bourgeois Utopias,* especially chapters 2–4.

48. Gwendolyn Wright, *Moralism and the Model Home* (Chicago: University of Chicago Press, 1980), p. 83.

49. Ibid., pp. 86–9; Gwendolyn Wright, *Building the Dream; A Social History of Housing in America* (New York: Pantheon, 1981), pp. 100–102; Alan Gowans, *The Comfortable House; North American Suburban Architecture 1890–1930* (Cambridge, Mass.: MIT Press, 1986), pp. 46–8.

50. Wright, *Moralism and the Model Home,* pp. 81–2.

51. I have drawn here on Wright, *Moralism and the Model Home* and *Building the Dream;* Gowans, *The Comfortable House;* Cohn, *The Palace or the Poorhouse;* Handlin, *American Homes;* and Jackson, *Crabgrass Frontier.*

52. In addition to sources mentioned in the last note, see Clifford Edward Clark, Jr, *The American Family Home, 1800–1960,* (Chapel Hill, N.C.: University of North Carolina Press, 1986), and Colleen McDannell, *The Christian Home in Victorian America, 1840–1900* (Bloomington, Ind.: Indiana University Press, 1986).

53. Wright and Gowans have been particularly helpful to me, here.

54. Wright, *Building the Dream,* p. 112.

55. Marsh, *Suburban Lives,* pp. 29–31; 84–6.

56. Wright, *Moralism and the Model Home,* pp. 89–90; Lynd and Lynd, *Middletown,* p. 97; Susan Strasser, *Never Done; A History of American Housework* (New York: Pantheon, 1982), pp. 93–7.

57. Beecher's remark is from an 1859 paper called "Building a House," quoted by Clark, *The American Family Home,* p. 104. Church's comes from an article of May, 1884, called "City Interiors," and is quoted by Wright in *Building the Dream,* p. 113.

58. Kenneth L. Ames, "Meaning in Artifacts: Hall Furnishings in Victorian America," *Journal of Interdisciplinary History,* vol. 9, Summer 1978, pp. 19–46.

59. Katherine C. Grier develops this idea at length in *Culture & Comfort; People, Parlors, and Upholstery, 1850–1930* (Rochester, N.Y.: The Strong Museum, 1988), from which I have learned much about the conventional vocabulary of parlor furnishings. Also revealing are the hundreds of photographs and the commentary in William Seale, *The Tasteful Interlude; American Interiors through the Camera's Eye, 1860–1917* (New York: Praeger, 1975).

60. See Grier, *Culture & Comfort,* chapter 3, on the "rhetoric" of parlor furnishing.

61. Sarah Orne Jewett, *The Country of the Pointed Firs and Other Stories* (Garden City: Doubleday Anchor Books, 1956), pp. 41–2. The novel was first published in 1896.

62. William Dean Howells, *The Landlord at Lion's Head* (New York: Dover, 1983), pp. 28, 54–5; original book publication, 1897. Mary E. Wilkins, *A New England Nun and Other Stories* (New York: Harper, 1891), pp. 4, 6, 455, 463.

63. Mary Antin, *The Promised Land* (Boston: Houghton Mifflin, 1912), 272, 274; Louise Bolard More, *Wage-Earners' Budgets; A Study of Standards and Cost of Living in*

New York City (New York: Henry Holt, 1907), pp. 132–3; Margaret F. Byington, *Homestead; The Households of a Mill Town* (New York: Russell Sage Foundation, 1910), pp. 55–6; see also Lizabeth A. Cohen, "Embellishing a Life of Labor: An Interpretation of the Material Culture of American Working-Class Homes, 1885–1915," *Journal of American Culture*, vol. 3, Spring 1980, pp. 752–75.

64. Esther Barrows, *Neighbors All; A Settlement Notebook* (Boston: Houghton Mifflin, 1919), p. 37; quoted by Cohen, "Embellishing a Life," p. 761. I have followed Cohen on several of these points; see especially pp. 756–8 and 767.

65. Grier, *Culture & Comfort*, pp. 136–7.

66. Seale's *The Tasteful Interlude*, juxtaposing photos of millionaires' rooms and of middle class interiors, shows graphically how the latter imitated the former, but without the services of artist, artisan, and professional decorator.

67. Louis C. Elson, *History of American Music* (New York: Macmillan, 1904), p. 279; quoted in Craig H. Roell, *The Piano in America, 1890–1940* (Chapel Hill, N.C.: University of North Carolina Press, 1989), p. xi. In fact, pianos advertised in the *Ladies' Home Journal* in 1896 cost from $40 up, close to 10 percent of an annual working class wage.

68. Seale, *The Tasteful Interlude*, p. 21. On this ecletic moment, see Gail Caskey Winkler and Roger W. Moss, *Victorian Interior Decoration; American Interiors, 1830–1900* (New York: Henry Holt, 1986), pp. 184–5.

69. Grier, *Culture & Comfort*, p. 193. On the transition from parlor to living room, see also Clark, *The American Family Home*, pp. 132, 144; and for a rich account, Karen Halttunen, "From Parlor to Living Room; Domestic Space, Interior Decoration, and the Culture of Personality," in Simon J. Bronner, ed., *Consuming Visions; Accumulation and Display of Goods in America, 1880–1920* (New York: W. W. Norton, 1989), pp. 157–90. I would locate the emergence of "personality" as a referent earlier than Halttunen does, in the efflorescence of eccentric taste through the high Victorian period.

70. Jean-Christophe Agnew, "A House of Fiction: Domestic Interiors and the Commodity Aesthetic," in Bronner, ed., *Consuming Visions*, p. 135.

71. Kenneth L. Ames, *Death in the Dining Room and Other Tales of Victorian Culture* (Philadelphia: Temple University Press, 1992), pp. 38–41.

72. John F. Kasson, *Rudeness and Civility; Manners in Nineteenth-Century Urban America* (New York: Hill and Wang, 1990), p. 173.

73. Ames, *Death in the Dining Room*, p. 38.

74. Halttunen, *Confidence Men and Painted Women*, pp. 102–3. Her first quotation is from D. Mackellar, *A Treatise on the Art of Politeness, Good Breeding, and Manners*, 1855; the other two are from *The Habits of Good Society; A Handbook for Ladies and Gentlemen*, anonymous, 1869.

75. Susan R. Williams, "Introduction," *Dining in America, 1850-1900*, Kathryn Grover, ed. (Amherst, Mass.: University of Massachusetts Press, 1987), pp. 11–14.

76. See Kasson, "Table Manners and the Control of Appetites," in *Rudeness and Civility*, chapter 6. Some of the essays in Grover, ed., *Dining In America*, spell out the dictates of refinement in temperance (W.J. Rorabaugh, "Beer, Lemonade, and Propriety in the Gilded Age"), dining room design (Clifford E. Clark, Jr, "The Vision of the Dining Room: Plan Book Dreams and Middle-Class Realities"), and utensils (Dorothy Rainwater, "Victorian Dining Silver"). Kenneth L. Ames's chapter, "Death in the Dining Room," in his book by the same title, explores the representation of culture and nature in the carved sideboard of the third quarter of the century.

77. Halttunen's chapter 5, "Mourning the Dead: A Study in Sentimental Ritual," in *Confidence Men and Painted Women*, nicely describes one of these ceremonies and the contradictions within it.

78. Halttunen, *Confidence Men and Painted Women*, pp. 115–16; I also draw upon Kasson, *Rudeness and Civility*, pp. 121–6.

79. I think of characters like Mrs Manson Mingott, in Edith Wharton's *The Age of Innocence.*

80. Karen Halttunen, "From Parlor to Living Room," in Bronner, ed., *Consuming Visions,* p. 169.

81. Ames, *Death in the Dining Room,* p. 237.

82. Katherine C. Grier, "The Decline of the Memory Palace: The Parlor after 1890," in Jessica H. Foy and Thomas J. Schlereth, eds, *American Home Life, 1880–1930; A Social History of Spaces and Services* (Knoxville, Tenn.: University of Tennessee Press, 1992), p. 67.

83. Lynd and Lynd, *Middletown,* p. 275.

84. I have been helped in these thoughts by Blumin, *The Emergence of the Middle Class,* pp. 284–5; Warner, *Streetcar Suburbs,* pp. 157–60; and Halttunen, "From Parlor to Living Room," pp. 168–9.

85. Robert H. Wiebe, *The Search for Order, 1877–1920* (New York: Hill and Wang, 1967), p. 119.

86. Margaret Marsh, *Suburban Lives,* p. 100.

87. Blumin, *The Emergence of the Middle Class,* pp. 220–21.

88. There is a large body of scholarship on this subject. A few works that have been of special help: Gilkeson, *Middle-Class Providence, 1820–1940;* Ryan, *Cradle of the Middle Class;* Marsh, *Suburban Lives;* Anne Firor Scott, *Natural Allies; Women's Association in American History* (Urbana, Ill.: University of Illinois Press, 1991); Karen J. Blair, *The Clubwoman as Feminist; True Womanhood Redefined, 1868–1914* (New York: Holmes & Meier, 1980); and Mary Ann Clawson, *Constructing Brotherhood: Class, Gender, and Fraternalism* (Princeton, N.J.: Princeton University Press, 1989).

89. Marsh, *Suburban Lives,* p. 109; Blair, *Clubwoman as Feminist,* p. 62.

90. See Clawson, *Constructing Brotherhood,* pp. 178–210.

91. Wiebe, *The Search for Order,* p. 128.

92. Faye E. Dudden, *Serving Women; Household Service in Nineteenth-Century America* (Middletown, Conn.: Wesleyan University Press, 1983), pp. 136–7; Blumin, *The Emergence of the Middle Class,* pp. 185, 238.

93. Blumin, *The Emergence of the Middle Class,* p. 238; Sheila M. Rothman, *Woman's Proper Place; A History of Changing Ideals and Practices, 1870 to the Present* (New York: Basic Books, 1978), pp. 19–21; Susan Porter Benson, *Counter Cultures; Saleswomen, Managers, and Customers in American Department Stores, 1890–1940* (Urbana, Ill.: University of Illinois Press, 1986), pp. 83–5, 89–90; William R. Leach, "Transformations in a Culture of Consumption: Women and Department Stores, 1890–1925," *Journal of American History,* vol. 71, September 1984, pp. 319–42; for the arrival of the bargain basement, see Leach, *Land of Desire; Merchants, Power, and the Rise of a New American Culture* (New York: Pantheon, 1993), p. 78.

94. Richard H. Brodhead, *Cultures of Letters; Scenes of Reading and Writing in Nineteenth-Century America* (Chicago: University of Chicago Press, 1993), pp. 125–31; William W. Stowe, *Going Abroad: European Travel in Nineteenth-Century American Culture* (Princeton, N.J.: Princeton University Press, 1994), especially chapters 1–3; Hugh De Santis, "The Democratization of Travel: The Travel Agent in American History," *Journal of American Culture,* vol. 1, Spring 1978, pp. 1–17; Horace Sutton, *Travelers; The American Tourist from Stagecoach to Space Shuttle* (New York: William Morrow, 1980), pp. 56–100; Donna R. Braden, *Leisure and Entertainment in America* (Dearborn, Mich.: Henry Ford Museum & Greenfield Village, 1988), pp. 295–320.

95. De Santis, "The Democratization of Travel," p. 7; James Gilbert, "Imagining the City," in James Gilbert, Amy Gilman, Donald M. Scott, and Joan W. Scott, eds, *The Mythmaking Frame of Mind; Social Imagination and American Culture* (Belmont, Calif.: Wadsworth Publishing Co., 1993), pp. 141, 147; Dean MacCannell, *The Tourist; A New Theory of the Leisure Class* (New York: Schocken Books, 1976), pp. 60–62; Braden, *Leisure and Entertainment in America,* pp. 299–301; John F. Sears, *Sacred Places; American*

NOTES TO PAGES 158 TO 166

Tourist Attractions in the Nineteenth Century (New York: Oxford University Press, 1989), pp. 12–30; Lawrence Levine, *Highbrow/Lowbrow; The Emergence of Cultural Hierarchy in America* (Cambridge, Mass.: Harvard University Press, 1988), p. 208. I have drawn some general ideas from MacCannell's and Sears's books.

96. Levine, *Highbrow/Lowbrow;* DiMaggio, "Cultural Entrepreneurship in Nineteenth-Century Boston: The Creation of an Organizational Base for High Culture in America," and "Cultural Entrepreneurship in Nineteenth-Century Boston, Part II: The Classification and Framing of American Art," *Media, Culture and Society*, vol. 4, 1982, pp. 33–50, 303–22; Trachtenberg, *The Incorporation of America; Culture and Society in the Gilded Age* (New York: Hill and Wang, 1982), especially pp. 140–81.

97. Lefebvre develops this idea of representations at length in *The Production of Space*, beginning on p. 38. I have also found helpful Part III, "The Experience of Space and Time," in David Harvey, *The Condition of Postmodernity; An Enquiry into the Origins of Cultural Change* (Oxford: Basil Blackwell, 1989), pp. 201–323.

98. I have been helped in this formulation by Stephanie Coontz, *The Social Origins of Private Life; A History of American Families, 1600–1900* (New York: Verso, 1988), especially pp. 11–14. I draw on her work for other ideas over the next few pages.

99. Ibid, p. 35; see also pp. 336–7. Earlier in this paragraph I allude to the familiar distinction between character and personality drawn by Warren I. Susman in *Culture as History; The Transformation of American Society in the Twentieth Century* (New York: Pantheon, 1984); see chapter 17, "'Personality' and the Making of Twentieth-Century Culture."

100. *Historical Statistics of the United States; From Colonial Times to 1970*, pp. 368–9. These numbers are not so firm as they sound: see Theodore R. Sizer, *Secondary Schools at the Turn of the Century* (New Haven, Conn.: Yale University Press, 1964), pp. 36–7.

101. Burton J. Bledstein, *The Culture of Professionalism; The Middle Class and the Development of Higher Education in America* (New York: W. W. Norton, 1976), p. 6.

102. See Barbara and John Ehrenreich, "The Professional-Managerial Class," in Pat Walker, ed., *Between Labor and Capital* (Boston, Mass.: South End Press, 1979), pp. 5–45; David Noble, "The PMC: A Critique," in the same volume, pp. 121–42; Dale L. Johnson, ed., *Class and Social Development, A New Theory of the Middle Class* (Beverly Hills, Calif.: Sage Publications, 1982), pp. 87–109; Magali Sarfatti Larson, *The Rise of Professionalism; A Sociological Analysis* (Berkeley, Calif.: University of California Press, 1977); Bledstein, *The Culture of Professionalism*; and Richard Ohmann, *English in America; A Radical View of the Profession* (New York: Oxford University Press, 1976), chapters 8–11. Many analysts have commented on the diversity of knowledges, practices, and statuses encompassed within some conceptions of the PMC (or the "new class"). See, for instance, Eliot Friedson, *Professional Powers: A Study of the Institutionalization of Formal Knowledge* (Chicago: University of Chicago Press, 1986), pp. 20–62. But the fact that a census category changes over time, and may comprise such diverse occupations as health administrator and bar manager does not call into question the validity of concepts like the PMC; Friedson, for all his empirical caution, has no trouble distinguishing the bar manager from the health administrator in his helpful analysis of credentialing and knowledge.

103. The best discussion, and my main source for these paragraphs, is Susan Strasser, *Never Done*.

104. Ibid., p. 45; David W. Miller, "Technology and the Ideal; Production Quality and Kitchen Reform in Nineteenth-Century America," in Kathryn Grover, ed., *Dining in America*, pp. 59, 71–3.

105. See for instance Delores Hayden, *The Grand Domestic Revolution: A History of Feminist Designs for American Homes, Neighborhoods, and Cities* (Cambridge, Mass.: MIT Press, 1981), p. 16 and elsewhere. But the material and domestic feminists whose

movements Hayden traces may have unintentionally made things tougher for the modernizing housewife, by hiking up the standards of domestic "science."

106. More, *Wage-Earners' Budgets*, pp. 211–27; Byington, *Homestead*, pp. 66–8; Robert Coit Chapin, *The Standard of Living among Workingmen's Families in New York City* (New York: Charities Publication Committee, 1909), pp. 154–66.

107. Lynd and Lynd, *Middletown*, pp. 169–70; Martha Bensley Bruère and Robert W. Bruère, *Increasing Home Efficiency* (New York: Macmillan, 1914), pp. 97, 298–313; David M. Katzman, *Seven Days a Week; Women and Domestic Service in Industrializing America* (New York: Oxford University Press, 1978), p. 61; Lucy Maynard Salmon, *Domestic Service* (New York: Macmillan, 1897), pp. vii–viii; Faye E. Dudden, *Serving Women*, p. 78. Kenneth Jackson estimates (without giving sources) that 10 percent of the residents of major cities could afford home ownership and at least one servant, in the 1880s (*Crabgrass Frontier*, p. 89).

108. There is now a lot of scholarship on these developments. Just a few of the studies that have influenced my brief summary are Strasser, *Never Done*, especially chapter 11; Wright, *Moralism and the Model Home*; Dudden, *Serving Women*, especially chapter 4; Barbara Ehrenreich and Deirdre English, *For Her Own Good; 150 Years of the Experts' Advice to Women* (New York: Anchor Books, 1979); Eleanor T. Fordyce, "Cookbooks of the 1800s," in Grover, ed., *Dining in America*, pp. 85–113; and William D. Andrews and Debora C. Andrews, "Technology and the Housewife in Nineteenth-Century America," *Women's Studies*, vol. 2, 1974, pp. 309–28.

109. Ellen H. Richards, *The Cost of Living as Modified by Sanitary Science* (New York: John Wiley & Sons, 1899), pp. 33, 34, 37. Richards, a Vassar graduate, taught Sanitary Chemistry at MIT, and campaigned for rational and thrifty middle class domesticity.

110. Bruère and Bruère, *Increasing Home Efficiency*, pp. 294, 298–313, 315.

111. Daniel Horowitz has written helpfully about these studies in *The Morality of Spending*, especially in chapter 6. He points out that the Bruères' attention to particular families' strategies and explanations of them itself individuates them, while studies of working class life tend to mass their subjects together (pp. 102–3). A recent historical study of personal consumption reveals that in 1900 the average per capita expenditure for recreation, education, religion, welfare, and travel was about 9 percent of total expenditures: Stanley Lebergott, *Pursuing Happiness; American Consumers in the Twentieth Century* (Princeton, N.J.: Princeton University Press, 1993), pp. 148–51. On the assumption that a quarter or so of the population accounted for nearly all expenditures in these categories, Lebergott's figures accord reasonably well with those of Richards and the Bruères.

112. I allude here to a burgeoning corpus of scholarship, including Kathy Peiss, *Cheap Amusements; Working Women and Leisure in Turn-of-the-Century New York* (Philadelphia: Temple University Press, 1986); Roy Rosenzweig, *Eight Hours for What We Will; Workers and Leisure in an Industrial City, 1870–1920* (Cambridge: Cambridge University Press, 1983); John Kasson, *Amusing the Million; Coney Island at the Turn of the Century* (New York: Hill and Wang, 1978); Richard Butsch, ed., *For Fun and Profit; The Transformation of Leisure into Consumption* (Philadelphia: Temple University Press, 1990).

113. Simon N. Patten, *The New Basis of Civilization* (New York: Macmillan, 1968); originally given as lectures in 1905 and published in 1907. Patten's whole chapter, "The Basis in Amusement," is remarkable for welcoming cheap commercial culture, along with edifying free schools and public lectures, while maintaining the condescension toward working class tastes that was shared by his fellow PMC reformers.

114. Blumin, *The Emergence of the Middle Class*, p. 11, and throughout.

115. Ibid., pp. 267–71, 290–97; Harry Braverman, *Labor and Monopoly Capital; The Degradation of Work in the Twentieth Century* (New York: Monthly Review Press, 1974), especially chapters 15 and 16.

116. Jurgen Kocka, *White Collar Workers in America 1890–1940; A Social-Political*

History in International Perspective, trans. Maura Kealey (London: Sage Publications, 1980), p. 77.

117. Anthony Giddens, *The Class Structure of the Advanced Societies* (London: Hutchinson University Library, 1973), pp. 111–12, 185–6. These terms, like everything else about class, are contested and problematic. I choose not to enter the theoretical debates on class, except in passing, but hope to contribute to them through this historical analysis of the PMC. Readers familiar with them will see that I accept the marxian premise of two fundamental classes in capitalist society, and understand middle classes in shifting relation to those two. But I take middle classes to be a permanent if always highly variable feature of such societies, not vestiges of older systems, nor necessarily precursors of new systems.

118. The first two of these phrases are from T. J. Jackson Lears, "From Salvation to Self-Realization: Advertising and the Therapeutic Roots of the Consumer Culture, 1880–1930," in Richard Wightman Fox and T. J. Jackson Lears, eds, *The Culture of Consumption: Critical Essays in American History, 1880–1980* (New York: Pantheon, 1983), p. 21. The other two are from Jean-Christophe Agnew, "A House of Fiction; Domestic Interiors and the Commodity Aesthetic," in Bronner, *Consuming Visions*, pp. 135, 153. Both Lears and Agnew, who have taught me much about these matters, distance themselves somewhat from what Agnew calls "the commodity aesthetic" and from the notion of the isolated self constructing identity from meanings supplied by advertising.

119. Michael Schudson, *Advertising, the Uneasy Persuasion; Its Dubious Impact on American Society* (New York: Basic Books, 1984), p. 155. Although I am critical of Schudson on this and some other points, he, too, has been influential in my thinking. These paragraphs also owe something to Mary Douglas and Baron Isherwood, *The World of Goods* (New York: Basic Books, 1979), who keep class and social standing alive throughout their analysis of how people "think with" goods.

120. Schudson, *Advertising, the Uneasy Persuasion*, p. 145.

121. William Leiss, Stephen Kline, and Sut Jhally summarize a large body of research along these lines in *Social Communication in Advertising; Persons, Products, and Images of Well-Being* (Toronto: Methuen, 1986), especially pp. 251–5.

122. Douglas and Isherwood, *The World of Goods*, chapter 6.

123. Mary Elizabeth Wilson Sherwood, *Modern Manners and Social Usage* (New York: Harper & Brothers, 1897), p. 314; quoted in John Kasson, *Rudeness and Civility*, p. 202.

124. More, *Wage-Earners' Budgets*, pp. 103, 142; Chapin, *The Standard of Living Among Workingmen's Families in New York City*, pp. 215, 218; Byington, *Homestead*, p. 88.

8. The Discourse of Advertising

1. William Leiss, Stephen Kline, and Sut Jhally, *Social Communication in Advertising; Persons, Products, and Images of Well-Being* (Toronto: Nelson, 1986), p. 175.

2. Daniel Pope, *The Making of Modern Advertising* (New York: Basic Books, 1983), p. 235. Probably the figures actually mean that 18 and 43 percent of ad pages carried single displays. The other reading of them doesn't jibe with evidence from my copies of *Century*.

3. David M. Potter, *People of Plenty; Economic Abundance and the American Character* (Chicago: University of Chicago Press, 1954), pp. 169–70; Potter bases this on an unspecified study by the 1920s advertising researcher Daniel Starch.

4. Richard Pollay, "The Subsiding Sizzle: Shifting Strategies in Twentieth-Century Magazine Advertising," History of Advertising Archives, University of British Columbia, Faculty of Commerce, May 1983; cited by Michael Schudson, *Advertising*,

the Uneasy Persuasion; its Dubious Impact on American Society (New York: Basic Books, 1984), p. 60.

5. I stress the simultaneity because recent scholars have tended to locate these changes in a later time, usually the 1920s. (This may be because turn-of-the-century magazine ads are hard to find.) Schudson, for instance, says that "ads with little or no written message . . . would have been unknown fifty or sixty years ago" (*Advertising, the Uneasy Persuasion*, p. 63). In fact, the 1890s audience knew them well; see the post-script to this chapter for discussion.

6. *J. Walter Thompson Advertising*, 1897, pp. 19, 20; *The Thompson Red Book on Advertising*, 1904–05, p. 13; H.C. Brown, "Art in Advertising," *Printers' Ink*, 7 January 1891, p. 10; *The Thompson Red Book on Advertising*, 1901, p. 10. The Thompson pub-lications are available in the J. Walter Thompson Company Archives at Duke University (Special Collections).

7. I adopt the terms "icon," "symbol," and "index" from Torben Vestergaard and Kim Schroder, *The Language of Advertising* (Oxford: Basil Blackwell, 1985).

8. Marchand, *Advertising the American Dream; Making Way for Modernity, 1920–1940* (Berkeley, Calif.: University of California Press, 1985), p. 165.

9. Judith Williamson, *Decoding Advertisements; Ideology and Meaning in Advertising* (London: Marion Boyars, 1978), p. 14. Those who know this rich study will recognize that its influence on the following pages is greater than indicated by my specific citations.

10. Earnest Elmo Calkins, *"and hearing not –" Annals of an Adman* (New York: Charles Scribner's Sons, 1946), p. 161.

11. James Playsted Wood, *The Story of Advertising* (New York: Ronald Press, 1958), p. 224.

12. Reproduced in Russell B. Adams, Jr, *King C. Gillette: The Man and His Wonderful Shaving Device* (Boston: Little, Brown, 1978), opposite p. 57.

13. It resembled the editorial persona of many of the magazines, whose voice Christopher P. Wilson describes as "colloquial, forceful, direct, and seemingly per-sonal," in "The Rhetoric of Consumption: Mass-Market Magazines and the Demise of the Gentle Reader, 1880–1920," in Richard Wightman Fox and T.J. Jackson Lears, eds, *The Culture of Consumption: Critical Essays in American History, 1880–1980* (New York: Pantheon, 1983), p. 55. But that is to anticipate a later part of my argument.

14. *J.Walter Thompson Advertising*, 1895, p. 16; emphasis added.

15. To my knowledge, no one from inside the industry has ever confirmed any one of Key's findings about subliminal erotic messages in ads: *Subliminal Seduction* (New York: Signet, 1972); *Media Sexploitation* (New York: Signet, 1976). Given the rewards an informant might claim, the failure of any to step forward makes Key's readings seem even more improbable than they originally did. Ads do not work chiefly by sneaking past conscious perception and addressing the unconscious; they work with and on what we do see and know, though much of that knowledge is tacit, so routine that we do not think of it as knowledge.

16. The most comprehensive study is Robert Jay, *The Trade Card in Nineteenth-Century America* (Columbia, Mo.: University of Missouri Press, 1987). Jay's 170 illustrations offer a fine sampling of trade card iconography.

17. See, for instance, figures 76, 89, 134, and 147 in Jay's book.

18. T.J. Jackson Lears, *Fables of Abundance: A Cultural History of Advertising in America* (New York: Basic Books, 1994); see especially pp. 102–13 and 142–53. Lears rightly notes that when agencies took over advertising they adapted some elements of the "older carnivalesque discourse" (e.g., the Quaker in the mirror) to their "util-itarian" purposes (p. 97), but most agency ads, like the ones reproduced in this chapter, bend imagery to commodification far more purposefully than did the designers of trade cards.

19. Looking back on the 1880s, an ad man at Wanamaker's (the Philadelphia

department store) said the staff knew the "value" of pictures in ads, but did not know how to "supply the demand"; "we were on entirely new ground then." Manly Gillam, interview in *Dry Goods Economist*, 17 September 1904; quoted by William Leach in *Land of Desire: Merchants, Power, and the Rise of a New American Culture* (New York: Pantheon, 1993), pp. 43–4.

20. The others are neatness, efficiency, modernity, and thriftiness. Obviously there is a good deal of overlap among these categories, hence some arbitrariness in my classification of individual ads; so I take my counts as suggestive, only.

21. The phrase is Marchand's (*Advertising the American Dream*, p. xxi), and he nicely explores this theme. His subtitle (*Making Way for Modernity, 1920–1940*) may imply that it was novel in the postwar period. It was not.

22. Servant and pickaninny were the two main positions for black people in ads. I will discuss conceptions of race in chapter 9.

23. Quoted by E.S. Turner, *The Shocking History of Advertising* (London: Michael Joseph, 1952), p. 168.

24. Stuart Ewen, *Captains of Consciousness; Advertising and the Social Roots of the Consumer Culture* (New York: McGraw-Hill, 1976).

25. Robert S. Lynd and Helen Merrell Lynd, *Middletown: A Study in American Culture* (New York: Harcourt, Brace & World, 1929), p. 82. Pope cites (*Making of Modern Advertising*, p. 243) a study claiming to show that negative ads were much less common in 1920 than in 1900. I find that hard to believe. Perhaps scare copy increased rapidly just after 1920; or perhaps the magazines covered by the study (*Harper's Weekly, Literary Digest, Collier's*) were different from the monthlies I have examined. Fear and anxiety leap out from the 1920s pages of the latter. E.S. Turner confirms my impression (*The Shocking History of Advertising*, pp. 184–5).

26. The phrase "compensatory fulfillment" is from Richard Wightman Fox, "Epitaph for Middletown; Robert S. Lynd and the Analysis of Consumer Culture," in Fox, Lears, eds, *The Culture of Consumption*, p. 125. Fox, speaking of the 1920s, is reserved about this view. Less so Sut Jhally, who makes the sad loss of traditional meaning central to his interesting last chapter in *The Codes of Advertising: Fetishism and the Political Economy of Meaning in the Consumer Society* (New York: St Martin's Press, 1987), pp. 173–205. The analysis is a strong one, but not for the period and the social class I am studying.

27. T.J. Jackson Lears, "Some Versions of Fantasy: Toward a Cultural History of American Advertising," *Prospects: An Annual of American Cultural Studies*, vol. 9, 1984, p. 392.

28. In an ad he placed in *J. Walter Thompson Advertising*, 1895.

29. Leiss, Kline, and Jhally, *Social Communication*, p. 47. For the next few paragraphs I join a kind of consensus emerging from their work and that of other recent scholars like Schudson, Marchand, Williamson, Lears, and Pope.

30. Raymond Williams, "Advertising: The Magic System," in *Problems in Materialism and Culture* (London: Verso, 1980), p. 188.

31. The last few sentences draw upon and add to some comments of Alan Trachtenberg in *The Incorporation of America; Culture and Society in the Gilded Age* (New York: Hill and Wang, 1982), pp. 135–9.

32. I respond here to Schudson, *Advertising, the Uneasy Persuasion*, pp. 175–7.

9. Charting Social Space

1. Alan Trachtenberg, *The Incorporation of America; Culture and Society in the Gilded Age* (New York: Hill & Wang, 1982), p. 143. Trachtenberg's discussion throughout his chapter 5, "The Politics of Culture," is most helpful.

2. "The Third Anniversary of the Founding of McClure's Magazine," *McClure's*, June 1896, p. 97.

3. "Cheap Magazines," *McClure's*, August 1895, p. 88.

4. A. H. Zander, "Living on $200 a Year," *LHJ*, March 1898, p. 6.

5. Salme Harju Steinberg, *Reformer in the Marketplace; Edward W. Bok and The Ladies' Home Journal* (Baton Rouge, La.: Louisiana State University Press, 1979), pp. 3–4.

6. Mrs D.B. Fitzgerald, "Buying and Cooking Terrapin," *LHJ*, February 1896, p. 31. (You do it by buying *small* terrapin.)

7. Henry Mills Alden, *Magazine Writing and the New Literature* (New York: Harper, 1908), p. 193.

8. George Britt, *Forty Years – Forty Millions; The Career of Frank A. Munsey* (New York: Farrar & Rinehart, 1935), p. 79.

9. Those magazines themselves gradually moved away from their old aristocratic formulas: they virtually dropped the "old-fashioned travel article," increased the number of timely articles, and printed more short stories. See Arthur Reed Kimball, "The Invasion of Journalism," *Atlantic*, July 1900, p. 124. The new magazines turned in this direction more abruptly, and led the way. From here on, until the last section of the chapter, I base my conclusions mainly on a survey of *Cosmopolitan* XX (November 1895–April 1896), *McClure's* VII (June 1896–October 1896), *Munsey's* XVI (November 1896–March 1897), and a more irregular sampling of the *Ladies' Home Journal* at about the same time. My aim is to discern patterns that held steady during these early years of the magazine revolution.

10. On this difference between newspapers and magazines, Anthony Smith is helpful, in *Goodbye Gutenberg; The Newspaper Revolution of the 1980s* (New York: Oxford University Press, 1980), especially pp. 29–30.

11. Arthur Sherburne Hardy, *Things Remembered* (Boston: Houghton Mifflin, 1923), p. 275.

12. Charles Hanson Towne, *Adventures in Editing* (New York: D. Appleton and Company, 1926), pp. 38–9.

13. *The Americanization of Edward Bok; The Autobiography of a Dutch Boy Fifty Years After* (New York: Charles Scribner's Sons, 1921), pp. 292–3; 163. The "real human being" Bok projected spoke in a hectoring and paternalistic voice, not just an intimate one. See Helen Damon-Moore, *Magazines for the Millions; Gender and Commerce in the Ladies' Home Journal and the Saturday Evening Post, 1880–1910* (Albany, N.Y.: State University of New York Press, 1994), pp. 66–71, for a good discussion.

14. "McClure's Magazine – Reminiscences and Forecasts," October 1897, p. 1101.

15. A rhetorical oddity in support of this claim: many or most articles came to a stop without what I would regard as a conclusion. They ended with just one more fact. An article on the country seat of the Tsars ended by saying that two reporters tried to interview the author as he left. One on the overland mail service finished with the news that it now had eleven divisions and seven thousand clerks. An article on the Lyceum: Anna E. Dickinson "had no rival among living orators" for "vituperation and denunciation." One on English silver: "The present year ends a cycle, and accordingly its date letter is U in a shield." (These from *Cosmopolitan*, March and April 1896. The feature was even more pronounced in *Munsey's*.) If an article's aim is enumeration, one stopping place is as good as another.

16. This point has been made in a somewhat different and quite powerful way by Christopher P. Wilson, "The Rhetoric of Consumption; Mass-Market Magazines and the Demise of the Gentle Reader, 1880–1920," in Richard Wightman Fox and T. J. Jackson Lears, eds, *The Culture of Consumption: Critical Essays in American History, 1880–1980* (New York: Pantheon, 1983), pp. 39–64. See also Wilson's *The Labor of Words; Literary Professionalism in the Progressive Era* (Athens, Ga.: University of Georgia Press, 1985), especially chapter 2, "'Magazining' for the Masses." Wilson says much

about the editorial methods practiced at the new magazines and about their "consumer rhetoric" that has influenced my thinking, and that parallels my argument.

17. I omit places – Venezuela, South Africa, China – represented not as potential holiday destinations but as politically and economically important societies on which a well informed (and imperially conscious) reader would want information and expert analysis.

18. In January 1896, he ran an article on "Ancient Lineage" by Edward Harlow, debunking the "common opinion" that European aristocracy and royalty can trace their nobility many generations into the past.

19. Except in a certain kind of fiction, to be discussed in the next chapter.

20. Of course the magazine printed much new fiction, but did not promote it in the way *McClure's* did; rather, it offered in effect cracking good stories and dependable generic experiences.

21. *Munsey's* came later to such forecasting. Articles on the automobile in 1903 predicted cheap cars, growth of suburbs, and the installment plan!

22. S.S. McClure, *My Autobiography* (London: John Murray, 1914), pp. 207–8.

23. Britt, *Forty Years – Forty Millions,* pp. 95–6.

24. Thanks to John Peckham of Meriden Gravure, who went over a number of illustrations with me and explained the mélange of techniques that had gone into their making.

25. I take this and much else from Estelle Jussim, *Visual Communication and the Graphic Arts; Photographic Technologies in the Nineteenth Century* (New York: R.R. Bowker, 1974), pp. 47–8. I have also learned from William M. Ivins, Jr, *Prints and Visual Communication* (Cambridge, Mass.: Harvard University Press, 1953), and, on the technical side, from Louis Walton Sipley, *The Photomechanical Halftone* (Philadelphia: American Museum of Photography, 1958).

26. On this debate, see for example Neil Harris, "Iconography and Intellectual History," in John Higham and Paul K. Conkin, eds, *New Directions in American Intellectual History,* (Baltimore, Md.: Johns Hopkins University Press, 1979), pp. 196–211. For an interesting account of how photographers as well as their audiences began to dichotomize the practice into art and documentary, see Allan Sekula, "On the Invention of Photographic Meaning," in Victor Burgin, ed., *Thinking Photography* (London: Macmillan, 1982), pp. 84–109.

27. Oddly, to the modern eye, photographs generally depicted lack of motion; for frozen "action," one must turn to illustrations and other art work.

28. These relations and feelings are thoughtfully explicated by Carol Shloss, *In Visible Light; Photography and the American Writer: 1840–1940* (New York: Oxford University Press, 1987); and Maren Stange, *Symbols of Ideal Life; Social Documentary Photography in America, 1890–1950* (Cambridge: Cambridge University Press, 1989).

29. Jussim, *Visual Communication,* p. 214.

30. John Tagg, "The Currency of the Photograph," in Burgin, ed., *Thinking Photography,* p. 133. McLuhan made this point about media, in a more generalized way.

31. Victor Burgin, "Photographic Practice and the Art Theory," in *Thinking Photography,* p. 41.

32. Robert Stinson, "McClure's Road to *McClure's*: How Revolutionary Were 1890s Magazines," *Journalism Quarterly,* vol. 47, Summer 1970, pp. 256–62.

33. Daniel Boorstin, "From Hero to Celebrity," in *The Image; Or What Happened to the American Dream* (New York: Atheneum, 1962), pp. 45–76.

34. For 1894–1903, his sample differs from mine only in including the *Century* instead of the *Ladies' Home Journal*; his working category is "general" monthly magazines with large circulations.

35. McClure, *My Autobiography,* p. 221. He attributed a 50 percent increase in one month to the first installment of Tarbell's biography.

36. Peter Lyon, *Success Story; The Life and Times of S.S. McClure* (New York: Scribner's, 1963), p. 134.

37. Likewise, *Munsey's* praised Tiffany for uniting "technical aims," successful business practices, utility, and "art," with no detriment to the latter (December 1896, pp. 266–8).

38. T.J. Jackson Lears, *No Place of Grace; The Quest for Alternatives in Modern American Culture, 1880–1920* (New York: Pantheon, 1981). I see in the ads of the period the same quest for self realization and "real life" that Lears finds there, but without much of the anxiety (see chapter 8).

39. See Steinberg, *Reformer in the Marketplace*, especially pp. 19–21. An unsigned article in *Cosmopolitan*, presumably by Walker, on "The Making of an Illustrated Magazine" boasts that the leaders "have been at all times untrammeled by any adverse advertising influence" (January 1893, p. 272).

40. James L. Ford, *Forty-Odd Years in the Literary Shop* (New York: E.P. Dutton, 1921, p. 118.

41. Quoted by Larzer Ziff, *The American 1890s; Life and Times of a Lost Generation* (New York: Viking, 1966), p. 126. Ziff's treatment of these matters is excellent, though with a disproportionate emphasis on sexual taboos.

42. A decade later, sex could also be treated as a *problem*, with a projected solution, as when Bok took on venereal disease and championed sex education in the staid *Journal.*

43. See for instance Mary Noel, *Villains Galore . . . The Heydey of the Popular Story Weekly* (New York: Macmillan, 1954), and Michael Denning, *Mechanic Accents; Dime Novels and Working-Class Culture in America* (London: Verso, 1987).

44. See, for instance, C. Vann Woodward's *The Strange Career of Jim Crow* (New York: Oxford University Press, 1966).

45. *Scribner's* (later the *Century*) was important in circulating these new myths, with a conciliatory series on the South as early as 1874 and a lengthy one on the Civil War in the mid 1880s.

46. See the account of this unpleasant bit of cultural gatekeeping in William L. Andrews, *The Literary Career of Charles W. Chesnutt* (Baton Rouge, La.: Louisiana State University Press, 1980), pp. 21–35. It may be worth remembering, in this context, that neither the genteel novelists associated with the elite magazines (Jewett, Howells, James, etc.) nor the bold, newer realists (Crane, Dreiser, Norris, etc.) took on the representation of black people or racial conflict during this period. Bellamy's *Looking Backward* made no gesture toward solving "the negro question," and represented an apparently negro-less United States in the year 2000.

47. Be it noted, however that in a "lost speech" of 1856 on the free-Kansas issue, printed in *McClure's* of September 1896, Lincoln made clear his acceptance of the negro's inferiority, while rejecting that as an argument for slavery (p. 325).

48. Scipio and the woolly-headed fireman look passive and pathetic in the illustrations. There is one photograph of a black man in my sample – a prisoner being coerced to have his picture taken in the article on identifying criminals (*Cosmopolitan*, November 1895, p. 36).

49. In one extraordinary tale from the 1902-04 period, a lynching is the central event, but only because of its dire psychological and moral impact on the *white* men who committed the crime. One of them gives from his memory our only glimpse of the dead man, pleading in the "piteous, childish language of his half-developed race" (Octave Thanet, "Beyond The Limit," *Cosmopolitan*, February 1903, p. 455).

50. I take encouragement in this hypothesis from one lengthy representation of African Americans in 1895–7, outside my sample, and outside of fiction. "Some Types of Dixieland," by Mrs D. B. Dyer, is a tourist's view of Augusta, Georgia, and the "types" are almost all black. "It is a most inspiring sight to watch these darkies, who are a happy, jolly throng of people": that passage adequately represents Dyer's tone,

and her grasp of negro lives entirely through clichés – comic dialect, love of water-melon and raccoon, laziness, loyalty to "ole miss" and "the doctor," superstition, and an addiction to gambling ("As soon as a pickaninny is big enough to do anything, he is big enough to play 'craps,' and he takes to it as naturally as does a duckling to water"). Although there is sadness over "the passing away of the old-fashioned negroes," the newer generation seems just as quaint and childlike. Numerous pho-tos, including posed ones of black youth "scrambling for pennies" and shooting craps, replay visually the text's repertory of cheerful stereotypes. No fiction could be more reassuring to the distant, urban reader than this supposedly descriptive account of black life (*Cosmopolitan*, January 1897, pp. 235–46).

51. I remind the reader that the volumes from which I have drawn my sample of articles, fiction, and so on, have had all the ads deleted for binding. The ads shown here come from my collection of old, individual issues of a variety of monthlies, from 1893 to 1907, so that the two samples do not correspond. But the number of issues in the two samples is about the same.

52. This imagery was widespread in other venues. Wayne Martin Mellinger traces the visual connections of child (pickaninny), contented slave, and happy darkey on postcards, which quickly became a fad when first sold in 1893: "Representing Blackness in the White Imagination: Images of 'Happy Darkeys' in Popular Culture, 1893–1917," *Visual Sociology*, vol. 7, Fall 1992, pp. 3–21. Doubtless, agencies prepar-ing ads for magazines drew upon the earlier use of comic negroes on trade cards; see Robert Jay, *The Trade Card in Nineteenth-Century America* (Columbia, Mo: University of Missouri Press, 1987), especially pp. 168–70. By contrast, Native Americans were often discussed and represented in the editorial pages, usually either as warlike and dangerous or as tragic victims. Correspondingly, advertisements rarely used images of Indians to sell commodities and promote good feeling about the social order.

53. Unpublished manuscript, "The Problem of the Color Line: Reading Segregation, Writing History." I learned from many discussions with Claire Potter and other Fellows at Wesleyan's Center for the Humanities during our colloquium on "Race and Culture," spring 1994. Much recent work has explored the imbrication of race in class formation and of class in the construction of race. See, for example, Barbara Fields, "Ideology and Race in American History," *New Left Review*, vol. 181, May/June 1990, pp. 95–118; David Roediger, *The Wages of Whiteness; Race and the Making of the American Working Class* (London: Verso, 1991); and Eric Lott, *Love and Theft; Blackface Minstrelsy and the American Working Class* (New York; Oxford University Press, 1993).

54. Other ads appropriate the New Woman for sale of Ivory Soap (she is "cleansed and beautified" after lifting weights and using the product [*Ladies' Home Journal* – June 1898]), S.H. & M. velveteen and bias (she uses them both for her "nice" gowns and her wet weather skirts [*Ladies' Home Journal*, June 1895]), and G-D bicycle waists (she is "graceful" always, "at work, a-wheel, in negligée" [*Ladies' Home Journal*, September 1896]). Thanks to Carla Willard for sending these ads; her University of Pennsylvania dissertation-in-progress brilliantly analyzes these strategies of contain-ment.

55. Letter from William V. Alexander (1901), quoted by Steinberg, *Reformer in the Marketplace*, p. 45.

56. William O'Barr examines the ways in which advertising's racial and ethnic par-adigms offer "an ideological guide for relations between the self and others, between us and them," and traces the representation of black people in ads through roughly the past eighty years: *Culture and the Ad; Exploring Otherness in the World of Advertising* (Boulder, Co.: Westview Press, 1994), pp. 2; 107–56.

57. Except that one of the three *Ladies' Home Journals* I am using is the issue of April 1893, and another is May 1898.

58. The article was called "The Bawling Brotherhood." Ellen Jordan says this was

the first use of the term: "The Christening of the New Woman: May 1894" (*Victorian Newsletter*, vol. 63, 1983, pp. 19–21; the date in her title refers to Ouida's capitalizing of the new phrase). "Sarah Grand" was the pen name of Frances Elizabeth Bellenden Clarke.

59. "Dies Dominae," *Saturday Review*, vol. 79, 18 May–22 June, 1895. My quotation is from p. 646. In tracing this genealogy I have drawn on Ann L. Ardis, *New Women, New Novels: Feminism and Early Modernism* (New Brunswick, N.J.: Rutgers University Press, 1990); Gail Cunningham, *The New Woman and the Victorian Novel* (New York: Harper and Row, 1978); Patricia Marks, *Bicycles, Bangs, and Bloomers; The New Woman in the Popular Press* (Lexington, Ky: University Press of Kentucky, 1990), and David Rubinstein, *Before the Suffragettes; Women's Emancipation in the 1890s* (New York: St Martin's Press, 1986).

60. This instability of "woman" was itself a very old story, one told to my own greatest illumination by Denise Riley, in *"Am I That Name?"; Feminism and the Category of "Women" in History* (Minneapolis, Minn.: Univesity of Minnesota Press, 1988). As Riley says, "the damage flows from the very categorization 'woman' which is and has always been circumscribed in advance from some quarter or other rendering the ideal of a purely self-representing 'femininity' implausible" (p. 107).

61. *Munsey's* XXIX, April–September 1903; *McClure's* XXI, May–October 1903; *Cosmopolitan* XXXIV, November 1902–April 1903. I did no comprehensive reading of the *Ladies' Home Journal* for this period.

62. Britt, *Forty Years – Forty Millions*, p. 93. Yet Munsey himself became a vigorous supporter of Roosevelt, contributing lavishly to the Bull Moose Campaign in 1912.

63. See Theodore Greene's balanced discussion in *America's Heroes*, especially pp. 169–77, and Christopher Wilson's treatment of Phillips, Steffans, and Upton Sinclair in *The Labor of Words*.

64. Briefly seconded by a short puff on "The Great St. Louis Fair" in *Munsey's*, August 1903, pp. 682–4.

65. A few years later some magazines – *Collier's*, *Everybody's*, *Cosmopolitan*, perhaps even *McClure's* – may have gathered readerships primarily around resistant anger and reformist hopes, but not the circulation leaders under scrutiny here.

66. Kolko makes this case most comprehensively in *The Triumph of Conservatism; A Reinterpretation of American History, 1900–1916* (New York: Free Press, 1963). He sees the muckrakers as people with "commonplace talents and middle-class values" who, through the whole period of their ascendancy, formulated "no serious social or economic theory" (pp. 160–61). I agree, but theory was not their game, and they articulated a coherent enough class ideology.

10. Fiction's Inadvertent Love Song

1. S.S. McClure, *My Autobiography* (London: John Murray, 1914), pp. 218–21. (Willa Cather actually wrote this "autobiography," more or less as McClure told it to her.)

2. Interview in the *New York Tribune*, 1897, quoted by Peter Lyon in *Success Story; The Life and Times of S. S. McClure* (New York: Charles Scribner's Sons, 1963), pp. 129–30.

3. See "'Magazining' for the Masses" in Christopher P. Wilson, *The Labor of Words; Literary Professionalism in the Progressive Era* (Athens, Ga.: University of Georgia Press, 1985). Also, Wilson, "The Rhetoric of Consumption: Mass-Market Magazines and the Demise of the Gentle Reader, 1880–1920," in Richard Wightman Fox and T. J. Jackson Lears, eds, *The Culture of Consumption: Critical Essays in American History, 1880–1980* (New York: Pantheon, 1983).

4. *Independent*, 1 October 1908, pp. 797–8.

5. George Jean Nathan, "The Magazine in the Making," *Bookman*, vol. 34, December 1911, pp. 414–15.

6. Charles Hanson Towne, *Adventures in Editing* (New York: D. Appleton, 1926), pp. 23, 26–7, 35.

7. I have tried elsewhere to ground its appeal in ideology; see "Advertising and the New Discourse of Mass Culture," in Richard Ohmann, *Politics of Letters* (Middletown, Conn.: Wesleyan University Press, 1987), pp. 164–7. For details of the novel's reception at *McClure's*, see Lyon, *Success Story*, pp. 154–6; James Woodress, *Booth Tarkington; Gentleman From Indiana* (Philadelphia: J. B. Lippincott, 1955), pp. 74–9; and Keith J. Fennimore, *Booth Tarkington* (New York: Twayne, 1974), pp. 38–41.

8. Salme Harju Steinberg, *Reformer in the Marketplace, Edward W. Bok and the Ladies' Home Journal* (Baton Rouge, La.: Louisiana State University Press, 1979), pp. 53–4.

9. *The Americanization of Edward Bok; The Autobiography of a Dutch Boy Fifty Years After* (New York: Charles Scribner's Sons, 1921), pp. 191, 233.

10. Quoted by George Britt in *Forty Years – Forty Millions; The Career of Frank A. Munsey* (New York: Farrar & Rinehart, 1935), p. 98.

11. Letter from Ormond Smith to William Gilbert Patten, 16 December 1895, quoted by Quentin Reynolds in *The Fiction Factory; Or, From Pulp Row to Quality Street* (New York: Random House, 1955), pp. 88–9. Patten's pseudonym for the Merriwell series was "Burt L. Standish."

12. I have read little of this fiction; for much richer characterizations of the four genres just mentioned, see the critics I have relied upon: John Cawelti, *Apostles of the Self-Made Man* (Chicago: University of Chicago Press, 1965); Jane Tompkins, *Sensational Designs; The Cultural Work of American Fiction, 1790–1860* (New York: Oxford University Press, 1985); Mary Noel, *Villains Galore . . . The Heyday of the Popular Story Weekly* (New York: Macmillan, 1954); R. Gordon Kelly, *Mother Was a Lady; Self and Society in Selected American Children's Periodicals, 1865–1890* (Westport, Conn.: Greenwood Press, 1974); Michael Denning, *Mechanic Accents; Dime Novels and Working-Class Culture in America* (London: Verso, 1987). Denning's discussion of formulas as "enactments of social conflicts and cleavages" (pp. 74–7) is extremely helpful.

13. Henry Mills Alden, long editor of *Harper's*, associates a "highly developed individualism" with "a large body of fairly well-educated readers" who have been "emancipated" from old, formulaic traditions such as the "silly love-romance" and "religious sentimentalism": *Magazine Writing and the New Literature* (New York: Harper & Brothers, 1908), p. 127.

14. Fredric Jameson, *The Political Unconscious; Narrative as a Socially Symbolic Act* (Ithaca, N.Y.: Cornell University Press, 1981), p. 75. In the whole analysis of "On the Way North," I loosely follow Jameson's scheme of interpretation, especially as developed on pp. 74–102 of that work. My analysis of "On the Way North" appears in an earlier version in "History and Literary History: The Case of Mass Culture," *Poetics Today*, vol. 9, 1988, pp. 357–75.

15. The little information I have about her early life comes mainly from "A Young California Author," *Munsey's*, November 1896, p. 211, and Flora Mai Holly, "Notes on Some American Magazine Editors," *Bookman*, December 1900, p. 367. Tompkins went on to become a popular novelist.

16. David Konstan, *Roman Comedy* (Ithaca, N.Y.: Cornell University Press, 1983), pp. 18, 25, 31.

17. Denning, *Mechanic Accents*, pp. 81, 77.

18. Letter references key to a list of stories in the Appendix; I adopt this notation to avoid cluttering the text with titles of stories mentioned only in passing. If a fiction runs through two or more issues, I cite the date of its first installment. But except where noted, I restrict the discussion to short and long stories; full-length novels

bring in different generic conventions, and there are not enough novels in my sample to encourage generalization. Perhaps this is the place to note that I am treating the stories of 1895–97 and those of 1902–03, and some in between, as a single group, since I cannot see major differences between earlier and later of the sort that marked the journalism in the two samples. One difference, though, is that in the 1895–97 period only *Munsey's* ran a lot of courtship stories, while in the later period all four magazines privileged the formula. This suggests that editors sensed a demand for it. Another stray piece of information: *Munsey's* printed much more fiction of all kinds than the other magazines in both periods, and that shows in my sampling.

19. Only one story in my sample presses against this boundary (r). The heroine, lonely and unfulfilled, yields to her married lover's wishes in a letter: "The almighty plans of the universe could not be cheated or changed by laws," is the drift of her thinking. But in her sleep that night she hears "*the cry of the other woman's child*," and tears up the letter. "Almighty plans of the universe" is not a bad phrase for the attitude readers were expected to have toward the union of matched lovers; those "plans" warranted the defeat of convention, but not of "laws."

20. That East meets West in these two stories partly explains their unusual class content; see the next section of this chapter. The second story, in fact, may be read as either a courtship story or a Western.

21. I can't resist quoting the narrator's gloss on Gervaso's melancholy thoughts, before Elinor becomes free to enter his arms: "Hymen and Pecunia must ever trot in harness, though little Cupid sit by the roadside and weep." As a foreigner, Gervaso could hardly be expected to know how Cupid makes things right with Pecunia in PMC fiction.

22. In Frye's scheme, courtship stories are high or low mimetic, and across the boundary they slide into the *ironic* mode (*Anatomy of Criticism* [Princeton, N.J.: Princeton University Press, 1957]).

23. To myself, I have also called it "looking down," but that implies a condescension that by no means always accompanies these narratives, though often it does.

24. As noted in the last chapter, these magazines establish a domain of cultural likeness that includes reputable English society.

25. He did print many stories with western dialect, to be considered later in this chapter, and some others that featured powerful or "funny" characters not of "our" class.

26. This last story amiably parodies the genre; the woman behaves pettishly, and henpecks the man.

27. "Schmoo": an adoring little animal, featured in the comic strip, "Lil Abner," during my youth. So obliging were schmoos that if they sensed hunger in a human being, they would fall dead and thus make their succulent, ready-to-eat flesh available. Literary theory needs a term for texts that submit cheerfully to the critic's every wish. I am happy to supply the need by resurrecting "schmoo," with credit to Al Capp.

28. Ellen Gruber Garvey describes this process of containment in a number of courtship stories that feature New-Womany bicyclists: "Reframing the Bicycle: Advertising-Supported Magazines and Scorching Women," *American Quarterly*, vol. 47, no. 1, March 1995, especially pp. 85–9.

29. So far as I can tell from about twenty stories, the conceptual West includes not only Texas and the mountain states, but the great plains, and also rough parts of the upper Midwest such as logging and Indian country. It excludes cities.

30. Some other types: historical romances, tales of endurance and courage pitting men against the elements, science fiction, Civil War stories, sketches of village life (especially in the *Ladies' Home Journal*), and so on until groupings shrink to the point where I am not sure whether I am perceiving a genre that readers and writers of the time would have recognized as such, or just incidental resemblances.

NOTES TO PAGES 335 TO 349

31. I have not spoken of religion, but will note in passing that it plays virtually no serious role in this fiction, save in a few stories about clergymen. Like politics, it is quietly excluded.

32. I quote from R. Gordon Kelly's *Mother Was a Lady* (p. 173) here, because his nice formulation suggests that the "gentry" ideal he finds in children's periodicals like *St. Nicholas* and the *Youth's Home Companion* from 1865 to 1890 may have a genetic relation to the fictional ideals of adult magazines a few years later.

33. They sold their labor power to corporate bosses. See the argument of Jack Weston's *The Real American Cowboy* (New York: Schocken, 1985).

34. Paul H. Buck's study, *The Road to Reunion, 1865–1900* (Boston: Little, Brown, 1937), gave major credit to magazine editors for guiding the process of reconciliation: "the cumulative effect of the literature of Southern themes was to soften the tension of sectional relations and produce a popular attitude of complacency to Southern problems" (p. 235). Twenty years later, Robert A. Lively disputed such a reading of Civil War *novels*, taken as a whole, but granted that fiction of the period in question here showed a predilection for "healing wounds between the sections," often through the device of "reunion by marriage" of a southerner and a northerner: *Fiction Fights the Civil War; An Unfinished Chapter in the Literary History of the American People* (Chapel Hill, N.C.: University of North Carolina Press, 1957).

11. Considerations

1. Perry Anderson, *In the Tracks of Historical Materialism* (Chicago: University of Chicago Press, 1983), p. 48. I have profited from Anderson's whole discussion of "Structure and Subject," in chapter 2.

2. Raymond Williams, *Marxism and Literature* (Oxford: Oxford University Press, 1977), pp. 125–6.

3. I refer (again) to the disputes gathered around Barbara and John Ehrenreich's ground-breaking essay on "The Professional-Managerial Class" in Pat Walker, ed., *Between Labor and Capital* (Boston: South End Press, 1979). For additional pertinent discussion see Dale L. Johnson, ed., *Class and Social Development; A New Theory of the Middle Class* (Beverly Hills, Calif.: Sage, 1982).

4. See pp. 60–61, 94–6, 157, 332–3 and other references in *Selections From the Prison Notebooks of Antonio Gramsci*, trans. Quintin Hoare and Geoffrey Nowell Smith, eds (London: Lawrence and Wishart, 1971). As with so many of his ideas, Gramsci never spelled this one out; it takes definition through repeated deployment. For a summary, see Ernesto Laclau and Chantal Mouffe, *Hegemony and Socialist Strategy; Towards a Radical Democratic Politics*, trans. Winston Moore and Paul Cammack (London: Verso, 1985), pp. 65–8.

5. According to research reported in George E. Mowry, *The Era of Theodore Roosevelt and the Birth of Modern America, 1900–1912* (New York: Harper Torchbooks, 1962), pp. 85–7.

6. For the best recent overview of ideology that I know, see James Kavanagh, "Ideology," in Frank Lentricchia and Thomas McLaughlin, eds, *Critical Terms for Literary Study* (Chicago, University of Chicago Press, 1990).

7. I adapt some of these thoughts from Stuart Hall, "Culture, the Media and the 'Ideological Effect,'" in James Curran, Michael Gurevitch, and Janet Woollacott, eds, *Mass Communication and Society* (London: Edward Arnold, 1977).

8. Ellen Gruber Garvey makes a good case for such collaboration in "Reframing the Bicycle: Advertising-Supported Magazines and Scorching Women," *American Quarterly*, vol. 47, March 1995, pp. 66–101. If she is right, I believe the bicycle is an exception.

9. And how we *change* the world, adds the ghost of Marx. I would not have undertaken this study or this kind of intellectual work, so distant from my early interests and training, had I not come out of the 1960s in solidarity with those on the socialist, feminist, and anti-imperialist left who wanted to change the world. Unfortunately, the study doesn't tell how to do that.

10. Neil McKendrick, John Brewer, and J. H. Plumb, *The Birth of a Consumer Society; The Commercialization of Eighteenth-Century England* (Bloomington, Ind.: Indiana University Press, 1982), p. 1.

11. Ibid., especially pp. 1–30.

12. Williams, "The Growth of the Popular Press," in *The Long Revolution* (New York: Columbia University Press, 1961), pp. 200–202.

13. Jan Cohn, *Creating America; George Horace Lorimer and the Saturday Evening Post* (Pittsburgh, Pa.: University of Pittsburgh Press, 1989), p. 21.

14. Benjamin M. Compaine and others, *Who Owns the Media? Concentration of Ownership in the Mass Communications Industry* (White Plains, N.Y.: Knowledge Industry Publications, 1979), pp. 131, 133.

15. Theodore Peterson, *Magazines in the Twentieth Century* (Urbana, Ill.: University of Illinois Press, 1956), p. 78.

16. Compaine, *Who Owns the Media?*, p. 133.

17. Ibid., pp. 67, 137.

18. Mark Edmiston, a friend with many years' experience in the magazine business, says, "*Reader's Digest* is not so much a magazine as a direct mail, list-gathering service. They test their articles . . . and . . . pick the highest ranking ones. Plus, it fits behind the toilet seat" (seminar at the Center for the Humanities, Wesleyan University, 1992).

19. My daughter, a kayaking enthusiast, knows of five magazines partly or entirely for paddlers.

20. Not only magazines, of course. Catalogs, clubs, and other kinds of direct mail promotion have contributed dynamically to development of specialized markets; and it seems likely that the Internet and the shopping channels on "interactive" TV will do so in the near future. Consider also the revival of fairs and bazaars, and their counterpart, the mall. Monopoly capitalism resurrects practices from its prehistory in its restless drive to make things new.

21. David Harvey, *The Condition of Postmodernity: An Enquiry into the Origins of Cultural Change* (Oxford: Basil Blackwell, 1989), pp. 147 and after. Harvey's argument has helped me think about these matters.

22. Peterson, *Magazines in the Twentieth Century*, pp. 386–96.

23. His work, executed at the "end of ideology" in the complacent 1950s, stands with the best liberal analysis of that time. Before popular culture became a reputable, not to say trendy, subject of study, Peterson treated one of its forms with both respect and critical distance. The honesty and breadth of his research make his one of the uncommon books that can serve as a reliable guide forty years after its publication, even for scholars and students with quite different premises.

24. Seminar with Mark Edmiston.

25. I allude here to the helpful analysis of John Clarke in *New Times and Old Enemies; Essays on Cultural Studies and America* (London: Harper Collins, 1991), especially pp. 92–7.

26. Peterson, *Magazines in the Twentieth Century*, p. 51.

27. The Lynds noted that in Middletown, "workers' habits . . . lag roughly a generation behind those of the business class" ((Robert S. Lynd and Helen Merrell Lynd, *Middletown; A Study in American Culture* [New York: Harcourt, Brace & World, 1929] p. 246). They refer to local activities like choral singing, but perhaps the rule of thumb applies to my topic as well.

Index

Le Gallienne, Richard 253
Lears, T.J. Jackson 202, 248–9; *Fables of
    Abundance* 201; promise of fun of
    living 211
Lease, Mary Ellen 266, 269
Leiss, William 175, 216, 217–18
Lerner, Daniel: literacy brings desires
    41; modernization theory 38–40
Leslie, Frank 26–7, 33
Lessing, Bruno: "The End of the Task"
    323
Lever, Charles 21
Levine, Lawrence 158
Li Hung Chang 240
Libby's 179, 180
Life (magazine) 354
Lincoln, Abraham 287; Tarbell's
    profile 241–2, 259
Lincoln, Mary J. 166
Lind, Jenny 19
Lindsay, Mary: "The House That Bobby
    Built" 317–18
Lindsey, N.A. 109
Linton, Lynn 270
Lippard, George 295
Literary Digest 354
London, Jack 289
Londonderry: class appeal 206, 208;
    connections 194–5
Longfellow, Henry Wadsworth 22
Looking Backward (Bellamy) 172, 227,
    250, 282
Lord & Taylor 66, 67
Lord and Thomas agency 104, 109
Lorenz, Adolf 275
Lorimer, George Horace 33
Lowell textile mill 64
Lynd, Robert S. and Helen Merrell
    Lynd 133, 153, 167, 210
Lyon (I.W.) and Son 72
Lyon, Peter 275, 290

Macy, Rowland 67, 73, 77
Macy's department store 67; hires
    female clerks 76; red star
    branding 77
Maeterlinck, Maurice 228
Magazine Writing and the New Literature
    (Alden) 254–5

Maggie (Crane) 245
The Magnificent Ambersons (Tarkington)
    219
Malraux, André 237
Marble Dry Goods Palace 66
Marble House 66
Marchand, Roland 216, 217;
    modernity 206; Parable of
    Democracy of Goods 208;
    personal relationship in
    advertising 193; scare copy 210;
    social tableaux 185
Marcuse, Herbert 43–4
Marks, Patricia 268
Marsh, Margaret 136
Marx, Karl: and Frankfurt School
    43–4; people making history 118;
    social production 41–3; unchosen
    circumstances 39
Marxism: and Gramsci's hegemony
    44–7
Mason & Hamlin Organ Co. 176, 177,
    186, 204; meaning system 193;
    writing style 187
Mason & Tuttle 95
Matthews, Brander 228
McCall's (magazine) 354
McClure, S.S. 25; commodification
    348; cultivates authors 287–91;
    displays the best of culture 245–7;
    magazine founders after death
    354; magazine office 224; one of
    "the people" 33; politics 250;
    popularity and worth 222;
    Standard Oil 214; technology 36,
    37
McClure's (magazine) 25; ads aim at
    women 76, 112; advertising style
    184–5, 190–91, 192; authors 296;
    celebrities 239–43, 245–6;
    circulation 344; class appeal 206;
    cultural field 232–5; departments
    225; domestic appliances 165–6;
    ends race moratorium 266; fiction
    33; fine writers 222; historical and
    literary slant 227; house design
    148; jingoism 277–8; mass market
    revolution 28–9; muckraking and
    reformism 273, 275, 282, 283–4,

THE HAYMARKET SERIES

Already published